CIVIL WAR

SUPPLY AND STRATEGY

CIVIL WAR SUPPLY AND STRATEGY

FEEDING MEN AND MOVING ARMIES

EARL J. HESS

Louisiana State University Press
Baton Rouge

Published by Louisiana State University Press
lsupress.org

Manufactured in the United States of America

Designer: Mandy McDonald Scallan
Typeface: Sentinel
Printer and binder: Sheridan Books, Inc.

Cover illustration: *A View in Williamsburg, Virginia, 1862,* by William McIlvaine. Courtesy Marian S. Carson Collection, Library of Congress Prints and Photographs Division, Washington, D.C.

Library of Congress Cataloging-in-Publication Data
Names: Hess, Earl J., author.
Title: Civil War supply and strategy : feeding men and moving armies / Earl J. Hess.
Description: Baton Rouge : Louisiana State University Press, [2020] | Includes bibliographical references and index.
Identifiers: LCCN 2020009006 (print) | LCCN 2020009007 (ebook) | ISBN 978-0-8071-7332-9 (cloth) | ISBN 978-0-8071-7447-0 (pdf) | ISBN 978-0-8071-7448-7 (epub) | ISBN 978-0-8071-8377-9 (pbk)
Subjects: LCSH: United States—History—Civil War, 1861–1865—Logistics. | United States—History—Civil War, 1861–1865—Equipment and supplies. | United States—History—Civil War, 1861–1865—Campaigns.
Classification: LCC E468.9 .H568 2020 (print) | LCC E468.9 (ebook) | DDC 973.7/3—dc23
LC record available at https://lccn.loc.gov/2020009006
LC ebook record available at https://lccn.loc.gov/2020009007

For Pratibha and Julie,

with Love

Contents

Illustrations

MAPS

FIGURES

Acknowledgments

My thanks go out to the many staff members at the archives listed in the bibliography who have helped access their holdings to support research for this book. The anonymous reader recruited by Louisiana State University Press to review this manuscript offered enthusiastic and very helpful suggestions for its improvement. I also wish to thank Terry Beckenbaugh for sharing with me some very useful studies of logistics his students have written. As always, my gratitude flows to Pratibha for all her love and assistance.

CIVIL WAR

SUPPLY AND STRATEGY

INTRODUCTION

"It is no small matter to feed three thousand men," confessed George Williamson Balloch to his wife. He served as commissary of subsistence for Winfield Hancock's Second Division, Second Corps, Army of the Potomac. Balloch sometimes felt overwhelmed, "almost discouraged" in fact, when encountering difficulties in the field. But he proudly informed his wife, "at no time yet have I failed to feed my men."[1]

Imagine the greatly enlarged difficulties encountered when feeding an army group of 100,000 men as William T. Sherman did during the Atlanta Campaign. With everything else on his mind, Sherman admitted that "the great question of supplies" was the most important component of his operations. "The 'feeding' of an army is a matter of the most vital importance," he wrote in his memoirs, "and demands the earliest attention of the general intrusted with a campaign." Like Balloch, Sherman admitted to a feeling of dismay when approaching this enormous task, for men and animals needed subsistence in a never-ending cycle. A good staff was essential but not sufficient. The general should never trust his staff members to do everything that was needed in this task. "He must give the subject his personal attention," Sherman concluded.[2]

Lines of Interpretation

One purpose of this book is to see how generals and their subordinates organized military resources to move both men and animals under their command and to feed and supply them with all manner of material along the way. It takes a chronological approach to the topic, looking at the major campaigns of the Civil War in each of the three major theaters of operations (eastern, western, and Trans-Mississippi).

More attention is devoted to the West, the region between the Appalachian Highlands and the Mississippi River, because that is where the problems of shipping material and moving large armies were most formidable. The western theater was immense, crisscrossed by numerous rivers and mountain ranges. The most severe test of military supply occurred in the West; the army that could master the environment in this complex region had a far better chance of winning the war than the side that failed to use technology, brains, and muscle power to achieve army mobility. Here is arguably where the Federals started to learn how to win the Civil War by solving the problems associated with army mobility.

This study looks at in-theater supply rather than the national lines of military transportation, which was the subject of my previous book *Civil War Logistics.* As I discussed in that study, the twin topics of logistics and supply are not only intimately tied together but also distinct. Supply concerns the process of procuring all manner of material, including food for men and for animals in the army, and distributing it to troops in the field. Between procurement and distribution, the food and material has to be transported to a variety of places—that is the job of logisticians.

Moreover, I pay more attention to Union than Confederate operations. As readers of *Civil War Logistics* will know, the main reason for this is because there is far more information available on Federal logistics and supply. Furthermore, as the offensive power, the story of Union efforts in this regard was much more complicated and important than that of the defending force. Confederate logistics and supply should have become easier as the war progressed because their lines of communications became shorter with retreat. But the Rebels suffered so many institutional and administrative problems with their system of logistics and supply that we cannot characterize it at any period of the war as simple or easy. Given that this study is concerned with supply in field operations, the Federal army's experience is far more instructive than that of the Confederates.

I spend a great deal of time on railroad management in contrast to river steamboats because river-based shipping constituted a self-operating system of logistics. Most of the boats remained in private control; the owners simply contracted with the government to haul a specified amount of material, men, or animals from one point to another and then sought another job. They did not have to invest money in infrastructure because the river systems were their highways and the Federal army did not have to own or operate any appreciable number of vessels.

In contrast, railroad companies were huge corporations for their day, and the infrastructure they created was expensive, expansive, and needed constant care. Moreover, only two Southern railroad companies, located on the fringe areas between North and South, were willing to work for the Federal government. All other companies in Southern territory abandoned their tracks, depots, and rolling stock when the Yankees came. The Union army was compelled to seize control of those resources and run the railroads for its own purposes. Thus learning how to manage railroads became a major focus of the war for Federal authorities, and it is impossible to tell the story of logistics and supply in the theater of operations without discussing that process in some detail. Railroad management, in other words, is at the heart of this study.

An important point of this study is that civilians working for the Federal government in the eastern theater led the way in developing the best method for managing railroads in wartime. Secretary of War Edwin M. Stanton initiated the idea of hiring railroad men to operate military lines early in 1862. He concentrated only on those lines operating near Washington, D.C., so as to exert personal influence on the process. This system worked so well that it expanded to other areas of the East, but Stanton did not insist on its use in the western theater. There, Union commanders tended to protect their turf by relying mostly on their quartermasters, engineer troops, and detailed infantrymen to repair and manage railroads, mostly excluding civilians. Their system barely worked in the best of times but completely broke down when the armies traversed the Appalachian Highlands in late 1863. As a result, the Stanton system was transferred to the West to fix the transportation crisis that developed and soon expanded to control virtually all Federal rail transport in the region. There was no substitute for hiring competent civilians to operate the military railroads if one wanted the trains to run on time.

In this context, it is worth repeating an important point that I made in *Civil War Logistics.* The Civil War in America was the first true railroad war in history. Rail transportation had played an important role in the Second War of Italian Unification (1859–61), but that conflict involved limited numbers of troops and was of short duration. Moreover, the rail lines that supported operations were very short. In terms of numbers of troops involved, duration of hostilities, and heavy reliance on railroads, the American Civil War overshadowed all previous conflicts and would continue to do so until World War I fifty years later. Not even the Austro-Prussian War of 1866 or the Franco-Prussian War of 1870–71 could match the Civil War in this regard. Federal success in railroad management was at least as good as in the Franco-Prussian War in every category and in many ways far exceeded the level of success that their Prussian counterparts achieved. Our war has rarely received the attention it deserves for this distinction, and a detailed study of how railroad management evolved in it is therefore justified and fits well with the topic of supply.

Upper South, Lower South

Logistics and supply came to empower Union offensive strategy and to limit it as well. The best way to understand this point is to consider how Federal armies moved and supplied themselves in the Upper South compared to the Lower (or Deep) South. Historians have long recognized the validity of compartmentalizing the Civil War into an east-west line of thinking, with the eastern theater offering different characteristics compared to the western theater, while the Trans-Mississippi constituted yet a third theater of war. But they have given scant attention to a north-south line of thinking. In reality, war in the Upper South was very different compared to operations in the Deep South, and the main differences lay in military transportation, army mobility, productive capacity, and health issues.

The Upper South offered the Federals railroads, improved pikes, and some rivers useful in their effort to occupy most of Kentucky, Tennessee, Missouri, Maryland, and the northwestern counties of Virginia. Union forces had essentially completed the conquest of the Upper South by the time the Tullahoma Campaign was completed in July 1863.

Beyond the west and central portions of Kentucky and Tennessee, Union logistical and supply problems worsened. The Appalachian Highlands cut across the Upper South and extend into major parts of the Deep South as well. They cover the eastern one-third of Kentucky and Tennessee, with mountains that provided an immense logistical and supply challenge for officers. The Chickamauga, Chattanooga, and Knoxville Campaigns witnessed unprecedented difficulties in railroad management for Federal quartermasters and commissaries. And the mountains yielded far less food to advancing armies than the lowlands and river valleys previously used by the troops. Only by revamping their concept of how to operate and manage railroads could the Federals cope with the increased difficulties in moving their forces through the Appalachian Highlands.

After coping with the mountains and contemplating the penetration of the Deep South, Federal commanders ran up against another logistical and supply problem. Their impressive railroad system, crafted under duress during the winter of 1863–64, could support large armies only down to Atlanta. In fact, Sherman had his hands full managing the railroads during his four-month drive toward that target city in the spring and summer of 1864. His army group of 100,000 men relied at the start of that campaign on a rail system stretching back 350 miles to Louisville, subject nearly the entire distance to guerrilla attacks and cavalry raids. Only through extraordinary effort could his support personnel keep the trains rolling. And only by detailing large numbers of troops was Sherman able to protect the line against heavy attacks.

Even so, the rail system only barely supported his army group during the campaign for Atlanta. The most serious medical problem Sherman's men suffered during the summer of 1864 was scurvy, brought on by the small amount of space left on the railroad cars for fresh vegetables. At times, the cars had no room at all for food, and there was little to be found in the devastated countryside of northwest Georgia. The rail line enabled the Federals to advance another 100 miles and capture Atlanta, but only barely.

Sherman felt he could not rely on that railroad to support a further penetration of the Deep South after Atlanta fell. Logistics and supply decisively influenced the shape of Union strategy afterward, serving as the most fundamental reason for cutting his supply line and conducting strategic raids in the form of his March to the Sea and through the Carolinas.

Railroads could not supply large Federal armies marching into the Lower South states. Only the Mississippi River allowed commanders to deeply penetrate the heart of the Confederacy. They did so along a narrow corridor of control, capturing all cities along the river's banks and severing the Confederacy in two. But moving any distance away from the Mississippi with the intention of permanently occupying territory was not deemed possible, which is why the Federals never mounted a campaign into Alabama from Vicksburg or Memphis. At most, their forces raided from those two cities into the central part of Mississippi on repeated occasions.

After Mobile was neutralized as a blockade-running port in early August 1864, Union generals viewed the capture of the city primarily as a way to mount an invasion of central Alabama from a secure place along the coast. They thought in terms of raiding in the Deep South to destroy resources, not to permanently hold that region because of the difficulties of maintaining long railroad supply lines in the face of a hostile population. The rivers of this region failed to offer the Federals any real logistical advantages, serving the needs of Confederate defense more than Northern offense.

The Confederates were well aware of the fact that the interior Deep South served as a kind of citadel of resistance to Union attack. Their strategy was focused on containing the enemy in the Upper South as long as possible, and they were surprisingly successful at doing this. In fact, in the eastern theater the war was fought entirely in the Upper South. In the western theater the overwhelming majority of Civil War battles and campaigns also took place in the Upper South. Only the Union conquest of the Mississippi River, Sherman's drive against Atlanta, and James H. Wilson's cavalry raid into central Alabama and western Georgia represented deep or near-deep penetrations of the Lower South originating from bases located in the Upper South. When Wilson sacked Selma, destroying what was left of Confederate industrial power, and then went on to Montgomery and Columbus at war's end, his troopers rode through territory that had never seen a blue-coated soldier before. In contrast, residents of Kentucky and Tennessee had seen so many of them as to be heartily sick of the war by this point.

Issues relating to health also played a role in contemporary views of how the Upper South differed from the Deep South. The latter region had a reputation for unusually severe diseases, especially yellow fever along the coasts. Several campaigns taking place early in the war seemed to prove that fact. Both Union and Confederate armies experienced unusual levels of illness during the Corinth Campaign of May 1862. The first Union strike at Vicksburg, in the summer of 1862, floundered, among other reasons, on the high levels of illness among the Federal infantry involved in that operation. Soon after, the armies that fought the Battle of Baton Rouge on August 5, 1862, could employ less than half their available manpower due to sickness. Federal armies did not suffer like this in Kentucky or Tennessee. Even Southern soldiers suffered severely from the unhealthy conditions in select areas of the Deep South.[3]

It is true that these startling problems of illness were not duplicated late in the war, when large Union forces actually penetrated the Lower South, but that was probably because those operations tended to be conducted in the healthier fall and winter months. During the early war period, campaigns took place in the hot months of summer, perhaps accounting for the discrepancy.

The Deep South was therefore a region set aside in the minds of both Union and Confederate strategists as a place of special difficulties for the North and special advantages for the South. Rebel observers considered it a bastion or citadel into which the Yankees dared not advance. They viewed the Lower South as a source of agricultural and industrial resources for the Confederate war effort, largely protected from enemy incursions by the Upper South states, the large distances to be traversed within it, and the lack of major rivers allowing Federal forces ready avenues to deeply penetrate the Confederate interior.

For the Federals, the Deep South was a region that posed many problems in terms of army mobility and accessibility. The railroad connections with the Northern states would be too long and vulnerable to allow easy access to the region. Many Federal commanders were leery of cutting off from their established lines of communication and freewheeling through the heart of enemy territory, although they recognized that the area produced a good deal of food and forage that could be utilized by an advancing force.

Logistics and Supply Cycle

There was a decisive link between supply and strategy during the Civil War. Decisions about where to strike and what line of approach to take toward desired targets were guided by logistics and supply issues because men could not fight if they were starving and animals could not pull artillery if they were reduced to skin and bones. Supply was closely tied to logistics, the ability to move men and material across long distances. The Federals developed a powerful logistical capability, utilizing river steamboats and wagon trains to a greater extent than during any previous period of American history and, at least in the area of river steamboats, greater than any other nation in world history. The North also was the first belligerent in world history to utilize railroads on such a large scale, over such an extended period, and over such long distances. Ironically, the Federal government received scant recognition for that premier success in the eyes of European military observers and latter day historians. Union victory literally was built on immense logistical power; it was the only way that Federal armies could penetrate Confederate territory and exert control over selected regions of the South. Strategy was therefore heavily dependent on lines of supply, road systems, preexisting railroad lines, and natural watercourses.

One can conceptualize the link between logistics and supply as a three-stage process, a continually moving cycle to procure, ship, and distribute food. In fact, as far as food was concerned, the process could never stop or armies would starve.

By the time of World War I (1914–18), only half a century following

Table 1. LOGISTICS AND SUPPLY PROCESS FOR CIVIL WAR ARMIES

Three-Stage Process	Method	Personnel Involved
Acquisition	Mostly by purchase in open market, with some government production, mostly in home country but some degree of impressment in theater of operations	Commissaries, Quartermasters, Ordnance officers, Medical officers
Transportation	By railroads, river steamboats, coastal shipping, wagon trains, pack trains, and mix of private and government ownership, mostly in home country but some degree of movement through theater of operations	Quartermasters
Distribution	Issuing within units in the field after arrival, mostly in theater of operations	Commissaries, Quarter masters, Ordnance officers, Medical officers

Appomattox, armies had grown to be huge, and industrialization had produced vastly improved material capacity and organizational concepts. As a result, armies involved in the Great War conceptualized field supply in a two-fold way. The old method was for commanders to request material by filing requisitions to be handed up the chain of command, timing them so the material would arrive when needed. This was the way the supply process worked during the Civil War. The other way, a new development in military supply, was for support personnel to anticipate the needs of units in the field, organize shipments (assuming the men would need food and a resupply of boots, for example), and dispatch it automatically. This process, called "push" in contrast to the old-fashioned "pull" method, mostly worked well and was more effective in meeting the needs of soldiers in the field. But it also could be wasteful and inefficient. Pull was more economical but often could break down because of delays in the processing of requisitions. Civil War America was not a fit place for the concept of push. That generation thought in terms of minimizing governmental expense instead of engaging in a practice that inevitably cost more money. But the Western world was a very different place in 1914 compared to 1861. It was more wealthy, more resource oriented, and more willing to employ expensive methods of winning a costly war.[4]

Army Mobility

Whether military systems used pull or push, the vital purpose of logistics and supply was to generate army mobility. Of course soldiers had to be supplied even if they remained in one place, but the real test of logistics and supply was in supporting offensive action into enemy territory. It is comparatively easy to feed an army that is retreating toward its base of supply; it is very difficult to support it while moving into hostile regions because the retreating enemy normally destroyed rail lines, bridges, and steamboats. They often ate up the available food supplies in the region before leaving, even if they did not deliberately burn provisions in a scorched-earth policy. Advancing armies moved away from their base of supplies and had to rebuild transportation infrastructure as they went. Then they had to protect that infrastructure against hostile civilians and enemy mounted raids.

It also must be emphasized that Civil War armies were improvised; they had little in the way of institutional memory to guide them about how to create long lines of communications for large forces. The American experience in the Mexican War (1846–48) did involve the deep penetration of a hostile countryside to capture the opponent's capital city. But Winfield Scott had to feed only 10,000 troops and march only 100 miles into Mexican territory, relying on wagon trains to link him with seaborne shipments at the Gulf coast. Sherman had to feed ten times more men and advance the same distance to reach Atlanta in only one of many campaigns of the Civil War. Moreover, his rail line of supply was exposed for 350 miles and more as the campaign progressed—not just 100 miles—before it reached friendly territory at Louisville, Kentucky. The scale, scope, and level of difficulties of the Union defeat of the South were unprecedented in American history, and the Mexican experience offered examples of only limited usefulness. River steamers were used only in a marginal way in the 1840s, and railroads apparently played no discernible role in logistical support during the Mexican War.

Historiography

Civil War historians have always known that logistics and supply were important to the effective use of military force, but no one had ventured a detailed study of these twin topics before the appearance of my *Civil War Logistics* in 2017. Previous to that book, a handful of scholars had discussed logistical and supply issues to some degree within the context of books that deal with many other issues associated with Civil War military operations. They included Edward Hagerman in *The American Civil War and the Origins of Modern Warfare* and Herman Hattaway and Archer Jones in *How the North Won: A Military History of the Civil War*. Mark A. Snell, Donald Stoker, Williamson Murray, and Wayne Wei-Siang Hsieh have also contributed to the scholarly discussion of logistics and supply issues associated with military operations in the Civil War.[5]

But compared to historians who examine other wars, the relative paucity of deep studies of logistics and supply in the Civil War is striking. Scholars working in the field of ancient Greek and Roman history have produced impressive studies of logistics and supply despite the fact that they have very few sources of information on those subjects.[6] In contrast, Civil War historians have at their fingertips literally hundreds of documents on logistics and supply readily available in the *Official Records*.

There are a few good studies of selected aspects of Civil War logistics and supply that have been produced by army officers in their postgraduate education within the current military system. These studies usually are not based on extensive research, but they offer some interesting points of interpretation.[7]

I make no claims to having written the final word on either logistics or supply—either with *Civil War Logistics* or with this book. Both are intended to introduce these important topics to the academic as well as the nonacademic reader. Even after the publication of these two studies, we still need more work on how the commissary system operated, how the procurement process interacted with the business community, and how food in general played a role in sustaining military operations and thus affected the course of the war. For that matter, we need much more work on how the military systems of both belligerents operated during the Civil War, from the government bureaus in Washington and Richmond down to the company level in the field. Such studies would greatly illuminate the interaction between the army establishment and the civilian community of both North and South, contributing to the developing "War and Society" trend in Civil War historiography.

International Context

The international context of logistics and supply is important in understanding those topics in the Civil War. Federal and Confederate commanders faced the same kind of problems and had to answer the same kind of questions that military leaders have dealt with since the dawn of organized warfare. They also have tended to answer those questions in roughly the same way, by a combination of relying on fixed lines of supply and of taking what was needed from the countryside. In terms of established lines of communication, historically carts, wagons, pack animals, and river boats have carried what was needed. In the modern era steam-powered transport (railroads, river steamers, and coastal shipping) came into play as well. In terms of living off the land, armies have gone all the way across the spectrum, from relying heavily on local stocks and stores to barely intruding on the civilian population.[8]

Alexander the Great's ruthless invasion of many territories was underwritten by extensive logistics and supply preparation. He paid a great deal of attention to feeding his army, especially when intruding upon relatively infertile or semiarid regions. He gathered information about an area's productive capacities, sent agents to arrange for depots of supply, or led portions of his army ahead to compel the populace to offer provisions under duress while the bulk of his troops rested in productive areas until called forward. Only through careful attention such as this could he feed upward of 60,000 troops and their dependents in sparsely populated regions.

Alexander and his father, Philip of Macedon, before him had stripped the army of transportation, so only the bare needs were met in that fashion. Soldiers carried much of their own baggage on their persons and used horses, mules, and camels rather than slower oxen and donkeys. They managed to virtually eliminate carts and wagons, the slowest form of land transportation, from the army. Alexander also maintained lines of communication by water whenever possible, but his troops could not depend on those avenues once they marched more than about eighty miles from them. "Supply was indeed the basis of Alexander's strategy," concludes historian Donald W. Engels.[9]

Why Total Reliance on Lines of Supply Failed

Reliance on established lines of communication became increasingly important over time, but complete reliance had never been achieved before the Civil War. Interestingly, Federal leaders generally agreed at the start of the conflict that it would be best to rely mostly, if not exclusively, on established channels of communications to feed, supply, and move their armies. While none of them ever explicitly stated this view, they all acted as if that was the best mode of operation. The Union developed such an efficient system of military transportation, and of procurement and distribution, to allow at least a chance of accomplishing that goal. Due to many and varied institutional and cultural problems, the Confederates never came close to this. Their military transportation system was weak to start with and deteriorated rapidly as the war lengthened; their institutional apparatus for procuring food and forage faltered from the beginning of the war and only worsened as time went on. The basic problem with Confederate logistics and supply was not that the South lacked resources, but that the Rebel government failed to develop effective methods of mobilizing and using those resources, especially compared with their opponents.

As a result, Confederate commanders relied more and more on feeding from the countryside. Their support systems were so weak that they never could invade Union-held territory with a real hope of conquering it and staying there. In every Confederate invasion attempt—Sibley's New Mexico Campaign, Bragg's Kentucky Campaign, Lee's Maryland foray, Lee's Pennsylvania raid, and Hood's Tennessee Campaign—Rebel forces lived off the land as they moved and were linked with their homeland by a string of wagons rather than secure rail lines or river-steamboat transportation. Their only hope was that the local population would rise en mass to support them, feeding their armies, or that they could capture enough supplies to enable their troops to remain in enemy territory. Southern commanders could not reasonably expect to be successful with a strategy such as this, especially when opposed by a larger, better-organized, and better-supplied army.

But even the Federals had to adjust their initial desire to rely exclusively on well-established lines of supply and came to feed off the countryside more extensively as the war progressed. The act of foraging inevitably loosened army discipline, allowing men to roam about with an assumed license to do as they pleased to civilians. This antagonized Southern citizens who might otherwise have been willing to accept Federal occupation of their homes.

If it was to be a short war, then a self-sustaining army moving quickly to victory without hurting the civilian population made a lot of sense. This neat conception began to unravel as the conflict not only lengthened but also proved to be more brutal than anticipated. At least four reasons account for the Union failure to rely completely on established lines of communications to win the Civil War.

Foraging

Soldiers defied their officers and began to forage from the countryside on their own hook. When officers failed to clamp down effectively on this lack of discipline, it created a feeling among many men that unauthorized foraging was acceptable. This kind of foraging grew in proportion to the length of the conflict until it seemed, as historian Joan Cashin has recently pointed out, almost endemic.[10]

Hard-War Philosophy

As the conflict lengthened, hard-core elements among Confederate soldiers and civilians stiffened their resistance to the Federal government. Prominent Confederate victories on the battlefield during 1862 highlighted the growing realization that it would be a long and tough conflict. As a result, Northern attitudes toward the proper way to conduct the war hardened by the summer of 1862, helping pave the way for the idea that it was useful to take food and forage from the civilian population as a way to punish Southerners and bring the fighting closer to an end through economic and psychological means.

Bragg's Kentucky Campaign

Union commanders adjusted their initial desire to rely heavily on lines of communications based on the example of their enemy. Confederate commanders tended to cut away from their own lines of communications, freeing up their field armies for rapid movement. This greatly impressed Union observers. Braxton Bragg's invasion of Kentucky in the late summer of 1862 was a turning point in their thinking. Federal Major General Gordon Granger called that campaign "a very extraordinary one" because it "certainly did violate, to a certain extent, some of the fundamental rules of war." General in Chief Henry W. Halleck remarked with candor that the "history of military campaigns affords no parallel to this, of an army throwing aside its transportation, paying no regard to its supplies, but cutting loose from its base, marching 200 miles in the face of and really victorious over an army double its size." Don Carlos Buell commanded the Union army that barely kept up with Bragg's fast-moving men. Two years after the Kentucky Campaign, Sherman was still referring to it as a model for what the Federals ought to be doing. "When Buell had to move at a snail's pace with his vast wagon trains, Bragg moved rapidly, living on the country. No military mind could endure this long, and we are forced in self-defense to imitate their example."[11]

Realities of Distance

Finally, Federal commanders discovered many problems associated with relying fully on established lines of communications during their extensive service in the field. While they often overcame these problems, they also realized that many of them were unsolvable and that living off the countryside was the only alternative.

The Atlanta Campaign is an instructive example of how the Federals, through an almost superhuman effort, barely managed to conquer the logistical and supply problems in supporting a large army group as it deeply penetrated Southern territory. Sherman had to feed 100,000 effectives and 35,000 animals at the end of a rail line that stretched 350 miles back to Louisville when the campaign started. The daily ration for every soldier weighed about three pounds. Sherman knew that he had to allow for more rations than the number of his effectives in order to take care of detailed men who did not fight, but he thought that 25 percent over the actual number of effectives would be sufficient. The total number of rations for his army group for 120 days, the duration of the campaign, therefore amounted to 22,500 tons of food for men alone.

The animals had to be fed as well. Each horse and mule needed—at full rations—twelve pounds of grain and eight pounds of hay per day. In other words, Sherman needed to transport 25,200 tons of grain and 16,800 tons of hay if he wanted his cavalry and artillery horses and his draft mules to be well fed during the length of the campaign. Adding all this up, his quartermasters needed to ship 64,500 tons of food for man and beast during the campaign.

To give some idea of the challenge to railroad management posed by these requirements, consider that each boxcar carried 10 tons and was on average thirty-two feet long. If all the cars necessary to carry this huge amount of food were placed end to end, they would constitute a string over forty miles long.

This does not take into account the amount of quartermaster stores, ordnance supplies, medical stores, and miscellaneous material needed by the Federals during this long campaign. But indications are that these items accounted for a relatively small percentage of space taken up on the rail cars. During the early months of 1863, the Richmond, Fredericksburg, and Potomac Railroad delivered from Aquia Creek Landing to Fredericksburg an average of 800 tons of material per day for the Army of the Potomac. A bit more than 75 percent of that material was food for man and beast.[12] If that proportion held true for Sherman, his nonfood needs would have lengthened his continuous boxcar chain another ten miles.

The alternative to hauling everything into the field was to acquire as much as possible from the countryside in the theater of operations. Sherman could expect little in this way from the counties he traversed in northwest Georgia because of their low population density, which in turn meant fewer farms and less produce. Historian John G. Moore has noted that Napoleon had been able to achieve a high level of army mobility because he lessened his transportation to the minimum and lived off the countryside as much as possible. He could do this because the population density of the European territory he largely operated in was high, as much as 140 people per square mile.[13]

But Federal commanders had no such luxury. Population density in the Southern states was much lower than in Europe. According to the 1860 census, it was 20 people per square mile in the Upper South and only 15 in the Lower South. In contrast, population density was 50 people per square mile in the New England states generally, with Massachusetts exceeding Europe at 157 people per square mile.[14]

It is difficult to determine exactly what level of density would have been required to feed a Civil War army, although we have some information on that matter concerning Sherman's March to the Sea and through the Carolinas (discussed in chapter 8). The conclusion is that much depended on the circumstances. Population density is a useful marker, but it is not a sufficient explanation in and of itself as to whether an army could live on the countryside. A sparse population could be unusually productive, and much depended on exactly when and how an army collected provisions. For example, if it entered even a modestly productive area just after harvest time, before the local populace had a chance to consume the collected crops, a bonanza could be found. Much also depended on whether an army stayed for an extended period of time in one region or continually moved on. It could eat out even a highly productive area quickly or survive quite well in a low-producing area if it marched swiftly through.

Europe is the best international comparison for American military operations, and the population density of that continent varied widely. By the early 1850s, this ranged from low levels such as Norway (13 people per square mile) to very high levels such as Belgium (397 people per square mile).[15] The generally high population densities to be found in the heartland of the continent (the Low Countries, France, and the German states), where so many wars had been conducted, helps explain why most European commanders throughout history had the opportunity to make war pay by feeding off the countryside rather than by heavily investing in established lines of communications.

In contrast, when Napoleon's armies left the heartland of high population density in Europe and ventured into areas such as Spain or Russia, they invariably suffered severely due to shortages of food, forage, and everything else needed to make an army work properly in the field.[16] American commanders have had to struggle in areas of similarly low-level population density throughout history. Perhaps that explains why Civil War commanders tended to rely on supply lines whenever possible.

And yet Civil War officers sometimes discovered that the Southern countryside could support large armies for limited periods. Following the Atlanta Campaign, Sherman found pockets of productivity in some parts of the Deep South. On cutting away from the railroad supply line and marching to Savannah, the Federals secured plenty of food in the central part of Georgia but found far less as soon as they neared the Atlantic coast. Only by quickly capturing Savannah and reestablishing their supply line via coastal ships could Sherman's men make the end of their March to the Sea a success without starving.

In order to deal with the Deep South, Federal commanders were forced to rely more heavily on feeding from the countryside than they had while campaigning in the Upper South. But they always used established lines of communications whenever possible.

Wagon Trains

In many ways Federal commanders came to realize that they labored under a burden of abundance in logistics and supply. They often were simply overloaded with material and had to trim down their transportation as time passed. This was almost entirely a problem of field transportation—in other words, military transport within the theater of operations. The strategic or national lines of communications were fully capable of carrying large amounts of material across the Northern states and through occupied Southern territory. But unloading that material from river steamers and railroads onto wagon trains for close support of mobile field armies was the chokepoint. The larger the wagon train, the slower the army moved, the more men had to be detailed to protect it, and the bigger the temptation for enemy cavalry to attack the wagons. Field armies could not dispense

Table 2. WAGON ALLOTMENT IN CIVIL WAR ARMIES

Unit	Baggage Wagons for Units	Baggage Wagons for Headquarters	Total Number of Wagons per Man
Napoleonic armies			12 wagons per 1,000 men
Army of the Potomac, 1861–summer of 1862	6 wagons per regiment		
Army of the Potomac, August 1862	6 wagons per regiment	3 wagons per brigade and division headquarters; 4 wagons per corps headquarters	
Army of, Virginia 1862	15 wagons per regiment		
Army of the Ohio, 1861–62	3 wagons per regiment		
General Order No. 160, War Department, headquarters Adjutant General's Office, October 18, 1862	6 wagons per regiment	3 wagons per brigade and division headquarters; 4 wagons per corps	
Army of the Potomac, 1863			30 wagons per 1,000 men
General Order No. 274, War Department, Adjutant General's Office, August 27, 1863	1 wagon per regiment (but poor compliance)	1 wagon per brigade and division head quarters; 2 wagons per corps headquarters (but poor compliance)	
Grant at Petersburg, 1864 (Army of the Potomac and Army of the James)	2 wagons per regiment		7 wagons in general train per 1,000 men

Table 2 *(continued)*

Unit	Baggage Wagons for Units	Baggage Wagons for Headquarters	Total Number of Wagons per Man
Army of the Shenandoah, 1864	1 wagon per regiment	1 wagon per brigade headquarters; 2 wagons per division, corps, and army headquarters	
Atlanta Campaign, 1864	1 wagon per regiment		
Army of Tennessee, August 1863			35 wagons per 1,000 men
Army of Tennessee, January 1864			26 wagons per 1,000 men
Army of Northern Virginia, April 1863			34 wagons per 1,000 men
Army of Northern Virginia, July 1863			28 wagons per 1,000 men
Early in Shenandoah Valley, 1864		1 wagon per division headquarters	1 wagon per 500 men
Pemberton's army, early 1863			27 wagons per 1,000 men
Maury's Division, Pemberton's army, early 1863			23 wagons per 1,000 men
Estimated average Civil War armies			25–35 wagons per 1,000 men

entirely with wagon trains—even Bragg took one along on his move into Kentucky. But they could learn to reduce the size of the train, to function without some items, and to live off the countryside as much as possible to achieve a higher degree of army mobility.

In fact, one of the consistent problems facing military administrators like Halleck was trying to convince field commanders to trim the number of wagons to the bare minimum. Those Federal trains were the largest, most efficient forms of wagon transportation ever formed by an army to date in world history because Americans had ample experience relying on wagons to supply far-flung outposts on the prewar frontier.

Civil War wagon trains were divided into three classes—baggage wagons for regiments; baggage wagons for brigade-, division-, corps-, and army-level headquarters; and a general class that included wagons hauling commissary, quartermaster, ordnance, and medical stores. The last named was the largest in number, serving the entire field army, and could hardly be reduced without injury to the army's efficiency. But the baggage wagons assigned to regiments and headquarters could be minimized, forcing men to do with fewer items for their personal comfort.

Officers allotted wagons using three methods of comparison. They assigned a certain number of baggage wagons for each regiment and each headquarters, but the general train was usually counted as so many wagons per 1,000 men. These three measures of how many wagons could safely be used for field armies fluctuated during the course of the war but, on the whole, went down with time. The biggest drop was in baggage wagons allowed for each regiment. The drag on army mobility posed by excessive numbers of vehicles in the field was at least partly resolved by the persistent effort of Federal officers to trim impedimenta, as the Romans called their baggage train, to more manageable levels.

Wagon trains were the final link in the logistical chain and provided the most immediate and flexible support of moving armies. How far the troops could rely on wagons from their nearest railhead, coastal port, or river town depended on many factors. Large forces had shorter wagon tethers than small forces. While George B. McClellan feared extending farther than 25 miles from his nearest railhead with the Army of the Potomac (about 100,000 men), Samuel Ryan Curtis's Army of the Southwest (12,000 men) managed to survive on a wagon tether 250 miles long during its march across Arkansas. Wagon trains could easily support the disparate columns of a large field army if the commander wanted to separate those parts from each other for complicated operational maneuvers. These types of "distributed maneuvers," as modern military terminology puts it, would rarely have been feasible if the army was tied to a static base such as a railroad town, a coastal depot, or a city on a major river.

Gradually, through a process of trial and error, the Federal army came to reduce its allotment of wagons per unit within a mobile field force as the war continued.[17] They particularly dealt with this issue once they had completed their occupation of the Upper South and began to contemplate the problems of penetrating the Deep South, where they could not count on railroad support. Prior to that point, Union generals merely yearned for lighter transportation so as to increase army mobility—they were not forced to do so. After that point, however, sheer necessity compelled them to cut down their transportation if they hoped to continue the process of destroying the Confederacy. Thus the last year of the Civil War witnessed a marked increase of strategic raiding, with Sherman's March to the Sea and through the Carolinas as the ultimate examples of living off the countryside.

Dual Strategy for Supply

The history of Federal army mobility is a story of change over time. Union authorities learned how to cope with challenges of both a technical and conceptual nature. They adapted to those challenges by crafting a strategy of mixing sources of supply, which meant combining reliance on a secure line of communications with living off the countryside. To a degree, Confederate authorities did the same, although from sheer necessity due to the many institutional problems affecting the Southern supply system. But, as indicated before, the Federals faced a far bigger and more important set of challenges to their ability to feed men and move armies than did the Confederates. They had to deeply penetrate a huge, hostile country while relying on ever-increasing lines of supply, crossing every manner of topographical obstacle along the way. Their achievement was simply unprecedented in American history and among the most impressive within the context of world history as well.

A Note on Mileage

Throughout this book, railroad miles are taken directly from reports by quartermasters when possible and sometimes by estimating modern mileage between cities. The latter roughly approximates railroad mileage. River miles are cited as straight-line miles because, as far as I know, there are no readily available statistics of actual distance traveled by boats along the twists and turns that often characterize rivers in the Mississippi Valley. In general, the main stem of the Mississippi curves so much that one can safely double the straight-line distance to get an understanding of how many actual miles a steamer had to travel from one point to another.

1

WAR IN THE UPPER SOUTH

The Civil War began as primarily a war for control of the Upper South. The secession of Virginia, North Carolina, Arkansas, and Tennessee in response to Lincoln's call for troops after the firing on Fort Sumter added a vitally important buffer zone for the original seven Confederate states, which were located entirely in the Deep South. The Upper South became the bloodiest battleground in American history as large armies traversed Virginia and Tennessee, with both states racking up the majority of pitched battles and campaigns to be fought in the four years of conflict.

As long as the war in the West was restricted to the Upper South, Federal armies had many logistical advantages. Kentucky and Tennessee were among the oldest states, with settlements dating back to the 1770s. By the time of Fort Sumter's fall, both states had modern turnpikes serving their heartlands—the Bluegrass of Kentucky and the Nashville Basin of Tennessee. Both also were crisscrossed with railroads. While the eastern portions of Kentucky and Tennessee consisted of rugged mountains, two-thirds of their territory had relatively even ground, and both states had rich agricultural regions that offered foraging opportunities to field armies.

After the collapse of Kentucky neutrality in September 1861, Confederate forces established a defensive posture running from the Mississippi River bluffs at Columbus; to Fort Henry and Fort Donelson on the Tennessee and Cumberland Rivers, just a short distance south of the Kentucky line; and on to Bowling Green on the Louisville and Nashville Railroad. More Rebel troops occupied the area around Somerset and held Cumberland Gap in the mountains.

Two natural arteries of transportation offered Union troops an approach to this position, and Federal forces were firmly in control of the northern

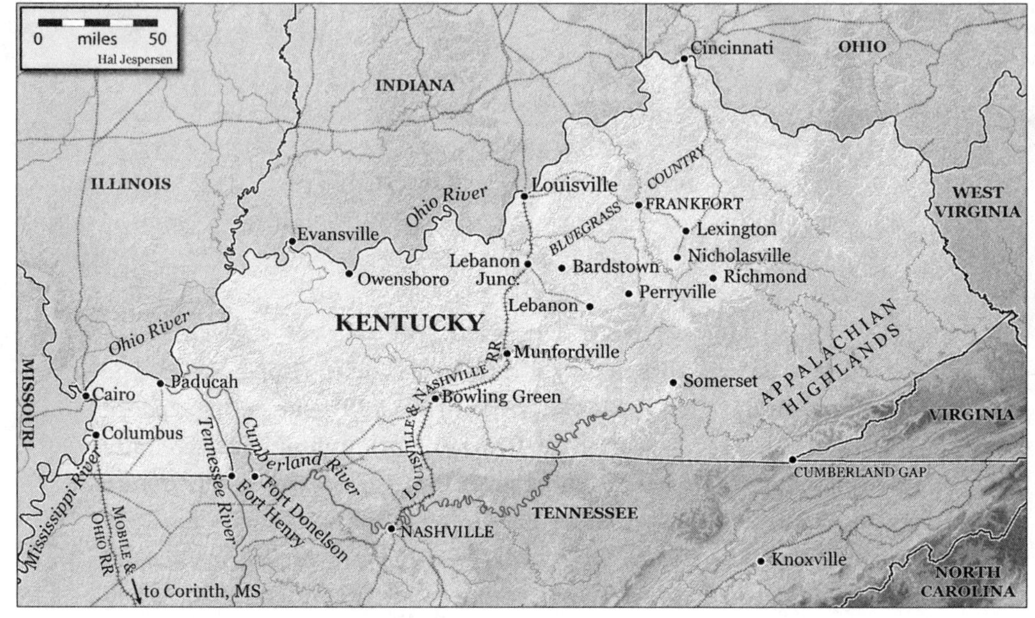

KENTUCKY

sections of these waterways. The Cumberland River was navigable from its junction with the Ohio River up to Nashville. At certain times of the year when the water level was low, boats could not go that far because of Harpeth Shoals, located thirty miles downstream from the state capital. The Tennessee River was navigable from its junction with the Ohio up to Eastport, Mississippi. In other words, both rivers had limitations as avenues of invasion, one extending only to the middle of Tennessee and the other only to northeastern Mississippi. Several hundred privately owned river steamers were available on the Ohio and Mississippi to move troops and supplies as far up the Cumberland and Tennessee as possible.

A third avenue of invasion presented itself in the Louisville and Nashville Railroad, headed by Pres. James Guthrie, who was eager to do business with the Federal government. It not only connected with Nashville but gave access to rail lines continuing on to Chattanooga, Atlanta, and points farther south. Unlike the two rivers, the Louisville and Nashville held the potential for deep penetration of the Lower South. That potential was limited by the fact that 473 miles of track would be used by the time Federal

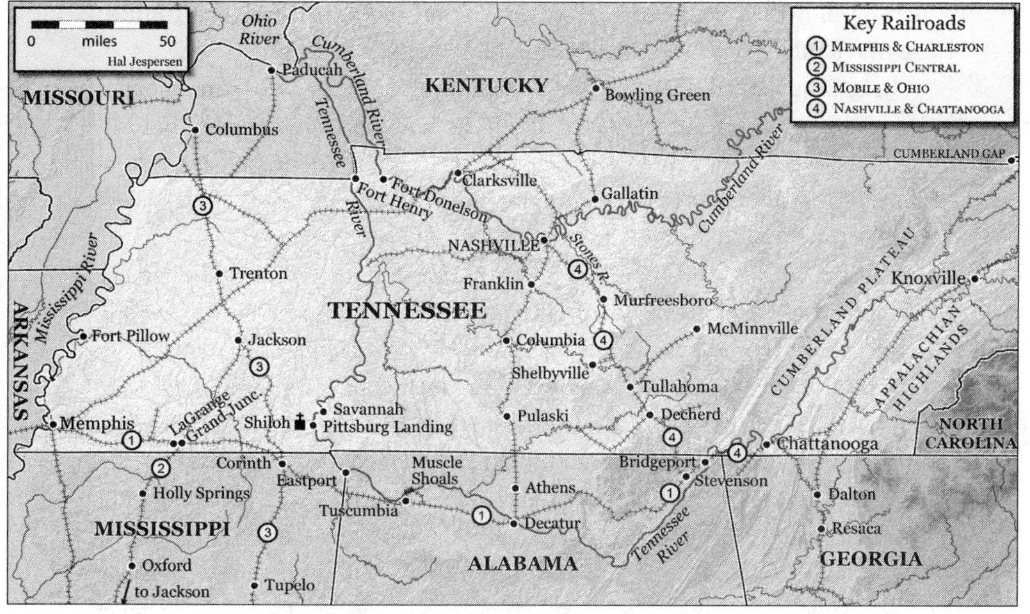

TENNESSEE

armies reached Atlanta. Whether they had the manpower to guard such a length of track and enough rolling stock to supply a large army that distance remained to be seen in 1861.

East Tennessee

As Federal commanders prepared to enter the Confederacy, the plight of loyalists living in the eastern, mountainous counties of Tennessee became an issue of political significance. Spurred by emotional stories of persecution by occupying Confederate troops, Lincoln and his general in chief, Maj. Gen. George B. McClellan, urged western commanders to enter the Appalachians and save those people.

But the difficulty of supplying even a modest number of troops in the mountains was not easy to solve. Railroads offered no help. The only line through East Tennessee ran between southwest Virginia and northwest Georgia and was not accessible to Federal troops. The dirt roads through the mountains ran along creek bottoms and were easily flooded by rain and melting snow. The scattered population of the region, except in the Tennessee River valley, produced barely enough food to feed itself.

Brig. Gen. William T. Sherman, who commanded the Department of the Ohio, knew that advancing south along the Louisville and Nashville Railroad was the correct line of advance. Militarily, East Tennessee was a sideshow. If Sherman was to penetrate the mountains from Kentucky, the best route was by wagon roads from the Confederate position at Somerset to the southeast. But the general pointed out that he did not have enough men or weapons even to capture Bowling Green, much less East Tennessee. Col. Robert K. Byrd of the 1st Tennessee Infantry (U.S.) advised Sherman that a column of at least 10,000 men would be needed to conquer and hold the mountainous counties of the east. "At no time had I a force at all adequate for such purpose," Sherman later told his brother.[1]

When Maj. Gen. Don Carlos Buell replaced Sherman in November 1861, he supported his predecessor's view. Buell resisted pressure from highly placed men to rush troops into the mountains. "Our people are oppressed and pursued as beasts of the forest," complained Andrew Johnson, the most vocal Tennessee loyalist. "The Government must come to their relief." McClellan warned Buell that Johnson had Lincoln's attention and urged his subordinate to act, noting it would be advantageous to cut the railroad that linked Virginia with Georgia.[2]

Buell informed McClellan that advancing along the railroad and the Tennessee and Cumberland Rivers were the best routes, but he was willing to move a column of 12,000 men into the mountains. He could not name a date for an advance and warned McClellan he needed at least 1,200 wagons and teams to support that column. His ratio of one wagon per ten soldiers is an incredibly high estimate, but we do not know the basis for his calculation. Buell also pointed out that he might need more than 12,000 men at the start, since he would have to detach troops to protect the wagon roads.[3]

By early January 1862, Buell had opted against the mountain thrust, telling Lincoln he was "decidedly against it." The president was stunned. "But my distress is that our friends in East Tennessee are being hanged and driven to despair," he told the general. Helping them was more important than the capture of Nashville, and surely cutting the rail line in East Tennessee was vital too.[4]

McClellan agreed with Lincoln, admitting that there were times when political interests outweighed purely military considerations. A strike into East Tennessee could inspire latent loyalism in North Carolina, South

Carolina, Alabama, and Georgia. Moreover, he wondered if Buell was too heavily influenced by "Louisville interests" clamoring to open up the rail line between that city and Nashville for their own benefit. McClellan had devised a comprehensive plan for breaking interior Confederate rail lines, and Buell was not doing all he could to promote it.[5]

Buell was now compelled to explain in detail the supply problems involved in an invasion of East Tennessee. The only feasible railhead was Nicholasville, Kentucky, 200 miles northwest of Knoxville. Buell would have to rely on Nicholasville for all the nonfood material his men needed and at least two-thirds of their sustenance as well. He calculated that 10,000 men needed at least 1,000 wagons, and the maintenance of the region's dirt roads required large resources. Already, Buell had five regiments repairing forty miles of road between Lebanon and Somerset. By that standard, it could take another 10,000 men to maintain the 200 miles of wagon roads between Nicholasville and Knoxville. Moreover, the general now estimated it would take 20,000 men rather than 10,000 to capture and hold the area. He now needed an army of 30,000 troops, one-third of them to repair and protect the roads, to secure East Tennessee.[6]

Lincoln was aware of the logistical difficulties in the Appalachians. Early in December 1861 he had asked Congress to fund the construction of a railroad from Nicholasville to Cumberland Gap or to Knoxville. He saw it not only as a temporary war measure but also as "a valuable permanent improvement" for the region. The War Department concluded it "could not probably be accomplished within the period required for military operations," so nothing came of Lincoln's proposal.[7]

East Tennessee is a good place to see how strategic objectives clashed with the problems of supply in the Civil War. The relief of mountain loyalists foundered on two rocks. One was the fact that the best way to penetrate the western Confederacy was not through the Appalachians but south along the Louisville and Nashville Railroad. There were yet not enough troops to conduct both moves.

The other rock was the difficulty of supporting even a modest column in the mountains without a railroad. The Confederates could use a rail line to occupy and control East Tennessee, but the Federals could not do the same until they captured both Nashville and Chattanooga first. Before that, any thrust into East Tennessee would have to be supported by wagons—and Buell shuddered at that prospect.

From Fort Henry to Corinth

Sherman remembered that sometime in January 1862 he joined a meeting held in Maj. Gen. Henry W. Halleck's room at the Planter House in Saint Louis. George W. Cullum, Halleck's chief of staff, drew a line across a map to represent the Confederate position in southern Kentucky. Halleck rhetorically asked them where they would cut it. Either Sherman or Cullum replied, "*Naturally* the centre." Halleck then drew a line north and south along the Tennessee River. "That's the true line of operations," he said. "I have always given Halleck the full credit for that movement," Sherman wrote in his memoirs, "which was skillful, successful, and extremely rich in military results."[8]

Halleck deserves credit for pinpointing the strategic center of operations in the region. "This line of the Cumberland or Tennessee is the great central line of the Western theater of war," he told McClellan on January 20. Halleck argued that 60,000 men would be needed to exploit it.[9]

Brig. Gen. Ulysses S. Grant took the lead in this movement. He told Halleck on January 29 that it was time to attack Fort Henry on the Tennessee River. He then could use it as a base for moving toward the Cumberland River, Memphis, or Columbus. "It will besides have a moral effect upon our troops to advance them towards the rebel states." After Halleck approved the plan, Grant found there were not enough steamers at Cairo, Illinois, to carry all of his 17,000 men plus artillery and animals. He managed to find enough boats for more than half the force and sent them on their way under Brig. Gen. John A. McClernand with instructions to send the boats back for the rest. Grant was compelled to leave his wagons behind and order his cavalry to march overland.[10]

As the campaign continued, more steamers became available. The Federals possessed the most secure line of communications possible for an invasion and captured Fort Henry on February 6. Then Grant moved sixteen miles overland to Fort Donelson on the Cumberland River. After several days of intense activity, that work fell on February 16. Grant captured enough supplies there to last his army twenty days, supplementing the material brought forward by the steamboats.[11]

The twin victories of Fort Henry and Fort Donelson broke open the Confederate position in Kentucky. Grant continued up the Tennessee until reaching Pittsburg Landing on the west bank, twenty miles from a key rail-

Mississippi River Steamers. These vessels were unique in American and world history, specially designed during the prewar decades for efficient operation along the Mississippi River and its major tributaries. More than 700 of them were available to Federal quartermasters at the start of the war, and those officers generally used about half of them at any given time during the conflict to transport men, animals, material, and all manner of supplies to far-flung posts along the river system. *Frank Leslie's Scenes and Portraits,* 94.

road junction at Corinth, Mississippi. Capturing Corinth would break the Confederate rail line between Memphis and Charleston, South Carolina.

Grant's victory also freed Buell to move with little opposition after the Confederates evacuated Bowling Green and gave up Nashville. When advancing, he relied on the Louisville and Nashville Railroad to supply his army. Sherman had already hired John Byars Anderson to superintend railroads in the Department of the Ohio on November 2, 1861. An educator who became involved in the management of several railroad companies during the 1850s, Anderson was superintendent of transportation for the Louisville and Nashville Railroad when Sherman recruited him to manage the railroads in his department as a civilian employee. Buell retained him when he replaced Sherman.[12]

As Buell occupied Bowling Green and then Nashville, Anderson found that the Confederates had left very little rolling stock behind. He used some cars owned by the U.S. government and borrowed engines and cars from the Louisville and Nashville Railroad. Halleck soon ordered Buell to move most of his troops to Pittsburg Landing so as to cooperate with Grant in the advance on Corinth. Buell relied on wagon trains to supply his men during the overland march until making contact with the river-based supply system on the Tennessee.[13]

Meanwhile, Anderson faced a difficult task restoring the rail system in Middle Tennessee. Many of the bridges and much of the track of the Nashville and Chattanooga Railroad and three smaller rail companies, together making up the line between Nashville and Decatur, Alabama, had been destroyed. Anderson created a civilian workforce consisting of ninety men and concentrated on repairing bridges. He divided the force into three groups and sent them to various locations as needed. "The rebuilding is tedious," Anderson told his brother on April 26. By then he finished repairing all bridges north of Nashville and hoped to complete the bridge over the Cumberland River at the capital by June 1. His men placed temporary bridges at seven locations along the Nashville and Chattanooga Railroad; five of them were between 250 and 700 feet long.[14]

Anderson obtained some cars from railroad companies in Ohio and acquired more stock from other lines in Tennessee. He could count on a small inventory of nine locomotives and fifty cars by the latter part of April, but Buell had left few troops behind to be supplied. Anderson's civilian workforce was barely adequate to rebuild the many bridges even in this quiet sector of operations.[15]

The bulk of Buell's army barely joined Grant in time to play a role in the Battle of Shiloh. Gen. Albert Sidney Johnston's Confederate Army of the Mississippi took Grant by surprise at Pittsburg Landing early on the morning of April 6. Johnston was killed, but the Confederates came close to crushing the Federals until stubborn fighting stalled them. Buell arrived that night to turn the tables on the exhausted Confederates, who received no reinforcements. The next day the Federals slowly pushed them back until Gen. P. G. T. Beauregard, who had succeeded the fallen Johnston, ordered a retreat to Corinth.

Halleck responded to Shiloh by concentrating troops in the West for a decisive move against Corinth. Several commands were shifted to Pittsburg Landing until the place hosted 100,000 Union troops, all of them supplied by steamers plying the Tennessee River. By early May, with Halleck in personal charge, this largest concentration of Federal might in the West thus far began a slow advance over muddy roads into northern Mississippi. Fortifying their position nearly every night at Halleck's insistence, the men of this army group were adequately supplied by wagon trains linking them with Pittsburg Landing. The river-borne system of supply was vindicated in this major test of its strength and vitality. Halleck drew material from as far away as Saint Louis, roughly 370 miles from Corinth, by way of the Mississippi, Ohio, and Tennessee Rivers. This secure supply line enabled Halleck to take his time, but Beauregard, fearing he could not match Halleck's numbers or his ability to flank the position, evacuated the railroad town on the night of May 29.

Confronting the Deep South

The Federals had achieved a great deal since Grant captured Fort Henry, but the big question now was what to do with the huge concentration of Federal troops Halleck led into Corinth. After the war the accepted line of interpretation argued that Halleck erred by dispersing his concentration, sending Buell back to Middle Tennessee to secure Chattanooga and spreading out Grant's forces to control Memphis and several railroad towns in northern Mississippi and West Tennessee. Critics argue that Halleck should have continued the advance into central Mississippi or moved down the Mississippi River to seize Vicksburg. "My opinion was and still is that immediately after the fall of Fort Donelson," wrote Grant in his memoirs, "the way was opened to the National forces all over the South-west without much resistance. If one general who would have taken the responsibility had been in command of all the troops west of the Alleghanies, he could have marched to Chattanooga, Corinth, Memphis and Vicksburg with the troops we then had." He further thought that Halleck could have detailed 20,000 men to hold the territory gained and moved 80,000 to any place he desired.[16]

Sherman also criticized Halleck in his memoirs, arguing that "he could have gone to Mobile, or Vicksburg, or anywhere in that region, which would by one move have solved the whole Mississippi problem." Sherman was certain after the war that "it was a fatal mistake" to disperse the troops into occupation duties, for Halleck had "the best materials for a fighting army that, up to that date, had been assembled in the West."[17]

John Pope also criticized his former commander after the war. "What, then, prevented an active campaign toward the Gulf and why was not the Confederacy cut in two and the Mississippi opened in 1862," he asked. Pope greatly exaggerated when claiming that Halleck had "scarce a ripple of opposition" before him after the fall of Corinth.[18]

Grant, Sherman, and Pope were guilty of injustice to Halleck in demeaning the difficulties of an overland advance to Vicksburg from Corinth. The largest concentration of Confederate troops in the West, the Army of the Mississippi, stood in the way. Its 46,000 men were outnumbered but far from defeated or demoralized. Taking position at Tupelo, fifty miles south of Corinth, the Confederates readied to resist a Union advance farther south.

Unfortunately historians have mostly followed the lead of Grant and Sherman (Pope's memoirs were not widely known) in their interpretation of Halleck's decision not to move deeper into Mississippi. Allan Nevins, for example, lamented Halleck's waste of "his irresistible concentrated force" in the summer of 1862.[19]

A few historians, however, have defended Halleck's decision. Stephen Ambrose accepted the need for dispersing troops to protect supply lines leading to Corinth and Memphis. He also recognized the strategic necessity of capturing Chattanooga. James M. McPherson has noted that the Deep South was correctly viewed by the Federals as a hazardous environment, with diseases cropping up in the summer months. Central Mississippi also experienced periodic droughts during the summer of 1862; indeed, Union cavalry, sent south to follow up Beauregard's retreat, suffered from lack of water. Guerrilla attacks already were taking place along the rail system that Halleck now began to use after the fall of Corinth. McPherson concludes that the decision to disperse was a legitimate way to deal with the many problems that resulted from this strategic success. Like McPherson, James Lee McDonough based his conclusions firmly on the evidence rather than on Grant's and Sherman's postwar comments. (I also supported this line of argument in a book published in 2000.)[20]

By June 9, 1862, Halleck began the process of fulfilling many strategic goals while postponing a further effort to clear the Mississippi River. He sent Buell toward the important rail center of Chattanooga, which was as significant to Confederate communications as Corinth had been. He prepared to help Federal troops under Maj. Gen. Samuel R. Curtis, then struggling across Arkansas toward the Mississippi. And he rehabilitated the Memphis and Charleston Railroad as part of a larger plan to create a rail-based supply system for his army group.[21]

Secretary of War Edwin M. Stanton approved these moves, but he urged Halleck to clear the Mississippi Valley down to Vicksburg. The general knew that other Federal forces were on their way upriver from New Orleans and offered to help them if needed. But for the time being, Vicksburg was low on his list of priorities.[22]

The bottom line in the strategic picture was that Halleck had put together the largest concentration of Federal troops west of the Appalachians. In fact, he overconcentrated, depleting troop strength from most other areas of his vast command. He postponed many important moves across the West to support his ponderous advance against Corinth. Halleck could not afford to keep that large army group together for long without losing other important objectives in his department. The North simply did not have enough troops to fulfill all of these goals simultaneously.

The Confederates also had overconcentrated their limited troop strength in the West to create the Army of the Mississippi at Corinth. Chattanooga was essentially undefended, and only about 10,000 troops under Maj. Gen. Edmund Kirby Smith held East Tennessee. Confederate leaders all but abandoned the central theater of operations in the West, the region along the line of railroad from Nashville to Chattanooga and Atlanta, in favor of defending the Mississippi Valley. For the time being, they continued that policy as Beauregard went on sick leave and was replaced by Gen. Braxton Bragg.

One might argue that Halleck misplaced his priorities, that crushing the only Confederate field army in the West was more important than all the other strategic considerations combined. If there was a realistic chance of doing so, that criticism would be justified. But military operations throughout the Civil War demonstrated how extremely difficult it was to "destroy" an enemy force in the field unless the opposing commander made so many mistakes as to allow it. More likely than not, such a campaign by Halleck into central Mississippi would have been prolonged as he advanced deeper into the Lower South for months, with no decisive battle destroying the Confederate army.

Moreover, Halleck justifiably viewed the Deep South as a different zone of operations compared to the Upper South. Environmental factors played a role in this. "If we follow the enemy into the swamps of Mississippi there can be no doubt that our army will be disabled by disease," Halleck declared. He preferred to establish garrisons at selected places in north Mississippi to create a frontier zone between Union-controlled and Confederate-controlled territory for the time being. The ideal sites for these military posts would be "high timbered ridges in the vicinity of clear streams and springs of water." Holly Springs, Hernando, and Ripley seemed to be good towns and were located in regions identified by his medical officers as the healthiest places in the state.[23]

In 1862 Sherman fully agreed with Halleck's decision not to chase Beauregard. "As to pursuing overland it would be absurd," he told his brother. He also worried about the slow progress of Federal forces in Virginia, where McClellan seemed stymied just outside the Confederate capital of Richmond. "We should not however go much further south till Virginia is possessed by the North," he told his wife on June 10. Sherman's 1862 comments in support of the decision to postpone a further invasion of Mississippi stand in stark contrast to his postwar criticism.[24]

Halleck was not the only Federal officer to hesitate about advancing into the Deep South. Americans had believed for decades that the Lower South, with its wetlands, stifling heat, and mosquitos, was a breeding ground for contagious diseases during the summer months. They worried that the region could ruin the health of their soldiers. At the start of the war, Maj. Gen. Winfield Scott warned of the need to wait for "the return of frosts to kill the virus of malignant fevers below Memphis" when planning an invasion down the Mississippi. Sherman contributed to fears by remarking on the scarcity of water in north Mississippi in June 1862. "This hot weather nearly kills our men on the march," he told Halleck while moving his division to Memphis. "Some are actually dead of sunstroke and very many prostrated and have to be carried in wagons."[25]

As historian Andrew McIlwaine Bell has noted in his study of mosquito-borne diseases during the Civil War, military operations provided proof of the health problems to be encountered in the Deep South. Even during the slow advance on Corinth, which took place along the border region between Upper and Lower South, Halleck's army group suffered terribly from disease. Thousands of men were afflicted, and malaria proved to be the second-most-serious health problem, next to diarrhea/dysentery. In Sherman's division 2,500 men out of 10,542 on the rolls were listed as sick. Even in Beauregard's Army of the Mississippi, nearly 6,000 men were ill out of 40,675. In other words, even Southerners were not immune to the disease environment of the region. The small Federal force sent up from New Orleans to attack Vicksburg in June and July suffered far worse, with up to 75 percent of the 3,200 infantry troops either ill or dying. The naval crews on the gunboats accompanying the expedition suffered 40-percent sickness rates.[26]

Federal fears that the Deep South could eviscerate a Northern army were not overheated fantasies. "I do not believe that Halleck will pursue or attack," concluded William Preston, the brother-in-law of the late General Johnston and a brigade commander in Beauregard's army. "A rough country of oak ridges, barrens uncultivated, without water, and traversed by muddy swamps intervenes between us for forty miles. The forage is exhausted, the people poor and ignorant, and it will require great labour & preparation for the enemy to advance under these circumstances."[27]

The sheer size of the Deep South impressed many observers as a barrier to invasion that steam-powered technology could not necessarily overcome. Georgia governor Joseph E. Brown envisioned the Lower South as a bastion of resistance that could hold out forever. "We can confine ourselves within the limits of the cotton and tobacco states, which should raise only grain, and defy the combined Federal forces for years to come," he wrote.[28]

Thus the notion that Halleck could have marched to the Gulf of Mexico in one stroke during the summer of 1862 is a fantasy. Sherman fully understood the difficulties in the summer of 1862 even though he went on to criticize Halleck for not ignoring them decades later because his former friend and commander had angered him over incidents connected with the ending of the war in North Carolina. Grant had an interest in portraying Halleck as a failure in order to enhance his own reputation as general in chief. Halleck never wrote a defense of his decision to break up his army group; those men who ended the war with the highest prestige—and who outlived Halleck—could write anything they wanted in their memoirs without fear of being contradicted.

Did subsequent efforts to do what Grant, Sherman, and Pope criticized

Halleck for not doing achieve any success? When Grant advanced into central Mississippi in November and December 1862, relying entirely on a rail-based system to support 40,000 troops, he failed. Rebel cavalry under Maj. Gen. Earl Van Dorn and Brig. Gen. Nathan Bedford Forrest destroyed a major supply depot at Holly Springs and tore up miles of track in West Tennessee. Grant was compelled to retreat and rely on transporting his army, as Sherman did during an expedition that resulted in the Battle of Chickasaw Bayou in late December, by steamers on the Mississippi. The great river offered the only sure avenue of approach to deeply penetrate the Lower South.

Railroads were advanced means of transportation, to be sure, but they had their limits as military tools. Vulnerable to disruption, every mile of track became a potential target for enemy guerrillas and cavalry. Sherman was only barely able to support 100,000 men during the Atlanta Campaign with a 350-mile rail line when he started from Chattanooga. Even he understood that he could not go on from northern Georgia in a further penetration of the Deep South while relying on a rail network. From Atlanta he had another 300 miles to march to reach the Atlantic coast and even farther than that to reach the Gulf coast. There were not enough Federal troops available to protect rail lines 650 miles and longer through hostile territory. By comparison with the European context, that is roughly the distance between Paris and Berlin.

In short, the Deep South was largely off limits to permanent invasion and occupation by Federal forces, but it was wide open to raids and temporary incursions. Due to logistical limits, Union commanders came to adopt strategic raiding as the best way to deal with the Lower South by 1864.

The only real solution to the problem Halleck and later Grant faced in planning an advance south from the border of Tennessee and Mississippi was to rely entirely on the Mississippi as the avenue of invasion. In the summer of 1862, Sherman agreed that operating large forces in the interior of the Deep South was a bad idea. "My own opinion is we ought not to venture too much in the interior until the River is safely in our possession, when we could land at any point and Strike inland. To attempt to hold all the South would demand an army too large even to think of." He thought Federal forces should view the Confederate interior as a fluid zone of operations rather than as a target of permanent occupation. "We should hold the river absolutely and leave the interior alone," he told Grant. "Detachments inland can always be overcome or are at great hazard, and they do not convert the people. They cannot be made to love us, but may be made to fear us, and dread the passage of troops through their country." Sherman envisioned marching from river towns into the interior, breaking railroads, taking slaves from plantations, and consuming property of all kinds. Gov. John J. Pettus of Mississippi feared the Federals would do just this, especially stealing slaves.[29]

Grant did not respond to Sherman's views, but he demonstrated his ideas about penetrating Mississippi using a railroad to support a large army in his North Mississippi Campaign (also called the Mississippi Central Campaign), which began in November 1862. He wanted to try it, and he had a railroad system—created by Halleck—to try it with.

Railroad Management under Halleck and Grant

Before he left for Washington to become general in chief of all Union armies, Halleck reoriented his supply lines away from steamboats on the Tennessee River. Federal quartermasters now used steamboats on the Mississippi to unload material at Columbus, Kentucky, and Memphis, Tennessee. From those points, several Southern railroad companies, now operated by the Federal army, hauled supplies to a number of posts in West Tennessee and northern Mississippi.

Four major railroads crisscrossed Halleck's area of occupation. The company personnel had fled, so the Federal army was compelled to take charge of these resources. The lines included the Mobile and Ohio Railroad, which started at Columbus, Kentucky, and stretched southward to Jackson, Tennessee, and on to Corinth and Tupelo, Mississippi. Another line, the Memphis and Charleston Railroad, started at Memphis and ran eastward to Corinth, then on to Tuscumbia, Decatur, and Stevenson, Alabama and finally to Chattanooga. The third line, the Mississippi Central Railroad, began at Jackson, Tennessee, and ran south into Mississippi, bypassing Corinth but passing through Holly Springs, Abbeville, and Grenada. The Memphis and Ohio Railroad started at Memphis and ran northeastward to bypass Jackson but connected with Clarksville, Tennessee, and ended at Bowling Green, Kentucky.[30]

Halleck chose to rely on military personnel to reconstruct and run these roads, appointing Brig. Gen. James B. McPherson to superintend all railroads in the area with Brig. Gen. Grenville M. Dodge to handle the reconstruction of the Mobile and Ohio Railroad between Columbus and

Corinth. These two men were infantry commanders, not quartermasters, and therefore reported directly to their superiors in the field rather than to Quartermaster General Montgomery C. Meigs in Washington. They relied on troops detailed from infantry units to work on the railroad.[31]

"We know exactly what is to be done," Sherman wrote of the work, "and not a minute shall be wasted. We labor under difficulties for want of tools, tackle." One regiment, Lt. Col. Edward H. Wolfe's 52nd Indiana, was referred to as "the Railroad Regiment" because it was dedicated to working on the lines. But Sherman also called on area planters for slave laborers to repair trestle work near LaGrange, Tennessee.[32]

By the end of June 1862, McPherson had opened 367 miles of railroad, including 143.5 miles from Corinth to Columbus, 95 miles from Corinth to Decatur, 20.5 miles from Corinth to Booneville, and 12 miles from Corinth to Chewalla. In addition, he operated 49 miles of line between Memphis and Grand Junction and 47 miles from Grand Junction to Jackson, Tennessee. There was not enough rolling stock, so McPherson asked for fifteen more locomotives, twenty-four passenger cars, eight mail cars, and 100 boxcars. Dodge, who had extensive experience at railroad work before the war, documented his men's accomplishments in reports that read more like corporate records than military dispatches.[33]

George G. Pride, a volunteer aide-de-camp on Grant's staff, took charge of organizing the Memphis end of this rail system. He found some machinery (planer and lathe) on the west side of the Mississippi River and used them to repair wooden water tanks and turntables. Pride obtained steel, iron, belts, and tools from Saint Louis to set up a blacksmith shop and a machine shop. He hired several local civilians as foremen and assigned six civilian carpenters to repair bridges. Pride also repaired engines and cars found near Memphis and obtained eleven new cars from Columbus.[34]

In one month, and with limited civilian help, the Federal army rejuvenated a rail system that traversed three states. "Without these roads our position here would have been untenable for the want of supplies," Halleck told Stanton.[35]

To protect this rail system, Halleck urged his subordinates to shoot anyone who tampered with the track or telegraph line, and he authorized them to assess the property of local citizens to cover repairs to damage caused by enemy attacks. The general also warned his officers to prevent their own soldiers from bathing in water tanks or using the water for their cooking.

On all lines operated by the army, military freight received top priority, but civilian freight and passengers were allowed if there was room. Railroad managers charged civilians the normal freight and passenger rates current before the war.[36]

Halleck established the rail system that supported his garrison troops in the area, and Grant inherited it during a time of increasing guerrilla activity. The Memphis and Charleston Railroad suffered "almost constant interruption east of Tuscumbia," with tracks torn up, men firing into cars, locomotives derailed, and water tanks and bridges burned. In August McPherson rebuilt seven bridges between Tuscumbia and Decatur.[37]

Despite the interruptions, McPherson increased rolling stock, acquiring five new locomotives and several freight cars in addition to repairing some stock that had been left behind by the owners of these roads. He could run two trains daily between Columbus and Corinth by late August and placed an extra train on the route between Columbus and Jackson three times per week. Under his master of transportation, Capt. Charles W. Lyman, McPherson thought he had more logistical capacity than needed. He had already added more sidings at Columbus for quicker loading and unloading and had appointed a civilian, Mr. W. J. Stevens, to manage affairs at Columbus. McPherson conducted more than $33,000 worth of private business on his railroads by the start of August and predicted it would increase to $40,000 by the end of the month.[38]

Grant recognized the wisdom of hiring more civilians to run the rail system. In October he requested permission to create "a corps of experienced railroad engineers and builders" to handle repairs. Halleck approved the plan, and Grant soon appointed J. D. Webster to replace McPherson as general superintendent of military railroads in the Department of the Tennessee, with Pride appointed chief engineer of those railroads. By this time Grant could dedicate the Engineer Regiment of the West to railroad work; the regiment reported directly to Webster.[39]

Railroad Management under Buell

Buell encountered many more difficulties in managing the supply lines to support his advance toward Chattanooga than did Halleck and Grant. He began to shift 40,000 men from Corinth on a broad front to cover two approaches to the mountain city. Both involved a combination of river and rail transportation. The Memphis and Charleston Railroad ran directly to Chattanooga across northern Mississippi and Alabama, roughly parallel to the Tennessee River. Upstream from Eastport, Mississippi, however, the Tennessee was essentially unreliable for all but the smallest boats during certain times of the year. Moreover, the Memphis and Charleston was exposed to enemy action, especially east of Tuscumbia, Alabama. Buell's other line of approach extended from Union-held Nashville. The Cumberland River could be used much of the year up to Nashville itself, and the Nashville and Chattanooga Railroad was open at least to Murfreesboro, thirty miles to the southeast. Between these two lines of approach, the one from Nashville was by far the best, but because he started from Corinth, Buell used both during his cautious advance.

The small forces Buell had left behind when he marched to join Grant at Shiloh had done little more than hold Nashville and a handful of other towns while he was away. A division under Maj. Gen. Ormsby Mitchel had penetrated north Alabama but could barely feed itself in the mountains. Another division, under Brig. Gen. George W. Morgan, was similarly situated at Cumberland Gap, seventy miles north of Knoxville. Anderson had not finished rebuilding all of the railroad bridges in the central zone of operations that Buell was beginning to fill. In short, the Federals faced the daunting task of restoring far-flung lines of transportation across a large contested zone while advancing to take Chattanooga, with scarcely enough men to accomplish both tasks simultaneously.

"The advance on Chattanooga must be made with the means of acting in force," Buell told Halleck, "otherwise it will either fail or prove a profitless and transient prize." Methodical in his approach, Buell spread out the Army of the Ohio in a wide arc from northern Alabama into Middle Tennessee. He incorporated Mitchel's division into the army and placed other divisions at McMinnville and Decherd, Tennessee, to form his center and left. Morgan's division at Cumberland Gap was separated from his left by one hundred miles. Altogether Buell arrayed six divisions in a line sixty miles long to screen his work crews. The closest contingent held a position at Battle Creek, only thirty miles from Chattanooga.[40]

Locking his units in stationary positions indefinitely, Buell defended his reasons for postponing the final push to Chattanooga. He needed secure lines of communications so as to ensure that he could hold the place once he got there. "It was desirable not to concentrate my force at a point which immediately threatened the enemy's position until I was prepared to move against him," he later put it.[41]

If Buell had been able to use a large corps of civilian railroad men, the huge task of restoring three railroads might have been accomplished rapidly. But he used only Anderson's small civilian force and detailed infantry troops to help them. The resources were far too few and scattered to complete the task quickly. Meanwhile, the troops suffered. Most units had to rely heavily on wagon trains to bring forward food and supplies. Those stationed in the mountains barely survived, "living from day to day" in "almost barren" territory. It was "impossible for my army to have advanced and depend on the resources of the country," Buell later stated.[42]

Buell's chief commissary, Lt. Col. Francis Darr, found that Muscle Shoals, located a few miles upstream from Eastport, prevented him from using the Tennessee to supply any part of the army. He employed wagons to haul everything from the slowly advancing railhead on the Memphis and Charleston to the arrayed troops. The railroad between Nashville and Decatur intersected this line, offering a possible alternate route, but it was cut in many places with repairs proceeding slowly.[43]

By July it was clear that the eastward approach from Corinth was hardly feasible and that the approach from Nashville was taking longer than expected. The Nashville and Chattanooga Railroad was not open to Stevenson, Alabama, until July 12, and then General Forrest captured Murfreesboro the next day, closing the line again until repair crews reopened it fifteen days later. Repairs on the route from Nashville to Decatur were not completed until the end of July.[44]

By then the Confederates had set into motion a bold offensive designed not only to protect Chattanooga but also to throw the Federals on the defensive by invading Kentucky. Primarily the work of Bragg but with the cooperation of Kirby Smith, Confederate forces set out in August to strike north. Grant later criticized Buell for taking so long in his approach to Chattanooga, arguing in his memoirs that he should have left two or three divisions behind to work on the railroad as he moved the rest of his troops to the city.[45]

One can also criticize Buell for trying to rebuild three lines simultaneously. He could have concentrated on only one, the Nashville and Chattanooga Railroad, as the most important. The other two were too exposed and had too many bridges in mountainous terrain for quick repairs. The Louisville and Nashville Railroad reliably brought supplies down to Nashville for his army, meeting quartermaster requests for 200 tons of material every day. The problem was getting it farther south to the troops. A concentrated restoration effort on that one line could have solved the problem more quickly.[46]

It does not appear that Superintendent Anderson was at fault for the delays in rebuilding Buell's rail lines. His ninety civilians had been working constantly since the general left to join Grant in March. Anderson simply had too few workers. Troops of the 1st Michigan Engineers and Mechanics were dedicated to full-time bridge work, but even that addition was not enough. Confederate guerrilla attacks and mounted raids soon began tearing up bridges and track, forcing crews to rebuild what they had only recently finished. Anderson's men also worked on the Louisville and Nashville Railroad, but Buell required him to charge that company for the repairs because it had not been seized by the government and was operating as a private entity. The railroad could deduct the amount from its charges to the government for hauling army freight and soldiers.[47]

Buell's troubles multiplied as the summer lengthened. Not only did Forrest briefly capture Murfreesboro on July 13, cutting the rail line for a couple of weeks, but also guerrillas cut the Memphis and Charleston Railroad east of Corinth on July 25. "The troops are on half rations, and even this supply is not altogether certain," Buell's chief of staff informed a division leader. Buell noted that he had 500 miles of rail lines to protect within a country that was "swarming with an immense cavalry force of the enemy, regular and irregular, which renders it almost impossible to keep them open, while every man that I can raise will be required toward the east." He planned to build wooden stockades at important bridges and detailed troops to pass over the tracks a couple of times every day. The Federals also began placing soldiers on every train as guards.[48]

These measures failed to solve the problem. Brig. Gen. John Hunt Morgan devastated Buell's logistics when he collapsed an 800-foot-long tunnel on the Louisville and Nashville Railroad near Gallatin, Tennessee, on August 12. Federal quartermasters created a wagon-train link twenty-five-miles long to bypass the destruction, which was not fixed for three months. "My advance has not been rapid," Buell admitted with understatement to Halleck, "but it could not be more rapid under the circumstances." The scale of work required on the rail system combined with effective attacks on it conspired to put the Union advance on hold.[49]

As Darr testified to the Buell Commission, Nashville was the chokepoint of the logistical network. He needed 75,000 rations to feed the army every day. There were only 45,000 effectives, but the other 30,000 rations were consumed by the sick in hospitals, teamsters, and other noncombatants. Nashville warehouses held 345,000 rations of salt meat and 1 million rations of bread by September 1. But these supplies only eked out of the city toward the south, and the troops subsisted on half rations. Darr focused on the essentials, shipping bread, meat, coffee, and sugar.[50]

The most fundamental of Buell's problems was that he had to improvise a railroad-management system in the field. "The means to overcome these difficulties had to be created, for they did not exist," as he put it to the commission.[51] Anderson was not an innovative, dynamic manager and hired far too few civilian workers. Soldiers detailed from regiments could not be expected to know the most efficient way to repair railroads.

Unfortunately the Federals did not take this difficult lesson to heart. When Maj. Gen. William S. Rosecrans, Buell's successor, planned his next two offensives along the railroad toward Chattanooga, he relied essentially on the same resources to maintain his rail system even though advancing into the heart of Appalachia, with its steep grades and bridges over treacherous mountain streams. The Federals in Virginia were far ahead of their western counterparts in putting together a large, vibrant, and responsive rail-based support system for field operations. Not until that system was adopted by the western armies could Sherman rely on adequate supplies for his huge army group as it penetrated northwest Georgia and captured Atlanta in 1864.

The Kentucky Campaign

Bragg's invasion of Kentucky in late August 1862 nullified Buell's cautious approach to Chattanooga and threw the Federals on the defensive. Confederate forces circumvented the Army of the Ohio, marching quickly while relying on wagon trains as a slim logistical support. Bragg's quartermasters had impressed hundreds of wagons and teams from civilian farms before departing Mississippi by rail. Each division carried enough food to feed the men for twenty days when they set out from Chattanooga.[52]

Before Bragg left the city, Kirby Smith commenced an invasion of Kentucky with his command. He bypassed Morgan at Cumberland Gap and cut off his line of communications when he reached Barboursville, Kentucky, on August 18, compelling the Federals to evacuate the gap. Then his Army of East Tennessee invaded the Bluegrass, severely defeating a force of Federals at Richmond on August 30. After that the heart of Kentucky fell into Confederate hands. Kirby Smith entered Lexington on September 2 and threatened Cincinnati. The state capital at Frankfort fell soon afterward, and there seemed to be nothing more to do except wait for Bragg.

Buell's first reaction to the enemy advance from Chattanooga was to draw back toward Nashville to protect that city. But Bragg had no intention of attacking the state capital. His hard-marching Army of the Mississippi crossed the state line into Kentucky by September 5, after which Bragg diverted the army briefly from its path to compel the surrender of a Union garrison at Munfordville on the Louisville and Nashville Railroad.

In giving chase to the Confederates, Buell lived off his wagon train too. He now engaged in a race for the northern terminus of his main railroad support. "The security of Louisville above all other points is of the most vital importance to our position in Tennessee," he told Maj. Gen. Horatio G. Wright. "It is the point the enemy will aim for, and should be protected by every possible means." Buell left a division of 5,000 men to hold Nashville and took the rest north in a desperate race to beat Bragg to the Ohio. All railroad work south of Nashville effectively ceased as quartermasters stored rolling stock within the confines of the city. The opposing armies confronted each other for a couple of days at Munfordville in mid-September, but with neither willing to initiate a battle, the race continued. Buell had hoped that some provisions could be shipped by rail from Nashville to meet his moving force, but that did not happen. He obtained some rations transported from Louisville via the Ohio River when his army reached West Point. By that time the Confederates had torn up sections of the Louisville and Nashville track south of Louisville, but Buell reached the city before his opponent. Bragg ended his long march by settling in at Bardstown, thirty miles southeast of Louisville.[53]

Lodged in central Kentucky, Bragg had no fully functioning supply line with the South but could obtain food from the largely pro-Confederate population of the area. For material other than food, he relied on periodic wagon trains reaching his army from the Confederacy.[54]

Frustration over the invasion boiled over in Washington, and Buell very nearly was fired. Halleck wrote instructions for his designated successor,

Maj. Gen. George H. Thomas, that expressed the view of Washington authorities. "The Government expects energetic operations," he told Thomas. "Operate against the enemy; find him and give him battle. Carry nothing with you which is not absolutely necessary. So far as you can subsist your army on the country passed over, paying or receipting for supplies. The immobility of our armies results from the excess of transportation," he concluded. At the last minute, the transfer of command was canceled; Buell had another chance.[55]

Washington authorities were impressed by the mobility of Bragg's invasion, especially the fact that he could move a large force a great distance with little apparent fuss and bother. That mobility underwrote the success of Bragg's invasion and contrasted sharply with Buell's sluggishness during the past summer. The authorities overlooked the fact that the Confederates barely had enough to eat along the way and could count their operation a success only insofar as they landed among people who were willing to sell them food. If the invasion was to result in permanent Confederate possession of Kentucky, Bragg needed much more than food and fodder—he needed a battlefield victory.

After resting, resupplying, and reorganizing his army to incorporate new regiments, Buell left Louisville on October 1 to confront the Confederates. Again he relied on wagon trains to supply his army. Bragg's men had decimated the railroads in the area, burning bridges on the Louisville and Nashville track, tearing up the branch to Bardstown, and destroying bridges on the branch to Lebanon. They also scoured the region for food and forage, leaving little for the Federals to find as they advanced. The Army of the Ohio had to subsist on wagon supply for the duration of the campaign, nearly wearing out teams and wagons alike.[56]

Logistically, the opposing armies were on a level playing field; Bragg continued to rely on wagon trains and foraging to feed both the Army of the Mississippi and the Army of East Tennessee. Buell advanced forcefully, caught a part of Bragg's army in battle at Perryville on October 8, and without realizing it, turned the corner in this complicated campaign. Although tactically indecisive, the Battle of Perryville resulted in a Confederate retreat. A few days later, after joining his force with Kirby Smith's and taking stock of the pros and cons, Bragg decided to evacuate Kentucky altogether as a lost cause for the Confederacy. Without large numbers of recruits from the state's population, he could not hope to stay very long in the face of Buell's army.

The Confederate retreat from Kentucky witnessed far more privations than the entry into that embattled state. Bragg and Kirby Smith moved toward the southeast by way of Cumberland Gap and Knoxville, taking their troops through mountainous terrain where they had no prospect of foraging. Only by moving swiftly through this region could the retreat be counted a success. Bragg's men lived on parched corn for several days. "The country is barren," noted John Euclid Magee of Stanford's Mississippi Battery. "Nothing but rocks and hills, and nothing can be had. Some are very near starved now." Kirby Smith estimated that 10,000 of his men straggled along the way searching for food.[57]

Bragg defended his campaign, pointing to the fact that he subsisted 40,000 men for two months on enemy-held territory. He also brought a great deal of material from Kentucky to stock Confederate depots. This included 1 million yards of cloth, 15,000 small arms, ammunition, horses, and other useful things. Bragg planned to shift most of his troops to Middle Tennessee, planting them as close to Union-held Nashville as possible, where he was confident enough food and forage could be found.[58]

In the aftermath of Buell's victory, bitter debate about how to follow up the success erupted. Once again the urge to secure East Tennessee cropped up. Once again Buell refused to do so. He characterized the mountain country as "almost a desert" and was certain the retreating Confederates would eat up everything in it as they passed through. "The enemy has been driven into the heart of this desert and must go on, for he cannot exist in it. For the same reason we cannot pursue in it with any hope of overtaking him." Buell was certain Bragg would wind up near Nashville; therefore his true course was to go there as soon as possible.[59]

Recognizing that he had devoted too few men to protect his supply lines in the past, Buell now devoted 20,000 troops to hold Kentucky and another 20,000 to protect Union-occupied zones in Tennessee. Perhaps in order to shock Halleck, he argued that an additional 80,000 men would be needed to advance on Chattanooga. Buell admitted there could be no security for Kentucky until East Tennessee was in Union hands, but he could see no prospect of conquering the mountainous region as yet.[60]

Halleck, like McClellan before him, represented Lincoln's opinion that "the capture of East Tennessee should be the main object of your campaign." He interjected his own view that Buell should "in a great measure live upon the country, paying for your supplies where proper and levying contributions when necessary." Halleck pointed out that Lincoln agreed with him. "He does not understand why we cannot march as the enemy marches, live as he lives, and fight as he fights, unless we admit the inferiority of our troops and of our generals."[61]

Buell rejected these views. He pointed out that Bragg had to give up Kentucky largely because he did not have a real line of supply with his home base and reiterated that a mountain campaign was not supportable. Currently, even the railroad to Nashville was not working fully, while Anderson had pulled his civilian crews up to Louisville to rebuild bridges and relay track in Kentucky.[62]

But Federal generals and politicians took lessons from Bragg's Kentucky Campaign. They used it as a marker to judge their own sluggish pace of army mobility and wanted to impart a greater degree of living off the land to improve their operations. "Bragg moved rapidly, living on the country . . . and we are forced in self-defense to imitate [his] example," Sherman later wrote. Halleck also was impressed by the high rate of mobility the Rebels achieved. But Buell pointed out that Bragg was praised for advancing without a supply line into a region filled with food and Confederate sympathizers, while he was condemned for refusing to advance in the same way into a region barren of resources.[63]

In the debate over what level of logistical support was optimal for Federal armies tasked with advancing into the Confederacy, both sides had good arguments. Obviously it was necessary to avoid extremes. An army too heavily burdened with wagons could not move swiftly, while an army that had too little support could not sustain itself in hostile territory. The Confederates operated at the extreme every time they ventured into Union-controlled areas, and the failure of those incursions was predictable on logistical grounds alone.

Yet Washington authorities were fed up with Buell. On October 24 they relieved him of command and placed Maj. Gen. William S. Rosecrans in his stead. Buell's fall was primarily due to logistical difficulties, plus the political weight attached to penetrating East Tennessee and rescuing mountain loyalists.

Ironically, Rosecrans fully agreed that moving his new army to Nashville rather than chasing Bragg through the Appalachians was the correct strategy. He implemented Buell's plan to shift back to the rail system of central Kentucky and Middle Tennessee. Rather than complain, officials allowed their new man to have his way.

Rosecrans was chosen to replace Buell because he had just achieved a defensive victory in protecting Corinth from a major attack. Bragg had left behind 16,000 troops to threaten Union garrisons in the northern part of Mississippi, otherwise they were to bypass those garrisons and move north to cooperate with his movements. A few other troops were added, and Earl Van Dorn wound up with a small but dangerous army in Mississippi. He vigorously attacked the defenses of Corinth on October 3 and 4 with about 20,000 men. Rosecrans's Federals put up fierce resistance. They barely held the town and compelled Van Dorn to retreat.

Van Dorn was the most cavalier general of the war when it came to supply. As during the Pea Ridge Campaign earlier that year, he was willing to risk all on the most slender thread of logistics. When searching the haversacks of Confederates captured at Corinth, Federal troops were stunned to find that many had little more than a handful of parched corn to eat. The Rebels claimed that Van Dorn had promised they could plunder Union stores after taking the town. George R. Elliott of the 2nd Missouri (C.S.) cooked some bread on a stick held over a campfire on the morning of October 3. That was all he had to eat until finding some potatoes three days later. Some Confederate officers refused to let Van Dorn get away with this. Brig. Gen. John S. Bowen preferred charges, among which was an accusation that the major general shamefully neglected to arrange the supply of his troops, "depending entirely upon captures from the enemy." In the ensuing court of inquiry, some witnesses confirmed that food shortages were serious, but others argued that this played no role in the outcome of the campaign. The court exonerated Van Dorn.[64]

Railroad Management under Bragg and Rosecrans

Throughout November and December, the opposing commanders repositioned their armies in Middle Tennessee. Bragg used a mostly intact rail system to move the Army of the Mississippi, soon to be renamed the Army of Tennessee, from Knoxville to Chattanooga and Bridgeport, Alabama. The railroad span over the Tennessee River at Bridgeport was a major building project; Bragg anticipated it would be finished by December 15, but the Nashville and Chattanooga Railroad had many breaks north of the river. Confederate quartermasters pressed rolling stock from lines in other parts of the country to operate the track when the line was ready.[65]

Bragg rebuilt the rail system to support his forward position at Murfreesboro, only thirty miles from Nashville, and to gather food and other material from the region. "The whole of Middle Tennessee south of the Cumberland is tributary to us," he told Adj. Gen. Samuel Cooper. "We are drawing immense supplies of subsistence, with considerable amounts of clothing, leather, & c., from the region just vacated by the enemy." Rebel quartermasters and commissaries purchased this material, Bragg preferring that his officers leave "a full and liberal allowance for domestic use," but he also authorized them to press supplies if needed. The general warned President Davis, however, that this largesse could not continue for long. "We are gleaning the country" so thoroughly that the region could not produce on this scale again "during the war."[66]

Repositioning his army in friendly territory, Bragg could rest easy about the security of his railroad. But Rosecrans had to complete the rebuilding effort inherited from Buell in a generally hostile country. Reaching Nashville by November 7, Rosecrans retained Anderson as superintendent of railroads, and his small corps of civilians continued working alongside the 1st Michigan Engineers and Mechanics. Anderson located two more locomotives, 100 boxcars, and 1,200 other cars of various types to supplement the rolling stock at Nashville.[67]

Railroad work consumed Rosecrans's energy for weeks. Forty-five miles of the 185-mile track between Louisville and Nashville were "so destroyed that it took all the forces we could [muster to] work on it night and [day] for twenty days." Even after that job ended, Federal quartermasters needed an additional twenty-five days to supply the immediate needs of the army and accumulate a stockpile of thirty days' rations before Rosecrans started his new campaign. He did not foresee living off the land because Bragg already was stripping the area, and the Federals did not have enough cavalry to protect large foraging trains.[68]

The collapsed tunnel near Gallatin remained the major rebuilding project in Middle Tennessee. It blocked railroad traffic forty miles north of Nashville, forcing quartermasters to move supplies around it by wagon. The garrison of Nashville had been on half rations for two months and had not received any mail delivery during that time.[69]

Rosecrans wanted to "get the road fully opened and throw in a couple of millions of rations" at Nashville before starting his campaign, but Washington authorities once again became impatient. "Take a lesson from the enemy," Halleck advised him. "Move light, and supply yourself as much as possible with provisions, animals, forage, transportation, etc., in the country you pass through." Rosecrans responded sensibly to this. "The delay is for the opening of railroads, and getting down ammunition and necessaries. Our advance will be wholly unlike the enemy's."[70]

To deal with his supply problem, Rosecrans reduced civilian travel on the railroads within his department. He requested officials at Louisville to stop giving passes to women and severely restrict those given to men on their way to Nashville. The express companies also were shipping large amounts of privately owned material on the cars, taking up valuable space. Rosecrans enjoyed the cooperation of President Guthrie of the Louisville and Nashville Railroad, who sent company workers to help the army repair the line to Nashville. Nevertheless, it took weeks to clean out the tunnel near Gallatin; then Guthrie recruited craftsmen from Virginia to rebuild the woodwork inside it as well as to replace dozens of water tanks at depots along the line. Once everything was ready, Guthrie felt he could shove seventy to eighty carloads of material into Nashville every day.[71]

Rosecrans's rail system spanned two states and two military departments. When his command around Nashville was renamed the Department of the Cumberland in November, the original Department of the Ohio was restricted to central and eastern Kentucky. Major General Wright, who commanded the Ohio department, recognized that his most important job was to protect the rails and support Rosecrans. He used 12,000 men to protect the Louisville and Nashville and to combat guerrillas. He had an additional 13,000 men at Richmond, Danville, and other locations in the Bluegrass. Without the railroad, Rosecrans's "army would be forced to retreat or starve," Wright told one of Halleck's staff officers.[72]

The Stones River Campaign

When Rosecrans finally was ready to advance on Bragg, his quartermasters made no plans to rebuild the Nashville and Chattanooga Railroad until after the fighting had stopped, mimicking the method they had used in previous campaigns. Ironically, even though the enemy lay only thirty miles away, the Stones River Campaign involved some of the worst logistical and supply problems encountered by any Federal army in the West. From almost the beginning of the move on December 26 until it ended with the occupation of Murfreesboro on January 4, 1863, the campaign devolved not only into a fight for possession of territory but also a fight for survival among the advancing Unionists.

Rosecrans's chief of staff encouraged the corps leaders to "move very light" at the start of the campaign, with three days' rations in the men's haversacks and two days' food in wagons. Additional supplies would arrive by wagon trains hauling material from Nashville to the advancing army. If the supply system had remained intact, this would have been adequate. But only a couple of days into the campaign, John Hunt Morgan mounted a raid on the Louisville and Nashville Railroad in Kentucky and caused serious disruption. Wright estimated it would take "some weeks probably to repair it." "Engage competent superintendents for the work, who can tell what timber is needed," he told Brig. Gen. Jeremiah T. Boyle, commander of the District of Kentucky, "and I will set quartermasters to procure and forward it." Wright also urged him to send rations to Nashville via the Cumberland River. Only light boats could negotiate the river, and Wright could find but one vessel at Cincinnati that was suitable. He hoped Boyle could find more at Louisville and detail guards to ride on the boats.[73]

By January 5, 1863, Wright sent off fifteen loaded boats from Cincinnati, Louisville, and Evansville. All of them ascended the Cumberland to Nashville with gunboat escort. But the general also managed to get a few light-draft steamers up the Green River to Bowling Green, bypassing the break in the railroad, then shipping the material by rail south to Nashville. The Federals were fortunate that the Cumberland and Green Rivers happened to be rising at this time.[74]

As Wright scrambled to the rear, Rosecrans scrambled at the front because Bragg launched his large cavalry force to find and destroy Federal wagon trains. In one of the most impressive examples of logistical raiding on the battlefield, Brig. Gen. Joseph Wheeler led a brigade of Rebel horsemen in a circling movement around the Union army and devastated Rosecrans's wagon trains. Wheeler destroyed 250 wagons, mostly on December 30–31, 1862, causing much suffering among the Yankees. Union soldiers resorted to cutting off chunks of dead horses on the Stones River battlefield when hungry.[75]

Despite these strategic and tactical interruptions of their supply system, the Federals stubbornly held on at Stones River when Bragg launched a surprise attack against their right wing on December 31. In one of the bloodiest battles of the war, the Confederates drove that wing three miles, inflicted enormous losses of manpower and material, but in the end failed to win a decisive victory. Over the next three days, the Federals continued to hold their position on the field. Bragg finally decided to withdraw to Tullahoma and Shelbyville on a report that Rosecrans was receiving large reinforcements.

Rosecrans's logistical problems did not end with the finish of this campaign. His army needed to replace 5,000 small arms and thirty-six field pieces lost on the battlefield. Virtually every category of material was reduced by the campaign, ranging from 1,762 camp kettles to 16,215 pairs of pants. It was estimated that nearly 20,000 sick and wounded men of both armies crowded the many hospitals in and around Murfreesboro.[76]

While the rainy season was current, quartermasters shoved as much material up the Cumberland River as possible. Fleets of steamboats arrived at Nashville, thirty of them on January 18, twenty-three on January 28, and forty-two on February 7. Each fleet was escorted by gunboats. This mode of supply proved so effective that Rosecrans wished he could dispense entirely with the railroad and its 185 miles of troublesome, exposed track. He estimated it would not only be more secure but also cheaper to transport material by steamer. The Louisville and Nashville Railroad was fully operational only for seven months and twelve days during the fiscal year that ended June 30, 1863, lending support to Rosecrans's contention that water-borne transportation was superior to rail-based logistics. But the steamboats were not immune to attack. Wheeler launched a foray against Cumberland River shipping early in January, capturing and burning several transports before they could reach Nashville. Not until mid-February did the Louisville and Nashville Railroad become fully operational.[77]

Federal troops had endured much privation since Buell left Corinth. Fred Knefler estimated his 79th Indiana had moved more than 700 miles from October 1862 to January 1863. For most of this time, the men existed on half rations, eating mostly fresh meat, with coffee and sugar to wash it down. At times two days' rations were issued to last for a week, the men supplementing these with parched corn. Half the troops were in need of shoes much of this time.[78]

Bragg's supply status weakened after his withdrawal from Murfreesboro. Once settled in their camps at Tullahoma and Shelbyville, Rebel soldiers scrounged around the countryside so that the general issued orders deploring their widespread pillaging. “Such wanton destruction would be a high military offense if committed in the country of an enemy,” read an order issued by the headquarters of Maj. Gen. Jones Withers’s division, “among our friends and fellow citizens it is an unpardonable outrage.” The fact that gray-clad men were eating out Middle Tennessee seemed to play into Confederate strategy. John Crittenden of the 34th Alabama assumed Bragg would lure the Federals deeper into the South to increase their logistical problems. “They cannot depend on getting supplies in this part of the country, for we have nearly consumed nearly all that can be found.”[79]

Federal soldiers also foraged without authority near Murfreesboro, eliciting similar orders from their generals condemning the practice. Meanwhile, material arrived at Nashville by steamboat and was carted to Murfreesboro by wagon. Before long the railroad operated between the two cities, and stockpiles of food and other material began to grow in preparation for the next move south.[80]

Conclusion

In the sprawling western theater of operations, a combination of geography, commercial railroads, and the placement of major waterways conspired to create two major zones of military operations. The Mississippi River valley was one, and the region embracing the line of railroads linking Louisville, Nashville, Chattanooga, and Atlanta, often called the central zone, was the other. Federal authorities had tacitly recognized this division early in the conflict, establishing separate troop concentrations in each, with Grant the major commander in the river valley and Sherman, Buell, and Rosecrans the major leaders in the central zone.

The Confederates arrayed their forces across the expanse of the western theater with no concentration at any one place early in the war. After the fall of Fort Donelson, Rebel authorities veered toward the opposite policy and concentrated all the men they could into one major field army. They shifted that force to defend the Mississippi Valley, virtually giving up the central zone. That move compelled Halleck to concentrate as well, shifting Buell’s forces west to the valley. From April to June, both sides overconcentrated until Halleck broke up his grand army and sent Buell back to the central zone of operations. Not long after that, Bragg took most of the Confederate army back to that zone as well.

The war in the West had finally settled down into a natural division of Federal forces in these two zones of operations. The major Confederate army in the West remained in the central zone for nearly the rest of the war, while a new field army assembled in Mississippi to protect Vicksburg.

The Federals had the best line of advance imaginable in the broad waters of the Mississippi River. All quartermasters had to do was contract with privately owned steamer captains for the transport of men, animals, and material. The river never ran dry, and guerrilla attacks on boats never stopped the flow of supplies.

Logistics in the central zone of operations were more complicated and difficult, however, because the Federals there heavily depended on railroads. The Tennessee and Cumberland Rivers provided some alternate modes of shipping up to Eastport and Nashville but not farther. Union troops aiming to take Chattanooga or Atlanta had no choice—they had to rely primarily on rail transport. Therefore it is in the central zone of operations that we must look for the main story of railroad management in the western theater from late 1862 to the end of the war.

Federal commanders struggled against a learning curve in 1861–62. They had to improvise methods of repairing, managing, and protecting rail lines, doing only a modestly successful job of it. Eastern commanders were already developing an effective system of railroad management based on the employment of skilled railroad men from civilian life, organized in large numbers and headed by railroad managers with military commissions. Unfortunately it was not until the early months of 1864 that this system came to the West.

Instead, western commanders worked under a spirit of improvisation rather than professionalism when it came to railroad management. They also guarded their turf by tending to vest control of their rail system in the hands of soldiers rather than civilians. John B. Anderson was an exception, to be sure, but he was not the dynamic, innovative manager that was needed for the job. He paled in comparison in these ways to Daniel McCallum and Herman Haupt in Virginia, who created and honed to near perfection a system of railroad management for military purposes unequaled in global history.

Stuck in an improvisational mode of thinking and a myopic focus on using military personnel, the Federals suffered a major logistical crisis in the central theater of operations during the latter half of 1863. After Stones

River their next step was to secure the remainder of Middle Tennessee, which did not prove too difficult. But then they had to ascend the Cumberland Plateau and enter the heart of the Appalachian Highlands. The mountains accentuated, enlarged, and intensified all the logistical problems Union forces had experienced thus far. No one at Federal headquarters anticipated this—no one was prepared for it—and instead they just reacted to crisis when it descended upon them in the fall of 1863.

2

GRANT AND VICKSBURG

When Halleck dispersed his large army group after the fall of Corinth, he postponed a Federal push into the Deep South for many months. He can be forgiven for not utilizing the Mississippi Central Railroad to support a land invasion of that state, but he can be criticized for not sending even a small force down the river against Vicksburg during the summer of 1862. At that time the city was more vulnerable than it would be in the fall or winter. Halleck did not believe he had enough troops to hit Vicksburg as well as do the many other things needed that summer. "As soon as the new troops are organized in the West the fall campaign will be opened there with energy," he told Sherman in late August. "All we can hope to do for the next month is to hold our positions and prepare for an onward movement."[1]

The Mississippi River was the true line of operations for any force trying to reopen its navigation. Frank P. Blair Jr. was so strongly convinced that clearing the Mississippi would bring down the entire rebellion that he had argued the Federals should put operations against Richmond on hold in the fall of 1861 while concentrating on the western river. He thought it would have been cheaper to transport and supply an army by steamers on the Mississippi than by railroads in Virginia. His arguments, of course, fell on deaf ears.[2]

Grant's North Mississippi Campaign, Chickasaw Bayou, and Arkansas Post

When Grant planned a major push against Vicksburg in the fall of 1862, rather than to the river, he looked primarily to the rail system as his support. Ever since June 1862 the Federals had been repairing and using the extensive rail system of western Kentucky, West Tennessee, and northern

Mississippi to support their garrisons. With so much invested in this rail system, Grant gave little thought to a river-borne advance toward Vicksburg. The Battle of Corinth greatly influenced him in this way. When Van Dorn attacked the Union-held town on October 3–4, the Confederates nearly overwhelmed the defenders. Some Rebel troops actually penetrated to the center of town before they were repulsed. In the end Rosecrans won a defensive victory as Grant tried to coordinate troops from other garrisons to intercept Van Dorn's retreat, nearly doing so at the Battle of Davis Bridge on October 5.

Corinth and Davis Bridge were two of many incidents in the border struggle between Union and Confederate forces in north Mississippi. The opposing sides had been sparring with each other in the upper counties of the state since early summer to forage from the countryside, gather intelligence, and temporarily occupy towns such as Holly Springs, evacuating them as soon as the enemy approached in force. This activity tended to draw Union commanders' attention away from the river and toward the rail system that supported their garrisons.

But the Battle of Corinth was far bigger and more dangerous than any other threat to the Federal presence in north Mississippi. In response Grant decided to resume the strategic offensive. His first step was to enlarge and strengthen the Union presence in the region. Towns like LaGrange and Grand Junction, Tennessee, had been temporarily abandoned in the early fall, but now Grant prepared to reoccupy them in force. Three divisions moved from Corinth and Bolivar, Tennessee. "If found practicable, I will go on to Holly Springs, and maybe Grenada, completing railroad and telegraph as I go," Grant announced. Finally, a Federal general was planning to start operations into the Deep South from this region. "I hope for an active campaign on the Mississippi this fall," Halleck told Grant. But note his phrase "on the Mississippi," meaning a river-borne expedition rather than a rail-based approach. From the beginning there was a divergence of opinion between the two generals about the proper logistical support for a strike against Vicksburg.[3]

On the move to LaGrange and Grand Junction, Federal troops engaged in widespread acts of plundering, leading to general orders condemning these acts. Grant authorized the holding of pay from all soldiers in a division that vandalized private property. "Confiscation acts were never intended to

GRANT'S NORTH MISSISSIPPI CAMPAIGN

be executed by soldiers, and if they were the General Government should have full benefit of all property." The Federals also gathered food for men and forage for animals through regular channels managed by officers, who issued receipts that could be redeemed at a future time if the owners proved to be loyal citizens.[4]

Grant concentrated his three divisions in the area of LaGrange and Grand Junction by November 8 and began to repair the rail lines north and south of the two towns. The Confederates reacted to this move by making

Holly Springs their main forward base. In an effort to take the next step—capturing Holly Springs and moving to the Little Tallahatchie River—Grant instructed Sherman to march three divisions from Memphis toward the southeast to meet his force somewhere near the river. "We will of course supply ourselves from the country with everything it affords necessary for the army," he told him. "I may occupy Holly Springs for the purpose of finishing the railroad as far south as possible and getting our supplies also as far in that direction as possible." Grant wanted to maintain a stockpile of 100,000 rations as a reserve for his large force, indicating a combination of fixed lines of communications supplemented by foraging from the countryside.[5]

Foreseeing his rail system stretching deeper into Mississippi, Grant requested more rolling stock. If he was to use the Mississippi Central Railroad as far as Grenada plus the line that ran southeastward from Memphis to join it, he needed around six more locomotives. He already had twenty-two engines, but only eighteen of these were operable. Halleck was concerned by this request. He told Grant that engines were in short supply and wondered why the general was contemplating a move along the rail line at all. "Operations in Northern Mississippi must be limited to rapid marches upon any collected forces of the enemy, feeding as far as possible upon the country. The enemy must be turned by a movement down the river from Memphis as soon as sufficient force can be collected."[6]

Grant acted as if Halleck's message was a suggestion rather than a clear directive. He continued to plan a major campaign down the railroad, forcing the Confederates to evacuate Holly Springs by mid-November. It seems as if he did not take seriously the notion of a river-borne expedition from Memphis until he began to hear rumors that Maj. Gen. John A. McClernand was raising new regiments in Illinois for such an operation. It is true that McClernand, a former division commander under Grant, had gone directly to Washington, D.C., where he talked both Lincoln and Stanton into supporting his effort to lead an expedition against Vicksburg. Grant did not trust him to command such a force and began to think of mounting an expedition of his own by way of the river, with Sherman in charge. Halleck helped Grant in this regard, telling him on November 12 that, as commander of the Department of the Tennessee, he had the right to use any troops or officers in his department as he chose. So long as neither Lincoln nor Stanton issued a direct order for McClernand to take command of the expedition (which they never did) or changed the date of his commission to predate Grant's, the latter had the upper hand in dealing with his overly ambitious subordinate.[7]

The best way to take the wind out of McClernand's sails was to mount the kind of expedition he was preparing before he left Springfield, Illinois, where he was then busy organizing the new regiments. Ironically, Sherman would use many of the newly raised units McClernand was sending down to Memphis. But Grant hesitated before committing himself to the river-borne expedition. It is ironic that the man who so brilliantly used river logistics on the Tennessee and Cumberland to capture Fort Henry and Fort Donelson was now so reluctant to do so on the Mississippi against Vicksburg. In fact, his first move after receiving Halleck's assurance of support regarding McClernand was to concentrate even more troops on the rail-based approach through northern Mississippi. He ordered Sherman to march three divisions from Memphis to join him in an attack on the Confederate defenses along the Little Tallahatchie River.[8]

Grant was helped by the fact that McClernand was stuck in Springfield until Halleck issued him orders to take the field, and the general in chief avoided doing that for as long as possible. Meanwhile, Sherman received fourteen new regiments at Memphis. "The new troops come full of the idea of a more vigorous prosecution of the war," he told Halleck, "meaning destruction and plunder."[9]

Pushing deeper into Mississippi intensified Grant's railroad focus. George Pride told Lewis B. Parsons, the quartermaster at Saint Louis, that Grant needed six locomotives and 200 additional cars. Pride suggested he go to Indiana, Michigan, and other states in the Old Northwest to find these vehicles because "our army cannot move without them." Halleck was irritated by this. He had already told Grant not to open up any more railroad mileage in north Mississippi.[10]

Grant moved his three divisions from Holly Springs with three days' rations in everyone's haversacks. Quartermasters stocked an additional five days' rations in each division's wagon train and transported 200,000 rations as far south as the railroad was operable. Ordnance officers kept two hundred rounds of small-arms ammunition available for every man, and Grant also authorized some limited foraging from the countryside to supplement his rail supply. In addition to Sherman's three divisions from Memphis, a large force of infantry and cavalry crossed the Mississippi River from Helena, Arkansas, to penetrate eastward toward Grenada, threatening railroads to the rear of the Confederate force lining the south bank of the Little Tallahatchie. This combination proved too much for the outnumbered Rebel army, which abandoned its position at the river in early December. Grant moved on to occupy Oxford without opposition.[11]

Sherman's men went a bit crazy with plunder as they moved into enemy territory from Memphis, compelling him to issue a stern order against "indiscriminate and extensive plundering." "Our mission is to maintain, not to violate, all laws, human and divine," Sherman continued. "Plundering is hurtful to our cause and to the honorable tone which characterized the army of a great nation." He reminded his men that the Federal government "undertakes to pay, clothe, and feed her troops well, and is prepared to do it. The officers and soldiers have no right to look to any other quarter for compensation and subsistence."[12]

As soon as Grant settled down at Oxford, he wondered if he should continue along the Mississippi Central Railroad. "How far south would you like me to go?" he asked the general in chief. Extending farther along the railroad might be beneficial, considering the Confederates had not offered much resistance thus far. Would it be possible to support several divisions all the way south along the Mississippi Central to Jackson and then attack Vicksburg from the east? For the time being Grant seemed to think not. With his present force, "it would not be safe to go beyond Grenada and attempt to hold present line of communication," he told Halleck on December 4.[13]

Halleck had definite ideas about this question—Grant should not think about moving all the way to Jackson by an overland route. He should destroy the railroad south of the Little Tallahatchie River, abandon all ground south of that stream, and move all the troops possible to the river for transportation by steamer to Vicksburg. Halleck set a date, December 20, for the start of this river-borne expedition. All Grant needed to do in north Mississippi was to secure a defensive line from Memphis to Corinth.[14]

Even with this second set of direct instructions, Grant continued to hesitate about his next move. By December 8 he knew it was not possible to hesitate longer. Grant estimated that with his present capacity for repairing and protecting railroads, he might be able to operate the Mississippi Central down to Grenada, but it would be impossible to do so farther south toward Jackson. He could stockpile supplies at Grenada, break away from a fixed line of supply, and march quickly to the Mississippi capital while living off the countryside. Once at Jackson, Grant felt certain that Vicksburg would be doomed. If a river-borne expedition also could threaten that city from the west, the combined weight of these two Federal approaches had a good chance of success.[15]

Missing from Grant's calculations was the question of Confederate reaction. If the enemy stopped his army part way between Grenada and Jackson, it could lead to disastrous consequences. His men could not afford to be cut loose from a line of supply for long unless they continued to move toward some point that offered them logistical support. The only solution to this problem was for the river-borne expedition to ascend the Yazoo River just north of Vicksburg and lodge on the high bluffs east of the bottomland. If Grant's mobile force could make contact with that Yazoo lodgment, it could be supplied by steamer at the end of its long march from Grenada.

Grant seriously considered this risky plan, banking on his ability to move fast and defeat any Confederates who stood in the way. It was a more dangerous plan than the one he actually adopted in May 1863 when moving east from the Mississippi River near Bruinsburg in the most mobile phase of the Vicksburg Campaign. But that bold move lay six months in the future, after a series of failed efforts to place his army in position to threaten the city. In December 1862 there was every reason to choose a less risky course, and Grant did so. In a letter to Brig. Gen. Frederick Steele, whose command at Helena, Arkansas, would play a role in whatever the general did in Mississippi, Grant declared that he would send a major force down the river as the main threat against Vicksburg. Interestingly, he did not indicate what the divisions remaining under his personal control in central Mississippi would do.[16]

On December 8 Grant instructed Sherman to return to Memphis, organize the river expedition, and leave the city by the twentieth. As late as December 19, Grant indicated he still was thinking about advancing his three divisions south, capturing Grenada and Jackson, and then approaching Vicksburg from the east. He sent Pride to Saint Louis and Chicago to acquire material "for a rapid construction and for running the railroad east from Vicksburg." The aide had authority to hire civilian railroad men, fix their wages, and provide transportation for them and the acquired materials to Cairo, where army transports would take everything south. Grant did not indicate how to get the men and material to the heart of Mississippi, whether by railroad or by the river.[17]

Grant knew the overland approach was hazardous. "I am extended now like a Peninsula into an enemies country," he wrote on December 15, "with a large Army depending for their daily bread upon keeping open a line of rail-road running one hundred & ninety miles through an enemy's country, or at least through territory occupied by a people terribly embittered and hostile to us."[18]

The Federals had been supplementing their army rations by foraging off the countryside since the start of the campaign. They found sweet potatoes, sheep, hogs, and beef cattle in abundance in some places. But Cyrus F. Boyd of the 15th Iowa knew it could not last. "We have eat out clean about one county since we came here and will soon have to move to new pastures," he wrote in his diary. A week later, with dwindling resources and trouble getting the rail system up to speed, his comrades received little more than two-thirds of what they needed to eat.[19]

Anyone familiar with the Federal capacity for repairing and operating the railroad in enemy territory that supported Sherman's Atlanta Campaign will recognize that the lack of this high level of logistical support hampered Grant's invasion of Mississippi. Although he had converted to the plan of hiring civilian workers, there is no evidence it had been done to a significant degree. Grant was still relying on soldiers to do a lot of labor on the railroad in late 1862.

Even though the Confederates had torn up little track when they left the area, mostly burning a few bridges, Grant's troops took a good deal of time to get the railroad in order. Brig. Gen. John McArthur detailed a large portion of his division to repairing railroad bridges near Abbeville, Mississippi, the first stop south of the Little Tallahatchie River. Large details were taken from every regiment in the division, supplemented by a company of Col. Josiah W. Bissell's Engineer Regiment of the West (the only engineer regiment in Grant's department). Only four of the ten bridges between Holly Springs and Waterford had been burned by Confederate forces, but it took much time to rebuild them. Engineers measured and estimated exactly what kind of timbers they needed for each bridge, after which the timbers were sawed and mortised at several sawmills along the track. Transported to bridge sites, these were then fitted together by soldier-laborers. It took almost three weeks to get the railroad working properly in this region, with the first train rolling into Oxford on December 18.[20]

Just when the task of rebuilding the railroad seemed finished, the Confederates dealt a devastating blow. Lt. Gen. John C. Pemberton authorized the consolidation of his cavalry forces under Major General Van Dorn, who would then bypass Union troops and hit the railroad at a vulnerable spot. Holly Springs was a major supply depot inadequately protected by a scratch force of detailed men from several regiments, under the command of a regimental colonel whose troops were not even part of the garrison. This situation was symptomatic of Grant's lax attitude toward protecting his rail system. He tended to accumulate all the manpower possible at the forward edge of his advance and neglected the protection of key points of his rearward communications, relying on small numbers of troops inadequately protected by fortifications. Van Dorn attacked Holly Springs early on the morning of December 20 with devastating effect. His cavalrymen overwhelmed the garrison, captured 1,500 troops, and destroyed 1.5 million dollars' worth of Federal property. Railroad resources, including the depot and a couple of trains, also went up in smoke. The Confederates evaded pursuing Union cavalry and returned to Pemberton's army with only light losses.[21]

The destruction of Holly Springs resulted in more than the need to rebuild an important supply depot; it also had an emotional and psychological effect on the Federals. Grant gave up any hope of continuing his approach to Vicksburg by land. He was out of immediate communication with Sherman at Memphis, and thus could not tell his subordinate of his decision, because Forrest was hitting the Union rail network in West Tennessee at the same time. Actually, Forrest did more physical damage than Van Dorn since he operated for a longer time, hit several towns, and tore up miles of track as well as burned depots and bridges. Grant could not even estimate the damage to his logistical network, much less hope to restore it quickly after these two mounted raids.

Federal troops reoccupied Holly Springs by December 22, but they were in a foul mood. The destruction of the depot broke their tolerance of local civilians, resulting in a notable increase in plundering for the rest of the campaign. The 11th Iowa, for example, went on half rations, so the men intensified their foraging. They also freely stole anything within reach, "carrying to their tents couches, rockers, tables, books, bric-a-brac—in fact, all kinds of household articles."[22] Van Dorn's raid worsened the tendency of many Union soldiers to view destruction and confiscation of private property as legitimate weapons. Buildings that had survived Confederate destruction now became targets of Federal vandalism.

Sherman, of course, was unaware of these developments. Having taken one of his divisions back to Memphis after receiving Grant's order to organize a river expedition, he busied himself with the preparations needed to move 30,000 men with their equipment and supplies 200 miles south to strike at Vicksburg. Sherman organized the largest river-borne expedition of the war. He was an excellent logistician and was well served by the quartermasters in charge of providing transportation and supplies. When Quartermaster Parsons received an order on December 11 to round up steamers for Sherman, he had a difficult time finding enough vessels for such a large force. There were no more than ten boats immediately available at Saint Louis, and coal was temporarily in short supply. With great energy, Parsons identified sixty-seven steamers at other locations, quickly made contracts and charters, and headed them toward Memphis. Acting Adm. David D. Porter, the newly appointed commander of the Mississippi Squadron, provided twenty warships of all sizes to accompany the expedition. Sherman left Memphis on December 22, only two days after Grant's target date, with 20,000 men. He picked up another 10,000 troops at Helena and was then off for Vicksburg.[23]

Each of Sherman's four divisions needed about a dozen steamboats to transport men, animals, and guns as well as a number of supply vessels and hospital boats. Parsons had been able to acquire enough coal and wood to get the fleet to the vicinity of Vicksburg and had arranged for 66,000 bushels of coal to be carried on boats and barges to follow the fleet. Sherman took along 1.6 million rations, 600,000 more than planned, in case he had to supply Grant's force if it made contact with his expedition on the Yazoo River.[24]

"General Sherman is a trump," Parsons told Halleck, "and makes things move. I like his business mode of doing things, his promptness and decision." The quartermaster accompanied the expedition to send empty boats upriver as soon as possible to continue the transportation of needed articles and men to other commands in the West. As the largest assemblage of vessels on the Mississippi River, Sherman's expedition made a "magnificent spectacle." The boat captains maintained a tight formation, stopping only to take on wood if needed or to release a shore detachment to find guerrillas who had fired on the boats as they glided past. Sherman ordered retaliation for every such incident, and his men burned every building they could find in the vicinity, often without any act of violence to justify it.[25]

The operation started with an attempt to cut the only railroad leading toward Vicksburg from the west. After making his first landfall near the city, Sherman sent a brigade from Milliken's Bend, on the Louisiana shore, to wreck the Vicksburg, Shreveport, and Texas Railroad. The few Confederates in the area fled as the Federals marched twenty-five miles into the interior, tore up bridges and track, and destroyed a lot of material before returning to Milliken's Bend.

Sherman's fleet entered the Yazoo River on December 26 and landed troops on the bottomland stretching eastward toward Walnut Hills, the high bluffs upon which Vicksburg is located. The Federals struggled through the tangled, swampy bottomland against a small but well-positioned enemy who offered stiff resistance. Although outnumbering the Confederates under Brig. Gen. Stephen D. Lee, Sherman foundered for several days before launching an attack on December 29 that was a bloody failure. Heavy fog forced the Federals to cancel a planned assault on Haynes' Bluff a few miles up the Yazoo. Then rain descended, portending a rise in the river. Sherman evacuated his position on the Yazoo and gathered the boats at Milliken's Bend.

It was fortunate that Sherman refused to let Parsons send away empty boats, for he needed them to evacuate his men from the bottomland. These steamboats served as the temporary home of his troops for a full month as Sherman and then McClernand, who superseded him on January 4, 1863, tried to figure out what to do next. Their attention turned to Arkansas Post, a Confederate stronghold forty miles up the Arkansas River. Troops from the post had seized a supply vessel called the *Blue Wing,* loaded with ordnance stores and mail, and thus posed a threat to the expedition's supply line.

The Federals had all the advantages in their strike against Arkansas Post. On January 11 they cut off the 5,000-man garrison by land while the gunboats engaged Fort Hindman, disabling its guns. McClernand's troops approached the fort and a connecting outer line of trenches. By late afternoon the garrison surrendered, resulting in a rich haul of prisoners, weapons, and supplies falling into Union hands.

But capturing Arkansas Post was no compensation for the failure to reopen Mississippi River navigation. McClernand took his command back to Milliken's Bend and Young's Point, only a few miles upstream from Vicksburg. The relative ease with which Sherman had transported 30,000 men down the Mississippi and kept them supplied with a string of river steamers contrasted sharply with Grant's logistical and supply problems on his overland attempt at Vicksburg. The Holly Springs raid had left Grant's forces "almost *rationless,*" in the words of David Herrick Gile, a member of McPherson's staff. This forced the Federals in northern Mississippi to feed off the countryside to a great degree. Heavily guarded foraging parties roamed twenty miles from garrison towns to strip the countryside of edibles, using mills within reach to grind corn and other grains. The Federals intended "to get along some way" rather than starve.[26]

The lesson of Holly Springs seemed evident to everyone. The Mississippi River was a more secure line of operations than the Mississippi Central Railroad. Within hours of Van Dorn's raid, McPherson had suggested to Grant that he shift most of his men to Memphis for transport down the river while the rest retired farther north. He also urged Grant to go down the Mississippi and supersede McClernand, whose competence was questioned by many. "Some plan of operations other than that of keeping up long lines of railroads should be adopted," wrote division commander John W. Denver.[27]

Grant needed no convincing. The combined effects of Van Dorn and Forrest "have cut me off from supplies so that farther advance by this route is perfectly impracticable. The country does not afford supplies for troops, and but a limited supply of forage." His army was able to live for a short time by relieving citizens of their goods, but that could not last long. Grant also tried to provide for civilian needs in the area. He mandated that foraging parties allow families enough food to last sixty days, but if army needs worsened, troops need not follow that directive. "If suffering must fall on one or the other, the citizen must bear it."[28]

Many of Grant's units found ample food and made the most of it. "We were ordered to subsist upon the country," noted J. P. Coulter of the 12th Iowa, "and as the people seemed to have an abundant supply we helped ourselves without much reluctance, the men faring rather sumptuously." But many of Grant's men occupied areas already cleaned out during the past month. Lucius Barber of the 15th Illinois recalled that his comrades spent several days in the Abbeville area on quarter rations after the Holly Springs raid. "The pangs of hunger actually began to gnaw at our vitals. The country round about was poor and barren. All we could find was the small pea-beans."[29]

Grant now repositioned his divisions to restore the static defense that had prevailed for months prior to the beginning of his Mississippi Central campaign. Adhering to Halleck's directive, he sought to maintain a position along the Memphis and Charleston Railroad to Corinth. It took several weeks to complete this repositioning and to rebuild the tracks torn up by Van Dorn and Forrest. A cavalry brigade destroyed the Mississippi Central south of the Little Tallahatchie River, so the Confederates could not use it for a while after the Union pull back. Grant also abandoned the railroad between Columbus, Kentucky, and Jackson, Tennessee, shifting all troops from LaGrange and Grand Junction. He continued to hold the rail lines out of Memphis to Corinth and then from there to Jackson. This represented a reduction of the Union stance in West Tennessee compared to the days of Halleck the previous summer.[30]

Before completing this repositioning, the Federals worked hard to rebuild the rail system wrecked by Van Dorn and Forrest. On December 23 Grant thought it would take only five days, but at that time the Confederates had not even finished their raids. By the twenty-eighth, when Van Dorn retreated but Forrest was still at large, Grant feared that the line between Columbus and Jackson would take several weeks to rebuild. This was a major factor in his developing plan to concentrate on Memphis as the fountain of all rail traffic in his department, with reports indicating that the Memphis and Charleston Railroad had suffered little damage during these raids.[31]

Van Dorn had torn up little track and few bridges in northern Mississippi—Forrest on the other hand had committed extensive damage across a wide area of West Tennessee. The latter became the heart of the reconstruction program that kicked into gear in late December and lasted until late January. Brig. Gen. Thomas A. Davies, commander at Columbus, organized a construction train and crew that left town on December 24 with four preconstructed bridges and 1,500 feet of trestle work. Davies held that crew at Columbus a couple of days on reports that Forrest and some guerrillas were still on the loose. "Accounts vary so much that it is hard to tell how long it will take to get through," he told Halleck. His earliest estimate for the completion of work was January 15. After Brig. Gen. James M. Tuttle replaced Davies as district commander, he pressed area civilians to provide a larger workforce. The Federals also hired black refugees. Work crews finished repairs in northern Mississippi by about January 10 but continued to labor on those in West Tennessee.[32]

When Grant moved his headquarters to Memphis on January 10, he found that a shortage of steamers hampered his plans to shift large numbers of troops to the Vicksburg area. McClernand had held on to all his boats, so Grant instructed him to discharge any not absolutely needed. There were twenty-five steamers at Helena, but eight of them were loaded with supplies for McClernand and six were occupied with the cotton trade. Coal stockpiles were almost depleted, so Brig. Gen. Willis Gorman, the commander at Helena, recruited one hundred blacks to cut timber and stack it in wood yards along the river. From Saint Louis, Quartermaster Robert Allen sent messages for all available steamers on the Mississippi and Ohio to go to Memphis and transport 16,000 troops downriver.[33]

Should Grant have risked a continued forward advance after the destruction of his depot at Holly Springs, hoping he could find enough food in Mississippi to feed his army on the march to Jackson? This depended on how much food could be obtained from the countryside. While some of his men found ample provisions in some areas of north Mississippi, many others suffered. There was enough food for only part of Grant's army, and even that lasted but a short while. It would have been a high risk to march the entire distance to Jackson or Vicksburg without a viable line of supply.[34]

Placing all his strategic hopes on the river was the right move for Grant to make, but that does not mean he experienced no logistical problems with river steamers. The accumulation of troops and animals in the Sherman-McClernand expedition was the largest seen on the Mississippi, and it strained the steamboat resources. McClernand tried to retain as many vessels as possible. "To be caught without such stores, particularly, *ordnance Stores,* at so remote a point as the vicinity of Vicksburgh, with the river infested by guerillas in the rear, would indeed be a dilemma," he told Grant. Likewise, Porter had to employ most of his gunboats to cooperate with the expedition and protect the steamers that supplied it. He could barely send a handful of armed vessels up the Cumberland River to help Rosecrans in Middle Tennessee.[35]

Bottomlands

Only by diligent work on the part of quartermasters in Saint Louis, Cairo, Louisville, and Cincinnati could enough steamers be found to transport Grant's men from Memphis by January 20, 1863. When the first contingent landed near Vicksburg, it found glutinous black mud lining the banks of the great river. In many places the only camping ground lay on top of the levees that lined the banks. Cyrus Boyd of the 15th Iowa noted that one levee, which stood ten feet tall and twenty feet wide, was "all the dry ground we can find." As he walked for two miles along its top, he found everything from hospitals to graves planted on it. Everything soldiers needed, from stockpiles of supplies to living quarters, was perched on the levee, with a long string of steamboats unloading stores onto its narrow confines. Grant agreed with McClernand that it was best to retain as many steamboats as possible in the area to evacuate the troops from their precarious campground if needed. Without the boats, disaster was a short step away.[36]

But Grant could not afford to stay in the bottomlands forever. His first thought was to bypass Vicksburg and operate south of the city, where the Confederates had not fortified the bluffs on the east side. A canal the Federals had started the previous summer across the neck of land called De Soto Point offered some promise. The general ordered work resumed on it early in 1863. Few observers had much faith in the canal since it was not located to take full advantage of the river's current. The Confederates also could erect batteries to cover its southern end.[37]

Bypassing Vicksburg rather than attacking Walnut Hills from the Yazoo River was the right course to pursue, but exactly how to do it was the problem. Grant detached units to explore several possible routes east and west of the Mississippi, all of them through miry, flooded bottomlands. None of those options panned out. The rest of Grant's troops continued to live precariously along the levees a few miles north of Vicksburg, surviving the winter rains and chilly temperatures. They depended on a string of chartered and contracted boats to keep them supplied, to transport their sick to Northern hospitals, and to evacuate everyone if spring rains threatened to inundate or isolate their camps. Illness soared among the troops, cooped up as many were along the narrow levees, living in mud and exposed to the cold spells that swept in from the west.[38]

Grant knew that levees were the saving of his men. When the weather dried now and then, some soldiers moved their camps onto the bottomland just west of the levees. Observers predicted, however, that this ground would be inundated by six feet of water if someone cut the levee upstream and let the river flow in. No Rebel sympathizer managed to do that, but spring rains could easily flood wide expanses of the bottomlands on both sides of the river. During a slow rise in water level in late February, Sherman warned Porter: "Our Camps are almost afloat and the road worse than I can describe. We are literally mud bound. Should the River rise one foot more we will be almost forced to take to the Levee and trees." The general feared there were not enough boats to evacuate his entire Fifteenth Corps in case of emergency. "We had no sure place of refuge except the narrow levee, and such steamboats as remained abreast of our camps," he remembered in his memoirs.[39]

Reports of widespread illness among the troops circulated in Northern newspapers, compelling Sherman to assert that the steamboat link provided food, medical supplies, and evacuation of the sick without major problems. "Our army is admirably supplied in all respects," he told a correspondent on March 15. Three chartered steamers were fitted up as hospital boats, with another stationed at Helena. As far as they could, Federal foragers penetrated the interior and found food, horses, and mules. Grant relied mostly on the countryside for animal forage because that was the most bulky and expensive item to transport on steamboats. His men found enough horses and mules to replace those lost in the Army of the Tennessee and shipped many north for issue to other commands.[40]

But it can only be said that quartermasters were barely able to supply the civilian steamboats Grant's operations against Vicksburg demanded. When he began the Yazoo Pass expedition through the Mississippi Delta beginning in February and extending into March, Grant imposed an additional burden on these officers. The expedition consisted of gunboats and steamers to transport troops through a torturous system of narrow rivers. The steamers had to be small and capable of negotiating the twisting waterways extending from a point opposite Helena to the Yazoo River. Quartermaster Parsons noted that Grant needed boats less than 200 feet long. These smaller craft were capable of carrying only 500 to 800 troops. In contrast, larger river steamers of more than 200 feet in length could carry from 1,200 to 2,000 soldiers. Such small steamers could only be found on the upper reaches of the Ohio River and were already in short supply. Rosecrans needed material shipped up the Cumberland River to Nashville for quite a while in the early months of 1863, and only these small vessels could handle that route.[41]

A steamboat shortage clearly had developed in the West by March 1863 due to the many demands of Grant's operations against Vicksburg. Parsons was frustrated. "Everybody is complaining of me here for want of boats," he told the general from Saint Louis. Parsons listed twenty-five large steamers he knew were being constantly used by the river expedition. These vessels had a total capacity for hauling 25,200 men. This created a shortage of available boats everywhere else. "It is extremely difficult doing our necessary business here," Parsons complained.[42]

Grant wanted no fewer than thirty small boats for the Yazoo Pass expedition, preferably sidewheel steamers because they could navigate the twisting waterways better than sternwheelers. Robert Allen reported that there were none to be had at Saint Louis, however, and he found it difficult even to procure boats of any size. He asked permission to seize vessels engaged in private business, but Halleck was reluctant to authorize such a measure. "I cannot direct the seizure of steamers on the Ohio River unless in case of absolute necessity, and that necessity must be certified to by the Quartermaster's Department. Where boats can be procured for reasonable hire, violent measures should be avoided. General Grant's last dispatches to me do not indicate any necessity for violent seizures." Boat owners became aware of Grant's needs and raised their rates to take advantage of it; this was the reason Allen had asked Halleck for authority to seize vessels in the first place.[43]

Without authority to press steamboats, Allen and Parsons talked Major General Wright into releasing a handful of small vessels from the Kentucky supply routes. Parsons managed to find three small boats and sent them down the Mississippi to Grant. Five small boats arrived at Saint Louis, and a few showed up at Cairo and Memphis. Two or three small boats were undergoing repairs at Saint Louis, and Parsons made arrangements for their service as soon as they were ready. He also found three other small vessels operating north of the rapids on the upper Mississippi and set into motion efforts to secure their services. Parson discovered an additional three small boats working on the Illinois River, but the owners refused to leave their profitable trade and join the war effort.[44]

Alerted by Allen, Halleck told Grant not to tie up so many steamboats with the downriver expedition. "We cannot otherwise supply our armies in Tennessee and Kentucky." This sparked a dispatch from Grant explaining why it was important to retain so many boats in constant service. His large army needed them if the Union hoped to take Vicksburg.[45]

Grant tried to alleviate the problem by using barges and yawls to supplement the small steamers in the Yazoo Pass expedition. "There is required with the greatest dispatch 30 yawl of 6 to 10 oar each and [a] number of flat boats, and scow that can be towed upon which I can place troops and Artillery," he wrote on March 26. "I must have not less than 25 flat boats and more if possible and also get me if possible from Chicago through the canal four or five of their tugs for towing."[46]

Parsons contacted people not only in Saint Louis but also in Cincinnati, Chicago, and Cairo. He quickly found ten to fifteen flatboats and scows at Saint Louis and about the same number at other places. The quartermaster was unsure if Grant literally meant that he wanted flatboats and scows; he could more easily procure coal barges to haul troops and artillery. As it was, "almost everything of the boat line has already been pressed into service and sent south." Parsons continued, "It will take a little time to get these boats from Chicago, and to get them here in condition to go below." In a week he managed to find most of the vessels Grant wanted and sent them south, with carpenters and a supply of lumber to make needed repairs on them. Ironically, the yawls, scows, and flatboats did not reach the army before Grant called off the Yazoo Pass expedition, having encountered a Confederate fort placed at a key location far short of the Yazoo River.[47]

The Yazoo Pass expedition created the worst shortage of suitable riverboats for Federal operations during the war. This was due, in part, to the already huge demand for vessels imposed on quartermasters by Grant's sustained presence on the Mississippi River just north of Vicksburg. But Yazoo Pass demanded not just more vessels but specifically small boats capable of navigating narrow and twisting channels. Those craft were in short supply. It was impossible for the Federal government to finance the construction of more such vessels because building them would take far too long for Grant's purposes. Moreover, despite their difficulties, quartermasters actually found a decent number of small craft and barges to help Grant by the time he called off the expedition.

All shortages of steamboats were temporary; there was no need to construct new ones or even to commandeer a significant number of civilian boats during the war. Most civilian steamboat owners operated on the contract system, hauling a specified amount of material for their customers and looking for another job when it was done. So there was a constantly regenerated supply of available vessels. If too few were available today, more would be available tomorrow.

With the end of the Yazoo Pass effort, Grant committed his resources to a more promising plan. Running gunboats and transports loaded with supplies past the Vicksburg batteries at night, while opening a line of march for his infantry and artillery along the Louisiana side of the river, could crack open the hard shell surrounding Vicksburg. The levee system provided a roadway, and spring floods would inundate the lowlands west of those levees to protect the moving Federals from attack. Not until he conducted a scout toward Haynes' Bluff on April 1 did Grant once and for all rule out any attempt to approach Vicksburg from upriver and firmly set his gaze on the southward move.

The passage of the Vicksburg batteries deliberately thrust civilian steamers under government contract directly into enemy fire for the first and only time in the war. Grant initially planned to use six boats loaded with 300,000 rations for his army, two batteries, and between 6,000 and 8,000 infantrymen to run the Rebel gauntlet. He did not want the boats to haul ammunition for fear of explosion if set on fire. McClernand's Thirteenth Corps would lead the way along the Louisiana side, moving from Milliken's Bend across De Soto Point and down the river to secure New Carthage. If all was successful, Porter's gunboats would spearhead an attack on Confederate batteries at Grand Gulf, thirty miles south of Vicksburg. Then the transports would ferry McClernand's men downstream to help Maj. Gen. Nathaniel Banks capture Port Hudson. After the fall of that stronghold, all Federal forces could concentrate on Vicksburg.[48]

Grant had to adjust his thinking for the passage of the Vicksburg batteries. He possessed only three tugs and fifteen barges by mid-April and realized the land route in Louisiana would have to bear more of the logistical burden than planned. Grant also reduced the number of steamers to three and protected their boilers with hay bales and sandbags. The land route would be no more than twenty inches above the surrounding swamp in many places and needed improvement to handle heavy wagon traffic. McClernand wanted to take along 300 rounds of small-arms ammunition per man, totaling 6 million rounds for 20,000 troops. Sixty rounds could be carried on each person, but 4.8 million rounds would be hauled by wagons for thirty-five miles from Milliken's Bend to New Carthage. With 150 vehicles available, half the number needed, McClernand planned to make more than one trip with the teams. He also needed 90 additional wagons to haul 300 rounds of artillery ammunition for each piece in the ten six-gun batteries of his corps. Since McClernand calculated it would take thirteen days to haul all this material, he asked Grant if a specially protected steamer could be packed with the ammunition; the answer was no.[49]

Given the obvious danger, civilian crewmembers of the steamers were very reluctant to risk their lives in the passage. One of the three boat captains refused to go, and the entire crew of his boat also refused to participate in the move. Grant could not order them to do it, so he recruited volunteers from infantry regiments to replace them. When the small fleet of eight gunboats and three steamers set out on the night of April 16, one of the most spectacular river engagements of the war ensued. The vessels took two and a half hours to pass the gun emplacements on the eastern bluffs, the gunboats returning fire as they steamed south. But the *Silver Wave, Forest Queen,* and *Henry Clay* all were hit by Confederate fire. The *Henry Clay,* last in line, burned up, along with the 50,000 rations on board. No other vessel was seriously damaged or sunk. Soon the fleet joined two divisions of the Thirteenth Corps at New Carthage.[50]

The passage stunned the Confederates, particularly since the Rebel guns had inflicted surprisingly little damage on the boats. "I regard the navigation of Mississippi River as shut out from us now," solemnly declared Pemberton. "No more supplies can be gotten from trans-Mississippi department." Grant was very encouraged by the relatively easy passage, the first tactical success he enjoyed in his efforts against Vicksburg. He therefore organized a second passage. Having transported 160,000 rations on the night of the sixteenth, he now planned to move 600,000 rations. On the night of April 22, six steamers without gunboat escort ran past the batteries, although with much difficulty and all suffering damage. The *Tigress,* hit by fourteen rounds, some below the waterline, was sunk. Six of the twelve barges also were lost to enemy fire. Apparently all of the transports were fully manned by army volunteers, mostly from Maj. Gen. John A. Logan's division of the Seventeenth Corps.[51]

The April 22 passage was not as successful as the one six days earlier, a lesson not lost on Grant. He decided it would be too risky to send one-third of his army to help Banks at Port Hudson. The general now planned to cross the Mississippi south of the Confederate batteries and operate against Vicksburg from the east. Carpenters repaired the transports that had run past the batteries, putting five of them into good working order and using the other two as barges to ferry troops. There were still six actual barges that had survived the passages.[52]

From a logistical and supply viewpoint, the passage had been the most innovative and decisive event of the Vicksburg Campaign. Grant used civilian steamboats with military crews to provide transportation power for operating on and across the river south of Vicksburg, well protected by a fleet of gunboats. Although small, the assemblage of seven steamers and six barges was the key to getting his army across the river and onto high ground so he could engage Confederate forces east of the Mississippi. Grant now could turn months of frustration into a quick march through west-central Mississippi, arriving outside Vicksburg not by railroad from the north, but by foot power and river steamers from the south. His brilliant strategic and tactical accomplishment was made possible only by control of the river and some daring use of steam transportation.

Grant now focused on securing a foothold on the east side of the river, with Grand Gulf, outside of Vicksburg's fortified zone, as the target. Heavy Rebel guns mounted on the bluff there posed another obstruction to river navigation, but Grant was convinced that capturing Grand Gulf would constitute "virtual possession of Vicksburg and Port Hudson and the entire Mississippi river." Seven ironclads bombarded the batteries as 10,000 troops of McClernand's corps waited on transports to land and assault the place on April 29. While Porter's gunboats silenced the lower batteries, the higher batteries on top of the bluff continued to fire. Grant decided against an infantry landing and called off the battle after five hours of artillery exchanges. That night his troop transports ran past the batteries, with gunboats providing support. Yet another nocturnal passage of Confederate guns came to the rescue in Grant's evolving plans for taking Vicksburg.[53]

The next day McClernand found a usable landing place near Bruinsburg, about fifteen miles south of Grand Gulf. On April 30 the Federals finally set foot on the east side of the Mississippi River in an uncontested landing. Grant later admitted to a huge feeling of relief. "I was now in the enemy's country, with a vast river and the stronghold of Vicksburg between me and my base of supplies. But I was on dry ground on the same side of the river with the enemy." With more Federal troops arriving by way of the wagon road from De Soto Point, the small fleet of steamers worked overtime to transport them across the river. Amid this frenzied activity, there was a terrible accident. The *Moderator* ran into the *Horizon* at 3 A.M. on May 1, sinking the latter vessel. Three soldiers and most of the equipment of Battery G, 2nd Illinois Light Artillery were lost.[54]

Overland

Grant now faced the question of supplying 30,000 men as they penetrated the countryside of west-central Mississippi, marching farther from the river and lengthening their tenuous supply line that ended near Bruinsburg. Fortunately they would be moving toward Walnut Hills north of Vicksburg. Once secured there, Grant could regain contact with his river-borne line of communications via the Yazoo. But feeding his men and supplying them with ammunition until that occurred would be the key to his overland march to the rear of Vicksburg.

The line of supply had a solid stem, the string of river steamers coming from Saint Louis, Cairo, Memphis, and Helena, bearing supplies of all kinds and bound for forward depots located at Milliken's Bend and Young's Point. This stem had been in existence since Sherman's Chickasaw Bayou expedition but was now extended via the wagon road linking Milliken's Bend with the area opposite Bruinsburg. This road ran for seventy miles over Louisiana bottomland, sometimes on firm ground but often along the top of the relatively narrow levees. The wagon road needed constant repair, but with the spring rains over by this time, the Federals could count on dry weather and firm ground. A small fleet of river steamers completed the supply line by ferrying material across the Mississippi to Bruinsburg.[55]

Grant planned to partially disengage his army from its line of supply for his march toward Vicksburg, relying mostly on the countryside to feed men and animals. He would maintain an irregular wagon link with Bruinsburg and perhaps Grand Gulf, if the Confederates evacuated that place. A conservative plan of action would have been to march his force directly north toward Vicksburg, hugging the east bank of the Mississippi as much as possible. But Grant knew that a daring drive into the interior offered more strategic possibilities, so he chose that course even though it worsened his logistical and supply problems.

To enlarge his bridgehead near Bruinsburg, Grant moved east from the landing and engaged a small Confederate force at Port Gibson, sent there to observe Federal movements. The battle on April 1 was touch and go for a while, but the Federals compelled their opponents to evacuate the area. Grant then took several days to arrange his logistics and accumulate troops. Pemberton, meanwhile, was distracted by the movements of Sherman's corps, which seemed to threaten a resumption of Union attacks on Walnut Hills north of Vicksburg. He did not pay enough attention to the threat posed by the Union concentration to the south.

Grant specified his men should carry only two or three days' rations when the overland march began. He also shortened the wagon road along the Louisiana side of the river, instructing subordinates on May 3 to move the starting point a few miles downstream to Young's Point and aim at reaching the west bank of the Mississippi somewhere below Warrenton, a town on the east bank. This new route would make his supply road only

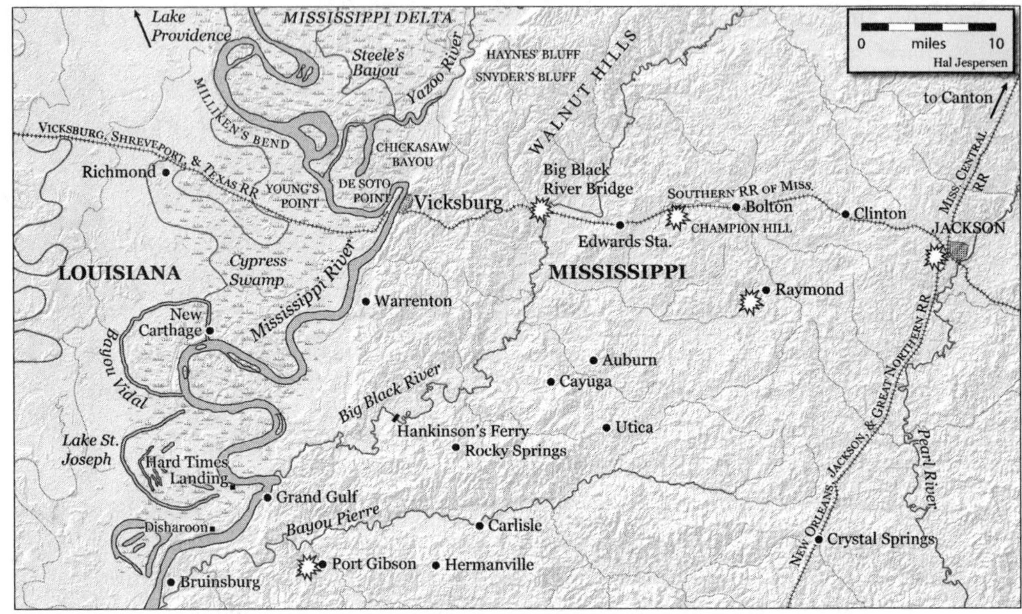

OVERLAND MARCH AND SIEGE OF VICKSBURG

about eight miles rather than seventy miles long. "Everything depends upon the promptitude with which supplies are forwarded," he told them. By early May the Rebels had evacuated Grand Gulf, and Grant ordered Sherman to assemble a train of 120 wagons loaded with 100,000 pounds of bacon and ample amounts of coffee, sugar, salt, and hard bread for the army.[56]

The third passage of the Vicksburg batteries also occurred at this time. Sherman was in charge of superintending it, and as with the earlier passages, army volunteers largely manned the vessels. Two steam tugs towing two barges each ran past on the night of May 3–4 but met with scant success. When a shell hit the boiler of the *George Sturgess,* that tug and both of its barges were destroyed. The other tug made it through the gauntlet. With 50-percent losses, it was the most dismal passage yet.[57]

Grant scarcely paid attention to the fact that passing the batteries had played out. "The road to Vicksburg is open," he excitedly told Sherman on May 3, "all we want now are men, ammunition and hard bread—we can subsist our horses on the country, and obtain considerable supplies for our troops." He told his wife that same day that "management I think has saved us an imense [*sic*] loss of life and gained all the results of a hard fight. I feel proud of the Army at my command. They have marched day and night, without tents and with irregular rations without a murmur of complaint."[58]

Sherman remained upstream from Vicksburg for a while before bringing his corps along the circuitous route west and then south of the city to join Grant. He fretted over the supply problems to come. "I apprehend great difficulty in the matter of food," he told a division commander on the fifth, "and caution you to give the subject your whole attention. Instruct all regimental commanders that every ounce of food must be economized."[59]

Grant delayed the start of his overland march for several days until he could stockpile three days' rations and enough small-arms and artillery ammunition to fight large battles along the way. He instructed a staff officer to procure one hundred wagons at Memphis and ship them south by steamer. Grant reminded another staff member, who was at Young's Point, to push the shipment of rations "with all dispatch." He demanded accurate reports of goods stored at various depots. "I want to know near as possible how we stand in every particular for supplies," he wrote.[60]

By May 7 the road to the river near Warrenton was still not open, but Federal quartermasters directed wagon trains from Young's Point to the river opposite Grand Gulf to be ferried across the Mississippi. This greatly shortened the line of communications. These wagons now rolled directly from Grand Gulf to the army's position near Rocky Springs. Grant told McClernand to pack three days' rations in the men's haversacks and send the empty vehicles back to Grand Gulf with a heavy guard of at least two men per wagon. Grant looked on Grand Gulf as only a temporary base of supplies on the east side of the river. But to secure it he ordered earthworks dug for a garrison of 2,000 men and made sure all wagon trains from there were escorted by infantrymen.[61]

Grant was allowed to make logistical arrangements for several days in an area of Union control from Bruinsburg to Rocky Springs and Grand Gulf. Pemberton's lack of concern about interfering with these preparations is astonishing, even if he believed there was only a small Union presence in the area rather than a substantial army. Grant took advantage of this opportunity to lay the foundation of success in his overland march to Vicksburg.

During this time, the Yankees fed themselves from the countryside as much as possible in addition to receiving army rations. But after a few days, the readily available supply of food and forage in the countryside began to dry up. Grant knew that as soon as he began his forward movement, the men would be marching through territory not yet visited by hostile armies where food would be more abundant. He expected to find ample amounts of corn and fresh beef but needed to rely on the line of supply for hardtack, coffee, and salt. His chief commissary of subsistence, Robert Macfeely, reported that he had sent 300,000 "small rations" of hardtack, sugar, coffee, and salt to the army from Milliken's Band and Young's Point as of May 8. In addition, Macfeely planned to maintain a steady inventory of 3 million complete rations, shipping them to the roving army by whatever route was feasible. With troops still moving toward Grant's concentration east of the river, it was possible to send supplies with those columns so as to have an ample escort for the wagons. "I will use every exertion to keep your army supplied," Macfeely assured his superior.[62]

As Grant began his advance in the direction of Jackson, he impressed on his subordinates the need to be concerned about supply problems. "We must fight the enemy before our rations fail," he told Major General McPherson, "and we are equally bound to make our rations last as long as possible."[63]

The overland march to Vicksburg was characterized by rapid movement, keeping one step ahead of the befuddled enemy, and outfighting the Confederates when engaged. Grant separated the small force held by Gen. Joseph E. Johnston near Jackson from Pemberton's much larger army in the vicinity of Vicksburg. Union forces captured the state capital of Jackson and held it a few days before turning to confront Pemberton at Champion Hill on May 16. Winning every engagement of the campaign, the Federals were able to drive Pemberton's forces into the city and lay siege to Vicksburg. The result was a stunning watershed in Grant's long campaign against the city.

Federal quartermasters seized only a few opportunities to supply Grant's army during the overland march. By May 12 they had completed the road between Milliken's Bend–Young's Point, on the one end, and a point five miles below Warrenton, on the other. But Confederate forces still held that small Mississippi town. Consequently, supplies were loaded onto steamers at the end of this new road and transported downstream to Grand Gulf, from where wagon trains rolled to seek out Grant's moving force. Still, as the Federals maneuvered and fought up to May 18, quartermasters were able to provide only five days' rations during twenty days of rough campaigning.[64]

Foraging from the countryside saved Grant's army from starvation. The men found enough fresh beef and pork for themselves and enough hay and grain for their animals. They could not hope to find enough of everything that was normally part of their army rations. The Federals also rounded up extra wagons and mule teams and used refugee blacks picked up along the way to drive them.[65]

Grant and his quartermasters overcame logistical and supply problems in a way to sustain the rapid movement of the army. Nevertheless, they achieved an uneven level of success. Some units suffered from hunger, while others fared rather well. Brig. Gen. Frank P. Blair's division of the Fifteenth Corps started late, crossing the river at Grand Gulf and moving inland on May 12. Blair escorted a train of 200 wagons, which slowed his men so much he was unable to participate in the fighting. The troops "got very hungry on that march to the rear of Vicksburg," according to John J. Kellogg of the 113th Illinois. "I heard men say that they partially subsisted by chewing newspaper advertisements of provisions."[66]

James Tuttle's division of the Fifteenth Corps had no wagons when it crossed the river at Grand Gulf; quartermasters loaded ambulances with spare ammunition. His men found "an abundance of beef-cattle, sheep, hogs, corn, molasses," according to the general. But one of his subordinates told a different story. Brig. Gen. Ralph P. Buckland could not take any rations along when his brigade crossed the river on May 7, and his men suffered from hunger. Only now and then could they find enough food along the way to alleviate their problem.[67]

Lt. Col. John E. Tourtellotte's 4th Minnesota in McPherson's Seventeenth Corps received five days' rations when it left Milliken's Bend to march seventy miles and cross the river at Bruinsburg. It received four days' worth of hardtack on May 1 and three-fifths rations of hardtack, sugar, and tea for five days on the fourth. From that date the regiment drew nothing from the government for nearly two weeks. Foragers gathered molasses, cornmeal, and bacon from the countryside until Tourtellotte received five days' rations of hardtack, sugar, coffee, and flour on May 17. The 4th Minnesota did not begin receiving full rations until the twenty-third, after Grant's supply line had been firmly reestablished by way of Walnut Hills north of Vicksburg.[68]

Grant's men needed no lessons in how to live off the countryside, for they had been doing it for a long time. The difference now was that officers encouraged it. Col. Norman Eddy told the men of his 48th Indiana "to Jayhawk all we could as the products of the country were about all we had to depend upon for several days." They found enough chickens and cornbread to sustain them.[69]

For the troops in Grant's army, foraging during the overland march was unusual only in the extent to which they had to rely on their own resources for sustenance. For troops of other armies, with less experience at this sort of campaigning, foraging was a novelty. Two divisions of the Ninth Corps arrived in June to help Grant, and these troops heard wonderful stories about the foraging that had occurred. Henry Tisdale of the 35th Massachusetts listened to Illinois and Iowa men camped near his regiment. "They say General Grant in his late march through Mississippi supplied his troops by foraging alone. They carry but little baggage, scarce any knapsacks, and no tents a good part of the time, sheltering themselves when in camp with bough houses shanties made from rails and sheds and barns torn down for the purpose." "Grant lives on the enemy," reported William A. Barnard of the 20th Michigan, and "while on the march takes . . . all their horses & all the mules, cattle, grain, & provisions he can find."[70]

The Civil War saw no other campaign with such a convoluted, risky, yet successful line of communications as Grant's circuit west, south, and then east of Vicksburg. It became during the overland march a porous rather than a solid line of communications, flexible and constantly on the move to match the rapid marches of his infantry force. By mid-May Grant had demonstrated his skill as a masterful logistician, taking risks with his obligation to supply the men, trusting heavily on their ability to find food on the march. Much of the credit for this success has to be given to his quartermasters and commissaries, not to mention the rank and file.

The marvel of Grant's Vicksburg Campaign is that he ended the overland march exactly where he needed to be in order to reconnect with the river steamers north of Vicksburg. As soon as the Confederates evacuated all positions along the Yazoo River and Sherman's corps occupied Walnut Hills, the campaign had come full circle. Steamboats moved up the Yazoo and opened landings on the eastern bank while Grant's engineers cleared roads from those landings to the besieging army. Some units, such as those in Sherman's command only a couple of miles from the hills, received full rations quickly, but others, such as those in McPherson's corps in the center of the Union siege line and those in McClernand's on the far left, did not receive full rations until May 23 because of the need to cut new roads.[71]

Soon the steamboat link between the Federals and their major supply centers at Saint Louis, Cairo, and Memphis was firmly established. Reinforcements flooded in until Grant's troop strength doubled and all manner of material flowed to the siege line outside the city. Timothy Phillips of the 19th Iowa, a regiment in Maj. Gen. Francis J. Herron's division shipped in from Missouri and Arkansas, counted no fewer than forty-seven steamers at the Yazoo River landing. The activity at that landing, along the road ascending Walnut Hills and extending to all sections of Grant's line, impressed everyone.[72] The Federals ate well and had more than enough ammunition to dominate no-man's land with their artillery and small-arms fire. In contrast, Pemberton's Confederates were short of virtually everything, from food to ammunition.

To a greater degree than usual, Grant's campaign against Vicksburg pivoted on logistical and supply issues because of its deep penetration of the Lower South. Only by using the Mississippi River and a fleet of civilian transports, supported by a large and powerful gunboat fleet, was the campaign possible. In contrast, the Confederates operated on their own turf and for months were largely unhindered in their access to richly productive sections of the country. Despite such advantages, they did no more than accumulate enough food for Pemberton's army to last a few weeks rather than for an extended siege. The contrast in logistics and supply between Union and Confederate forces in the long campaign for Vicksburg is startling.

3

STOCKPILING FOOD AT VICKSBURG

By the time Grant laid siege to Vicksburg, he had reestablished a secure line of supply with his Northern bases, connected to them by a reliable string of river steamers. Material of all kinds flowed to his army, enabling it to tighten the cordon around the doomed city for six weeks until Vicksburg gave up on July 4, 1863. A severe shortage of food was the primary cause of its surrender. Lieutenant General Pemberton's men had enough ammunition and weapons to withstand the Federals, but they were weakened by short rations, resorted to eating mule meat, and began to show signs of incipient rebellion. Hunger brought the garrison down on July 4 more than any other factor, even though Union siege approaches had gotten so near that an all-out attack planned for July 6 likely would have busted the Rebel earthworks wide open and given Grant the city by assault rather than by starvation.

The Confederate food shortage became an issue of heated public discussion in the weeks following the fall of the city. Even today it is a wonder that Pemberton failed to stockpile enough food in Vicksburg to withstand a lengthy siege. He had taken command of the Department of Mississippi and Eastern Louisiana in October 1862 and had plenty of time to fill the city warehouses with provisions.

In fact, accumulating food should have been the easiest task on his long list of things to do. Vicksburg was located south of the Mississippi Delta, one of the richest agricultural regions of the South. It consists of a wide alluvial bottomland bordering the east bank of the Mississippi River, starting just north of Vicksburg and stretching nearly to Memphis. Two hundred miles long and seventy miles wide, the Mississippi Delta was home to many large plantations connected by a system of rivers and creeks, many of which were navigable by steamers.

In addition to the Mississippi Delta, Confederate commissaries could collect food from the equally rich plantations on the Louisiana bottomlands west of the river. And as long as they held Jackson, forty-five miles east of Vicksburg, they had access to a system of railroads that tapped into north, south, and east Mississippi.

But the apparently easy task of accumulating provisions became impossible even before Grant ran the Vicksburg batteries in April and seized control of the river south of the city, cutting off access to the Louisiana bottomlands. When Grant crossed the Mississippi and campaigned overland to Jackson, the Confederates no longer could transport food by rail to Vicksburg. When Grant closed in on Vicksburg from the east, Pemberton abandoned all points north of the city and cut himself off from the Mississippi Delta. By then it was far too late to do anything about the fact that his 20,000 men had barely enough food to last a month or two.

Pemberton's failure to stockpile enough provisions to withstand a long siege involved a variety of factors, but most of them point to the inefficiency of the Confederate system of finding, purchasing, and transporting commissary supplies. In short, the issue showcases nearly everything that was wrong with the institutional apparatus of the Confederate military system. It did not work well because competing interests fought with each other rather than cooperated. In addition, a creaky transportation system broke down more often than it delivered. Pemberton tried to do something about these problems but failed at nearly every turn.

Administrative Turf Battles

Soon after taking command of the department, Pemberton set out to prepare the logistical and supply foundation to hold Vicksburg. He wanted to stockpile enough food for a garrison to last sixty days in case of a siege. His staff members were fully aware that the sources of food lay north, west, and east of the city as evidenced in a postwar article written by his adjutant general, R. W. Memminger.[1]

From the beginning, administrative conflict threatened Pemberton's efforts. The Confederacy's commissary general, Col. Lucius B. Northrop, had developed a scheme to gather supplies on a nationwide basis by dividing the South into districts, each overseen by its own commissary with the power to supersede the jurisdiction of local commissaries attached to the staff of military commanders. It was a necessary plan to nationalize the process of food gathering, but it met a lot of resistance from local commanders who resented any interference with their authority.[2]

Northrop appointed Lt. Col. William A. Broadwell to the area that encompassed Pemberton's supply areas. Broadwell had lots of cash supplied by the Confederate government to purchase food. His charge was to buy and ship to central depots that could supply armies far afield from Vicksburg based on decisions made in Richmond. But Broadwell also was amenable to supporting the goal of stockpiling siege supplies at Vicksburg.[3]

Pemberton's chief commissary, Maj. R. H. Cuney, shouldered responsibility only for the Department of Mississippi and Eastern Louisiana. He tasked Maj. T. B. Reed to oversee the work of civilian purchasing agents along the Louisiana side of the Mississippi in mid-November 1862. Specifically, he charged the major with buying "corn, meal, pease, and potatoes" before the Federals descended the river and cut Pemberton off from this area. Reed arranged for transportation of these purchases to both Vicksburg and Port Hudson by steamer, although some of it was destined to go on to Jackson as well, indicating that thus far Cuney's own efforts were not yet oriented toward favoring the depots at Vicksburg.[4]

By early December 1862, Northrop appointed W. H. Johnson as a general agent of the Commissary Department and sent him to Vicksburg, where he worked under Broadwell's direction. A civilian without an army commission, Johnson received wide authority to procure 300,000 bushels of corn and ship it to Vicksburg, but he soon ran into transportation difficulties. After struggling for a month with those problems, Pemberton issued Special Order No. 4, which forbade any commissary agent from purchasing supplies within his department except those managed by his own chief commissary; by this time Maj. Theodore Johnston had supplanted Cuney in that staff role. This special order indicated to W. H. Johnson that "so much jealousy and opposition" stood in his way as to negate his effectiveness in accumulating supplies for Northrop's national plan.[5]

Pemberton had soured on Broadwell after learning that the commissary agent had been trading across the lines in an effort to procure supplies within Union-occupied territory. The general complained to Secretary of War James A. Seddon that this activity demoralized civilians and weakened their allegiance to the Confederacy. Seddon was not convinced of this point but admitted to having authorized trade across the lines. Explaining why it was

Table 3. COMPETING CONFEDERATE COMMISSARIES AT VICKSBURG

Central Governmental Agency	Regional Military Department
Lucius B. Northrop, Commissary General, CSA	Lt. Gen. John C. Pemberton, Department of Mississippi and East Louisiana
Lt. Col. William A. Broadwell, Chief Purchasing Commissary in region of Vicksburg	Maj. R. H. Cuney, Chief Commissary*
W. H. Johnson, General Agent of Commissary Department (a civilian with no army commission), assigned to Broadwell	Maj. T. B. Reed, Assistant Commissary
	Maj. Livingston Mims, Chief Quartermaster

* Maj. Theodore Johnston replaced Cuney as chief commissary by the end of 1862.

necessary, he argued that "internal resources of supply for these articles had either not been judiciously managed or were deficient," resulting in "actual suffering" among soldiers in the Army of Northern Virginia and the Army of Tennessee. Even so, Seddon felt compelled to take Pemberton's concerns seriously and allowed him to maintain his Special Order No. 4 in effect.[6]

Ironically, Pemberton wrote to Broadwell on January 14, ten days after issuing Special Order No. 4, asking his help in the accumulation of food for his department. He also ordered all his subordinates to cooperate with the lieutenant colonel. What he meant by this turnaround is unclear, for the special order had taken away Broadwell's most effective mode of operation—to work with a completely free hand. The most likely explanation for Pemberton's plea was the undeniable fact that his own commissary officers were incapable of supplying his department. T. B. Reed wrote a rather desperate letter to Theodore Johnston early in January begging for help in finding bacon, soap, salt, rice, vinegar, coffee, candles, and flour for the depot at Vicksburg—Cuney could not help him in this effort. Late in January Reed also complained to Pemberton that no commissary officer in the department had sufficient money to pay farmers for the supplies they were trying to purchase. As the general well knew, most farmers refused to sell corn to the government unless they were paid in cash up front, and Reed encountered great difficulties in procuring the needed funds.[7]

By late February, members of Pemberton's staff adopted a desperate tone in their communications about food. Major Reed bemoaned "the unfortunate and deplorable condition of the commissariat" at Vicksburg. "I do not feel the least responsible for the present state of affairs," he wrote to Maj. Gen. Carter L. Stevenson, one of Pemberton's division leaders, who also commanded the post of Vicksburg. Not only did Special Order No. 4 fail to give the major any advantages but he also was even more severely hampered by the lack of funds. From mid-December 1862 to early March 1863, Reed received from Pemberton only $113,000 with which to purchase supplies. Broadwell received from Northrop $318,000 in funding, which he doled out to Reed and several other individuals during the same period. This differential indicates how much more financial power Northrop's agent could employ compared to Pemberton's staff members, yet the department commander insisted his people remain in charge of purchasing.[8]

Pemberton alienated the most efficient commissary agent available to him, William A. Broadwell, and severely hampered his ability to purchase food. As a result, Broadwell went across the Mississippi to Louisiana in early February and did not return to the Department of Mississippi and Eastern Louisiana. On March 19 Pemberton told Seddon of plans to push forward the accumulation of supplies by using his own staff members. "I propose to endeavor to subsist my army as hitherto—have agents with large amount of funds to make purchases of corn, beef, and bacon west of [the] Mississippi River, and also collecting some supplies in this State." He had already authorized his chief commissary, Theodore Johnston, to send purchasing agents into Louisiana even though it lay outside his department. Northrop, upon learning of this, told Johnston to withdraw those agents and work solely through Broadwell to get food out of Louisiana. This was "impracticable" in Pemberton's view. Because Broadwell did not cooperate with him and was not even physically near Vicksburg, Pemberton wanted to have a commissary he could control. The general refused to rely on Broadwell for anything by this stage in the game.[9]

The Richmond authorities supported Pemberton rather than Northrop. Given the importance of holding Vicksburg and the lack of success in accumulating supplies, they allowed the general to stop all shipments of commissary stores out of his department to other commands, a decision that limited the food supply of Maj. Gen. Simon Buckner's Department of the Gulf.[10]

These administrative turf battles played out for five months and severely hampered the ability of commissaries to accumulate supplies at Vicksburg. Within a month after Pemberton was allowed to take control of purchasing food, Grant ran transports and gunboats past the water batteries at Vicksburg, securing control of the Mississippi south of the embattled city. "I regard navigation of Mississippi River as shut out from us now," Pemberton told a subordinate. "No more supplies can be gotten from [the] Trans-Mississippi Department." But for another month, until mid-May 1863, the rich farms in the Mississippi Delta remained open to Pemberton. His staff members accumulated reports that those farms were bulging with corn, bacon, and cattle. All that was needed was transportation to bring the supplies into Vicksburg.[11]

Transportation

Therein lay another problem hampering Confederate efforts to supply their Mississippi Gibraltar. "It was one thing to purchase supplies," Pemberton later wrote, "but another to transport them." There were a significant number of river steamers available to Confederate authorities at this time, but most of them had moved up the Yazoo River when Federal warships approached Vicksburg from north and south in the summer of 1862. Union domination of the river was temporary, however, and by October Pemberton felt it was safe to allow these vessels to reenter the Mississippi. His quartermasters began to charter some boats and seize others for permanent service to the Confederacy, "notwithstanding the violent opposition of private parties." Nevertheless, there were not enough steamers to meet Pemberton's needs. T. B. Reed complained in late November that his requests for boats were not met even though he had corn waiting for transport.[12]

Pemberton noted that a few larger boats, with greater carrying capacity, became available by early January 1863, but they were not sufficient to meet the great demand for transportation. Later that month a purchasing agent named B. Roach told Reed that he knew several planters along Deer Creek in the Mississippi Delta who had up to 400,000 bushels of corn in storage and were willing to sell it to the government for a dollar a bushel. Any transaction needed to be done soon, however, as the rivers would rise and many levees were breached. Roach even knew the capacity of several steamers and indicated which ones were essential in carrying out his plan. Major Johnston authorized Roach to move ahead but pay a dollar a bushel for only 100,000 bushels. He allowed him to purchase more than 100,000 bushels if the price did not exceed seventy-five cents a bushel. Johnston said nothing about the steamers because that was a matter for Pemberton's quartermasters to arrange.[13]

For reasons that have never been made clear, the quartermasters mostly failed to deliver the goods. Other men besides Roach told Johnston that immediate attention was needed to this issue, for the corn was stored along the Rolling Fork and Bogue Phaliah in addition to Deer Creek, waiting for transportation; any undue delay would lead to exposure to rain and flooding. "There should be reliable, energetic men sent up who should be instructed to collect these stores at the shipping points," read an unsigned memorandum submitted to Johnston in late January.[14]

Some of this corn was shipped to Vicksburg, but most of it dropped through the cracks of the Confederate transportation system. When the *Charm* and *Paul Jones* steamed to Saint Joseph to pick up corn that W. H. Johnson had arranged for them to haul to Vicksburg, the boat captains could not locate it and returned empty.[15]

To a degree, commissary officers tried to arrange for transportation directly with boat owners, a process that should have been conducted by quartermasters. Reed discussed terms with the owner of the *Edward J. Gray* to use his vessel as a storage boat at Haynes' Bluff for the same rate as Pemberton's quartermaster department had arranged for the *Scotland.* Reed thought mills could be attached to the engine of the *Edward J. Gray* to grind corn on board the vessel.[16]

By late March Pemberton was concerned about the transportation problems. He instructed his chief quartermaster, Maj. Livingston Mims, to create "a complete organization of the boat system on the Yazoo" to provide steamers for transporting supplies and troops. Pemberton envisioned using large boats on that river and small ones on the Tallahatchie. It is extraordinary that Pemberton should have to tell his chief quartermaster to work on such a basic task as this, and so late in the campaign for Vicksburg as well.[17]

Throughout March and April, Confederate documents mention at least twenty steamers that hauled mostly commissary supplies for the department. That is a modest number, especially considering that most of them were small boats. If managed efficiently, those twenty vessels could have had a chance of meeting Pemberton's needs, but there is plenty of evidence that Mims did not manage them well.[18]

The entire blame cannot be laid at Mims's door. Pemberton admitted after the fall of Vicksburg that many boat owners did not cooperate with his quartermasters. "Most of the boats were engaged in carrying sugar, molasses, and salt either for private parties or for the Government. There was great opposition on the part of owners at every attempt to divert them from these purposes. The Government was appealed to against what was styled the violation of the rights of the citizen by the military authorities."[19]

Use of the available steamers was severely compromised by this attitude among boat owners and by a lack of stern measures exercised by Pemberton's quartermasters. Widespread seizure of boats could have alleviated private reluctance to serve the real needs of the army, but that did not take place. Steamboat owners and quartermasters alike contributed to the problem.

But poor conditions on the railroad system serving Vicksburg also contributed to the failure to accumulate supplies. Pemberton characterized the Southern Railroad of Mississippi, which linked Vicksburg with Jackson, as in "wretched condition" during the early months of 1863. Writing after the war, Memminger thought it "was in a miserable and even dangerous condition. Accidents occurred almost daily, engines being broken up, and there being a lamentable scarcity of any species of cars." He admitted that more food came into Vicksburg by rail than by river steamer, but the wretched conditions severely limited the flow. "This, the great thoroughfare to Vicksburg, was entirely out of repair and almost impassable."[20]

Not only the Southern Railroad but also the Mobile and Ohio Railroad suffered hardware problems. This line ran north and south through the eastern portion of Mississippi by way of Meridian, which was at the eastern end of the Southern Railroad of Mississippi. In other words, it was a major feeder of shipments into Jackson and Vicksburg. When Pemberton traveled to Jackson to look into the situation during mid-March, he telegraphed Stevenson to make sure all railroad cars on the Southern line were unloaded at Vicksburg as fast as possible. The empty cars needed to be rushed back to help the Mobile and Ohio line, where transportation was "almost stopped for want of cars." Pemberton followed up this directive by ordering Mims to compile reports on the exact number of carloads entering Vicksburg from the east, listing what type of material was contained in them, so he could keep track of this vital transportation link.[21]

Hardware problems and car shortages were not the sum total of Confederate challenges. Pemberton had to deal with resistance on the part of railroad officials to ship what was truly needed by the army. "The obstacles that were continually thrown in the way by railroad authorities, and the clamor raised at any attempt of mine to make private interests subservient to Government necessities" created major roadblocks to his logistical effort. This was a pervasive problem across the Confederacy because the Richmond government had doggedly insisted on a policy of paying minimal freight rates. Railroad companies preferred to ship private freight, for which they were paid more. Although the Confederate Congress had authorized governmental seizure of railroad companies if needed, President Davis was so reluctant to violate the sanctity of private property that it was never done. All the government did was to pressure the railroad companies into a limited, temporary agreement to give priority to army freight for a couple of weeks. Pemberton tried to do that with the Southern Railroad of Mississippi, suggesting the company restrict itself to shipping private freight only one day per week, but there is no indication its president, Victor F. Wilson, agreed to the suggestion.[22]

Problems with steamboats and railroads constituted the major part of Pemberton's logistical troubles but not all of them. Corn shipped from the Mississippi Delta had to be unloaded at Haynes' Bluff rather than at its ultimate destination. The reason was a massive raft that had been constructed downstream from the bluff to hinder Union vessels attempting to steam up the Yazoo River. Pemberton did not want to dismantle the raft, so it continued to pose as much of a hindrance to Confederate river traffic as to Federal movements. From Haynes' Bluff the corn had to be hauled in wagons eleven miles to Vicksburg, and the heavy traffic along this route led to severe damage to the roadbed. Up to one hundred wagons were used for this purpose by late February, and in the wet winter months, they cut deep ruts with each passage until the road itself became a major impediment.[23]

Storage

In addition to administrative turf battles and transportation problems, Pemberton's men faced additional hurdles in terms of storing food. Those issues started with inadequate provision for protecting food at the point where steamers were supposed to pick it up. Storage facilities at the point of departure, along the levees that lined the many streams of the Mississippi Delta, were almost nonexistent. Farmers tended to dump bags of corn and other commissary supplies on the levees and hope the government steamers would arrive soon. The vessels very often failed to do so. Winter rains did their worst on exposed bags of corn, peas, and loose fodder thus deposited in this fashion at places such as Saint Joseph, Ashwood, and Waterproof. As a result, much of the grain and hay were "in a rotting condition," according to Reed.[24]

Similar problems troubled the commissaries trying to assemble food for the Port Hudson garrison. George Cammack reported that forty barrels of salt stood exposed to the weather at the river landing of Port Hudson for a full month before someone finally hauled it to a storehouse. He saw soldiers detailed to logistical duty who did not take their jobs seriously. Some men shelled the kernels of corn to get cobs, which they threw at each other out of boredom, while others helped themselves to the supply, filling their haversacks. What was left of the corn rested at the landing for a week, and much of it became spoiled by rain. Maj. Joseph P. Carr, the post commissary at Port Hudson, vigorously denied Cammack's report, but another man named Walt S. Wingate added his own statement supporting Cammack's observations. Wingate watched as detailed soldiers unloaded corn from boats at the landing so carelessly that much of it fell into the river. To Wingate's statement, Carr simply responded that he was overwhelmed with duties and could not oversee everything.[25]

Even near the end of the Vicksburg Campaign, the Confederates suffered from the combined problems of storage and transportation. When they evacuated Snyder's Bluff north of the city upon Grant's approach from the east, the Rebels left behind 30,000 bushels of corn that Pemberton's army, horses, and mules would soon desperately need.[26]

Ironically, even if additional corn could have been moved to Vicksburg, it is possible there would have been no place to store it properly. In late November T. B. Reed had to plead with another officer for help in moving commissary supplies from the levee at Vicksburg to the few storehouses in the city. He suggested that details be sent through the countryside to round up wagons and teams to carry the material only a few hundred yards. This short trip constituted the final link in the logistical chain that funneled supplies to the stockpile.[27]

Reed was harried to find adequate lumber and nails to construct storehouses in the city, pleading with Mims in early December for a supply of these necessary materials. He also asked Mims for sixty mules plus harness to move supplies from the levee to the intended storage facilities. By January 20 Reed again pleaded for help, this time to the post quartermaster, to provide twenty-five kegs of nails and much more lumber. By this time he had contracted to procure 100,000 pounds of bacon, 100,000 pounds of flour, and 1,000 bushels of salt that he hoped would soon be arriving at Vicksburg. In addition, Reed knew of 40,000 bushels of corn waiting along various streams in the Mississippi Delta for shipment to the Gibraltar. He was keen to point out that the captain of the *T. D. Hine* was doing his best, having already delivered 107,467 pounds of salt, 40,166 pounds of flour, 2,738 pounds of lard, 6,556 pounds of bacon, and 460 hogs weighing 200 pounds each.[28]

Placing all this material in secure and watertight storage proved a problem that never seemed to end. By late January reports of the storage issue reached Richmond, where Northrop complained to Seddon that about 60,000 bushels of corn had to be condemned as unfit for consumption.[29]

Northrop probably received those reports from W. H. Johnson, his man in Vicksburg now that Broadwell had elected to work in Louisiana. Major General Stevenson held a conference with Johnson on March 10 in which he expressed his concern that the stockpile was not taking shape. "I understood him to say that he considered the holding of Vicksburg simply a question of subsistence," Johnson later wrote of Stevenson. The post commander was frustrated. "General Pemberton would neither provision the post nor give him authority to do so," according to Johnson. Stevenson had heard that Broadwell was accumulating commissary supplies in Louisiana and Texas and asked Johnson's help in getting it to Vicksburg. Johnson was able to ship some of it by steamer across the Mississippi and part way up the Big Black River before Grant passed the Vicksburg batteries and cut off the flow.[30]

Other Richmond authorities besides Northrop heard reports concerning the lack of storage facilities. Secretary of War Seddon instructed Pemberton in March to fix those problems and store sugar and molasses at Vicksburg to last his army four to six weeks in case of a siege.[31]

Stevenson, Northrop, and Seddon brought up an interesting point—Pemberton had lost his focus on the goal of stockpiling food at Vicksburg. There is no doubt that he at times understood this to be an important goal but then allowed himself and staff to be diverted by the many other supply needs of his large department. On December 23 Pemberton told Reed to maintain a food store of five months for the garrison of Vicksburg. But soon after that Theodore Johnston placed an urgent call for 20,000 bushels of corn to feed troops in the Jackson area. Reed asked Maj. Gen. Martin L. Smith, current commander of post at Vicksburg, if he should comply, but Smith's answer is unavailable. The fact that Reed had to ask this question indicates that he did not consider stockpiling as his number-one priority.[32]

Pemberton went from wanting to stockpile supplies to simply requiring his commissaries to maintain enough food at Vicksburg to feed 25,000 men on a short-term basis.[33] One cannot blame him too much for these variations. The problems already described—from turf battles to shortages of transportation and storage facilities—severely restricted his logistical preparations. All too often the exigencies of the moment compelled Pemberton and his staff to deal with short-term goals that diverted them from long-term stockpiling.

Confederate commissaries provided detailed statistics on the food at Vicksburg to defend themselves in the face of raging public controversy after the fall of the city. To feed 20,000 troops would require a stockpile of 600,000 rations of all food articles for every month of the siege. Commissaries were able to accumulate respectable amounts of most items on the ration list, although only enough for short-term use rather than quantities that would constitute a real stockpile. The only item they had difficulty finding was beef, considered an important element in the soldier diet. Bacon was relatively easy to find, but "meat is difficult to be got at any price," Pemberton wrote in April. He authorized commissaries to pay up to fifty cents a pound and to impress the staple if farmers refused to sell, "always leaving sufficient for family use."[34]

A "List of stores in Vicksburg, Miss., December 15, 1862," does not even list beef but includes 7,570 rations of bacon. The amount of flour consisted only of 1,098 rations, but peas were in abundance, with 2,033,906 rations available. Sugar and salt also were in good supply at 485,833 rations and 1,108,608 rations respectively, but then those two items always were doled out in sparing portions to the men.[35]

A month later, in mid-January 1863, the amount of bacon remained essentially unchanged at 7,466 rations (measuring two pounds per ration). There was still no beef on the list, and peas had dropped a great deal to

690,633 rations (at fifteen pounds to every 100 rations). Sugar and salt had also dropped a great deal to 235,250 rations (at twelve pounds to every 100 rations) and 325,222 rations (at four and a half pounds to every 100 rations) respectively. Flour had risen dramatically to 47,138 rations (at one and a half pounds to each ration).[36]

No list exists for February, but the March report indicates little change in the supply. Bacon rested at only 2,200 rations (listed now as half a pound per ration), and salt pork appears on the list at only 400 rations (at half a pound per ration). Bulk pork consisted of 370 rations (also at half a pound per ration). For the first time, beef appears on the list in the form of salt beef at 3,060 rations (at the rate of one pound per ration). Flour had dropped dramatically to 24,451 rations (at one and a half pounds per ration), and peas remained on the inventory with 153,333 rations (at fifteen pounds per 100 rations). No sugar was listed, but salt stood at a hefty 2,709,200 rations (at four and a half pounds per 100 rations).[37]

By early April the stocks had risen across the board to more respectable levels. Bacon stood at 319,728 rations; the storehouses contained 302,400 rations of bulk pork, 120,314 rations of flour, 4,220,000 rations of peas, and 5,646,190 rations of salt. By late April the stocks were higher, with bacon standing at 526,468 rations. And by May 14, only four days before Grant's arrival, the Vicksburg storehouses contained 239,862 rations of flour, 3,506,698 rations of peas, and 10,546,400 rations of salt.[38]

These statistics indicate that nothing was done to stockpile a large amount of commissary stores at Vicksburg during the period December 1862 through March 1863. What was stored in the warehouses really was about the normal level needed for the near-future use of the troops in and around the city. But by late March there is evidence of progress in trying to create a true stockpile. It never reached the level needed to withstand a long siege of five months or thereabouts—perhaps that was an unrealistic goal in any case—but at least there was enough food in Vicksburg by May 14 to last several weeks.

From April 30 to May 14, a total of 413,130 rations of bacon were shipped to Vicksburg, with most of it (240,000 rations) transported from collection depots near Jackson. An additional 153,130 rations came from Meridian and another 20,000 rations from Snyder's Bluff. When supplying corn, 42,771 rations came from Jackson, while 31,590 rations came from Meridian, and 360,000 rations came from Snyder's Bluff, a total of 434,361 rations shipped to the Mississippi Gibraltar.[39]

In the last few weeks before the siege, Confederate commissaries began to redeem themselves by accumulating stores mostly from the interior of Mississippi rather than from the delta (except for corn). They were able to overcome at least some of the railroad problems and draw supplies more readily from inland rail than from the Mississippi bottomlands by steamer.

This logistical and supply effort saved Pemberton at the last minute. It accumulated enough food in the city so that he could choose to stand a siege inside Vicksburg rather than evacuate as his superior, Gen. Joseph E. Johnston, strongly urged him to do.

Pemberton seemed pleased with the efforts of his commissaries. On May 2 he told Davis that Vicksburg had a supply of food to last the garrison for thirty days. He also told his chief commissary, Major Johnston, that he "did not think it necessary to have a larger accumulation of stores at Vicksburg." Pemberton obviously had given up on accumulating a true stockpile to last several months and felt ready to risk the army and the city while standing a siege. He had to hold out only long enough for Johnston to mount an effective relief effort with troops assembled by the Richmond government at Jackson.[40]

The Fall of Vicksburg

In the end Pemberton and his commissaries failed to create a true stockpile at Vicksburg. A combination of problems led to this failure. Ironically, the administrative turf battles were all generated by Pemberton himself, needlessly alienating a good commissary officer in William A. Broadwell because he did not like trading across enemy lines. Winning the right to purchase food as the sole preserve of his departmental commissaries, those officers failed to accumulate a stockpile because of many problems associated with transportation and storage. Only by dint of supreme effort could they gather enough food by mid-May for Pemberton to stand a siege of about six weeks.

Ironically, the Confederates possessed so many advantages in the game of gathering food that one would expect them to be able to stockpile whatever they wanted, but that did not happen. Even more ironic, the Federals labored under many disadvantages in supplying Grant's army during the Vicksburg Campaign yet overcame all of them brilliantly. Union logistical power was immense; commissaries and quartermasters alike were adept at their jobs, and the result was that Grant could more easily feed 30,000 men perched at the tail end of a long tether of steamboats linking him with cities more than 200 miles away than Pemberton could feed his 20,000 men located only a few miles from rich corn-producing regions of his own territory.

Siege operations pin opposing armies in one spot for a long period of time, making firm logistical support imperative for success. The Federals far outperformed the Confederates in this regard. Their steamboat landings on the Yazoo River teemed with activity. Edward Jesup Wood, major of the 48th Indiana, counted more than fifty steamers at one landing, while Edwin C. Obriham, detached from the 9th Iowa to work on an ordnance boat, counted 112 vessels at and near the landings. Obriham marveled at the sight of wagons from many regiments lining up to take supplies back to their units. "It is one Grand circus all the while Sundays not excepted," he wrote. A contract surgeon on one of the hospital steamers heard that Grant was spending $90,000 a day on transportation alone to feed and supply his army during the siege of Vicksburg.[41]

While Pemberton's men stretched out their meager food stocks inside Vicksburg and Grant's men ate well during the siege, Confederate authorities struggled to find commissary stores for the troops assembling under General Johnston as a relief force. Theodore Johnston asked H. P. Atkins to assess food supplies in several Mississippi counties, including Panola, De Soto, Tunica, and Marshall. Atkins reported by May 27 that the citizens had surplus stores of corn, beef cattle, bacon, and wheat. The problem was that Grant had already begun disturbing these areas with raids coming out of Union-held posts in southwest Tennessee, which made it difficult to gather the surplus stocks. Atkins needed 5,000 Confederate troops to protect the region and to help move the commissary stores. He advised that a uniform price be offered to everyone and that the government should impress material if necessary. Atkins was particularly worried by the fact that some citizens were eager to sell cotton to Northern merchants based in Memphis. He argued that food could be pressed from these Southerners to punish them for doing so. "They now estimate our currency by the Yankee standard greenbacks. In fact, to say in moderate language, they are demoralized."[42]

Walter Goodman, president of the Mississippi Central Railroad, was keen on getting the wheat crop of north Mississippi down to Jackson, but the track was in poor shape north of Panola. He suggested running only small cars on that section, a tactic already practiced by the Mississippi and

Tennessee Railroad between Grenada and Panola and by the Mobile and Ohio Railroad north of Okolona. Goodman's company ran cars regularly up to Oxford but only small cars pulled by mules between Holly Springs and that town. Between Oxford and Water Valley, it used only wagons to haul material for twenty miles. Goodman was impressed by the use of mules to pull rail cars. Although small, these cars still transported much more material than an ordinary wagon pulled along a dirt road. But he also pointed out to General Johnston that his company could repair two major stretches of track. It would cost $25,000 to $30,000 to put the rails between Abbeville and either Oxford or Water Valley back into full operation. He estimated it would cost $50,000 to extend the working track all the way to Holly Springs. But Goodman made it clear that the government would have to foot the bill for this work. His company was "unwilling to do it at its own cost. It would not be a source of profit or any benefit to it, while to the Government it might be of great benefit."[43]

General Johnston did not take up Goodman's suggestion, and the problems of transportation continued to plague Confederate efforts to feed the relief army. T. L. Maxwell, an assistant commissary officer, reported that the men stationed at Jackson had only three days' rations left by May 29. He had a mill located six miles from the city that was grinding corn twenty hours each day, processing twenty-five bushels daily.[44]

Commissary officers had accumulated stocks of food at various locations in Pemberton's Department of Mississippi and Eastern Louisiana, an area that General Johnston commanded now that Pemberton was isolated in Vicksburg. They had knit together a storage network consisting of fifteen depots, all of them located on the rail lines of the department. As of June 20, the total amount of food stored in those depots included 499,526 rations of bacon, 104,970 rations of flour, 1,336,703 rations of corn, 217,650 rations of peas, and 1,552,470 rations of salt. Johnston's commissaries worked to accumulate these stores essentially on their own, without cooperating with Northrop's agents.[45]

Ironically, in some categories Pemberton had more food stored inside Vicksburg than General Johnston had outside the city. On June 7 Stevenson reported 964,000 rations of bacon, 742 barrels of flour, 20,000 rations of beef, and 2,365,211 rations of beans. The difference was that Pemberton had no hope of replenishing his supply, while Johnston's commissaries could find ways to replace their stocks. As the siege lengthened, food shortages began to strangle soldiers inside the beleaguered city. In a statement sent to Pemberton's headquarters signed by "Many Soldiers" and bearing the date of June 28, the sentiments of many men were starkly expressed. A biscuit "and a small bit of bacon per day, not enough scarcely to keep soul and body together, much less to stand the hardships we are called upon to stand," was their fare. "If you can't feed us, you had better surrender us, horrible as the idea is, than suffer this noble army to disgrace themselves by desertion." The authors of this statement made their point clearly. "This army is now ripe for mutiny, unless it can be fed."[46]

After waiting several days and consulting his commanders, Pemberton took the final step and entered into negotiations for surrender. The siege ended on July 4, 1863. At that time Pemberton's commissaries reported that the Vicksburg storehouses contained 76,482 rations of bacon, 2,400,000 rations of peas, 523,400 rations of rice, and 731 rations of flour. That stock represented no more than 3 days of bacon, 120 days of peas, and 26 days of rice. The men felt that their stamina would not be supported by a diet of peas and rice alone. The shortage of meat loomed foremost in their plight. Pemberton reported that he had reserved 40,000 pounds of pork and bacon to feed his men in case he tried to break through Grant's siege lines, but it is unclear whether that amount was included in the commissary report.[47]

"Our rations were reduced to little more than sufficient to sustain life," Ashbel Smith, colonel of the 2nd Texas, wrote in his report of the Vicksburg siege. "Five ounces of musty corn-meal and pea flour were nominally issued daily. In point of fact, this allowance did not exceed three ounces. All the unripe, half-grown peaches, the green berries growing on the briars, all were carefully gathered and simmered in a little sugar and water, and used for food. Every eatable vegetable around the works was hunted up for greens." As his men thinned and weakened, Smith noticed signs of incipient scurvy. Ralph J. Smith, who served in the 2nd Texas, argued that such hunger would have been an incentive to fight in order to capture commissary stores from the defeated enemy. But the Federals were protected by strong earthworks, precluding any offensive action; the result was widespread discouragement.[48]

"In the commissary department there has been a great want of foresight and energy," concluded John W. C. Watson in a report to Adjutant General Cooper in Richmond. "The troops at Port Hudson and Vicksburg should never have been reduced to short rations. These strongholds, by proper management, could have easily been provisioned for six or twelve months."[49] Speaking theoretically, Watson was correct. But theory often is interrupted by reality. Given the multifaceted problems of administration, transportation, and storage, Pemberton's commissaries deserve some credit for doing as much as they did to support his army.

That certainly was Theodore Johnston's viewpoint. He was upset that public opinion condemned his actions after the fall of Vicksburg and Port Hudson. "All officers connected with the Commissary Department were assailed by newspaper editors after the fall of those two places, and the failure" was attributed first to Pemberton and second to his chief commissary. Major Johnston tried to document the many problems and partial accomplishments of Pemberton's commissariat. "There was in Vicksburg when it surrendered half as much bacon as there was in the whole Department of Mississippi and Eastern Louisiana when I was assigned to duty," he informed Northrop.[50]

And yet self-serving comments only go so far. In the middle of the siege, Silas Hemphill of the 22nd Iowa wondered how long his opponents could hold out inside Vicksburg as far as their food supply was concerned. "I *would not* be surprised if they had *enough for* Six *months yet,*" he wrote his brother and sister. "I don't Know why they should *not* as they have *been* preparing for this long *enough* to be prepared."[51] As Hemphill so plainly put it, there was every reason to believe Pemberton would have stockpiled plenty of food for his men during the long months that led up to the siege.

But that did not happen, and Confederate supply during the Vicksburg Campaign stands in stark contrast to Federal supply efforts. To a large degree this is a reflection of general weaknesses in the Confederate military system and of general strengths in the Federal military system.

Every problem associated with Pemberton's effort to stockpile food at Vicksburg was reflected by similar problems other Rebel commanders faced. Personality clashes intermingled with wretched institutional conditions to combine with a culture of laissez faire in the undoing of Confederate logistics and supply throughout the South. It was not a shortage of resources but a boiling mix of conflicting tendencies in the culture and ideology of the South that was the problem. When you add bristling personalities jealous of their turf, you have the makings of a Confederate military system that did not work very well.

The most generous conclusion is that Confederate commissaries worked hard against these problems and managed to pull out a level of success that minimally supported Pemberton's defensive strategy of holding Vicksburg long enough to be helped by a relieving force. In the end Vicksburg's fall was triggered by food shortages rather than by any other cause. As a result, the commissaries' limited success was ignored, and they received the blunt end of criticism for the Gibraltar's fall.

4

TRANSPORTATION CRISIS IN APPALACHIA

The Appalachian Highlands posed a major threat to logistics that Federal commanders and quartermasters did not appreciate until they began to move through the mountains. As long as they operated in the relatively level country of central Kentucky and Middle Tennessee, they could deal with nature fairly easily. The underpowered locomotives of the day could handle shallow slopes, but mountainous terrain was a different story. When railroad companies ran lines across the Appalachian Highlands in the 1850s, they sought routes of least resistance. The Nashville and Chattanooga Railroad crossed the Cumberland Plateau, the first range of elevated ground in the highlands, at its most narrow point. Even so, an extra engine had to be stationed at the foot of the western slope near Cowan, Tennessee, to help trains go up, and the long downslope on the other side often produced frightening speeds because the engine could barely hold back the following cars. Railroad companies were forced to reduce the number of cars because of these problems. Carrying capacity was automatically reduced to negotiate Appalachian terrain.

In addition to this automatic decrease in hauling capacity, the countryside of Appalachia offered less food for foraging. The population of the mountainous counties of Tennessee and every other state that shared the highlands was less dense than the population of the low-lying areas east and west of the Appalachians. The mountains also restricted the amount of arable land available, with only the creek and river valleys providing viable farmland. Even small columns of advancing troops found it difficult to live off the countryside; large armies found it impossible.[1]

The Confederates were the first to experience these logistical and supply problems. Most residents of East Tennessee remained loyal to the U.S. government, forcing the Richmond authorities to send troops into the region soon after Tennessee left the Union in June 1861. For more than two years, Rebel regiments were disgusted with the Unionist attitude of the people and fed up with the lack of food and other resources in the region. "We are going to a starvation country," James E. Rains of the 11th Tennessee put it. Thomas B. Hall of the 17th Alabama referred to the Unionist sentiment of the natives and the supply problems his regiment faced in East Tennessee when writing that "Gen. Bragg ought to feed his army on them. The truth of it is that the men do not get half enough to eat now; nor have they since we got into Tennessee."[2]

The same was true of other Appalachian areas. Horatio G. Wright warned against any hope of conducting military operations in the mountainous counties of western Virginia by November 1862. "Bridges are all gone, boats broken up, and roads will be impassable as soon as bad weather sets in." Between Columbia and Cumberland Gap in Kentucky, no food or forage could be found. "I am satisfied that operations cannot be carried on in that direction at this season," he told General in Chief Halleck.[3]

Rosecrans and the Mountains

Rosecrans would have to deal with the mountains if he hoped to restart his campaign along the rail line linking Murfreesboro with Chattanooga, but the first step in that process was to clear Bragg's army from the rest of Middle Tennessee. He began the Tullahoma Campaign on June 24, 1863, with a brilliantly conceived plan to push the Army of Tennessee from its extended position anchored on the towns of Tullahoma and Shelbyville. The Federals outmaneuvered and outfought their opponents and compelled Bragg to abandon the rest of Middle Tennessee with minimal loss of life and comparatively little fighting. Not only was this in stark contrast to the bloody nature of the Stones River Campaign, but Rosecrans also suffered nothing like the logistical and supply problems of that previous effort. Bragg did not unleash his cavalry to strike the Federal wagon trains; in fact, at one point in the Tullahoma movement, Rosecrans threatened Bragg's railroad supply line and convinced the Confederates to retire from an intermediate position all the way to the edge of the Cumberland Plateau.

After the Tullahoma Campaign Rosecrans faced the challenge of moving his army across the most rugged terrain feature faced by any Civil War force. As his engineers and quartermasters repaired the railroad up to his waiting army, the troops struggled to find food in the countryside. There

APPALACHIA

was little to be acquired near McMinnville, already cleared out by the Confederates. "We can not get a bit of old corn or hay," reported T. C. Honnell of the 99th Ohio, "so we cut grass & oats take wheat & rye out of the shock drive in all the cattle for beef and just sweep everything before us. I don't know how the citizens are going to live."[4]

Rosecrans explained to his superiors that he already relied on 260 miles of railroad back to Louisville and faced "sixty miles of barren mountains, traversed by a few poor roads—to cross not the little Shenandoah a few miles from the Potomac." The Tennessee River, 800–1,800 yards wide, was a major barrier to his advance. "We have [no] gun-boats to aid us, and if our communications are interrupted no broad Mississippi, covered with transports, to supply us." Rosecrans was sensitive to the results of failing to sustain his army of 56,000 men while dealing with these problems. "It would be better for us to go a mile a day and [be] sure," he told Lincoln on August 1. "It takes time [to] organize the means of success."[5]

But even though he tried, Rosecrans failed to prepare adequately for the challenge posed by the mountains. Because there were just enough cars on the Nashville and Chattanooga Railroad to "barely suffice to keep us day by day," he purchased fifty additional cars, but it would take some time for them to arrive. Worse than shortages of rolling stock, Rosecrans rearranged his railroad management just before the army started to climb the highlands. On August 10 John B. Anderson resigned as superintendent of military railroads in the Department of the Cumberland. Both Sherman and Buell had been satisfied with Anderson's work since the fall of 1861. Whether Rosecrans eased him out or Anderson left on his own is unclear. The general then assigned Col. William P. Innes of the 1st Michigan Engineers and Mechanics to replace him. Several other army officers were assigned to subordinate positions within the railroad-management team as well. The effect was to thoroughly militarize the logistical system, stepping away from the earlier use of civilians.[6]

In addition, Rosecrans failed to anticipate the logistical needs of his army as it entered the mountains. He failed, as one historian has noted, to properly inform his railroad managers what was needed and what had to be done before the army resumed its forward march.[7]

What Rosecrans needed was a huge increase in rolling stock, not just fifty additional freight cars. More importantly, he needed a much larger corps of experienced railroad workers armed with construction trains, tools, and material to repair bridges of all sizes. One could expect many structures to be burned after the Confederates retreated. Rather than diminishing his reliance on civilians, Rosecrans should have increased it. Civilians with railroad experience were the key to meeting the logistical challenges posed by the mountains, yet Rosecrans denuded his department of this vital asset.

It is difficult to understand this development because Rosecrans normally acted like a thoroughly good military manager. In this case he understood the problem but not the solution. "It is necessary to have our means of crossing the river completed, and our supplies provided to cross 60 miles of mountain, and sustain ourselves during the operations of crossing and fighting, before we move," he wrote on August 6. "It is a stupendous undertaking. The Alps, with a broad river at the foot, and not fertile plains, but 70 miles of difficult and mostly sterile mountains beyond, before reaching a point of secondary importance to the enemy, in reference to his vital one, Atlanta" was what lay before the Army of the Cumberland.[8]

Ironically, Bragg also saw the mountains as a problem while replying to pressure from his government to take the offensive. "To 'fight the enemy' is a very simple operation when you have the means and can get at him," Bragg complained to General Johnston. "But with less than half his strength, and a large river and 50 to 100 miles of rugged, sterile mountains, destitute even of vegetation, between you and him, with our limited commissariat, the simple fighting would be a refreshing recreation."[9]

Crossing of the Tennessee River at Bridgeport, Alabama. Although the original caption for this photograph indicates it was taken in 1864 and that the Federals are constructing a pontoon bridge in the foreground, neither can be true. The Confederates gave up this area in the late summer of 1863, and Union engineers constructed a wagon bridge here by September 2. Looking closely at the bridge under construction in the foreground, it does not rest on pontoons but on wooden supports sunk into the river bottom. This photograph must have been exposed in late August 1863, when the Federals had just begun building the wagon bridge. The McCallum Bridge Company of Cincinnati rebuilt the railroad structure by mid-January 1864, and it was never destroyed again during the war, another reason to assume this photograph was taken in 1863. Judging by the driftwood collecting on the upstream side of the piers, this view was taken from the north bank of the river looking south. LC-DIG-ppmsca-33490.

Federal preparations for the push across the highlands were impeded by slow repair work on the Nashville and Chattanooga Railroad. Crews restored the line down to Wartrace, about halfway between Murfreesboro and Tullahoma, by July 6. Four days later they were at Tullahoma. When Confederate troops raided the section between Nashville and Murfreesboro, crews had to repair that damage. It took "several weeks" to get the line working to Stevenson, Alabama. Meanwhile, because heavy rains caused the Cumberland River to rise above the norm for summer, quartermasters could ship large amounts of material to Nashville by steamer until late July.[10]

The purchase of fifty additional freight cars provided some help. The Army of the Cumberland required forty-one cars of material to meet its daily needs and sixty cars per day to exceed them in order to accumulate a stockpile that could enable it to operate away from the railroad. That stockpile began to slowly build up at Stevenson.[11]

If nothing unusual transpired, Rosecrans's preparations seemed adequate thus far. But soon after he began to move across the mountains on August 16, the logistical and supply situation deteriorated. The Louisville and Nashville Railroad, for reasons not clearly explained, reduced its Nashville shipments to only twenty cars per day. By this time, early September, river steamers found it impossible to reach Nashville due to falling water levels. Quartermasters also began to realize that the Nashville and Chattanooga Railroad, even though comparatively new, had been constructed with the cheapest and least reliable type of rails. The road was so bad that in places engines ran at no more than 8 miles per hour. It took some trains twenty-four hours to travel 130 miles from Nashville to Bridgeport, Alabama, the last stop north of the Tennessee River. Although Federal engineers constructed a wagon bridge over the river by September 2, the long railroad bridge was a daunting structure to rebuild. Rosecrans hired a civilian contractor to restore it, with consequent delays and frustrations.[12]

Rosecrans had failed to anticipate these problems, which a good railroad man could have foreseen. Historian Douglas H. Galuszka has concluded that the general "was a poor logistician" who impaired the ability of his army to deal with the challenges posed by the mountains. Because Rosecrans had thoroughly militarized his logistical system, officers and men had to perform dual jobs. Many high-ranking officers such as the chief commissary, the superintendent of railroads, and the chief quartermaster stayed at Nashville rather than accompany the army because they had to wear two hats instead of one. They were responsible not only for the 56,000 men in the field but also for all problems within the entire Department of the Cumberland.[13]

Burnside and the Mountains

To complicate matters, the railroad system within the Department of the Cumberland also had to supply the troops of Maj. Gen. Ambrose Burnside's Department of the Ohio when they entered the heart of East Tennessee in the late summer of 1863. Finally, after two years of agonized waiting, the loyalists of the region would be placed high on the agenda of both President Lincoln and his generals. The primary reason for this was the transfer of two divisions of Burnside's Ninth Corps to the West following that general's defeat at the Battle of Fredericksburg the previous December. Burnside's primary goal was the conquest of East Tennessee, but he was compelled to divert both divisions to aid Grant at Vicksburg in June. With the western regiments stationed in his department, Burnside set out in late August to penetrate the mountains.

The supply problems associated with a strike into East Tennessee had not disappeared during the past two years. Col. Samuel A. Gilbert explained them very well to a Ninth Corps general in May 1863. Taking the region was comparatively easy, Gilbert argued, but holding it was the problem. When Morgan's Federal division had held Cumberland Gap from June to September 1862, his men were able to forage for half the meat they needed in an area extending 50 miles in all directions from the gap, but this area was largely denuded by the summer of 1863. Gilbert concluded that nearly everything a Union garrison would need at Cumberland Gap would have to be carried 120 miles by wagon from the nearest railhead at Nicholasville, Kentucky. Each wagon could carry 400 rations plus food for its team, needing sixteen days to make the roundtrip. A garrison of 5,000 men would need 13 wagons every day, and if that force had 1,000 horses, it would need an additional 22 wagons per day to feed the animals. Gilbert estimated an additional 5 wagons would be needed per day to carry quartermaster and ordnance stores. The total logistical power to supply a garrison of 5,000 men and 1,000 horses at Cumberland Gap came to 924 wagons and 5,544 mules to pull them. He added an additional 20 percent of wagons to cover losses due to breakdowns and guerrilla attacks. "This mountain country was poor then," Gilbert concluded, "it is utterly exhausted now, and its destitution forms a very fair barrier to an invasion."[14]

It was impossible to extend the railroad from Nicholasville to Cumberland Gap and Knoxville earlier in the war, but Rosecrans's campaign now offered a rail route to the heart of East Tennessee from the south. Capturing Chattanooga would allow the Federals to use the East Tennessee and Georgia Railroad between that city and Knoxville. Burnside started 8,400 men from several points in south Kentucky, crossing the Cumberland Plateau and making his way directly toward Knoxville. He relied entirely on 200 wagons to supply them. Because he moved simultaneously with Rosecrans in late August, the Confederates stripped East Tennessee of troops to concentrate on the defense of Chattanooga. Burnside occupied Knoxville on September 1 without a struggle and compelled the surrender of Cumberland Gap on the ninth.[15]

Burnside's men went on half rations from the moment they ascended the Cumberland Plateau and continued on less than full rations after occupying Knoxville. It proved more difficult than expected to open the East Tennessee and Georgia Railroad. Rosecrans occupied Chattanooga without a battle on September 9 but then was defeated just south at Chickamauga on September 20. The Army of the Cumberland took refuge in Chattanooga and could offer no support to Burnside. There were five locomotives and twenty cars along the 100 miles of intact railroad southwest and northeast of Knoxville, but the Confederates had destroyed the long and high railroad bridge over the Tennessee River at Loudon, a few miles southwest of the city.[16]

By mid-September two Federal armies were planted in the most important cities of East Tennessee, but neither had secure lines of supply. The rail line from Louisville operated at diminished capacity down to Bridgeport, with no working link to either Chattanooga or Knoxville. There was scant hope that more than 70,000 men could feed themselves in this region.

In addition to food, both Federal armies needed a variety of supplies of all kinds. The defeat at Chickamauga robbed Rosecrans of much valuable material. His subordinates submitted requisitions that included 45,000 coats, 75,000 pairs of shoes, 25,000 shirts, 5,000 blankets, 26,000 pairs of socks, 5,000 axes, and 768 wagons. Quartermasters had little hope of transporting that amount of material to where it was needed.[17]

Supply Crisis

A supply crisis descended over Union military operations in East Tennessee. Washington's immediate reaction was to do what the Confederates had earlier done when they shifted two divisions under Lt. Gen. James Longstreet from the Army of Northern Virginia to help Bragg win at Chickamauga. The Eleventh and Twelfth Corps were detached from the Army of the Potomac, placed under Maj. Gen. Joseph Hooker, and transported by rail to Middle Tennessee. The troops performed occupation duty along the functioning part of the rail line to ensure the flow of supplies down to Bridgeport. From there, the material was transported in wagons toward Chattanooga.[18]

Washington authorities also began to examine Rosecrans's personnel decisions. Thomas A. Scott, railroad executive and current assistant secretary of war, began to wonder why Anderson had resigned as superintendent of the department's military railroads in August. Scott knew Anderson and considered him to be a skillful manager and a man of integrity. He recommended Anderson be reinstalled as superintendent, and Secretary of War Stanton was easily persuaded. Anderson was currently helping find rolling stock for the move of the Eleventh and Twelfth Corps but could be sent to the Department of the Cumberland as Scott suggested.[19]

The eastern soldiers found Rosecrans's logistical arrangements in terrible shape. "This Department was completely 'out of joint' when we first arrived," complained Maj. Gen. Oliver Otis Howard, commander of the Eleventh Corps, to Sen. Henry Wilson. "A *most complete* and *perfect want* of system prevailed from Louisville to Chattanooga. . . . You ought to have ridden with us from Nashville to Bridgeport to see the results of bad management." To his wife Howard wrote, "just think of hauling all the supplies for an army over fifty miles of road, over mountains & through muddy valleys. . . . When you come here and find us as far from Nashville as Portland is from Boston and that every article must come by a single poor rail road running over a high mountain valley with different grades at best and that the main army is forty or fifty miles further on, and that the country is too impoverished to support the inhabitants, the wonder is how the army can remain & sustain itself."[20]

Brig. Gen. Alpheus S. Williams, a division commander in the Twelfth Corps, was even more surprised. "This is a monstrous line over which Gen.

Rosecrans has to supply his army, over 300 miles of railroad, crossed every few miles by broad streams and valleys and running through and around and across high mountains. This beggars anything we have seen of lines of operations in the Army of the Potomac." Williams's division was responsible for maintaining and protecting twenty-two miles of railroad south of Tullahoma. "Of course we can guard only the bridges, tunnels, culverts, water-tanks, etc."[21]

Thomas A. Scott was appalled when he reached Nashville. He found too little rolling stock to supply Rosecrans and called for twenty-five to thirty additional engines from the roads in Virginia. This request illustrates how much Rosecrans had failed to anticipate his logistical needs.[22]

Confederate guerrillas began to burn small bridges that had to be replaced. They dropped rocks through two shafts into the tunnel near Cowan, Tennessee, forcing railroad crews to clear up the debris. Charles Henry Howard, Oliver's brother and a member of his staff, reported that even without interference, the underpowered engines had difficulty negotiating the grades of the region. He rode on a train that stalled "on a heavy *up-grade* between Wartrace and Tullahoma."[23]

Grant and the Mountains

Rosecrans put it mildly when he told Halleck: "Our future is not bright. . . . This army with its back to barren mountains, roads narrow and difficult, while the enemy has the railroad and the corn in his rear, is at much disadvantage." On that day the general in chief issued orders to appoint Grant commander of a newly created Military Division of the Mississippi. "One of the first objects requiring your attention is the supply of your armies," Halleck told him. Grant relieved Rosecrans and replaced him with Maj. Gen. George H. Thomas. "Hold Chattanooga at all hazards," he telegraphed the new commander on October 19. "I will be there as soon as possible." By a great effort Grant reached Chattanooga on the night of the twenty-third "after a ride on horseback of fifty miles, from Bridgeport, over the worst roads it is possible to conceive of, and through a continuous drenching rain." He saw enough to conclude, "it is bearly [*sic*] possible to supply this Army from its present base."[24]

In addition to sending Grant to Chattanooga, Washington authorities rearranged the support staff in the region. Quartermaster General Meigs went to Chattanooga to see if he could help. Quartermaster Robert Allen was shifted from Saint Louis to Louisville to mastermind procurement and shipping in the entire Mississippi Valley. James L. Donaldson was appointed quartermaster, Department of the Cumberland, while Langdon C. Easton was sent from his post at Fort Leavenworth to Chattanooga to serve as the new chief quartermaster, Department of the Cumberland. Lewis B. Parsons was promoted to superintend all river-borne transportation in the western theater of operations. This was the most impressive team of experts in logistics and supply ever assembled in the higher echelons above that of field armies in the Civil War.[25]

"Your difficulty will not be in the want of men," Halleck told Grant, "but in the means of supplying them at this season of the year." He suggested moving all animals not needed at Chattanooga back to Nashville and sending forage for animals and food for men on the backs of soldiers marching from Bridgeport to Chattanooga. Grant, however, refrained from using his soldiers as mules.[26]

Halleck's suggestion was tied to a shortage of wagons in the area. In the aftermath of Chickamauga, Rosecrans needed 768 wagons but there were no more than 135 available at Nashville. Four hundred wagons were in need of repair and being fixed at the rate of 40–50 per week, which would not meet the army's needs. Making the situation worse, Maj. Gen. Joseph Wheeler raided behind Union lines and destroyed 300 wagons in the Sequatchie River valley that were on their way to Chattanooga loaded with supplies. Quartermasters scrambled to find replacement animals, more easily procuring mules than horses.[27]

Fall introduced the worst season for traveling in the mountains. "The roads from here to Chattanooga are terrible," wrote William P. Lyon of the 13th Wisconsin from Bridgeport. Grant agreed with that assessment. "This is one of the wildest places you ever saw, and without the use of rail roads one of the most out-of-the way places." Hauling capacity was reduced because wagons had to be loaded with less freight for the mules to have a chance to navigate the roads. Grant estimated that about 10,000 animals had already died in trying to supply the army. Thomas did not have enough artillery horses to pull his batteries for operations outside the confines of Chattanooga. "When I got here it was impossible to move a peg," Grant reported, "worst roads you can conceive of. There was not another trip left in the mules," and it would have taken all the horses of a battery to move even one artillery piece. "I have never felt such restlessness before as I have at this fixed and unmovable condition of the Army of the Cumberland," Grant confessed to Halleck.[28]

Although immobile, enough food came in through wagon trains to keep the troops alive. But the supply route was grueling. Beginning at Bridgeport, it extended to the northeast along the bottomland of the Tennessee River and its tributary, the Sequatchie River. Then the wagons turned east and ascended the 1,400-foot western slope of Walden Ridge, moved across its top, and descended the eastern slope of 1,300 feet. Six miles away lay a pontoon bridge to take the trains across the Tennessee into Chattanooga. The entire trip included sixty-one miles of dirt mountain roads, two very difficult slopes, and two river crossings. On average it took ten days to go from Bridgeport to Chattanooga. Historian Phillip Kemmerly has estimated that only thirty-one men could be fed each day by every wagon that made it through. That would require 1,677 wagons pulled by 10,000 mules to supply the army for just one day. But Thomas had only about 800 wagons left after Wheeler's raid in October. The Army of the Cumberland was reduced to half rations by this time.[29]

Thomas's troops endured this crushing lack of food. "Men are starving here," reported A. G. Wilcox of the 105th Ohio. "Saw a man today picking Kernels of corn out of the dirt, and eating them. He was the picture of misery. Men go to bed tonight without supper and get nothing more until day after tomorrow. Mule-meat is considered a luxury."[30]

But soon after Grant's arrival, improvement took place. He approved a plan worked out by Rosecrans to shorten the wagon link with Bridgeport by clearing Confederate troops from the area south of the Tennessee River downstream from Chattanooga. This operation worked smoothly on October 27, and the Federals defended the new route when Longstreet tried to cut it on the night of October 28–29 in the Battle of Wauhatchie. What soldiers fondly dubbed the "Cracker Line," about thirty miles long, now alleviated the worst suffering. Sixty carloads of material arrived at Bridgeport every day, most of which was stored until wagons became available.[31]

The presence of two large armies, Union and Confederate, soon stripped the region of provisions. "The country is exhausted beyond conception," wrote Capt. William Wheeler of the 13th New York Battery. "The army has to struggle with the citizen for his mouthful of corn." Many civilians were "on the very border of starvation," while the army was "moderately well provisioned" after the Cracker Line opened.[32]

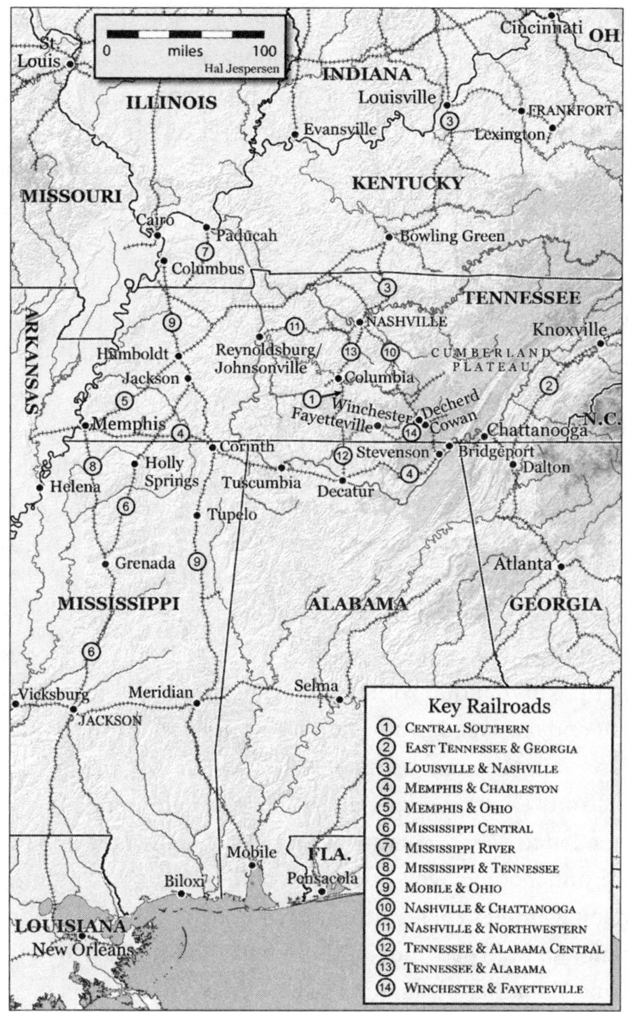

RAILROAD SUPPLY LINES IN THE WEST

Creating a New Logistical Network

The key to solving this problem was to repair and expand the railroad system, and the new team recently appointed worked hard to do so. When Donaldson moved from Baltimore to become chief quartermaster, Department of the Cumberland, he found that the Nashville and Chattanooga Railroad could haul only forty cars per day to Bridgeport, while, according to his estimate, Thomas needed one hundred cars each day. It took a week to deliver mail 151 miles from Nashville to Chattanooga, and Donaldson noticed that much government property was stolen along the route. "I confess I felt appalled and almost disheartened at the magnitude of the work before me," he admitted. Donaldson consolidated all offices of his department previously scattered throughout Nashville. He installed his subordinates in an entire city block so they could occupy contiguous buildings. Donaldson examined every officer under his charge, determined each man's strengths and weaknesses, and reassigned them to positions where they could work well. He also assigned a reliable man with an assistant to take charge of the mail system and deliver dispatches more quickly to Chattanooga. After about a month, Donaldson returned the delivery of the mail to the army post office, having improved the process so much that it had no trouble managing the system.[33]

Donaldson saw the Nashville and Chattanooga Railroad as the all-important stem of his rail system, but it was "a rickety, stringer-tie, dilapidated affair, never worth much before the rebellion, and well used up in supplying Bragg before he fell back across the Tennessee." As of November 1, 1863, he had only thirty engines and 350 cars on the line. Donaldson could depend on no more than half of that rolling stock because the rest "had been off the track, upset, and damaged generally, so seriously that they could hardly be reckoned as among the resources of the road." In fact, one officer told him the Nashville and Chattanooga line "was a vast cemetery of rolling-stock." The road needed to be refurbished with entirely new rails and the infusion of more cars and locomotives, but that would take several months.[34]

Donaldson wanted to open alternate routes to supplement the Nashville and Chattanooga Railroad. One of them was the line that linked Nashville with Decatur, Alabama, which in turn was linked to Stevenson and Bridgeport by the Memphis and Charleston Railroad. Not one but three railroad companies constituted the line between Nashville and Decatur. The Tennessee and Alabama Railroad controlled the track from Nashville to Columbia, while the Central Southern Railroad ran from Columbia to the Alabama state line, and the Tennessee and Alabama Central Railroad continued the route from the state border to Decatur. Together these three companies totaled 133 miles of track spanning some of the most mountainous terrain in the United States. But when put into operation, the line between Nashville and Decatur could help a great deal to supplement the flow of supplies to Bridgeport.

Another supplemental line was the Nashville and Northwestern Railroad, which ran seventy-five miles west from Nashville to Reynoldsburg (later called Johnsonville) on the east bank of the Tennessee River. It had been started before the war and was yet unfinished, but if opened, steamers could ascend the Tennessee and deposit material at Reynoldsburg for rail shipment to the state capital.

A third alternate route of supply involved the Edgefield and Kentucky Railroad. It started from the Louisville and Nashville Railroad at a point called Edgefield Junction, ten miles north of Nashville, and continued forty-seven miles northwest to Graysville, Kentucky, very near the Tennessee state line. At Graysville, the road connected to the Memphis, Clarksville, and Louisville Railroad only fifteen miles northeast of Clarksville. Using this roundabout rail connection between Clarksville and the state capital allowed Federal quartermasters to bypass Harpeth Shoals on the Cumberland River, which often prevented steamers from reaching Nashville in times of low water levels.[35]

Donaldson envisioned a logistical system for the Department of the Cumberland that could truly solve the problems posed by the mountains. It would supply the Federals at Knoxville, too, and eventually make possible a further push south from Chattanooga. But it would take months to create this expansive network.

Joining the new management team was a member of the old one. Washington authorities held a good opinion of John B. Anderson and seem not to have known why he had resigned in August. When Stanton placed Anderson in a supervisory role over the railroads in Thomas's department on October 19, he made sure that Meigs had authority over him. This was a significant change in Anderson's status because, before his dismissal, he had reported only to the commander of the department.[36]

Anderson began working at Nashville on November 2 to provide the Army of the Cumberland with at least thirty carloads of rations every day; at least ten had to be filled with beef cattle. Initially Anderson promised to send fifty cars each day and increase it to as many as one hundred after a while. He could dispatch a total of four trains per day and hoped soon to increase this to five. When he inspected the line between Nashville and Decatur, Anderson reported that many trestles were flimsy and liable to be washed out by the next heavy rain. He wanted to prebuild trestles at Nashville and store them for use when needed, a plan Grant heartily approved.[37]

But Anderson soon found that his job was more difficult than anticipated. By mid-November he was unable to increase the flow of cars to Bridgeport. Fewer than fifty per day were arriving due to bad tracks. The Army of the Cumberland had a stockpile of only ten days' rations at Chattanooga but less than the standard ration of forage for its animals, which were "still suffering." Anderson complained that his engines were in bad shape but hoped to receive new ones from the North very soon. His major worry was the poor condition of track on both lines extending south and southeast from Nashville. One thousand tons of railroad iron was shipped from Washington, D.C., to help him repair the tracks. Meigs urged him to take up the rails from the Winchester and Fayetteville Railroad and use them to repair the Nashville and Chattanooga line. Anderson was willing and targeted the thirty-nine-mile stretch between Fayetteville and Decherd, but he needed infantrymen to guard his work crews.[38]

Grant was impatient. "There is so much dependent upon geting [*sic*] up everything promptly, (and all the means of carrying on War here have to pass through Nashville)," that he stationed two of his staff members at the Tennessee capital to help Anderson funnel material past that chokepoint.[39]

Grant lost his patience when it seemed that Anderson was not pushing bridge reconstruction fast enough. Anderson contracted with L. B. Boomer to rebuild spans along the line between Nashville and Decatur. "He is the only builder who could procure the timber," Anderson explained. Born in upstate New York, Boomer had moved to the West in 1851 to become one of the major bridge builders in many states. But Grant fumed as Boomer dallied. "Already several weeks of valuable time have been lost," he complained on November 23. The general told Anderson to replace trestles using his own men and assign Boomer only to the larger projects. When Anderson asked if he should offer new contracts to civilians who lived in the area, with the intent of getting the job done in ninety days, Grant lost all faith in him. He severed Anderson's connection with the Nashville to Decatur route and looked for someone else to push that work forward.[40]

Sherman and the Mountains

The arrival of Sherman with six divisions from the Department of the Tennessee gave Grant more personnel to devote to railroad work. Sherman started with four divisions of the Fifteenth and Seventeenth Corps from the Big Black River in central Mississippi as part of the major effort to reinforce Rosecrans soon after Chickamauga. He marched his 20,000 men, 8,000 animals, and 600 wagons to Vicksburg, where river steamers transported them to Memphis. The Memphis and Charleston Railroad was not operational beyond Corinth, but Sherman's men tried to repair it as they moved east. That effort caused unacceptable delays. By October 24 Grant ordered him to drop the railroad work and march the troops across country to Stevenson. Sherman picked up two additional divisions of the Sixteenth Corps, commanded by Brig. Gen. Grenville M. Dodge, from north Mississippi as well.[41]

Sherman organized shipments of supplies for his roving column. The Tennessee River was on a slow rise, which enabled steamers to transport food to Eastport, Mississippi. Commissaries shipped a quarter million rations and 250 beef cattle to that place. Sherman's troops were crossing the Tennessee at Eastport by October 30, using three steamers, a small ferry boat, and two gunboats. "I can only carry ten days' rations, and will draw liberally of meats and corn of the country," he told Grant.[42]

Sherman intended to avoid the mountainous section of northern Alabama by marching north and east, traversing southern Tennessee by way of Fayetteville. This town was located halfway between the Central Southern Railroad and the Nashville and Chattanooga Railroad. A line called the Winchester and Fayetteville Railroad connected Fayetteville not only with Winchester but also with nearby Decherd on the Nashville and Chattanooga line. This gave Grant an opportunity to detach part of Sherman's command and devote it to railroad reconstruction. He ordered him to detach Dodge's 8,000 men of the Left Wing, Sixteenth Corps to rebuild the line between Nashville and Decatur. Dodge's area of responsibility would be from Columbia south to Decatur, the most difficult part of the rail network supplying Chattanooga. Dodge already was working on the line for two weeks when Grant became fed up with Anderson's and Boomer's delays in rebuilding its bridges.[43]

"Sherman will reach Fayetteville to-morrow without anything to eat," Grant told staff member T. S. Bowers on November 7. He wanted Bowers, who was stationed at Nashville, to send 100,000 rations by the Nashville and Chattanooga Railroad and the Winchester and Fayetteville Railroad. Sherman reached Fayetteville on November 8 with four Fifteenth and Seventeenth Corps divisions. He had cut off his connection with Eastport much earlier and now relied entirely on the railroads running south from Nashville to support his column.[44]

It would not be easy to supply Sherman at Fayetteville. Frank Thomson informed Grant that the "track is in bad order and covered with grass so that an engine would have great difficulty in getting along." In addition, there were no water or wood stations along the line. Federal forces had had no reason to use the line thus far and thus had not rectified these problems. Meanwhile, Dodge reported vicious guerrilla attacks were hampering his work on the line south of Columbia. He planned to feed his troops by rail shipments from Nashville and limit foraging because of the guerrillas.[45]

Dodge found that the Central Southern Railroad had a fine roadbed with lots of spare rails "and good cedar ties its entire length." The real problem was the numerous bridges, most of which needed work, and the many water tanks that had to be replaced. He estimated it would take at least ten days to redo the line between Columbia and Pulaski alone. When he reported that no work force was located between Columbia and Nashville, Sherman urged Grant to extend Dodge's zone to include that stretch.[46]

With time, Dodge became convinced that feeding his men from the countryside was the best policy. He wanted to do this in an orderly manner to maintain troop discipline. Foraging liberally off the countryside would deny food to roving guerrilla bands as well. "These people are proud, arrogant rebels," he told a subordinate. "They must support my command, respect and obey my orders, and that all they possess belongs legitimately to the U. S. Government." If local citizens brought food in, he would pay them for it, but if the Federals had to seize supplies, they would only issue certificates for future settlement if the owner was found to be loyal. Dodge tried to curb wanton destruction of property and warned civilians he would hold them responsible for guerrilla attacks on the railroad.[47]

Commissary officer Cyrus C. Carpenter was in charge of Dodge's new procurement process. He required that all civilians report the amount of provisions they had and then "apportioned it between the Government and themselves, including their negroes, and gave them vouchers." Carpenter was convinced this was the most judicious way to subsist an army from the populace. He used all the mills he could find six days a week to grind for the army and allowed civilians to use them on Sundays.[48]

Sherman's moving column also had procured food from citizens before reaching Fayetteville. W. G. Buck of the 17th Iowa told his cousin that the

Steamer *Chickamauga.* One of the thirteen purpose-built steamers constructed at Bridgeport by Arthur Edwards. These vessels were designed to be small with a shallow draft so as to negotiate the uncertain water levels of the upper Tennessee River. They could do no more than provide a supplement to the large amount of material shipped by railroad, which was the main supply line for any large army in the Appalachian Highlands. LC-DIG-ppmsca-33983.

troops "foraged through the country to Winchester. We got plenty of Fat Hogs Turkeys geese chickens and sweet potatoes. we Lived high. Besides the persimmons & Beach Nuts which could Be scraped up By handfuls along the Road there was thousands of Bushels of persimmons where we marched through the Country." But when the column reached Fayetteville, the men began to enter a zone already traversed by Union and Confederate troops. "The Country was Foraged Bare and we had to Come down to the Regular hard Tack and sow Belly with plenty Sugar & Coffee."[49]

Sherman began to ascend the Cumberland Plateau on November 17, his men marching close to the Nashville and Chattanooga Railroad as they climbed the rocky slope near Cowan. In places, horses and mules collapsed from the strain, and the men pushed wagons and artillery carriages up the grade. That night they bivouacked on top and the next day "went Tumbling off the Mountain on this side," as Buck described it.[50]

Sherman's arrival at Chattanooga added another 20,000 mouths to feed, but the rail system still needed work. "It is almost impossible to get sufficient to supply this army," Grant told Maj. Gen. Stephen A. Hurlbut, ordering him to send rolling stock from West Tennessee. Grant also wanted Hurlbut to strip several lines of rails and ties for shipment by river to Nashville. He pointed to the Memphis and Ohio Railroad between Memphis and Humboldt, Tennessee; the Mississippi and Tennessee Railroad between Memphis and Grenada, Mississippi; and the Mississippi Central Railroad south of Grand Junction, Tennessee, as suitable sources. Grant advised that the crews start as far away on each of these lines as they could to procure the maximum amount of material.[51]

Steamboats

Grant's supply problem eased only a little as quartermasters began to use the upper reaches of the Tennessee River. Muscle Shoals, located 130 miles downstream from Bridgeport, blocked passage for most steamers used on the lower part of the river. Rosecrans had assigned Arthur Edwards to find a solution to this problem on August 9. Edwards recommended constructing small, light-draft vessels at Bridgeport for use on the river from that point to Chattanooga. Rosecrans approved the plan, and Edwards began to transport virtually all boat-building tools as well as machinery from the North, relying on the local area for timber. He repaired an old sawmill at Bridgeport and constructed fourteen barges that were later used as pontoons before beginning work on the steamboats. Rosecrans authorized him to cannibalize machinery on government-owned vessels on the Cumberland River. Edwards raided the *Conway, Cottage,* and *Glenwood* and shipped their machinery by rail to Bridgeport in September.[52]

Edwards completed his first boat, *Chattanooga,* in late October. Its maiden voyage occurred right after the Cracker Line opened. *Chattanooga* towed two barges with 34,000 rations for Thomas's men, making the roundtrip in twenty-four hours. Edwards soon completed the *Paint Rock,* which could carry 200 tons of material in addition to towing barges. Meigs directed Edwards to repair a civilian steamer on the upper Tennessee named *Dunbar* and use it for military purposes. Eventually, Edwards constructed four light-draft gunboats, partially clad in iron, in addition to nine other transports. All told, his builders made thirteen steamers in nine months, an average of one every twenty-one days. His sawmill produced 750,000 feet of lumber from trees cut one to three miles away. Edwards mounted an interesting experiment in government shipbuilding to fill a specialized need in military transport.[53]

Another steamboat effort farther north also played a marginal role in dealing with supply problems. The same rains that began to raise the water level in the Tennessee River, enabling Sherman to cross at Eastport while receiving supplies by boat, also raised the water level in the Cumberland River. Rosecrans had requested 10 million rations to be stockpiled at Nashville, and commissary H. C. Symonds thought it would be possible to use the river for a short time in this effort. The general's order amounted to 25,000 tons of commissary stores, but Symonds also thought Rosecrans would probably want 40,000 tons of ordnance supplies, medical stores, and a variety of quartermaster stores. He cooperated with quartermaster officers to ship as much as possible in ten days while the water lasted, estimating that thirty to forty boats of 500-ton capacity could be obtained between Cairo and Pittsburgh. It was unlikely any of them could make more than one trip in the time allotted. Symonds managed to get many boatloads into Nashville during his short window of opportunity.[54]

Weak Links to Knoxville

Federal quartermasters and commissaries also worked to supply Burnside at Knoxville. With the addition of two divisions of the Ninth Corps to supplement his western troops, the general now had 12,000 men to feed. Those troops had been on half rations since August. Until the railroad from Nashville to Chattanooga and then to Knoxville became operable, they depended on wagon trains, some small shipments by river steamer, and a lot of foraging from the countryside.[55]

The wagon-train link was Burnside's primary supply channel. Trains were organized at Camp Nelson, 160 miles from Knoxville, and moved along rugged roads that snaked through creek bottoms subject to flooding at high water. One man counted 114 dead mules during one day of travel along the route in November 1863. Frederick W. Fout of the 15th Indiana Battery thought the bones of animals like these would have corduroyed the entire road from Camp Nelson to Cumberland Gap. "Any thinking man could have seen that it was absolutely impossible to supply an army in East Tennessee by wagons over the mountains," he concluded.[56]

Some degree of river transport was employed to help the Army of the Ohio. T. S. Bowers organized a few light-draft steamers at Nashville to take advantage of a rise in the Cumberland River. These boats could make it to the Big South Fork by following the Cumberland upriver into southeast Kentucky, about 140 miles from Nashville. From here the supplies could be hauled by wagon 70 miles to Cumberland Gap and then another 60 miles to Knoxville. The steamers needed gunboat escorts of similar draft. Pilots told Bowers that the Cumberland above Nashville was too narrow and had too many sharp turns for boats to tow barges. "Above Burkesville [100 miles above Nashville] it is barely wide enough for small class steam-boats," Bowers informed Grant.[57]

An alternate route was to send steamers up the Cumberland River from Nashville and take a turn into Caney Fork Creek at the town of Carthage, about forty miles east of the state capital. Caney Fork flows from the southeast toward Carthage and the Cumberland, and for the time it was navigable by small boats. Meigs thought such vessels could make it to Sligo Ferry, located twenty-five miles upstream from Carthage. From there a wagon road extended due east for sixty-five miles by way of Sparta and Crossville before reaching Kingston on the Tennessee River. It was only another thirty miles before the wagons would roll into Knoxville from the southwest. Meigs was informed that the road between Sligo Ferry and Kingston was "tolerably good," but he advised that each train be well escorted by troops. The teamsters could use axes, spades, and picks to repair rough places in the road.[58]

Battle at Chattanooga

The expansive Union posture in East Tennessee placed sizeable numbers of troops in several locations within Appalachia by late November 1863. All of those troops suffered supply problems. The only sure way to properly support them was to improve the rail network. That difficult task was not yet finished when Grant took the offensive against Bragg at Chattanooga on November 23. Thomas's troops moved forward a short distance to take

Orchard Knob, a prominent hill between the lines. The next day three Federal divisions attacked Lookout Mountain and cleared it by evening. The climactic day of battle on November 25 witnessed an inspiring attack by four divisions of Thomas's army against the main Confederate position on Missionary Ridge. To the amazement of many observers, the Federals crumpled Bragg's position, drove the Army of Tennessee from the ridge top, and administered a dismal defeat on the Rebels.

Inadequate supplies did not prevent Grant from winning a decisive victory that reversed the strategic situation around Chattanooga in one stroke. But after the battle, the Federals were still underfed and undersupplied. The level of deprivation could not last much longer without irreparable harm to troop effectiveness.

Starving in East Tennessee

Grant dispatched a relief column of 30,000 men under Sherman to help Burnside at Knoxville. Since mid-November, when Bragg sent 12,000 men under Longstreet to recapture the mountain city, the Federals there had been penned up behind their defenses. Sherman's command consisted of troops from his Department of the Tennessee plus the Eleventh Corps and the Fourth Corps from the Army of the Cumberland. The troops lived off the denuded countryside with no regular supply lines, spurred on by the thought that Burnside was starving in Knoxville.[59]

Sherman's relief march impressed the eastern soldiers. "It was the wild project of *ignoring our base* so ridiculous in the terms proposed by Pope in Virginia and capable of being successfully carried through only by the most resolute and fertile of Commanders," commented Charles Henry Howard.[60]

Grenville Dodge did not participate in the relief march to Knoxville, but he heard about it early in 1864. When Maj. Gen. Gordon Granger, commander of the Fourth Corps, hosted Grant, Sherman, and Dodge in Nashville, Granger's mother upbraided Sherman for letting his men forage so liberally. "Madam, my soldiers have to subsist even if the whole country must be ruined to maintain them," Sherman retorted. "There are two armies here; one is in rebellion against the Union, the other is fighting for the Union—if either must starve to death, I propose it shall not be the army that is loyal."[61]

Merely marching toward Knoxville was enough to lift the "semi-siege" of the city. Heavily outnumbered, Longstreet broke away on the night of December 4 and retired toward the northeast. Sherman stayed only a few days before taking most of his force back to Chattanooga, leaving Granger's Fourth Corps to support Burnside. Granger was not happy. He saw the heart of East Tennessee as a wasteland and wanted to return to the Cumberland army. He stressed the supply problems suffered by his men as the best way to convince Thomas to call him back. "The sufferings and privations now being undergone by our troops are most cruel," Granger wrote on December 19. "Rations have been very irregular and limited," and sickness was on a sharp increase.[62]

Capt. William N. Buckley of Battery D, 1st Rhode Island in the Ninth Corps, felt his troops suffered more at Knoxville than during any other campaign.

> Some of the men are quite ragged, and hardly any have stockings. The weather is getting quite cold, and they are in great need of all kinds of clothing. In addition to this, they have not drawn over one-half rations of coffee and sugar since the 28th day of August, and a great part of that time it has been but one-quarter rations, and sometimes none at all. They have had but very little hard bread; it has been flour and fresh beef, and the flour they can only cook to make it hardly eatable, as they have nothing to mix it with. Beans, rice, and vegetables, they have had none since leaving Cincinnati, and, only once in a great while, candles and soap.[63]

An inspection of Col. William Humphrey's Ninth Corps brigade took place in early January 1864. Of 1,015 men, 374 needed underclothing, 386 had no shoes, 65 needed blankets, 471 had no overcoats, 218 had no tents, 657 had no socks, 295 needed pants, and 186 needed coats. The men barely subsisted on food from the countryside and the wagon trains coming from outside Appalachia.[64]

Brig. Gen. William B. Hazen thoroughly documented the supply problem of his Fourth Corps brigade in a report to Thomas's headquarters. From September 20 to November 28, his men were on short rations, often less than half the standard issue. From November 28 to December 20, "their subsistence was precarious, sometimes ample and at others scant." From December 20 to January 8, 1864, the men had from one-half to two-thirds rations.

Foraging parties traveled thirty miles to find a little hay for animals. By early January Hazen's men were understandably tired, hungry, and cold.[65]

The Federals became so harsh in their efforts to find food that they alienated many Union loyalists in East Tennessee. "Hungry men are difficult to control after fasting for five months on half and quarter rations," admitted E. E. Potter to General Granger.[66]

Meigs explained the lingering supply problem to Maj. Gen. John G. Foster, who replaced the ailing Burnside at Knoxville. "The Nashville and Chattanooga road will not be reliable until entirely reconstructed. Trains are off the track every day." The many bridges along the line between Nashville and Decatur were the cause of the delay in opening that alternate route to Chattanooga. Meigs did not even mention the bridge over the Tennessee at Loudon, which was taking a long time to rebuild.[67]

Wagon trains from Chattanooga and Kentucky provided a slim flow of material for the time being. Joseph S. Fullerton, one of Granger's staff officers, organized a train of 80 wagons for the Second Division from Chattanooga. Thirty wagons carried camp and garrison equipment, 45 wagons transported commissary stores, and 5 wagons hauled animal forage. He also organized another train of 55 wagons for the Third Division with a similar proportion of camp equipment, commissary stores, and forage. The total came to 135 wagons escorted by 3,584 troops.[68]

Confederate Logistics and Supply

Confederate forces suffered from serious supply deficiencies during the Chattanooga Campaign. The primary reason Bragg placed the Army of Tennessee on top of Missionary Ridge and Lookout Mountain rather than bypass Chattanooga after his victory on September 20 stemmed from logistical and supply issues. Longstreet urged an offensive, deeming it imperative that the army march across the mountains and strike Union lines of communication in Middle Tennessee, perhaps recapture Nashville, or even invade Kentucky. Bragg considered this option for several days but then discounted it. "Such a move was utterly impossible for want of transportation," he explained to Richmond authorities. "Nearly half of our army consisted of re-enforcements just before the battle without a wagon or an artillery horse, and nearly, if not quite, a third of the artillery horses on the field had been lost." He had no pontoon bridge to cross the Tennessee River.

Even if successful at reaching Middle Tennessee, Bragg was appalled at the thought of severing his army from its line of communications. Instead he hoped Rosecrans would soon evacuate Chattanooga, opening a line of advance through the mountains that would allow him to maintain his line of communications. Meanwhile, the Confederates reconstructed bridges on the railroad near Ringgold as the general tried to get more food to his army.[69]

Bragg seemed to be as stuck in the mountains as Grant would be, having lost the bold strategic vision that had driven him to invade Kentucky with no real line of communications the year before. The Federals gained all the advantages with their massive infusion of reinforcements and by upgrading their supply arrangements, both of which enabled them to remain in and near Chattanooga. This was the basis of their brilliant victories on November 23–25. Bragg retired to Dalton, Georgia, and resigned his command, replaced temporarily by Hardee and then by Joseph E. Johnston.

"Hard work bad weather & scarcity of food have been the lot of the Army," reported division leader Micah Jenkins to his wife. "I only get one meal a day and not enough at that on 1/4 pound of meat," wrote William Wesley Welborn of the 1st South Carolina. "There is nothing to buy in this country. Everything is destroyed." He concluded "that starvation will end this war."[70]

Federal Logistics after the Battle of Chattanooga

While both sides suffered supply problems, the Federals invested more resources than the Confederates to solve them. The weakest link was the Nashville and Chattanooga Railroad because of its outdated track. Donaldson reported to Thomas on December 23 that it "has failed me for the last three days."[71]

"Since our arrival here we have been on but little more than half supplies," Joseph Hooker told Secretary of the Treasury Salmon P. Chase, "and it is telling fearfully on men and animals. The great embarrassment lies between Bridgeport and Nashville. The capacity of the road is insufficient for present wants. The continuation of that road from Bridgeport to Chattanooga is yet unfinished, and will remain so for weeks to come."[72]

The major bridges in the system were far from finished. That at Bridgeport, 1,450 feet long, was the biggest on the rail network. The bridge over the Tennessee River at Loudon was 900 feet long, and the bridge over the Hiwassee River at Charleston was 500 feet long.[73]

Dodge continued to push efforts on the Nashville to Decatur link. "The work upon the railroad has been immense," he assured Sherman, relying on a mix of soldiers and black laborers. Col. Henry R. Mizner of the 14th Michigan told Grant he had 300 men working on the Duck River bridge near Columbia but that he could use 50 more and 100 blacks. Dodge relied so heavily on black laborers that he refused to allow recruiters to enlist them for army service; Grant supported him. By December 21 Sherman assigned Dodge and a civilian contractor to finish the work on the entire Nashville to Decatur route and assigned Maj. Gen. John A. Logan's Fifteenth Corps to repair the Memphis and Charleston Railroad between Decatur and Stevenson. "We will then have a triangle of railroad, Nashville the apex and the base along the Tennessee," he told Logan. On the day after Christmas, Sherman estimated it would take six weeks to finish this work.[74]

With winter weather turning dirt roads into quagmires, Grant repositioned his large command as close to railroad depots and steamboat landings as possible to decrease reliance on hauling material in wagons. Sherman's troops from the Army of the Tennessee were parceled out at many locations across north Alabama.[75]

Federal Strategy

While waiting for the rail network to become fully operational, Grant weighed all the options for his next campaign. He had contemplated an attack on Mobile since the fall of Vicksburg, but events at Chickamauga had prevented it. Now he entertained a proposal to move on the Alabama city by way of New Orleans, using coastal shipping, and attack it from the mouth of Mobile Bay. After securing the Gulf port, he wanted to move troops into the interior of Alabama and Georgia.[76]

But Halleck pressured Grant to give first attention to Longstreet, who continued to occupy a position northeast of Knoxville. "The holding of East Tennessee, and the prevention of the enemy from getting supplies there, is deemed of the greatest importance," the general in chief wrote. Grant considered a campaign to drive Longstreet out of the state. He felt "deeply interested in moving the enemy . . . so as to be able to select my own campaign in the spring instead of having the enemy dictate it for me."[77]

But Grant's contemplated drive through East Tennessee foundered on logistics and supply. A personal inspection that took him to Knoxville convinced the general he would not have enough logistical support for such an effort. He then planned to hold Federal troops there, now under Foster, to protect Knoxville while assuming that Lee would recall Longstreet before the opening of the spring campaign in Virginia.[78]

Ignoring Longstreet, Grant again envisioned Mobile, Atlanta, or Montgomery as the next target. Sherman saw Chattanooga as "the base of operations for the next grand campaign," no matter what the target. One of Grant's staff officers told commissary Symonds to accumulate supplies for 100,000 men who were to advance toward Atlanta. For the first time, Federal commanders seriously contemplated penetration of the Deep South along a railroad with a large force meant to permanently occupy that region.[79]

Much of this new Federal interest in Deep South operations grew out of an increasing desire to acquire the services of able-bodied black men. Maj. Gen. David Hunter pointed out that 2 million African Americans lived in Alabama and Georgia. They could provide 400,000 men of military age, according to his calculation. If a column of 10,000–20,000 Union troops penetrated this region, "subsisting on the country" and taking weapons along to arm blacks, it could do what John Brown had envisioned when he raided Harpers Ferry in 1859—free thousands of slaves and create an army of angry black men in one stroke. Such a column "could go without serious opposition directly from Vicksburg to Charleston," Hunter continued. "The Southern heart could thus be beautifully fired and in a very short time consumed. A general rebellion among these crowded negroes would certainly produce great demoralization throughout the rebel army."[80]

No Federal commander tried to implement Hunter's scheme, but they continued to envision efforts to penetrate the Deep South. Ironically, the Confederates also grappled with supply problems as they contemplated mounting a quick offensive to upset enemy preparations for a spring offensive. For Joseph E. Johnston, who replaced Bragg and Hardee as commander of the Army of Tennessee, those logistical problems nullified the thought of a strategic offensive. The army's wagon trains were so small that at best they could haul eight days' rations and some baggage but no forage or stores. By early February 1864, the army's railroad link with Atlanta had increased its capacity while Johnston had acquired more wagons. But these improvements merely made the stay at Dalton more comfortable rather than enabled his troops to take the offensive.[81]

Johnston resisted pressure from Davis to move forward. William Whann Mackall, his chief of staff, cited supply problems and pointed out that the Federals maintained a strong defensive posture at Chattanooga. "The enemy were never so well posted on any frontier opposite the Army of Tennessee as at present," he wrote. "Chattanooga a fortress, and Knoxville fortified, and their line of communication barred to us by a river and a chain of barren mountains."[82]

Longstreet's idea to mount his 12,000 men and ride around these fortified positions into Kentucky appealed to Richmond authorities, but it also ran aground on supply difficulties. As the president pointed out, he would never be able to find that many horses or mules in the Confederacy.[83]

Struggling to Improve

Finally, some signs of progress could be detected in Union railroad work. By January 14 the line between Bridgeport and Chattanooga opened. A total of thirty engines and 240 cars were available on the Nashville and Chattanooga Railroad to run into the latter city, but Thomas still was not satisfied. His men had been on short rations so long, and he faced the task of stockpiling at Chattanooga to support a further push, that logistical needs were even greater now. He wanted quartermasters to double the logistical capacity on the Nashville and Chattanooga. Moreover, this route had to supply not only the Army of the Cumberland but also Sherman's large force and, as soon as the railroad between Chattanooga and Knoxville was complete, the troops near the latter city. Thomas wanted at least thirty-six trains per day to roll into Chattanooga and an additional twenty-four per day to feed the troops at Knoxville. If the Federals hoped to advance on Atlanta in the spring, they would need thirty-six trains per day to follow them as they penetrated Georgia. Those were tall orders. Merely meeting Thomas's immediate needs would require more than 100 carloads of material every day at Chattanooga, but the railroads could manage no more than 50 at this time.[84]

If more rolling stock was needed, it had to come from less important lines. Sherman ordered the dismantling of the Memphis and Charleston Railroad east of Memphis and gave up Corinth, held since the city had been captured in late May 1862. Virtually all rolling stock was shipped by river steamer to Nashville. Sherman allowed for retaining only two engines and ten boxcars at Memphis.[85]

McCallum and the Mountains

By mid-December Meigs realized something drastic was needed to solve the logistical problem in the mountains. He urged Daniel McCallum to send some of his experienced crewmembers from Virginia to lend a hand. "All the construction corps could be most profitably employed upon this road, with its full organization and equipment and tools," Meigs wrote without exaggeration.[86]

McCallum and some of his men journeyed to Nashville and reported to John B. Anderson, who assigned them to finish work on the rail link between Bridgeport and Chattanooga by mid-January. But when McCallum offered to work on the rest of the Nashville and Chattanooga Railroad, Anderson refused. Thomas instead arranged for McCallum's men to work on the line between Chattanooga and Knoxville, while Anderson superintended work on the Nashville to Chattanooga route. McCallum examined the Nashville and Chattanooga Railroad, however, and considered it "in bad condition." He urged Anderson to strip secondary lines, such as the McMinnville branch and the Trenton branch, to secure rails and ties, but Anderson refused. Locomotives could go no more than eight miles per hour between Nashville and Chattanooga; even so, "accidents are frequent."[87]

McCallum evaluated the entire rail system in the region. His report included all lines serving Union needs in the mountains along with his estimate of their length in miles: The Nashville and Northwestern Railroad, 72 miles linking Nashville with the Tennessee River; the Nashville and Chattanooga Railroad, 151 miles long; the Nashville to Decatur route, 133 miles; and the Chattanooga to Knoxville route, 111 miles. His construction corps was fully capable of rehabilitating the aggregate 467 miles of track. The network had seventy engines and 600 cars, but McCallum considered this rolling stock to be "entirely inadequate." At times he could recall running sixty engines and 800 cars on the 70-mile line between Culpeper and Washington, D.C., although admitting that was an extreme case. For the line between Aquia Creek Landing and Fredericksburg, Virginia, he regularly ran fourteen engines and 165 cars for a track that was only 14 miles long. On average, American railroad companies used one engine and twelve cars for every 2 miles of track.[88]

By these standards, Anderson was running far too little rolling stock. He had enough engines only for 100 miles of track and enough cars for only

140 miles of line, according to that formula. This did not take into account the losses to guerrilla attacks and accidents or the need to increase hauling capacity to support a further advance. McCallum thought Anderson should have at least 200 engines and 3,000 cars to handle current needs plus emergencies, as well as future military operations.[89]

McCallum went on to criticize Anderson himself to Stanton, viewing "the railroad organization of this department as decidedly defective." There was "a lack of well-directed energy and seeming want of ability to comprehend the magnitude of the undertaking." He recommended a construction corps of at least 1,000 men for the area. "The experiment of supplying an army over a long line of railroad, through an enemy's country, is yet to be tested," he wrote. "The most perfect organization and the best practical talent in the country will be indispensable to success."[90]

McCallum was right—Anderson was part of the problem. A crippling lack of vision had dogged the Federals since August 1863. After firing Anderson, Rosecrans reverted to the old policy of relying on army personnel instead of civilian experts to operate and maintain the railroads. Chaos was the result when the Army of the Cumberland entered the mountains. Both Anderson and Rosecrans were guilty of lack of vision. When the former was rehired after the latter was replaced, he failed once again to meet the challenge of running an expansive rail network.

Grant fired Anderson and placed McCallum in charge, designating him general manager of the U.S. Military Railroad in the Military Division of the Mississippi on February 4, 1864. McCallum transferred in many of his most dependable men from Virginia. William W. Wright came and served the needs of western armies for the remainder of the war. Eben C. Smeed transferred from Alexandria, Virginia, to Bridgeport and worked on the rail link to Chattanooga. He later rebuilt the line to Knoxville. The company of Construction Corps men assigned to repair tracks moved west by rail, taking all its tools and supplies along. The company assigned to work on bridges had to use western wagons to reach Charleston, Tennessee, because the track was not yet finished to that point. There the bridge force reconstructed the span over the Hiwassee River and finished it before the track force reached Charleston. Then the bridge men went on to Loudon to help with one of the biggest reconstruction projects in the West, the long and high span over the Tennessee River, which already was being rebuilt at a slow pace by a private contractor.[91]

McCallum also hired some experienced railroad men from the North. Leonard Eicholtz accepted a commission as captain of engineers and left home on March 27. While his train journey demonstrated that the track to Louisville was in good shape, Eicholtz found the line farther south to be troublesome. "Road in very bad condition," he noted before reaching Chattanooga on April 2. Eicholtz became an important element in railroad work in the department. McCallum and Wright assigned him to the Chattanooga area as division engineer, in charge of the 1st Division, Construction Corps.[92]

The true turning point in the transportation crisis in the West had been reached with the ascension of McCallum over Anderson and the consequent infusion of eastern Construction Corps resources into the mountains. Those easterners would eventually spread out over the West, taking with them their talent and can-do attitude. One of the more important differences between McCallum and Anderson was the former's keen recognition of the dimensions of the transportation problems facing Federal commanders in the West, not to mention his willingness to expend whatever money and resources were needed to fix them as fast as possible. The problem-solving experiences of McCallum and his people in the East had been a necessary preparation for handling the far larger difficulties to be solved in the West.

River-Borne Transport

While McCallum and his men worked on the rail system, quartermasters supplemented the trains with steamboats. Severe ice on the Mississippi and Ohio Rivers prevented success during most of January, but by the end of the month steamers began to arrive at Nashville. Large vessels could not navigate Harpeth Shoals, which had only about five feet of water at that time. They usually unloaded at Clarksville, where quartermaster Frederick S. Winslow moved the material to the state capital on eleven light-draft boats. During the month of February, Winslow recorded 178 steamboat arrivals at Nashville, carrying a total of 35,860 tons of material. Despite fluctuations in the water level of the Cumberland during March (Harpeth Shoals went from three and a half feet to fifteen feet at various times in the month), he moved 213 boats into the city carrying 62,666 tons of material.[93]

To help the Federals at Knoxville, Winslow loaded eight light-draft steamers with 1.25 million rations, obtained four small gunboats as escort,

Whiteside Bridge. Located near Whiteside, Tennessee, fifteen miles west of Chattanooga, this span took the Nashville and Chattanooga Railroad over Running Water Creek, which runs through a narrow valley in the mountains. The original bridge was covered, with a wooden roof overlaid with sheet-iron plating, but the Confederates destroyed it before evacuating the area in August 1863. L. B. Boomer, a noted bridge builder based in Chicago, rebuilt the structure in late 1863 at a cost of $95,000. The bridge was 500 feet long (780 feet including the trestle work) and rose to a height of 95 feet. This photograph is attributed to George N. Barnard. LC-DIG-ppmsca-33483.

and pushed the convoy from Nashville up the Cumberland River to the mouth of the Big South Fork River. Guerrilla attacks and sandbars posed major obstacles. The fleet sometimes had either to wait several days for enough water to rise over channel obstructions or to lighten its load so one boat could pull another over bad places. Crewmembers gathered rails from nearby farms when they ran out of fuel. After six weeks of hard work, the convoy reached the mouth of the Big South Fork on February 19, unloaded its material, and returned to Nashville.[94]

The Tennessee River provided only a marginally better route of supply into the heart of East Tennessee. Thomas sent the *Lookout* with a cargo of shoes and clothing to Loudon when the water level was high in January. Federal troops moved this freight by wagons from there to Knoxville. "It was very little," admitted division commander Jacob D. Cox, "but it was greatly encouraging."[95]

Completing the Federal Network

For the Federals, months of ceaseless labor on the rail network gradually paid off. McCallum infused the area with three to four times more construction workers than had been available in the fall. Dodge, using his own soldiers, finished rebuilding 182 bridges on the 133-mile line between Nashville and Decatur by mid-March. Before he was fired by Grant, Anderson got the Nashville and Chattanooga line working at a minimal level, but McCallum's people conducted a thorough overhaul of the track that greatly improved its carrying capacity that winter.[96]

The two most important bridges on the western railroads were finally rebuilt. The first and biggest was the span over the Tennessee River at Bridgeport. A private concern, the McCallum Bridge Company of Cincinnati (apparently no relation to Daniel McCallum), finished rebuilding it in January. The second, the long bridge over the Tennessee at Loudon, took longer. It had been broken by retreating Confederate cavalry when Burnside entered the area early in September 1863. When Sherman's relief column neared Loudon early in December, a small Confederate force ran three locomotives and forty-eight cars off the bridge to litter the river bottom with tons of wreckage. The result necessitated much cleanup work before reconstruction could begin. The army had contracted with a civilian named W. H. Bristol early in February 1864 to rebuild the bridge. Quartermasters transported Bristol's workers, tools, and building material from Nashville to Loudon free of charge.[97]

Major General Granger, Fourth Corps commander, superintended progress on the Loudon bridge. Bristol's civilian workers grew rebellious in late March, probably sensing how desperately the army needed the structure. They staged a strike on March 27 for more pay, but Granger refused to consider their demands. Instead he sent troops to round them up and confine them on the nearly finished bridge, stationing armed guards at both ends of the span. The workers were forced to stay on the high, exposed middle section of the bridge without shelter, eighty feet above the Tennessee, with no food or fire. Still they refused to cave in, but the first cold night weakened the resolve of many. One by one they came to the bank and resumed work until the entire crew gave up the strike. Granger continued to post armed guards for several days to make sure they understood his position.[98]

Three weeks later the long structure was finished. Railroad engineers ran a locomotive called the *Greenville,* pulling one passenger car, over the bridge on April 13. No mishaps occurred, so through traffic between Chattanooga and Knoxville resumed.[99]

The completion of the bridge at Loudon ended a long transportation crisis in Federal operations. The Army of the Cumberland had failed to meet the challenge posed to field logistics by the Appalachian Highlands. Rosecrans was primarily responsible for that failure, although Anderson played a close second to him. Neither man anticipated the increased need for rolling stock to handle the capacity drain of running trains through mountainous territory. Neither man foresaw that a larger construction corps filled with civilian experts was the key to repairing and maintaining tracks dotted with more than the usual number of bridges. Rosecrans compounded the failure by trying to use his army personnel to run the lines after Anderson left government employment. Only the railroads offered a hope of proper logistical support in the region. Neither the rivers of Appalachia nor wagon trains could substitute for the iron horse.

Even without the terrible defeat at Chickamauga, Rosecrans's army would have been on half rations or worse for an extended period of time that fall and winter. But that setback led to the infusion of many more troops into the mountains, further compounding the logistical and supply crisis. In early September 1863 Federal quartermasters had to ship food for 68,000 men in and around Chattanooga and Knoxville. By early November Hooker and Sherman had brought an additional 48,000 men to the region. All of these 116,000 troops relied primarily on a rail system that operatives were still trying to rebuild and improve.

The transfer of McCallum and his Construction Corps was a watershed in the history of logistical support in the western campaigns. The easterners had excelled the westerners in their learning curve about managing military railroads thus far in the conflict. Importing their way of war to the West transformed military railroading in the theater of conflict where the rails played a more vital role than in any other area of operations. McCallum had the experience, the foresight, and the managerial skill to handle the far-flung rail system that spanned Appalachia. He completed the rail system early in 1864 and then repaired and managed it for the rest of the war.

This was the system that made Sherman's Atlanta Campaign possible. After two years of operating on rails through the Upper South, the Federals were now poised to penetrate the Deep South, at least in a limited way, through the use of railroads.

5

SHERMAN AND ATLANTA

The Atlanta Campaign was the only attempt by the Federals to penetrate the Deep South while relying on a railroad to support large forces. It would not have been possible except for the massive railroad work conducted from September 1863 through April 1864, work that rehabilitated the lines traversing the Appalachian Highlands and opened up two rail routes between Nashville and Chattanooga.

But that was not enough. To supply 100,000 men for a persistent drive to Atlanta, relying on 350 miles of track from Louisville at the beginning of the campaign, demanded huge stockpiles of supplies at several points, additional rolling stock, and a dedicated corps of personnel able to repair the inevitable breaks in the system. Everyone involved in Sherman's supply during the Atlanta Campaign had to exert themselves in an extraordinary way to make the operation possible—they barely were able to accomplish the task of supporting the army group's capture of the city after four months of continuous campaigning. Never before had such a large field army relied on such a long line of railroad for so long while on active campaign. The logistical history of the Atlanta Campaign was unprecedented not only in the Civil War but also in world military history.

Logistical Preparations

Sherman was keenly aware of the need for extraordinary effort. After replacing Grant as commander of the Military Division of the Mississippi, he inspected transportation facilities for the "big fight in Georgia," traveling to Nashville, Chattanooga, and Knoxville. Along the way he consulted George H. Thomas, James B. McPherson, and John M. Schofield, who commanded the major departments in his command. On landing back at

Nashville on April 2, 1864, Sherman gave his "personal attention to the question of supplies." He acquired the government's 1860 census tables for Georgia and the tax compilations assembled by the controller of the state government to get an idea of the productive capacity of the counties he intended to traverse.[1]

Northwest Georgia was partially Appalachian terrain, thus sparsely populated and not overly productive. Sherman would have to rely on the railroad for nearly everything needed, and he devoted his primary attention to railroad matters for a full month before the campaign opened. He was determined that there would be no starving time in the drive to Atlanta, no repetition of the transportation crisis that had nearly wrecked Union strategy the winter before.

Fortunately Sherman could rely on a new set of men to handle his logistics. Daniel McCallum had become general manager of railroads in the Military Division of the Mississippi in February 1864. Unhappy with having only 30 usable engines and 400 usable cars, he requested more to reach a goal of 200 engines and 3,000 cars. Stanton told Northern manufacturers of railroad stock to provide him with whatever he needed. By the end of April, McCallum had received 30 new engines and 675 new cars, far fewer than his goal. The manufacturers of the North continued to supply him with new equipment after the start of the Atlanta Campaign so that by May 1865 he had received a total of 110 engines and 1,898 cars.[2]

Federal authorities supplemented the new equipment by pressing rolling stock from Kentucky companies, including nineteen engines and 135 cars from the Louisville and Nashville Railroad and two engines and 60 cars from the Kentucky Central Railroad. The government later purchased most of this pressed rolling stock from the companies. McCallum realized that the most important element in his operation was the creation of a large and efficient construction corps, organized on "a much broader development" than anything he had managed in the East.[3]

As chief quartermaster of the Department of the Cumberland, James L. Donaldson was largely responsible for managing the flow of supplies on the railroad. Donaldson was told to be ready to supply all of Sherman's troops and animals and to feed the soldiers in East Tennessee garrisons as well. His most immediate task was to stockpile up to six months of supplies in various depots before May 1, 1864. Donaldson, in turn, relied on Quartermasters Robert Allen and Lewis B. Parsons to send him material for the storehouses.[4]

The most concentrated acquisition and shipment of supplies to be conducted during the war now kicked into gear. Throughout February, March, and April, Donaldson received 2,000–3,000 tons of freight every day, mostly from steamers plying the Ohio and Cumberland Rivers to Nashville because, for the time, the water level was high. Donaldson employed 3,000 men and 500 wagons to haul material from the levee at Nashville to warehouses in the city, the men and teams working seven days a week in shifts. A total of 178 boats and barges arrived at the state capital during February, amounting to more than 6 per day, with 213 arriving in March and 158 in April. The levee was no more than half a mile long and quite steep and rough. Quartermaster Frederick S. Winslow found it inadequate for the volume of traffic. He often had to hold a steamboat for a day until room could be made at the levee to offload its stores, with the government paying an additional $225 to boat owners for this delay. While the Cumberland River was most navigable from February to May, its water level fluctuated during that time so as to "baffle all calculations," as Winslow put it.[5]

Donaldson constructed three new warehouses to accommodate the influx of material. At 1,709 feet long and 140 feet wide, one of these was devoted to animal forage. Another, called the "Bread Shed," was 600 feet long and 112 feet wide. The Taylor Depot was 517 feet long and 190 feet wide but had a basement that proved to be the equivalent of another story in terms of storage space. Two other new warehouses constructed in Nashville were devoted to commissary supplies.[6]

Donaldson had asked for 108 million pounds of animal feed, and Robert Allen in Saint Louis sent it all to him by May 1. Even with the new Forage House, Donaldson was compelled to store some fodder outdoors, "raised from the ground and well covered with tarpaulins." He admitted to losing some of it to bad weather, but the proportion was small compared to "the whole amount poured in upon me." Allen warned him that the effort to get this much grain to Nashville had "drained the whole Northwest" of available stocks, and he would have to wait until the spring harvest before sending more.[7]

At Nashville Sherman found that "crowds of idlers, Sanitary agents, Christian commissioners & all sorts of curiosity hunters" were taking up space in the railroad cars. Other civilians were paying the military railroads to transport their private freight. "It was the Gordian knot," he told his foster father, "and I cut it. People may starve, and go without but an army cannot & do its work."[8]

Quartermaster Warehouse in Nashville, March 1864. Warehouses such as these contained the vital supplies Sherman needed to support his huge army group during the drive toward Atlanta. Nashville had become the most important Federal depot in the western theater by this stage of the war. LC-DIG-ppmsca-33613.

Sherman cut that knot with General Orders No. 6, prohibiting private citizens and private freight from all government-controlled railroads except by special permit. He allowed one car per day to be used by the express companies for the shipping of parcels sent by Northern families to his soldiers and one car per day to haul sutlers' goods and the baggage of his officers. All this related to southward-traveling trains; empty cars on northbound trains could haul private freight if it did not impede military needs.[9]

Sherman continued to pursue efficiency by ordering every garrison within thirty miles of Nashville to haul supplies by wagons rather than by train. All troops in his military division were to march rather than ride the rails and drive their beef cattle on land rather than haul them in cars. All this "naturally raised a howl," Sherman admitted, but he exaggerated when claiming that these measures doubled the "daily accumulation" of supplies.[10]

Donaldson clamped down on thievery along the rail lines as part of Sherman's efficiency drive. He printed orders on cardboard to be displayed in every railroad car and at every station along the line to ward off thieves. He also hired civilian agents, placing one on every train to watch the supplies.[11]

Sherman curtailed issuance of army food to civilians on April 29, an order that undoubtedly hurt many people. "I was compelled to stop this, for a simple calculation showed that a single railroad could not feed the armies and the people too, and of course the army had the preference. At first, my orders operated very hard," but then spring vegetables became available, and bread and meat arrived by ox-drawn wagons from Kentucky. As a result, "no actual suffering resulted," he concluded.[12]

Banning civilian travel on military railroads produced the most reaction from frustrated citizens. More than 100 people had been requesting permission to use the rails before Sherman curtailed the practice. He had grown sick of these requests and, now that the ban was on, told Thomas to "be as severe as possible with citizens who smuggle themselves into the cars." When Lincoln asked him to relent on this policy, Sherman absolutely refused. "The railroad cannot supply the army and the people too," he told the president. "One or the other must quit, and the army don't intend to." Sherman understood that the immense logistical power of his government had its limits.[13]

The Louisville and Nashville Railroad was exempt from the order prohibiting civilian travel because it had never been seized by the government. President James Guthrie strove to meet the army's needs in order to retain control of his company. Sherman tried to convince him to stop civilian business temporarily in order to get his men to the front after their veteran furloughs.[14]

Sherman also had to deal with turf battles within his command. The Army of the Tennessee was a visitor to the Department of the Cumberland, entirely dependent on Thomas's command for the use of railroads, but some members developed an impression that their needs were slighted by Thomas's quartermasters. Maj. Gen. John A. Logan, commander of the Fifteenth Corps, complained that guards refused to recognize passes issued by his own headquarters for travel on the line. Thomas was very surprised when Sherman informed him of this and other complaints. He felt bad that Logan did not inform him rather than complain to Sherman. Thomas issued orders rectifying the situation, but Sherman was not satisfied. He decided to take a more personal interest in such matters to avoid friction among his high-level subordinates.[15]

One of the many jobs Sherman devoted personal attention to was the running of trains between Nashville and Chattanooga. He concluded that there had to be 130 carloads, at ten tons of freight each, arriving at Chattanooga every day for his 100,000 men and 35,000 animals. His quartermasters told him they had only sixty engines and 600 cars early in April but needed one hundred engines and 1,000 cars to accomplish his goal. New rolling stock arrived (as we have seen), but not enough to make up this shortage. Sherman told his quartermasters that when Louisville and Nashville cars arrived at the latter city, they should keep them rolling on to Chattanooga. Of course Guthrie protested this arbitrary use of his equipment but accepted it, borrowing extra engines and cars from railroad companies in the North. It was an emergency measure that the robust Northern companies could afford to accommodate. A few months later Sherman was tickled to see many railroad cars scattered along the rail line to Atlanta that, according to their markings, belonged to a number of Northern companies. He often wondered in later years if those companies ever retrieved them.[16]

Sherman tried to facilitate the flow of supplies by urging his people to run loaded cars from Nashville to Decatur and Chattanooga while moving only empty cars on the direct line from Chattanooga to Nashville. But he met resistance to this idea, reporting that the superintendent preferred to run his trains on the old system of a timetable to avoid accidents on a two-way line.[17]

There was some question about whether the stockpiling of supplies should guide the timing of the Atlanta Campaign. John M. Brannan, Thomas's chief of artillery, predicted that the troops would not be able to move out until late May at the earliest. "Our supply of provisions for man & beast this side of Nashville is very limited yet," he added. Sherman optimistically predicted in mid-April that he could increase the flow from 73 cars per day to 115—even to 157. But several factors caused the actual numbers to be much lower than Sherman's goal. Beginning with 75 loaded cars rolling into Chattanooga each day in February, traffic rose a bit to 79 in March and 114 in April, with the peak occurring in May at 121. This rate then dropped to 107 loaded cars in June, after the campaign was long underway. Jacob Cox, a division commander in the Twenty-Third Corps, noted in his memoirs that the locomotives were limited to pulling no more than 20–30 cars from Nashville to Chattanooga with about ten tons of freight per car. There was no possibility of increasing the amount of supplies hauled by adding more cars to each train.[18]

The army group suffered from a shortage of draft animals due to the high rate of attrition over the past winter. According to Quartermaster General Montgomery Meigs, 30,000 mules had perished during that terrible time of suffering. Those still alive in the Chattanooga area had to be dispersed to far-flung posts in hope of finding forage in the local areas. Donaldson had enough artillery horses but was short of cavalry mounts as well as draft animals. He impressed all horses within twenty miles of Nashville, netting about 1,000 usable mounts, but was still "largely short" of horses for the cavalry.[19]

Sherman stripped his command's baggage to the bare minimum to increase its mobility. "When we move, we will take no tents or baggage," he told Thomas, "but one change of clothing on our horses or to be carried by the men and on pack animals by company officers; five days' bacon, twenty days' bread, and thirty days' salt, sugar, and coffee; nothing else but arms and ammunition, in quantity proportioned to our ability." Sherman implemented this in General Orders No. 7, mandating no more than one wagon per regiment and foraging off the countryside whenever possible.[20]

As Sherman dramatically put it, his objective was "to convert all parts of that army into a mobile machine, willing and able to start at a minute's notice, and to subsist on the scantiest food. To reap absolute success might involve the necessity even of dropping all wagons, and to subsist on the chance food which the country was known to contain." He set an example by stripping his headquarters to the bone. Thomas refused to do this at his own headquarters despite numerous recommendations, but Sherman knew his example influenced other subordinates. "Soldiering as we have been doing for the past two years, with such trains and impediments, has been a farce," he complained to Meigs, "and nothing but absolute poverty will cure it."[21]

Most of Sherman's subordinates took his order for streamlining transportation seriously. Col. William H. Gibson, a brigade leader in the Fourth Corps, saw to it that his men sent their knapsacks and extra clothing to storage. They were allowed an extra shirt, a blanket, and a shelter tent half while Gibson allowed himself two shelter tent halves, an overcoat, a blanket, an oilcloth, an extra undershirt and outside shirt, in addition to a small box for provisions. Officers of the 15th Indiana Battery in the Twenty-Third Corps "literally carried out" Sherman's order. The gunners "learned to do without any surplus," even though the "greatest sacrifice had to be made."[22]

By April 26 Sherman was frustrated that he could do no more to logistically prepare his campaign. "If I only could count on a few more days," he told Meigs, "I would have a thirty days' start, but I may have to move on the 2d of May, with barely enough to warrant the move." It is true that he had not met his goals, but the situation was not as gloomy as it seemed. Donaldson noted that the accumulation of supplies at Nashville had been a roaring success. "Five months' supplies of all kinds are at Nashville," he told Meigs on May 1. "The great work on this side is nearly done." But the problem lay in the route from Nashville to Chattanooga. Donaldson recognized that the latter place was the crucial link in the network. "A failure there, and all that is accomplished is a failure." As of May 1 there were but seven days of food and one day of grain for animals stockpiled at Chattanooga.[23]

Donaldson took personally the responsibility for feeding Sherman's host. "On the whole I feel encouraged," he told Meigs. "I think I shall be able to supply the army." When last speaking with Donaldson before the campaign began, Sherman gave him a memorable thought that bordered between familiarity and a threat. "I have no orders to give you," Sherman frankly told him. "Only supply my army or I will eat your mules."[24]

Of course Donaldson and his subordinates deserve credit for their extraordinary accomplishment in stockpiling enough supplies to enable the campaign to begin on schedule during the first week of May. We must also give credit to Sherman. While Thomas was ultimately responsible for the rails within his department, Sherman temporarily overrode that authority to meet the unusual supply challenges of a major invasion of the Deep South. As historian Larry Daniel has put it, "If Thomas got the trains moving, it was Sherman who enabled the army to get beyond a hand-to-mouth existence to stockpiling."[25] The Atlanta Campaign probably would not have been possible without that extra effort in April and early May 1864.

Sherman's Rail-Based Supply Line

The rail network that Sherman's army group relied on was the longest used by any Civil War force. From the primary supply base at Louisville, the Louisville and Nashville Railroad (still under private control) stretched 185 miles to Nashville. The Nashville and Chattanooga Railroad (under government management) ran 151 miles between those two cities. As the Federals penetrated northwest Georgia, they would depend on the Western and Atlantic Railroad (under government management), which stretched an additional 137 miles between Chattanooga and Atlanta. Sherman relied

SHERMAN'S SUPPLY LINES

on 350 miles of track at the start of the campaign but by its end used 473 miles of vulnerable rail lines.[26]

The three companies named above constituted the main stem of Sherman's supply line, but it was supplemented by additional lines of supply. By 1861 the Nashville and Northwestern Railroad, designed as a link between Nashville and the Tennessee River to the west, had been completed to Kingston Springs, about twenty-five miles from the state capital. Some work had also been done on the remaining right of way to the Tennessee River. Grant had ordered the line put into operation in February 1864, work that was completed by May 10, making a line seventy-eight miles long. The

Nashville and Northwestern Railroad began to support Sherman's operations on June 9. At the river terminus at Johnsonville, extensive facilities were constructed to offload material from steamboats onto railcars. Andrew Johnson, the military governor of Tennessee, had played a key role in the development of this line and continued to oversee operations on it until Sherman insisted that his officers take full control of the road on August 5. Johnson acquiesced, and Donaldson took over four days later. This line was especially helpful in supporting Sherman from August to October, when low water on the Cumberland River interfered with steamboat traffic to Nashville. Quartermaster Walter Howland noted that nine steamers landed supplies at Johnsonville on August 26 and six more arrived the next day, contributing much to the stockpiling effort at Nashville.[27]

As mentioned earlier, quartermasters also utilized a secondary route between Nashville and Chattanooga. The three small railroad companies that had built the line between Nashville and Decatur provided a link between the state capital and the Memphis and Charleston Railroad, which joined the Nashville and Chattanooga Railroad at Stevenson, Alabama. This alternate route was eighty-seven miles longer than the more direct line between Nashville and Chattanooga, but it helped the Federals move material to the latter city until June, when all trains going to and from Chattanooga were shifted to the direct line with Nashville.[28]

Sherman wanted yet another rail link between Nashville and a navigable part of the Cumberland River as insurance against periods of low water. McCallum used parts of two companies to create a bypass of Harpeth Shoals, located between Nashville and Clarksville on the Cumberland River. The Edgefield and Kentucky Railroad (forty-seven miles) started from the Louisville and Nashville Railroad at Edgefield Junction, a spot ten miles north of Nashville. It ran northwest to join the Memphis, Clarksville, and Louisville Railroad at Graysville, Kentucky, near the Kentucky-Tennessee state line, fifteen miles northeast of Clarksville. (The name of Graysville was changed to Guthrie in 1867.) The Federals could use these two stretches of rail to bypass the shoals. McCallum's Construction Corps repaired those two stretches, and cars started rolling in August 1864. Quartermasters continued to use it for the rest of the war.[29]

There was also some discussion about opening the Memphis and Charleston Railroad all the way from Memphis to Decatur. Meigs viewed this as a daunting task but expressed willingness to try if Grant, now Union general in chief, approved. The long line was especially vulnerable to enemy attack, and McCallum had no rolling stock to spare for it. Grant wisely told Meigs on July 9 to forget the idea.[30]

The final link in Sherman's supply arrangement was the Western and Atlantic Railroad. Funded and owned by the state of Georgia a few years before the war, McCallum's men had to rebuild all of the major bridges and some of the track as the Federals advanced into Georgia. Given its close proximity to the Army of Tennessee, it was subject to Confederate raids by small parties and cavalry attacks during the campaign. McCallum claimed it was more difficult to operate this line, so close to the fighting front, than any "military railroad operation during the war."[31]

Donaldson firmly supported Sherman's desire to supplement the main railroad stem from Louisville to Chattanooga. He pushed steamboat transportation so that 300–500 tons of freight arrived every day at Nashville. The greatest challenge to this remained Harpeth Shoals, thirty miles below Nashville. Before the June rains caused a rise in the river, there was only ten to twelve inches of water over the shoals. Donaldson acquired 100 oxen and used them to tow shallow-draft boats over the shoals. It was "a novel feature in river navigation and unheard of here before," he reported. When heavy rains fell in June, river levels rose "several feet" above the shoals for up to two weeks, and Donaldson pushed heavily loaded steamers to Nashville during that time.[32]

Supplying an Army on Campaign

The Federals constructed depots along their line of communications from the beginning to the end of the railroad. They started with Louisville, the primary supply base where all material bound for the troops left friendly territory and entered the South. Nashville became the main supply depot for the Atlanta Campaign, the place where more material was stored than anywhere else. Chattanooga was the forward supply depot at the start of the campaign. It became a chokepoint because the flow of supplies had to constrict when crossing the Cumberland Plateau, plus its storage facilities were more limited than those in Nashville. As the armies advanced, Sherman established small forward depots in appropriate towns along the Western and Atlantic Railroad.

Getting things past that chokepoint became a major problem as the Fed-

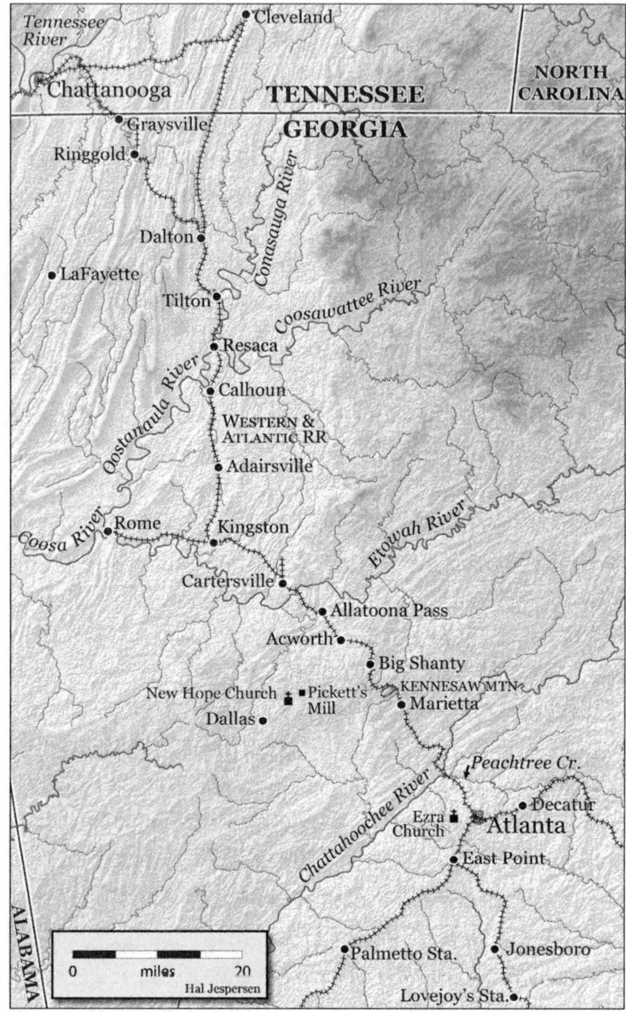

ATLANTA CAMPAIGN

erals fought their way south. Edward L. Hartz was in charge of managing this movement at Chattanooga and often received brusque orders from Langdon C. Easton, Sherman's chief quartermaster in the field. "Don't let it remain at Chattanooga a moment," Easton told Hartz about 150 cars loaded with grain for Sherman's mounts. "Report to me as often as trains arrive & leave Chattanooga." Hartz became a lightning rod of complaint anytime

Commissary Depot at Rocky Face Ridge, Dalton, Georgia. Sherman established depots at key points along his line of advance toward Atlanta, the first at Dalton. Unlike the large, specially designed warehouses at Chattanooga, this depot was located at a civilian house. These forward depots appeared soon after Sherman's army group occupied the towns, keeping pace with the progress of his campaign. LC-DIG-ppmsca-33616.

trouble appeared in the system. Donaldson told him he could not afford to let work crews at Chattanooga unload cars only during the day, which created a twelve-hour delay in returning empty cars to Nashville. Donaldson urged Hartz to hire more civilians and unload trains around the clock. "You know we have not a car to spare," he lectured Hartz. "I am straining every nerve to supply you fully."[33]

Quartermasters established the first forward depot at Dalton, Georgia, by May 15. "Send forward supplies to that place as rapidly as possible," Easton told Hartz. Sherman announced in special field orders that his quartermasters could ship material almost "to the very rear of the army." Nevertheless he instructed subordinates to keep a ten-day supply of meat and bread on hand in case the flow broke down.[34]

As the men advanced, so did the logistical system. Resaca became the forward depot after the Confederates evacuated the town on the night of May 15–16. Easton told Hartz to shove twenty days' worth of food for men and ten days' worth of feed for animals into storage facilities there. After more than a month of campaigning, Sherman then maneuvered the enemy out of Allatoona Pass. "I regard Allatoona of the first importance in our future plans. It is a second Chattanooga." He ordered the erection of earthworks and the planning of a major supply depot after the burned railroad bridge over the Etowah River was rebuilt. As the Federals continued to creep forward during June, smaller depots sprang up at places like Big Shanty and Acworth.[35]

Track and Bridge Repair

An important element of success was a vibrant repair capacity. McCallum put William Wierman Wright in charge of construction, with Adna Anderson to oversee track repair and Eben C. Smeed to repair bridges. All these men had honed their skills in the Virginia campaigns. Wright held the rank of colonel and had been a civil engineer before the war. He controlled 2,000 workers.[36]

From the start of the campaign, Sherman refused to be delayed by logistical issues. He pushed his supply team to repair the track as close to the

William Wierman Wright. As chief of construction, U.S. Military Railroad in the West, Wright was a key player in working out the process of making war on a large scale with railroads. LC-DIG-ppmsca-23721.

advancing lines as possible. The result was an unusual example of close rail support of troops engaged in combat.[37]

It was Wright's job to fulfill Sherman's goal. Very early in the campaign, the colonel suspected the Confederates might have planted torpedoes inside the tunnel at Tunnel Hill, so he slowly ran an unmanned locomotive through it. The engine came out safely. As the campaign progressed, the Confederates made Wright's task easier by failing to destroy or booby trap the rail line. He reconstructed 18.75 miles of track early in the campaign, but that was a small proportion of the mileage covered by Sherman's rapid advance during May. In general the Confederates only burned major bridges, leaving the track and the telegraph wire intact. This limited damage helped Wright a great deal.[38]

Wright was able to push railroad cars loaded with animal forage into Resaca on May 16 only hours after Johnston evacuated the place. The Confederates burned the railroad bridge over the Oostanaula River but left the wagon bridge intact. They tore up only two miles of track in two places, one section north of Marietta and another south of town, before Johnston pulled away from his Kennesaw Mountain Line on the night of July 2–3. Wright's men repaired the damage by July 6, helped by the fact that ties had not been disturbed. Leonard Eicholtz repaired the track literally up to the Union skirmish line on the seventh. He reported that two bullets whistled past by the time his crews called it a day. As Sherman put it, his enemy could hear the sound of locomotives from the safety of their own line of fortifications.[39]

Smeed, one of Wright's most valuable crew supervisors, was in charge of rebuilding railroad bridges. He organized his workers into twenty-man squads for greater flexibility in assigning them tasks, appointing one foreman for each squad. The squads worked like the units of a well-practiced drill team. Axe men cut logs from forests near a burned-bridge site, squared the timbers, and loaded them on flatbed cars for transport to the work area. Other squads of framers and raisers cleared debris from the destroyed structure. When the first load of timber arrived, raisers and framers assembled the bridge from the bank outward, using a raft if needed to place timbers across the stream. The teams then assembled the bridge in sections from the bottom up.[40]

These methods enabled Smeed to rebuild large structures with speed. "The bridges built in this way were rough and strong," he admitted after the war, "they would sometimes settle out of line and surface under the

Eben C. Smeed. Ace bridge builder of the U.S. Military Railroad in the West, Smeed honed the art of reconstructing spans to a high level of efficiency. LC-DIG-ppmsca-33989.

weight of the first trains, but they were easily relieved and surfaced again." Herman Haupt took credit for this method of bridge construction, claiming he developed it while working on the rail line between Aquia Creek and Fredericksburg during the spring of 1862. Smeed worked as his assistant on that project.[41]

The railroad bridge over the Oostanaula just south of Resaca took only five days to rebuild. The span crossing the Etowah River south of Cassville, 600 feet long and 67 feet tall, required five and a half days to reconstruct. Eicholtz worked on the Etowah bridge with three crews of several squads each. On June 9 the men worked from 4 A.M. until midnight in a race to finish it two days later. Eicholtz and his men completed the Etowah bridge at noon on June 11 and then ran a construction train over it an hour later as a test. He moved the train another twenty-eight miles down to Big Shanty, the last stop currently held by the Federal army, and "gave a loud & long whistle in face of the Rebels some 3 miles distant & returned to Etowah." On the twelfth he sent all three crews off to other projects.[42]

The bridge over the Chattahoochee River was the biggest along the rail line to Atlanta. Johnston's men burned it when the Army of Tennessee retreated south of the Chattahoochee on July 9. Because the defenses of Atlanta were only ten miles away, Sherman hesitated before ordering Wright to rebuild the span. The general used pontoon bridges at various locations to cross his army group by July 17. For several days he continued to cross supplies on a captured Confederate pontoon bridge and two wagon bridges that his engineers built. Not until August 2 did Wright receive authorization to rebuild the railroad bridge. It was 780 feet long and 92 feet high, yet the crews needed only four and a half days to complete it by August 5. The men worked "daylight till dark," but not at night, and took one hour each day for lunch. Haupt was impressed by Smeed's work. "This bridge I regard as the most extraordinary feat in military bridge construction that the world has ever seen," he concluded in his memoirs.[43]

Given the heavy volume of traffic on the line between Chattanooga and the advancing army group, accidents were bound to happen. Freight trains, hospital trains, and troop transports were involved in such mishaps on a fairly regular basis, usually resulting in damaged rolling stock as well as a few casualties.[44]

Targeting Sherman's Supply Line

The occasional accident was to be expected even on a Northern railroad during peacetime, but the Western and Atlantic was subject to attack by guerrillas and roving bands of Confederate cavalry as well. Joseph Wheeler, Johnston's cavalry commander, sent small parties of mounted men behind Union lines armed with "torpedoes and other contrivances" to tear up tracks and run engines off the road, causing a number of small, temporary breaks in the line. Detailed cavalrymen from Brig. Gen. Frank C. Armstrong's brigade were captured near Kingston and Rome as early as June 11. An estimated force of one hundred Confederate cavalry burned a bridge near Tunnel Hill later that month.[45]

"I have to make allowances for our road being broken one-third the time," Sherman told Halleck. "Keep Colonel McCallum advised that he must be prepared to lose half a dozen or more trains every month by guerrillas and dashes at the road which cannot be prevented." These small breaks were only interruptions rather than campaign-breaking disasters because Wright was on top of his job. "This army . . . has been wonderfully supplied," Sherman exulted to a colleague on July 7. "Though repeatedly broken, our railroad and telegraph are in good order to the rear, and I have depots of supplies accumulated at fortified points to my rear."[46]

But Confederate attacks on the rail line intensified in early July. An estimated 300 men hit a train between Tilton and Dalton on the evening of July 5, removing one rail and causing an engine to slide off the track. They then burned all sixteen cars. On July 14 a group of men stopped a train on its way to the front and burned a dozen cars containing commissary stores. They held a section of the track for one and a half hours before Federal troops chased them away.[47]

Confederate attempts to interrupt the flow of supplies increased in August. "Our telegraph wires are cut so often that it is prudent to have signal telegraph back as far as Allatoona," Sherman wrote. The railroad was cut so badly in mid-August that nothing reached the army for five days. All told, Wright estimated that his crews relaid ten miles of track during the Atlanta Campaign as the result of attacks by Confederate cavalry detachments and guerrillas.[48]

Sherman took extensive measures to protect his rail line. The governors of Indiana, Illinois, Iowa, and Wisconsin raised several regiments of short-term troops to garrison important posts along the line north of Chattanooga. To protect the more vulnerable area south from Chattanooga, Sherman placed Maj. Gen. James B. Steedman in charge of the newly created District of the Etowah on June 10. Steedman was responsible for garrisons as far away as Bridgeport and Rome in addition to the line down to Sherman's army. The garrison guarding the crossing of Chickamauga Creek near Graysville, Georgia, for example, consisted of 108 men and five officers. Kingston, which served as the advanced railhead for Sherman's army group in late May and early June, was held by 900 men, while Allatoona had 1,500 troops after the Federals turned it into a major depot. Sherman posted three regiments at Marietta, with instructions to be ruthless in scouring the country near his railroad and deporting suspicious persons who threatened to damage it. "The bridge, the stores and the Allatoona depot must be held, cost what it may," he asserted.[49]

Maj. Gen. Lovell H. Rousseau's District of Nashville was responsible for protecting the rail line between the capital, Decatur, and Bridgeport. He was convinced that mounted patrols along the track could disrupt or divert guerrilla attacks but not eliminate them. Protection coupled with rapid repair work was the only solution.[50]

The guerrilla and small-unit strategy failed to decisively break the Union rail line, but the possibility of mounting a big attack on it burned brightly in the eyes of Confederate officials. Many people urged Jefferson Davis to send Nathan Bedford Forrest's cavalry into Tennessee, but the president told them Forrest could not be spared from protecting valuable country in Mississippi and Alabama from Federal raids. Johnston persistently urged a cavalry strike on the railroad but did not feel he could commit the Army of Tennessee's limited number of mounted troops to the task.[51]

After Gen. John Bell Hood succeeded Johnston on July 18, he took the offensive against Sherman, resulting in battles at Peach Tree Creek on July 20, east of Atlanta on July 22, and at Ezra Church on July 28. These engagements only temporarily halted Union efforts to snip the rail lines feeding Hood's army in Atlanta and resulted in at least 11,000 Confederate casualties. But unlike Johnston, Hood was willing to commit his cavalry to a major attack on the Union railroad.[52]

When Wheeler led 4,000 mounted men northward in mid-August, he proved that Federal protective measures had not been taken in vain. His large force committed only limited damage to the railroad system. The least amount occurred on the line between Chattanooga and the advancing army, where the Confederates only tore up a few sections of track, requiring only three days for Wright's squads to repair. Wheeler failed to capture Dalton because the small garrison there held a well-placed earthen fort. He veered away and crossed the Tennessee River to hit the line between Chattanooga and Knoxville. Here the Confederates found the railroad less heavily guarded and destroyed a total of twenty-five miles of track and nine bridges. When Wheeler's command rode to the area between Nashville and Chattanooga, they also committed significant damage. Rousseau marshaled his troops and chased them away, averting a catastrophic result. In the end Wheeler's raid failed to deliver a campaign-crushing blow to Sherman's lifeline.[53]

The Federals never had to face the worst-case scenario, a catastrophic breakdown of their logistical system, but Grant worried that this might happen. If the Confederates decisively cut the railroad in Tennessee, he hoped Sherman's troops could hold out a while, feeding from the stockpiles at Chattanooga and depots farther south. If needed, Grant wanted Sherman to ruthlessly take everything from the countryside and issue food to prevent civilian starvation.[54]

The combined use of cavalry, small detached parties, and guerrillas failed Confederate strategy. The Federals had the advantage in three areas: an effective system of static defense (garrisons and blockhouses at key points); a mobile reserve of troops capable of meeting these small Confederate forces in the field; and a highly effective repair capacity to take care of the breaks. Federal commanders did not have well-developed resources in any of these three categories the year before—they were all developed just in time for the Atlanta Campaign.

Targeting Confederate Logistics

Sherman also tried to disrupt his enemy's rail supply line, but the Confederates devoted far fewer resources to its protection. The Rebel rail system lay in friendly territory, so there was no need to worry about guerrillas. When Sherman launched cavalry raids behind enemy lines, Southern commanders responded with their own mounted force to counter the threat.

Rousseau mounted a raid from Nashville to the rail system in Alabama with 3,000 cavalry in mid-July. He took the Confederates by surprise, kept one or two days ahead of them, and tore up thirty miles of track east of Montgomery before joining Sherman's army group on July 22. He had a modest effect on the flow of Confederate supplies—the damage was repaired in two weeks.

Sherman launched a major attack on Hood's rail lines in late July, sending 10,000 cavalrymen in three columns to hit the Macon and Western Railroad, which entered Atlanta from the south. Hood responded by sending Wheeler and 10,000 cavalry to chase those Federals down. In a series of engagements, Wheeler prevented them from doing much harm to the railroad. The Confederates defeated one column on July 28, another the next day (resulting in the capture of 700 Federals), and a third column on the thirtieth. With a loss of 2,000 troopers, Sherman witnessed one of the most dismal Union cavalry operations of the war.

Even so, the Federals tried one more time to use mounted troops to cut Confederate supply. Brig. Gen. Hugh Judson Kilpatrick took his cavalry division to raid the line south of Atlanta in late August. He duplicated Rousseau's limited success, tearing up only a short stretch of track that was quickly rebuilt.[55]

Sherman realized that mounted raids could not carry the force needed to destroy an enemy's rail support. Only large infantry forces could tear up enough track to have a decisive effect. Thus he broke away from his rail line temporarily in late August and took most of his army group on a flanking march to land on the two rail lines that supported Hood's army. The result was decisive in opening the gates of Atlanta by September 2.[56]

Working the System, Day by Day

On the strategic level, Union logistical support avoided a catastrophic collapse and survived the minor breaks inflicted upon it. On the tactical level, Sherman's rail-based supply line worked well enough to keep the army group moving. The logistical flow, according to Sherman, consisted normally of ten cars per train, four trains operating in a sort of convoy system, or as a "gang" in his terminology. Trains moved normally at ten miles per hour from Nashville to Chattanooga and on to the armies. "Four such gangs of trains daily made one hundred and sixty cars, of ten tons each, carrying sixteen hundred tons, which exceeded the absolute necessity of the army, and allowed for the accidents that were common and inevitable." There could be some degree of accumulation in the most forward depots in a flow such as this, but the safety margin was not large.[57]

Anytime the troops needed something, Easton telegraphed Hartz for it. For example, Sherman wanted ten days' worth of all supplies for the army group as "soon as possible" on June 28. The horses and mules were in need of 200 cars of forage as well. A few days later Easton was keen on not only supplying the men but also accumulating ten days' worth of supplies at the forward depots, yet not enough cars were arriving to make that happen.[58]

This was a problem that still needed to be worked out. As early as May 6, Donaldson had complained to Hartz that not enough empty cars were returning to Nashville. He was able to send only thirty-seven loaded cars the day before and only thirty-four that day. "This is murderous & will starve the army if it continues," he warned. "You will have forage if I can get cars but you must help me." On May 26 he again complained to Hartz that he heard the Chattanooga crews were not unloading them fast enough. "I . . . could do but little with 10000 cars unless you unload & return them. I have supplies here in abundance for six 6 months of nearly all important articles & can send you 200 car loads per day if you will only return the cars."[59]

Rapid unloading was a problem that was never completely solved, and Sherman had to accept the fact that his men were likely to suffer temporary supply shortages. He therefore set priorities. "First, ammunition; second, clothing; third, provisions for men; fourth, forage for horse." He allowed the

Quartermaster's Office at Chattanooga. Here is where Edward L. Hartz worked hard to keep the flow of supplies moving forward to the advancing army group during the Atlanta Campaign, fielding stern telegrams from superiors both at Sherman's headquarters and at Nashville when the flow faltered or slowed. LC-DIG-ppmsca-35062.

shipment of newspapers to the troops, but no newspaper vendors would be allowed and only a limited number of passes for other civilians to travel the line between Nashville and Chattanooga. Under no circumstances would he allow civilians to travel south from the latter city, "for I find them useless mouths that we cannot afford to feed."[60]

Easton told Hartz to load animal forage into separate trains from the other material for faster unloading, but Hartz was reluctant to adopt this practice. Complaints about it surfaced for a few days and then disappeared by the end of June, indicating that he must have eventually agreed with Easton that it helped streamline the process of loading and unloading.[61]

Despite Sherman's report about an orderly procession of trains flowing to his army in convoys, Julius E. Thomas indicated the flow was far from regular. From his post at Bridge Number 4 over Chickamauga Creek near Graysville, Thomas counted five trains going south and five going

Federal Boxcars at Chattanooga. In cars such as these rode the viability of Sherman's campaign for Atlanta, carrying food, material, returning soldiers, and all manner of supplies to the army group as it advanced. Returning empty or filled with wounded men and civilians who wished to escape the zone of operations by moving north, the same cars provided roundtrip logistical power to Federal quartermasters. Julius L. Thomas spent a good deal of time watching these cars go back and forth while performing guard duty near Graysville, Georgia. LC-DIG-cwpb-02122.

north on May 22. "A continuous train of cars" streamed north on June 1, mostly loaded with wounded men, and those heading south contained provisions from the storehouses of Chattanooga. At times the flow dried up almost to nothing. On June 8 "no trains from Chattanooga and only two from the front" crossed the bridge. Later that month Thomas normally counted seven trains going north and five heading for the army each day. The cars heading south contained food and ordnance stores, while those heading north carried prisoners, wounded men, and troops whose term of service had expired. By mid-July Thomas counted ten to twelve trains moving along the line every day, with an increase in the number of prisoners transported north. By late July the number increased to a maximum of twenty trains per day but varied widely over time. He noted that on days of heavy rain there were few trains, while on clear days the number increased dramatically.[62]

When Sherman set priorities for shipping during times of railroad disruption, he gave priority to ammunition and other ordnance stores because such material could not be obtained in the countryside. Clothing received second priority for the same reason, but food might be found among civilians. When the logistical system worked normally, quartermasters gave priority to subsistence stores because the men consumed food at a faster rate than any other item in the field. Quartermasters gave second priority to forage for animals. Easton estimated Sherman needed at least thirty cars of subsistence stores for men and forty cars of grain for animals every day.[63]

Quartermasters tended to pack in other types of supplies, whenever they had room on the cars. Easton told Hartz to send a few boxes of new shoes when the Twentieth Corps asked for them, but only "without interfering with the supply of forage & provisions." Requisitions for clothing often were huge because the men wore it out so fast while living in the field. Twenty-Third Corps quartermasters not only asked for 3,000 pairs of shoes but also 5,000 pairs of stockings, 1,500 pairs of pants, and 500 canteens. Other commands in Sherman's army group filed even bigger requisitions for hats, underwear, rubber blankets, haversacks, knapsacks, writing paper and envelopes for headquarters staff, horseshoes, mule shoes, and harnesses. Hartz sent 10,000 blouses, 38,000 shirts, and 15,000 infantry trousers to Big Shanty in late June.[64]

The heavy earthwork construction during the Atlanta Campaign led to loud calls for picks, spades, shovels, and axes. "The army is badly in need of them," wrote a quartermaster in the Sixteenth Corps. On more than one occasion requested tools did not arrive promptly, leading to testy telegrams received by Hartz, who scrambled to get them to the field as soon as possible.[65]

Quartermasters sent in unusual requests for items such as rope, wagon wheels, nails, and pontoon trains. Officers of the 48th Ohio wanted to replace their colors and asked Easton to arrange it. He described to Hartz what was needed: "one silk Regtal national color that is the Reg tal Color that is composed of the Stars & Stripes."[66]

As the system of forward depots lengthened during the campaign, Easton pressed Hartz on June 9 to send civilian laborers south to unload cars at various stations. Hartz contacted people as far away as Washington, D.C., and got the reply that no workers were available in the East. W. D. Wood Jr. suggested he could find laborers at Saint Louis, but they would expect thirty-five dollars per month. Hartz had no choice but to pay this exorbitant salary for common laborers, a rate more than double the monthly salary of privates in the army.[67]

The variety of shipments demonstrated the complex needs of an army in the field. On August 27 several trains hauled a total of twenty-six cars of forage, six cars of subsistence stores, one car of ammunition, three cars of baggage, two cars of quartermaster stores, four cars of lumber, one car of express packages for individuals in the army, one car of mail, and two cars of railroad supplies out of Chattanooga for Sherman's command.[68]

Not surprisingly, Federal troops took what they could from the countryside during the course of the Atlanta Campaign. The 124th Indiana, a new regiment assigned to the Army of the Ohio, did so more than other units because it acted as an escort for the army's wagon trains and had more opportunity to roam about. Division commander Milo S. Hascall was sickened by the plundering he witnessed during the campaign. On more than one occasion he counted half a dozen burning buildings while standing at one spot, witnessed the "wanton destruction of fine paintings," and felt these acts were enough "to disgrace and render worthy of defeat any army in the universe." He despaired of serving "with an army where the fundamental principles of civilized warfare are so shockingly violated at every step in our progress."[69]

Most of the destruction that overwrought Hascall was done by a relatively small percentage of men, but its effect was highly visible. Other observers tended to overstate the plundering. "As we pass through the country," wrote John W. Geary to his wife, "we leave it as though all the locusts of Egypt had been upon it. There is not a single blade of grass left upon the earth. Wheat fields are eaten to the ground, and the rising corn is beginning to yield its quota to the sustenance of our animals. The provisions of the people is also taken without compunction, and they are left in utter want." Tennessee Unionist Alexander Hammontree called northwest Georgia "a desetet county the sitoyens all flees before our armey & leaves all they have they are bound to starve every thing is tore up the wor[1]d left bare."[70]

Some degree of suffering was visited upon the citizens by the retreating Confederates as well. The enemy "always sweeps the country clean," reported Manning F. Force in the Seventeenth Corps. Two women who had driven their milk cows into the woods to keep them out of Confederate hands came to Force begging for food. He offered them army hardtack, and they were grateful for it. More women showed up asking the Federals to transport them north from the war zone, and they obliged. Hood issued instructions to his subordinates to remove all hogs and cattle from the reach of the enemy before giving up territory. The Confederates pillaged the civilians they were pledged to protect, as witnessed by Hood's general order calling on his men to stop plundering. In both armies infantrymen tended to blame their own cavalry for most of this pillaging because the mounted troops had more opportunity to roam the countryside.[71]

By mid-July civilian refugees seeking safety in the North appeared on trains heading toward Chattanooga. Two months before that, cotton began to be shipped north as well. Easton mandated it be moved to Nashville, where Donaldson could release it to Treasury Department officers. But in June Sherman began to crack down on this kind of freight because "our railroad must be exclusively used for the supplies of the army till the war is over." Lincoln urged Sherman to let cotton flow north, and the general allowed what little was available in northwest Georgia to be shipped if it did not interfere with military needs. "The trouble about cotton is the time consumed in loading and unloading," he complained to Halleck. "It is all we can do to get supplies up."[72]

Sherman was increasingly frustrated that Thomas had not taken his order to streamline transportation in the field seriously, maintaining a large and comfortable headquarters establishment. McPherson had cut his Army of the Tennessee headquarters transportation to the bone, not even allowing shelter tent halves for his staff until they complained about it. Added to the difficulties of getting Thomas's Fourteenth Corps to act aggressively in the field, Sherman felt the Army of the Cumberland was not performing as well as his other armies. "They still think and act as though the railroad and all its facilities were theirs," he complained to Grant about Thomas's staff officers.[73]

Sherman relied heavily on wagon trains, each vehicle pulled by a six-mule team, for hauling material from the railroad to his deployed troops. Pack mules were available but little used. Each corps utilized 800–1,000 wagons plus 200 ambulances, the latter of which were pulled by two horses each. The canvas covering of each wagon was marked to designate whether it carried ordnance stores, forage, subsistence, or camp and garrison equipage. Corps transportation placed in a single line would stretch at least ten miles, making a total of seventy miles for the seven corps in the army group. There were 6,000 animals in each corps eating twelve pounds of grain and eight pounds of hay every day, if they could get it. Quartermasters tried to hold at least 200 wagons as a reserve for Sherman but were able to locate only about half that number at various depots such as Bridgeport and Stevenson, which could be called on if he needed them.[74]

Sherman placed ordnance stores at the top of his priority list at times of emergency not only because they could not be obtained in the countryside but also because his troops expended prodigious amounts of ammunition. Large battles were relatively few, but heavy skirmishing occurred every day. The 92nd Ohio detailed 200 men to the skirmish line on June 21. They expended 24,000 rounds in twenty-four hours even though instructed to keep their fire to a minimum, a rate of 120 rounds per man. "The army is getting out of amm.," Easton reported on June 24. "For[war]d all ammu promptly it must have preference over everything." In the Army of the Tennessee, ordnance officers maintained a reserve in their wagon train amounting to 140 rounds per man and 200 rounds for every artillery piece. The Third Division, Fourth Corps used on average 421 rounds per man during the four-month campaign. The entire Army of the Cumberland expended 3,051,943 rounds of small-arms ammunition during August alone and 11,815,299 rounds during the entire campaign.[75]

There appeared only slight fears among some Union commanders that the ammunition supply might fail. Schofield warned his subordinates to guard against useless firing of artillery on May 10. Six weeks later he reported that his artillery chests were full but that he had no more than one-third the number of rounds needed to refill them.[76]

Feeding Horses and Mules

The worst supply shortage for the Federals lay in forage for animals, an item placed low on Sherman's priority list. Hay and grain were the most bulky items to transport, and each animal needed twelve pounds of grain and eight pounds of hay every day. The shortage was felt by mid-May among Thomas's mounted units. William H. Jennings reported that the horses of the 7th Pennsylvania Cavalry had to eat "the leaves and short grasses to be found on the hills around Adairsville," and 76 of them literally "died of starvation" or were abandoned as too weak to carry mounted men by May 22. They had no feed at all from May 26 to June 2, leading the regiment to abandon an additional 101 mounts. Details roamed as much as thirty miles but could find no forage. The 7th Pennsylvania Cavalry received half its feed ration from June 13 to 18, none from June 19 to 22, half from June 23 to July 17, and none from July 18 to 19. Sporadic shortages continued into August.[77]

Sherman downplayed the significance of this shortage by telling Halleck his animals subsisted on grass. But Brig. Gen. Edward M. McCook pointed out that "green wheat and leaves, the only food we can procure, neither strengthens nor nourishes" horses. Five mounts in one company of his command literally dropped from exhaustion one morning while on picket duty. Many of the others were "absolutely dying from starvation."[78]

Clifford Stickney of the Signal Corps pointed out that along the Mississippi River, steamers were well fitted to handle large, bulky material in contrast to the railroad system, which was "utterly unable to transport enough forage." As a result "the horses and mules are becoming so lank, weak and their ribs show so like those of a skeleton."[79]

Easton was aware from the start of the campaign that forage shipments were a problem. He needed forty carloads every day but received only eleven in a period of thirty-six hours on May 5. The problem worsened afterward. "I have just seen Gen Sherman," Easton told Hartz on the twentieth, "we must have 300 car loads of Grain here in 3 Days." By May 30 Easton had 300 wagons waiting at Kingston to be loaded with animal food and urged Hartz to hurry up the shipments. Those wagons could carry an estimated 2.5 million pounds of grain, which the horses desperately needed. Hartz was able to ship 1,106,250 pounds of grain on May 30 alone, and he pushed forward ten carloads of forage on June 7 and fifty-five the next day. But by June 14, shipments amounted to only 262,105 pounds daily. "We are getting out of forage," Easton sternly told him on June 16. Only by shortchanging the shipments of human food could Hartz come close to the required number of cars containing forage by the twenty-sixth.[80]

By dint of enormous effort, Hartz achieved a level of adequacy in shipments of forage in late June but soon began to lose ground again. Only fourteen carloads of animal food arrived on June 29. "That is not enough to supply Daily issue," he was told. Hartz learned that 400 empty cars were sitting idly at and near Marietta. "I cannot return cars fast enough to Nashville," he complained.[81]

Contributing to the problem was a fall in the water level of the Cumberland River that reduced steamboat traffic to Nashville, although using the rail route between Nashville and Clarksville helped a good deal. When the water level rose by late August, it finally ended the worst phase in the crisis of forage delivery. The new oat crop began to provide fresh supplies of grain in the North as well. Donaldson complained that officers in the Army of the Ohio and the Army of the Tennessee did not submit proper estimates of the number of horses in their commands. He had good estimates from the Army of the Cumberland, the field force he was primarily responsible for, but the "visiting" troops from the other two departments were lax in their paperwork.[82]

Compounding the forage problem was the periodic shipment of damaged grain that could not be used at the front. Easton told Hartz, "this is very wrong stop it at once." A week later "ten car loads of worthless grain arrived at Acworth this morning the army is out of grain & the sending of this trash to the front is intolerable." Donaldson thought the grain probably was damaged in transit from Chattanooga to the army. He knew that sacks often had to be shipped in open flatcars because of shortages of boxcars, and any sudden rain shower could ruin dozens of them within minutes. Donaldson issued instructions never to ship grain on flatcars again. But the problem was deeper than that. Easton admitted that he had two million pounds of grain lying in an exposed place at Resaca due to lack of storage facilities, and he needed empty cars to shift it to Big Shanty before the next rain. When Hartz acknowledged that one of his clerks had allowed damaged grain to be sent forward, Easton had the man fired.[83]

Donaldson had small reserves of horses at Nashville to replace animals worn out by the campaign. There were only 108 artillery horses and eleven cavalry mounts as of June 8. He also had 281 mules, 326 wagons, and 560 sets of mule harness. That number fluctuated over time as requisitions from the field arrived. Hartz kept a few cavalry mounts at Chattanooga, but they were in need of rehabilitation with feed and rest. When replacement animals were sent to Sherman, Easton required they go on foot rather than take up space in the cars. Only when Sherman needed four mules for his headquarters did Easton tell Hartz to "pick out good ones" and send them by rail. The same applied when Sherman needed two wagons and an ambulance for his headquarters a few days later.[84]

The army group needed horseshoes by the thousands, but these took up little space in the cars. Easton not only asked for 4,000 pounds of horseshoes on May 30 but also included a long list of other small items, such as wagon covers, nails, harness and bridle leather, blacksmith coal, thread for sewing saddles, axle grease, and wagon wheels.[85]

Feeding Men

Sherman often worried most about shipping human food. "The task of feeding this vast host is a more difficult one than to fight," he told his wife. Sherman examined statistics comparing how much food was issued and the reported number of effective soldiers in the army group. He found that the number of issues were 50–75 percent higher than the effectives. That was intolerable. "The question of supplies to an army of this size is one of the greatest possible importance, and calls for a most rigid economy," he stated in a field order. Only cooks, teamsters, pioneers, and laborers could be defined as noneffectives. Sherman allowed up to 25 percent of effective strength as "a large and reasonable limit" to issue for all noneffectives accompanying his command.[86]

Amos Beckwith, Sherman's chief commissary, reported the army group consumed 20 million rations from late May to late August, all of them coming from stockpiles in the Nashville depot. But that depot needed an additional 10 million rations as soon as possible to keep up. Beckwith recommended that 15 million rations of salt meat (pork) be added to the stockpile because, until late August, commissaries had arranged to drive beef cattle to the army. That was now becoming almost impossible given the long distance from the corrals at Nashville and Chattanooga. To keep things in perspective, Beckwith told the commissary general of subsistence in Washington that Sherman's men consumed less food than "the various garrisons, camp, hospitals, employees & c., everywhere between the Ohio and Chattahoochee River, including East Tennessee."[87]

Because of the difficulty of getting food to the troops in the field, Sherman reduced rations when they advanced beyond easy reach of the railroad. Federal soldiers were happy one day and complained the next as a result. And there always were some men who were never satisfied with their rations. "Our only trouble is, that we do not get half enough to eat," wrote Thomas Christie of the 1st Minnesota Battery, "a little hard bread, a little coffee, and occasionally a very little meat—day after day that is all; so there is not much variety." After enduring half rations for two weeks, David Watts of the 88th Illinois admitted to his wife, "there is a good deal of complaint about it." These shortages did not last forever, but they were more frequent than historians have reported.[88]

The period embracing late May and early June was particularly difficult because Sherman temporarily cut himself off from direct contact with the railroad to flank the Allatoona hills. For two weeks his men relied on wagon trains to bring all manner of supplies from the railroad at Kingston to the battle lines. When heavy rains set in, the wagons had difficulty making headway on the dirt roads. The men in the field were "almost shelterless, and subsisting on short rations of hard tack, pork and coffee," complained F. Y. Hedley of the 32nd Illinois. The effect on their spirits "was most depressing." For a very few of them, a ration of whiskey provided by the Western Sanitary Commission on rainy days helped ease the depression a bit.[89]

Sherman's army group suffered shortages of many items needed for effective operations in the field during June. Due to repeated short breaks in the railroad, the logistical system seemed able to provide only "bread, meat, coffee, and ammunition. The men are even cautioned to be sparing of cartridges," reported Hedley. "No soap is to be had; the men have no clothing except that upon their persons, and there is great suffering on account of vermin." Craving tobacco, some soldiers used dried coffee grounds in their pipes as a substitute. Henry G. Ankeny of the 4th Iowa told his wife, "Clothing and shoes are in great demand." In fact, forty men in his regiment were barefoot. "All together this so far is the hardest campaign that we have yet experienced." Because his 76th Ohio was stationed quite far from the railroad, Quartermaster John J. Metzgar found it difficult to transport supplies with the few wagons available since shortages of forage weakened his mules.[90]

A natural result of limited food supply was the appearance of scurvy. Extended periods of operations while subsisting on field rations of bread and pork denied soldiers vitamin C, which they mostly got in the vegetables that made up the full ration. "In a short time scurvy will make its appearance among us on account of the diet we are necessarily confined to," anticipated Charles Blank of the 32nd Missouri in May. The condition became serious by July. Surgeon George Martin Trowbridge of the 19th Michigan thought scurvy "one of the loathsome diseases," and he kept an eye open for its signs. "The blood seems dissolved & exudes from the whole mucous surface," Trowbridge explained to his wife, and "the skin looks as if [it] had been bruised all over, gums spongy teeth loose, diarrhea general failure of vital powers emaciation & death." As of July 25 he noticed only mild cases. Victims had a "great desire for something sour, which should be a vegetable acid, good vinegar, fresh vegetables, dried better than none." Trowbridge saw no sign of scurvy in any of the Confederate prisoners or deserters gathered by the Federals.[91]

The extent to which scurvy affected Sherman's men is not easy to pin down because no one compiled statistics, but the evidence indicates the condition was widespread. "The Atlanta campaign had confined our army so long to a diet of hard bread and salt meat that it had become greatly infested by scurvy," concluded a veteran of the 150th New York. Surgeon John Bennitt of the 19th Michigan argued that "the largest proportion" of men in Sherman's command "have scurvy in some degree. This is due to a want of a mixed diet and cannot be very well remedied by medication, but the use of vegetable food with fruits indulged freely will relieve this scorbutic condition very promptly."[92]

Fourth Corps troops admitted that scurvy affected their units to a considerable degree. Col. Luther P. Bradley thought friends and family back home would gladly send vegetables to relieve the problem, but there was no room on the cars for it. "This scorbutic condition is very unfavorable for wounded men," Bradley noted, "and we lose a good many from this cause."[93]

Surgeon John W. Lawton, chief medical officer of Hascall's command, reported that "scorbutic tendency . . . has generally pervaded the troops of this division." Lawton believed his Twenty-Third Corps men had been predisposed to the condition by months of privation in East Tennessee during the previous fall and winter. On inspecting the division early in July, he found on average that 20 percent of the men exhibited "marked cases of scorbutics," while more than 50 percent showed "a taint" of the condition.[94]

"Scurvy has been the great cause of sickness" during the campaign, concluded Surgeon H. Earnest Goodman, chief medical officer of Geary's division. He had noticed it in early May, and the condition worsened steadily. Goodman was convinced that two-thirds of the 1,000 men he sent to the rear due to illness during the campaign showed "scorbutic affections." He admitted at least 150 advanced cases of it into the division hospital during July and August but could only guess at how many other cases existed.

Goodman knew that the men had received few rations of vegetables during the winter encampment. Even though commissaries issued vegetables "freely during three weeks before" the onset of the campaign, it did not make up for the prolonged deprivation. Goodman left 250 men of the division behind in Chattanooga due to scurvy.[95]

Sherman recalled that Edward D. Kittoe, his medical inspector, warned him that scurvy was spreading through the army group as the campaign unfolded. In late June, when it was impossible to get up enough potatoes and other vegetables, blackberries and green corn "providentially" became available in the countryside, according to Sherman. He also noted that "lime-juice, sauerkraut, and pickles" arrived on the cars to counter the condition. From the countryside one could also count on persimmons, sassafras root, wild mustard, agave, turnip tops, and "dandelion cooked as greens, and a decoction of the ordinary pine-leaf" as antiscorbutics.[96]

It is interesting to read Sherman's list of natural antidotes for scurvy but frustrating that he so casually dismissed the problem. There is no evidence that any Union soldier roamed through the countryside looking for these plants. Even if they had the opportunity to forage, it would have been impossible to obtain more than limited supplies of these potential remedies. As we have seen, scurvy did not disappear in late June when blackberries became ripe—it actually grew more widespread.

Agents of the Western Sanitary Commission called for hundreds of barrels of sauerkraut by late June, saying it was "more needed than anything else at present for distribution among regiments in the field." The list of antiscorbutics included dried apples, cranberry sauce, citric acid, and canned tomatoes. It was easier to ship desiccated vegetables than fresh vegetables, and now and then soldiers found some in their rations. What the men did not need was more salted food, but for some reason commissaries experimented with smoked herring during the Atlanta Campaign. It was obtained at Boston to the tune of 100,000 boxes, but few men appreciated the fish.[97]

To some degree Sherman was right that the ripening of area fruit helped alleviate the scurvy problem. Blackberries and peaches were the mainstay reliance in Georgia, and green corn helped too. "Our men are in better health now than they were six weeks ago," asserted John Moore, medical director of the Army of the Tennessee. Members of the 85th Illinois stewed blackberries into "a somewhat novel but very palatable dish" to be eaten with hardtack. "But the great number of men," recalled Henry Aten, "all ravenously hungry for fruit or berries of any kind, soon exhausted the supply, and men wandered in search of berries too far from camp for safety."[98]

It is obvious that the limitations of Sherman's supply line affected the health of his fighting men. Luther P. Bradley also complained that it affected the care of those men who were wounded and fell ill. He indicated that fewer medical stores were shipped than surgeons needed. Accidents affected the care of the wounded too. A locomotive ran into a hospital train on May 18, killing one man and seriously hurting half a dozen wounded soldiers.[99]

Confederate Logistics and Supply

The Army of Tennessee faced far fewer logistical challenges than did the Federals during the Atlanta Campaign. Its line of communications lay entirely within friendly territory. The base of supply at Atlanta was only a few dozen miles away, and the army constantly fell back toward that city. Rebel commanders fended off a handful of mounted Federal raids that failed to disrupt the rail system very much. Most of their problems stemmed from the inherent weaknesses of the Confederate supply system—a shortage of rolling stock, the lack of a strong governmental presence on the rail system, and the tendency of railroad companies to favor private freight and passengers over government business since Richmond authorities did not pay their bills on time. As one frustrated Confederate officer noted, it took seventy hours to haul wounded soldiers 130 miles from Atlanta to Macon, on average only 1.8 miles per hour.[100]

The best that can be said is that Confederate soldiers got by with their logistical support. Benedict Joseph Semmes was placed in charge of the wagon trains of the Army of Tennessee and spent many hours every day superintending the issue of rations from the farthest point north on the Western and Atlantic Railroad that Johnston controlled. While he was able to issue enough to avert hunger, many soldiers complained that it was a monotonous and unsatisfying diet. "We have had nothing but bacon & corn bread & I fear that if it is continued much longer we will all have the scurvy," complained Col. Newton N. Davis of the 24th Alabama. "The Soldiers are all crazy for vegetables." Some of them knew enough of nature to find the vines of sweet and Irish potatoes, but that could not solve the problem for everyone. Despite Davis's concern, there is no evidence that scurvy became a major problem in the Army of Tennessee.[101]

When Hood evacuated Atlanta on September 2, his commissaries and quartermasters left behind large amounts of material for want of time and carrying capacity. Semmes reported that twenty-seven days' rations were abandoned at the depot after 550,000 pounds of meal had been given to the citizens. A total of five locomotives and eighty-one cars were left in the city, including twenty-five cars loaded with ammunition that were burned before the Confederates abandoned Atlanta. Semmes evacuated a train of eighteen cars loaded with various stores out of the city on the night of August 30 and barely made it to Jonesboro before the advancing Federals caught up with him. From there he rode on a train filled with Confederate wounded, which slammed full force into another train loaded with wounded, killing twenty men and wounding many more near Barnesville.[102]

Supply and Strategy

While both sides endured supply problems during the Atlanta Campaign, the Federals faced more challenges than their opponents. As the campaign deepened in intensity, many of Sherman's men became sharply aware of just how much their existence depended on the railroad. Some wondered if the rail system could support the army group during the long campaign. "I doubt whether it can be maintained," worried brigade leader James Sidney Robinson in late May. Charles F. Morse, lieutenant colonel of the 2nd Massachusetts, had spent the first half of the war in Virginia where the Army of the Potomac enjoyed "an unlimited amount of transportation for public and private supplies." But Sherman's men were "in the midst of an enemy's country as completely cut off from the smallest luxury of civilised [*sic*] life as if we were in the middle of the African desert."[103]

As we have seen, the slender line of iron barely managed to meet Federal logistical needs. At times Sherman felt compelled to break away from it temporarily to mount big turning movements because he could find no other way to deal with strong Confederate positions. But he always sought to regain contact with the railroad as soon as possible. The first time occurred on May 23, when he left the rail line with twenty days' rations, supplemented by authorized foraging, and crossed the Etowah River. By June 7 he had regained contact with the railroad south of the river and reestablished his supply line, but (as we have seen) his horses and mules suffered enormously during that period for lack of feed. Sherman prepared to do the same thing early in July to deal with the Kennesaw Mountain Line, but the Confederates pulled out of their trenches just after the flanking movement began, resulting in no disruption of Union supply arrangements. The third and last time Sherman prepared to cut away from his line of supply occurred in late August as he sought a way to pounce on the last two railroads feeding Hood's army. This movement by six of his seven corps finally opened the gates of Atlanta and brought the campaign to an end.[104]

After the fall of Atlanta on September 2 and an inconclusive standoff at Lovejoy's Station, Sherman called off further operations and retired to the Gate City. Macon was 103 miles away, and the drive toward that city would have nearly doubled the Georgia section of his already extended supply line. He knew the railroad would not support his command for such a drive—it had barely supported it to Atlanta. Hood and his subordinates, unaware of the limitations of their enemy's logistical thread, assumed the Federals would continue moving south.[105]

Easton admitted to Quartermaster General Meigs that it had been a very difficult task to keep the army group going in Georgia. But, even though aware of the limitations in his supply arrangements, Sherman uniformly praised its success to everyone. "We have been wonderfully supplied in provisions and ammunition," he told Grant, and "better than I expected," as he wrote to another officer. "I esteem this a triumph greater than any success that has attended me in Battle or in Strategy," he boasted to his foster father. "Rosecrans had his army starving at Chattanooga, and I have brought an army double its size 138 miles from there."[106]

The commissaries and quartermasters themselves looked on the Atlanta Campaign as an unusual triumph of their military art. Noting the distance to the primary base at Louisville, the fact that the rail line ran through hostile territory the entire way, and quoting figures for the size of Sherman's manpower and his large collection of animals, Daniel McCallum called the success "without precedent in the history of warfare." It required "an enormous outlay for labor and a vast consumption of material, together with all the forethought, energy, patience, and watchfulness of which men are capable." Donaldson gushed in his report to Meigs that it was "the proudest joy of my life" to have played a key role in its success. "From the bottom of my heart I thank God that I have been able to supply" Sherman's troops in an "illustrious campaign, so big with the destinies of the Republic."[107]

Sherman knew the Atlanta Campaign would have been literally impossible without the railroad. He calculated that it would have required at least 36,800 wagons with six mules each (a total of 220,800 mules) to supply his army group during the campaign—that is, if every wagon could have carried two tons of supplies at least twenty miles per day. Sherman realized that this was "a simple impossibility on roads such as then existed in that region of country."[108]

McCallum put it well when he described the objective of his logistical team during the campaign. "The design and aim was to make the railroad a transportation machine to aid in working out the combinations of the commander of the military division," he wrote.[109] Through a combination of hard work and expertise, the Federals accomplished that goal.

6

HOOD AND SHERMAN IN NORTH GEORGIA

By the summer of 1864, there was a noticeable shift in strategic emphasis in the campaign for Atlanta. Opposing commanders increasingly targeted each other's supply lines. Using mounted forces in such actions was not a new idea, but the size of those forces increased and the strikes occurred more often and with more intensity. Wheeler's raid in August was unusually long, and he hit three rail lines rather than just one. Moreover, Sherman pioneered in the use of large infantry forces to cut enemy supply lines that summer. He utilized nearly all his army group in late August to devastate Hood's railroads and isolate Atlanta from the outside world.

Freed from defending the city, Hood sought to duplicate Sherman's heavy use of infantry forces to attack his opponent's supply line. He needed time to see if the Federals intended to continue advancing south of Atlanta, time to rest his own troops, and time to obtain approval from Richmond for an offensive into northern Georgia. After working out all these preparations, Hood was ready to see if targeting railroads could reverse Confederate failure by the beginning of October 1864.

Railroading or Raiding?

For a month after his capture of Atlanta, Sherman had no idea he would soon be on the defensive. Instead he contemplated the next move in his deep penetration of the Lower South. He could not continue to rely on the slender rail line to Louisville, which had barely sustained his army group to the gates of Atlanta. Strategic raiding was the only recourse, leaving a garrison behind to hold Atlanta and the rail link to Chattanooga, while he moved most of his troops through the Deep South, living off the land. The only real question lay in exactly what route to follow, when to start, and where to end.[1]

The need to cut from the railroad and march through the countryside was apparent to all. Thomas told Sherman, "it would not be prudent for us to go much farther into Georgia because of our already long line of communication," as Sherman recalled. Fourth Corps brigade commander Luther P. Bradley told his sister, "our line of communications at present is too long, too expensive and uncertain, and it takes an army to guard it." Oliver O. Howard pointed out that 8,000 of his troops were guarding railroads already. According to Sherman, Thomas was compelled to assign more than five times that number of men to railroad duty within the Department of the Cumberland.[2]

Even so, the supply line barely supported the Federals. Surgeon John Bennitt of the 19th Michigan shuddered at the thought of continuing to Macon, while relying on this fragile line, in contrast to a fast march, feeding from the countryside, that ended up at Mobile, where he could "get some fresh tropical fruits and vegetables."[3]

Sherman contemplated turning Atlanta into the last Federal bastion on the railroad before leaving, which meant stockpiling supplies and building a new line of earthen defenses for a sizeable garrison. As early as July 15, Grant had a similar idea, suggesting to Halleck that Sherman "devote himself to collecting the resources of the country" after capturing Atlanta. "He will take everything the people have, and will then issue from the stores so collected to rich and poor alike."[4]

The harsh measures Grant outlined were within Sherman's contemplation. In his mind Atlanta would become a huge depot like Chattanooga and Nashville, self-sufficiently operated by its garrison after he left the railroad on his raid farther south. Federal quartermasters began to collect food and forage from the area around the city, offering receipts and letting the government decide who was loyal and deserving of reimbursement. Sherman told Maj. Gen. Henry W. Slocum, who was in charge at Atlanta, to secure "all good buildings for Government purposes." He encouraged Unionist families to refugee north and secessionist families to go south. Sherman told Joseph Webster in Nashville not to allow civilians to travel south to the city. He intended to "remove all the present population and make Atlanta a pure military town."[5]

The Federal experience at Memphis, Vicksburg, Natchez, and New Orleans had convinced Sherman to depopulate Atlanta as the best way to eliminate civil-military problems. On September 7 he informed Hood of the need to accept the citizens he intended to remove from the city to Rough and Ready. "Atlanta is no place for families or non-combatants," he told him. Hood and Mayor James M. Calhoun bitterly protested, but Sherman continued his plan to turn Atlanta into a "pure Gibraltar" by October 1. His policy, more harsh than any adopted in previously occupied cities, met with approval in Washington. "Your mode of conducting war is just the thing we now want," Halleck told him. "We have tried the kid-glove policy long enough."[6]

The question now was where to go on this raid through the Deep South. Halleck preferred the Montgomery-Selma route. "There is a section of country from fifty to one hundred and fifty miles wide extending from Selma west to Meridian, and thence north on both sides of the Tombigbee to Columbus, Aberdeen, and Okolona, more rich in agricultural products than any equal extent of country in the Confederacy," he told Grant. "Slave labor has been but very little disturbed in this section, and the large crops of this year are being collected at Demopolis, Selma, Montgomery, and other points for the use of the rebel army."[7]

Halleck saw the Deep South as a rich agricultural region ripe for exploiting by a roving force of Union troops. Every agricultural region of the South also had a large population of slaves and Federal authorities wanted to harvest black human resources for service with the U.S. Colored Troops and for government laborers. Halleck failed to mention that Selma had become, by this stage of the conflict, an industrial center that produced a wide variety of ordnance and other supplies vital to the Confederate war machine. There was more to be gained economically by driving into the industrial heart of Alabama on the way to the Gulf coast than through the agricultural region of central Georgia on the way to Savannah.

Grant seemed to have no preference in this matter. His only concern was that Federal quartermasters accumulate a store of supplies waiting for Sherman on the coast no matter which direction he took from Atlanta.[8]

So authorities prepared for either strategic raid. Engineer Miles D. McAlester consulted a man who had been supervising inspector of steamboats for the U.S. government before the war. From his information, McAlester reported on the conditions of the Apalachicola River, the Chattahoochee River, and the Flint River, all part of the drainage system of western Georgia, eastern Alabama, and the Florida Panhandle into the Gulf of Mexico. The report included details about the number and type of steamboats operating on these small streams. The Federal high command wanted to be ready for supplying Sherman if he chose to head south to the Gulf—they already knew that Savannah was easily accessible by coastal shipping once its port facilities were secured by Sherman's men.[9]

Hood and Confederate Strategy

The necessary delay in Union operations after the fall of Atlanta gave Hood the chance to seize the strategic initiative. He would use the entire Army of Tennessee to wreck Sherman's railroad and draw him from Atlanta. For the first time in the Civil War, the focus of a major campaign would be on logistics. Along the way, Hood planned to feed his men off the countryside as much as possible and arrange for wagon trains to follow as best they could until regaining contact with a secure supply line. If successful, his campaign could reverse all that had been lost with the fall of Atlanta.

The Army of Tennessee rested during September while still connected to its rail support. After Sherman broke off contact at Lovejoy's Station on the Macon and Western Railroad on September 4, Hood advanced north to Jonesboro but then shifted his troops westward to Palmetto Station on the Atlanta and West Point Railroad twenty-four miles southwest of Atlanta. Jefferson Davis came to visit the army, giving a speech at Macon along the way that irritated Sherman for months to come. "Sherman cannot keep up his long line of communication, and retreat sooner or later, he must," the Confederate president proclaimed. "And when that day comes, the fate that befell the army of the French Empire and its retreat from Moscow will be reacted. Our cavalry and our people will harass and destroy his army as did the Cossacks that of Napoleon, and the Yankee General, like him will escape with only a body guard."[10]

In consultation with Hood, Davis approved his proposal to move north against the rail line between Chattanooga and Atlanta. Then Davis left the army on September 29. On his way back to Richmond, he gave another speech at Goldsboro, North Carolina, in which he said that Hood "expected to select his own position on the railroad, and if once he laid his paws on Sherman's rear, he expected to hold there, wait for him to attack and then whip him." Davis predicted that Rebel troops would not only drive the enemy from Georgia but also all of Tennessee and Kentucky, then advance north of the Ohio River.[11]

HOOD'S NORTH GEORGIA CAMPAIGN

In preparation for the campaign, Hood ordered the rails removed from all lines that ran to Atlanta to prevent the enemy from advancing toward Macon and Augusta. He ordered a bridge constructed over the Chattahoochee River at LaGrange, Georgia, to move his wagon trains. Engineer John W. Green initially built a wooden span but soon replaced it with a pontoon bridge to get the wagons across more safely.[12]

The Army of Tennessee set out on September 29 and moved fast. Striking the rail line between the Etowah River and Kennesaw Mountain constituted the first phase of Hood's North Georgia Campaign. He instructed Lt. Gen. Alexander P. Stewart, whose corps was given the job of tearing up track, to do a thorough job of destruction. All cuts in the roadbed were to be filled up with brush, rails, and dirt. Even the wagon road that ran parallel to the track was to be blockaded as much as possible. Stewart occupied Big Shanty on October 3 and began to wreck track from there to Allatoona.

After two days Hood thought Stewart had done a good job, capturing 350 Federals to boot, and had compelled Sherman to begin moving toward the Army of Tennessee.[13]

Hood also sent French's Division of Stewart's Corps to capture the large depot at Allatoona. It was defended by a sizeable force of Federals who put up the toughest fight of the campaign on October 5. The Battle of Allatoona was a particularly bitter battle. Outnumbered by 3,276 Confederates, Brig. Gen. John M. Corse's 2,000 Federals fought for hours and barely held on to the position. French failed to capture the depot and was forced to break away because of a report that Union reinforcements were close by. He lost 800 men while inflicting a loss of 706 Federals. The van of Sherman's army group was only a few miles south near Kennesaw Mountain when the battle ended.[14]

After the bloodletting at Allatoona, Hood moved northwest rather than plant the Army of Tennessee on the Western and Atlantic Railroad. Instead of challenging his opponent to a make-or-break battle, he hoped to draw Sherman from Atlanta in a cat-and-mouse game through the hills. Whether this was the more effective strategy is questionable, but Hood, without consulting anyone, elected to pursue it.

The army's wagons trailed behind Hood during this first phase of his campaign. Federal officers were impressed by his celerity of motion and attributed it to the fact that he had no concerns about protecting a line of supply. They assumed he had "very few wagons" and carried "scarcely anything except ammunition." Yet they also realized that Hood *had* to march fast precisely because he had no supply line. There were too few provisions in this region, already devastated during the Atlanta Campaign, for the Army of Tennessee to dally long at one place. In fact, this was one unstated reason for Hood's decision not to stop and offer battle. He had no secure line of communications to stay in one place very long in a denuded country. But already there were signs that Hood's ultimate goal would not be realized. Sherman detailed the Twentieth Corps to hold Atlanta while taking the other six corps to chase the Army of Tennessee.[15]

Davis wanted a new head of affairs in the West to supervise Hood's actions. He placed Gen. P. G. T. Beauregard as commander of the Military Division of the West, encompassing two departments, Hood's Department of Tennessee and Lt. Gen. Richard Taylor's Department of Alabama, Mississippi, and East Louisiana. That appointment took place on October 2, after Hood started out from Palmetto Station. It was another week before Beauregard caught up with the Army of Tennessee at Cave Spring, Georgia, on the ninth. There he learned of Hood's intention to draw Sherman farther from Atlanta by initiating the second phase of his campaign, striking the Western and Atlantic Railroad around Resaca and Dalton.[16]

Beauregard approved Hood's plan and then rushed off to arrange logistical support for the army. He wanted to shift Hood's base from Jonesboro, Georgia, to Jacksonville, Alabama. Until this time wagon trains had hauled supplies from Jonesboro to Palmetto Station while the army had rested at the latter place. Then they tried to keep up with the fast-moving Confederates. Jacksonville was much closer to the developing theater of operations. It was located at the eastern end of the Alabama and Tennessee River Railroad, which stretched 135 miles from Selma to Blue Mountain, a small town fifteen miles south of Jacksonville. The company had constructed an additional 22.5 miles of track toward Dalton, Georgia, in 1862. Beauregard also wanted to consult with his other department commander, Taylor, about getting his help in supporting Hood.[17]

Even before he met Beauregard at Cave Spring, Hood had mapped out the second phase of his campaign. He planned to cross the Coosa River ten miles from Rome, Georgia, then march along the west side of the Oostanaula River to hit the Western and Atlanta Railroad at Resaca. For some reason Hood thought Sherman might move south; if so, he would backtrack and attack the Federal rear. If Union forces moved north instead, then Hood would defer battle and move to the Tennessee River by way of La Fayette, Georgia, and Gadsden, Alabama, where he would meet his wagon trains. Hood also began to think of building an expansive rail system of supply to support his army's fast-paced campaign. The Mobile and Ohio Railroad, running north and south through Mississippi, could constitute the stem of a new supply line that could support either one of two rail lines that ran west to east. One linked Montgomery with Jacksonville, and the other connected Corinth with Decatur. Hood might wind up at the end of either line. Setting his army in motion for the second phase of the campaign, Hood issued orders to Maj. Gen. Arnold Elzey, now in charge of the army's wagon trains. Elzey was to send provisions and ammunition to La Fayette and the rest of the train plus the army's pontoons to Jacksonville.[18]

The Army of Tennessee devastated a long section of track during this second phase. Lt. Gen. Stephen D. Lee's corps partially invested Resaca by

Members of the Construction Corps, U.S. Military Railroad, at Chattanooga, 1864. These men and their colleagues provided the talent and skill needed to keep the expansive Federal rail system operating. They have displayed many of their tools and pieces of equipment for the photographer. As soon as Hood's Army of Tennessee moved out of the way, they set to work repairing the damage to track and bridges in northern Georgia and later in Middle Tennessee. LC-USZ62–62364.

October 12, but the small Federal garrison refused his demand for surrender. Lee decided it would cost too many men to assault the place, so he broke contact and concentrated on destroying track. Farther north at Dalton, Maj. Gen. Benjamin F. Cheatham's corps compelled the 800-man garrison there to surrender without a fight. For several days the Confederates tore up Sherman's lifeline for many miles before the Union army group moved near.[19]

"We have completely destroyed the enemy's railroad from Resaca to Tunnel Hill," Hood boasted on October 16. He urged Taylor to send Forrest on a raid to destroy the line between Nashville and Chattanooga. Hood also ordered his own cavalry, consisting of Brig. Gen. William H. Jackson's division, to hit the rail line between the Etowah River and the Chattahoochee River. Neither cavalry thrust took place, but the Confederates consoled themselves with the knowledge that they had inflicted far more damage to the Union rail system than anything they had done during the Atlanta Campaign.[20]

Hood's Railroads

The Confederates were adept at moving large armies with little logistical support, but reconstructing a long, dilapidated rail line was something new to them. Support personnel tried to put two rail lines back into working order—the Mobile and Ohio Railroad, from Mobile to Corinth, and the Memphis and Charleston Railroad, from Corinth to Tuscumbia or some other point—a total of 150 miles of deteriorated track. This was a kind of work that the Federals accomplished with regularity, but Hood charged his support personnel with a daunting task by requiring a real supply line to support his presence in north Alabama.

Corinth, the junction of these two lines, became the lynchpin of the Confederate rail system. The Federals had evacuated the northeastern Mississippi town in early 1864 because it was no longer useful to them. Lt. Gen. Leonidas Polk, commander of the Department of Mississippi, East Louisiana, and Alabama, had started to rehabilitate the railroads by late April 1864. He wanted to get trains rolling northward to Corinth and eastward from there to Cherokee or Tuscumbia, intending to use the line to support operations by Forrest that threatened Memphis and West Tennessee. But most of Polk's manpower was soon after ordered to join the Army of Tennessee in Georgia (along with the general himself), and these plans fell apart.[21]

Confederate troops now began to make Corinth an important post along their new line of supply. Forrest filed a report about this matter on October 12 after he inspected the area. He concentrated on the Memphis and Charleston Railroad, noting that it was utterly destroyed for several miles between Cherokee and Tuscumbia. Forrest recommended placing a pontoon bridge over the Tennessee River at Florence, which lay only a couple of miles from Tuscumbia. Here the pontoons could be tied to the masonry piers of a bridge for a railroad spur that ended on the north bank of the Tennessee. Forrest envisioned using this crossing to strike at both the

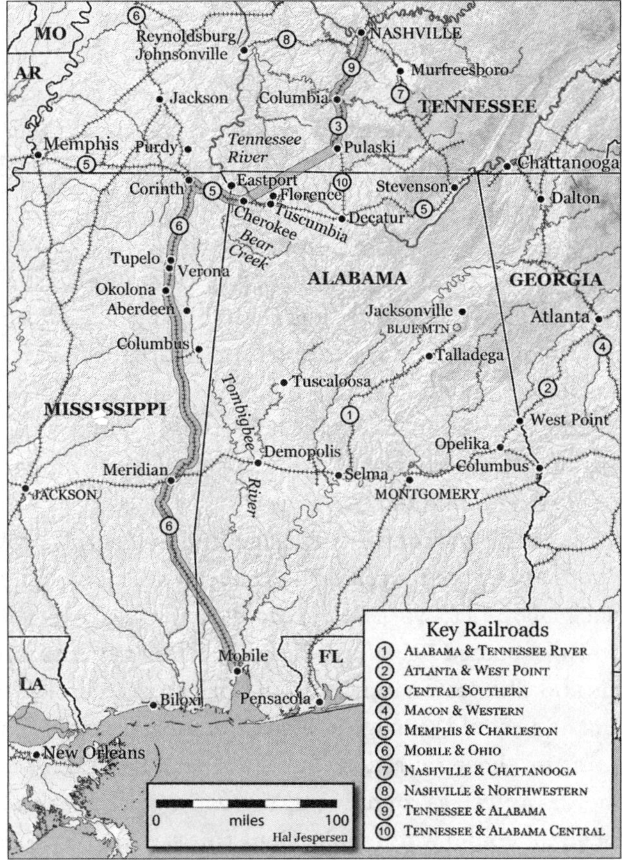

HOOD'S SUPPLY LINES

rail line between Nashville and Decatur and the Nashville and Chattanooga Railroad in the near future. Taylor had suggested that Forrest move into West Tennessee to collect provisions, forage, and recruits. If he could stay some time, the cavalry commander might even rebuild the Mobile and Ohio Railroad between Corinth and Jackson to support his stay. Forrest believed that line could be reconstructed, but he admitted that there were far fewer resources in West Tennessee than imagined.[22]

Beauregard, whose authority was needed for this railroad reconstruction, decided to concentrate on the route from Corinth to Tuscumbia rather than the road to Jackson. He urged Taylor to get the Mobile and Ohio and the Memphis and Charleston into running order soon. That meant establishing garrisons at Corinth and Bear Creek as well as constructing earthwork defenses at all significant places. He wanted Forrest to raid the Nashville and Northwestern Railroad between Johnsonville and Nashville before joining Hood's army. Martin L. Smith, chief engineer of the Army of Tennessee, was to place torpedoes and other obstructions in the Tennessee River between Eastport, Mississippi, and Florence, Alabama, to hinder Union gunboats from ascending the waterway and interfering with the crossing at the latter place. By this time Confederate engineers had begun to repair the Alabama and Tennessee River Railroad between Montgomery and Jacksonville, but now that Hood's plans had changed, that line was no longer needed. Beauregard mandated that the repairs continue anyway but wanted the rolling stock on the line reduced to the bare minimum and the excess shifted to the Mobile and Ohio line.[23]

After two years of wartime destruction and neglect, it proved to be more difficult to repair the railroads than expected. Taylor gathered tools and some black laborers to work on the Mobile and Ohio between Okolona and Corinth. He expected Brig. Gen. Philip D. Roddey to find laborers for the Memphis and Charleston repairs from Corinth to Cherokee or farther to Tuscumbia, if he could manage it. The Confederates rarely referred to whites working on these railroads, and they had a habit of pressing free blacks as laborers as well as rounding up slaves for work such as this. Roddey also needed to rebuild water tanks along this stretch. Grass had grown on the roadbed, which tended to cover the rails and reduce the friction needed for the iron wheels to propel the train. Many new ties had to be put in place as well. Taylor assigned his superintendent of railroad transportation to oversee all the work on both rail lines and press more black laborers from Demopolis and Mobile, transporting them by rail as far as possible to work areas. Most slaves in the region had already been pressed or had been taken away by their owners, so Taylor felt compelled to use black Union soldiers captured by Forrest and Hood in their raids on Union supply lines. "General Hood's movement is intended to extend to the occupation of Middle Tennessee," Taylor told Forrest as early as October 23.[24]

The biggest part of the job lay in the fifty-two-mile stretch between Corinth and Tuscumbia. W. J. Ross, superintendent of the Memphis and Charleston Railroad, could not even estimate how long it would take to repair this line, although he admitted that a good labor force could rebuild about three-fourths of a mile per day. The workers had to be divided into gangs, one to cut timber, another to straighten rails and collect small pieces of iron such as chairs and spikes. Many more tools, especially shovels, were needed, and the available hands had to work constantly if there was to be a hope of getting the line into shape reasonably soon.[25]

As far as repairing the line from Corinth to Jackson for the purpose of procuring supplies in West Tennessee, Forrest admitted it would not be feasible. He traveled along the track and told Taylor that the road was utterly devastated. Virtually every bridge and trestle was gone, and the telegraph wire had been stolen by local farmers to use in baling cotton. Most of the telegraph poles were rotting as well.[26]

While Taylor's men sought a way to make the rail system work, Hood decided in late October not to risk a general engagement with Sherman. He had hoped the Federals would divide their large force so he might strike one part in detail, but Sherman kept his six corps together during the move from Atlanta, always one or two steps behind the Confederates. Hood marched into north Alabama, reaching Gadsden by October 20. Here Beauregard joined him a few days after assuming command of the Military Division of the West on October 17. Initially Hood wanted to quickly cross the Tennessee River and attack Bridgeport but concluded the Army of Tennessee did not have enough cavalry to protect its flanks while crossing because Forrest had not yet joined the army.[27]

Hood therefore marched west to Florence. Along the way he threatened the 3,000-man garrison of Decatur on October 27 and 28 but decided it would cost too many lives to capture the place by storm. This demonstrated the worth of Federal efforts to construct strong defenses at key points on their rail system. The Army of Tennessee continued to Florence, where Lee crossed some of his troops on pontoon boats to drive away a Federal cavalry force on the north side of the Tennessee. Then in early November Rebel engineers lay a pontoon bridge, following Forrest's earlier recommendation, by tying the boats to the masonry piers of the unfinished railroad spur. Hood now had a secure crossing and was eager to move northward, but he was compelled to wait for his quartermasters to finish restoring the railroad so he could refurbish his army.[28]

Hood's march from Palmetto Station had been impressive. His army moved swiftly, accomplished significant damage to Sherman's rail line, and got away without punishment. The Army of Tennessee accomplished this logistically in the same way that Bragg had supplied the Army of the Mississippi during the Kentucky Campaign—and the same way Robert E. Lee had supplied the Army of Northern Virginia during the Maryland and Pennsylvania Campaigns—mostly by living off the land and supplementing that source with intermittent wagon supply from the nearest railhead. This mode of operating imparted great mobility to a field army, but only for a short time. Hood reached the end of his North Georgia Campaign when he arrived at Florence. If the railroad had been put into shape much earlier and he had found a stockpile of supplies at Tuscumbia, his wait would have been short. But the railroads were not in shape and there was no stockpile.

Hood's pause at Florence was the turning point of the war in the West. A similar pause by the Federals after the fall of Atlanta had given the Confederates an opportunity to seize the strategic initiative. Now it was Sherman's turn to take advantage of a pause in the pace of operations. He had worried that Hood might cross the Tennessee and strike at his main rail line near Wartrace, Tullahoma, or Decherd. Now the danger of a quick strike was averted by Confederate logistical problems, and Sherman seized the initiative in a way to suit his own strategic goals rather than simply reacting to Hood's movements.[29]

Hood's Wagon Trains

What Sherman did will be detailed later in this chapter; for now, we need to round out the story of Hood's supply arrangements as he prepared for the contemplated invasion of Middle Tennessee. During the time when the Army of Tennessee began to move into north Alabama, its support personnel had shifted the line of supply from Jonesboro to Jacksonville, Alabama, a town linked by rail to Montgomery. Jacksonville was about eighty miles west of the Western and Atlantic Railroad that linked Chattanooga with Atlanta. Hood's wagon trains had traveled from Palmetto Station to Jacksonville by this time and were employed in shuttling supplies from the railhead to the roving army. The roads were very bad, snaking among mountains, and the mules were taxed to their limit. As his army moved toward Gadsden, Guntersville, and Decatur, Hood ordered Elzey to bring the wagon trains along, shifting the rail support from Jacksonville to Tuscumbia.[30]

Commissary officer Benedict Joseph Semmes was in charge of feeding Hood's army with 580 wagons during the campaign. It tasked his considerable energy to the utmost. On the march toward Florence, Semmes found the roads to be particularly bad, "many mules gave out," and a lot of his wagons broke down along the roadside. Those that did not break down "were more or less used up." He had to cross several large mountains, taking eighteen hours to negotiate one that was especially high and rugged. A brigade of infantry was detailed to escort the train. Upon receiving word that the army's food had run out, Semmes managed to meet it at Decatur by detaching the better wagons and rushing them ahead of the rest of the column.[31]

The journey of Hood's wagon train from Palmetto Station to Tuscumbia was a minor epic, especially for the resource-strapped Confederates. Maj. E. H. Ewing, an officer of the national field-transportation office assigned to accompany the Army of Tennessee, reported that the journey required more than a month of hard traveling. The wagons averaged between twenty and twenty-five miles each day, and the teams did not stop for feed or water until the end of the day's journey. The black teamsters often neglected their mules even at the end of the day, and the animals were in terrible shape by the time they reached Tuscumbia. For one seven-day period, they were never unharnessed. "1,500 animals have been utterly used up on this march," Ewing reported, "and the number will be doubled if we make as hurried a trip into Tennessee as it is expected we will." He believed the Army of Tennessee had captured 100 horses and a few mules and wagons on the campaign, but none were turned over to the wagon trains for use. "General Hood steadily refused to let us have anything to do with them" complained Ewing, "and nobody else takes any interest about it. Many of the horses are being constantly sold and traded off by parties capturing them." After reading his report, Ewing's superior, A. H. Cole, warned the secretary of war that the land transportation of the Army of Tennessee could collapse entirely. Be ready "for the possible total loss for all useful purposes of the magnificent equipment of field transportation with which the Army of Tennessee started on its recent campaigns."[32]

Confederate Railroad Management

Hood's supply problems persisted despite a great deal of activity on his railroads. He realized that a major problem lay in the different gauges of the Mobile and Ohio Railroad and the Memphis and Charleston Railroad, which compelled quartermasters to shift all material from one train to another at Corinth. Probably because of that problem, Hood suggested that his railhead be shifted from Tuscumbia, Alabama, to Purdy, Tennessee, located twenty-five miles north of Corinth on the Mobile and Ohio line. Beauregard ignored that suggestion—there already was too much effort being expended on the route to Tuscumbia, and as Forrest reported, the track north of Corinth was in far worse shape than the line to Tuscumbia.[33]

Work on the Mobile and Ohio and the Memphis and Charleston continued at a desperate pace. Beauregard authorized Taylor to impress as many workers from the civilians in his department as possible. It was thought 200 black laborers were needed to get the line running to Tuscumbia, but they could not be procured because the few available were already on their way to Corinth to dig a new defensive line for a small garrison. Rolling stock also was a problem. Such a weak engine pulled one train carrying black laborers and tools that quartermasters had to reload the tools into the passenger car of another train to get them to Corinth.[34]

In fact, much freight of all kinds was shipped to Corinth in passenger cars because there were not enough freight cars available. This material came from depots at Mobile, Meridian, Columbus, and Macon along the Mobile and Ohio Railroad. Maj. George Whitfield urged subordinate quartermasters to roam along the line and expedite these shipments. "Allow no stores to lay on the road," he wrote, "particularly commissary stores." By November 6 Whitfield reported that the Mobile and Ohio Railroad was "in tolerably safe order to Corinth." He thought the Memphis and Charleston Railroad was "about the same to Cherokee." He needed more laborers, however, to get the stretch from Cherokee to Tuscumbia into a similar condition. "Taking into consideration the short notice we had and the amount of stores we have transported I think we have done well with the roads in such bad condition."[35]

Corinth continued to be a chokepoint. Not only was the garrison small and lacking proper earthworks but also stores could not be shifted from one train to another quickly enough. Hood had sent quartermasters there to forward material to his army, but the place needed more officers and laborers than were available in Taylor's department.[36]

During early November, a trickle of supplies began to move uncertainly to the Army of Tennessee, but it was far less than Hood needed to prepare for his next move. As of the fifteenth, Beauregard predicted it would take another three weeks to finish work on the railroads so they could run at full capacity. He warned, however, that it might be five weeks if the weather turned bad. The first shipment of material reached Tuscumbia by rail on November 21, but not at full capacity.[37]

Confederate quartermasters failed to support Hood's strategic needs. Sherman set out from Atlanta on his March to the Sea on November 15. The Federals fully understood Hood's supply arrangements. They knew he was drawing from depots at Selma, Montgomery, and other places by way of the Mobile and Ohio Railroad and the Memphis and Charleston Railroad to Cherokee, then by wagon to the army. Sherman urged raids by Union forces out of Memphis and Vicksburg to cut the Mobile and Ohio line. Grant and Halleck agreed, but arrangements proceeded slowly, and the raid did not occur until weeks later.[38]

Meanwhile, Hood waited impatiently at Tuscumbia. On November 12, three days before the start of Sherman's march, the frustrated commander explained to Davis that not only supplies but also the long delay in Forrest's arrival postponed his move. Hood wanted the cavalryman, who belonged to Taylor's department, to screen his flank and protect his wagon train on the drive northward. But Forrest was still busy raiding Union supply arrangements at Johnsonville. "This circumstance, high water, and the fact that I had to draw supplies from and through a department not under my command, involving delay in their reaching me, have retarded my operations," he complained to Richmond.[39]

With the onset of Sherman's march, Davis and Beauregard urged Hood to do something. Hood and Beauregard agreed that it would be impracticable to pursue Sherman; the only alternative was to move north into Middle Tennessee. Hood had hoped to accumulate three weeks' rations before starting this campaign. But by November 17 he had only one week's accumulation. Four days later, despairing of getting the additional two weeks' rations, he set out from Florence anyway on his risky invasion of Tennessee.[40]

Forrest and the Railroads

The delay caused by logistical problems was something the Confederates could not avoid at this stage of the war. Their logistical capacity had always been limited by a number of factors too big for any one man to solve; those limitations worsened as the war progressed until they came close to paralyzing Rebel commanders. But the fact that Forrest took so long to join Hood was something a man could control. Forrest had been very busy from

September to November, inflicting destruction on Sherman's railroads. In fact, with only 4,500 men, he succeeded in damaging Federal transportation facilities far more than Hood's 35,000-man Army of Tennessee had during that same period. His work, however, had far less consequence on the course of events because the lines that Forrest targeted in Alabama and Tennessee were of only secondary importance to the Federals, rather than the main stem line that Hood wrecked in north Georgia.

Forrest started his railroad campaign two weeks before Hood left Palmetto Station. On September 16 Taylor ordered him to hit the line between Nashville and Decatur. Leaving Verona, Mississippi, Forrest rode by way of Cherokee, crossed the Tennessee River near Florence, and reached Athens, Alabama, by September 23. The next day he bluffed the Federal commander of the post, Col. Wallace Campbell of the 110th USCT, into surrendering 400 men without firing a shot. Then he rode to Sulphur Creek Trestle, four miles north of Athens. Here the Union garrison put up a fight, but the Confederates were able to place eight artillery pieces on advantageous ground and pound the two blockhouses protecting the bridge. After two hours of punishment, the Federals surrendered. Forrest then burned one of the more important trestles in Sherman's rail system, 1,100 feet long and 90 feet high, on September 25.[41]

As Federal authorities began to realize what was happening, Forrest already had a couple of days' head start on them. He capitalized on that advantage by burning the bridge and connecting trestle work over the Elk River, where the small Union garrison had already abandoned its blockhouse, on September 26. Riding farther north to Richland Creek near Pulaski, Tennessee, he compelled the Federals to give up a blockhouse and bridge after a short fight.[42]

By September 27, however, Forrest began to encounter stiff resistance. Lovell H. Rousseau had gathered 3,000 Federal cavalry and now confronted him near Pulaski, but Forrest decided to break off contact. His mission was to tear up track, not fight a major battle. He rode northeast to hit the Nashville and Chattanooga Railroad, reaching Fayetteville by September 28. From there, Forrest sent two small parties to tear up track north and south of Tullahoma. The next day Forrest learned from his scouts that 15,000 Federals were in the area to protect the line. He decided this was too many for his small force, recalled the two parties, and retired to the railroad linking Nashville with Decatur, which was less heavily defended.[43]

In this second phase of his campaign, Forrest once again achieved a high level of destruction. He detailed Brig. Gen. Abraham Buford's brigade with some artillery to move south toward Huntsville while taking the rest of his force to hit the railroad between Pulaski and Columbia. On October 1 Forrest talked Lt. E. F. Nixon of the 7th Pennsylvania Cavalry into ordering three blockhouses under his command to give up without a fight. These positions protected the rail line as it crossed a winding stretch of Carter's Creek a few miles north of Columbia. Another blockhouse, commanded by Lt. J. F. Long of the same regiment, refused to give up, and a small fight ensued for ten hours. The Confederates were able to set fire to one end of the bridge that Long was protecting and destroy it. Even though Long had held out, Forrest managed to destroy three blockhouses and three bridges in the area.[44]

Forrest demonstrated against Rousseau at Columbia on October 2 but then ended his raid, retiring south by way of Lawrenceburg until reaching Florence on the fifth and Cherokee the next day. On the expedition he captured 1,274 Federal troops, 800 horses, seven guns, and 2,000 small arms. Forrest claimed "the complete destruction of the railroad from Decatur to Spring Hill" except for the large bridge crossing the Duck River. For all this he lost 340 men, while 500 more Confederates had dropped out along the way and were now straggling back to their units. Forrest thought it would take at least two months for the Federals to repair what he had burned.[45]

This was one of the more destructive cavalry raids of the war, but Forrest exaggerated the level of destruction. It is true that the loss of Athens and Sulphur Creek Trestle were major blows to the rail line between Nashville and Decatur. McCallum called the latter "the most formidable trestle on the Decatur and Stevenson line." But at Carter's Creek the Confederates burned only small structures and five miles of track. Rousseau was able to save the line between Pulaski and Columbia, and Forrest did not try to hit the Duck River bridge. The Federals reoccupied Athens on September 28 and planted a garrison of 500 men and two guns. When Buford tried to attack it again on October 2, he was handily repulsed.[46]

Forrest had destroyed a lot along the line between Nashville and Decatur with comparatively few troops, but this success failed to further Confederate strategic goals. The Nashville to Decatur route was a supplementary line to the main stem of Union supply, the Nashville and Chattanooga Railroad. Sherman could afford to lose it for a time without endangering his position in Georgia. This was why there were so many more Federal troops guarding the Western and Atlantic compared to the Nashville and Decatur line. That was in turn why Forrest was able to so heavily damage the latter railroad. When he tried to do the same to the Nashville and Chattanooga, he backed off upon learning of the Union force he would have to contend with and did not make the attempt.

On October 13, several days after Forrest's raid, Grant told Halleck it would be best to abandon the Nashville and Decatur line from Columbia southward in order to obtain more troops for the defense of Tennessee. Acting on this directive, the Federals converted a defeat into an advantage.[47]

W. W. Wright, head of construction for the U.S. Military Railroad, left all the bridges that Forrest destroyed south of Pulaski in ruins. North of Pulaski, he rebuilt the spans and blockhouses at Carter's Creek. When Hood finally entered Middle Tennessee in late November, he found the railroad working from Nashville down to Pulaski but not south of that town. He needed that stretch of railroad to support his army in its close-in position at Nashville following the Battle of Franklin but did not have it. Ironically, the immense destruction exacted by Forrest in September and October actually hurt the Confederates more than the Federals.

If Forrest had been content with his raid on the Nashville to Decatur line and joined the Army of Tennessee in late October, Hood would not have had to complain about his whereabouts while waiting for the supply line to be opened to Tuscumbia. But the cavalry commander was even further delayed by conducting yet another mounted raid on a secondary and therefore nonessential Union supply line. This time the target was the Nashville and Northwestern Railroad linking the state capital with Johnsonville on the east side of the Tennessee River. Johnsonville was isolated, vulnerable, and an easy target. Forrest also was motivated by an erroneous report he heard while on the previous raid "that it is by this route that the enemy received most of their supplies at Atlanta."[48]

Forrest left Corinth and arrived near the target by November 3. "The wharf at Johnsonville was lined with transports and gunboats," he reported. "An immense warehouse presented itself." He set up artillery on the west side of the Tennessee and opened fire the next day. The bombardment rattled the small Union force of 1,000 troops. Positioned on higher ground, the Confederate guns dominated the supply depot, which was located in a basin. The Federals panicked and did more destruction than their enemy. A navy lieutenant ordered four gunboats to be burned, while the post commander ordered eight transports worth $300,000 and ten barges valued at $35,000 to be torched. Material worth a total of $1.5 million also went up in smoke; one-third of it consisted of commissary stores. Forrest broke off contact on November 5 and returned to Corinth five days later.[49]

Again the level of destruction was immense, and it neutralized Johnsonville and the Nashville and Northwestern Railroad as a supply conduit. But once again it was far from a campaign-winning blow. McCallum admitted that a lot of supplies had been funneled through that line from August to October, yet Sherman was correct to point out that it was only of secondary importance. "But you know," he wrote Grant, "that that line of supplies was only opened for summer use when the Cumberland is not to be depended upon. We now have abundant supplies at Atlanta, Chattanooga, and Nashville, with the Louisville and Nashville Railroad and the Cumberland River unmolested."[50]

Compared to Hood's campaign of destruction along the Western and Atlantic Railroad, Forrest's campaign received secondary priority as far as the Federals were concerned. Sherman had sent Thomas to Middle Tennessee as early as September 29 to organize the railroad guards against Forrest's raid. The very next day word filtered into Atlanta that Hood had left Palmetto Station and crossed the Chattahoochee River. Sherman knew that "desperate efforts will be made to render our roads useless" as the Army of Tennessee became the main focus of defensive measures.[51]

Sherman and Federal Strategy

Sherman was forced to react to Confederate initiatives, but he refused to give up plans for an offensive into the heart of the Deep South. His first reaction to the news of Hood's movement from Palmetto Station was to launch a quick countermove east or southeast of Atlanta to draw the Confederates away from his railroad link with Chattanooga. But Sherman quickly gave up that notion. While informing Grant of developments, he stated that if Hood got to the Western and Atlantic Railroad south of the Etowah River, he would pursue him. But if the Confederates aimed at a point farther north, he would prefer that Thomas deal with the Army of Tennessee while he set out for Savannah or Charleston. "We cannot remain on the defensive," he told the general in chief. To complicate the situation, heavy rains descended by October 2 and washed out several bridges along the Western and Atlantic.[52]

Leaving the Twentieth Corps to hold Atlanta, Sherman led six corps northward, but Hood was at least a couple of days ahead of him. By October 7 the Confederates had broken the rail line south of the Etowah River. Based on initial reports, Thomas assured Sherman that Wright could repair these breaks in a week. But the news of Forrest's raid on the secondary line between Nashville and Decatur worsened Thomas's concerns. The track between Pulaski and Athens was "pretty thoroughly destroyed," he reported. Sherman ignored the wrecking of that line and urged the speedy reconstruction of the Western and Atlantic Railroad, pushing some repair crews north from Atlanta as Thomas pushed others south from Chattanooga. These crews not only repaired Hood's damage but also rebuilt the washed-out bridges over the Chattahoochee, Etowah, and Oostanaula.[53]

It is ironic that Hood thought he could force Sherman into playing his game by moving into north Alabama. Actually, that move played into Sherman's own thinking. The Federals had enough manpower in Georgia to divide their forces, dealing with Hood and at the same time raiding through the Deep South. The farther Hood moved away from his pursuing column, the better Sherman's chances of gaining approval from Washington authorities for the splitting of his army group.

On October 9, only four days after the bloody fight at Allatoona, Sherman told Thomas he wished to reclaim control of the flow of events. "I want to destroy all the road below Chattanooga, including Atlanta, and make for the sea-cost. We cannot defend this long line of road." For the first time Sherman talked of giving up Atlanta and its rail link with Chattanooga rather than turning the former city into a military base. Wright had to continue repairing the Western and Atlantic Railroad for now because it was needed as Sherman prepared for his raid through the Deep South. Supplies had to be accumulated, unnecessary material shipped north along with sick and wounded men, and troops ready to report for duty in the field transported to Atlanta. After that Wright would have to tear up the track. Sherman also confirmed that Thomas should not repair the line between Nashville and Decatur as it would be of no use to him.[54]

On October 10 Sherman sought Grant's approval for his plan to move from Atlanta to the coast if Hood's army veered off into north Alabama. He assured the general in chief that Thomas would have ample manpower to deal with the Army of Tennessee.[55]

"On mature reflection," Grant wrote to Secretary of War Stanton on October 13, "I believe Sherman's proposition is the best that can be adopted. With the long line of railroad in rear of Atlanta Sherman cannot maintain his position. If he cuts loose, destroying the road from Chattanooga forward, he leaves a wide and destitute country to pass over before reaching territory now held by us." Grant sent a cipher telegram to Sherman approving his plan, but the cipher was "imperfect," and Sherman could not tell whether Savannah or Mobile was Grant's preferred target. Actually, Grant was willing for Sherman to make that decision. He arranged through Halleck to have large amounts of supplies shipped by coastal steamers to the area near Savannah and to Pensacola to accommodate either the Atlantic coast or the Gulf coast as Sherman's objective. Interestingly, Grant specified to Halleck that Sherman should take 30,000 men with him, obviously expecting him to leave behind the rest for Thomas to use. In the end Sherman took 60,000 men without Grant's explicit approval.[56]

By October 16 the Federals were hurrying repairs on the Western and Atlantic Railroad, especially the larger break near Resaca. "We must finish the road to prepare for the future," Sherman wrote. "I want to make a raid that will make the South feel the terrible character of our people." Wright employed 1,500 men but needed additional rails. McCallum not only arranged for 3,000 tons of new rails to be shipped to Nashville but also suggested taking up rails from little-used auxiliary lines. Slocum detailed men to tear up the line between Atlanta and East Point for Wright's use. Sherman learned that the break at Big Shanty was rebuilt by October 19, but the damage at Resaca took longer. Not until the twenty-eighth did the first train roll into Atlanta from Chattanooga with supplies.[57]

The six corps that chased Hood into north Alabama relied on wagon trains until reaching the area of La Fayette, Georgia. Then Sherman organized a supply line by rail from Chattanooga to Ringgold so his wagons could refill from stores shipped south from the major depots. Chattanooga alone held a stunning amount of material by mid-October. A quartermaster's report indicated that 3 million meat rations (120 days' supply for 25,000 men) was stored there. The quartermaster also had 3.5 million bread rations (140 days), 3.5 million coffee rations (140 days), 7 million sugar rations (300 days), and 500,000 rations of beans and rice (200 days each). The list included 250 days' worth of small rations (soap, salt, candles) and 1 million rations of whiskey. Even with this large accumulation so close to his command, Sherman allowed his men to scrounge food from the depleted countryside of north Georgia. When civilians complained about it, he told them to blame it on Hood for breaking his railroad.[58]

Although Sherman was willing to do battle if the Army of Tennessee made a stand, he preferred to see the Rebels move off into Alabama. "I want the first positive fact that Hood contemplates an invasion of Tennessee," he told Schofield on October 16; "invite him to do so. Send him a free pass in."[59]

As soon as Hood reached Gadsden, Alabama, Sherman broke off pursuit and concentrated on preparing for his raid. "I want the road repaired to Atlanta, the sick and wounded sent north of the Tennessee, my army recomposed, and I will make the interior of Georgia feel the weight of war." By October 19 he had decided to send the Fourth Corps to Thomas and move the rest to Savannah, "destroying all the railroads of the State." Previously seen as remote and inaccessible, the Deep South now was open and vulnerable. "I am going into the very bowels of the Confederacy," Sherman wrote, "and propose to leave a trail that will be recognized fifty years hence."[60]

Despite his reference to Savannah on October 19, Sherman kept his choice of target open for several days. He penned a long letter to Halleck that day pondering this important question. Sherman sensed that Grant preferred he head for Savannah, while Halleck liked Selma and the central region of Alabama. He believed his army could hit many cities while marching toward Savannah, including Macon, Milledgeville, and Augusta, and possibly cause Charleston to be cut off and fall into Union hands.[61]

To Thomas, Sherman wrote that the Fourth Corps and all miscellaneous troops in the West would be enough for him to deal with Hood's estimated 40,000 men. Thomas must have been stunned to learn that Sherman wanted to take with him not only the five corps but also Brig. Gen. Edward McCook's division of cavalry and the mounted troops that Brig. Gen. James H. Wilson was then organizing for the Military Division of the Mississippi. Sherman wanted Thomas to command all assets of the military division, except the units he personally took on the raid, during his absence. He was planning to take the lion's share of those assets, even though the only large enemy force in the region was heading directly toward Middle Tennessee. Sherman was so obsessed with his raid that he divided his resources unwisely, favoring the movement that would have the least resistance instead of the most.[62]

On October 20 Sherman told Thomas he wanted to take 60,000–65,000 men on his raid, double the number Grant expected him to use. He was more firmly committed to Savannah as a target but still wanted to keep open Mobile or the mouth of the Apalachicola River as options. "To pursue Hood is folly, for he can twist and turn like a fox and wear out any army in pursuit. To continue to occupy long lines of railroads simply exposes our small detachments to be picked up in detail and forces me to make counter-marches to protect lines of communication." "We have now a good entering wedge and should drive it home" by moving south or east of Atlanta rather than chasing Hood.[63]

Sherman was impatient to get the Western and Atlantic Railroad repaired as soon as possible. He wished to move sick and wounded men, as well as "surplus trash," to the north. "I want nothing in front of Chattanooga save what we can use as food and clothing and haul in our wagons," he told Quartermaster Easton. Guerrillas harassed Wright's crews, killing or wounding sixty men by October 23 and destroying a train loaded with ties. This delayed Wright's timetable, but he hoped to finish repairs by the twenty-seventh.[64]

The delay in repairs led to some degree of suffering by the Twentieth Corps in Atlanta. Animal food, the bulkiest material to convey, became so scarce that many horses and mules were "actually dying from starvation" while others were rendered of little use for field service. In many brigades almost an entirely new supply of artillery horses had to be procured before the onset of the march. Troops went on half rations early in October. "Famine began to look the corps squarely in the face," recalled Wisconsin soldier Edwin Bryant.[65]

Sherman told Slocum to forage from the countryside, predicting he would discover "fine corn and potato fields about Covington and the Ocmulgee bottoms," areas yet to be visited by Federal troops. On October 11 Alpheus Williams's division set out in large foraging parties to harvest the bounty of rural Georgia. Five hundred wagons escorted by 2,500 men moved fifteen miles east of Atlanta to collect potatoes and hogs. On the thirteenth troops of John Geary's division escorted 420 wagons to collect 352,800 pounds of corn and 28,299 pounds of forage for animals. James Robinson's brigade of Williams's division took 671 wagons into the countryside for more than 500,000 pounds of corn on October 20, while Brig. Gen. Thomas Ruger's brigade penetrated the area southeast of Atlanta to collect 800 wagonloads of corn on the twenty-third. Similar foraging expeditions took place on October 24 and 29 as the Twentieth Corps gathered in the civilian harvest within reach of their base at Atlanta. In many cases the soldiers themselves harvested the standing crop in the fields. Robinson warned all his men to keep their guns slung over their shoulders because Confederate cavalry lurked about. "We take everything from the people without remorse," Geary told his wife. Sherman approved. "If Hood breaks our road Georgia must pay for it," he wrote.[66]

After absorbing the import of Sherman's plan for the upcoming raid, Thomas gently criticized him for taking away so many troops. On October 17 he suggested that Wilson's cavalry should be used in the defense of Tennessee. Three days later he suggested that an additional corps of the Army of the Cumberland be loaned to him so he could, in conjunction with Wilson, deal with Forrest effectually.[67]

By October 28 Sherman agreed to send the Twenty-Third Corps to Thomas and allowed him to retain Wilson. He also urged Halleck to send additional manpower to Tennessee. Sherman predicted that Thomas would have 40,000 infantrymen and 12,000 cavalrymen in a short while, more than enough to deal with Hood, he thought, but Thomas disagreed. The 12,000 troopers were nothing more than a prediction by Wilson, who in reality was able to mount only 5,000 men by mid-December. Thomas also thought his superior underestimated the number of troops needed to protect the main depots and railroads but was able to convince him to adjust his plans only a little. When Thomas complained that he could not guarantee the safety of the rail line between Chattanooga and Knoxville unless the Western and Atlantic Railroad was kept in operating condition down to Dalton, Sherman agreed and cancelled orders for its destruction to that Georgia town.[68]

As far as Sherman saw it, there was a possibility that Hood might pursue him once he started from Atlanta. In that case he wanted Thomas to move south, penetrate Alabama, and capture Selma. Thomas thought this a good idea after hearing reports that the "country through Middle Alabama . . . is teeming with supplies this year, which will be greatly to our advantage."[69]

Everything seemed to be settled for a unique divergence of opposing forces in the West, with one army heading north and the other heading south. But then Grant raised a question. On November 1 he asked Sherman if it was wise to rely on Thomas's scratch force alone to oppose the Army of Tennessee. "Now that Hood has gone so far north," he wrote, why not "settle him before starting on your proposed campaign." After that Sherman could "go where you please with impunity." Sherman reiterated the same arguments he had used earlier. If he pursued, the Army of Tennessee most likely would evade him and nothing would be resolved. He assured Grant that Thomas would have enough manpower to handle the enemy, estimating Hood had 30,000 infantrymen and 10,000 cavalrymen. The Fourth and Twenty-Third Corps together numbered 25,000 men, and he believed Thomas could gather up to 25,000 additional troops from various sources. Grant was finally convinced. "I do not really see that you can withdraw from where you are to follow Hood, without giving up all we have gained in territory. I say, then, go as you propose."[70]

Sherman was delighted. By November 3 he firmly fixed Savannah as his target and considered moving on from there to reinforce Grant at Petersburg. But three days later, less than a week before leaving Atlanta, he again considered marching in other directions, knowing there was "no serious" force to oppose him in any of those directions. First, to aim at Charleston or Savannah would allow him to cut the only east–west rail lines serving the Confederates and make it easier for him to go to Petersburg. Second, to head for the Apalachicola River would be the easiest march as it would take his men through the "very fertile and well supplied" valley of the Flint River. He could free the Union prisoners at Andersonville along the way, but this route would not facilitate the next move to Petersburg. Third, he could march down the valley of the Chattahoochee River to Opelika, Montgomery, or Pensacola and help Maj. Gen. E. R. S. Canby capture Mobile. But this move would negate any chance of getting to Petersburg in the foreseeable future.[71]

The Railroad's Part in Preparations for the March

While Sherman pondered this last-minute question, his subordinates finished repairs on the Western and Atlantic Railroad. Quartermaster Easton was charged with supervising this work. He deployed the 1st Michigan Engineers and Mechanics from Tilton to Adairsville to help Wright's Construction Corps by cutting new ties and hauling them to the roadbed. Easton also ordered rails removed from sections of the Atlanta and West Point Railroad southwest of the city for use farther north. Wright's men worked on the ten-mile break near Big Shanty and the twenty-five-mile break near Resaca. In addition, they rebuilt 455 feet of bridging. It took them thirteen days to do all of this.[72]

For three weeks Slocum's 21,000 men and 9,400 horses and mules at Atlanta received nothing from the north. The men suffered little because of the heavy foraging they conducted, but the animals began to weaken. By October 30 the trains were again rolling into Atlanta from the north in regular fashion.[73]

Easton became burdened with multiple transportation tasks as soon as the rail line was reopened. He moved Schofield's Twenty-Third Corps to Thomas while transporting hundreds of sick and wounded men from Atlanta to hospitals at various cities along the line to Louisville. Many white refugees and blacks wanted to go north, and Easton also evacuated garrisons at dozens of locations along the railroad that had to be abandoned. He detailed two officers to roam along the line making sure civilians did not load private property such as furniture and tobacco for shipping north. Sherman's men needed more supplies transported to Atlanta to prepare for the march. In addition, Easton had to move what Sherman referred to as "trash"—meaning a variety of baggage, equipment, and stores not needed for his march—from Atlanta. In all Easton was busier than ever trying to coordinate this array of shipments. "It was the most arduous and difficult duty to perform successfully that I have ever had to do in the same period of time," he admitted.[74]

The Western and Atlantic Railroad was operable by October 31, but not at peak capacity. Not all the sidings, switches, or water tanks were finished, and the roadbed was not properly ballasted. "Trains have to move slow," Chief Commissary Beckwith told Sherman, "there is much freight to come forward, and much material to go back, and no calculation can be made as to time." Guerrillas continued to harass the road as quartermasters geared up for a hectic two weeks of work in November.[75]

The transport of Schofield's command represented the biggest drain on the railroad's capacity. In fact, Easton estimated it would take half his available railcars operating between Chattanooga and Atlanta to move the Twenty-Third Corps to Nashville. He feared he would have to stop all shipments of people and material out of Atlanta for several days to accomplish this goal. Sherman was adamant, insisting the corps be shipped by rail rather than march on foot and that everything else be moved as well. If Easton could not get enough supplies to Atlanta, his men would do without the material on the march. If he could not move the "trash" out of Atlanta, the quartermaster would have to burn it.[76]

When Easton examined this surplus material, he was astonished that so much had accumulated at Atlanta. Slocum's men gathered "more plunder in the last two months than I supposed could have been got here in six," he told Sherman. By November 4 Easton requested 500 cars to transport everything from Atlanta and from the various posts along the way to Dalton. Sherman wrote to James B. Steedman to assemble 300–400 cars and send them to Atlanta right away. He also wanted him to take personal charge of supervising the passage of trains along the Western and Atlantic Railroad to expedite movement. Steedman jumped to the task, assuring his superior that 370 cars would be on their way to Atlanta by noon on November 5. Sherman was willing to give his railroad men until the ninth to finish the task of transporting everything.[77]

Easton encountered several hindrances to the smooth working of his transportation system. "We have been very seriously delayed the past three days by small run-offs, slippery tracks, bunching of the trains ten and twenty together, and telegraphic communication imperfect from the storm blocking road," he wrote on November 5. Three days later Sherman offered his quartermaster more time, feeling less anxious now that it seemed Hood was stalled at Tuscumbia. Easton devoted full attention to shipping material north from Atlanta once he got Schofield's troops out of the way on the sixth. He managed to move most of the "trash," but a good deal of it was burned nevertheless.[78]

In fact, the Second Brigade, Third Division, Fourteenth Corps destroyed a surprisingly large amount and variety of commissary stores at Atlanta on November 14. This included 60,500 pounds of bacon, 15,556 pounds of peas, 408 gallons of whiskey, 148,766 pounds of salt, and much smaller amounts of a dozen other items on the ration list. This indicates that Easton was not as successful as he pretended in saving usable stores. He reported that only a little useless material was destroyed.[79]

By November 11 Easton said he was ready to begin tearing up the Western and Atlantic Railroad. Five days earlier Sherman had adjusted his plan and now intended to destroy only all track south of the Etowah River and north of the Chattahoochee River. Howard divided up the task among his troops, assigning the Seventeenth Corps to the stretch from Big Shanty to a point eleven miles south and the Fifteenth Corps to work on the tracks from there to the Chattahoochee. Not only were the troops to burn the ties but also to twist the rails. Sherman did not, however, do the same with the railroad between Dalton and the Etowah River. The Federals took up the track between Dalton and Resaca, a total of sixteen miles, and stored the rails at Chattanooga for future use. Of course all rolling stock was moved north.[80]

Railroad crews and large masses of infantrymen more or less completed Sherman's logistical preparation for the March to the Sea by November 15. The previous six weeks had seen unusual developments in the strategic course of the war. A defeated Confederate army had turned the tables on its opponent, breaking the logistical lifeline of the Federal army group and getting away without punishment. But that move failed to compel Sherman to give up Atlanta or to reverse the course of his own strategy. The key lay in manpower differentials—he could afford to divide his force and set into motion two operations to deal with Hood's threat and continue Union penetration of the Deep South at the same time. Thus we are treated to the bizarre spectacle of two opposing main armies facing away from each other while a scratch force of Federals assembled to deal with the Army of Tennessee.

The role of railroads in all this unusual strategic maneuvering was paramount. As the Confederates scrambled to rehabilitate two decrepit rail lines to support their offensive into Middle Tennessee, the Federals scrambled to repair a rail line that they had relied upon for months only to tear it up a few days later and live off the countryside in their own campaign through the heart of Dixie.

7

HOOD'S TENNESSEE CAMPAIGN

Hood's invasion of Tennessee in the late fall of 1864 was the last Confederate incursion onto Federal territory in the Civil War. It was a desperate gamble by an army that was capable of moving swiftly with few material resources. But that paucity of material was exactly the reason why it had little prospect of permanently staying in whatever territory it managed to occupy. In contrast to previous Confederate commanders who penetrated Union territory, Hood at least tried to create a viable logistical system to support his army in Tennessee. His failure to do so played a decisive role in the failure of the campaign. But despite their immense logistical power, the Federals found it impossible to catch Hood's army during their hot pursuit following the Battle of Nashville.

Confederate Logistical Problems

The Army of Tennessee waited in vain near Tuscumbia for three weeks to allow Confederate personnel to rehabilitate its supply line. As it turned out, Richard Taylor did not have the resources to complete repairs on the Mobile and Ohio Railroad and the Memphis and Charleston Railroad. That three-week waiting period shifted the strategic initiative back to Sherman, who set out from Atlanta on November 15 on his March to the Sea. Finally, after criticizing the "bad condition" of the railroad between Okolona and Cherokee and the miserable "dirt road" between Cherokee and Florence, Hood began his invasion of Tennessee on November 21. Issues concerning logistics and supply would deeply affect its outcome.[1]

Before leaving Florence, Hood warned his men that "there may be a scarcity of the bread ration" and called on them to be patient. "The fruitful fields of Tennessee are before us," he proclaimed in general orders. Hood wanted Forrest to send small parties of cavalry out "to break the enemy's railroad and telegraphic communications from Nashville to the north." His objective was to prevent the Federals from shipping out food and other supplies from the state capital, intending to capture everything there for the use of his army. Hood sent Col. Hylan B. Lyon's Kentucky cavalry brigade to "destroy the railroads between Nashville and Clarksville, and between Bowling Green and Nashville."[2]

Schofield opposed the Confederate advance with the Fourth and Twenty-Third Corps near Pulaski, fifty miles northeast of Florence. The Army of Tennessee began to flank Schofield on the west as the Federals evacuated Pulaski on November 24 and took position at Columbia, thirty miles away. As soon as Hood occupied Pulaski on the twenty-fifth, he asked Beauregard to repair the rail line northward from Decatur, the same railroad Forrest had destroyed only two months before. Meanwhile, he planned to grind his own meal by utilizing the mills near Pulaski. Hood hoped to break the Nashville and Chattanooga Railroad in a couple of days, targeting the stretch between Cowan and Nashville. He also ordered Brigadier General Philip D. Roddey, commander of the District of North Alabama, to destroy the Memphis and Charleston Railroad between Decatur and Stevenson, apparently to prevent the Federals from sending troops by rail from Chattanooga to interfere with his use of the line north from Decatur. Even as the Army of Tennessee advanced, it continued to rely on wagon trains to move supplies from Cherokee to the roving units. Hood instructed the commander of the post at Corinth to organize 1,000 convalescent soldiers as an escort for a wagon train loaded with salt to his army.[3]

"All the country south of Columbia, Tenn., is now open to collect supplies," Hood told Richmond on November 27. He requested the services of James F. Cummings and some agents to collect this material, all reporting to the commissary general of the Army of Tennessee. "I have had no difficulty about supplies," Hood reported the next day, "and anticipate none in the future."[4]

That may have been Hood's official report, but there is plenty of evidence that his men suffered for want of supplies. When the Confederates maneuvered Schofield out of Columbia, they ransacked the town without mercy on the morning of November 28. Hood issued a general order expressing his pain at witnessing such an act. He pleaded with the men to restrain their

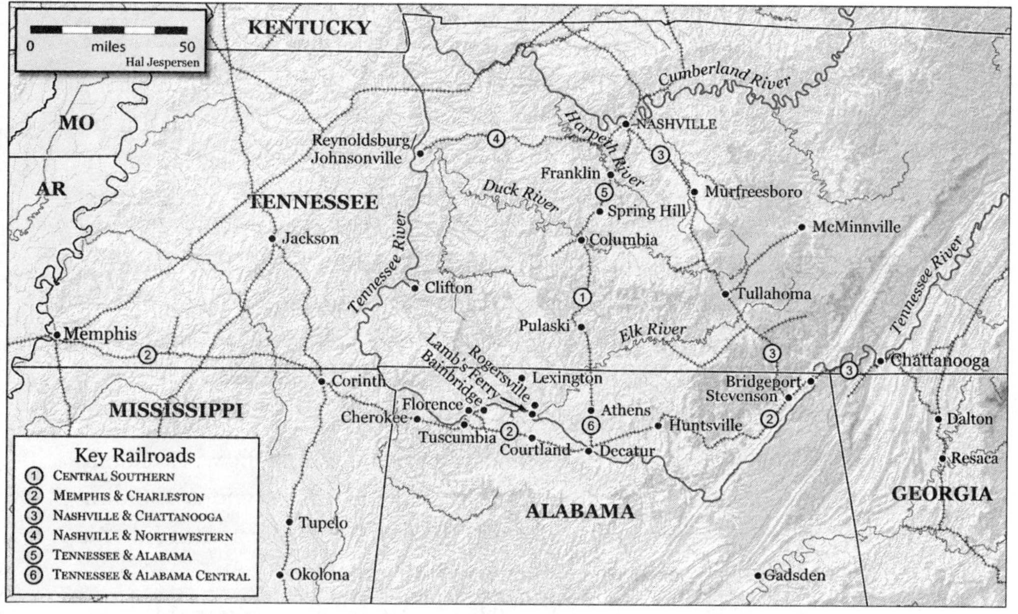

TENNESSEE CAMPAIGN

"unbridled spirit of plunder." Missing in this plea was an acknowledgement that the army's supply situation was precarious at best.[5]

Hood continued to hope the rail system could be made to supply his army, and Beauregard did his best with "the limited means of the engineer and quartermaster departments." On November 15 he anticipated it would take another fifteen to twenty days if the weather remained good. If heavy rains set in, he warned Hood to expect an additional one to two weeks of work time. Two days later, on November 17, George W. Brent reported that a major bridge only three miles west of Tuscumbia would take at least six days to finish due to a shortage of laborers. By the next day Beauregard thought the cars would be running at least to Barton Station, six miles east of Cherokee and ten miles west of Tuscumbia. But the dirt road that Hood complained of east of Cherokee, the only available supply link with the Army of Tennessee, was "almost impassable."[6]

Logistical problems were not confined to the short stretch between Cherokee and Tuscumbia. Beauregard found trouble nearly everywhere along the rail system. Empty cars sat idle at several depots because there were no supplies for them to haul. Beauregard could find no more than sixteen loaded freight cars on their way to Corinth early on the morning of November 28, a pitifully small number for the Army of Tennessee. Jackson, Mississippi, had no garrison. Even Corinth, a much more important link in the transportation chain, had an inadequate garrison. As late as November 22, Brent urged subordinates to construct blockhouses and other defenses at bridges and trestles along the line. By November 29 the Corinth depot had enough bread to meet Hood's needs for ten days, but nothing else. The post commander complained of a severe shortage of wagons. He could not even provide transportation for the members of Hood's military courts, who arrived at Corinth with all their records, wanting to rejoin the army. Beauregard promised to find 150 wagons, but it would take some time for any of them to become available. He wanted to begin rebuilding the wrecked rail lines near Atlanta in late November, specifically the Atlanta and West Point Railroad from Fairburn to the city and the Georgia Railroad between Atlanta and Augusta. Beauregard hoped Hood could secure the rail line from Nashville to Chattanooga and all the way back to Atlanta for Confederate use.[7]

In other words, Hood started his risky invasion of Tennessee with the most slender logistical support, his rail system not yet complete, too few wagons to meet his needs, and too few support personnel to repair, maintain, and operate it all. As with Lee's invasion of Maryland and Bragg's invasion of Kentucky in 1862, the Confederates relied on luck and foraging from the countryside to pull through. They were opposed by a Federal force in Tennessee that had a reliable supply system to draw upon. That fact alone did not preordain Confederate defeat or Union victory, but the huge gap between Southern and Northern supply heavily shifted the advantage to the Federals.

Thomas and the Management of Federal Resources

In contrast to Confederate efforts, Union management of logistical resources moved along smoothly. After Forrest's destructive raid and before Hood entered Tennessee, Thomas had tried to start repairs on the rail link between Nashville and Decatur. Leonard Eicholtz took a division of the Construction Corps to Pulaski, arriving by the night of November 18. The next day he built platforms and sheds for unloading and storing construction supplies and began to inspect one of the burned bridges at Richland

Creek. Also, Thomas directed Wright to take up the Western and Atlantic Railroad from the Etowah River northward toward Dalton as Sherman's men tore up the line south of the Etowah in preparation for the abandonment of Atlanta. Steedman, commander of the District of the Etowah, was in charge of the latter process. He also evacuated garrisons along the line as the wrecking crews reached them. By November 19 the track had been taken up nearly to Tilton, ten miles from Dalton. Wright shipped the rails to Chattanooga for future use.[8]

The start of Hood's incursion into Middle Tennessee forced the Federals to revamp their posture. It became apparent they had to abandon much of their rail network and save all the rolling stock from falling into enemy hands. Wright sent a division of trackmen to Louisville to lay more sidings to accommodate the "large number of cars and engines" to be sent there for safekeeping. Thomas ordered the evacuation of Athens, Huntsville, and Decatur, Alabama, providing more than 120 cars to move all that had been accumulated at Huntsville by November 25. Brig. Gen. Robert S. Granger was in charge of this job, with instructions to move the garrisons to Stevenson. There he was to replace the Stevenson garrison, which was instructed to move to Murfreesboro. Eicholtz was told to stop work at Pulaski and move his workers to Columbia to make sure the track there was in good shape in case Schofield had to retreat quickly to Nashville. By November 30 Thomas had decided to abandon the Nashville and Northwestern Railroad too.[9]

Thomas gave up all the railroads that lay within easy reach of Hood's army, but he also worried about the security of the Nashville and Chattanooga Railroad, which was on the margin of Hood's range. When Schofield evacuated Columbia, Thomas ordered the evacuation of Tullahoma as well. The garrison there, under Maj. Gen. Robert H. Milroy, was to join the growing concentration at Murfreesboro. Thomas instructed Milroy to keep the garrison at Elk River bridge on the Nashville and Chattanooga Railroad because it was a large and expensive structure, but the track and attendant stations between the Elk and Murfreesboro would be abandoned. Thomas felt that Murfreesboro was the best citadel along the line—Fortress Rosecrans, a massive, enclosed earthwork, had been constructed by the Army of the Cumberland after the Battle of Stones River and now could serve a useful purpose.[10]

The Federals smoothly evacuated posts and transported troops and supplies in preparation for Hood's arrival. Granger removed almost all materials from several towns, although he destroyed some government property

Duck River Bridge. Facing Hood's vigorous advance into Middle Tennessee, Thomas evacuated some sections of rail lines to draw in garrisons for the defense of Nashville and Murfreesboro. But he mandated that the garrison at the Nashville and Chattanooga Railroad crossing of Duck River stay in place to protect this long, high bridge. LC-DIG-ppmsca-33387.

at Decatur due to lack of transportation. Five regiments of infantry took up the march to Murfreesboro. "Negroes by the thousand, from contraband camps, Government plantations and all other plantations, are filling the road for five or six miles behind us," Granger told Thomas. "I have ordered them to stop here; they block the road so that the column cannot get along." Granger destroyed his pontoon boats at Decatur, forcing Thomas to find others at Chattanooga in case he needed some in the near future.[11]

Thomas continued to worry about Hood lodging on the railroad between Nashville and Chattanooga. He wanted Steedman to move a force from the latter place to strike any Confederates who approached the track. Steedman thought he needed to keep 1,300 men in the Dalton area, 1,200 to protect the line between Chattanooga and Knoxville up to Loudon, and 3,000 at Chattanooga itself. Even with these garrisons, he could spare 5,000 men as a mobile column to hit Hood. Two divisions of the Sixteenth Corps under

Maj. Gen. Andrew J. Smith were on the way from Missouri to Nashville, and Thomas was prepared to shift them to Murfreesboro if needed. Steedman planned to keep garrisons at the Duck River bridge near Shelbyville and the bridge near Manchester, with orders to burn the spans if an overwhelming force of the enemy appeared.[12]

But Thomas also began to think of using Steedman's 5,000-man mobile column in an offensive capacity. He asked the general if he thought it possible to strike at Tuscumbia and destroy Hood's pontoon bridge, a vital link in the Confederate supply line. Thomas proposed moving the troops by rail via Chattanooga and Stevenson as far as Decatur, then laying pontoons over the Tennessee River and marching swiftly to Tuscumbia. Steedman was optimistic, but he preferred to cross the river with four steamboats escorted by two gunboats rather than pontoons. He suggested moving some cavalrymen on the steamers, while transporting the infantry by rail. In fact, Steedman planned to be ready for this move by November 29. Thomas told him to put the plans on hold for the time—Steedman was to remain at Cowan and be ready to hit the Confederates if they lodged on the railroad nearby. The next day Thomas ordered Steedman to bring his men to Nashville. The strike at Tuscumbia was postponed.[13]

On November 30 Milroy completed the evacuation of Tullahoma and began to move to Murfreesboro. At the latter town Maj. Gen. Lovell H. Rousseau commanded a scratch force of troops from the region. Thomas counted on Rousseau to hold the place against anything Hood sent against Fortress Rosecrans. He also sent westward four trains with ten cars each to evacuate material from Johnsonville.[14]

Schofield and Hood

While all this was going on, Schofield's column bore the brunt of dealing immediately with the Army of Tennessee. Eicholtz had barely started the job of repairing the Central Southern Railroad at Pulaski before he was ordered to stop and return to Nashville. On November 29 he went to Franklin with his crew and five carloads of building timber to reconstruct the wagon bridge over the Harpeth River. The railroad bridge was down there, and Schofield needed help. Eicholtz arrived at Franklin at 7 P.M. to find Union forces in retreat toward the town. The Federals took up a strong defensive position south of Franklin, their retirement delayed by the hours it would take Eicholtz's men to provide a crossing of the Harpeth. The next day, November 30, Eicholtz put planks on the railroad track approaching the river and then started to make a small bridge, eight feet wide, for infantry but that also was capable of crossing artillery. By 3 P.M. he was able to get the Fourth Corps and Twenty-Third Corps wagon trains to the north side of the river. According to Eicholtz's watch, Hood attacked Schofield's position at 4:15 P.M. Forty-five minutes later, Eicholtz was told to take his construction crew back to Nashville. They arrived at the state capital at 7:30 P.M., when the bloody battle at Franklin was sputtering to a close. "Had a good view of the fight" before leaving Franklin, Eicholtz noted in his diary.[15]

After repulsing the Army of Tennessee, Schofield's two corps retreated to Nashville to protect the capital. Hood followed up that retreat and established his weakened army in a defensive posture just south of town. His success at penetrating Federal territory was deceptive; the Army of Tennessee was vulnerable, holding a precarious position in the heart of Union-held Tennessee without a secure line of supply. While Hood's troop strength was little less than the combined forces of the Fourth and Twenty-Third Corps, additional Union troops were arriving at Nashville, and Thomas would soon have a much larger army at hand.

Confederate Strategic Vision

Despite his many problems, Hood acted as if it were possible to secure the territory he had captured and stay the winter in Middle Tennessee. But he had to continue the process of trying to create a viable supply line if he hoped to accomplish those goals. His first objective was to take Murfreesboro and with it the Nashville and Chattanooga Railroad. Incredibly, Hood seems to have thought he could follow that up by capturing Chattanooga and the entire rail network south and east, writing of opening "communication with Georgia and Virginia." If Thomas attacked his army in the interim, Hood was confident his troops could repel the assault and follow it up by seizing Nashville and the "abundant supplies" in the city. "This would give me possession of Tennessee," he predicted.[16]

His strategic vision was typical of many Confederate dreams of victory in the Civil War—bold, grandiose, and utterly unrealistic. Barely matching the current Federal troop strength in Middle Tennessee, Hood was struggling to rehabilitate the rail system he already possessed to link his starving army with home bases in Mississippi and Alabama. The notion that he could capture the rest of the western rail network from the stronger Federals and operate it into Georgia and Virginia was a fantasy.

How much of a fantasy it truly was can be encapsulated in the miserable attempt to capture Murfreesboro. Hood assigned Maj. Gen. William B. Bate's infantry division and Forrest's cavalry to the task. Thomas felt secure with the sizeable forces stationed at Murfreesboro, Chattanooga, Bridgeport, Stevenson, and the Elk River bridge. Rousseau also maintained small garrisons at other locations along the railroad to protect bridges. Even if Bate had been able to capture Murfreesboro, he would have had to deal with all those other garrisons. But the Confederates had no luck from the start. They unsuccessfully attacked a blockhouse at Overall's Creek, five miles northwest of Murfreesboro, on December 4, after which 2,500 Confederates demonstrated against Fortress Rosecrans on December 5, 6, and 7. The 8,000 Federals there had no trouble holding the post. Milroy led seven regiments out on the seventh and drove the Confederates away. And with that, all hope of capturing the Nashville and Chattanooga Railroad evaporated.[17]

Even when it came to rehabilitating the rail system he possessed, Hood had scant success. The Confederates captured two locomotives and three cars on the railroad, but the track was usable only down to Pulaski. From there south to Decatur and west to Cherokee existed a huge rail gap that could only be filled by wagon trains. Hood expected this wagon link to rapidly deteriorate as soon as winter battered the dirt roads of Tennessee. That is why he urged the rapid reconstruction of his rail link with Corinth. "The permanent occupation of this country absolutely requires that this road be repaired," he wrote on December 6.[18]

Before he became aware of Bate's failure at Murfreesboro, Beauregard continued to urge work in the Atlanta area so as to reach Hood's army if his attack succeeded. He wanted subordinates to press at least 900 black laborers for the job. They had already pressed some 3,000 blacks for work on the rail system by December 6, and yet Martin L. Smith could report that the Mobile and Ohio Railroad was only "in fair running condition." Only "fair progress" was being made in work on the Memphis and Charleston Railroad. At that rate it would take many weeks if not months to complete the rail system to Pulaski.[19]

By the end of the second week of December, the Confederates had not even provided a proper garrison for the post of Corinth, the key point in their rail system. Hood wanted to have one million rations stored there as a reserve for his army, but Taylor thought it a bad idea. He had heard that Hood's chief commissary believed it possible to feed the troops from the countryside south of Nashville, and if the Army of Tennessee had to retreat, it was not likely to march by way of Corinth. That would make it impossible to get these rations to the men, while the retreat would leave Corinth vulnerable to Union attack. Taylor preferred to keep smaller amounts of provisions at thirty-three small depots in Mississippi and Alabama that were linked by rail.[20]

Problems continued to plague Confederate efforts to rebuild the railroad to Pulaski. Maj. George Whitfield complained that he could not find enough workers or material. More engineers who knew how to build a railroad also were needed. Hood now gave up the idea of using the Nashville and Chattanooga Railroad. His headquarters sent orders to Roddey to destroy the track from Huntsville to Stevenson and also from Stevenson to Murfreesboro.[21]

Federal Prospects after the Battle of Franklin

In contrast to the Confederates, Federal efforts to strengthen their position in Middle Tennessee after the bloodletting at Franklin proceeded without interference. Wright had most of the Construction Corps at Chattanooga, with one division under Eicholtz at Nashville. Eicholtz worked on the fortifications of the city for a while as Thomas's situation improved rapidly. On December 1, the day after the battle at Franklin, 5,000 Sixteenth Corps troops under Smith arrived at Nashville. Later that evening Steedman arrived with another 5,000 men. Although he had fewer cavalry than expected, Thomas now had enough infantrymen to deal with Hood. He also received urgent telegrams from Grant to attack Hood before the Confederates bypassed Nashville and rampaged farther north, but he took his time to prepare a strike at the Army of Tennessee.[22]

By December 5 Thomas had accurate information as to how Hood was supplying his army. Prisoners told him of the rail system to Cherokee and the wagon link with the Army of Tennessee. Thomas suggested to Halleck that Union forces from Memphis strike at that rail system. The Federals had some difficulty with their own supply system when Confederate artillery planted downriver from Nashville fired on steamers approaching the capital. Navy gunboats, however, moved in to clear the stream.[23]

North of Nashville, James H. Wilson positioned his cavalry on the

Louisville and Nashville Railroad to protect Thomas's link with the North. Lyon's brigade of 800 Kentucky cavalrymen and two guns represented the main Rebel threat to this link. Hood had dispatched Lyon on this mission before starting from Florence, and the small force caused some trouble. Thomas assigned McCook's cavalry division to chase the Confederates as they rode by way of Hopkinsville, Greensburg, Elizabethtown, and Glasgow in Kentucky. Several fights occurred in which the Federals were unable to deal a lethal blow to Lyon, but the overall result was that the Confederates failed to cut the rail link in any serious way. A few burned trestles and some rails taken up represented the total damage. The most serious effect of Lyon's raid was that Thomas could not use as much cavalry in his confrontation with Hood as he had wished.[24]

That confrontation took place on December 15 and 16 after delays that nearly led Grant to relieve Thomas from command. The delays were at least partially excusable, given the improvised military force Thomas assembled for the defense of Middle Tennessee. Then very bad weather descended over the region to further delay the attack. When Thomas advanced on the fifteenth, Hood fell back some distance to a new defensive position. The next day the Federals dealt a crushing blow to the Army of Tennessee. It is completely wrong, as many historians have contended, that the Confederate army was "destroyed" that day, but it certainly suffered one of the more devastating battlefield defeats of the war. Hood immediately gave up all hopes of success and, his army organization still intact, began an effective retreat south.[25]

The Pursuit of Hood

The Federals mounted a massive follow up to Hood's retreat with most of their available manpower, creating one of the largest pursuits of a beaten army during the Civil War. They were greatly impeded by logistical problems stemming from burned bridges, swollen streams, and bitterly cold rain. The Confederates merely had to run; they possessed few resources to protect and destroyed what they could of the railroad and wagon bridges along their line of retreat. But the Federals not only had to chase their enemy but also reconstruct crossings and the railroad track to supply their mobile columns.

In the long term the Federals also had to provide the wherewithal to permanently reoccupy ground they had given up when Hood began his invasion of Tennessee. And even beyond that they needed to think of the next step in their strategy, no matter whether they caught Hood's fugitives. Commanders needed a secure line of railroad communications stretching as far south as possible for that next stage. Union logistical power was immense, but so were the strategic and tactical requirements facing Thomas.

The best way to understand the Federal pursuit of Hood is to divide the topic into modes of moving troops and wheeled vehicles during the chase. That pursuit covered ninety miles, from Nashville down to the Alabama state line, and centered on the railroad stem that linked the state capital with Decatur. Several streams served as major impediments to the Federals. The Harpeth River at Franklin was the first. Farther south the railroad crossed twelve bridges within a distance of six miles at Columbia, with the last one spanning the Duck River. Still farther south at Pulaski, the railroad crossed four bridges over Richland Creek and one over Pigeon Roost Creek before traversing the Elk River. By destroying all these structures, the Confederates created three major chokepoints in the Federal pursuit.

Of course Thomas did not need to rebuild railroad or wagon bridges in order to cross infantry. His pursuit was led by Wilson's cavalry and Maj. Gen. Thomas J. Wood's Fourth Corps. Both commands were capable of improvising bridges for foot crossings. Yet this proved to be more difficult than usual because of heavy rains that caused water levels to rise quickly, turning rivers and creeks into raging torrents. Even when across, Fourth Corps troops pushed ahead without artillery or wagons, which had to wait for pontoon trains or Construction Corps personnel to create bridges. Lacking fire support and rations, the infantry lagged behind in their strenuous efforts to catch up with Hood. Schofield's Twenty-Third Corps; A. J. Smith's Right Wing, Sixteenth Corps; and Steedman's troops from the District of the Etowah followed the Fourth Corps in the pursuit column.

The process by which Thomas's command tried to overcome all these obstacles can best be seen in sequence. First, Wilson's cavalry and Wood's troops improvised stream crossings. Next, the pontoon trains managed to catch up with the advance and provided a readymade method of traversing streams. Then, Construction Corps personnel arrived on the scene to repair wagon and rail bridges along the main stem of rail line linking Nashville with Decatur. While all this was going on, Thomas sought to rebuild the rail network linking Nashville with Chattanooga. He wanted not only to reestablish garrisons the Federals had earlier abandoned but also to use the railroad as a way to flank Hood from the east. He hoped to send troops on a mission to destroy the Confederate pontoon bridge over the Tennessee River and cut off their escape into the Deep South.

The Army of Tennessee conducted its retreat effectively, adding to Federal pursuit problems. On the first night of the withdrawal, December 17, Hood's army bivouacked at Spring Hill, twelve miles south of Franklin. Pressed hard by Wilson's cavalry, the Confederates destroyed bridges over the Harpeth River. Hood continued moving south from Spring Hill on the eighteenth, placing Stewart's Corps behind Duck River at Columbia. He positioned Cheatham's Corps and Lee's Corps at Rutherford Creek, three miles north of Columbia.[26]

Improvised Stream Crossings

The pursuit of Hood witnessed some of the most difficult improvised crossings of streams to be found during the Civil War. Federal infantry and cavalry struggled to find ways to cross dangerous waterways in bad weather in order to maintain army mobility, with time their most pressing concern. They succeeded to a remarkable degree, but it was not enough to catch the fleeing enemy.

The Harpeth River posed the first obstacle. When Wood reached Franklin at 1:20 P.M. on December 17, he saw that the bridges had been destroyed. Heavy rains that morning and the previous night had raised the water level. Col. Isaac C. B. Suman of the 9th Indiana took charge of constructing a foot bridge over the swollen stream, but he was hampered by a shortage of tools and material and a lack of boats. Driftwood came roaring down the river to interfere with his work, but his men managed to erect a footbridge by 7:30 A.M. on the eighteenth.[27]

When Wood advanced to Rutherford Creek near Columbia on the morning of December 19, he found that stream "a perfect torrent" due to the recent rains. The water was fifteen feet deep and rising, the current "very swift." There were no trees tall enough near the bank to cut down in order to form a footbridge, and the corps had no tools or materials to make a wagon bridge. Rain fell mercilessly all day. Although Wood assigned two subordinates to find some way to cross the creek, they reported by 11:30 P.M. that it seemed impossible.[28]

Fourth Corps personnel struggled with Rutherford Creek throughout the night of December 19–20. They improvised rafts, but these craft were swept away, drowning at least two men in the process. Their comrades tried cutting some trees for spans, but the current tore them from the bank as soon as the trunk fell into the water. At 8:30 A.M. corps headquarters instructed all division commanders "to do everything possible to get over," and an hour later one of them reported that a footbridge had somehow been finished. An hour after that another division leader completed a second footbridge. With two crossings, the corps began to resume its march south. Cavalry commanders also improvised a crossing, using debris from the burned railroad span to make a "floating bridge" of sorts.[29]

But when Wood reached Columbia at 2 P.M. on December 20, he was stymied by the Duck River. The Confederates had taken up their pontoon bridge at dawn that day, leaving a channel that was "very much swollen," as Joseph S. Fullerton, Wood's assistant adjutant general, described. "It is too deep and swift to bridge with timber, and we will have to wait for the pontoon train to come up." Fullerton estimated the corps had already been delayed thirty-four hours by the Harpeth River, Rutherford Creek, and now the Duck River because of trouble getting the pontoons up. Wood took position on the north bank and waited. He did not have his trains or artillery at this time because there were no resources to build a wagon bridge over Rutherford Creek.[30]

As of the evening of December 20, wheeled vehicles could cross the Harpeth River at Franklin but not Rutherford Creek. Schofield's headquarters remained at Spring Hill. The railroad bridge over the Harpeth at Franklin also was not ready, but Construction Corps men were repairing track down to Spring Hill. Thomas's headquarters urged Quartermaster James L. Donaldson to send three trainloads of forage for Wilson's cavalry so it would be available to cross the bridge at Franklin as soon as the span was ready. The countryside was too devastated to expect the horses to feed from farms along the line of march.[31]

Pontoons

The only positive news on December 20 was that Thomas's pontoons began to reach the front. Schofield had a small pontoon train, and it caught up with his corps at Spring Hill that day. But Thomas had another, much larger pontoon train of sixty wagons and 500 mules that also appeared, crossing the

Harpeth River over the flimsy wagon bridge. The mules pulling the larger train were exhausted and needed forage, so the train bivouacked two miles south of Spring Hill that night.[32]

Fullerton found out why this general train had been delayed. Thomas had ordered it to leave Nashville on December 17, but Asst. Adj. Gen. Robert H. Ramsey had made a mistake when writing out the order, sending the train toward Murfreesboro rather than Franklin. The pontoons had already moved fifteen miles before the mistake was discovered. By the time a dispatch rider caught up with it, the train was forced to move across country on very bad roads to reach the Franklin Pike. Ramsey exonerated himself by explaining that Thomas woke up from a very deep sleep to dictate the order and named the wrong road. "By this mistake we have been delayed about three days in the pursuit of the enemy," Fullerton fumed, "and have missed many splendid opportunities to inflict severe blows upon the enemy, perhaps to annihilate him."[33]

Fullerton fixated too much on only one problem marring the Union pursuit; there were many obstructions to Wood's close pursuit besides the delay in getting the pontoon train forward. Making the best of these problems, Thomas ordered Schofield to focus on providing a way to cross artillery and wagons over Rutherford Creek. He did that by using the Twenty-Third Corps pontoon train. The general pontoon train had orders to push on to Columbia, where it would span the Duck River. Thomas wanted Wood over that river before dark of December 21 in a desperate bid to catch up with the Confederates before they found safety on the south side of the Tennessee River.[34]

The weather continued to deal unkindly with the Federals. Ever since December 17 rain or snow had fallen on them. The general pontoon train struggled along mud-engulfed roads toward Columbia on December 21. Ramsey warned Wood to collect forage for the 500 mules so they would have something to eat on arrival. The general promised to try to provide the feed, but Wilson's cavalry had already stripped this war-torn area, and the ground was so soft that forage wagons could hardly move if they left the macadamized pike. Wood also asked Thomas for 15,000 pairs of shoes and 15,000 pairs of socks for his troops.[35]

At Rutherford's Creek A. J. Smith's Right Wing, Sixteenth Corps crossed over Schofield's pontoon bridge just behind the large pontoon train but before the Twenty-Third Corps infantry on December 22. Ramsey told Schofield that when he crossed the creek, he should use the improvised footbridge "to save the pontoon bridge" from wear and tear. The corps commander also detailed a company of one officer and thirty men to guard the span. These troops were charged with superintending the movement of wheeled vehicles since so many of them were waiting to cross. First, the Fourth Corps artillery had the lead, then Wilson's cavalry train, followed by the Fourth Corps wagon trains, then Smith's wagon trains, and last Schofield's wagon trains.[36]

The large pontoon train finally reached the Fourth Corps, after a long and grueling march, early on the morning of December 22. Wood positioned Col. Abel D. Streight's brigade on the north bank of Duck River so the men could deploy the canvas boats. Streight sent a detachment of the 51st Indiana over the stream in a few of them to establish a bridgehead on the south bank, losing one killed and eight wounded in skirmishing with Confederates posted there. The soldiers began laying the pontoon bridge at 8 A.M., but the colonel had only three trained pontoniers, the rest of his troops being completely inexperienced at the task. The water level fell rapidly during the day, forcing them to adjust the end of the bridge attached to the north bank. The weather continued to be bitterly cold, which did not help matters.[37]

Nevertheless the bridge was finished by the evening of December 22. The first Fourth Corps troops began to cross at 7 P.M., and the last were over Duck River by midnight. It had become apparent by then, however, that the pontoon bridge was "a very poor one, and may break down before all of our artillery and trains pass over it," as Fullerton wrote. It was important to get all the wheeled vehicles over before 5 A.M. of the twenty-third to allow Wilson's cavalry to cross. Thomas wanted Wood to move his corps rapidly along the pike as Wilson's troopers spread out to either side to protect his flanks. Schofield and Smith would follow at a more leisurely pace.[38]

But the wheeled vehicles were delayed by a new development. The river banks had become very slippery and steep now that the water level had fallen, making it difficult for wagons and artillery to negotiate the approaches to and from the bridge. From midnight of December 23 until 5 A.M., only three batteries and some wagons managed to cross. The rest of Wood's guns and trains were ordered to wait on the north bank because Wilson needed to cross his cavalry and take position guarding the flanks of Wood's infantry column. Fullerton expected Wilson to finish crossing by 9 A.M., but even at 2 P.M. the horsemen were still using the bridge. In fact, it was nearly dark on the twenty-third before the last of his 5,000 troopers negotiated the rickety span and were out of the way.[39]

The worn-out pontoon bridge broke many times during the next morning. Following several quick repairs, it seemed to hold together throughout the afternoon of December 24. Sixteenth Corps troops crossed that day, but not their artillery. Wilson's cavalry train followed Smith's infantry, while Sixteenth Corps artillery crossed during the night to be followed by Fourth Corps artillery. By the evening of the twenty-fourth, Schofield reached Columbia and began to lay a second bridge, using his Twenty-Third Corps pontoon train again. This work finished on Christmas Day. Looking ahead, Thomas wanted to take the general pontoon train away from Columbia and move it to the Elk River, anticipating that the bridges there would be burned.[40]

Railroad Reconstruction, Nashville toward Decatur

The Federals could maintain their pursuit of Hood by using improvised methods to cross infantry over swollen streams and follow that up with pontoons to cross wheeled vehicles. But if they hoped to secure their control of territory abandoned to Hood since the start of the campaign, they needed to rebuild the rail system. The three small railroad lines that collectively linked Nashville with Decatur became the main focus of Union restoration efforts. The sector from Nashville to Pulaski had been intact at the start of that pursuit, but the Confederates made sure that all of the bridges they could reach were in ruins before they left the area. Rebuilding this stem not only served the immediate purposes of the Federals but also their long-range strategy.

From the start of his pursuit, Thomas wanted to push forward with railroad reconstruction on an expansive scale, and he had the resources to do it. On December 18 he told Wright "to put the railroads of the military division in running order" and authorized him to seize "any timber which may be necessary for making ties or bridge timbers that may be standing near the lines of roads." When the present emergency was over, he could revert to the normal practice of contracting to acquire timber and ties. Wright was optimistic. He reported to McCallum that the road could be open to Franklin within a few hours, "and we will follow General Thomas as fast as possible." As Wright correctly put it, "There is a very large amount of work blocked out for us ahead."[41]

Thomas shared Wright's optimism when his headquarters reached Spring Hill on the evening of December 18. He also urged Quartermaster Donaldson to shift working parties to Franklin and construct a proper wagon bridge over the Harpeth River. Donaldson sent Eicholtz and his Construction Corps men.[42]

The rail line from Nashville was operable only as far as Franklin by December 19. When Eicholtz arrived at Franklin around 3 P.M., he used some of his men to save the wagon bridge over the Harpeth from collapsing due to rising water. Three trainloads of workers and material arrived with him, but most of those resources were devoted to restoring the railroad bridge over the Harpeth. Donaldson pushed supply trains down to Franklin to wait for the completion of the rail bridge.[43]

Eicholtz had a tough day at Franklin on December 20. He continued to work with a small crew to strengthen the improvised wagon bridge so it would not collapse under the weight of carrying literally everything the Federals needed to cross the Harpeth. The water was then nine feet deep, the current was still rapid, and Eicholtz discovered a great deal of scrap iron littering the river bottom. "Very cold & snowing & raining all day," he recorded in his diary.[44]

Construction Corps men struggled with terrible working conditions at Franklin. "This morning every thing frozen up," Eicholtz wrote on December 21. "The ropes froze stiff and the men can scarcely go out on the scaffolding. Have the greatest trouble in getting a foundation" for the wagon bridge. Conditions were better in the afternoon, and his men worked until 9 P.M., well after darkness had closed in.[45]

The railroad bridge at Franklin also was delayed by the bad weather, much to Thomas's disappointment. William Whipple of his staff complained to Eicholtz, who explained, "we are making but slow progress, on account of the high water and the mass of wreck and iron to remove." The engineer shifted all his workers from the wagon bridge to the railroad structure to move it along to completion. He believed the railroad bridge would be ready on the morning of the twenty-second.[46]

Meanwhile, reports indicated the track was in good shape down to Columbia. Quartermaster William Le Duc suggested that a company of pioneers be sent to the Duck River to prepare facilities at the nearest railroad station north of it for unloading supplies as soon as the first train reached the area. Construction crews of the military telegraph also accompanied Thomas's column to reconstruct the line along the railroad whenever they had a chance.[47]

At Franklin, Eicholtz and his workers completed the railroad bridge over the Harpeth River on December 22, having worked all the previous

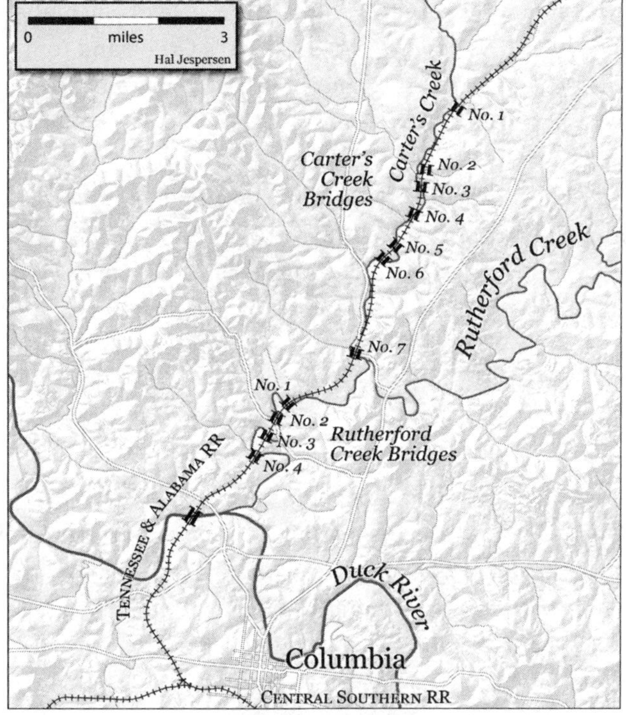

CARTER'S CREEK AND RUTHERFORD CREEK AT COLUMBIA

night. "Got all the small trestles set on logs & the stringers on by daylight," he reported, "ready to put iron by 10 A.M." The first train crossed the river at noon that day. "It has been an awful job to complete it," admitted Wright to Thomas's headquarters.[48]

Thomas sent scouts down the railroad to examine its condition farther south. They reported the first two bridges over Carter's Creek as "but little damaged," while the third bridge was "all gone but the debris," which had washed up three-quarters of a mile downstream. The fourth bridge was down, but its debris remained in place, while the fifth bridge was destroyed, with a part of the wreckage in place. "Duck River bridge gone, but trestle on south side of the river complete to the bank of the river," as Ramsey put it. The scouts found piles of timber between the third and fourth bridges and between the fourth and fifth bridges, evidence that the Confederates had begun to reconstruct those spans before the Battle of Nashville. A total of seven bridges had to be repaired over Carter's Creek and four more over Rutherford Creek before the railroad could reach the Duck River at Columbia. It was estimated that task would take about five days, a crushing delay in following up a beaten enemy.[49]

The hard-working Eicholtz had no rest on December 23. Only the day after finishing the large railroad bridge at Franklin, his men began repairing the first Carter's Creek span. The stringers were "burnt off the bridge," and his men replaced them all day. Eicholtz started work on several bridges during the twenty-fourth, moving men to the second and third span, both of which they restored before nightfall. Other men found the fourth bridge completely gone. Eicholtz sent still others to start clearing wreckage at the sixth bridge.[50]

Now that locomotives and cars could run south of Franklin, Donaldson pushed supplies by rail from Nashville. He sent a quartermaster "to take charge of advance depot of army." No sooner was the depot at Spring Hill opened than the quartermaster there began to complain that Federal soldiers were stealing his supplies. He called for troops to guard the depot from his own army.[51]

Eicholtz and his men continued working at a steady pace. They finished framing the sixth bridge over Carter's Creek by dusk of December 26 and then started to place stringers in the dark. Wright was on the scene and reported to Thomas that the fifth bridge was finished except for laying the track. He planned to start reconstructing the first bridge over Rutherford Creek at dawn on the twenty-seventh and predicted it would be finished by the evening. A force of 300 workers who specialized in bridge building was on its way to the front, but the blockade of wheeled traffic at Spring Hill delayed their wagon train. Wright promised to push them on to the Duck River bridge at Columbia as soon as possible. But there was a blockage of wheeled traffic at Columbia as well. Schofield reported on December 26 that both pontoon bridges over the Duck River were frequently breaking due to heavy loads. Smith's 200 wagons had not yet crossed, and the Twenty-Third Corps wagons were also waiting to move. Schofield thought it best to throw together some trestle bridges rather than rely on the worn-out pontoons; Thomas approved.[52]

By 2:30 P.M. of December 27, Eicholtz managed to place stringers and rails on the fifth Carter's Creek bridge and got the first train across the stream. His men finished the first Rutherford Creek bridge that day as well, and some of them joined those who were clearing up the wreckage of the second bridge spanning Rutherford Creek before dark. Wright called the second-bridge job "quite a formidable affair. I have had 200 men on it for two days, and it will take at least till night to get it out of the way." He also sent "a large force to work on the south end of Duck River bridge" on the twenty-seventh.[53]

The next day, December 28, Eicholtz put four gangs to work clearing away the wreckage at the second and most troublesome bridge over Rutherford Creek as other men finished laying track at the first bridge, allowing a train to cross it by midafternoon. Other workers were busy cutting trees from nearby forests to provide building timber for the artificers. A bit farther south, where Schofield was constructing trestle bridges over the Duck River to replace the rickety pontoons, progress was so swift that the general predicted Thomas could take both pontoon trains to other locations the next day. Railroad engines and their cars could safely roll from Nashville as far as Spring Hill, where the depot was growing in size.[54]

With nearly 1,000 men at Carter's Creek and Rutherford Creek, "nearly as many as can work to advantage," Wright felt he could spare laborers for other locations. He was ready to send a division to help Sherman, who by now was besieging Savannah, and to send other men to restore the railroad near Decatur. Orders shifting Wright and one division of the Construction Corps to the East were issued on December 28, and they left Nashville on January 4, 1865. It also was easy to restore the telegraph line along the heavily damaged railroad running south from Nashville to Columbia and Pulaski so that Thomas's headquarters could be in touch with the outside world as the commander waited for his crews to rebuild the many bridges along the line.[55]

Eicholtz's crews finished "digging out [the] wreck" of the second Rutherford Creek bridge by 10 A.M. of December 29. He then sent men to clear the debris at the third bridge. The next day his men finished framing the new structure of the second bridge at noon. By dark they had set up stringers and ties, even though it started to rain, and began laying rails after dusk, working by the light of torches until 11 P.M.[56]

"Mr. Eicholtz is doing his best," reported Wright on December 29. But the colonel estimated it would take at least ninety days to complete repairs all the way to Decatur. Progress slowed on New Year's Eve as two inches

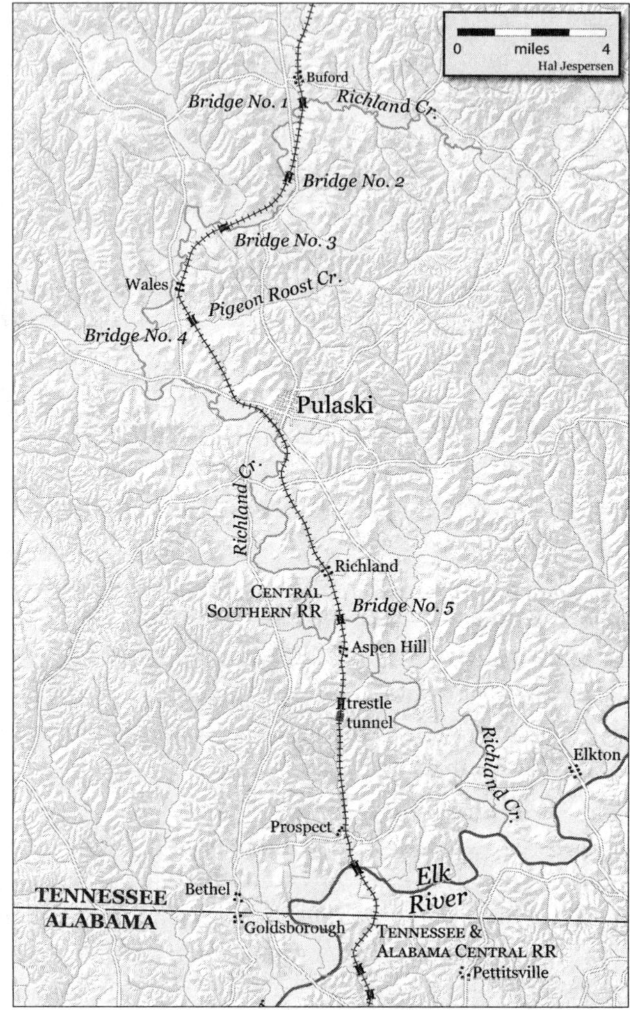

RICHLAND CREEK AT PULASKI

of snow blanketed the region. The cold caused many problems. "Nothing working right this A.M.," Eicholtz noted in his diary. When he went to the Duck River, he discovered that nothing was being done on the railroad bridge because of a shortage of material. It still was not rebuilt by January 11, 1865, when a heavy rain washed away the pontoon bridge that had been in use for a couple of weeks. Two days later telegrapher John C. Van Duzer reported to Washington, "work of repairing railroads to the Tennessee goes on slowly, if it can be said to go at all."[57]

As Van Duzer surmised, the steam had gone out of the restoration effort along the difficult rail link between Nashville and Decatur. It had always been a troublesome line because of the many bridges and the exposure to Confederate raids. Reconstructing the line yet another time failed to aid the pursuit of Hood, but it was necessary if the Federals wanted to reestablish control of southern Middle Tennessee as a jumping off place for a thrust into the Deep South.

Railroad Reconstruction, Nashville to Chattanooga, and Attacking Hood's Logistics

From the start of the pursuit, Thomas pushed the restoration of all major rail lines that had been given up when Hood initially entered Tennessee along with the garrisons along those lines. This effort continued simultaneously with the work to restore the difficult line between Nashville and Decatur. In addition, Thomas saw the Nashville and Chattanooga Railroad and the connecting Memphis and Charleston Railroad as a route of approach to Hood's bridge at Florence. If Thomas could move a sizeable force quickly enough to Stevenson and Decatur, it might be able to cut that vital crossing point and isolate the retreating Rebels north of the Tennessee River. He also envisioned the navy spearheading an effort to reach the bridge at Florence by steaming up the Tennessee, knitting together a double envelopment of Hood's line of retreat.

Thomas's staff sent an order on December 17 to give high priority to the Nashville and Chattanooga Railroad. Also that day another order instructed Robert S. Granger at Stevenson to reopen the rail line to Decatur and stockpile supplies there to support a sizeable force of troops. Thomas also urged Rear Adm. Samuel P. Lee at Clarksville to send gunboats up the Tennessee River.[58]

The next day, December 18, Thomas detached Steedman's 5,000 men from the pursuit column and sent them marching cross-country to Murfreesboro. Steedman had orders to move by rail to Stevenson and Decatur, picking up Granger's garrisons along the way, and to take the offensive against Hood's supply line at Florence. It would take some time for Steedman to make headway, but the wheels were set in motion.[59]

By December 19 Wright had organized "four strong working parties" and set them laboring on various parts of the rail system. Eicholtz worked southward along the line toward Decatur to support the pursuit of Hood, while another party worked its way from Nashville toward Stevenson. A third work party started from Stevenson toward Nashville, and the fourth restored the railway from Stevenson toward Decatur.[60]

Work on the line between Nashville and Stevenson proceeded smoothly. Rousseau began laying track and building trestles out of Murfreesboro both north and south as soon as he received word of Thomas's victory at Nashville. Working throughout the night of December 19, his crews finished repairs south of Murfreesboro and allowed ten trainloads of material to reach the town from Chattanooga. This also allowed Steedman's 5,000 troops, recently arrived after their cross-country march to Murfreesboro from Thomas's pursuit column, to move south. Rousseau predicted the track between Nashville and Murfreesboro would be reopened "in a few days" after the twenty-first. He planned to repost guards along that line even before the tracks were repaired, meanwhile transporting needed material from Nashville to Murfreesboro by wagon.[61]

In addition to sending Steedman to intercept Hood at the Tennessee River from the east, Thomas wanted to send other forces to intercept the enemy by a western approach. He needed the aid of the navy for this because it was possible to steam up the Tennessee from the Ohio at least as far as Eastport in the northeastern corner of Mississippi. Initially he asked naval commanders merely to ship rations and forage to Eastport and for a barge that could be used to ferry troops and artillery over the river, expecting his infantry and cavalry to meet that naval contingent. Moreover, Thomas's earlier suggestion to Halleck that Federal forces from Memphis should hit the Mobile and Ohio Railroad paid dividends. On December 21 a force of 3,500 cavalrymen under the able leadership of Brig. Gen. Benjamin H. Grierson set out to tear up the track.[62]

Hood's retreat was facilitated by a pontoon train, which gave his army a decisive edge in running away. It had been completed in November when Samuel H. Lockett gave twenty of Taylor's pontoon boats to Stephen W. Presstman so the Army of Tennessee's pontoon train could be completed. Then Lockett, under Beauregard's orders, began to assemble a reserve train of 100 new pontoons for Hood. Half of them were made at Demopolis and the rest at Mobile. The Demopolis depot could not start production until after December 1 due to a shortage of seasoned wood, but the Mobile depot built two pontoon boats every day.[63]

Yet the reserve train was far from ready when Hood began his retreat from Tennessee. He sent the only train available to Lamb's Ferry on December 22. Located on the north side of the Tennessee River equidistant between Florence and Decatur, the ferry lay three miles south of Rogersville. Hood chose it as his crossing point so he would not have to cross the Elk River, which bisected the main wagon road and railroad twenty-five miles north of Decatur and emptied into the Tennessee east of Lamb's Ferry.[64]

Ironically, it was easier for the Federals to make end runs around Hood's fleeing army than to pursue it directly south. Donaldson moved steamers loaded with supplies and forage down the Cumberland River and up the Tennessee, heading for Eastport and a projected rendezvous with Federal troops threatening the Confederates' flank from the west. From the east Granger started on his way from Stevenson to Decatur before Steedman joined him. He had a few small transports capable of navigating the upper reaches of the Tennessee. Riding on the *Stone River,* Granger directed the boats as they neared Decatur by noon on December 22. But he learned that the town was held by Roddey and 2,000 men with nine guns. Granger had only 1,200 troops and called on Steedman for help.[65]

But Steedman needed time, and whether he could intercept the Confederates depended on how fast Hood traveled. As of December 24, the Army of Tennessee was only one day away from the Tennessee River, and Steedman had not yet combined with Granger to retake Decatur. There was no hope that the steamers Donaldson sent down the Cumberland River could get to Eastport soon. In fact, Whipple told Donaldson to stop those boats when they reached Paducah, Kentucky, at the mouth of the Tennessee, until Thomas had a better idea of where Hood was going. There now seemed to be little prospect of intercepting the retreating Confederates by an end run, although Thomas remained optimistic.[66]

The Federals did not yet know that Hood had decided not to cross the Tennessee River at Decatur. In fact, he had also decided against crossing at Lamb's Ferry. Instead he now aimed to cross opposite Bainbridge, a small town on the south bank of the Tennessee eight miles upriver from Florence at the western end of Muscle Shoals. Here the water level would be low, making it easier to lay the pontoons. Hood moved southwest after passing Pulaski and rested his headquarters six miles north of Lexington, Alabama, on the evening of December 23. By the following evening, Army of Tennessee headquarters stopped for the night eleven miles north of Bainbridge. The next day, December 25, the army was on the north side of the Tennessee opposite Bainbridge and laying its pontoon bridge.[67]

The Federals were very far behind. Having crossed the Duck River, Wilson's cavalry ranged southward on December 24. The troopers stopped seven miles south of Pulaski and thirty-seven miles northeast of Hood's headquarters the next day. There was no railroad leading directly to Bainbridge, thus necessitating a march over the countryside, but the Federals were at least aware that the Army of Tennessee was moving toward Bainbridge. Wilson sent this important bit of intelligence to Thomas at 10:10 A.M. on Christmas Day.[68]

Logistical problems became so pronounced by this stage of the pursuit that they decisively impeded Federal movement. Both Wilson's cavalry and Wood's infantry stopped seven miles south of Pulaski on the evening of December 25. The infantrymen were out of rations, and Wood was compelled to wait for more to come up. Rain set in that afternoon, making it difficult for the wagon train to reach the hungry troops and issue food before 5 P.M. on the twenty-sixth. The roads were in terrible shape, compelling wagons to move only half a mile per hour. While Wood's men had some food, Wilson cited a severe shortage of forage for his horses as the reason for prolonging the delay.[69]

As the Federals struggled with their logistical problems, the Confederates reached an important watershed in their retreat. Hood's engineers laid his pontoon bridge over the Tennessee at Bainbridge on Christmas as the Army of Tennessee formed a bridgehead to protect it. The span was finished by dawn of December 26, and the army crossed over during the next two days; Cheatham and Lee on the twenty-sixth and Stewart and the cavalry on the twenty-seventh. The engineers took up the span on the twenty-eighth.[70]

Two days before that crossing was completed, Wood's Fourth Corps left its bivouac seven miles south of Pulaski on the evening of December 26 after receiving a resupply of provisions. It crawled to Sugar Creek by 2 P.M. on December 27, having negotiated twelve miles of "the worst road that, perhaps, an army every [*sic*] marched," according to Fullerton. At this point the Federals were still twenty-five miles from Hood's army, which by that evening had nearly completed its crossing of the Tennessee River.[71]

By December 26 Thomas had accepted the fact that there was no hope of catching the Confederates. Now he focused on securing control of the territory down to the Tennessee River and preparing for a projected spring campaign into the Deep South. He considered sending Wilson's Cavalry Corps and A. J. Smith's Sixteenth Corps to Eastport to meet the transports loaded with supplies. The other troops could cross the Tennessee at Decatur, meeting Steedman's column coming from the east. After that the Federals would occupy the line of the Tennessee River until spring.[72]

Neither Wilson nor Schofield cared much for Thomas's plan. Wilson chafed at the idea of pushing his cavalry force across a countryside barren of food and forage. He recognized that Thomas had to send his men somewhere because they could not live where they were without a secure line of supply. Schofield, however, preferred to take his Twenty-Third Corps to the East and help Grant deal with Robert E. Lee at Petersburg. Bypassing Thomas on December 27, he suggested this idea directly to Grant.[73]

Thomas stuck to his plan despite objections. On December 27 he ordered Wilson to march for Eastport and sent the Sixteenth Corps there as well by a combination of marching and steamboat travel. Smith was to move his infantrymen to Clifton, on the east bank of the Tennessee River fifty miles northwest of Pulaski. Transports would haul the troops from there to Eastport.[74]

Thomas's end runs to intercept Hood from west and east failed by wide margins. Admiral Lee pushed his gunboats up the Tennessee, engaging some Confederate batteries along the way. He reached Florence by December 27, but Hood was crossing the river eight miles farther upstream that day. Lee could do nothing more except protect the transports that carried supplies from Nashville and Smith's troops from Clifton once they arrived at Eastport to establish a depot there.[75]

The column from the east, led by Steedman and Granger, also failed to intercept Hood. Steedman's 5,000 men had a long distance to travel. They initially accompanied Thomas's army in the pursuit from Nashville but then were detached at a point somewhere between Franklin and Spring Hill on December 18. This column, marching overland on country roads, reached Murfreesboro by the evening of the twentieth. Delayed by the lack of empty cars, Steedman did not leave town until the morning of December 22. His troops reached the mouth of the Limestone River on the evening of the twenty-sixth and joined Granger's command, which included four gunboats, an armed transport (the *Stone River*), and five steamers loaded with food and forage dispatched from the Chattanooga depot. Steedman loaded his men onto the transports and steamed down the Tennessee on December 27. The Federals landed three miles above Decatur, bridged a lagoon, and drove off a small force of Confederates to recapture the town that day.[76]

Steedman by then had lost any opportunity to intercept Hood's army. The next day, December 28, when Rebel engineers took up their pontoon bridge at Bainbridge forty miles away, the Federals left Decatur and headed for Courtland, located halfway between the two places. Steedman's small mounted force led the way, skirmishing with Confederate cavalry, until the main Union force lodged securely at Courtland on the thirtieth. The Federal cavalry rode farther and intercepted Hood's pontoon train as it struggled south, Col. William J. Palmer of the 15th Pennsylvania Cavalry capturing seventy-eight pontoons and 200 wagons. Palmer was unable to bring the train back to Courtland and had to burn everything. Steedman left Courtland on January 3, 1865, and returned to Chattanooga ten days later.[77]

The last Federal force to play a role in efforts to interrupt Hood's retreat was highly successful at destroying the weak Confederate supply line to his army. Benjamin Grierson conducted an effective campaign against the Mobile and Ohio Railroad. Leaving Memphis on December 21, his 3,500 troopers tore up track for several miles down to Egypt Station, Mississippi, where they fought a sharp battle on December 28. The Federals destroyed a total of fifty miles of track along the Mobile and Ohio Railroad, then rode over to the Mississippi Central Railroad, tearing up thirty miles of track on that line. Grierson ended his raid by riding to Vicksburg on January 5. His men had destroyed a total of eighty miles of railroad, including thirty-five bridges, and a large amount of rolling stock.[78]

The Confederates had never gotten their rail system into full working order before this raid, and now Grierson abruptly stopped all traffic. Hood's first response was to repair the damage. Beauregard optimistically reported it could be done by mid-January. One officer estimated that, by then, the rail system in Mississippi had the capacity to haul up to 2,500 men per day. It is not clear if this indicates that Grierson's damage had been repaired, but the Confederates had certainly abandoned Corinth by that time, giving up the rail system that had been designed to support Hood in Tennessee.[79]

Although the Federals failed to stop Hood, they easily repaired the damage inflicted on their own transportation system during the Tennessee Campaign. Donaldson dispatched work crews to repair wagon roads and bridges in the Nashville area, especially along the pikes leading south to Franklin and southeast to Murfreesboro. He also reopened the Nashville and Northwestern Railroad and rebuilt the depot at Johnsonville, expending a full month in cleaning up the wreckage left by Forrest's attack of early November. The Confederates had destroyed all bridges along a seventy-five-mile stretch of the railroad. Federal crews began working on the line by January 2 and finished on February 13, rebuilding 2,200 feet of bridges only to see them washed out by heavy rains in late February and early March. Those spans were once again rebuilt, this time as permanent truss bridges. The original owners received this boon when the government transferred ownership of the railroad to them on September 1, 1865.[80]

Hood Ends His Retreat

Hood led the shattered Army of Tennessee out of the pincers that Thomas set in motion from west and east, and he managed to keep ahead of the main Federal column struggling along mud-engulfed roads from Nashville. But he failed to keep his superiors and colleagues informed of his line of retreat. Beauregard and Taylor wondered for days where the army would show up. As of December 27, Beauregard had not received any word from Hood since the fifteenth and did not know of his terrible defeat at Nashville. Later that day Taylor learned about the battle and organized a wagon train loaded with supplies at Blue Mountain in case the army retreated in that direction. He also planned to move cattle herds toward the area. Beauregard, however, assumed the defeated troops would retire by way of Corinth. "Be good enough to let us know your plans so that we may provide for you accordingly," George Brent asked Hood late on the twenty-seventh.[81]

By January 5 Hood had lodged the remnants of his army at Tupelo. His logistical support was slender at best. "We are rapidly running out of breadstuffs at Tupelo and Okolona," wrote his inspector general. Confederate soldiers were using their weapons to steal food from civilians in the area, and desertion was on the rise. The Army of Tennessee became "a demoralized wreck," according to Douglas J. Cater of the 19th Louisiana. "Nearly all without shoes & with worn out garments and added to this a *ear of corn* in each man's haversack to check the awful *epidemic—hunger.*"[82]

Hood's effort to use his cavalry against Thomas's supply line failed to produce results. Lyon's small brigade rode into Kentucky after November 18, but Thomas dispatched McCook's cavalry division to deal with him. McCook split his command and pursued, harassing Lyon enough to limit the damage the Confederates could inflict. Lyon managed to evade a crushing defeat and tore up at least one bridge near Elizabethtown, but he was repulsed in an attack on a small garrison at Scottsboro, Alabama, on his way back south. Lyon reached safety in central Alabama by mid-January 1865. The superintendent of the Louisville and Nashville Railroad repaired the damage his mounted men had caused by December 30, long before Lyon finished his raid.[83]

Assessment

Few Civil War armies were as badly defeated on the battlefield as the Army of Tennessee at Nashville. Afterward it faced a daunting task in trying to escape from a very vulnerable position. Halleck was well aware of the golden opportunity to deal a death blow to Hood's army. "A most vigorous pursuit on your part is therefore of vital importance," he told Thomas on December 21. Thomas responded with a tone of strained exasperation. His men were moving forward "as vigorously as it is possible for one army to pursue another," he wrote the same day. "We cannot control the elements." Thomas explained that "pursuing an enemy through an exhausted country, over mud roads, completely sogged with heavy rains, is no child's play." He pinpointed the key chokepoints in his advance—the Harpeth River, Carter's Creek, Rutherford Creek, Duck River, and Richland Creek.[84]

By the simple expedient of making sure every bridge was burned before leaving an area, the Confederates gained a decisive edge on their pursuers. Coupled with their own pontoon bridge to cross the Tennessee, Hood's army saved itself by a few adroit measures and fast marching.

The Union pursuit of the Army of Tennessee was foiled by logistical and supply problems that greatly impaired mobility even for the resource-rich Federals. "It is without a parallel in this war," wrote Thomas J. Wood, the Fourth Corps commander. "It was continued for more than a hundred miles at the most inclement season of the year, over a road the whole of which was bad, and thirty miles of which were wretched, almost beyond description. It were scarcely an hyperbole to say that the road from Pulaski to Lexington was bottomless when we passed over it."[85]

Federal Strategy for the Spring Campaign

As he repositioned troops to occupy the Tennessee River valley, Thomas also began to plan a spring campaign. "I have made diligent inquiries concerning the resources of the country, and believe that an army would find ample resources on two or three routes south." Those routes were the line of the Mobile and Ohio Railroad, a march directly south from Decatur "through the middle of Alabama," and an advance "along the west side of the Coosa" River. Thomas felt it was impossible to utilize any of those routes in winter and planned to place Wilson's cavalry and A. J. Smith's infantry at Eastport, Wood's corps at Huntsville, and Schofield's corps at Dalton, Georgia, for the winter.[86]

Thomas's wait for better weather produced frustration in Washington. "This seems to me entirely wrong," Halleck complained to Grant. "In our present financial condition we cannot afford this delay." He suggested detaching Schofield or Smith to Canby so he could capture Mobile by a coastal route, then move inland to Selma or Montgomery. "If Thomas was as active as Sherman, I would say march directly from Decatur to Talladega, Montgomery, and Selma, living upon the country, and anticipating Hood, should he move by Meridian. But I think Thomas entirely too slow to live on the country." Halleck could not support the idea that Schofield or Smith march east from Vicksburg into central Alabama because that route was already stripped of food. The route from Mobile toward Selma and Montgomery had never been used.[87]

Wood agreed that the time to strike was now. The Army of Tennessee was disorganized and suffering for want of provisions; it was more vulnerable now than it would be in the spring. He urged Thomas to organize a push south from the Tennessee River as soon as possible. A column of 40,000 infantry and 10,000 cavalry taking along wagonloads of hard bread, sugar, coffee, and salt to last for forty days, along with ammunition, was all that would be needed. The column could carry some forage for emergencies and drive along a herd of beef cattle, "trusting the country to supply the remainder of the meat ration and forage for daily use." Wood guaranteed, "we could eat our oysters in Mobile" within forty days.[88]

Grant told Halleck to order Thomas into an offensive from the Tennessee River as soon as possible. He also instructed him to send the Twenty-Third Corps to Eastport rather than Dalton. That order started Schofield marching overland to Clifton, following Smith's route to the Tennessee and the Federal transports on the river.[89]

While Thomas started the troops where Halleck instructed, he put his foot down on the timing of an offensive into the Deep South. Word reached his headquarters that the dirt roads of Alabama were impracticable for wheeled vehicles during the winter months. Not even a letter written by Sherman to Montgomery Meigs, exulting in how easy it was for his columns to live off the land during the March to the Sea, persuaded Thomas to change his mind when one of Meigs's assistants sent him a copy. Sherman also wrote directly to Thomas urging him to conduct a penetration of central Alabama as soon as he could. But nothing moved the stolid commander to action.[90]

Ironically, Thomas found it difficult to feed his men even when they were stationary in the Tennessee River valley. Wood complained that the area around Huntsville was already eaten out. He requested 60,000 pounds of forage every day for the animals in his Fourth Corps and had to send parties up to forty miles from town to find anything. That kind of foraging wore out wagons, teams, and men alike, and it did not gather enough food to feed his animals. Guerrillas constantly attacked outposts and troops who were posted as safeguards for houses around Huntsville. This danger, and the problem of feeding his men, could not have been any worse if the Fourth Corps was ranging south toward Selma or Montgomery during the winter.[91]

Frustrated with Thomas, Grant decided to take as many troops from him as possible. He approved Schofield's suggestion of shipping the Twenty-Third Corps to the East, and those troops departed from Clifton on the Tennessee River. He sent Smith's Sixteenth Corps troops to Canby, and they participated in the capture of Mobile a few weeks later. Wilson was eager to conduct a penetration of central Alabama with his cavalry command, so Grant gave him free rein to plan one even if Thomas was not pushing it. In addition, Grant mandated that Thomas's available pontoon trains be given to Smith and Wilson.[92]

Wilson was forced to accede that Thomas had a valid point in at least one respect. While it would be easier for an infantry column to feed itself on the country, a large cavalry force such as the one he wanted to assemble (up to 25,000 men) had a more compelling logistical need. Horses ate a lot of hay and grain. While moving through virgin territory, a large mounted column could feed itself even though leaving behind a devastated countryside. The Tennessee River valley and the territory for some distance south of it was not very productive; it would take a few days of riding to reach the fertile grounds of central Alabama. Wilson's troops were exhausted from the Tennessee Campaign, and the general contemplated resting them for some time in camps scattered along the Tennessee River, where steamers navigating to Eastport could provision them. After resting and feeding for seventy to ninety days, the column could more easily handle a campaign through the less-productive regions until reaching central Alabama than if he set out immediately.[93]

As a result, Thomas's plan to advance into Alabama with a large force of infantry and cavalry in the spring evaporated. All that remained was a cavalry raid by Wilson as the infantry diverted to the eastern theater and the Gulf coast. Thomas would remain behind in Nashville to manage the Union presence in the western theater, while the energetic Wilson led his mounted men in the largest and most devastating cavalry raid of the war.

8

STRATEGIC RAIDS IN THE DEEP SOUTH

When Sherman resisted Hood's attempt to pull him from the Deep South in the fall of 1864, he pursued a course already mapped out by months of operational experience in the war. The drive to Atlanta was unusual; no other military force had penetrated the Lower South using a railroad. But that line of communications had barely supported Sherman's large force on its way to Atlanta, and he had no intention of trying to make it work beyond the city. If he was to retain the offensive, then abandoning the railroad and living off the countryside was the only recourse.

The March to the Sea

Sherman needed several weeks of preparation to conduct a strategic raid out of Atlanta, and Hood's attack on the Western and Atlantic Railroad delayed that task. Even as he chased the Army of Tennessee northward, Sherman argued for his plan with Grant, eventually convincing the general in chief of its wisdom. He also arranged for the defense of Tennessee in the face of what appeared to be Hood's intention to invade that state. In the end Sherman got his way on all fronts—Thomas reluctantly accepted his role as protector of Tennessee, and Sherman was able to take 60,000 men rather than the 30,000 that Grant initially approved. Sherman chose the easiest line of march—directly from Atlanta toward the Atlantic coast at Savannah. As his men moved through central Georgia, they would find abundant resources of food and animals but less-productive farms as they neared the seacoast. Federal quartermasters could bring in food by ship and other material as soon as the port facilities at Savannah were secured.

True to form, Sherman prepared for the march in detail. His wagons were loaded with plenty of ammunition, twenty days' bread rations; thirty days' coffee, sugar, and salt; five days' salt meat; and four days' forage for animals. His quartermasters drove a herd of 5,476 beef cattle capable of feeding his men for forty days. But Sherman intended these provisions to serve as a reserve. He wanted his men to forage liberally from the countryside as their main source of subsistence.[1]

How to organize this feeding off the enemy's resources was a point of importance. Sherman knew that in previous European wars commanders made requisitions on civil magistrates to gather food and forage from the inhabitants. This practice tended to minimize confrontations between occupying soldiers and civilians. That system worked well enough in densely populated Europe, where the local government remained intact and cooperative. But these conditions did not exist in the South. The population was much more dispersed, and the local governments, weak even in the best of times, were anything but cooperative. It was necessary for the army to take what it needed directly from farmers and plantation owners whether they cooperated or not. Such a situation could easily have devolved into a brutal mess.[2]

Sherman established a system to minimize suffering for civilians and maintain discipline in the ranks. He authorized each brigade to send out fifty men ahead of its column to collect food and forage in wagons. These parties were to deliver the material to their brigade commissary when the command caught up with them. These foragers acquired the name of "bummers" and amounted to 1,950 troops for Sherman's thirty-nine brigades.[3]

According to John McWilliams, commissary of subsistence for the First Brigade, Third Division, Twentieth Corps, Sherman's orders were followed, but his own brigade leader gave him more simple instructions. "You are to do nothing in this campaign but forage. Take what men you want and a guard to look after what you get. I expect you to keep your wagons full of the products of the country." McWilliams was assigned to take charge of foraging for the 3,000 men of the Third Division. He chose twenty-five soldiers he could rely on plus a squad to guard the wagons. By the third day of the march, these men had secured enough horses to mount all twenty-five foragers.[4]

The bummers devised methods of gathering food quickly. Quartermasters scouted and planned the route the night before, opening fences along the way to drive wagons through. They placed men at the food source ready to load when the wagons arrived, then rushed those wagons to the road ahead of their unit's arrival. Sherman watched one day as a group of bummers tilted a loaded corncrib and drove a wagon next to it. Several men crawled into the crib, lay on their backs on the corn, and kicked it out into the wagon with their legs. John Billings of the 10th Massachusetts Battery had served in the Army of the Potomac but studied the March to the Sea after the war and was amazed at this industrial method of foraging. Sherman's operation illustrated "in a *wholesale* way the kind of business other armies did on a *retail* scale," he concluded.[5]

In addition to regulating the process of foraging, Sherman tried to maintain discipline by issuing Special Field Order No. 120. Soldiers were forbidden to enter private dwellings. Only corps commanders could authorize the destruction of buildings, and they were not supposed to do so as long as the citizens were peaceful. If they offered resistance, "enforce devastation more or less relentless according to the measure of such hostility." Federal foragers were also to "refrain from abusive or threatening language" and offer certificates documenting what was taken if they felt it was appropriate. But Sherman forbade them from offering receipts that could be used to obtain automatic reimbursements from the government after the war. Given that this was the heart of the Confederacy, there was little chance these civilians could prove they had been loyal to the U.S. government. In the end there is no evidence that any Federals gave certificates to civilians during the March to the Sea. Sherman wanted the bummers to leave enough food behind for the families to live on and authorized his subordinates to collect able-bodied black men.[6]

Sherman's careful organizing of a select group of foragers to bear the burden of collecting foodstuffs paid many dividends. It was far more efficient than allowing units to forage in any way they wished, minimized the negative effects on the civilian population, and was reminiscent of previous foraging methods to be seen in eighteenth- and early nineteenth-century European practice. It allowed fewer opportunities for members of the rank and file to plunder, although one could never entirely eliminate that unfortunate outgrowth of army operations. The bummers also brought back intelligence about the countryside that often proved useful in planning the next day's march. In no other campaign of the Civil War did the Federals adopt such an effective system of food gathering in the field.

For the most part, the rank and file acted relatively well during the march to Savannah. Twentieth Corps commander Alpheus Williams admitted that "repeated instances of wanton pillage" had taken place but con-

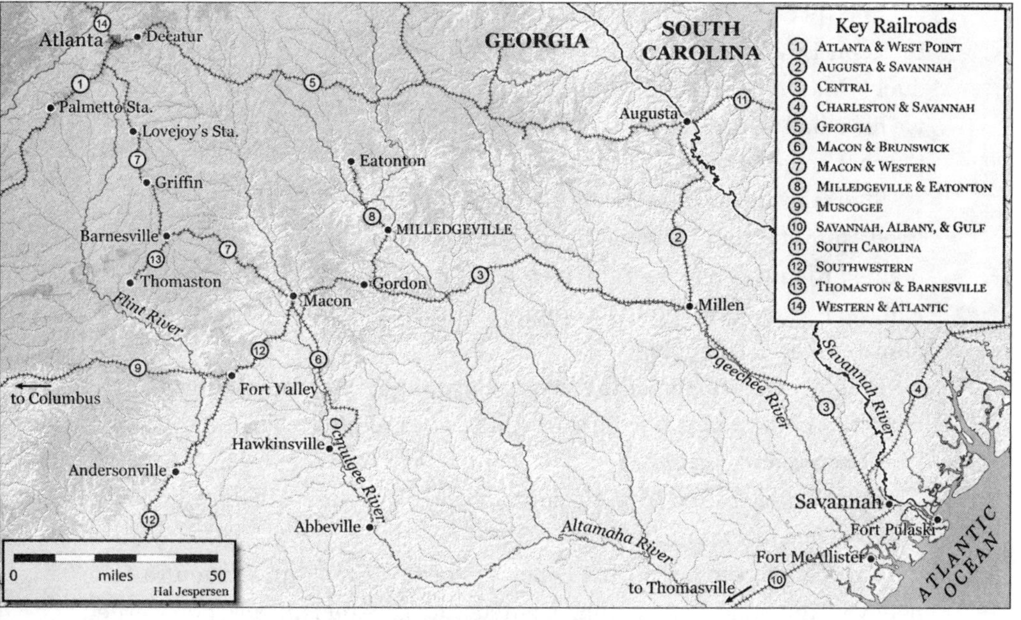

MARCH TO THE SEA

cluded that the "general conduct" of his men was good. "The nature of the march was calculated to relax discipline," he judged, yet "comparatively" little trouble ensued. He blamed what problems did occur on the few "disorderly and vicious" men in every unit.[7]

Away from Atlanta, the Federals entered a region of rich farms that had never been visited by the contending armies. The harvest had just been gathered, creating an ideal situation for living off the land. On the way to Milledgeville, the Yankees found "corn, molasses, meal, bacon, and sweet potatoes, oxen, cows, mules" in abundance, Sherman recalled in his memoirs. "We enjoyed a continual Thanksgiving," exulted O. P. Johnson of the 33rd Massachusetts. Along the way, normally under orders of their superiors, the troops burned cotton bales, cotton presses, and cotton gins as well as public buildings. "A great many of the large planter's houses were destroyed, as a general thing the dwelling houses in the towns & villages were not destroyed," reported Thomas Howland. During the month-long march to Savannah, the 33rd Massachusetts drew only five days' rations from the wagon train.[8]

The "privates in the ranks have lived like princes everyday," reported Surgeon Edwin Hutchinson of the 137th New York. "Chickens, turkeys, ducks, butter, flour, meal, sweet potatoes and every thing you can imagine we have had in profusion. It is all nonsense to talk about starving out the South. I never saw such quantities of good things."[9]

Sherman agreed with Hutchinson, telling his wife, Ellen, that the men lived "sumptuously" during the march to Savannah. When civilians complained to him about the raid, he told them to look toward Richmond. "If Jeff Davis expects to found an empire on the ruins of the South, he ought to afford to feed the People."[10]

Roughly two-thirds of the way to Savannah, the topography changed from the piedmont environment to the coastal plain. The land became "more sandy and barren" as Sherman put it, "and food became more scarce." The men's diet shifted from turkey to hardtack as the reality of campaigning returned in a familiar way.[11]

Throughout the march, the Federals tore up a lot of infrastructure. "His policy is universal destruction," Confederate general Howell Cobb warned Davis about Sherman. But there was no wide-scale destruction of Milledgeville during Sherman's two-day stay in the Georgia capital. Certain rogues in Union ranks burned dwellings without authority, but Twentieth Corps commander Alpheus Williams correctly blamed it on a small percentage of the men. Officially authorized destruction of buildings was kept to a minimum.[12]

In contrast to buildings, Sherman was almost obsessed with tearing up rail lines. "I attached much importance to this destruction of the railroad, gave it my own personal attention, and made reiterated orders to others on the subject," he wrote after the war. The Federals tore up 310 miles of track during the march to Savannah, representing more than 22 percent of the total railroad mileage in Georgia.[13]

By the time Sherman's march ended, his enemy had an opportunity to assess the damage to Southern railroads across the state. Engineer chief Jeremy F. Gilmer reported that the Federals destroyed the track and all bridges of the Western and Atlantic Railroad from Atlanta up to the Etowah River, a total of forty-six miles, in early November. On the Georgia Railroad, which linked Atlanta with Augusta, there were thirty-eight miles of track and three bridges out. Gilmer estimated that the rails left behind could be reused quickly along twenty-three miles of the Georgia Railroad, but the rest needed new rails. New ties were required for between twenty-five and thirty miles of that road as well. All this damage, however, had been done before the March to the Sea.[14]

Sherman's raid to Savannah tore up 100 miles of the Central Railroad, which linked Macon with Millen and Savannah, with the most serious damage between Gordon and Millen. Gilmer noted that no repairs had yet started on the Western and Atlantic Railroad as of mid-December 1864, but he hoped to get the Georgia Railroad operable by mid-February 1865. The Atlanta and West Point Railroad between Atlanta and Palmetto Station could be repaired by that time too, but he could not estimate when the Central Railroad in the heart of Georgia could be operational again.[15]

Sherman not only isolated Atlanta, the state's most important transportation center, but also cut the east–west rail link between the Atlantic coast and the rest of the ever-shrinking Confederacy. It is therefore astonishing that 7,000 men from the Army of Tennessee were shifted more than 1,000 miles from Mississippi to North Carolina in the early months of 1865 to oppose Sherman's columns. Those men rode the rails wherever lines were still operable and walked across the break in central Georgia until they were able to participate in the final stages of the war in the Carolinas.[16]

Much of the resource destruction taking place during Sherman's March to the Sea was performed by the Confederates. Joseph Wheeler's cavalry division conducted a scorched-earth policy in a vain attempt to starve the enemy as they traversed central Georgia. "You have now the best opportunity ever yet presented to destroy the enemy," boasted Sen. Benjamin H. Hill in a proclamation to the people of Georgia on November 18. He urged them to remove food from the path of the advancing host and to set up obstructions along the roads to delay its march. "Every citizen with his gun, and every negro with his spade and axe, can do the work of a soldier," Hill continued. Beauregard and six other members of the Confederate Congress issued similar appeals.[17]

Wheeler instructed his troops to tell civilians in Sherman's path that they had to drive all their livestock out of the way. W. C. Dodson, a historian of Wheeler's campaigns, estimated that the country through which the Federals marched contained ten million pounds of meat and one million barrels of corn. In other words, Wheeler faced a huge task if he wanted to deny food to the Federals. Dodson argued after the war that the Confederate general believed his actions "entailed great suffering upon the people without giving Sherman more than temporary inconvenience."[18]

Nevertheless, Wheeler's men tried to fulfill the directive. According to P. A. Lawson, a resident of Griffin, Confederate cavalrymen burned corn and fodder and pressed livestock for ten miles north and south of the Central Railroad, even going into areas that were not directly in Sherman's path. A planter near Grahamville named William F. Robert complained to Davis that "Wheeler's cavalry—are far more terrible to Confederates—than to Yankees." Wheeler tried to curb this tendency by appealing to the fair name of his command, but it did not help. He vigorously defended his men against charges of wanton destruction by blaming much of it on the citizens themselves. Wheeler asserted that the proclamations urging them to resist Sherman inspired footloose men to hover around the enemy and commit depredations on civilians while claiming to be part of the Confederate cavalry.[19]

The organized collection and destruction of resources by the Federals was enormous. Brig. Gen. Jefferson C. Davis's Fourteenth Corps burned 12,000 bales of cotton along the way and collected 1,770 draft animals to replace worn-out horses and mules. Davis's men also collected 1,500 cattle along with several hundred sheep. They found 1,000,730 pounds of fodder and 1,474,834 pounds of grain. His commissaries issued only three and a half days' rations from November 16 to December 11; the men ate from the countryside the rest of the time, with sweet potatoes being the staple item.[20]

Sherman's animals also lived off the countryside. Langdon C. Easton estimated that the horses and mules consumed eleven million pounds of grain and fifteen million pounds of fodder and hay from the countryside. The herd of beef cattle also grazed along the route. Many animals gave out during the move. having been weakened from lack of food during October and early November due to Hood's cutting of the Western and Atlantic Railroad, and had to be shot. As they died off, the Federals replaced them with fresh animals taken from farms and plantations. The Twentieth Corps lost 402 horses and 524 mules killed or abandoned along the line of march, but its bummers more than compensated by taking 410 horses and 1,020 mules. Easton argued that Sherman's draft animals were in "far better" condition at the end of the march than at the beginning.[21]

Throughout the March to the Sea, Sherman estimated that his men destroyed or consumed $100,000,000 worth of property, using $20,000,000 of it for their own purposes. That represented 18 percent of the $600,000,000 worth of taxable property in Georgia. Of course, this destruction was confined to a corridor some 300 miles long and 60 miles wide from Atlanta to

Savannah. Twenty-one counties were affected by Sherman's march, with a total of $162,592,366 worth of real and personal property combined. The Federals therefore burned or consumed 61.7 percent of that property during their move to Savannah, an unusually high level of resource destruction spread over an unusually large area of the countryside.[22]

The population density of those twenty-one counties can be estimated by using the county-level population reports contained in the 1860 census. That census did not, however, report the square miles contained in each county, but since all of those counties still exist, their current areas will have to suffice. Population density in the twenty-one counties was 22.2 people per square mile in the 1860s. One must, however, consider that the timing of Sherman's march was perfect, allowing his men to gather recently harvested crops and abundant food for the first two-thirds of the march. Once they began to enter the heart of the coastal plain, that abundance quickly declined. The population density of the counties composing the first two-thirds of the marching route was 26.3 people per square mile; for the rest of the counties, those closer to the coast, this fell to 13.9 people per square mile.[23]

If we merely look at the overall population density of the twenty-one counties, it suggests that a density of 22 people per square mile was sufficient to feed a large army in the Civil War. Yet one must consider this with caution. One reason is that the density was higher in the first two-thirds of the march. Second, as mentioned, Sherman's men hit a very productive pocket of territory lying southeast of Atlanta and west of the coastal plain, an area not previously entered by the Federal army. And they entered it at exactly the right time to collect the current crop. Moreover, they did not tarry in this region but continually moved through it. If Sherman had stayed any length of time even in this relatively rich region, his men would have eaten it out very quickly. The last one-third of the march took the army group through less populated and less productive regions, with consequent suffering by the men.

Savannah

As the Federals neared Savannah, they began to experience food problems. The coastal plain yielded fewer provisions than the piedmont, and Savannah blocked Union access to coastal ships. The city was protected by a ring of earthworks and garrisoned by 10,000 men under William J. Hardee. To avoid risky frontal assaults, Sherman conducted his operations against Savannah with caution.[24]

The first step was the reduction of Fort McAllister, an earthen fort on the south bank of the Ogeechee River southwest of the city. It was designed to prevent Union seagoing vessels from ascending the river and flanking the city defenses. Sherman devoted his old division, now led by William B. Hazen, to attack the fort on December 13. The men captured it in splendid style after some sharp fighting.[25]

The fall of Fort McAllister allowed Sherman to reestablish a supply line with the outside world. Transports that had been waiting at Port Royal and Hilton Head, South Carolina, could now steam up the Ogeechee River to King's Bridge, where Easton used 2,500 detailed troops to construct a dock for them. But quartermasters could only use coastal vessels that drew less than seven feet of water, and as Easton reported, it was "very difficult to supply" Sherman's army group that way. Even before the city fell, the Federals began removing obstructions planted at the mouth of the Savannah River. The city docks were located several miles upstream.[26]

Before Sherman's men closed in on Savannah, Grant devised a plan to bring his them to Petersburg and help defeat Lee. The most expeditious way was for Sherman to create a fortified base on the coast near Savannah; leave his artillery, cavalry, and some infantry to protect it; and ship the rest of the troops to Petersburg by coastal vessels. "Select yourself the officer to leave in command, but you I want in person," Grant directed.[27]

Sherman received these instructions after the fall of Fort McAllister but before the capture of Savannah. He felt it was necessary to take the city before starting this next move but told Capt. Orlando M. Poe, his chief engineer, to plan a fortified camp somewhere near Fort McAllister. Sherman estimated it would take 100 vessels to move his men to Virginia and assumed the quartermasters needed some time to assemble such a fleet. He could proceed with operations against Savannah in the meantime.[28]

Moving his men to Virginia would have been the biggest military transportation job of the Civil War, but there simply were not enough coastal vessels for it. Quartermasters told Grant it would take two months to move the 60,000 troops from Savannah to City Point, Virginia. Sherman, in contrast, promised he could march his command to Petersburg in only six weeks (an overly optimistic guess). Grant caved in and changed his plans—

Sherman could capture Savannah and then prepare for a march through the Carolinas en route to Virginia.[29]

By the time this was settled, Sherman had maneuvered so as to threaten all exits from the city, and Hardee evacuated on the night of December 21. Ironically, the Federals fared worse for provisions now than when marching through Georgia. General Williams complained that "few supplies have reached us. The country has none, and we are almost starving our animals on rice straw." His artillery horses and mules were "reduced to a dying state." Williams argued that his troops were suffering from food shortages more severe than any they had endured since the war began.[30]

The problem lay in the condition of the Savannah River. The Confederates had planted a number of obstacles in the main northern channel, consisting of "heavy cribs filled with stones and brick." Easton hired Orlando Bennett, a civilian contractor formerly employed by the Federal government in Florida, to remove these obstacles. Meanwhile, Easton used a handful of small vessels on the shallower southern channel of the river to bring in provisions. The dry spell in shipments of food and forage lasted until February 3, 1865, when Bennett opened "a practicable passage" for large boats through the northern channel. He finally cleared the entire northern channel by the twentieth.[31]

Easton utilized some rail power in supporting the troops. When Hardee evacuated Savannah, he left behind eight locomotives and 213 cars in working order. Easton organized trains to roll ten miles southwest from town along the Savannah, Albany, and Gulf Railroad to gather wood for both the army and the civilians in the city.[32]

Sherman was enormously pleased with Quartermaster Easton and Commissary Beckwith during the March to the Sea. "All through the campaign this army of mine has looked to Beckwith for its rations," the general said. "He has never failed them."[33]

Sherman was not shy about pinpointing the reason his raiding strategy worked. "I have a Singular Capacity for knowledge of *Roads,* the resources of a Country, and the Capacity of my Command," he assured his brother. This was not mere bragging. Sherman was one of the most impressive logisticians among Civil War generals and made that skill the foundation of his success as a commander.[34]

"My marches have demonstrated the great truth that armies, even of vast magnitude, are not tied down to bases," he told Montgomery Meigs.

"In almost any quarter of the South armies of from 30,000 to 50,000 may safely march, sure to find near their route forage of some kind or other for their animals."[35]

Carolinas Campaign

Not surprisingly, when contemplating his march through the Carolinas, Sherman gave full thought to logistics. "The question of supplies remained still one of vital importance," he wrote in his memoirs. Grant assured him he would find enough provisions and forage south of the Roanoke River, while north of that stream Federal quartermasters could accumulate stockpiles for his use.[36]

It was important to arrange a reserve supply of food and forage in case resources south of the Roanoke River proved inadequate as well, but that was not easy. Bennett did not fully open the Savannah River before the Carolinas Campaign began. The supply vessels that had been sent to Pensacola in case Sherman decided to march to that point were ordered to come around to Savannah, but only two of them made it in time to help Easton before the march began. According to the quartermaster, Sherman planned to take 66,000 men, 35,000 animals, 2,690 wagons, and 503 ambulances; Easton was barely able to accumulate enough material to support them before they started.[37]

Meigs was involved in the preparation for Sherman's move as well. Beckwith estimated that the army group would use 80,000 rations a day on the march through the Carolinas and wanted to start with no less than fifteen days of food, or 1,200,000 rations. He requested 1,000,000 rations of Meigs to reach that target.[38]

If these figures seem to represent overpreparation for a force that was supposed to live off the countryside, they show that Sherman hedged his bets in every way possible. Just as on the March to the Sea, he meant to take along as much as his powerful wagon train could haul and keep it as a reserve in case the countryside proved inadequate to feed his men and animals.

Sherman recalled the statistics of his army group differently than did Easton. According to his estimates, troop strength amounted to 60,079 men. A total of 2,500 wagons, pulled by six mules each, and 600 ambulances, pulled by two horses each, carried what he needed on the march.

CAROLINAS CAMPAIGN

There was enough ammunition "for a great battle" and forage for the animals to last seven days. His men could count on twenty days' rations in the wagons, "mostly of bread, sugar, coffee, and salt, depending largely for fresh meat on beeves driven on the hoof and such cattle, hogs, and poultry, as we expected to gather along our line of march." He wanted to make it to Goldsboro, North Carolina, in one sweep, a total of 425 miles from his starting points in the vicinity of Savannah.[39]

Sherman authorized stringent regulations for foraging. Howard ordered his corps leaders to exert more control over the process and warned bummers not to use their firearms except at the enemy. Brig. Gen. John M. Corse instructed his division to take only the material actually needed, "without the destruction of private property or the unauthorized burning of houses, fences." The bummers encountered far more resistance in the Carolinas than in Georgia, and many were captured or killed by the enemy. This led Federal commanders to increase the size of foraging parties to at least twenty men each. All parties were mounted by pressing horses from farms and plantations in order to give them greater latitude in dealing with the enemy.[40]

The wisdom of such measures became clear when eighteen men of Kilpatrick's cavalry division were killed on February 21. Some of those men had their throats cut as well. Kilpatrick also found eight foragers from infantry units who had been shot the same day. Their bodies had been mutilated after death, and notes written on paper pinned to their clothes that read "Death to foragers."[41]

Sherman protested in a dispatch to Lt. Gen. Wade Hampton, who commanded Confederate forces in the area. "Of course you cannot question my right to 'forage on the country.' It is a war right as old as history. The manner of exercising it varies with circumstances." Sherman warned Hampton that he held 1,000 Confederate prisoners and was prepared to kill some of them as retaliation for the bloody deeds. Hampton refused to back down, threatening to kill some of the fifty-six Union prisoners he held if Sherman followed through on his threat.[42]

Federal officers tried to clamp down on plunder. Brig. Gen. Giles A. Smith, commander of the Fourth Division, Seventeenth Corps, admonished his men to recall their families back home before they mistreated civilians and to "leave a fair share of provisions" for residents. John A. Logan, commander of the Fifteenth Corps, called plundering "disgraceful in the extreme" and ordered his officers to watch their men carefully.[43]

But it proved impossible to eliminate all pillaging. No one tried harder than Oliver O. Howard, yet he admitted that some of his men simply refused to obey orders. He fielded complaints that soldiers stole watches and jewelry. When one of Corse's men was arrested for pillaging, his friends rescued him with guns in their hands. "I am inclined to think that there is a regularly organized banditti who commit these outrages and who share the spoils," Howard told one of his corps commanders. Later in the campaign Howard issued a circular forbidding the wanton burning of mills and grain that his troops needed for their subsistence as it endangered the viability of the campaign.[44]

Brig. Gen. James D. Morgan, commander of a Fourteenth Corps division, complained that some men "have mistaken the name and meaning of the term foragers, and have become under that name highwaymen, with all their cruelty and ferocity and none of their courage; their victims are usually old men, women, and children, and negroes, whom they rob and maltreat without mercy." Morgan wanted to put on record his "detestation and abhorrence of their acts."[45]

This small group of men performed most of the private, unauthorized acts of violence on the people of the Carolinas, while most of the authorized, restrained violence against the transportation system was done by obedient troops. "As a rule" Sherman mandated that bridges, depots, water tanks, switches, and sawmills be destroyed. "The utter demolition of the railroad system of South Carolina, and the utter destruction of the enemy's arsenals at Columbia, Cheraw, and Fayetteville are the principles of the movement. These points were regarded as inaccessible to us, and now no place in the Confederacy is safe against the Army of the West," he told Stanton.[46]

Sherman united the Army of the Tennessee (his right wing) and the Army of Georgia (his left wing) by February 11 on the South Carolina Railroad between Charleston and Augusta. From that point the combined force moved along the line for fifty miles, tearing up the road thoroughly. Then the Federals marched to the track linking Charleston and Columbia to continue their work of destruction.[47]

When the Federals entered the state capital of Columbia on February 17, the city erupted into flames due to a number of factors. It started with well-meaning civilians who greeted entering soldiers with offers of liquor to appease them and save their town. This had the opposite effect, however, with drunken soldiers causing trouble. The retreating Confederates set fire to an enormous amount of cotton before leaving the city. That fire spread to buildings as Howard organized an effort by his men to contain the flames. Thousands of Federal soldiers worked hard to do so, but their efforts failed because the wind picked up dramatically during the night, creating a holocaust that destroyed 265 residences in Columbia before morning. It is true that the incorrigibles in Union ranks ransacked buildings and helped spread the conflagration, but the majority of Federal soldiers were appalled by the burning of the city and made efforts to help the residents. In fact, provost guards reportedly shot forty Union soldiers who refused to stop plundering and spreading the flames. Several drunken Federals were burned to death as well.[48]

The level of destruction during the campaign intensified, and the Federals met much more resistance as they continued through the Carolinas. Confederate authorities scrambled to assemble troops in Sherman's path. Hood had finally exhausted his stock with the dismal failure of his Tennessee Campaign and was relieved on January 23, 1865. Lt. Gen. Richard Taylor temporarily replaced him. Davis then authorized the transfer of part of the army from Mississippi to the Carolinas and caved in to public pressure that Joseph E. Johnston command the Army of Tennessee on February 22.[49]

Johnston also was charged with managing the concentration of Rebel troops in the Carolinas. While waiting for the Army of Tennessee troops, he took charge of Hardee's Savannah force and Maj. Gen. Robert Hoke's command. The latter had lost Wilmington, North Carolina, when Schofield brought his Twenty-Third Corps from West Tennessee to the mouth of the Cape Fear River and maneuvered Hoke out of the city. Schofield now sought a junction with Sherman at Goldsboro.[50]

The Confederate concentration in the Carolinas was hampered by poor logistics. "This road," Hardee complained of the Northeastern Railroad from Cheraw, "like all others in the Confederacy, is wretchedly managed. With proper management I ought to have had everything there by this time." Robert E. Lee fully recognized the problem when he urged Johnston to rely on foot power rather than rail transport to concentrate his available troops for a showdown with Sherman.[51]

Wheeler continued to struggle with his cavalrymen, complaining that officers did not give proper vouchers to civilians when they pressed supplies. He issued several circulars to standardize the acquisition of food, requiring officers sent on foraging details to carry a written order issued by a brigade or division commander and presenting it "on demand" to civilians. "Utmost courtesy and kindness to every citizen" was the rule, "only cowards insult the weak." But civilian complaints continued to pile up until Wheeler began to catalogue them as a record of transgressions by his men. When Hardee advised that food should be left for civilian families to subsist on, Wheeler thought one bushel per person every month would be enough.[52]

Although moving through hostile country, Sherman's army group experienced fewer supply problems than the Confederates. The key lay in his large and well-organized wagon trains, which carried all the nonfood material the army needed as well as a sizeable reserve of provisions for the men. The Twentieth Corps train moved a total of 456 miles during the campaign, crossing a dozen rivers. Pioneers corduroyed 275 miles of that route for the wagons, which averaged a speed of 10.3 miles per day. In the sixty-seven-day campaign, it rained twenty-one days, and the route lay along the seam between the coastal plain and the piedmont, mostly low-lying ground prone to flooding and muddy conditions. The train left early in the morning and continued moving until late, "wet and dry, over swamps, sometimes in sight and sometimes sunk in the mud nearly out of sight," wrote Henry M. Whittelsey, chief commissary of the Twentieth Corps. Only four wagons and five ambulances broke down along the way and were abandoned because repairs were impracticable.[53]

Combining Lines of Supply with Foraging

Sherman utilized coastal shipping to a limited degree during the Carolinas Campaign. He transported Blair's Seventeenth Corps from Thunderbolt Landing near Savannah to Beaufort, South Carolina, where the troops started their march. Sherman left Easton behind to arrange coastal shipping at appropriate ports along the coast in case the infantry was compelled to meet supply vessels. Easton inspected various points and chose Morehead City, North Carolina. He started to build a depot there and created another at Wilmington soon after its capture in January 1865. Only ships that drew no more than twelve feet of draft could use either port.[54]

After leaving Columbia and reaching Fayetteville, North Carolina, Sherman received oats for his animals from vessels steaming up the Cape Fear River. Later, a boatload of clothing reached the troops before they left Fayetteville. The vessels went back down the river loaded with sick and wounded soldiers. By the time Sherman joined Schofield's command at Goldsboro, he could use the railroad link with Wilmington.[55]

Montgomery Meigs reported that a total of ninety-eight vessels supplied Sherman's army group with 37,539 tons of material. That may have represented the total effort beginning with the initial assembly of coastal ships to stockpile supplies while Sherman was still marching through Georgia. But one wonders how differently the course of the war might have been if those ninety-eight vessels had been used to transport Sherman's men from Savannah to Petersburg rather than relying on the slow process of marching.[56]

Living on the Countryside

The Carolinas Campaign "tested most thoroughly the power of endurance and elasticity of spirit among American soldiers" than any other movement, argued John W. Geary. During fifty-six days of marching, his division received five days' supply of salt meat, twenty-seven and three-quarters days' hard bread, forty-nine days' coffee, twenty days' sugar, thirty days' salt, fifteen days' pepper, ten days' soap, three days' beans, and seven days' forage for their animals. Geary estimated that his division ate or destroyed $2,960,143 worth of property during the Carolinas Campaign. That included 2,000,000 pounds of corn, 2,000,000 pounds of corn fodder for animals, 50,000 chickens, 100,000 pounds of sweet potatoes, and 1,400,000 fence rails.[57]

If Geary's experience was typical, Sherman's fourteen divisions consumed or destroyed a total of $42 million worth of Southern property during the march through the Carolinas. That was less than the army group ate or destroyed during the March to the Sea, even though it traveled more than 100 additional miles and took twice as long to do it. In both marches Sherman was traveling through areas not yet visited by hostile armies.

Ironically, the area he traversed through South Carolina was far wealthier than the Georgia counties his troops had moved through during the March to the Sea. The twelve counties of South Carolina affected by his march, on average, contained three times more wealth in real and personal property compared to the twenty-one Georgia counties. This is probably because South Carolina was divided into a relatively few number of counties, which were called "districts" in the state. The average size of those dozen South Carolina counties was 771 square miles compared to an average of only 490 square miles among the twenty-one Georgia counties. The seven North Carolina counties involved in the Carolinas Campaign, however, were only slightly wealthier than the Georgia counties. Of the combined $260,351,799 worth of real and personal property in the South Carolina and North Carolina counties traversed by Sherman's men, the Federals were able to access only $42 million worth, or no more than 16.1 percent of the total.[58]

Population density in those Carolina counties that Sherman traversed was markedly lower than in Georgia. The twelve South Carolina counties held on average only 9.9 people per square mile, while the seven North Carolina counties had 12.7 people per square mile.[59]

Timing could well account for this differential in accessing material wealth in Sherman's two campaigns. In Georgia the march took place at exactly the right moment to maximize Federal access to the fall crop, just after it had been harvested and stored and before it could be requisitioned or purchased by the Confederate government. In contrast, the move through the Carolinas started two months later. Lee's Army of Northern Virginia was drawing heavily from the Carolinas to support its position at Petersburg by this stage of the war and may well have already drawn much food from the farms and plantations Federal bummers visited.

"At times the men were reduced to living on parched corn," reported Brig. Gen. Manning F. Force of his Seventeenth Corps division, and "at times they feasted upon abundance." By the time they joined Schofield at Goldsboro on March 23, the Federals had been surviving "precariously upon the collections of our foragers, our men 'dirty, ragged, and saucy,'" Sherman told Grant. Now at last he could rely on a combination of coastal shipping and railroads for supplies. The two forces combined totaled 80,000 men, so the demand on quartermasters and commissaries was great. Nevertheless, Sherman's subordinates discontinued their foraging parties—the day of the bummer was over.[60]

Using North Carolina Railroads

"As long as we move we can gather food and forage," Sherman declared to Grant, "but the moment we stop trouble begins." That trouble could only be solved by his quartermasters. The coastal-shipping link was not a problem, but rehabilitating wretched Southern railroads was difficult. McCallum ordered a division of the Construction Corps from Middle Tennessee to the Carolina coast. It left Nashville on January 4, reached Morehead City by February 5, and began to rebuild the Atlantic and North Carolina Railroad from that point for forty-four miles to Batchelder's Creek, just a few miles west of Union-occupied New Bern. Wright found that all sidings along the line were inadequate for handling the traffic he expected and the wharf at Morehead City was only half as big as needed. He found no more than three locomotives and sixty-two cars in working order, plus two locomotives and nine cars in need of repairs. Wright was forced to call for a good deal of rolling stock and other railroad material from the North.[61]

Wright plunged into one of the most difficult construction jobs of the war to make this line ready for Sherman. First he constructed a new wharf at Morehead City comprising 53,682 square feet of wood, making one and a quarter acres of flat space. Seven or eight coastal vessels could unload at this new wharf at the same time. Then moving along the Atlantic and North Carolina Railroad toward New Bern, his crews rebuilt a dozen bridges and relaid 111,100 railroad ties and thirty-three miles of new rails.[62]

A column of troops under Major General Jacob D. Cox advanced along the railroad from Morehead City, Wright's men keeping up with them as they worked. Cox's goal was to link with Schofield's column advancing from Wilmington along the line of the Wilmington and Weldon Railroad. Both columns were to join at Goldsboro and meet Sherman. Wright found that the Confederates had begun to take up rails and ties and to destroy water stations and bridges between Batchelder's Creek and Kinston on the Neuse River, a distance of twenty-five miles. Kinston was located a bit more than halfway between New Bern and Goldsboro. Wright obtained another division of the Construction Corps to help the one already on the job. Schofield also sent troops to cut 5,400 ties for Wright's use. With help such as this, Wright was able to repair the Atlantic and North Carolina Railroad to Kinston by March 20, rebuild the railroad bridge over the Neuse River three days later, and get the line running to Goldsboro by March 25, only two days after Sherman reached that city.[63]

After his march through the Carolinas, Sherman now relied on a fully functioning supply line with the outside world. Morehead City served as the focal point where coastal ships unloaded all manner of material for his enlarged army group, with the Atlantic and North Carolina Railroad carrying it all to New Bern and Goldsboro. "Every wheel we had was kept turning night and day" to get supplies to the army, as Wright put it. He could use only five locomotives and eighty-seven cars before April 1, adding only one more engine after that date.[64]

Sherman was convinced his strategic raids through Georgia and the Carolinas had accomplished a great deal. "I regard my two moves from Atlanta to Savannah & Savannah to Goldsboro as great blows as if we had fought a dozen successful Battles," he told his wife. But by the time his army group rested, refitted, and prepared to resume the march on April 10, the war had essentially ended. Grant broke Lee's line at Petersburg on April 2 and then pursued the fleeing Army of Northern Virginia until cornering it at Appomattox on the ninth. Its surrender signaled the collapse of organized Rebel resistance to the Federal government.[65]

Meanwhile, Sherman set out on April 10 and occupied Raleigh three days later without a fight. Only two or three days before the fall of the city, the Confederates had torn up eight miles of track and filled in several cuts, which delayed the task of rebuilding. Cars did not start to roll into the state capital until April 19, with two trainloads of supplies steaming up just behind the construction crews. Further delay ensued as Wright rebuilt bridges over Little River and Neuse River.[66]

The immediate needs of Sherman's army group were now satisfied. The Federals found additional railroad cars in Raleigh with enough locomotives to pull them. They had pressed into service a total of 262 railroad cars and an uncounted number of locomotives from different Southern lines since February to support Sherman's operations in North Carolina. Material continued to roll into Raleigh from Morehead City, which remained the primary base of supply for the army group. Easton allowed only staff officers and couriers to ride the cars so as to provide more shipping space for material. He also supplemented the flow of supplies by directing coastal shipping to unload grain at New Bern, where it was transferred to river steamers and barges for shipment to Kinston or to the Neuse River bridge. Wagons then hauled it from there to the army at Raleigh. In addition, 850 carloads of material unloaded from steamers at New Bern were shipped directly to Raleigh. And, after the Wilmington and Weldon Railroad was reopened on April 4, Easton used it to transport a small amount of material to Sherman from Wilmington, amounting to only 110 cars total by May 1. In contrast, Easton moved a total of 1,841 cars loaded with supplies from Morehead City to the troops by that same date.[67]

After Appomattox Sherman prepared for further moves against Johnston. He told Wright and Easton to plan how to support a drive toward Greensboro and Salisbury, but Wright warned him that he did not have enough rolling stock to do this. To compensate, Wright arranged a deal with the president of the Raleigh and Gaston Railroad on April 21. The line would loan the army four locomotives if the Federal government rebuilt the Cedar Creek bridge, but this became unnecessary after Johnston agreed to surrender terms on April 26. Easton continued to supply Sherman's army group in the Raleigh area until it marched for Virginia on the thirtieth.[68]

Wright's accomplishment was impressive. Moving construction crews from Middle Tennessee to the coast of North Carolina, he relied on whatever rolling stock could be found in the state, rebuilt track quickly, and met Sherman's host before its supply needs caused it to veer offcourse to seek relief. He resurrected a system of supply for one of the largest concentrations of Union manpower in the country. "In no railroad operations during the war was the efficiency of the military railroad organization more fully demonstrated than in North Carolina," Wright concluded a year later. Railroad historian Thomas Weber has called the work of Wright and Easton "a practically perfect small-scale demonstration of what could be done to supply an army in the field by rail."[69]

Deep South Strategy

It must be emphasized, however, that this "practically perfect" support took place in the Upper South over relatively short distances from the coast to Sherman's army group. As the Carolinas Campaign played itself out, other Federal commanders wrestled with the problem of penetrating the Deep South during the final months of the war. The region of central Alabama, especially along the Selma–Montgomery corridor, still remained untouched. By this stage of the conflict, that area had developed into a major industrial base for Confederate war production. The region had long been a potential target of the Federals, but how to get troops into it had always been the problem.

Neither Grant nor Halleck had any faith in Thomas's ability to conduct a deep penetration of central Alabama following the Battle of Nashville. Halleck suggested that Thomas defend Tennessee along the line of the Tennessee River while more aggressive commanders penetrate the Deep South. He suggested that Schofield's Twenty-Third Corps or A. J. Smith's Sixteenth Corps divisions reinforce Canby for a combined drive to take the port city of Mobile, followed by a march from that point to Selma and Montgomery. Halleck wanted to push operations as much as possible; the financial cost of the war was staggering, and the country could not afford to keep troops idle even during the winter months.[70]

Sherman had tried to urge Thomas on before he set out from Savannah. On January 21 he suggested taking 25,000 troops plus Wilson's Cavalry Corps from Eastport and Decatur to hit Columbus, Mississippi, and Tuscaloosa and Selma, Alabama.[71]

But Thomas found many excuses for not taking up Sherman's suggestion. The dirt roads of the region would become horrible in winter months, Schofield's command was taken away and shipped to North Carolina, while Smith's troops were taken away and sent to Canby. He suggested moving the Fourth Corps and Wilson's cavalry through East Tennessee in order to shield Sherman's flank during the Carolinas Campaign, then move on to Richmond to help Grant. There was no possibility that Grant would approve this. He became frustrated at Thomas's obstinacy. "There is no better man to repel an attack than Thomas," Grant had written to Halleck before the Battle of Nashville, "but I fear he is too cautious to ever take the initiative."[72]

Mobile

Canby moved before Thomas, mounting a large campaign against Mobile. The city had already been closed to blockade runners by Rear Adm. David G. Farragut, who had run his seagoing fleet past the forts guarding the entrance to Mobile Bay on August 5, 1864. The city itself lay on the northwest corner of the bay thirty miles from the entrance. If the Federals wanted to use Mobile as a jumping-off place to penetrate central Alabama, the city and its array of earthen defenses had to be taken.

Thomas agreed to send Wilson's cavalry south from its camps near Eastport, Mississippi, to divert Rebel attention. Grant wanted Canby to organize his force into two corps under Frederick Steele and A. J. Smith. "Both these officers have had experience in subsisting off the country through which they are passing," he wrote. Grant ordered Canby to prevent the citizens from planting their spring crop; to "destroy their railroads, machine shops &c"; and to collect all the able-bodied black men "before the enemy put them in their ranks." For the inland strike, "what is wanted is a Commander who will not be afraid to cut loose from his base of supplies and who will make the best use of the resources of the Country," Grant asserted.[73]

Canby managed the campaign with skill and caution. He assembled 45,200 men and transported them by coastal shipping from New Orleans in late February and early March 1865. By March 17 he was ready to advance from two places on the coast, with one column marching directly toward the southern fortified position on the east side of Mobile Bay (Spanish Fort), and another moving in a wide sweep from Pensacola toward the northern fortified position on the east bay (Blakeley). Because of a shortage of coastal vessels, Canby's quartermaster used eleven Mississippi River steamers to transport troops to the mouth of Mobile Bay. Only because the weather was calm and these craft hugged the coastline could this work. Even so, the frail rivercraft barely survived their trips along the coast. "Sudden and violent storms" forced repairs after each squall. These rivercraft also supported the Federal strike inland after the fall of Mobile by moving supplies along the Alabama and Tombigbee Rivers.[74]

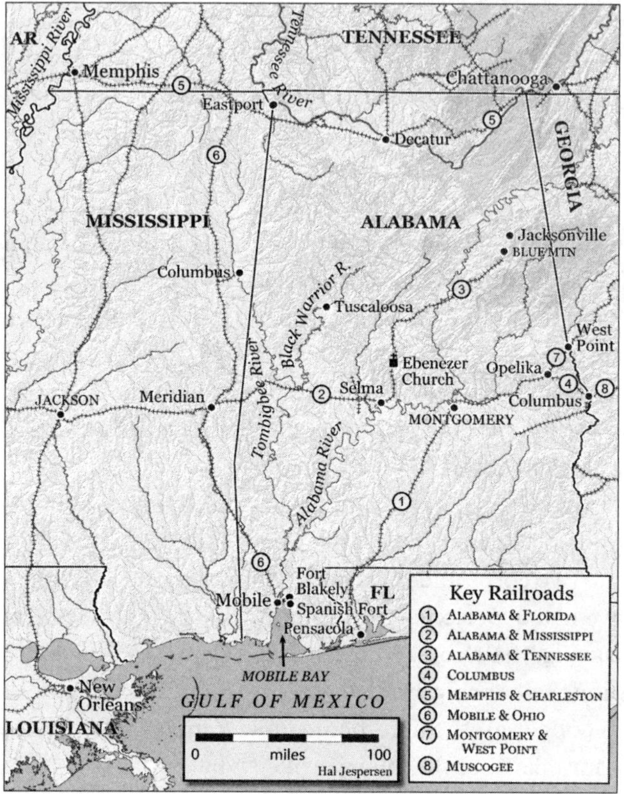

MOBILE AND WILSON'S RAID

Canby ran vessels between New Orleans and Mobile Bay and established depots on the coast to support his siege of Spanish Fort and Blakeley. But he also sent foraging expeditions into the coastal lowlands. Up to 10 percent of the manpower of every regiment was detailed to foraging. They were instructed to range widely across the countryside so as not to overburden civilians in any area, avoid the poorest people, and refrain from wanton destruction.[75]

The Confederates evacuated Spanish Fort on the night of April 8, and the Federals captured Blakely the next day by assault. On the twelfth Federal troops entered Mobile. Now Canby organized three columns to penetrate the interior of Alabama. Sixteenth Corps troops left the city on April 14 and started for Montgomery, 160 miles away. Benjamin H. Grierson led a force of 4,000 cavalrymen to screen the right flank of this column, leaving Blakeley on the seventeenth. By the time Grierson ended his tour of central Alabama, he had paroled more than 10,000 Confederate troops, secured 300,000 bales of cotton, and fed hundreds of destitute civilians from government stores shipped up the rivers from Mobile. Canby also sent Steele's command to Montgomery by steamer up the Alabama River, escorted by navy gunboats.[76]

Wilson's Raid

The infantry columns from Mobile met Wilson's Cavalry Corps, Military Division of the Mississippi. As early as February 23, Thomas had urged Wilson to plan a strike toward Selma to divert attention from Canby's operations. Initially the plan involved 5,000–6,000 troopers, but Wilson wanted to take his entire command and to not stop at Selma. Thomas and Grant gave him free rein, and Wilson mounted the largest cavalry raid of the war. He assembled 13,480 men in northern Alabama, which had been trammeled by the past two years of war. "In all directions for 120 miles there was almost absolute destitution," Wilson wrote. Only by shipping large amounts of forage and other necessities up the Tennessee River to the head of navigation at Eastport, Mississippi, could Wilson feed his command until ready to set out south.[77]

Each of Wilson's men carried five days' rations in their haversacks. In addition, his train of 250 wagons, escorted by 1,500 dismounted men, conveyed twenty-four pounds of grain for each horse, one hundred rounds of ammunition for each man, and one extra pair of shoes for every horse. Wilson also organized a pack train of mules because the wagon train might not be able to keep up with the troopers. Each mule carried five days' supply of hard bread and ten days' sugar, coffee, and salt, along with eighty rounds of ammunition.[78]

Wilson left his winter camps near Eastport on March 22 and moved southward, hitting industrial targets along the way. He fought several battles with Nathan Bedford Forrest's cavalry until capturing Selma on April 2. Wilson then decided there was little need to help Canby at Mobile. After resting and waiting for detached columns to rejoin his command, he set out for Montgomery, entering the state capital on April 12 without a battle. Canby's infantry reached Montgomery soon afterward. Wilson then continued to Columbus, Georgia, capturing the place and its important industries on the sixteenth, where confirmation that the war was ending reached his command.[79]

Wilson's raid devastated the heart of the Deep South. The first major Union incursion there also was the last, much of it taking place beyond the ending of the war. Wilson traveled 525 miles, captured 6,820 prisoners, and destroyed 100,000 small arms; twenty-one ironworks, foundries, and machine shops; two rolling mills; five collieries; thirteen factories; four niter works; three arsenals; a navy yard; a powder magazine; and five river steamers. His men also wrecked thirty-five locomotives and 565 railroad cars. By this stage of the conflict, the Confederates had few resources to protect these assets, while the Federals had overwhelming resources to find and destroy them.[80]

The Confederates had managed to restrict most of the fighting in the Civil War to their Upper South states. Even as late as December 1864, a major battle took place just south of Nashville. Except for the Union conquest of the Mississippi River and Sherman's penetration of north Georgia during the Atlanta Campaign, the Deep South was largely untouched by Union hands until the last months of the conflict. When the Yankees did come, they intensely destroyed military resources and food supplies. Sherman's March to the Sea and Carolinas Campaign, along with Wilson's raid, may have destroyed as many resources as all previous campaigns combined.

Western Railroads

Ironically, the Federals later repaired some of the damage they inflicted on the countryside for humanitarian reasons. When evidence of widespread starvation began to appear around Atlanta in the spring of 1865, Thomas authorized the rebuilding of the Western and Atlantic Railroad to ship government corn to the residents.[81]

This was no small or inexpensive job. Partially damaged by Johnston's retreating Rebels and restored by Sherman's construction crews during the Atlanta Campaign, Hood's army again tore up thirty-five and a half miles of it in October 1864. After quick repairs the Federals then destroyed the line from the Etowah River to Atlanta, leaving the track north of that river partly operational.

Starting on May 10, 1865, Leonard Eicholtz used 1,200 workmen to rebuild the road and was able to open it down to the Etowah River by June 1. But the line south of the Etowah had been thoroughly devastated. Eicholtz organized his men into a division dedicated to clearing away the debris, cutting timber, and straightening bent rails, while another division replaced track and still another rebuilt bridges. Even though the Etowah bridge had three spans down, it took the Federals only four days to repair it. On June 5 they started to work their way south toward Marietta. Eicholtz sent his bridge crews ahead to rebuild structures in time to meet the track crews as they completed their work. The line was open to Acworth by June 20, to Marietta nine days later, and to Atlanta by July 4. A private firm called Grant and Company rebuilt the railroad bridge over the Chattahoochee River at a cost of $15,670. Black troops also helped the Construction Corps by relaying some track, but Eicholtz thought they did a poor job of it.[82]

To put the much-abused Western and Atlantic Railroad back into operation, Eicholtz's crews cut 3,000 cubic feet of timber to provide the raw material for 42,000 ties. They also placed 14,794 rails of twenty feet length, using 1,140 kegs of railroad spikes to secure them to the ties. All told, the Federals rebuilt sixty-six and a half miles of track in less than two months. There was no military need for this project—it was entirely driven by humanitarian concerns. Moreover, the Western and Atlantic Railroad was given back to its prewar owner (the state of Georgia) on September 25, 1865, although Eicholtz thought the state should be forced to pay Grant and Company's bill for rebuilding the Chattahoochee River bridge. Wright estimated the government had spent a total of $2,569,318.69 on the line during the course of the war.[83]

The other important line constituting the main stem of logistical support in the West was the Nashville and Chattanooga Railroad. McCallum noted that 115 miles of its 151-mile extent had been completely refurbished at government expense from February 1864 to the end of the conflict. This was necessary because the original owners had constructed the line with out-of-date U-rails laid on stringers, which quickly deteriorated with the heavy loads the army needed. McCallum's subordinates put new ballast on the roadbed, new ties, and new rails along almost the entire length of the line. They also added many new sidings so there would be one at least every eight miles to accommodate the heaviest traffic possible. Each siding was long enough for five to eight "long freight trains," and most of them also had a telegraph station. Federal crews, in short, built a total of nineteen miles of new sidings along this line in addition to forty-five new water tanks. As W. J. Stevens, the general superintendent of military railroads in the West, put it, the line went "from one of the worst and least available" to "one of the best under my control." When the government restored the Nashville and Chattanooga Railroad to its prewar owners on September 15, 1865, the corporation received a line that was in far better shape than the one it had constructed.[84]

The rail line from Nashville to Decatur was in terrible shape after the Confederate offensives of 1864. In the last phase of his raid against Sherman's railroad, Wheeler had managed to get onto the track between Nashville and Columbia in early September and tear up "several miles" of it. Then Forrest hit the line in late September, burning many bridges and wrecking a good deal of track between Pulaski and Athens. The two raids combined destroyed almost thirty miles of the railroad. Federal crews repaired Wheeler's break between Nashville and Columbia, but the rest of the line had to wait until after the end of Hood's Tennessee Campaign. It then took two months for the Federals to restore that line from Columbia to Decatur, finishing by February 10, 1865. But in late February and early March, torrential rains washed away many of the new bridges. Construction crews had to rebuild them yet again, this time with "permanent truss bridges" that would withstand such natural forces. The line was restored to its owners on September 15, 1865.[85]

The East Tennessee and Georgia Railroad, linking Chattanooga with Knoxville, had been used by the Federals since it was fully repaired in April 1864. But the East Tennessee and Virginia Railroad between Knoxville and Bristol, Virginia, lay mostly in contested territory during the final year of the war. The Federals used part of it to establish forward positions in the region. They repaired the road up to Bull's Gap, fifty-six miles from Knoxville. When Grant urged Thomas to prepare for a push into the southwestern part of Virginia in case Lee abandoned his position at Petersburg and retreated to that area, repair crews were called into action. They began to work from Bull's Gap forward on March 4, 1865, and opened the line to Carter's Station, 110 miles from Knoxville, on April 23. By this time there was no longer a need to reopen the road. All told, the crews had completely relaid twelve miles of track and repaired another ninety-four miles that spring, in addition to rebuilding 4,400 feet of bridging. The army gave the East Tennessee and Virginia Railroad back to its owners on August 28, 1865.[86]

While military operations in the Upper South continued to be dominated by the need for creating and sustaining major lines of supply, operations in the Deep South witnessed the fulfillment of a dream in the minds of most high-level commanders in the Federal army. They had finally achieved the goal of creating large mobile columns that could smash through the protected regions of the inner South and deal a mortal blow to the rebellious states. Union forces had demonstrated an ability to move quickly, with minimal trains and baggage, and to live off the land as much as possible. They had achieved a high state of army mobility.

9

RAILS AND RIVERS IN THE TRANS-MISSISSIPPI

The Trans-Mississippi states of the Confederacy were on the margins of the Civil War, both geographically and demographically. Situated west of the great river and bordering the frontier, Arkansas, Louisiana, and Texas played the role of poor cousins to Cis-Mississippi states such as Virginia, Georgia, and Alabama. Ironically, the Trans-Mississippi constituted 49 percent of the Confederacy's square miles but contained only 20 percent of its population. That statistic highlights another important fact—the Trans-Mississippi states were relatively underdeveloped in terms of modern transportation facilities and of cultivation of arable land.

Large-scale military operations were, therefore, even more problematic west of the Mississippi than east of it. With fewer railroads, fewer farms, and seemingly trackless expanses, it represented an operational environment somewhere between the wilderness of the frontier and the largely settled regions of the Eastern Seaboard. The Trans-Mississippi is an interesting case study of military logistics and supply. The slave border state of Missouri should be included in any discussion of these topics, even though it never officially left the Union. Along with Arkansas and Louisiana, these three states witnessed most of the major campaigns that took place in the Trans-Mississippi.

Whether there could be much strategic influence on the general course of the war in this region is still a matter of debate. But at the very least the Federals needed to protect their access to the Mississippi River from Confederate attacks coming from the west. And they needed to hold at least the central part of Missouri, the Missouri River valley, to have access to Unionist Kansas and U.S. territories on the frontier. Any other areas of the Trans-Mississippi open to military occupation on a long-term basis were

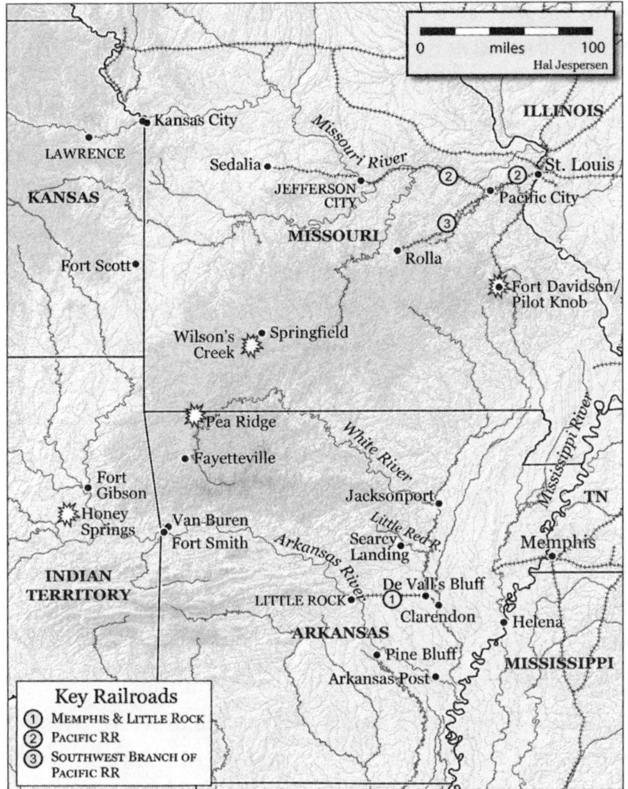

MISSOURI AND NORTH ARKANSAS

worth the effort to secure by Federal authorities if for no other reason than simply to plant the flag and rally loyalists to the Union cause.

Rails and rivers, or more properly the severe limitations of those lines of advance, dominated the logistical and supply story of the war west of the Mississippi. The Missouri River, which begins in the Rocky Mountain region, sweeps toward the southeast until reaching the western border of its namesake state, where it runs nearly due east to join the Mississippi just north of Saint Louis. The Missouri was the artery of advance for Brig. Gen. Nathaniel Lyon when he led a small force from Saint Louis to capture the state capital at Jefferson City in June 1861. Lyon then advanced southwest toward Springfield by overland marches. A railroad provided some hope of logistical support for his army in the southwestern part of the state. The Pacific Railroad started at Saint Louis and ran west to Jefferson City, but it provided a less reliable line of communications for Lyon than did the Missouri River. A line called the Southwest Branch of the Pacific Railroad broke off from this line at the small town of Pacific City, about one-third of the distance from Saint Louis to Jefferson City, and stretched southwest toward Rolla, located sixty miles from Pacific City and one hundred miles northeast of Springfield. Federal quartermasters made the South Pacific Railroad the primary logistical link between Saint Louis and Lyon's forces at Springfield, with wagon trains moving between Rolla and Springfield. When the Federals were defeated and Lyon killed at the Battle of Wilson's Creek on August 10, the Federals retired to Rolla, where they spent the winter of 1861–62.[1]

In Arkansas no major railroads offered Federal commanders an opportunity to enter the state. The Arkansas River flows southeast through the heart of the state and links Fort Smith in the western part of Arkansas with Little Rock near its center. Pine Bluff is located farther downstream from Little Rock, with Arkansas Post even farther down the river. The Arkansas joins the Mississippi about forty-five miles south of Helena, Arkansas, a town located about forty-five miles south of Memphis.

If the Arkansas River had reliably high levels of water most of the year, it could have served as a good line of invasion into the center of the state. But like most Trans-Mississippi rivers, the water levels fluctuated widely during the seasons. Most of the time they were too low for any but the smallest craft. During the spring-thawing season, water levels rose quickly and provided floating power for large boats—but only for a while.

The same was true of the White River, the only other major stream in the state. It flows southeast from Missouri and then nearly due south through the northeastern part of Arkansas until joining the Mississippi a few miles upstream from the mouth of the Arkansas. De Vall's Bluff, a small community on its west bank, is fifty-five miles up from the mouth of the White and forty miles due east of Little Rock. The Memphis and Little Rock Railroad linked De Vall's Bluff with the state capital, but one needed to use the White or the Arkansas to reach either point in order to make use of it.

In Louisiana the Red River cuts through the state much as the Arkansas slices through its namesake state. Flowing toward the southeast, the Red River links major towns such as Shreveport in the northwestern part of

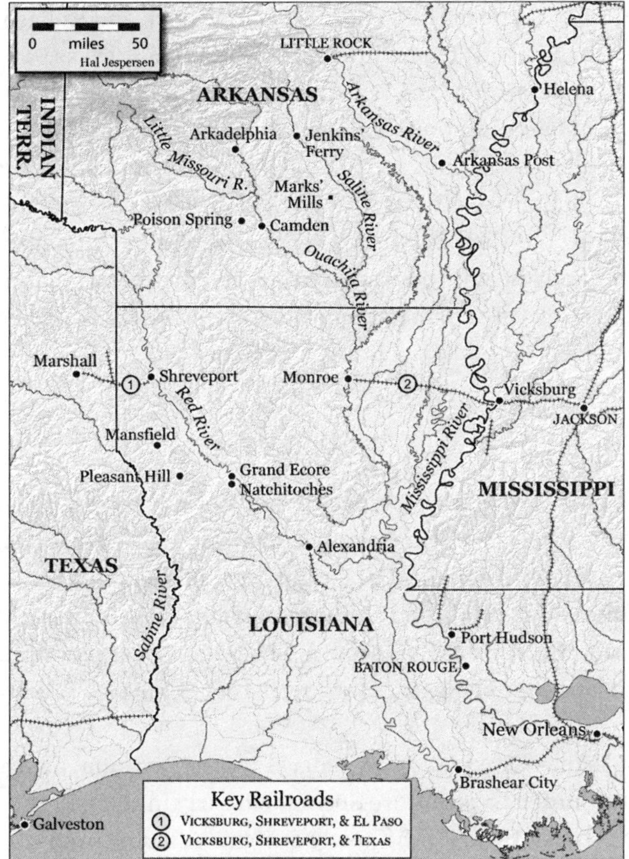

SOUTH ARKANSAS AND LOUISIANA

Louisiana with Alexandria, located 120 miles downstream. From Alexandria the river flows another forty miles to join the Mississippi at a point thirty-five miles south of Natchez, ninety miles south of Vicksburg, and thirty miles north of Port Hudson, Louisiana.

A railroad was under construction to link Shreveport with Vicksburg, but the onset of war curtailed its completion. The Vicksburg, Shreveport, and Texas Railroad started at a point across the Mississippi River from Vicksburg and went to Monroe, Louisiana, sixty-five miles due west. It was finished along this stretch, but no track had yet been laid on the 105-mile extension between Monroe and Shreveport. The line continued under the slightly modified name of the Vicksburg, Shreveport, and El Paso Railroad another forty miles west from Shreveport to Marshall, Texas.

With the exception of the Southwest Branch of the Pacific Railroad and the incomplete Vicksburg, Shreveport, and Texas Railroad, no rail line offered the Federals a hope of supporting campaigns into the Trans-Mississippi. Several major rivers flowed in the right direction and connected with the Mississippi, but they were not usable most of the year. Federal armies would have to rely heavily on wagon trains and feeding from the countryside, but the relatively sparse population offered only bleak prospects in that regard.

Pea Ridge Campaign

During the summer of 1861, before the Battle of Wilson's Creek, Lyon's army of 10,000 men rested at Springfield, Missouri. Federal quartermasters supported it with depots at Rolla and other places along the Southwest Branch of the Pacific Railroad and wagon trains running 100 miles from Rolla to reach the army at Springfield. The region was "mountainous and barren," according to Chester Harding. "Teams have to take their own forage."[2]

After Wilson's Creek and the Federal retreat to Rolla, another major thrust was mounted to recapture Springfield early in 1862. Brig. Gen. Samuel R. Curtis took charge of the newly designated Army of the Southwest. Giving instructions to Col. Eugene A. Carr, slated to lead a cavalry thrust beyond Rolla, Curtis told him to "carefully husband your supplies . . . using whatever you can procure on the way." Ironically, Curtis also forced his officers to give up large amounts of stores accumulated during the winter because the army "had thus become unmovable." His quartermaster took away more than 200 wagonloads of material to lighten the trains in preparation for a winter campaign.[3]

Henry W. Halleck, Curtis's superior in Saint Louis, supported his efforts to streamline the command. "Cut down regimental transportation as much as possible," he wrote. "Get as many hand-mills as you can for grinding corn." Halleck feared that the Southwest Branch of the Pacific Railroad would "break down" under the strain of feeding Curtis's small army of 12,000 men. The company was "greatly distressed for money to pay their operatives and fear a strike."[4]

"We must strip for a forced march and final conflict," Curtis told his men. He wanted the wagon train to carry six days' rations of "hard bread, flour, hominy, rice, desiccated potatoes, and mixed vegetables, sugar, coffee, and salt. Pinole (ground parched corn and sugar) ought to be procured." Curtis instructed his commissaries to obtain fresh pork and beef if they could find any along the way. The beef should be jerked to make it last longer and carried more conveniently in haversacks.[5]

Because of these preparations, and because he led a small column by Civil War standards, Curtis achieved a resounding success. Starting on February 10, he outmaneuvered the Confederates and captured Springfield. Then, continuing the advance despite harsh winter weather, Curtis entered northwest Arkansas and established himself near Pea Ridge, thirty miles north of Fayetteville. Confederate forces combined with pro-Confederate Missouri State Guard troops to form the Army of the West under the command of Maj. Gen. Earl Van Dorn, who attacked Curtis at Pea Ridge on March 7 but was repulsed. Curtis mounted a counterattack the next day that drove the Rebels from the field, making a significant Union victory out of the Battle of Pea Ridge.[6]

After that success, Curtis's logistical problems did not change much. He was still dependent on the Southwest Branch of the Pacific Railroad (60 miles long), and a wagon-train link between Rolla and his army in the field (stretching 175 miles). "Some exertion is required to avoid the alternative which is constantly presented, starve or steal," he told one of Halleck's staff officers. Curtis needed enough usable wagons or his army could not survive. Halleck had to admit that the supply of wagons was limited due to heavy demands for them from Grant's operations in West Tennessee, but he scrambled to find some for Curtis.[7]

Curtis's Little Rock Campaign

The transfer of Van Dorn's Army of the West from Arkansas to Tennessee opened the possibility of Curtis advancing toward Little Rock, even though he was dependent on a supply line that would lengthen as he marched. Halleck arranged for a supporting column of 5,000 men under Brig. Gen. Frederick Steele to move 150 miles from Pilot Knob, Missouri, into northeast Arkansas. He urged Steele to take only "small stores" along in his wagons (meaning sugar, salt, etc.), and rely on the countryside for meat, forage, and flour. Steele's quartermaster should take along cash for immediate payment of needed supplies, but if the money ran out, he could issue certificates for future reimbursement. "If the people will not sell at reasonable prices or if you have no money to pay, you will make forcible requisitions." Halleck advised him to arrange a mix of wagons and pack mules to increase his mobility. Steele estimated he could find at least half rations of meat and flour in the country. He reached Jacksonport on the White River by May 4. Two days earlier Curtis had reached Batesville, a few miles upstream.[8]

The Federal approach to Little Rock was based on a precarious line of communications. By late May Curtis stopped in the area of Searcy Landing on the Little Red River, forty-five miles northeast of the state capital. Carr explained the situation to Sen. Lyman Trumbull of Illinois when he noted that over 250 miles separated the Federal rail head at Rolla from Little Rock, with a few dozen wagons providing the only link to the Army of the Southwest. "In this region, we are obliged to carry on war on purely American principles," he told Trumbull. "Our deep lines of communication, the absence of Depots and magazines, the sparseness of the settlements, . . . [create] the necessity of taking what we can get in the way of arms, ammunition, food, clothing camp equipage, and all the material of war."[9]

The Federals failed to capture Little Rock at this time because of their logistics problems. It was impossible to supply the Army of the Southwest all the way from Rolla, Missouri, to central Arkansas by wagon trains. After combining with Steele's column, Curtis cut his supply line and marched seventy-five miles toward Helena on the Mississippi to make contact with river steamers. He fed his men off the countryside before reaching Helena by July 12.[10]

Curtis considered another try at Little Rock after settling in at Helena but decided against it. He had inadequate wagon transportation and felt that securing the Mississippi River as far to the south as possible was more important. "All my generals concurred with me in the necessity of establishing our power on the river . . . before we depart" for the interior, Curtis reported to Halleck early in August.[11]

Steele's Little Rock Campaign

Steele mounted a second drive toward Little Rock more than a year after the Army of the Southwest reached Helena. Much had changed during the course of that year. Grant had captured Vicksburg on July 4, 1863, and soon after Steele, who had commanded a division in the Army of the Tennessee, was given the task of moving against Little Rock. This decision was sparked by a failed attack on Helena on July 4, which alerted Federal commanders to the danger of ignoring Rebel troops in the state. It sparked a series of moves that restarted Federal efforts to dominate Arkansas.

John M. Schofield, commander of the Department of the Missouri, suggested to Grant that an advancing force could use the Arkansas River as a line of communication. Alternatively, it could steam up the White River to De Vall's Bluff and use the Memphis and Little Rock Railroad to reach the state capital. The wagon road that paralleled the rail line also could be used if the rolling stock of the company proved inadequate. Grant did not think the Arkansas River would have enough water to support the kind of steamers needed by Steele, but the White River up to De Vall's Bluff would do. Schofield began to send 500 wagons and teams for the column, which was to consist of troops from the Department of the Tennessee. Grant felt he could spare the men more readily than Schofield.[12]

Steele arrived at Helena by July 31 to begin preparations. He commanded 12,000 men; nearly half of them were mounted troops. Steele began to move the cavalry overland toward Little Rock on August 17 by way of Clarendon, a town fifty miles northwest of Helena, sixty miles east of Little Rock, and thirty-five miles south of De Vall's Bluff. Steele moved his infantry by steamer up the White River to De Vall's Bluff by the twenty-third and began to construct depots and fortifications to turn the tiny settlement into his forward base.[13]

The Memphis and Little Rock Railroad had only one locomotive and a "few cars" available, so Steele asked Maj. Gen. Stephen A. Hurlbut to send more from Memphis. The level of the White River dropped steadily during September. By the third week of the month, it was too low for most steamers even up to De Vall's Bluff.[14]

Nevertheless, Steele pushed ahead. His infantry left De Vall's Bluff on September 1 but could not rely on the railroad to haul everything it needed—extra cars did not arrive for several weeks. His quartermasters relied on wagon trains to support the infantry advance. The Federal cavalry also relied on wagon trains as it moved cross-country from Clarendon. The two columns joined at Brownsville on September 2 and reached the Arkansas River downstream from Little Rock five days later. Steele planned an effective approach toward the city, crossing his cavalry to the south of the river as his infantry approached from the north. This combination threatened the Confederate line of retreat, and the city fell on September 10.[15]

The capture of Little Rock took place after a successful campaign by Federal troops farther west. Maj. Gen. James G. Blunt took command of a Union column at Fort Gibson, Indian Territory, on June 11. He defeated the Confederates in battle at Honey Springs on July 17 and moved against Fort Smith, just inside the Arkansas border and on the south bank of the Arkansas River. He maneuvered the small Confederate garrison out of the fort without a battle on September 1. Nine days later, when Little Rock fell, the entire length of the Arkansas River was in Federal hands, severing central Arkansas from the Confederacy.[16]

Relying on the Arkansas River

Now began the problem of supplying Union garrisons at Little Rock and Fort Smith. "Arkansas River is frozen over," reported Brig. Gen. John McNeil on January 4, 1864. Horses could walk over the frozen stream and six inches of snow covered the ground. McNeil's troops at Fort Smith were on half rations of bread, and even at that had enough to last only one week. He suggested that Union quartermasters assemble loaded boats at the mouth of the Arkansas ready to steam up as soon as the weather warmed. Three weeks later Adolf Engelmann informed his sister that the river was not yet navigable even up to Little Rock. The Memphis and Little Rock Railroad proved to be inadequate for the support of the city's garrison, forcing the troops to live on half or three-quarter rations for months. The difference was that last fall the countryside had provided good foraging opportunities, and now it was largely stripped bare.[17]

Provisioning river posts through central Arkansas depended a great deal on the state of the river. Capt. John R. Graton of the 1st Kansas Colored Infantry, stationed at Roseville forty miles downstream from Fort Smith, watched eagerly for every rain shower. He heard that three steamers were waiting seventy miles downriver from Roseville for a sudden increase in the water flow. But these rises often were accompanied by equally sudden decreases. If that happened, the boats could be stuck at either Little Rock or Fort Smith for many months. J. V. Lewis, a quartermaster at Memphis, reported that, given the threat of guerrilla attacks, naval officers refused to let any boats ascend the Arkansas unless they were protected by gunboats.

That only complicated the supply arrangements along this shallow and eccentric river.[18]

Throughout February, the river strengthened its reputation for unreliability. When a convoy of eleven boats entered the Arkansas from the Mississippi, three of them grounded at different places between Pine Bluff and the capital. The smallest steamer in the convoy grounded five miles short of Little Rock. The rest of the boats were compelled to unload their stores at Pine Bluff as quartermasters tried to find wagons to haul their material the rest of the way to the capital. A herd of 200 cattle left at Pine Bluff by the convoy was captured by Confederates before it walked to Little Rock. Forage for animals proved to be a bigger problem for the garrison than human food. Half of Steele's draft animals had already starved to death by late February. "The Arkansas has been a miserable stream," Engelmann complained to his sister.[19]

Samuel R. Curtis, now commander of the Department of Kansas, suggested that quartermasters stockpile supplies at depots along the Arkansas whenever high water allowed them to compensate for the low-water seasons. "It is only a few days or weeks in a year that the upper Arkansas can be navigated," he lectured a quartermaster at Fort Scott, who also was dependent on the river. In a theoretical sense this was sage advice, but in a practical sense it was virtually impossible to accomplish. The few weeks of navigation barely allowed quartermasters to get up to daily standard rations, much less to stockpile food and feed the troops and animals at the same time.[20]

"As a river—the Arkansas is a Humbug," concluded Adolf Engelmann once again in late March. "Now it will barely float a flatboat. I have 110 men guarding boats aground on sand bars." R. B. Brown, a quartermaster serving in the District of Southwest Missouri, fully agreed. "Twenty years' acquaintance" with the Arkansas and White Rivers led him to conclude "that, at best, they will furnish a doubtful source of supply, and cannot be calculated upon as means of transportation for any considerable period of time in the year."[21]

Yet the Federals had no choice but to rely on the Arkansas River. When the water did rise, it created an air of excitement and feverish activity to take advantage of every day. On May 26 Brig. Gen. John M. Thayer at Fort Smith telegraphed his superior that the river rose three feet the night before. "There is every indication that it will be navigable through June. Now is the time to get supplies to this post." Forage for animals was exhausted in the area around Fort Smith, and Thayer hoped to accumulate eight months' worth of it. Two days later he informed a colleague that "the river is in good boating condition. We have nothing to fear if we have supplies." In addition to feeding his own troops, Thayer had to care for about a thousand destitute refugees from the area. He could not feed them, so he decided to send some of them to Fort Scott in Kansas and others downstream on empty boats to Little Rock.[22]

The Arkansas gave quartermasters another rise in the water level during December 1864. This led to frantic orders for tons of material to be shipped immediately, sucking the flow of supplies up the river channel. Thayer wanted 120,000 pounds of hard bread, 9,600 pounds of coffee, 18,000 pounds of sugar, and 5,000 pounds of salt shipped to Fort Smith "as soon as possible." Even so, the water level did not allow boats to pass a point called Moore's Rocks twenty miles below Van Buren, but Thayer was determined to haul the stores by wagon the rest of the way. "If I do not receive commissaries from Little Rock I will be without rations for at least five days" before an emergency wagon train of supplies was due to reach him from Fort Scott.[23]

With drafts on the supply system like this, it is no surprise that steamboats loaded with food and forage bypassed many lesser posts farther downstream. Brig. Gen. Powell Clayton, a cavalry commander at Pine Bluff, complained of being neglected. "Our horses are absolutely perishing for want of long forage," he reported, yet nine-tenths of the forage shipped up the Arkansas was diverted to posts upstream from Pine Bluff. "Last winter the fleet brought up a large amount of hay," Powell told Steele. "Our half-starved horses looked at it as it passed by with longing eyes, but not a mouthful did they get."[24]

Engelmann noted that a dozen steamers had made it up to Little Rock by December 30, 1864, and were unloading their stores. But the Arkansas was "again falling very fast and the boats will have to be in a hurry if they want to get out again."[25]

Quartermasters could not rely on the Memphis and Little Rock Railroad to compensate for the river's defects. By the end of the war the line was "in very bad condition," wrote Daniel McCallum, "in consequence of the nature of the soil and neglect or want of skill in keeping up the necessary repairs." In fact, it was the only railroad in the Trans-Mississippi that the U.S. Military Railroad operated.[26]

Federal commanders charged with holding posts in the Trans-Mississippi had to accept the fact that their men and animals hardly ever enjoyed full rations. If not for the sparse pickings in an increasingly denuded countryside, they would have starved altogether. Logistical and supply conditions shaped the nature of operations in the Trans-Mississippi. Large troop movements were rare, but mobile concentrations of mounted troops that could move across the landscape without staying in one place very long were common. Small garrisons at permanent posts rather than large concentrations at one place were the rule.

Rivers had to bear the weight of supply in the Trans-Mississippi, but they were inadequate to the task. Even the tributaries that drained into the Mississippi from the east were reliable only for certain distances upstream. The Mississippi basin supplied one fully reliable river, the main stem itself, and only partially usable watercourses east and west.

Red River Campaign

Despite the logistical and supply problems, Federal authorities sanctioned a large campaign deep into the Trans-Mississippi while relying solely on a tributary river. The Red River campaign of March and April 1864 was launched with only a slim logistical chance of succeeding. Halleck cited the need to shorten lines of control across the occupied portion of the Trans-Mississippi and the desire to "secure the navigation of the Mississippi from interruption from the western side, and to prevent any large forces from penetrating into Arkansas, Missouri, or the Indian Territory." He hoped afterward to thin the garrisons at Mississippi River towns and free more troops for active operations elsewhere.[27]

Sherman was dismayed by the campaign. "The whole movement on Red River was predicated on the fact of high water and prompt movements," he wrote. But Maj. Gen. Nathaniel Banks, who commanded the expedition, had to rely on wagon trains to hedge against the limitations of the river, and that slowed his movement. "Small boats navigate the Red up as far as Shreveport all June and July," Sherman told Rear Adm. David D. Porter, based on his personal knowledge of the area, "but the big boats cannot venture above Alexandria later than May."[28]

This information was important to Porter because he led a large contingent of gunboats up the Red in cooperation with Banks. The narrow, shallow stream would have to support a sizeable fleet of civilian steamers in addition to the warships, and all of these vessels had to take advantage of whatever window of opportunity the water level presented. Porter kept a keen eye on the river before the onset of the campaign in early March 1864. It was very low, with no more than four feet of water over a bar located four miles up from its mouth. Heavy boats could not negotiate that level. "All we can hope for is a rise," Porter told Sherman.[29]

Banks allowed each regiment in his 32,000-man force to have two six-mule teams and wagons plus two ambulances, double the allowance Sherman stipulated for his army group during the Atlanta Campaign. Banks's men would start with five days' provisions, which included only half the allotted amount of most categories in the official ration but full amounts of coffee and salt.[30]

By mid-March the water level had risen enough to allow boats to operate on the river. S. B. Holabird, Banks's chief quartermaster, saw to the creation of storehouses at Alexandria, where he wanted to accumulate at least 600,000 rations. He planned to use the larger boats up to this city but only lighter boats between it and Shreveport. The Right Wing of the Sixteenth Corps under A. J. Smith traveled on its own fleet of fifteen transports, carrying along thirty days' rations for the men but scouring the countryside for animal forage. For the time being, the river was cooperating with the Federals. Five feet of water flowed over the rapids just upstream from Alexandria, enough for all boats, including the warships. By March 20 there were forty-seven transports unloading material at Alexandria, although the levee was "very bad for landing stores," according to one of Banks's quartermasters.[31]

The rapids located just above Alexandria posed a major obstacle, but on March 21 Porter estimated that six feet one inch of water covered them and that the current flowed at a rate of six miles per hour. Four days later it had risen to seven feet and was expected to remain at a minimum of six feet for more than a week. Banks's staff also estimated that by this date enough food had been brought to Alexandria to constitute eighteen days' rations for the army. With all these hopeful signs, Banks unwisely decided to leave the Red River by marching to Natchitoches, fifty-six miles to the northwest of Alexandria and seventy-five miles southeast of Shreveport, as the best way to approach his target city. Charles P. Stone, Banks's chief of staff, believed the quartermasters could find enough forage in the countryside to fill one-third of the ration for the army's horses and mules, but the rest would have to be shipped from New Orleans to Alexandria and then hauled to the advancing troops.[32]

As the infantry left Alexandria, slowed down by its large wagon train, Federal quartermasters and commissaries began to move material sixty miles upstream from Alexandria to Grand Ecore. They planned to store 440,000 rations there and 400,000 at Alexandria so that Banks's army would have enough food to last two weeks at either location. Commissaries at New Orleans were told to gather another 800,000 rations at that city for shipment to the army in a couple of weeks.[33]

As the campaign progressed, Banks's supply line lengthened. "You must be prepared for very heavy transportation of subsistence and ordnance stores from New Orleans to the upper Red River," Stone told Holabird on April 4. The strain began to tell three days later. The water level fell slowly over the rapids upstream from Alexandria, causing quartermasters to hesitate about risking boats in the passage. They also noted that the army's wagon train stretched fifteen miles along the dirt roads of Louisiana, roads that were rapidly become "awful" with ruts and mud holes. Mules also were becoming worn out struggling with their loads. Wagon masters ordered drivers to throw out tents and other material to lighten the wagons by one-third so the trains could keep moving.[34]

Then the campaign took a disastrous turn. Banks failed to keep the elements of his force within supporting distance of each other, and Maj. Gen. Richard Taylor, the Confederate commander opposing him, took advantage of it. With 8,800 men, Taylor defeated 7,000 Union troops in battle three miles southeast of Mansfield on April 8, capturing twenty guns and 150 wagons. The Federals retreated to Pleasant Hill, seventeen miles to the southeast, where they met reinforcements. On the ninth Taylor also received reinforcements and offered battle with 12,000 Confederates against an equal number of Federals. This time Union forces repulsed Taylor's men, but Banks retreated to Grand Ecore that night, giving up all hope of reaching Shreveport.

Banks lost 3,500 casualties and a huge amount of stores and transportation in the two battles. Once settled at Grand Ecore, he called for more food to be shipped from Alexandria, but the river now was falling at the rate of four inches every day. Quartermasters scrambled to find light-draft vessels and send them to Alexandria.[35]

The boats already upstream from the rapids that lay near Alexandria were having difficulty navigating the falling water level. Many of them had already steamed upriver from Grand Ecore and now retraced their path to join Banks's army at that place instead. Brig. Gen. Thomas Kilby Smith, an infantry officer on board one of the boats taking A. J. Smith's command downstream, watched as vessels ran aground, broke their rudders and paddlewheels, and were fired upon from the banks by roving Confederate cavalry. The fleet was delayed an entire day when one large boat, the *John Warner,* ran aground in midstream on April 13. "The river was exceedingly narrow and torturous," Kilby Smith reported, "the bottom covered with logs and snags, and the banks full of drift, rendering the navigation most difficult and dangerous." The Federals were lucky not to lose a single transport in this perilous retreat to Grand Ecore.[36]

Porter was caught up in this worsening crisis with eleven gunboats and twenty-six transports. Upon reaching Grand Ecore, another ten transports were added to his worries. On April 19 Banks decided to evacuate Grand Ecore and retreat to Alexandria, which meant that all the vessels had to go with him. Quartermaster D. N. Welch had twenty-six steamers below the rapids at Alexandria and another thirteen transports above, which he had to unload before hoping to get them downstream over the shallow passage. As of April 23, Welch reported losing only one boat, which hit a snag so hard that it "tore out her bottom." He hired "a falls pilot" who seemed essential in his effort to save the transports. For the time being, there were enough rations stored at Alexandria to feed Banks's men, but already by the twenty-third guerrillas were shooting at steamers twenty-five miles downstream from Alexandria. "Affairs do not look promising at all," Welch frankly told Holabird, who had by now gone back to New Orleans. "Everything has the appearance of a failure in the object of the expedition, provided it had one."[37]

In the retreat from Grand Ecore to Alexandria, discipline in the Federal ranks deteriorated. The men plundered indiscriminately, and the Nineteenth Corps commander offered a reward of $500 to any soldier willing to testify as to the guilty parties. As Taylor followed up the Union retreat, he was appalled at the destruction that "exceeds anything in history," he reported. "For many miles every dwelling-house, every negro cabin, every cotton-gin, every corn-crib, and even chicken-houses have been burned to the ground; every fence torn down and the fields torn up by the hoofs of horses and wheels of wagons. Many hundreds of persons are utterly without shelter."[38]

The key problem for the Federals lay in the rapids upstream from Alexandria. The water level by late April had fallen so much that there was a real prospect of having to destroy the gunboats and remaining transports stuck above the falls. But the situation was saved by Lt. Col. Joseph Bailey of the 4th Wisconsin, a civil engineer before the war. He proposed a plan to construct a series of dams above and below the falls to funnel the water and raise its level enough to get the boats over the rapids. With infantry details to provide the labor, along with teams of mules and even oxen to haul material, Bailey worked feverishly on his plan. He estimated, as of May 4, that it would take ten days to finish the project.[39]

For the time being, Alexandria seemed to hold enough food to feed the 39,000 men now congregated at that city after Maj. Gen. John A. McClernand brought up boatloads of reinforcements to help Banks on April 26. Twenty-one days' rations were available, but quartermasters were told to ship even more in case of necessity. The transports up the Red River could only move in convoys protected by gunboats because of guerrilla attacks. Food for men seemed to be no problem, but forage for animals was becoming "a serious one." By May 6, Confederate artillery had been placed at two or three spots along the Red River, and several transports were lost or seriously damaged.[40]

The accumulation of vessels upstream of the rapids compelled Banks to remain at Alexandria longer than he wanted. By May 9 the water was rising in an encouraging manner thanks to the dams, and Porter urged Banks to have patience. It was better to have the horses and mules suffer due to lack of forage for a few days rather than to lose even one of the eleven warships then north of the rapids. These boats began to pass the obstacle because Bailey had increased the water level by six and a half feet. Six of the gunboats passed by May 11, and the rest were over by the end of the next day. The crisis was over.[41]

Even though Banks had lost 175 wagons and 920 mules during the campaign, his wagon train still stretched for twelve miles along the road as his army retreated from Alexandria. Although Banks had only 900 wagons when he had advanced toward Shreveport, due to replacement vehicles and those of the fresh units that joined him later in the campaign, the train now contained 976 wagons and 105 ambulances. With the draft animals plus cavalry mounts and artillery horses, 12,000 animals accompanied the retreat.[42]

Banks's drive up the Red River was the largest campaign in the Trans-Mississippi. It foundered on inadequate means of transportation. The Red River simply was unreliable as a line of communications, and everyone knew it before the campaign started. Union commanders gambled that the boats could take advantage of a window of opportunity when nature cooperated with Federal military plans. How the vessels could be expected to remain so far up the river after the fall in water level never was explained, and Banks made the situation far worse by his delays and inept handling of the enterprise.

Steele's Camden Expedition

Banks had hoped for support from troops marching from Little Rock under Frederick Steele, who was burdened by even worse logistical problems. Steele was compelled to march his 7,000 men 200 miles toward Shreveport through a region already visited by contending armies. His only logistical supports were wagons and the mules that pulled them. "The roads are most if not quite impracticable," he warned Halleck, and "the country is destitute of provision on the route we should be obliged to take." The troops carried only two days' rations, a blanket, a poncho, one shirt, one pair of socks, and forty rounds of ammunition. He allowed one wagon for each regiment, half the allotment of Banks's troops and the same as Sherman allowed for his army group in Georgia.[43]

Steele left Little Rock on March 23, but his quartermasters found no animal forage for the first leg of the journey to Arkadelphia. The forage brought out from Little Rock was consumed in four days. After reaching Arkadelphia on March 29, Steele waited for several days as details managed to find some forage in the area. He wanted his men to gather provisions, too, but instructed them to leave something behind for the civilians and to give proper receipts. "The taking of household stuff or the immediate provisions of families is nothing less than downright robbery," read Steele's order. But the need to forage was imperative. "The greatest danger in this expedition is that our horses and mules will starve enroute," reported Engelmann. "We are to live off the land as we go and it has already been stripped bare by the war."[44]

Resuming the march from Arkadelphia, another column under John M. Thayer from the Department of Kansas joined Steele at the crossing of the Little Missouri River, twenty miles southwest of town. Consisting of only nine regiments and two batteries, but 300 wagons, Thayer's column was bloated with transportation, some regiments having twenty-two wagons. Such an allotment would slow any column, and Capt. Charles A. Henry, Steele's chief quartermaster, convinced the general to reduce Thayer's train to a more manageable level. The combined columns reached Camden by April 15 after considerable skirmishing. The Federals lost no wagons, but 200 animals collapsed or died due to the hard pulling they exerted along the swampy roads. Henry counted 800 wagons and 12,000 animals when he reached Camden, and it would not be an easy matter to feed them.[45]

Hearing reports that the area had corn to spare, Henry sent large foraging parties, heavily escorted by troops, to find it. The day after reaching town, 177 wagons traveled sixteen miles. The Federals found much corn that had been burned by the enemy but nevertheless filled 141 wagons with usable grain. On its return journey, the train was attacked by Confederate troops near Poison Spring, sixteen miles west of Camden, on April 18. After a sharp fight the Confederates defeated the escort and captured or destroyed many of the wagons.[46]

The battle at Poison Spring proved that relying on wagon trains would be unusually dangerous during this campaign, but waterways failed to provide an alternative. The Ouachita River was large enough to allow a small steamer to reach Camden, but the narrow stream also provided ample opportunities for the enemy to fire on boats. Confederate troops captured a steamer loaded with 3,000 bushels of corn thirty miles downstream from Camden on April 16.[47]

Henry continued to find some forage in the countryside. His details discovered caches of corn, and the captain operated every mill within reach to grind it. A train of 150 wagons from Pine Bluff, sixty miles northeast of Camden, arrived on April 20 with enough provisions to feed Steele's men for ten days at half rations. Federal patrols also captured 5,000 bushels of corn on a Confederate steamer named *Homer*. Still, the net result of all this was bare survival for Steele's men and animals. He concluded it would be impossible to continue to Shreveport.[48]

In fact, Steele's situation was far worse than he realized. The general would be lucky to get his command out of the Arkansas wilderness intact. Henry took the 150 wagons from Pine Bluff, added 61 wagons already in Camden, and sent the 211 vehicles with an escort of 1,600 infantry, 400 cavalry, and four guns. The train set out from Camden on April 22, heading back to Pine Bluff for more supplies, but 6,000 Confederate cavalry attacked it near Marks' Mills, thirty miles north of Camden on April 25. Again a sharp fight resulted in Federal defeat. This time 1,300 members of the escort and the entire train were captured.[49]

By striking at the enemy's vulnerable supply line rather than Steele's fortified position at Camden, the Confederates achieved one of the most devastating logistical victories of the war. Steele felt it was impossible to feed his men and animals at Camden and decided to retreat to Little Rock.[50]

While Steele dallied in the heart of the Arkansas wilderness at the end of a vulnerable line of supply, his superiors scrambled to provide help. Halleck asked Robert Allen at Saint Louis if he could get small boats up the Ouachita River, which Allen thought might be possible. Rivermen told him that the Ouachita was navigable when the Red River was high, but he refused to order boats into the stream until he could find out what Steele needed. By that time the Federals had decided to leave Camden, and there was not enough water in the Ouachita anyway.[51]

At Little Rock Federal quartermasters assembled a train of sixty wagons loaded with supplies, although they had to seize horses and mules from the area. Col. Christopher C. Andrews took charge of an escort of four regiments, some cavalry, and two batteries, totaling 2,200 men. He had instructions to feed his men and animals from the countryside so as not to reduce the 30,000 rations and forage carried in the wagons. But even before the train left Little Rock, a dispatch arrived that Steele had evacuated Camden.[52]

Steele's retreat became a minor epic of endurance for the Federals. Henry's biggest problem was that his draft animals were undernourished. He left most of them behind and destroyed ninety-two wagons because he did not have enough teams to pull them. The 43rd Illinois, consisting of 428 men, received three-quarter rations of coffee for four days, full rations of salt and sugar, but only a quarter ration of bacon just before leaving Camden on the night of April 26. Within four days most of this was consumed, and the men got by "almost exclusively on coffee," according to Engelmann. Col. John A. Garrett, commander of the 40th Iowa, reported that his troops "had a coffee supper on the night of the 29th" and "a coffee breakfast, a part getting a little meat, on the morning" of the thirtieth.[53]

The Federals were compelled to conduct a difficult, fighting retreat on these slender rations. A large force of pursuing Confederates caught up with Steele at the crossing of the Saline River near Jenkins' Ferry, forty miles north of Camden, on April 30. Here a critical battle developed as Steele's engineers tried to deploy an old India-rubber pontoon bridge one last time. It had been issued to Steele when he moved south from Pilot Knob in 1862 to join Curtis in Arkansas and was nearly worn out. The structure held up enough to enable Steele to cross his troops while his rear guard repelled vigorous attacks on the bridgehead that rainy day. By winning the Battle of Jenkins' Ferry, the Federals saved themselves and turned the corner in this dismal campaign.[54]

From the Saline River to Little Rock, a distance of thirty-five miles, the only thing the Federals had to contend with was starvation. Rations had essentially disappeared, so Henry destroyed many of the wagons. He retained enough to carry ordnance stores and headquarters records and baggage, and of course he kept the ambulances. But the Federal column was now stripped down to only 200 wagons, an unusually low number for 8,000 men.[55]

Setting out from the Saline River on April 30, the Federals had to march fast. "Though we hurried as much as possible our men nearly starved to death," reported Engelmann, "and the 1000 dead horses and mules lying between here and the Saline show the necessity of burning our trains. If we had not—we all—men and animals would have stuck in the swamp on the Saline and starved."[56]

Steele counted himself lucky as his hungry men marched into Little Rock on May 4. "The whole command had been on short rations during the whole campaign," he told Halleck, "except when occasionally supplies could be obtained in the country." Steele's chief engineer reported that the troops were issued half rations of hard bread and quarter rations of bacon during the campaign but received full rations of coffee and salt. They relied "on the country for the filling out of the ration" when that was possible, but the area through which the Federals marched was "nearly barren of forage and exhausted of supplies."[57]

The loss of logistical material during the Camden Campaign was staggering. The Confederates captured 298 wagons and destroyed 90 more, while the Federals destroyed 247 themselves for a total of 635 wagons lost. The Confederates captured 2,000 mules, and another 500 were lost due to overwork, undernourishment, or abandonment, for a total of 2,500 animals. Halleck instructed Allen to send agents to Saint Louis, Cairo, Memphis, and other cities to purchase wagons and mules and send them to Steele.[58]

Both Banks and Steele were operating deep in enemy territory with desperately insecure lines of supply. Steele's situation was much worse. Even though he had fewer than one-third the troops compared to Banks, he could not feed them adequately from the countryside, and his efforts to supply them by wagon trains came to disaster because of aggressive enemy action. Banks's campaign was a major embarrassment, but Steele's was a virtual catastrophe. The Trans-Mississippi was an unforgiving environment for the movement of large forces deep into enemy territory.

Canby and the Railroad Alternative

Maj. Gen. Edward R. S. Canby tried to find a railroad solution that could restart the drive toward Shreveport. To build a more coordinated approach to operations in the Trans-Mississippi, Federal authorities created the Military Division of West Mississippi, which embraced the Department of the Gulf and the Department of Arkansas. They appointed Canby to take charge of it on May 7, 1864, to oversee Banks and Steele.[59]

Canby saw the unfinished Vicksburg, Shreveport, and Texas Railroad as a potential line of approach to Shreveport and was determined to put it into full operation, using soldiers to do the heavy labor and mechanics for the skilled work. He assigned Joseph Bailey, builder of the Alexandria dam, to manage the enterprise. Canby wanted to advance 15,000 troops to Shreveport, using the railroad as their logistical support.[60]

But Washington authorities had no enthusiasm for Canby's plan. Halleck pointed out that it would cost $4–5 million and take up to five months of hard work to complete the railroad, and there would be great difficulty finding rolling stock east of the Mississippi to handle the flow of material. "All shops are now pressed for locomotives and rolling stock to supply Sherman's army," Halleck told him.[61]

Even more sobering was a report by C. G. Sawtelle, a quartermaster who made a close examination of the roadbed west from Vicksburg. Only three miles of iron in the first nine miles of track were usable, all the bridges and trestles between Vicksburg and Monroe were destroyed, many sections of rails were gone, and major bridges over the Tensas River, Bayou Macon, Bayou Boeuf, and the Ouachita River had never been completed by the company. Even the wagon road that paralleled the track between Vicksburg and Monroe ran along mostly low and swampy ground and would be difficult for large wagon trains.[62]

Putting the railroad into usable shape would be a huge undertaking. Yet, in deference to Canby, the authorities submitted his proposal to Grant. Meanwhile, Bailey started to work on the railroad. The civil engineer turned army officer began to stockpile material, thirteen boxcars, and two engines at Vicksburg. Bailey was optimistic; apparently he had not read Sawtelle's report when he told Quartermaster General Meigs the stretch between Vicksburg and Monroe could be put into operation relatively quickly. He thought that all but 25 miles of the 105-mile stretch between Monroe and Shreveport had already been graded.[63]

Canby lobbied vigorously, telling Halleck that he could find enough rolling stock east of the Mississippi without hurting Sherman. "The reconstruction of this road is necessary," he asserted, and would be less expensive than any other means of transportation. "I put the rivers out of question," he told Halleck, "for they cannot be relied on." Canby reiterated his plea for support of the railroad approach, apparently fired with a determination to overcome the humiliation of Banks's failure.[64]

But Grant put an end to all hopes of restarting the campaign toward Shreveport. On June 23 he told Halleck that all efforts should be devoted to supporting the campaigns in Virginia and Georgia. Canby's job was to protect the navigation of the Mississippi. In fact, Grant wanted him to send the Nineteenth Corps to Virginia. Halleck relayed this information to Canby, who finally gave up his plans to complete the railroad.[65]

Grant probably was correct to focus on the major campaigns in Virginia and Georgia, but he did not appreciate the hard logistical problems faced by his subordinates in the Trans-Mississippi. Looking over returns in the spring of 1864, he was astonished to find that William S. Rosecrans had 1,600 wagons and teams operating in the Department of the Missouri. Rosecrans complied when asked to spare 500 of them for more important operations east of the Mississippi, but he explained that circumstances dictated heavy reliance on this form of transportation in his department.[66]

The quartermaster at Springfield backed up Rosecrans by reporting that he needed at least 20 wagons to haul 13,000 pounds of grain to feed his troops and many local civilians who were dependent on the army for subsistence. In addition to his own garrison, the quartermaster also fed troops at Fayetteville and other posts. With 220 wagons, he barely had enough to handle these wants and constantly received requests for more transportation than he could supply.[67]

The last major campaign in the Trans-Mississippi exemplified the logistical and supply issues discussed thus far. Maj. Gen. Sterling Price entered Missouri late in September 1864 with 12,000 mostly mounted troops. He had no intention of maintaining a functioning supply line with Arkansas but relied entirely on feeding his men and animals from a countryside that had already witnessed three years of warfare. Price therefore had to carefully plan his route of advance to traverse pockets of territory that reportedly still had some food and forage. By planning the route and moving quickly, Price's Missouri Raid became possible. Moving into southeast Missouri, threatening Saint Louis, and then advancing west, the Confederates were stopped near the Kansas border and pursued by large forces of Federals. Price retreated south through eastern Kansas. He decided to cross the Arkansas River by moving through Indian Territory, where he hoped to obtain fresh beef, knowing that crossing between Fort Smith and Little Rock would take his army through a country devoid of adequate food, forage, or even grass. Price traveled a total of 1,434 miles during his two-month campaign on the most slender logistical plan imaginable.[68]

Going Hungry in the Trans-Mississippi

By the latter half of the Civil War, Union and Confederate troops increasingly suffered from hunger in the Trans-Mississippi. From November 17, 1863, until February 22, 1865, the men of Company B, 12th Kansas had "not drawn quite half rations of provisions and never within that time but twenty days' full rations and that of an inferior quality," according to the man who kept the company's record of events. "The men have spent nearly half of their wages in that time for provisions." While hunger was no stranger to all Civil War soldiers, the problem was more intense west of the Mississippi. It must be pointed out that the 12th Kansas was a Federal regiment—hunger knew no distinction of uniform.[69]

Yet there is no doubt that Confederate soldiers in the Trans-Mississippi suffered more from hunger than Federals. A voracious demand for land transportation afflicted Rebel quartermasters, and they could not fill it. Although the Confederates captured many wagons and mules from Banks and Steele during April and May 1864, most of the captures were in bad shape. The Southerners had to repair the wagons and graze the mules before using either, and even then the number did not compensate for all shortages of land transportation in the vast region. Moreover, civilians, Confederate cavalrymen, and "Choctaw Indians" stole many of the mules while they were grazing. Rebel officers expressed their frustration at not being able to move subsistence stores to troops desperately in need of them. To a limited degree they used a few steamers to ship food during periods of high water, but that fell far short of demands.[70]

Moreover, the need to move men by marching rather than riding added to the problem. Capt. Elijah P. Petty of the 17th Texas complained of the many miles of marching he experienced. "This would not be so hard if we had steam boats & Rail Road transportation over here but when we have to make long forced & weary land marches it wears the soldiers down."[71]

As the Trans-Mississippi Confederates staggered toward war's end, hunger gripped them ever more tightly. An inspector reported troops poorly supplied with everything they normally should have possessed. Lt. Gen. Theophilus Holmes reviewed and inspected Price's troops in January 1864 and found them poorly clothed, many "in their shirts and drawers" with no jackets or pants. The fall of Vicksburg and Port Hudson hurt the Trans-Mississippi in serious ways. While 51,336 pants had been shipped from east to west in 1863, quartermasters were able to transport only 7,742 pants to the Trans-Mississippi in 1864. Similar statistics can be seen in blankets, drawers, and shirts. The Trans-Mississippi Confederates were starving for a variety of needed articles in addition to food as the war dragged closer to an end.[72]

One result was a noticeable rise in plundering of civilians. Rebel cavalry raids in Arkansas and Missouri resulted in so many indiscriminate depredations as to sour the loyalty of civilians sympathetic to the Confederate cause. "In fact, sir," wrote C. Franklin to Jefferson Davis, recent Rebel raids had "transferred to the Confederate uniform all the dread and terror which used to attach to the Lincoln blue." General orders condemning such actions failed to arrest the growing practice. Systematic efforts to scour the countryside for food in a more orderly fashion failed to arrest the slide toward civilian demoralization. "We ask to be saved from our friends," pleaded one civilian who lived in Drew County, Arkansas. "The Yankees are friends and protectors when compared to the vandalism of" Confederate foraging parties. "The Yankees have been down here twice, but they have left enough of horses and mules to farm with and enough provisions to live on."[73]

Hunger characterized soldier life west of the Mississippi River more thoroughly and deeply than in any other theater of operations during the

Civil War, even more so than in Appalachia. Large-scale infantry operations were severely limited west of the Mississippi because of these logistical and supply problems. Small groups of foot soldiers or highly mobile concentrations of mounted troops could operate effectively even though they often suffered food shortages. But large concentrations of slow-moving infantry could not be supported in a reliable way except by rail or river, and neither transportation option was available to commanders deep inside the Trans-Mississippi. Federal authorities had more resources and a stronger and more flexible support system than their opponents. They eventually came to dominate enough areas to lay claim to winning the war in the Trans-Mississippi.

10

SUPPLYING THE ARMY OF THE POTOMAC

When the Confederate government moved its capital from Montgomery to Richmond in May 1861, it put a straitjacket on Union and Rebel operations in the eastern theater. Logistically the East posed different problems and advantages for the Federals compared to the West. While Union operations west of the Appalachian Highlands were characterized by multiple objectives spread over a huge area of diverse topography, operations in the East were centered on one goal—the capture of Richmond. There certainly were divergent moves now and then, but the Army of the Potomac's main task was the reduction of that city and the field army that protected it. The Federals found the task more difficult than imagined, and the Confederates (as we shall see in the next chapter) found it troublesome merely to obtain food for troops locked into a small theater of operations on the edge of their territory.

The logistical and supply history of the Army of the Potomac has four main themes. First, geography offered it some degree of latitude in choosing modes of supply as it advanced 100 miles south from Washington to Richmond. Both cities were located at or near the geographic line separating the coastal plain from the eastern edge of the piedmont. That meant that oceangoing vessels were capable of sailing up the tidal zone of several rivers. Both Washington and Richmond were linked by rail lines as well. Federal commanders could employ either coastal shipping, railroads, or both to support a forward move.

In fact, Maj. Gen. George B. McClellan chose to rely solely on coastal shipping for his approach to Richmond in the spring of 1862, moving and supporting the Army of the Potomac entirely by this method for several months. A concurrent move by Maj. Gen. Irvin McDowell to Fredericksburg, fifty miles south of Washington, was supported by a combination of coastal shipping and railroads. When future operations veered inland away from the tidal zone of the coastal plain, the Federals depended entirely on railroads. In 1864–65 Grant relied on a combination of coastal shipping and railroads during the Overland Campaign and entirely on coastal shipping for his operations around Petersburg and Richmond. Inland from the tidal zone, the rivers of the East were not deep or wide enough to support a fleet of commercial steamers. As a result, riverboats were hardly used by either side in Virginia.

The second theme of Union logistics and supply in the East is railroad management. It was in Virginia where the working out of many problems associated with using railroads to support large masses of troops in the field took place. Herman Haupt was largely responsible for starting this process, but other railroad managers hired by the Federal government, especially Daniel McCallum, were responsible for its further development. Haupt started his work by supporting McDowell's occupation of Fredericksburg in the spring of 1862, creating a reliable corps of railroad managers and workers, all hired from the civilian railroad industry, to operate rail support in the East. This system was transferred to the West by early 1864 to replace the haphazard method of railroad management in that theater of operations, where it ballooned into a huge corps of men.

A third theme is managing excess. The Army of the Potomac rarely suffered supply shortages because of its high-profile mission and its proximity to the national capital. It usually got what it wanted, and sometimes more than it needed. Even though its supply lines were short (normally under 100 miles), sometimes they were engorged with more material than could easily be managed.

Finally, the Army of the Potomac operated entirely in the Upper South. Its strategic mission did not require the troops to penetrate Deep South territory. If it had captured Richmond early in the war, the army probably would have been devoted to some sort of Deep South campaign as a follow up. But that never happened because the war in the East only came to an end with the surrender of the Army of Northern Virginia a week after the fall of Richmond in April 1865. As a result, the main Federal force in the East never stretched its supply lines to the breaking point, never resorted to strategic raiding, and never had to live off the land as a main support to its existence.

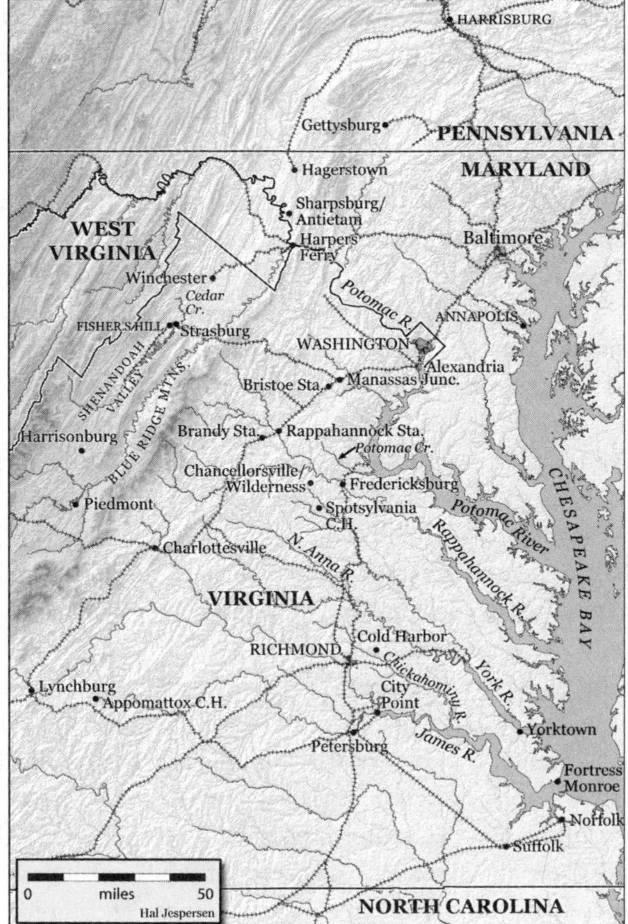

THE EAST

The Peninsula and the Seven Days

Federal arrangements to support McDowell's "On to Richmond" drive in the summer of 1861 were slight, admitted Quartermaster D. H. Rucker. Everyone assumed the city would fall, and major depots could be established at the former capital for further drives into the Deep South.[1] But that first offensive came crashing to a halt on July 21 with a humiliating defeat. The First Battle of Bull Run was followed by the creation of a large army of

100,000 men under McClellan, tripling the size of McDowell's force. Not only the lesson of First Bull Run but also the nature of McClellan meant that the new Army of the Potomac had to create a solid, long-term logistical and supply system if it hoped to fulfill Union objectives in the East.

Stewart Van Vliet, McClellan's chief quartermaster, found it difficult to feed the many horses and mules the army used. He established a major depot at Perryville, on the Susquehanna River, in northern Maryland. It was connected by rail with Baltimore and Philadelphia. Van Vliet organized a huge train of 1,500 wagons to haul fodder for animals from Perryville to the army encamped near Washington. He also created huge depots at Washington itself and supplied them by coastal shipping coming up the Potomac River. Henry F. Clarke, McClellan's chief commissary of subsistence, obtained food from depots at Alexandria, Fort Corcoran, and Fort Runyon. After the Confederates erected artillery along the south side of the river and cut off that supply route on October 19, Van Vliet relied on a railroad between Baltimore and Washington to take up the slack, shipping in 400 tons of forage every day for the army's animals. Only because the rail line was short and well protected was this possible.[2]

When McClellan moved the army to begin his Peninsula Campaign, Van Vliet's rail supply line became unnecessary. McClellan had long wanted to approach Richmond by using coastal shipping to transport his army to a point along the serrated Chesapeake coast between Washington and Richmond. He even thought of moving the Army of the Potomac all the way to New York City because that was the center of the North Atlantic coastal shipping industry. "All sea steamers (not otherwise chartered), the large sound steamers, the large North River, sound, and coasting propellers can be had there," he reported, "and there all the appliances to fit them for troops, horse, &c, can be quickest made." But he wisely decided to have all this shipping and material sent down to Washington instead.[3]

The advantage of relying on a water-based line of supply was that the Confederates had no opportunity to interfere with it. Railroads were always vulnerable to attacks by guerrillas or cavalry raiders, but the enemy had no naval power. Moreover, the tidal zone allowed these vessels to unload at convenient locations miles up the many rivers that drained toward the southeast from the mountains.[4]

Secretary of War Stanton assigned John Tucker, one of his assistants, to round up civilian vessels for the transfer of 100,000 men from Washington to the Yorktown Peninsula. McClellan assigned Maj. Rufus Ingalls, an assistant quartermaster, to manage the embarkation. "Operations of this nature on so extensive a scale had no parallel in the history of our country," McClellan proclaimed in his report. He mounted the largest troop movement by boat to be seen in the Western Hemisphere. Initial plans to march the men to Annapolis and Baltimore to meet the boats due to the Confederate blockade of the lower Potomac were changed when the Federals conducted a move that forced the enemy to raise the blockade in March 1862. A motley fleet assembled at Alexandria for the army, including seventy-one sidewheel steamers, 187 sailing vessels, fifty-seven propeller-driven craft, and ninety barges. Tucker assembled a total of 405 vessels of all kinds for the move. Many of these vessels were capable of holding fewer troops and animals than the typical Mississippi River steamboats. Depending on their size, each could carry 100–1,200 men. Van Vliet also shipped 3,600 wagons and 700 ambulances and spring wagons with the army.[5]

For the first leg of the journey, from Alexandria to Fortress Monroe, the sailing vessels were often towed by the steamers for faster progress. Leaving Alexandria in mid-March, the transports consumed twelve days in getting the army to Fortress Monroe, at the tip of the peninsula. McClellan left his camps and depots in the Washington area so abruptly that the troops abandoned lots of government property. D. H. Rucker, in charge of the depot at Washington, spent a month collecting the material and hauling it to storehouses in the city.[6]

Commissary Clarke loaded six propeller-driven craft with 600,000 complete rations at New York City to join the flotilla "for immediate use." He shipped another 2,500,000 complete rations from New York to Fortress Monroe to use as a food reserve. Clarke also put rations on barges and towed them from Washington to Fortress Monroe, believing barges would be handier to deposit food at temporary field depots located along the rivers of the Peninsula. The enterprising commissary also shipped beef cattle from New York City to Fortress Monroe and drove them in herds to keep pace with the army's advance.[7]

Van Vliet decided to retain most of these coastal vessels indefinitely to support the army as it moved up the Peninsula. This was an easy but costly solution to his supply challenge. The government racked up enormous expenses on daily charges in keeping hundreds of ships tied up for months on end. Van Vliet was ready to discharge most of them as soon as McClellan fixed on a permanent depot, but that never happened. Clarke took charge of all vessels in the fleet that carried subsistence stores, and McClellan's ordnance officer probably did the same for those that carried ammunition and weapons. The Federals found that detailed soldiers had trouble working in the hot, humid climate, so they relied mostly on black laborers to unload vessels. Toward the end of the Seven Days Campaign, the army employed 2,500 black workers, each paid twenty dollars per month, and provided food and rudimentary shelter for their families as well.[8]

Van Vliet established temporary depots along the banks of the Peninsula, abandoning them as McClellan moved forward, until he established a major base at White House on the Pamunkey River. Located twenty-three miles east of the Confederate capital, the Richmond and York River Railroad crossed the Pamunkey there. Supplies could be offloaded from the coastal vessels at White House and shipped west along this track. Described as a light "country railroad," the line was strained by the movement of 600 tons of material every day, more than half of it food for animals. Material had to be offloaded at its western terminus for shipment by wagons to the various units in the Federal line. The wagon link was short, only seven miles to the right end of the line and two miles to the left end. Rain fell nineteen days during the forty-four-day period from May 15 to June 28, turning the roads into mud that forced teamsters to lighten their wagonloads. Much road repair became necessary, and a washed-out portion of the track was rebuilt to support the army's lodgment east of Richmond.[9]

By the end of the Seven Days, White House on the Pamunkey supported an army of 115,355 men, including noneffectives, plus 25,000 horses and mules, then located fifteen to twenty miles west of the landing. Ingalls constructed a dozen wharves by using barges and canal boats, running them on the bank at high tide and then bridging them over. McClelland arranged for six locomotives and eighty boxcars to be purchased from Northern railroad companies and transported by boat to White House for use on the railroad. Clarke established three depots along the line for unloading and kept a cattle herd at White House.[10]

Gen. Robert E. Lee's offensive in the Seven Days Campaign dashed McClellan's hope for a war-winning campaign. The base at White House had to be evacuated quickly, and while Ingalls had to destroy all the rolling stock of the railroad, he managed to evacuate 400 vessels from the area. "It seems almost a miracle, our successful escape from White House," he later reported. If any vessels had "entangled at some of the narrow bends, the consequences to the army would have been fatal." The ships had no room for wagon trains, so these were driven under escort overland to the James River. Clarke also drove his herd of 2,518 cattle overland. There was so little time to evacuate that he told subordinates to give all the food in the depots along the railroad to the troops without proper paperwork and burn what they could not take away. He also destroyed a lot of subsistence stores at West Point for lack of transport.[11]

McDowell at Fredericksburg

When McClellan moved south from Washington to clear the lower Potomac of Confederate river batteries, he also forced the enemy to evacuate Manassas Junction and all of northeast Virginia. Upon leaving for the Peninsula, McClellan left behind a considerable force to hold this area, protect Washington, and serve as a strategic reserve for his operations farther south. Federal officials established a logistical system to support this occupation of northeast Virginia. They took control of the Orange and Alexandria Railroad, opening it to Manassas Junction, twenty-five miles from Alexandria, by the latter part of March. Then they opened it to Warrenton Junction, thirty-nine miles from Alexandria, the next month and continued to extend it to keep pace with Union military needs.[12]

When McDowell's corps occupied Fredericksburg in April 1862, quartermasters opened a depot at Aquia Creek Landing, fifteen miles northeast of town. Coastal vessels could deposit material there for shipment along the Richmond, Fredericksburg, and Potomac Railroad to McDowell's men. Quartermasters constructed wharves at the landing, relaid track, and rebuilt bridges along the line.[13]

Northeast Virginia saw a managerial innovation in railroad work. Stanton had already appointed a professional to direct and superintend the U.S. Military Railroad, created when Congress authorized the War Department to seize any railroad company in the country for military use. Stanton had the foresight to find one of the best railroad executives, Daniel McCallum, to head the organization. As general superintendent of the New York and Erie Railroad, McCallum had pioneered the process of railroad management. Thus far he had a small job, limited mostly to the Orange and Alexandria Railroad and ancillary lines near Washington.[14]

Federals Rebuilding Railroad Bridge at Fredericksburg. In this interesting depiction of a railroad bridge under repair, one can see many of the typical methods used by Civil War engineers to access the damaged parts of a long and high structure. This scene most likely illustrates Herman Haupt's repair of the bridge in May 1862, when McDowell held Fredericksburg. *Frank Leslie's Scenes and Portraits,* 211.

Then Stanton found another professional to supplement McCallum, Herman Haupt. An engineer, inventor, and expert in rail management, Haupt was assigned to support McDowell's occupation of Fredericksburg. He and McCallum, both strongminded and forceful men, worked out an arrangement so that Haupt would largely work in the field while McCallum would manage things from a central office.[15]

Although only a short line, the Richmond, Fredericksburg, and Potomac Railroad linking Aquia Creek Landing with Fredericksburg became a laboratory for Haupt to work out an effective method of rail support for an army in the field. He arrived at Aquia Creek Landing on April 29 to find a gap of three miles in the track and three bridges down. He assigned D. Stone to rebuild the bridges while he organized a gang to unload ties and rails from boats and move them to the break. Laying the track at night with the aid of lanterns, Haupt's people repaired the breaks, even though they were all "green hands" of detailed soldiers.[16]

Haupt applied his talents to getting the bridges in working order quickly. The structure over Potomac Creek was the biggest job, with three spans of 150 feet in length each and all resting 85 feet above "a frightful look-

Potomac Creek Bridge, First Version. Haupt rebuilt this bridge on the Richmond, Fredericksburg, and Potomac Railroad to support McDowell's occupation of Fredericksburg early in May 1862, using detailed infantrymen to cut local timber. The structure had three spans, each 150 feet long and with two stone piers, and stood 85 feet tall. When Abraham Lincoln saw the bridge, he marveled at how Haupt had been able to create a serviceable structure so quickly with local resources, stating, "there was nothing in it but bean poles and cornstalks." The structure was used until the Federals abandoned their rail link between Fredericksburg and Aquia Creek Landing in early September 1862. LC-DIG-ppmsca-33392.

ing chasm." With 300 soldiers available, Haupt told the officers to make a list of what each man had done before the war, then he organized them into squads of carpenters, woodchoppers, teamsters, and the like, placing a noncommissioned officer in charge of each squad and holding officers responsible for tools and the overall performance of the men. In addition to the structure over Potomac Creek, Haupt's men rebuilt a bridge 150 feet long and 40 feet tall over Accokeek Creek in fifteen working hours. They also reconstructed the bridge over the Rappahannock River at Fredericksburg.[17]

To solidify the division of labor between Haupt and McCallum, Stanton appointed Haupt chief of construction and transportation in McDowell's Department of the Rappahannock, with the rank of colonel. When McDowell was diverted toward Front Royal due to the operations of Stonewall Jackson in the Shenandoah Valley, Haupt shifted his crews to the Manassas Gap Railroad, which ran from Manassas Junction west to Mount Jackson in the Valley, by June 1. Here he relaid track and reconstructed seven bridges. McDowell used the Richmond, Fredericksburg, and Potomac Railroad and the Manassas Gap Railroad to support his troops.[18]

Haupt regularized the running of trains with an efficient system of management. He broke away from the civilian practice of running trains by telegraph (using telegrams to clear the track for the next train) and insisted on running each train on a fixed time schedule with no deviations so as to avoid collisions. He battled against the interference of army officers who commandeered cars for storage of material or for their personal use. Haupt also cracked down on the slow unloading of cars at the delivery point because this greatly disrupted running schedules.[19]

Stanton authorized Haupt to organize a permanent body of railway workers because the railroad man realized that relying on detailed soldiers had its limitations. Troops went on strike in early May, but McDowell authorized their mass arrest and even shooting, which brought them back to work quickly. A dedicated corps of professional railroad workers would be far more efficient in every way. Haupt created such an organization on July 11, 1862.[20]

This probably was Haupt's most important contribution to logistics during the Civil War. Hiring professional civilians was not a new idea. As we have seen, Sherman had been the first to do so by employing John B. Anderson in the fall of 1861, to be followed by McCallum and then Haupt in 1862. But creating an entire corps of railroad workers was a true innovation. Moreover, it has to be noted that the quality of personnel hired in the East far exceeded those hired in the West. Anderson was less skilled and energetic than McCallum and Haupt. It took the western generals much longer to realize that good managers and a large corps of professional railroad workers was the best way to keep the trains running.

One can see Haupt's talent by looking at how he reconstructed bridges. He made a study of this problem and wrote a book on it. Haupt pointed out that the need was for speed not permanency, and any method adopted should be so simple that semitrained laborers could do it. He rebuilt the Potomac Creek bridge in nine working days, utilizing untrained soldiers and

Potomac Creek Bridge, Rebuilt. The Federals burned the "bean poles and cornstalks" bridge when they abandoned the Richmond, Fredericksburg, and Potomac Railroad in early September 1862. After Burnside brought the Army of the Potomac to Fredericksburg, quartermasters reopened the railroad, and Haupt rebuilt the bridge, once again using local timber. Several months later he was not certain the bridge could withstand the possibility of a freshet sweeping along the stream now that most of the trees had been cut from its watershed. He quickly rebuilt the structure on April 1–3, 1863, using prefabricated trusses that were shipped to the site. This photograph was taken by Andrew J. Russell on April 18, 1863. LC-DIG-ppmsca-11744.

using material they cut two miles away and then hauled to the site by oxen. The structure had a flimsy appearance, but ten to twelve trains passed over it every day without incident, including one carrying Abraham Lincoln. The president was impressed, telling some congressmen, "Upon my soul, gentlemen, there was nothing in it but bean poles and cornstalks."[21]

Because local commanders had authorized the clearcutting of timber in the valley above Potomac Creek bridge, Haupt decided to rebuild it to withstand the floods he expected to come in the spring of 1863. This time he preconstructed trusses long enough to rest on the stone piers. Construction Corps personnel replaced the span on April 1–3, causing minimal disruption in the supply of the Army of the Potomac, which at this time was heavily dependent on the line to Aquia Creek Landing.[22]

By the summer of 1862, the Federals had worked out a highly advanced system of railroad reconstruction and management. It would be expanded to include all theaters of operations east and west. In fact, the Stanton system, or perhaps better termed the Haupt-McCallum system, was the most advanced concept for managing military railroads in the world because the Civil War created the largest, most demanding need for rail support of large armies in global history up to that time. Relying on soldiers detailed from the ranks simply did not work. Grant was working slowly and uncertainly toward that goal by late 1862 in the Department of the Tennessee, but with men of less skill in charge of the civilian crews. Anderson also applied less skill in the management of his small force of civilian workers in the Department of the Ohio during the latter part of that year.

Second Bull Run

The new system of railroad management faced a severe test in the late summer and fall of 1862. After the Seven Days the Army of the Potomac rested on the north bank of the James River a few miles from Richmond from July 2 to August 15. It was abundantly supplied by coastal vessels that transported beef cattle from Washington; fresh vegetables from New York, Baltimore, and Norfolk; and soft bread from Fortress Monroe. Because fresh vegetables often became spoiled in the Virginia heat, Clarke obtained desiccated vegetables as well as dried peaches and apples. He maintained a stockpile of sixty days' rations for the army at depots on land and on board ships along the James River. In fact, the coastal vessels had been in service so long that much of the animal forage had deteriorated. Hay had rotted and corn had become moldy, causing suffering among the horses and mules. Ingalls, who replaced Van Vliet as chief quartermaster of the army, assigned Alexander Bliss to inspect all transports on the James and report on what they carried and how long they were in service. Ingalls then began to discharge as many boats as possible, beginning with those longest in service. Before that was done the transports also resupplied the army with a wide variety of material lost during the Seven Days.[23]

McClellan began shifting the Army of the Potomac from the Peninsula to the Washington area by August 15, but such a large force needed three weeks to complete the transfer.[24] As a result, most of the army missed the Battle of Second Bull Run. Fought primarily by Maj. Gen. John Pope's Army of Virginia, the campaign was characterized by massive logistical problems stemming from too much material combined with incompetent management. Pope allowed his wagon supply to balloon out of proportion to his army's needs. With fifteen wagons per regiment, it was more than double McClellan's allotment of six wagons per regiment. Moreover, Pope ignored Haupt because he did not think a civilian railroad organization was necessary, preferring to rely on his quartermasters to handle rail support. He wanted his troops to feed off the countryside, even though Virginia already had been trampled by contending armies for months. Halleck encouraged him in this policy.[25]

Both Pope and Halleck were western generals transplanted to the East. They continued for the time to adhere to western attitudes about railroad management, which essentially was to favor military control over the rail system rather than involve civilians. Stanton had started the process of heavy reliance on civilian experts to operate military lines, and he pushed that concept vigorously in the East, where he could exert personal influence on the generals. But Stanton never insisted that western commanders do the same, and thus the implementation of the Stanton model for railroad management took a long time to cross the Appalachians.

Pope would soon find that relying on competent civilians was the best way to manage his rail supply. The Army of Virginia depended on the Orange and Alexandria Railroad and drew mostly from Rucker's Depot of Washington. With 45,000 men to feed, it was not a large army compared to McClellan's, but Pope's quartermasters mishandled the supply. The logistical incompetence of Maj. Gen. Franz Sigel and Maj. Gen. Nathaniel Banks, two of Pope's corps commanders, contributed to the problems. Citing the "grossest possible carelessness somewhere in the Quartermaster Department," Pope bemoaned the waste and mismanagement that became apparent by mid-August. He concluded that Robert E. Clary, his own chief quartermaster, was "too old and too easy."[26]

The problem with Pope's logistics was a combination of too many wagons, too much unnecessary baggage carried in them, no faith in civilian management of the railroads, and a set of incompetent quartermasters incapable of dealing with those problems. Pope was beginning to realize all this just when Lee launched an offensive, and the Union general wanted to strip his army of transportation so he could maneuver more quickly. He sent back most of his army's wagon trains, required his men to carry three days' rations, and prepared the Orange and Alexandria Railroad for shipping his baggage back to Washington while keeping twenty carloads of supplies moving forward every day. All this was a recipe for trouble. The animals suffered most, many literally dying for want of forage even though operating only a few dozen miles from the Washington depot.[27]

Pope was forced to ask Haupt for help, calling him back from his Massachusetts home in mid-August. Haupt dealt with conflicting instructions from the general to move his baggage back and from Halleck to move McClellan's army forward to help the Army of Virginia. Pope seemed unable to set priorities in these shipments. It was "a regular mess," as Haupt put it. The railroad man had to cut through the chaos, giving top priority to moving troops to the front, then forage for animals, and finally food for men. Delays in unloading everything at the forward end vexed his schedule. When Stonewall Jackson temporarily captured Manassas Junction, the Confederates wrecked track and burned rolling stock and supplies. Haupt called up his Construction Corps to repair everything as fast as the Federals could reclaim the area.[28]

Haupt was still working to create order out of chaos when Pope's campaign ended in defeat on the old Bull Run battlefield at the end of August. This disaster created a military crisis, with Federal forces abandoning virtually all positions in northeast Virginia to protect Washington. Maj. Gen. Ambrose Burnside ordered Col. William W. Wright to give up the Richmond, Fredericksburg, and Potomac Railroad and evacuate Aquia Creek Landing. Wright was able to get off seven locomotives worth a total of $50,000 within two days but left behind fifty-seven cars. He destroyed that rolling stock plus the buildings and a pier that stretched 870 feet into the river, covering one and a half acres of floor space. The Federals also burned bridges over the Rappahannock River, Potomac Creek, and Accokeek Creek, but Wright was careful to record their dimensions for easier rebuilding.[29]

The Maryland Campaign

McClellan was put in charge of operations as Lee invaded Maryland in September, but there was a great deal of confusion in his supply arrangements. Only some of his wagons were brought up from the Peninsula in time for the campaign, but fortunately 2,500 wagons from Pope's now-defunct Army

RAILROADS IN THE EAST

of Virginia were available. Ingalls supplied McClellan with these wagons directly from the Washington depot as the Federals advanced west to meet Lee. The Baltimore and Ohio Railroad operated from Washington to the Monocacy River, where Ingalls created a temporary depot. When the bridge over this stream was finished, he established additional depots at Frederick and later at Hagerstown, on the Cumberland Valley Railroad, to supplement the wagon train link with the capital. Supplies also were brought from New York, Philadelphia, and Baltimore through this pipeline that kept pace with the army's advance.[30]

And yet the supply system did not run smoothly. Complaints reached Quartermaster General Meigs of delays in material reaching the troops, which seemed to conflict with other reports that McClellan had 6,000 wagons and 30,000 mules to pull them. The problem appeared to be improper management of abundant resources. Meigs suggested that only two or three wagons be allowed for every regiment and the rest placed in a reserve. "Until it is done, the army will not be a movable one, and will not be effective."[31]

On September 18, the day after the savage Battle of Antietam, Haupt was placed in charge of managing the supply arrangements for the Army of the Potomac. He held a conference with officials of the Baltimore and Ohio Railroad in which all agreed that this line would handle most of the work, supplemented by two smaller lines. Haupt had complete faith in the Baltimore and Ohio, which had great capacity and good executives. The two smaller lines were barely able to cope, but Haupt delayed seizing them until it became absolutely necessary. He mandated that all three lines put aside hauling civilian freight or passengers for the immediate future and concentrate only on government business. Haupt found the tracks blocked at Hagerstown and worked to clear them. He also found it necessary to temporarily seize the Trunk Line Railroad between Hagerstown and Chambersburg. When he was told that 200 cars had been idled for a week on a siding at Monocacy, he sent a staff officer to see that they were unloaded and forwarded to receive more material.[32]

With Haupt on the job, the rail system quickly improved. The Ordnance Department in Washington sent a special train with 2,500 rounds of 20-pounder ammunition on the Northern Central Railroad. It left Baltimore at 6:57 A.M. on September 18 and was transferred to the Cumberland Valley Railroad at 10:20 A.M. The train made eighty-four miles in two hours and fifty-three minutes. "It will be put through at same speed to Hagerstown," announced a government official to Stanton. Meigs sent 1.1 million rations and enough grain to create a pile of 50,000 bushels to Hagerstown. "Dispatch is important to the success of the army," he told superintendents of the two small lines. But there still were problems. Dispatchers of the Cumberland Valley Railroad erroneously made out orders for material to be sent to Harrisburg rather than Hagerstown, creating much delay in its arrival.[33]

After Antietam and Lee's retreat into Virginia, Ingalls had to figure out how to supply the Army of the Potomac there. He reported that the countryside north and south of the Potomac River was devoid of provisions and suggested that the bridges at Harpers Ferry be restored so he could use the place as a forward base of operations. McClellan refused to move more than twenty-five miles away from his forward railhead. He reasoned that if Lee offered battle at Winchester, he could accept, but if the Confederates moved farther up the valley, he would not pursue.[34]

The Federals opened a depot at Harpers Ferry and began to refit the Army of the Potomac. Alexander Bliss was in charge of this effort, with a staff of thirty clerks and more than 100 black laborers and detailed soldiers. But Lee did not offer battle at Winchester or elsewhere, so McClellan shifted operations farther east. Bliss was told on November 5 to diminish the Harpers Ferry depot, leaving enough behind to supply the Twelfth Corps, which was to remain in the area. In assessing the possibilities for supplying his army, McClellan found the Manassas Gap Railroad "in such poor running order" as to be unreliable. He told Haupt to restore the Orange and Alexandria Railroad as far as the Rappahannock River, but that line had a limited capacity of no more than 900 tons daily, assuming no accidents or unwarranted detention of cars at the receiving end. The Army of the Potomac demanded 1,500 tons each day. Haupt needed 550 cars but had only 300 on the line.[35]

This became Burnside's problem when he replaced McClellan on November 9. Haupt explained it bluntly to him. The Orange and Alexandria Railroad's "ordinary working capacity . . . is not equal to the half of your requirements," but he believed it could suffice if properly managed. The first priority was rapid unloading of cars; the next was not stopping trains along the way to partially unload in order to save wagon hauling. The Federals needed depots every thirty to forty miles along the line in case of breaks in the track. Burnside had to issue stern orders to implement these directives and make sure they were obeyed. "Without this, the supply of your army is impossible." Burnside understood and complied with Haupt's recommendations, but the Orange and Alexandria barely fulfilled its mission as far as Warrenton, sixty miles from Alexandria.[36]

Haupt urged Burnside to restore Aquia Creek Landing and the Richmond, Fredericksburg, and Potomac Railroad as a supplemental line of supply, but McClellan had already ordered that to be done before he left the army. Only two months after the hasty destruction of that depot and line, the government began to rebuild them. When Burnside moved the army to Fredericksburg later in November, Federal quartermasters gave up the Orange and Alexandria Railroad and concentrated on making Aquia Creek Landing and the Richmond, Fredericksburg, and Potomac his primary supply line.[37]

Meigs thought it necessary to lecture Stanton on the larger picture, telling him that the flow of supplies to an army like Burnside's had to be continuous "like that of a great city whose population it equals in number." Statistics bear this out. The army received 97,700 pairs of drawers, 34,500 forage caps, and 76,120 pairs of trousers during the second week of October alone.[38]

Even though it operated only a few miles from railroads, the Army of the Potomac was engulfed with horses and mules. Meigs complained that he sent 13,000 horses to McClellan from September 1 to October 25 with great difficulty. When asked to explain the need, McClellan detailed why he required 31,000 animals in order to feed 110,000 troops (122,000 men, if one counted teamsters and citizen employees). Ten days' food for the army required 1,830 wagons (carrying 2,000 pounds of freight each). He claimed to need 17,832 mules just to haul the forage to feed all the animals in his army.[39]

Haupt speculated that the army was awash with resources because the process of requesting material was not centralized enough. Quartermasters assigned to units had too much leeway in making requisitions, requiring only their immediate commander's approval.[40]

Halleck was in a good position to obtain perspective on McClellan's and Burnside's supply situation. He thought the Army of the Potomac was better provisioned than those in the West. "The latter have operated at much greater distances from the sources of supply, and have had far less facilities for transportation."[41] And yet the western armies had achieved far more in their strategic objectives than the Army of the Potomac thus far in the conflict.

Rebuilding the line from Aquia Creek Landing toward Fredericksburg began on November 18 and required a great deal of work. McCallum found that the Confederates had added to the destruction wrought by the retreating Federals by thoroughly burning everything at the landing after they occupied the area on September 7. The Federals took ten days to rebuild the facility, in part by using river barges to create a temporary floating wharf. Then they began to build an entirely new wharf one mile below the old one, which was finished in February 1863. This allowed for the use of coastal vessels that drew ten and a half feet of draft as opposed to only eight and a half feet. McCallum thought the difference was well worth the time and expense.[42]

As soon as the first locomotive reached Aquia Creek Landing from Alexandria, it began running cars along the rail line without intermission. The Federals added more engines as soon as possible. Haupt laid tracks on barges so rolling stock could be shipped more expeditiously by coastal vessels. The line was operable up to Potomac Creek, where the Federals created a depot and began repairing the bridge.[43]

Meigs estimated that 150–200 sutlers accompanied the Army of the Potomac, and all of them wanted to ship their wares to Aquia Creek Landing and along the railroad. He thought this would take 100 vessels and refused to tie up so many craft. Meigs recommended to Burnside that he detail troops to escort sutlers' material by wagons from Alexandria. "The supply of regulation rations and forage and clothing to such an army is a herculean task," Meigs told the general. "That of luxuries cannot go on at the same time without delaying and interfering with the other."[44]

As Burnside planned to cross the Rappahannock River at Fredericksburg in the face of Lee's army, he also looked ahead to providing mobility to his ponderous command while advancing south of the river. He wanted to ship most goods by riverboats up the Rappahannock to Fredericksburg, but Haupt thought the railroad would be more efficient. Haupt heard that the enemy was moving trains northward to Fredericksburg, so the track was at least operable south of town. Burnside thought Lee could not destroy much of the railroad if he quickly flanked him out of Fredericksburg. But Haupt began to accumulate ten miles of track material in case of need and instructed Wright to be ready to rebuild the railroad bridge over the Rappahannock at Fredericksburg. If any bridges south of town had to be rebuilt, Haupt planned to do what he had done to support McDowell in 1862—cut timber from the local area and use oxen to haul it to the construction site. He refused to take up valuable space on the cars with bridging material.[45]

The question of how to supply the Army of the Potomac when it advanced south of Fredericksburg became a moot point after Burnside's attempt to throw Lee out of the city resulted in a bloody failure. Crossing the river on December 11 under heavy fire, Burnside attacked the strong Confederate position on the thirteenth with heavy losses. He retreated to the north side of the river, delivering one of the most depressing defeats the army ever suffered.

Burnside was stuck north of the Rappahannock, and with winter coming on the problem of supplying forage for his animals became acute. Ingalls had recommended that the Quartermaster Department stockpile forage the previous September, when the price of oats had been sixty-five cents per bushel. By December it had risen to eighty-nine cents per bushel, and Burnside's stock was running out by Christmas Day. He needed 6,000 tons of hay and 225,000 bushels of oats and corn to endure bad weather or ice closing the Potomac River. Already the water level at Aquia Creek Landing was falling due to seasonal variations in the tide, and Ingalls was increasingly "at the mercy of contractors with a constantly increasing price."[46]

The main problem was that the army remained immobile in one place, with the countryside around it devoid of provisions and forage. Meigs urged Burnside to move forward as soon as possible. The Treasury was feeling the strain of war expenses as prices rose. "Every day's consumption of your army is an immense destruction of the natural and monetary resources of the country. The country begins to feel the effect of this exhaustion, and I begin to apprehend a catastrophe."[47]

Several of Burnside's subordinates thought the overland approach to Richmond was too difficult. They advocated a return to McClellan's use of coastal shipping to move the army back to the Peninsula. Maj. Gen. William B. Franklin and Maj. Gen. William F. Smith further advocated stripping the army of nearly all its land transportation so it could move more quickly once ashore. It would be turned into something "like an immense partisan corps than a modern army," as Franklin put it. His suggestion is a telling comment on the disadvantages of an army having too much material.[48]

But Burnside could not find a way to restart his failed offensive. Meigs suggested that he detail foraging parties into the five counties near his army. "Were the support of only 10,000 men and their animals transferred from our Treasury to the rebel people and lands, it would be an important economy." The war was becoming a struggle to be decided by exhaustion, "and every pressure we can put upon a rebel is so much toward the end."[49]

By late January 1863 Burnside still had not moved, and Meigs was even more worried. He cited enormous figures as the size of the army, with

186,000 men, 62,000 animals (including 18,000 cavalry and 9,800 artillery horses), 6,000 wagons, and 1,400 ambulances. The problem of feeding such a host increased with the deepening of winter and the rise in prices.[50]

Chancellorsville

With the passing of winter, Maj. Gen. Joseph Hooker replaced Burnside and promised an offensive as soon as the weather allowed. Meanwhile, Hooker rejuvenated the spirit of the army. Haupt once again prepared for a deep penetration of the territory south of Fredericksburg. Back in December he had planned to divide his personnel into separate construction and transportation departments. Halleck had no problem with that idea, but he balked at the hiring of 500 civilian railroad workers, suggesting the use of engineer troops instead. Haupt was willing to do that if necessary, but he much preferred civilian experts because even engineer troops would have to be trained how to lay tracks and build bridges. Haupt won this argument, creating separate construction and transportation departments on January 17, 1863, and appointing Adna Anderson chief of construction and William W. Wright chief of transportation. He moved forward with hiring civilians to fill both departments and urged Anderson to prepare for close cooperation with Hooker once the army pushed Lee out of the Fredericksburg area.[51]

Hooker relied so much on Haupt to assist him as he advanced south that he refused to let Stanton send him west to supervise railroad management. By this stage of the conflict, Washington authorities had the impression that Federal generals in the West were not doing a good job with their railroads. If Haupt could not go, then someone else had to be sent. Haupt recommended F. H. Forbes of Massachusetts, a newspaper reporter he trusted, and Meigs wrote the order sending him on April 23, 1863. Forbes made extensive investigations and by June 23 began to report a good deal of waste and mismanagement, although nothing was done about it.[52]

Meanwhile, Hooker's new offensive came to grief at Chancellorsville. Noteworthy in this campaign was the sheer waste of government material above and beyond the norm in other military operations of the war. Roads were littered with knapsacks and overcoats that had been thrown away by the men. Third Corps commissaries issued a total of thirteen days' rations during a campaign that lasted only eight days, indicating how much the men wasted. Quartermasters carefully calculated the loss of other material as well. The Twelfth Corps requested replacement of half of its shelter tents, one-fifth of its canteens, and three-eighths of its woolen blankets, haversacks, and rubber blankets. And this on a campaign that lasted a bit more than one week and extended no more than a few miles from the starting point of the movement.[53] At Chancellorsville the Army of the Potomac wasted more material than most other armies actually used in much longer operations. The main problem was abundance—the men knew they could get whatever they wanted and took little care in preserving what they already possessed.

This campaign also stressed management of the rail line from Aquia Creek Landing to Fredericksburg. Medical personnel shipped wounded along the track but stopped trains to unload them at many locations along the way instead of moving the cars off to a siding. As a result, one train consumed three hours in traveling only fourteen miles. Wright was tried by such practices. He had to ship 200 loaded cars every day to supply Hooker besides moving troops and wounded men. In addition, the telegraph along the line did not operate efficiently, making his job even more difficult.[54]

Gettysburg

When Lee launched his raid into Pennsylvania in June 1863, the Army of the Potomac was compelled to move away from its established lines of supply in northern Virginia, dismantling the Aquia Creek Landing facilities by the eighteenth. The army survived on the contents of its wagon trains while on the move. Halleck instructed area commanders in the path of Lee's advance to seize all manner of supplies to prevent them from falling into Rebel hands. If the supplies were of no immediate use to their own men, they should be shipped to the nearest depot for storage. These inactive districts normally had few wagons available, so commanders faced the problem of transporting the impressed material. Meigs suggested they hire civilian teams, wagons, and drivers to haul it at a rate of fifty cents per day for horses or mules and one dollar per day for each driver, plus one government ration. Maj. Gen. Darius Couch, commander of the District of the Susquehanna, did not like the idea of pressing resources from Northern people and also reported that the civilians were not inclined to work for the government. Consequently, Halleck's and Meigs' ideas were never fully implemented.[55]

By the time the opposing armies met for battle at Gettysburg, Meigs began to reestablish supply lines to Maj. Gen. George G. Meade, who replaced Hooker as commander of the Army of the Potomac on June 27. He planned to use the Baltimore and Ohio Railroad and several smaller lines north of it, including the Western Maryland Railroad, the Northern Central Railroad, and a branch of the Baltimore and Ohio that linked Baltimore with Westminster, Maryland. "We have plenty of supplies, I think, to answer, until after the battle," Meade told Meigs on July 1.[56]

The Federals won an important victory at Gettysburg, and Lee broke contact to retreat toward Virginia. Feeding the Army of the Potomac as it slowly followed became a problem. It was moving through areas temporarily controlled by the enemy and found much destruction of the transportation facilities. The Confederates burned nineteen bridges between York Haven and Hanover Junction, and three more between the latter place and Gettysburg. They also tore up several miles of track on the Cumberland Valley and Franklin Railroad between Hagerstown and Harrisburg. Moreover, the Western Maryland Railroad, which stretched for twenty-nine miles from Baltimore to Westminster, had no sidings, telegraph facilities, turntables, or water and wood stations. Haupt brought in Wright, Anderson, and construction crews from Virginia to effect repairs and improvements on all lines needed by the army.[57]

The Western Maryland Railroad proved to be the biggest challenge. It was set up to run no more than three or four trains each day, but Haupt needed to move fifteen trains daily to help Meade. He shipped locomotives and cars from the Orange and Alexandria Railroad, loading many of them with wood as well as buckets, with which the crews filled the boilers of their engines with water dipped from streams along the track. Haupt organized convoys of five trains each and ran them eight hours apart from each other since there was no telegraph along the line that could be used to coordinate the schedule. Because there were no sidings, trains could not bypass each other. Only by convoying could he avoid head-on collisions. With efficient management, Haupt moved 150 cars carrying 1,500 tons of material in three convoys each way along this short line every day.[58]

Even though Haupt set his construction crews to rebuilding the nineteen bridges along the Northern Central Railroad between Harrisburg and Hanover Junction, he had little faith in the line. On examining it he found that the track and grade were poorly planned and constructed. Curves were too sharp for most modern engines to handle. In contrast, the Baltimore and

Ohio Railroad offered its usual hearty response to logistical calls by the government. Its operatives pushed themselves for seventy-five to ninety hours without sleep to keep the trains running. "Some rest must be had," reported John W. Garrett to Halleck, "or sleep on duty and accidents will follow."[59]

Moving the many wounded from Gettysburg to hospitals farther north became a confused mess due to breaks in the rail lines. Haupt brought order to the process, but medical officers complained about the callousness of the private railroad company. It provided ordinary freight and stock cars for the wounded, not taking the time to clean them and not providing straw, water, or lanterns. Edward P. Vollum reported sarcastically that the company made sure a man was there to count the number of wounded who were loaded so it could file proper vouchers for reimbursement, but it did nothing else. As a result, wounded men often had to lie in cars littered with cattle dung. McCallum authorized the seizing of thirty miles of railroad between Gettysburg and Hanover Junction on July 9 to conduct the transfer more efficiently. By the time he released the line back to its owners on August 1, the Federals had removed 15,580 wounded to Harrisburg, Baltimore, and New York; more than 3,000 were Confederates.[60]

The rail system also moved enormous amounts of material to refurbish Meade's army after Gettysburg. Shoes were badly needed, especially in the Eleventh Corps, and horses had suffered heavily in the campaign and the battle itself. Ingalls urgently requested 2,000 cavalry mounts and 1,500 artillery horses the day after the engagement. Two days later Meigs started 5,000 fresh horses toward Meade from several depots while Rucker moved 750,000 pounds of grain and 250,000 pounds of hay daily toward the army. Rucker also shipped 25,000 pairs of boots and 25,000 pairs of stockings plus horseshoes and nails.[61]

In the wake of Gettysburg, the transport of voluminous amounts of material over these short rail lines was astonishing. When Lee pulled back across the Potomac River by July 14, Meade's army continued to follow up, and quartermasters planned new lines of support. Haupt began to move his construction and transportation crews out of Pennsylvania back to Alexandria because both the Manassas Gap Railroad and the Orange and Alexandria Railroad would once again become the army's reliance. Ingalls had doubts the latter road could support Meade. The army took position across the Orange and Alexandria near the Rappahannock River by July 25 and stayed there until mid-September. Ingalls noted that the track appeared in bad condition and remembered that, in the summer of 1862, many observers had considered it was not capable of supplying more than 40,000 men.[62]

McCallum and Haupt put their energy to the job of making the line work for Meade's army. They started to effect repairs on July 18, finding that the Confederates had done little damage at least to Culpeper. Depots were constructed at Warrenton, Warrenton Junction, and Bealeton. Responsibility for protecting the track was divided between troops of Maj. Gen. Samuel P. Heintzelman's Department of Washington (from Alexandria to Bull Run) and Maj. Gen. Oliver O. Howard's Eleventh Corps (from Bull Run to Catlett's Station). With guerrilla attacks on the rise, Meade wanted at least twelve men to guard every mile of track. Along the sector guarded by Heintzelman, there were 1,362 men for eighteen miles of track, making seventy-five men per mile. Every culvert and bridge received special attention, and blockhouses began to spring up at these locations.[63]

Ingalls was impressed by the improvements on the Orange and Alexandria Railroad by mid-September. McCallum and Haupt repaired the track and added many new sidings to increase traffic on the line. Fourteen stations were in operation along the sixty-two miles between Alexandria and Culpeper, with a telegraph operator at each station. The capacity by mid-September was sixty engines and 600 cars. Ingalls believed the line could have supported an army of 300,000 men at Culpeper, although that seems an extravagant claim.[64]

Bristoe Station and Mine Run

The Orange and Alexandria Railroad became a target of Lee's operations in the fall of 1863. Spurred by a need to transfer two divisions to help the Army of Tennessee defend Chattanooga, Lee took the offensive to distract Meade. The Federals fell back to Centreville by mid-October, allowing Lee access to many miles of track, which the Confederates destroyed very thoroughly before retiring. When the Federals recovered the lost ground, they found that everything had to be rebuilt from Bristoe Station to Culpeper. The task was daunting, and Meade suggested instead that his army shift to the area near Fredericksburg to use Aquia Creek Landing as a base or even move back to Washington and send part of the Army of the Potomac to operate elsewhere.[65]

After consultation with Meade, Washington authorities decided the army should continue to operate along the Orange and Alexandria Railroad, repairing the extensive damage as fast as possible. They were impelled by a desire to prevent Lee from sending more reinforcements to the West. McCallum reported that twenty-two miles of track had been "thoroughly destroyed" from Manassas almost to Brandy Station. He started repairs on October 23, reopening the line to Warrenton by the thirtieth and to Culpeper by November 16. As crews worked on the line, Meade advanced to the Rappahannock River, capturing many prisoners when his troops secured the rail crossing of that stream on November 7.[66]

When Meade launched the Mine Run offensive in late November, his quartermasters supplied the troops with six days' rations carried in their haversacks and ten days' rations, along with ten days' forage for animals, carried in wagon trains. The army was ready for several days of campaigning without relying on the railroad. But the operation foundered when Meade encountered the Army of Northern Virginia in a strongly fortified position and canceled his plans for a major assault at the last minute. After Mine Run, both armies went into winter quarters.[67]

Fall operations ended, but Haupt had already left government employment. The authorities, alarmed by Forbes's report of railroad mismanagement in the West, had wanted Haupt to go there and straighten things out. He was very reluctant to do so, recognizing that the "labor would be excessive and the result problematical." Also, Haupt had always seen government service as a temporary role during a national emergency. He had most of his enormous skill, energy, and personal finances invested in the Hoosac Tunnel project in Massachusetts and was eager to go back to tend to that business, especially when he learned that his enemies were working to circumvent him by influencing Gov. John Andrew to divest him of control of the project. That is why Haupt refused to accept the commission as brigadier general that Stanton had long before offered him. Now Stanton, egged on by Andrew, tried to coerce Haupt into accepting the commission by refusing to pay his expense accounts. Haupt continued to refuse the commission, however, and Stanton dismissed him on September 14, 1863.[68]

Haupt never regretted the year and a half he devoted to the Union war effort. His legacy was enormous, and it mostly lay in creating an efficient system of railroad management. He was not the sole originator of using civilian employees to build, repair, and run railroads, but he did push that concept farther than anyone before him. Haupt also became fascinated with the problem of bridging streams for army use, writing a book on the subject early in 1863, which was published with numerous engravings.[69]

His influence was felt in many ways. Haupt drew a fine line in the smallest details. When Stanton wanted railroad officials to take responsibility for the freight they hauled, he refused, arguing that they should only run the trains while army quartermasters would be responsible for handling freight receipts. Haupt possessed a keen eye for talent. "Stowe understands the operation of the road," he told Maj. Gen. Daniel Sickles of a railroad operative at Manassas, "and can run the trains by telegraph without running them into each other, we have few men who could take his place." Haupt wanted railroad men to control the drawbridge apparatus at the Long Bridge over the Potomac between Washington and Arlington because the bridge people tended to keep it open too long for passing ships, greatly interfering with railroad travel over the span. "Movement in everything and everywhere is essential," Haupt lectured Burnside one day. "Trains must not stand still, except when loading and unloading, and the time for this should be measured by minutes, not by hours."[70]

Haupt further illustrated the principles of his approach to railroad management by complaining to Halleck of the three major problems inhibiting smooth transportation of military goods. First was a tendency of quartermasters to send too much material too early to the most advanced positions, where personnel tended to delay in unloading them. "Nothing should be sent to the extreme front until it is actually needed," he wrote. Next, cars were not unloaded fast enough even at intermediate points between the forward units and the base of supplies. Quartermasters ought to maintain enough laborers at every depot to unload an entire train at once and never use cars as storehouses. Finally, army officers were often guilty of interfering with railroad management and throwing train schedules off kilter. Haupt believed that a set schedule was better than using telegraph messages to clear the track for individual trains. He viewed the telegraph apparatus as delicate and liable to break down, and with it broke down the system of running trains by telegram. If a set schedule was posted and adhered to, it would be much more efficient as long as all officers refrained from interfering with it.[71]

Not shy about his accomplishments, Haupt listed them in a letter to Lincoln a month before his dismissal. "The transportation of loaded cars on floats; of bridge trusses to be erected whole; the various new plans for military bridges; the blanket boats for crossing streams and forcing a passage of rivers in the face of an enemy; the torpedoes for destroying bridges; the appliances for destroying track at the rate of five miles per hour; and the plans for rapidly reconstructing roads that have been destroyed by the enemy are among the most valuable results of my operations."[72]

Even though impressive, Haupt's accomplishments should not be allowed to overshadow those of his colleagues. Many men, including McCallum and Wright, labored far longer than he did on the problems associated with railroad transportation in the East. They did not innovate as much as Haupt, who was undeniably the great idea man of railroad management in Civil War America, but they created effective support throughout the long years of the conflict without tooting their own horn as much as Haupt was prone to do.

The Overland Campaign

When Grant was elevated to the position of general in chief in March 1864 and given responsibility for directing operations against Lee, the war in the East entered a new phase of intensity. He was determined to move the Army of the Potomac overland to Richmond and wanted to use a combination of coastal shipping and railroads to supply it along the way. Moreover, his plans called for assembling troops from the southern Atlantic coastal enclaves for a new field force called the Army of the James under Maj. Gen. Benjamin F. Butler. Meigs sent Col. George D. Wise to Philadelphia and Baltimore to round up fifty schooners and forty barges to effect this concentration. All steamers within reach of Washington were corralled on short notice, and those working in the New York area were chartered and sent to the Potomac River. Within a few days Wise found twenty-eight coastal vessels capable of hauling 20,000 men along with eight steam tugs and fifty canal barges to transport Butler's troops.[73]

Meade prepared the Army of the Potomac for the coming campaign so it would have enough supplies without impeding its movements. He arranged for 150 rounds of small-arms ammunition per man, 50 to be carried on the person and 100 in the ordnance trains. Sixteen days' marching rations, four days' salt meat, and twelve days' beef on the hoof would be taken. Drawing a lesson from Chancellorsville, where each man was loaded with eight days' rations on his person and threw much of it away, Meade mandated that only three full rations be carried in haversacks and three small rations in knapsacks. The animals of the army had ten days' forage carried in the trains. The artillery could count on 100 rounds per gun readily available, and the medical department was prepared with enough supplies to treat 12,000 wounded. Meade told Grant that if a battle occurred early in the campaign, the army could use the Orange and Alexandria Railroad for resupply. Farther south, it would be best to rely on coastal shipping. To that end he arranged for the loading of one million rations on ships for delivery wherever needed.[74]

Grant was careful not to let the mass of material derail his plans for movement. When Meigs told him that Burnside wanted more than the 500 wagons allotted to his Ninth Corps, Grant refused to comply. Burnside should give up all material he could not haul with 500 wagons and make do with less.[75]

"Probably no army on the earth ever before was in better condition in every respect than was the Army of the Potomac on the 4th of May, 1864," concluded Ingalls. For 125,000 men he counted 4,300 wagons; 835 ambulances; 29,945 artillery, cavalry, ambulance, and wagon horses; 4,046 privately owned horses; and 22,528 mules. A herd of more than 6,000 cattle accompanied the army to provide fresh beef for the men.[76]

Ingalls reduced operations along the Orange and Alexandria Railroad, breaking up depots back to the Rappahannock River on May 4 and sending extra supplies to Alexandria for storage. His subordinates prepared to cut back operations still further in the near future when it became apparent that the army was moving south beyond the line's reach. They also prepared to establish temporary depots at selected points near the coast "as the army fought its bloody way along and approached within striking distance of these points," as Ingalls described it.[77]

The supply officers waited for the result of the Overland Campaign's first engagement at the Wilderness to see what their next move would be. When Grant conducted a short march around Lee's right flank after two days of combat, they started to repair the Aquia Creek Landing facilities and the railroad to Fredericksburg on May 9. McCallum used Haupt's innovation of placing tracks on barges to transport rolling stock to the line, which was operable by the seventeenth. Crews repaired the much-abused Potomac Creek bridge in forty hours. Grant used this line of communication from May 17 to May 22, mostly to transport wounded men from the battle at Spotsylvania Court House. It was never used again for military purposes after that. The Federals also opened a secondary landing for coastal vessels at Belle Plain, near the junction of Potomac Creek and the Potomac River. It proved to be much less efficient than Aquia Creek Landing, with a smaller, weaker wharf and bad roads leading inland. The Federals abandoned the Belle Plain depot on May 22.[78]

After Aquia Creek Landing and Belle Plain, supply officers next established a temporary depot at Port Royal, on the south bank of the Rappahannock River, from May 22 to May 31. During this time, the army was at the North Anna River, thirty miles away, linked to the depot by its wagon trains. Those trains carried wounded and sick men to Port Royal and came back loaded with provisions and other needed items. The wagons moved continually back and forth in an effort to keep the supply up to the army's demand.[79]

The Federals next established a depot at White House on the Pamunkey River, the same place McClellan had used two years before during the Peninsula Campaign. They opened the Richmond and York River Railroad by June 1 as far as Dispatch Station and used this as the army's main line of supply until June 12, while the army suffered in the trenches at Cold Harbor.[80]

As Grant continued south, Halleck carefully thought out the pros and cons of his line of approach. He consulted officers who had participated in the Peninsula Campaign and warned Grant that to approach Richmond from the northeast, using White House as his base, would duplicate McClellan's problems. The chief of these challenges was the wide, swampy course of the Chickahominy River, which had to be crossed. It was a major impediment to the movement of a large army and the transportation of supplies in addition to being very unhealthy in the summer. Halleck thought it better for Grant to shift farther west and approach Richmond from the north, using other rail lines to obtain supplies either directly from Washington or from depots along the coast.[81]

Petersburg

But Grant had no intention of approaching the capital from the north. In mid-June he planned a shift of operations to the south side of the James River, thereby avoiding the Chickahominy River and casting Petersburg as the key to the Confederate capital. He also was motivated in this by a belief that it would be too difficult to protect the railroad back to Fredericksburg, "a long, vulnerable line which would exhaust much of our strength to guard," as he told Stanton.[82]

Several days of preparation were necessary to cross this wide tidal river. Most of the available coastal vessels were currently moving material to White House, but they could be diverted to ferry the army over the James. Meigs also began to detain other vessels, and as Halleck pointed out, the barges and tugs already in the area could be used for ferrying purposes. By June 12, orders went out to push all craft toward the James River. The crossing took place almost flawlessly and, for several days, without Lee's certain knowledge of what was taking place.[83]

South of the river, Grant's plan for capturing Petersburg foundered on a number of factors during fierce fighting on June 15–18. The army then settled down outside the city, building earthworks and establishing a permanent presence. Ingalls focused on developing the small community of City Point, eight miles east of Petersburg, as Grant's forward supply base. Extensive wharves were constructed for all supply departments. The combined armies of the Potomac and the James assembled a total of 100,000 men and 60,000 animals in the area, demanding the biggest, busiest field depot of the war at City Point. It was fed entirely by coastal shipping from Washington, New York, and other cities of the Eastern Seaboard. "City Point was one of the great seaports of the world," concluded historian Russell Weigley. Ingalls boasted that he could have supplied an army of 500,000 men from it, another extravagant claim.[84]

P. P. Pitkin was in charge of the depot at City Point until November 7, 1864, when he was succeeded by George W. Bradley. Both men discharged their duty well in Ingalls's view. They also were in charge of all transportation on the James River. Ingalls now supervised quartermaster duties for both the Army of the Potomac and the Army of the James, requiring the quartermasters of each force to submit their requisitions by the twenty-fifth of every month. He kept pretty tight control over the process of issuing material to limit waste. Ingalls also established repair shops at City Point in charge of E. J. Strang, who hired 1,800 carpenters, blacksmiths, saddlers, and wheelwrights to repair more than 3,000 wagons and 2,000 ambulances. What Strang could not fix he shipped to the Washington depot.[85]

To get material out to the units, Ingalls built the most famous military railroad of the war. A civilian line called the City Point and Petersburg Railroad already existed, and four miles of it was operable when the Federals came to the area. Ingalls changed its gauge to suit Northern rolling stock. He then built new track from the four-mile stretch along the rear of the Union line, setting up stations and depots about every five miles for disbursement to the troops. "I will have a cheap temporary track laid down that will not cost much nor take much time," Ingalls reported. Engineers estimated it would take four weeks to build four to five miles of track for only $75,000, less than half the cost of building the average Northern railroad in the 1850s. As Grant extended his lines westward, the railroad kept pace, the Federals at times using ties and rails from the inactive Norfolk and Petersburg Railroad. By late August Ingalls requested that McCallum bring in his personnel to run the line, which eventually stretched for eighteen miles behind Union lines.[86]

The supply arrangements for the Army of the Potomac drastically changed from early May to midsummer. It had relied on "an ever-shifting base" during the Overland Campaign but shifted to a firmly planted, gargantuan base for the Petersburg Campaign.[87] Quartermasters did a magnificent job of mixing coastal shipping with limited rail transport and effective management of wagon trains to keep the army going during the earlier operation. Then they constructed the most impressive forward base of operations to appear in any theater of the war at City Point. That base enabled Grant to stay at Petersburg as long as necessary to work out a solution to the tactical problem facing the army—defeating a tenacious enemy protected by heavy earthworks.

Shenandoah Valley

The Army of the Potomac and the Army of the James may have been stuck in the trenches at Petersburg, but other Union forces engaged in free-wheeling operations that spanned Maryland and the lower Shenandoah Valley during the summer and fall of 1864. Lee sent Lt. Gen. Jubal Early with the Second Corps, Army of Northern Virginia to clear the valley of Federal troops and invade Maryland, threatening Washington in mid-July; Grant shifted the Sixth Corps from Petersburg just in time to save the capital. As long as the opposing forces remained in Maryland, supply was a simple process for the Federals. They received material directly from Washington. In fact, the Sixth Corps left its wagon trains behind at City Point and did not need them for three weeks before Ingalls began to shift them to Maryland while the corps inched farther from the capital.[88]

As operations moved from Maryland to the lower Shenandoah Valley, the question of supply became more problematic. Federal authorities consolidated several departments into the Middle Military Division and assigned Maj. Gen. Philip Sheridan to command it. Sheridan had at his disposal the Sixth Corps, Eighth Corps, and Nineteenth Corps plus the Cavalry Corps of the Army of the Potomac. Such a large force needed rail-based logistics, but there were no reliable railroads going directly into the lower valley. The Winchester and Potomac Railroad stretched from the thoroughly reliable Baltimore and Ohio Railroad at Harpers Ferry to the major city of the lower valley thirty-two miles south, but it was one of the worst lines in the country. Badly graded and constructed with obsolete strap iron, its wooden supports had rotted, and engines frequently ran off the track. McCallum's crews began to rebuild the line on August 14 and pushed it through to Stephenson's Depot, twenty-eight miles from Harpers Ferry, by early November, taking rails from the Manassas Gap Railroad to do so.[89]

Sheridan relied on large wagon trains to feed his army from wherever the rail line ended. Brig. Gen. John D. Stevenson was in charge of the post at Harpers Ferry, which served as the army's main field depot. He wanted to maintain a post reserve of 300 wagons there, independent of Sheridan's trains, to ensure there would be enough vehicles to handle the job. "The loss of one train by a careless officer would defeat a campaign," he told Stanton. "Certainty in delivery" was a guiding principle. Stevenson felt that no army the size of Sheridan's could rely on wagon transport beyond 100 miles from its nearest railhead.[90]

As long as Sheridan operated in the lower Shenandoah Valley, this supply arrangement was adequate. If he was to advance up the valley to Lynchburg, then some other arrangement was needed. For weeks everyone from Grant on down was uncertain as to how far Sheridan should go, and just to be safe they began to plan logistical support for his farther advance. The only practicable way was to rely on the series of rail lines that stretched southwest from the Washington area. That meant the Orange and Alexandria Railroad as far as Manassas Junction, then from there the Manassas Gap Railroad to Piedmont, Front Royal, and Strasburg. The last town was only twenty miles from Winchester.[91]

Relying on wagon trains from Winchester to Strasburg was not only expensive but also dangerous. Guerrilla and partisan attacks on Federal wagons picked up alarmingly in late September after the twin Union victories at Third Winchester on the nineteenth and Fisher's Hill on the twenty-second. Initially Stevenson did not have enough troops to protect the trains he sent south.[92]

By early October, with his infantry near Harrisonburg, Sheridan confirmed that he could not advance up the valley by depending mostly on wagon trains back to Winchester and urged Grant to reopen the rail lines from Washington. He predicted it would take an entire corps to guard them. The only alternative was to forget about a permanent line of support and raid as far up the valley as possible with a smaller but more mobile force. Sheridan also suggested sending the Sixth and Nineteenth Corps to Petersburg and holding the Eighth Corps in a defensive position in the lower valley, devastating the countryside to create a barren wasteland through which Early would hesitate to move.[93]

While the generals debated how to proceed, Stevenson increased the size of his wagon trains from Harpers Ferry to the army and assigned more men to escort them. The size of his trains varied from 200 to 300 wagons early in October, reaching a maximum number of 560 wagons guarded by 2,000 troops.[94]

Meanwhile, McCallum started to reopen the Orange and Alexandria Railroad on September 28 and pushed repairs as far as Rappahannock Station, fifty miles from Alexandria, by October 2. Immediately after that Grant decided to shift the Sixth and Nineteenth Corps back to Petersburg by the rail system. Orders went out to rejuvenate the Manassas Gap Railroad as far as Front Royal. Halleck would arrange for coastal vessels to transport the two corps from Alexandria to City Point. Ever since July Grant had wanted his subordinates to devastate the Shenandoah Valley, and he now urged Sheridan to make it a wasteland. McCallum worked on the Manassas Gap Railroad starting on October 3 and opened it to Piedmont, thirty-four miles from Manassas, by the eleventh.[95]

A week later Early met his final defeat in the Battle of Cedar Creek on October 19. Federal officials then settled their defensive posture in the region. Based on reports that the Manassas Gap Railroad would need many guards, Sheridan opted instead for marching the Sixth and Nineteenth Corps to Stephenson's Depot and then entraining them on the Winchester and Potomac Railroad and the Baltimore and Ohio Railroad. That plan changed slightly when it was decided that the Nineteenth Corps needed to stay to help the Eighth Corps protect the region. Sixth Corps troops headed for Stephenson's Depot early in December. "Our little road is taxed almost to its full working power," reported J. J. Moore of the Winchester line. Only by using cars loaned to it by the Baltimore and Ohio could the company move the understrength Sixth Corps as planned. McCallum's crews had already taken up the rails they had so recently laid on the Manassas Gap Railroad from October 27 to November 10, sending them back to Alexandria for storage.[96]

Petersburg and Appomattox

As the confrontation at Petersburg lengthened, Ingalls and his subordinates intensified their supply efforts at City Point. Eventually Wise, who was in charge of all coastal shipping for the Federal government, either chartered or purchased a total of 190 steamers, sixty tugs, forty sailing vessels, and 100 barges to supply the Army of the Potomac and the Army of the James in their lines outside Richmond and Petersburg. This amounted to a grand total of 390 craft of all kinds at 120,000 tons capacity. Wise doled out $48,000 every day for this assemblage of military transportation.[97]

Everyone who came within sight of City Point marveled at the enormous activity. Joseph H. Goulding, an officer of the 6th USCT, observed it while passing by to participate in the first Fort Fisher expedition in December 1864. "Schooners by the hundred anchored off the point waiting to be towed back down the river," he wrote after the war. "Baled hay is piled mountain high; long storehouses are crammed with all things needed to feed or clothe a great army, or to provide it with means for offence or defence. Long trains of freight cars go almost hourly out to the front, swaying to and fro on the rough uneven track up toward the lines."[98]

The military railroad that took those swaying cars to the Union lines had grown by February 1865 to include a total of twenty-two miles of track, including the sidings and branches. Quartermasters ran fifteen to twenty-three cars in each train and included two passenger trains every day. It was in effect a real railroad, constructed to serve a temporary military purpose.[99]

The one exception to the story of abundance at City Point involved forage for animals. Meigs reported that his department expended more than one million dollars to provide for the horses and mules of the Federal army at Petersburg during the winter of 1864–65. A shortage of forage and feed had developed, driving up prices. City Point had no hay in stock, and the armies had only four days of grain and two days of hay as of January 5, 1865. Grant put the animals on half rations until the quartermasters managed to bring more to the field. "We are entirely out of hay," Ingalls reported on March 20, when another wave of shortages hit the supply system. But with the coming of spring, the problem eased.[100]

As long as Grant's men remained in the Richmond-Petersburg lines, their supply was assured in virtually all categories. When Lee gave up his position under the hammering of Federal attacks on the night of April 2, operations in Virginia once again became fluid. Grant organized the most effective pursuit of a fleeing army to be seen in the war, feeding his men by wagon trains because there was no possibility of repairing railroads fast enough to keep up with the rapid pace of movement. If the Federals retained Grant's allotment of wagons from the Petersburg Campaign, then they were moving with only two wagons per regiment and seven wagons in the general train for every 1,000 men, a low allocation that facilitated their rapid marching. Lee's inability to find food in the countryside plus the destruction of provisions waiting for him at Appomattox Station, 100 miles west of Petersburg, were factors in the Union success.[101]

After Lee surrendered on April 9, Ingalls inspected the Confederates' land transportation. He found the wagon trains to be "in a horrible condition" and ordered forage for the starving animals. Grant had allowed private animals to be taken home by the Rebels, and as Ingalls expected, most of the better government animals were claimed as privately owned and taken away. In the end Ingalls turned over to Federal quartermasters a total of 400 horses, 1,300 mules, 101 wagons, and ninety ambulances from Lee's disbanded army.[102]

Even after the end of fighting, Federal operatives restored some rail lines in Virginia to support occupying Union troops. McCallum repaired the Richmond and Petersburg Railroad by April 4 and then worked on the South Side Railroad, reopening it from Petersburg to Burkeville, 62 miles from City Point, by the eleventh. The latter was the main line of supply to Meade's army in the field. The Federals had to change the gauge of this road to suit their rolling stock. McCallum also opened the Richmond and Danville Railroad as far as 140 miles to Danville to be in touch with Sherman's army group in North Carolina.[103]

The government returned these rail lines to their prewar owners as soon as possible. Quartermasters used the Richmond and Petersburg Railroad until July 3 and then transferred it to the Virginia Board of Public Works to sort out legal issues concerning ownership. They used the Richmond and Danville Railroad until July 4 and then did the same with it. Because the South Side Railroad supported the largest concentration of troops, it served Union needs longer. By July 24 that concentration broke up, and the government gave the line to the board as well.[104]

Because Lee had been prevented from escaping south from Petersburg, the Army of the Potomac and the Army of the James never had to conduct operations in the Deep South. They never outran their supply lines to a dangerous extent and never suffered unusually for want of food, equipment, or supplies like Union armies sometimes did in the West. Its line of operations from Washington to Richmond meant the Army of the Potomac could employ a combination of coastal shipping and railroads as its primary mode of supply. Operating so close to the national capital, the Army of the Potomac was the only field force on either side of the conflict that suffered from too much material, although it has to be pointed out that this occurred only sporadically during the course of the war. Of all its campaigns, the overland drive and the Petersburg Campaign developed the most impressive supply story. During the last year of the war, with few exceptions, quartermasters and commissaries gave the army what it needed without glutting the men with too much. They also anticipated well, developing supply lines and field depots in time to meet needs. Then they built up a huge but temporary forward base of supplies at City Point that surpassed anything to be seen in prior military experience in this country. Victory in the East rode on their work.

11

FEEDING THE ARMY OF NORTHERN VIRGINIA

When the Confederate government, in a burst of enthusiasm for the secession of Virginia, decided to remove its national capital from Montgomery, Alabama, to Richmond in May 1861, it created a very difficult mission for its army. Located only 100 miles south of the opposing capital, Richmond was on the margin of Confederate territory and too close to the political heart of the Union. When Rebel legislators settled at Richmond, the strategic course of the war in Virginia was set in stone—the Army of the Potomac would be doomed to strike at Richmond, and the Army of Northern Virginia would be foreordained to oppose it.

In short, freedom of movement for the Army of Northern Virginia was highly circumscribed. It had to operate in roughly the same small area of Virginia countryside indefinitely, eating up the local resources of food and relying on long-range shipments of commissary stores and an array of quartermaster material, horses, and mules from points hundreds of miles away. At the same time, the Confederacy was shrinking due to important Union conquests in the western theater, reducing the available country from which the army defending Richmond could draw material. Moreover, the Army of Northern Virginia was served by a railroad system that rapidly deteriorated as the war continued.

It was a poor strategic situation for the Confederates. They were forced to mass a large field army to defend their capital and found that the problems of supplying it increased the longer the war lasted. That army was so successful at fulfilling its mission, despite the worsening supply situation, that the war eventually caught up with it. The approach of 80,000 veterans of the western campaigns under Sherman would have ended its career even if Federal attacks on April 2, 1865, had failed to dislodge the army from its fortifications protecting Petersburg and Richmond.

Stunning battlefield victories such as those at Fredericksburg and Chancellorsville characterized the history of the Army of Northern Virginia, but persistence by its soldiers under the burden of food shortages was another aspect of its history. Limited Confederate resources were only a small part of this problem; far larger was a pervasive ineffectiveness that characterized every aspect of Confederate administrative life, especially its logistical and supply arrangements. Many areas of the South were highly productive, but effecting cooperation between the army, the Commissary Department, the Quartermaster Department, and the many privately owned railroad companies that the Army of Northern Virginia heavily relied on was the key problem.

1861–1862

Originally named the Army of the Potomac and commanded by Gen. Joseph E. Johnston, the army defending Richmond had relatively few supply problems during the first year of the conflict. Northern Virginia contained areas of high agricultural productivity, especially in the lower Shenandoah Valley. The railroad system serving the new Confederacy was at the height of its effectiveness early in the war, and suffering in the ranks was sporadic and temporary.

But even early in the war, there were periodic examples of inefficiency. While evacuating the area around Manassas Junction, thirty miles south of Washington, Johnston and his subordinates failed to save all the food that had been processed and stored in warehouses nearby. Commissaries had established a large meatpacking plant at Thoroughfare Gap, fifteen miles west of Manassas Junction. When quartermasters received word that it was time to evacuate the area, they could not find more than seven empty railroad cars to haul the material away. The quartermasters rounded up thirty wagons belonging to local civilians and gave the owners a total of 200,000 pounds of meat in exchange for them, managing to move more stores in this way. But in the end they had to burn 169,819 pounds of meat and left behind an additional 369,819 pounds intact. Even minimal preparation to move this supply of food could have saved every pound of commissary stores processed at Thoroughfare Gap.[1]

In contrast to logistical breakdowns such as this, the Confederates sometimes enjoyed huge windfalls of supplies captured from the Federals. While operating in the lower Shenandoah Valley in the spring of 1862, they secured an enormous amount and variety of material at Front Royal. Even here administrative foul-ups bedeviled Confederate quartermasters. They were frustrated that officers and enlisted men simply took captured property without authorization, making it impossible to account for or distribute the material where it was most needed. Orders were issued to turn in all captured property, but they were not followed. Maj. John A. Harman processed no more than $125,185 worth of this material and knew there was much more that had already found its way into the unofficial inventory of various units. Harman especially blamed the cavalry regiments for taking property at an alarming rate.[2]

Food represented a large proportion of Confederate captures in Maj. Gen. Thomas J. "Stonewall" Jackson's Valley Campaign of 1862. At Front Royal, Winchester, Martinsburg, and Harpers Ferry, his troops secured a total of 161,954 pounds of hard bread, 103 head of cattle totaling 92,700 pounds, 14,637 pounds of bacon, and 4,930 pounds of coffee. But, as Harman put it, "large amounts of supplies were carried off by division wagons" at all of these places with no report submitted to him. Another quartermaster estimated that Maj. Gen. Richard S. Ewell's division took 20,000 pounds of bacon and 40,000 pounds of hard bread without accounting for it. Added to what other commands pilfered, the entire stock of captured goods quickly dwindled as if it had never existed.[3]

Of course, it found its way into the haversacks of the soldiers, but in a way so that those in charge of the army had no idea how much was used or how long it would last. Efficient supply had to be based on control by officers in charge of the process; they could not anticipate needs on a long-range basis if they had no idea what the army already was consuming. Irregular feast-and-famine supply was not the way to run an army. Supply could be supplemented by foraging from the countryside, and the Army of Northern Virginia engaged in this activity when possible. For example, Ewell planned sweeps through Page and Rappahannock Counties in May 1862.[4]

Even before taking command, Gen. Robert E. Lee was concerned about the army's long-term supply arrangements. As Jefferson Davis's military advisor, he outlined the logistical system designed to support the army of 50,000 men as it confronted the Army of the Potomac on the Yorktown Peninsula in May 1862. At that time the storehouses in Richmond contained enough food for 100,000 men for ten days. Quartermasters had constructed depots at various places along the rail network linking Richmond with the South, such as Danville, Virginia; Charlotte, North Carolina; and Atlanta, Georgia. For example, five million rations were stored at Lynchburg, Virginia. With Confederate forces in the Shenandoah Valley largely feeding from the countryside, the storehouses along the rail system could be relied on (as long as the trains ran properly) to feed the Army of Northern Virginia on the Peninsula for the immediate future.[5]

Although the supply situation seemed good in May, Lee changed his tune one month later after replacing Johnston. "The subject of subsisting this army having become one of the gravest importance," he wrote in general orders issued on June 14, officers were enjoined to check their provision returns to see that the number of troops needing food coincided with the number of men listed as present for duty. Subsistence officers needed accurate information about the number of mouths to feed, and Lee worried that many men not due provisions were being listed on the requisitions.[6]

Feast and famine continued to occur. When elements of the army captured Manassas Junction in late August 1862, mounds of food fell into Confederate hands once again. The haul included 50,000 pounds of bacon, 1,000 barrels of corned beef, 2,000 barrels of salt pork, 2,000 barrels of flour, plus a variety of quartermasters' stores. But provisions like these would feed only a handful of units for a few days and could never make up for the increasing shortages to be seen along the rail network that was the mainstay of supply for the Army of Northern Virginia.[7]

Gathering food was one of the more significant problems associated with Lee's incursion into Maryland in September. He admitted that the army was "not properly equipped for an invasion of an enemy territory. It lacks much of the material of war, is feeble in transportation, the animals being much reduced, and the men are poorly provided with clothes, and in thousands of instances are destitute of shoes. Still, we cannot afford to be idle." Two points worried him more than any others. One was the supply of ammunition, and the other was subsistence for the troops. He planned to live off the land as much as possible and therefore issued orders that food should be taken only by authorized officers who would purchase the stores. Lee planned to cut off his rail communications with Richmond while moving north, but ammunition would have to be sent to his army in some way because, unlike food, that was a necessary item he could not acquire from the civilian population.[8]

Once across the Potomac River by September 7, Lee reported that "there is plenty of provisions and forage in this country." He intended to pay for it "on the spot" and, if needed, could offer "certificates of indebtedness of the Confederate States for future adjustment" to civilians. Two days later Lee adjusted his optimism by informing Davis that forage was no problem but food for his men was in short supply because the wheat crop was not yet harvested. "I shall now open our communication with the valley, so that we can obtain more supplies."[9]

Even though his stay in Maryland was short and his army lodged only thirty miles from Winchester, Virginia, the major city of the lower valley, Lee was unable to establish a viable supply line with the South. McClellan moved on him, and the resulting battle of Antietam on September 17 proved to be a tactical draw. But Lee elected to return to Virginia the next day, extricating his army from a precarious situation. "In one month," Maj. Gen. James Longstreet wrote, "these troops had marched over 200 miles, upon little more than half rations, and fought nine battles and skirmishes." Maj. Gen. Daniel H. Hill believed that no more than 30,000 Confederates actually were engaged in the big battle at Antietam because of excessive straggling. He further believed that want of food was one of the chief reasons for that unusually high level of absenteeism from the ranks. A severe shortage of shoes contributed to the straggling. Longstreet's divisions reported 6,648 barefoot men by mid-November 1862.[10]

In the wake of the stressful campaigns of Second Manassas and Maryland, the Army of Northern Virginia rested for several months as officials took stock of its supply situation. It is likely true, as suggested by one modern historian, that quartermasters in the army failed to file requisitions in a timely manner to anticipate material shortages, such as those encountered with footwear. The hallmark of a good quartermaster and commissary was being able to anticipate needs, and that could be done only if he was armed with up-to-date paperwork coming from his subordinates and the infantry commanders he served. An army that failed to keep its paperwork up to date suffered the natural consequences of neglect.[11]

Even more importantly, as far as the food supply, was that the region was being eaten out. "The second year of the war exhausted northern Virginia of subsistence," recalled Texas senator Williamson S. Oldham. The Army of Northern Virginia increasingly relied on areas far afield from Richmond, stretching deep into the southeastern and southwestern portions of the

Confederacy even though those areas supported separate field armies of their own. The high-level importance of the mission assigned Lee's men led Richmond authorities to give them priority over all other field armies as the war continued, disrupting supply arrangements everywhere. No other field force in the Confederacy received such preferential treatment.[12]

And yet the needs of Lee's army still were not met. Col. Lucius B. Northrop, commissary general of the Confederacy, worried enormously over the problem. The Army of Northern Virginia consumed 1,000 cattle every week, but Northrop knew of no more than 8,500 head that were available for it. Half of them were more than 250 miles away from the army and needed to be transported over a rail system that was fast losing its modest level of efficiency. The Confederate government had been successful at slaughtering and packing the meat of 40,000 beeves during the winter of 1861–62, but that number declined to only 4,000 beeves during the winter of 1862–63. This had largely been caused by the loss of valuable country in the West. "The future of beef supply for the Army is so nearly exhausted that this Bureau does not know whence more is to be obtained," Northrop complained.[13]

One response to the problem was to economize, which the Confederates did. In fact, as early as April 1862 the army ration was reduced. In November Secretary of War George W. Randolph suggested it was necessary to reduce it even more. He cited the failure of corn crops in what was left of Confederate Tennessee and in north Georgia, the reduction in beef supply that Northrop already was aware of, and the fact that the wheat crop in Virginia appeared to be less than half the volume of last year's harvest. Transportation problems prevented quartermasters from shipping the corn of the Deep South to Virginia.[14]

"The future supply of subsistence for the army is to me a source of great anxiety," Lee wrote in mid-November. "I have endeavored all in my power to economize that that now exists, and to provide for our future wants." But he pointed out that economizing could go only so far. When the previous ration reduction went into effect, Lee received so many complaints from subordinates that he increased the allowance of flour and beef. Even so, he received many reports that food shortages led to widespread straggling. By the fall of 1862, his army lived mostly on bread and beef; there were no fresh vegetables available. Lee planned to sweep selected areas, such as Culpeper, Greene, and Madison Counties, that reputedly had good crops. Quartermasters who traveled through those areas reported encouraging amounts of corn, wheat, and pork available for purchase.[15]

But then there was always the problem of shipping. When reports reached the capital that grain was not being transported along the Virginia Central Railroad, President Davis sent a personal aide to investigate. Abraham Lincoln never had to send his personal staff on such a mission—he had no need to worry about fundamental matters of supply for his armies.[16]

Lee's problems were not confined to food. Even though 5,000 pairs of shoes were shipped by mid-November 1862, he still had 2,000 barefoot soldiers and an estimated 5,000 additional men who soon would be. This problem continued into December.[17]

1863

After the army achieved its defensive victory at Fredericksburg on December 13, 1862, its supply situation worsened until a genuine crisis developed that was far worse than any yet suffered. More strenuous efforts to locate what few commissary stores remained in northern Virginia became necessary, but Lee was reluctant to cooperate with the commissary general. Northrop appointed James R. Crenshaw as the department's commissary agent for Virginia, but Crenshaw had great difficulty obtaining help from army headquarters. Northrop sent Crenshaw to consult with Lee in mid-January 1863, but the general did not make time to talk with him. Instead Crenshaw discussed the situation with R. H. Chilton, Lee's assistant adjutant general. Crenshaw had purchased up to 400,000 bushels of wheat in Rappahannock and Madison Counties, and parts of Culpeper and Fauquier Counties as well, but needed transportation to haul it out. Lee had earlier obtained authority to secure all wagons available for his own use, so Crenshaw could not find a single one to haul his wheat. If Lee would authorize the detail of some wagons in possession of the Army of Northern Virginia, the grain could be secured. But Chilton could only refer him to James L. Corley, chief quartermaster of the Army of Northern Virginia, who informed Crenshaw he could do nothing unless Lee gave him an order. Crenshaw was understandably frustrated and informed Northrop of his troubles.[18]

A week later Lee finally consented to release fifty wagons from his train to help Crenshaw gather the purchased wheat and suggested the quartermaster general in Richmond take responsibility for finding more. "Our necessities make it imperative that every exertion be made to supply the army with bread," he told Davis, even as he dallied for days before loaning his wagons to Crenshaw.[19]

Lee's reluctance to cooperate with Northrop's agents is not easy to understand. After all they were working for the same goal, keeping the Army of Northern Virginia effective as a field army. Lee probably thought he would never get those wagons back if he loaned any to the Commissary Department. The reluctance to cooperate stands in stark contrast to the Federal army, where officers of various branches did not hesitate to work together to achieve their common goals.

The Army of Northern Virginia continued to suffer shortages in many categories of quartermaster supplies in the early weeks of 1863. Out of 1,500 men in Hays's Louisiana Brigade, 400 were completely barefoot and many had no blankets. A few possessed no underwear, shirts, or socks, while overcoats had become "objects of curiosity," according to the brigade's assistant adjutant general. The commander of the 5th Louisiana decided not to drill his men because so many were without shoes that their feet were "in horrible condition . . . from long exposure."[20]

In late January Lee expressed continued concern about the food supply and wondered why commissary stocks in Richmond were so low. This led Northrop to explain that, as Lee suggested, the problem lay in the increasingly inefficient rail system coupled with decreasing territory from which to draw stores. Northrop pointed out that, as early as the latter part of 1861, he had predicted the beef supply would dwindle quickly. He therefore started a plan to obtain cattle from Texas and feed them on grass in East Tennessee and southwestern Virginia. This failed due to a draught in those regions. Secretary of War Randolph had reduced the beef ration on April 28, 1862, by one quarter, but Northrop had reserved beef held in many areas outside Virginia for the use of the Army of Northern Virginia, telling local commissaries to fend for themselves. In addition, he refused to let anyone except Lee's commissaries have any food stockpiled in the Atlanta depot. These draconian measures helped stave off an even worse food shortage, but when Lee unilaterally increased the beef ration to the previous level because of complaints from the men, it made the problem worse. According to Northrop, Lee's commissaries ignored his suggestion that they use the necks and shanks of the beeves rather than throw them away.[21]

Lee was not impressed by these explanations. "The question of provisioning the army is becoming one of greater difficulty every day," he wrote to the new secretary of war, James A. Seddon, on January 26, 1863. His army had on hand only one week of food, which included four days' supply of fresh beef and four days' salt meat. "After that is exhausted, I know not whence farther supplies can be drawn." The only recourse was further effort to scour northern Virginia, with Lee expanding the list of counties that commissaries suspected had some stores of food beyond the immediate needs of the civilians.[22]

As Seddon told Lee, the main problem was transporting supplies from far-flung areas that had food. By early February the army needed 180,000 pounds of hay each day for its horses and mules but received only 30,000 pounds. The Virginia Central Railroad had promised to move 90,000 pounds each day but failed in that commitment because it had many other customers who paid higher freight rates than the Confederate government. Those civilian customers also paid their bills on time. Lee was forced to send his wagons foraging into the countryside up to seventy miles away from army headquarters to secure what could be found.[23]

Food shortages began to drive strategy by March 1863. Longstreet learned from his commissary that several counties near Federal enclaves in Virginia and North Carolina had ample supplies of commissary stores. He wanted to take a portion of his First Corps to near Suffolk, Virginia, and collect all he could find. "If we can supply our army otherwise the expedition should not be made. If it is a case of necessity we should lose no time." Lee responded well to the idea. "I consider it of the first importance to draw from the invaded districts every pound of provision and forage we can," he told Longstreet. "It will lighten the draught from other sections and give relief to our citizens." Longstreet used two divisions on a campaign that netted quite a bit of material while threatening the Union garrison of Suffolk through April and early May 1863.[24]

Meanwhile, Lee pressed forward with efforts to find cattle, sheep, and pork in the Shenandoah Valley. When symptoms of scurvy began to appear in his troops by late March due to a severe shortage of vegetables, he ordered each regiment to gather "sassafras buds, wild onions, garlic, lamb's quarter, and poke sprouts, but for so large an army the supply obtained is very small." His men had been living on severely reduced rations for some time already. "I do not think it is enough to continue them in health and vigor, and I fear they will be unable to endure the hardships of the approaching campaign." He heard reports that the Army of Tennessee and the troops under Beauregard in South Carolina were more bountifully provided. "I think this army deserves as much consideration as either of those named," he protested to Seddon, "and, if it can be supplied, respectfully ask that it be similarly provided."[25]

But was Lee doing all he could to alleviate his supply problem? In late March Northrop complained that the army leader still had not cooperated with his agent in getting the 400,000 bushels of wheat hauled out of Rappahannock, Madison, Culpeper, and Fauquier Counties. He needed 200 wagons to accomplish the task, but Lee had earlier promised only 50 vehicles. Whether even those wagons were ever sent is unknown. But the fact remains that the Confederates had purchased wheat to make bread for the Army of Northern Virginia and could not even transport it to the mills and bakeries for several months. Lee has to bear much of the blame for this situation.[26]

The Confederates never discussed the possibility of making more wagons, which suggests they felt they did not have the productive capacities to do so. Philadelphia had been the center of wagon production before the war, and many cities in the Ohio Valley and along the Atlantic coast developed that capacity to meet the expansive needs of the Union army. Yet a similar growth in wagon production seems not to have taken place in the Confederacy.[27]

The railroads continued to pose an almost insurmountable problem, worse than any reluctance on Lee's part to loan his wagons. The basic issue was that civilians were better customers than the Confederate government, and railroad officials preferred to serve the citizens. "This army is living from hand to mouth as to meat and bread," wrote Northrop of the Army of Northern Virginia. He suggested the Richmond government flex its muscles and compel the railroad companies to cut their hauling of private freight in half to make room for government material. Seddon understood the problem, writing that "our railroads are daily growing less efficient and serviceable," but like Davis he was deeply averse to compulsion when it came to private companies. Even though the Confederate Congress had authorized the seizure and operation of railroads by the army if needed, Seddon could only suggest a conference with railroad officials designed to convince them to voluntarily cooperate with the government. He assured

Lee that other Confederate armies were suffering food shortages similar to that of his own.[28]

As if he needed more trouble, Lee learned from his chief of artillery that the army was in desperate need of more horses to pull the guns. Many had been killed or had died of exhaustion in the heavy battles of the previous year, and those left were suffering greatly from the shortage of grain and forage during the winter of 1862–63. Moreover, the army was shifting from lighter to heavier guns, replacing the older 6-pounders with 12-pounders, in an effort to match the heavier Federal artillery. These new pieces needed more horses to pull them. Lee reported that the army required 1,200 additional animals.[29]

Longstreet found a lot of food in the southeastern counties of Virginia and eastern North Carolina during his campaign around Suffolk, but he also found that his own purchasers were forced into competition with Northrop's agents. As soon as Longstreet moved into the contested region, the commissary general sent in his people to buy up stores to be deposited in general depots under his control. These agents offered double the price that Longstreet's purchasers could pay, one dollar per pound for bacon. Of course the result was that Longstreet's men could find few sellers. He was forced to authorize them to offer seventy-five cents by April 10 but knew that soon he would have to increase it to one dollar.[30]

Longstreet's inability to cooperate rather than compete with Northrop's agents mirrored Lee's own reluctance to cordially accept the Commissary Department as a partner in his efforts to feed the Army of Northern Virginia. It would seem to be an easy matter to have a conference between the army and the department to coordinate purchasing in southeast Virginia, but that did not happen. Even when it became apparent that the two agencies were working at cross-purposes, no conference took place. The Confederate military system consisted of parts that barely spoke to each other. As we have seen in relation to the stockpiling of food at Vicksburg, turf battles were endemic to the Confederate military system.

Back at army headquarters, Lee resorted to inventive ideas that had little effect on his problem. He issued an order that his men should leave fences standing so that farmers could grow crops to feed the army. The order pointed out that the "contracted limits of cultivated country render it more difficult to procure subsistence." Whether this order worked is unknown, but the tendency for soldiers to pilfer fence rails for firewood was very strong.[31]

On April 17 Lee told Seddon that the army had had no sugar for the past ten days. Its current daily ration consisted of a quarter pound of bacon and eighteen ounces of flour, ten pounds of rice for every 100 men every third day, and "some few peas and a small amount of dried fruit occasionally." It was a pitiful allotment for young men in uniform. "This may give existence to the troops while idle, but will certainly cause them to break down when called upon for exertion." He heard reports that, for the previous two weeks, 100 carloads of sugar and other commissary stores had been detained at Raleigh and Gaston, North Carolina. "The time has come when it is necessary the men should have full rations," he warned Seddon. "Their health is failing, scurvy and typhus fever are making their appearance, and it is necessary for them to have a more generous diet."[32]

This was the supply situation faced by the Army of Northern Virginia just before its great battle at Chancellorsville. Fought without the two divisions that Longstreet had detached, it was even more outnumbered than usual when Hooker's Army of the Potomac, rested, well fed, and well equipped, descended on the rear areas of the Confederate position at Fredericksburg. Lee's handling of his troops during the campaign has been termed the most brilliant of his career, but it was done with largely empty stomachs as far as the rank and file were concerned. Stonewall Jackson's famous flank march on May 2 barely happened because of the weakness of his troops. "This march was a trying one for the men," asserted C. T. Zachry of the 27th Georgia. "The day was very warm; many fell out of ranks exhausted, some fainting and having spasms; only a few had eaten anything since the morning before."[33]

Jackson's attack that evening rolled up Hooker's right flank but stalled in the darkness that night. The next morning Confederate commanders tried to provide rations for their hungry troops. Food arrived for Maj. Gen. Robert Rodes's division, and Rodes "was extremely anxious to issue" it, but circumstances prevented him from doing so. Maj. Gen. J. E. B. Stuart, who replaced Jackson after the latter was wounded during the night, issued an order to adjust unit positions that was misinterpreted as an order to attack. Thus the battle began on May 3 earlier than anticipated, and Rodes had to go in without issuing the rations to his men. The only compensation was victory; the Federals abandoned a great deal of commissary and quartermaster stores in their retreat.[34]

The army also acquired a large amount of Federal commissary and quartermaster stores when Ewell's Corps captured Winchester on June 15, 1863, as part of the preparatory phase of Lee's raid into Pennsylvania. The Federals managed to retreat with considerable amounts of material but lost a great deal as well. Out of 354 wagons, for example, Ewell captured 198. Once again officers and enlisted men pillaged the captured material, taking away what they wanted without authorization. This grew to be such a problem that Ewell issued a general order requiring all officers to turn over public property to their quartermasters and commissaries except what was "needed for present consumption." He enjoined the provost marshal to police the captured material to stop "individual appropriations of what belongs to all." Ewell was aware of the grinding shortages in his command but was determined to suppress plundering, otherwise, he warned, "our discipline is gone; the prospect of victory which has hitherto marked our course will be lost, and we will become, like our enemies, a band of robbers, without spirit to win victories."[35]

This large haul of supplies captured at Winchester would be the last Lee's army enjoyed during the war. But his raid into Pennsylvania offered an opportunity to forage from a fresh and productive countryside. Lee cut his rail communications with the South on June 25, when he crossed the Potomac River. He set regulations for provisioning his army "in the enemy's country" in General Orders No. 72. Lee insisted that his men not wantonly destroy or take private property without authority. His commissaries and quartermasters should offer "the market price" for all material and keep duplicate receipts. If an owner refused to sell, they had authority to seize the material but nonetheless had to offer a receipt, listing the market price and name of the owner, and forward a copy to their superior officer.[36]

General Orders No. 72 read exactly like dozens of similar orders issued by Federal commanders who entered Southern territory. Everyone wanted to make "living off the countryside" as clean and orderly as possible. Such a process, if done right, not only treated the local inhabitants with respect but also went a long way toward maintaining discipline among the troops involved in the process.

But like Federal commanders, Lee would learn that there was a difference between intent and practice. By June 27, when his headquarters reached Chambersburg, Pennsylvania, so many violations of General Orders No. 72 had occurred that he issued General Orders No. 73. "No greater disgrace could befall the army, and through it our whole people, than the perpetration of the barbarous outrages upon the unarmed and defenseless and the wanton destruction of private property, that have marked the course of the enemy in our own country," it read. Lee strongly urged his men to stop emulating their example and "abstain with most scrupulous care from unnecessary or wanton injury to private property."[37]

As soon as the Confederates crossed the Potomac, the gathering of provisions began, and it was conducted in some cases according to Lee's instructions but in most others according to the urges of officers and men. The troops did not live up to their commander's high ideal of soldierly conduct when it came to feeding off the countryside. They fought and lost the Battle of Gettysburg on July 1–3, then retreated back to Virginia, desperately gathering everything they could along the way. The army's train consisted of 6,000 wagons pulled by 30,000–40,000 mules and horses. Confederate forces gathered 30,000 head of cattle, 25,000 sheep, and thousands of hogs along with thousands of tons of hay and grain.[38]

This was an impressive haul of valuable material, but one must keep in mind that Lee essentially had no supply line with the South during the raid into Pennsylvania. Much of this material had to be consumed on the spot or on the march. As a result, Lee continued to face the same supply problems after returning to Virginia that had existed before the Pennsylvania raid.

By July 29, less than a month after Gettysburg, Northrop told Lee that he had tried for months to accumulate a stockpile of food in Richmond. Transportation problems had prevented him from acquiring flour and wheat, however, although he was able to accumulate almost half a million pounds of bacon from various pockets of productive territory in northern Virginia. Much of the corn shipped from Georgia arrived at Richmond spoiled because of carelessness and delays in transportation by rail. But Northrop honestly told the general that the railroads were not the only problem; he had persistent trouble finding enough wagons to haul material. One of his agents needed 75 wagons to get some wheat and corn from Orange, Culpeper, Madison, Greene, and Albemarle Counties. Another needed 100 wagons at Staunton, and his agents in the valley of the Rappahannock River needed 150 wagons in addition to the 30 vehicles they already possessed. South of the James River his people needed 75 wagons. Northrop could think of nowhere to obtain additional vehicles except from the Army of Northern Virginia. He had heard that Lee intended to reduce his land transportation and hoped that any spare wagons could be given to his agents in the field.[39]

This time Lee readily acceded to Northrop's request by sending what he could spare to the Commissary Bureau agents. He made an exception, however, for those agents working in the Rappahannock Valley because his own commissaries were buying food there and needed all the wagons possible to move it out. Lee hoped it would not be necessary to reduce the men's ration because it was barely adequate already. "In all the operations of this army," he told Northrop, "I have endeavored to economize the supplies as much as possible, and to obtain as great an amount from the country occupied as could be collected." He agreed that the government should arbitrarily stop railroads from hauling all civilian freight for a short time to allow its own freight to have priority. He received only 1,000 bushels of grain each day for the animals in his army. Even if he gave all of it to the cavalry and artillery horses, it would not be enough to rebuild their stamina and strength, and there would be nothing for the mules. By late August his quartermaster promised Lee 3,000 bushels of corn per day, which brightened the general's outlook about the possibility of improving his animals.[40]

Railroad problems continued to plague the supply situation. Peter V. Daniel Jr., president of the Richmond, Fredericksburg, and Potomac Railroad, told Seddon that he needed to rebuild four bridges near Hanover Junction destroyed by Federal cavalry raids in June. He required two to three months to do so and warned the secretary that Lee may need to retreat to Richmond from the area around Culpeper if he could not restore the rail link. Daniel also pointed out that the Richmond facilities of his own company and of the Virginia Central Railroad had never been designed to handle such a heavy volume of traffic as was needed to supply an army of 60,000 men. His line's Richmond depot was the first constructed in Virginia several years earlier; it not only was comparatively old but also much smaller than newly constructed depots. His rolling stock also was wearing out from the strain. Lee's Pennsylvania raid was a welcome break because the army cut its connection with the rail system during that time, but Daniel was unable to effect repairs because of a shortage of mechanics. Now that Lee was back in Virginia, the strain resumed.[41]

Meanwhile, shortages of quartermaster stores worsened in the fall of 1863. Lee complained that the "want of the supplies of shoes, clothing, overcoats, and blankets is very great." These shortages influenced his decisions about where to move the troops to deal with Meade's Army of the Potomac. He avoided Loudoun County because of its rough roads subject to frosts in this season, which would produce great suffering among barefoot men. "I should otherwise have endeavored to detain General Meade near the Potomac, if I could not throw him to the north side."[42]

Quartermaster General A. R. Lawton scrambled to help him, shipping almost 10,000 pair of shoes to the army by telegraphing to various depots across the Confederacy. He knew that 12,000 blankets were in the Atlanta depot, but various commands in that area needed them too. Nevertheless, he managed to issue 4,000 blankets to the Army of Northern Virginia and found some horseshoes for the army as well. These shipments helped, but they did not settle the problem. Many men in the army were still barefoot by November 10, and the "weather has become very cold," Lee told Seddon.[43]

By mid-November the promised supply of corn had not arrived. Lee feared he would lose many animals as the weather turned cold. His scouts provided information that led him to believe Meade planned an offensive into a region that Lee knew to be "barren" of supplies. He had to move there in order to intercept the enemy but could not count on finding forage for his animals. "I fear our horses will die in great numbers, and, in fact, I do not know how they will survive two or three days' march without food."[44]

Lee also worried about the Virginia Central Railroad, his main link with the capital. The track was "very bad," and engines often derailed. Lee felt it was "next to impossible" to detail men from his regiments to repair the roadbed because of reduced troop strength. If the road could not be improved, "the only alternative will be to fall back near to Richmond." He suggested to Seddon that laborers of the Engineer Department could be shifted from working on the Richmond defenses to repairing the track; the government could charge the railroad company for their labor, deducting the money from freight costs of the army.[45]

Seddon tried to address these problems with increased energy and ideas. He hoped to lessen the Army of Northern Virginia's reliance on transporting corn from "such distant points as South Carolina and Georgia," although he did not explain how that could be accomplished. Seddon promised Lee that the Army of Northern Virginia would be given priority over other field forces not just for food but also for all kinds of supplies.[46]

Northrop's idea to impress material from the civilian populace in a wide, comprehensive fashion represented a new idea, but neither Lee nor Seddon liked it. "Impressment as a mode of supply for the army, even with the restrictions imposed upon the Department, is unequal and odious,"

Seddon concluded. Northrop explained that the impressment law allowed department commanders in times of emergency to press any material and argued that the situation had reached that stage. Extensive impressment over the whole of Lee's department would demonstrate how serious the army's problem was and "rouse the nation to a sense of its real condition."[47]

Lee flatly refused to do this. It would have "evil consequences" and would be unfair to the residents of his department. If it should be done at all, it had to be done all across the Confederacy. He preferred to keep the regular and emergency systems of procurement separate from each other, with the latter employed only as a last resort. Meanwhile, Lee continued to send foraging parties into counties that still had something to offer, avoiding regions already worked over by Northrop's agents and offering cash for food and horses. If the owners did not want to sell, his people could press the needed items but were to leave enough food for the civilian populace to survive.[48]

But the policy Lee preferred was inadequate to meet his army's needs. The alternative, drawing supplies from other parts of the Confederacy, was fast breaking down. Maj. S. B. French, a commissary officer in Richmond, reported that in September 1863 he had started to procure corn across the Confederacy because the wheat crop had produced less than anticipated. He acquired nearly 50,000 bushels of corn and began to ship it to Richmond, but none arrived by mid-January 1864. Moreover, no one could account for its whereabouts. French sent an associate named Welford to round up supplies for Lee's army in Georgia during the month of December 1863. Welford found lots of material and sent it to Augusta. But after that it "seems to have been 'swallowed up' somewhere between that point and Richmond, for we have but little trace of it," French admitted. There was evidence that quartermasters along the way took it for their own commands without authorization. A commissary at Columbus, Georgia, told French that he could supply 75,000 bushels of corn every month for Lee except for "the obstacle of transportation."[49]

As a result, Lee faced another food crisis in the early months of 1864 due to this breakdown in Confederate transportation, combined with scarce food resources in his own department. The cavalry attached to the Army of Northern Virginia had not received any beef from the commissary for eighteen months. It supplied its own beef by foraging from the countryside and, as of January 5, reportedly had enough to last until mid-February.

How the horsemen managed to do this was not explained, but Lee admitted that commissaries in his infantry units could not find any beef at all in the local areas.[50]

Despite his supply problems, Lee refused to bend his principles. When Northrop urged him to use the resources of the Commissary Bureau to create a dragnet for food throughout north Virginia, Lee stated that he had no authority to do so. "You wish me to do it continuously, to accumulate supplies for the troops, and to give orders to that effect to the officers and agents of your bureau, over whom I cannot legitimately exercise any control." Bending the rules could produce "nothing but evil and confusion if the armies are told to take care of themselves. The supplies must be obtained by a general system under a common control, so that there may be uniformity, and the burden made to fall equally upon all." Lee was hamstrung by respect for lines of authority within the supply system in contrast to Northrop, who was willing to bend any rule that constrained his ability to feed the army's hungry men.[51]

In addition to prudishly holding back from any hint of administrative conflict, Lee complained to Northrop that it looked as if the Army of Northern Virginia was the only Confederate force whose rations were reduced because of food shortages. He heard reports that the Army of Tennessee had "full rations of meat, bread, rice, molasses, and some whisky." In contrast, the Army of Northern Virginia stumbled along with only three-quarters of a pound of fresh meat, half rations of sugar and coffee, and one day's ration of fruit in addition to "some lard."[52]

Refusing to increase the range, comprehensiveness, and severity of impressment, Lee continued to seek information about available food in various counties within his department. "If I can learn of these in sufficient quantities to justify an expedition, I will send one, if it is in my power." But there was precious little evidence that large amounts of cattle, sheep, and hogs still existed in the war-wasted counties of northern Virginia. Lee found it very hard to find enough cattle to provide only half rations of beef to the troops. He also heard reports that 20,000 rations of bacon being shipped to his army disappeared between Richmond and Orange just before reaching the troops. He recalled that similar disappearances had occurred on the Richmond, Fredericksburg, and Potomac Railroad, and it was discovered that the food had been stolen by railroad employees. Lee considered putting a government agent on every train that hauled supplies for his army to end this pilfering.[53]

Not only did Lee have to fight for food but he also continued to deal with shortages of quartermaster stores. One of his regiments had only fifty men with "serviceable" shoes in late January 1864. "Several hundred" men in one of his brigades had such poor footwear they could not do picket duty without suffering in the cold weather.[54]

Lee endorsed a plan to detail men from the ranks who had experience at making shoes and set them to work within each brigade. His quartermaster thought this system could provide footwear for up to half the troops. To start the process Lee requisitioned 37,500 pounds of leather, but by late January the army had received only 9,000 pounds of it. He heard reports that speculators got wind of the requisition and began to horde leather to drive up the price. To circumvent the speculators, Lee sent quartermasters into the lower Shenandoah Valley to find leather, and they had some success, locating 2,880 sides of leather in the hands of original owners and 220 sides in possession of speculators. The upper valley also provided 400 sides of leather.[55]

But then a discussion arose as to whether the shoes could be better made in the field by men detailed from the ranks or by Confederate manufacturing establishments in the South. After his quartermaster showed him examples of Confederate shoes made at Richmond and Columbus, Georgia, Lee thought his own men could do better. Of the shoe from Richmond, he noted that "the side of the skin next the animal was turned out, which is contrary to the practice of the best makes and contrary to the arrangement of nature." In both shoes the soles were so slight they "would not stand a week's march in mud and water." He was confident that 500 shoemakers could be found within the Army of Northern Virginia, and they already had tools—he just needed leather.[56]

Quartermaster Lawton was miffed at the suggestion that Lee's men could make better shoes than his own people. He argued that the Richmond depot could turn out 500 pairs of serviceable shoes each day. Lawton continued to insist that it would be easier to rely on the fixed system than to create a new one in the field. Nevertheless, he pledged to cooperate with Lee if the general insisted on doing it his way, promising to help his quartermasters in transporting leather from the valley. Lawton knew of large shoe-manufacturing plants in Columbus and Atlanta that were privately owned and hoped to get them to increase their production to 1,000 pairs a day to meet the army's needs. But Lawton could do little to increase the supply of blankets, which also were wanting in Lee's army, because there were no manufacturing plants in the Confederacy to make them. The government had to rely on importations through the blockade.[57]

Lawton also felt a bit insulted at Lee's implied criticism of the Quartermaster Department for not supplying the army as it should. He complained that the army's requisitions did not arrive in proper form, dribbling in directly from regimental, brigade, and division commanders rather than being consolidated and sent in by the army's chief quartermaster. Lawton also argued that many of the requisitions from lower-level commanders were wildly unrealistic. He could not possibly supply everything asked for in these cases. Lawton felt he received no credit for providing what was sent, which embraced "thousands of pairs of shoes, blankets, and suits of clothing" that "must have filled some of the requisitions."[58]

1864

The Confederates could have engaged in a never-ending war of words because of their frustration with supply problems that difficult winter of 1863–64. Food shortages worsened until Lee targeted it as "the chief subject of anxiety for me." He finally concluded that private citizens did not trust Confederate currency and suggested agents use hard currency rather than paper money to entice them into selling provisions. He also suggested the agents offer cotton and tobacco to citizens as barter in exchange for food. Lee wanted to drop army regulations that allowed officers to purchase food for their families from the commissary and instead reserve the provisions for enlisted men.[59]

Northrop shot down every one of Lee's suggestions. He did not believe that offering coin rather than paper money would help, criticized Lee's views on the more severe impressment policy he had earlier suggested, and had no faith that preventing officers from purchasing commissary food would have much of an effect on the problem.[60]

The commissary general hit the nail on the head when he reminded everyone that the Confederacy grew enough food but the railroads could not or would not carry it to hungry soldiers. The Army of Northern Virginia lived "from hand to mouth" because it was dependent on provisions shipped from Georgia. "Over 100,000 bushels of corn demand transportation; not over one-third of what is already on the road has arrived. Unless all passenger trains are stopped the consequences may be fatal."[61]

For a while in March 1864, the government pressured railroad companies into reducing their shipments of private freight to give preference to government material. The result was stunning as corn and other provisions rolled into Richmond for several days. "Scarcely before during this war have so many public stores been moved within the same number of days by these roads," exulted Lawton to Lee. "But, like 'forced marches' in an emergency, these results cannot be kept up permanently."[62]

Lawton was right. As long as the government was reluctant to seize a railroad company (which it had the legal authority to do), the companies only cooperated for short periods in giving preference to army freight. Lawton pointed out to Lee that in 1863 the Army of Northern Virginia drew food only from as far away as North Carolina. Now, in 1864, it had to draw on sources deep in Georgia. The lines of supply had lengthened, and the conditions of the railroads had further deteriorated during that year. "Not a bar of railroad iron nor a single locomotive has been brought into the Confederacy."[63]

The spurt of government hauling that took place in March ended pretty quickly. By April 7 Northrop lamented that the depot at Richmond had no accumulation of provisions and sometimes was empty altogether. In contrast, he read reports that commissary depots farther south were full. Reports also indicated that one million pounds of meat were "on their way" to Richmond, but no sign of it could be detected. Gen. Braxton Bragg, Davis's new military advisor, endorsed Northrop's report by asserting that the "want of harmonious action between the roads is a great evil." No arrangements for easy transfer of bulk items from one railroad line to another had been set up, causing much delay at respective depots. Bragg suggested that the army take over the companies and run them according to its own priorities, restricting civilian travel to no more than one train each day to Richmond. Davis did not support this idea.[64]

Consequently, soldiers tightened their belts and suffered. Lee issued a general order assuring them that the reduced rations were unavoidable. The army's "welfare and comfort are the objects of [my] constant and earnest solicitude, and no effort has been spared to provide for its wants."[65]

That last sentence was not literally true. Lee could have sanctioned Northrop's draconian plan to scour his department for food and could have pressured Davis to exert governmental control over the railroads, but his philosophy, demeanor, and high ideals prevented him from doing so. He was reduced to the same old policy of carefully foraging from the countryside and pleading with Richmond authorities for help. "It is absolutely necessary that the army should be properly fed," he unnecessarily told Seddon. "I cannot see how we can operate with our present supplies," Lee confessed to Davis on April 12. "Any derangement in their arrival or disaster to the railroad would render it impossible for me to keep the army together, and might force a retreat into North Carolina. There is nothing to be had in this section for man or animals."[66]

What was to become of the army in the pending campaign against Grant worried Lee. "Short rations are having a bad effect upon the men, both morally and physically. Desertions to the enemy are becoming more frequent, and the men cannot continue healthy and vigorous if confined to this spare diet for any length of time. Unless there is a change, I fear the army cannot be kept effective, and probably cannot be kept together."[67]

Lee underestimated the stamina, loyalty, and perseverance of most enlisted men in his army. Probably their enormous respect for and trust in his leadership represented the key factor in this perseverance. Fortunately for Lee, the coming campaign would prove to be mostly a defensive one, which required less energy, stamina, and vigorous marching than offensive operations.

During the Overland Campaign, from May 4 until June 14, 1864, the Army of Northern Virginia was pressed south toward the capital while relying on two lines of supply. The Richmond, Fredericksburg, and Potomac Railroad was its direct link with the capital, while the Virginia Central Railroad kept it in touch with the lower Shenandoah Valley. South of Richmond several rail lines linked the army with the ever-shrinking Confederacy. The Richmond and Petersburg Railroad connected the capital with an important rail junction thirty miles to the south. The South Side Railroad linked Petersburg with Lynchburg to the west. The Virginia and Tennessee Railroad extended from Lynchburg to Bristol, connecting the capital with the few parts of East Tennessee still controlled by Confederate troops. The Petersburg and Weldon Railroad linked the capital area with Wilmington, North Carolina. The Richmond and Danville Railroad ran toward the southwest, and the Piedmont Railroad linked Danville with Greensboro, in essence extending the Richmond and Danville to link with the North Carolina Railroad at Greensboro. The Piedmont Railroad, built at the insistence of the Confederate government by May 25, could be used as an alternate line of supply in case the Petersburg and Weldon was cut by the Federals.[68]

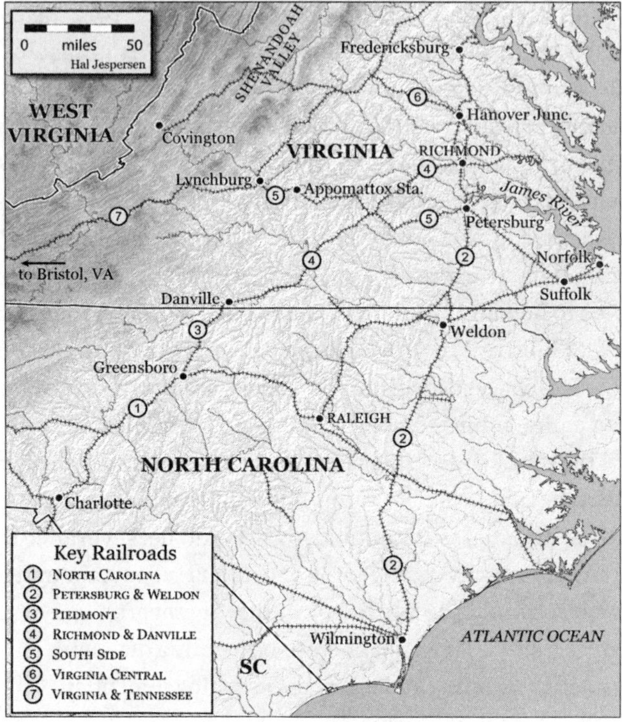

LEE'S SUPPLY LINES, 1864–1865

This rail network allowed Lee to draw supplies from far-flung areas, including the Shenandoah Valley, southern Virginia, North Carolina, Georgia, and Alabama. When the opposing forces lodged in semistatic positions at Petersburg, Grant tried to interrupt Lee's logistical network with cavalry raids and by extending his infantry lines west to cut off the rail links. It would prove to be an effective strategy in the long run, but the Confederates countered each move, often with success.[69]

"I am less uneasy about holding our position than about our ability to procure supplies for the army," Lee confided to Davis on June 26. The meat ration had been reduced to one-quarter of a pound, whereas other Confederate soldiers received one-third of a pound. Lee's subordinates requisitioned whiskey for the men "on the ground that they were broken down and needed the stimulant." It was not possible to fill the request, but Northrop obtained more coffee and sugar as a substitute for the liquor.[70]

Lee felt his food supply was adequate for the near future, but the rail system that brought it to his hungry men was vulnerable. Ironically, even though Grant's forces were lodged within sight of Petersburg and Richmond, the Virginia Central Railroad northwest of the capital remained in Confederate hands and allowed the shipment of some supplies from the Shenandoah Valley. It also allowed Lee to keep in touch with his Second Corps, which he had sent to that area in late June. In a small act of piracy, a Confederate cavalry force captured 2,486 Federal beef cattle in a daring raid behind Union lines in mid-September.[71]

But as the campaign around Petersburg lengthened, the Confederate supply situation worsened. The Army of Tennessee lost Atlanta, allowing the Federals to operate in the heart of the southeastern Confederacy. Access to productive regions decreased. Senator Oldham of Texas served on a joint committee to investigate the question of military supplies and recalled that the Richmond depots had no significant accumulation of food after the first of October. In fact, it normally had not over four days' rations on hand, sometimes no more than one day's. "It required all the efforts of the commissary department, to meet the daily demand and frequently the Department was unable to do so fully. It taxed the utmost capacity of the railroad, to transport the amount of subsistence required by the army as fast as required." There were still some pockets of productivity in what was left of the Confederacy. When Richard Taylor traveled through the Deep South in the fall of 1864, he noticed that the country east of Demopolis, Alabama, seemed fertile and concluded that Lee's army "could have been liberally supplied from this district but for lack of transportation."[72]

Instead of bringing this produce to Richmond, Davis and his supply officers were forced to draw food from the Confederate navy when Lee's men went for ten days without an issue of their scanty meat ration. The president and secretary of war borrowed 15,000 barrels of meat from the navy and more than that amount from the governor of North Carolina.[73]

Lee's logistical network weakened even more during the winter of 1864–65. The Piedmont Railroad, although only a short link between Danville, Virginia, and Greensboro, North Carolina, proved the weakest link of all. Senator Oldham rode along it in December and noted that it took him forty-eight hours to travel forty-eight miles. "Every few miles I met trains standing upon the road at stations and between them, with tenders without wood or water and boilers without steam, locomotives out of order, or cars broken down."[74]

When Lee shifted Hoke's Division from the Richmond-Petersburg area to Wilmington in December, he became aware of these problems on the Piedmont Railroad. It took three days to move one of Hoke's brigades forty-eight miles between Danville and Greensboro. Disgusted, Hoke marched his other two brigades the distance. He warned Lee to expect nothing but trouble from this line and suggested the officers of the North Carolina Central Railroad take over the Piedmont company. Sen. Gustavus A. Henry of Tennessee agreed that the managers of the Piedmont line were to blame for the worsening condition of the road.[75]

For the first and only time, Confederate authorities issued an order for the impressment of a railroad. Special Orders No. 309, Adjutant and Inspector General's Office, boldly declared that management of the Piedmont Railroad would be taken over by the government on December 30. But in reality Confederate officials did not "take over" the line. They merely required that the railroad management give priority to government shipping for a required length of time, something that they had often cajoled other railroad companies into doing without an order of impressment. Even that did not improve conditions on the line for long: heavy rains tore out long stretches of track less than two weeks later and closed the Piedmont Railroad for a long while.[76]

1865

As the transportation system continued to deteriorate, Seddon did not know what to do except resort to Northrop's earlier proposal for unrestricted impressment of food by Lee within his department. This course of action was distasteful to the secretary of war as well as to Lee. "I fear the extraordinary power reposed in commanding generals of impressing without limit will have to be resorted to by you," he warned Lee on January 11, 1865. "A call by you on the people would be more influential in inducing acquiescence, perhaps voluntary contributions, than from any other source."[77]

Northrop continued to support the idea to impress without limit. Special Orders No. 9, Adjutant and Inspector General's Office, gave Lee the authority to do so on January 12. Northrop went on to declare that a crisis had developed in the supply situation similar to what had existed a year before. Shipments of corn from Georgia had been disrupted by Sherman's operations. Northrop knew that meat and corn was available in southwest Virginia and

North Carolina, but he also noted that three things were needed to acquire them—money, wagons, and the "co-operation of the people." The reluctance to sell to the Confederate government was widespread because Richmond had developed a well-deserved reputation for not paying its debts.[78]

But by the winter of 1865, it was too late to implement the drastic policy of unrestricted impressment within the Department of Northern Virginia. In early January Lee issued an appeal to the farmers for volunteer contributions, which produced very little response. "There is nothing within reach of this army to be impressed," Lee told Seddon on January 11, "the country is swept clean. Our only reliance is upon the railroads. We have but two days' supplies." His men needed not only food but also soap, the lack of which had led to "great suffering in the Army. . . . The neglect of personal cleanliness has occasioned cutaneous diseases to a great extent in many commands."[79]

The Confederates were able to limit Federal progress in their Seventh Offensive, also known as the Battle of Hatcher's Run, February 5–7, 1865. Even so, Grant managed to achieve a new position he could later use to good effect in further efforts to turn Lee's extended line stretching west from Petersburg. During the offensive, Confederates "were suffering from reduced rations and scant clothing" in bad winter weather. Having eaten no meat for three days, there was no prospect of obtaining any in the near future. "The physical strength of the men, if their courage survives, must fail under this treatment," Lee warned the newly appointed secretary of war, John C. Breckinridge. His cavalry fared no better. The troopers were compelled to forage as much as forty miles to obtain food. "This is too sad to be patiently considered," wrote Davis when he read Lee's report, "and cannot have occurred without criminal neglect or gross incapacity."[80]

Northrop admitted that the Army of Northern Virginia "has been living literally 'from hand to mouth'" and that other Confederate field armies were in better shape. The counties of northern Virginia no longer had enough food for their civilian inhabitants, and the problems of transportation inhibited his ability to supply the army from remote areas. Northrop revealed that through barter and conducting "secret arrangements with the enemy, turning on their anxiety to get cotton," some food had been obtained from behind Union lines. Given all this, the commissary general admitted to Breckinridge that "the subsistence of the army rests on a most precarious foundation."[81]

During March, the final month of the Petersburg Campaign, Lee watched as his prospects for supply dwindled ever more. The only idea he could find to provide some hope was to issue a call for a "generous contribution" by the populace. Commissary T. G. Williams thought that might produce a substantial amount of food, but he urged the government to find more money and take control of the railroad system as better alternatives. Williams and other commissary officers knew that food was out there in Georgia, Alabama, and Mississippi, but the persistent problem of reliable rail transport continued to keep it there instead of in the camp kettles of Lee's starving troops.[82]

Federal moves continued to reduce that rail system. The capture of Wilmington, North Carolina, cut off shipments by way of the Petersburg and Weldon Railroad, and Lee had to rely mostly on the line from Danville. By March 18 there were still nineteen engines and 150 cars available to send food to the army, but how long they could roll was questionable given the steady advance of Sherman and his 60,000 men bearing down on Petersburg from the Carolinas.[83]

Supply issues affected the Appomattox Campaign in decisive ways. Lee was compelled to give up his trenches at Petersburg by Union victories at Five Forks on April 1 and the breakthrough achieved by the Sixth Corps on April 2. Moving his army due west to Amelia Court House, Lee halted for a whole day while fruitlessly looking for food in the countryside. This delay was priceless for the Federals, who were hot on his heels when Lee continued retreating westward. Hoping to find a promised shipment of food on the railroad at Appomattox Station, 100 miles west of Petersburg, Lee was disappointed when Federal cavalry got there ahead of his hungry troops and captured the supply, blocking his further retreat.

Conclusion

In the end it can only be said that the Confederate rail system managed to deliver just enough food to prevent actual starvation in the Army of Northern Virginia. Otherwise those railroads served the army very poorly. Placing the national capital so near the enemy and so far from the most productive areas of the South, combined with weak governmental control of the most modern means of transportation yet developed, doomed the Army of Northern Virginia to persistent food shortages and seasonal crises during the winter months. Its rank and file often had to fight on empty stomachs and endure Valley Forge–like conditions in winter camps. During the last winter of the war, food problems lead to threatening rates of desertion in Lee's army. That last winter narrowed the thin margin between food supply and soldier persistence almost to the breaking point.

All Civil War armies suffered periodic food shortages, enduring ups and downs in provisioning. But these fluctuations were more pronounced and persistent in the Army of Northern Virginia. According to Confederate officials, the Army of Tennessee rarely suffered as much as Lee's army, and it is certain that all Union field armies fared better than either of the two Rebel forces. The Army of Tennessee moved around all the way from Mississippi to Kentucky to Tennessee to Georgia and finally the Carolinas. It had opportunities to gather food from areas less well trodden than northern Virginia and usually did not need to rely on rail transportation from depots very far from its position. The peculiar situation of the Army of Northern Virginia—assigned the task of defending the national capital in a constrained geographic space—hampered Lee's ability to feed his army to an unusual extent.

As we have seen with the effort to stockpile food at Vicksburg in chapter 3, the Confederate military system failed to meet the supply challenge posed by the Army of Northern Virginia's mission, and for many of the same reasons. Half measures proved inadequate in solving its most fundamental problems—shrinking territory compounded by a worsening national transportation system. Lack of cooperation between the army and the Commissary Department contributed to the failure of supply in Virginia as did Lee himself, who complained a lot but always failed to act decisively to solve these problems. His refusal to enact draconian foraging policies spared the civilians but doomed his men to suffer, while his myopic hording of wagons impaired Northrup's ability to bring food to his hungry troops.

And one must remember that the Union naval blockade of the Confederate coast placed an added strain on the already fragile Southern rail system. It virtually stopped coastal shipping, which forced Confederate officials to rely on railroads to ship needed men and material along the coast.[84]

It is extraordinary that Confederate commissaries both at Vicksburg and in Virginia had so much difficulty stockpiling provisions and feeding hungry troops while in friendly territory. Normal practice would be for commissaries or their agents to purchase all that was needed from willing sellers. That often failed to happen in the Confederacy due to depreciated currency and lack of faith in the Richmond government's ability to pay.

Moreover, neither at Vicksburg nor with the Army of Northern Virginia could commissaries rely on transportation to move needed material from distant places. With Lee's army the only recourse was to press food from the few northern Virginia counties that still had something to offer. Rather than living off hostile countryside, Lee's army was living off friends through a sometimes harsh method of procurement.

Lee could not hope to live off his opponent's country because he did not have the strength or logistical support to occupy it for any length of time. Temporary raiding could net significant hauls of material, but it would be eaten up in little time. Also, capturing provisions on the field of battle occurred about half a dozen times during the first half of the war, but that source also yielded only limited amounts of food when considering the long-term need. The Army of Northern Virginia was doomed to maintain a largely static position in a country that could not support so large an army for four years of harsh war.

In the end it is true that food shortages never led to the collapse of the Army of Northern Virginia or directly to the failure of its strategic mission. But Lee and his governmental colleagues in Richmond could not know that. They certainly feared that this scenario might happen. It actually did happen in the case of hundreds of individual soldiers who deserted during the winter of 1864–65 because of persistent hunger. As a field unit, the Army of Northern Virginia barely survived its struggle with starvation.

CONCLUSION

In studying the history of logistics, supply, and army mobility in the Civil War, the potential as well as the limitations created by several factors are equally important. The conflict spread out over a huge geographic area that contained a variety of topography as well as a transportation infrastructure that also varied widely in form and quality. Viewing the theater of operations from east to west, the Appalachian Highlands, which cut across both eastern and western sections of the Confederacy, posed the most difficult challenge to large-scale army movement. Viewing the theater of operations from north to south, the Upper South possessed railroads and rivers that tended to facilitate the movement of Federal troops and supplies. But in the Lower South there were few advantages for an advancing Union army.

Geography, topography, and the built environment (the prewar construction of transportation venues) were all important during the Civil War. Population density and the ready availability of provisions were yet more factors of relevance to army mobility. As the advancing force, the Federals literally could not have won the conflict unless they found a way to deal with all these challenges impeding their mobility. Being able to move thousands of troops and material over hundreds of miles of contested territory became the key to Union victory. After all, army mobility was and is the foundation of success for any army in any war, especially one aiming to advance into hostile territory. It is the process of moving men and material in a reliable way and allowing those troops to stay in the areas they capture.

The first step in creating army mobility was the utilization of a national system of transportation, which was mainly located in friendly territory. This aspect is fully addressed in my previous book, *Civil War Logistics: A Study of Military Transportation.* In addition to transportation, it was necessary for the Federal government to create an effective system of procuring all manner of food and other supplies for its army of nearly three million men. A detailed study of that topic awaits a motivated historian. The next step in creating army mobility was to work out a system of transportation *within* the theater of operations, which is the main purpose of this study. There was a good deal of procurement of food and animals from Southern territory, and to a large degree that topic figures into this current study as well. Finally, army mobility depended on the ability of commanders, quartermasters, and commissaries to manage all the resources available to them, to coordinate effort, and to allocate materials so that everything came together at the right time and place to provide support for offensive operations. To a large extent, this aspect is also addressed herein.

There can be no doubt that the Federals generally did a magnificent job of creating army mobility. They did so in the most challenging arena of operations between the Appalachian Highlands and the Mississippi River, where it counted the most. There is every reason to believe that Union victory in the Civil War started in the West because of this logistical and supply achievement.[1]

And yet it is equally important to keep in mind that this immense logistical and supply capacity had its limits. The Deep South represented the most important such limit. Rivers failed to favor Union military operations in central Mississippi, all of Alabama, and all of Georgia, especially as compared to the immense natural highway offered by the Mississippi for deep penetration of Confederate territory. The area was well endowed with railroads, but Union authorities realized that the cost of maintaining and protecting long lines of rail supply through occupied country was prohibitive. Sherman managed to do so during the Atlanta Campaign only by extraordinary effort. Even so, the rail system stretching 350–473 miles just barely supplied his large army group. He had no intention of continuing this process south of Atlanta.

The Confederates fully realized that the Deep South created serious logistical and supply problems for Union armies and often commented on their own advantages in this area. The region became a citadel, an area largely protected by geography, disease, and logistical limitations.

In addition to their advantages in the Deep South, the Confederates made a strenuous effort to keep the Federals at bay by fighting hard in the Upper South. Union forces were able to make only limited and temporary incursions into the Lower South from 1861 to 1863. A division of Don Carlos

Buell's Army of the Ohio, under the command of Ormsby Mitchel, penetrated a few miles into north Alabama by the spring of 1862 but retired a few months later. Only the great campaigns along the Mississippi River, beginning with the fall of New Orleans in April 1862 and extending to Grant's capture of Vicksburg on July 4, 1863, offered the Federals the opportunity to operate deep into the Lower South with large forces and to stay there for the rest of the war.

When the Federals were finally able to enter the Deep South overland in 1864 and 1865, they adapted their strategy and tactics to meet the challenges of the region. Logistical and supply limitations led them to cut away from established lines of communications and conduct strategic raids through the heart of the western Confederacy. Sherman had no real supply lines during his Meridian Campaign of February and March 1864. Several smaller raids were launched from Memphis and Vicksburg into central Mississippi without a fully functioning supply line during the following summer, often for the purpose of keeping Confederate cavalry so busy they could not attempt to hit Sherman's rail line during the Atlanta Campaign. Sherman again conducted strategic raids when he left Atlanta in mid-November 1864 for his famous March to the Sea and then his Carolinas Campaign from Savannah. The war already was staggering to an end by the time the next and last round of Union raids, conducted by Wilson's large cavalry force and infantrymen operating out of Mobile, came roaring through the heart of the western Confederacy.

The Trans-Mississippi shared many of the characteristics of the West in terms of geography and topography, with the added factor of lower population density. It was a severe challenge to Union operations particularly because the railroads and rivers in this area failed to offer much advantage. Railroads were scarce in this underdeveloped territory, and the rivers tended to be unreliable in terms of water levels. Logistics and supply played larger roles in the campaigns of the Trans-Mississippi than many other factors, limiting Union offensives and producing starving conditions for Federals and Confederates alike. Major campaigns such as Banks's Red River foray and Steele's march to Camden, Arkansas, turned on logistical and supply issues that forced conclusions unfavorable to the Federals.

The conflict in the East remained an Upper South war almost exclusively throughout the conflict. The heart of that theater centered on the ground between Washington, D.C., and Richmond, Virginia, although campaigns spun out into the Shenandoah Valley and into Maryland and Pennsylvania. Until Sherman brought his western army to the area, campaigns in North Carolina, South Carolina, and Georgia were limited to coastal operations that failed to penetrate the interior. Union and Confederate troops in the East never had to face the logistical and supply difficulties that posed such challenges to operations in the West and in the Trans-Mississippi.

Everywhere Civil War armies tramped, they could collect food for themselves and for their animals from the countryside, but they could not collect ammunition, uniforms, replacement weapons, or readily serviceable fresh troops from occupied territory. In fact, most items on the long list of material needed to support an army were unobtainable from the countryside. Only food and forage were possible, and the effort to secure them involved many difficulties. The process of foraging off the countryside, if conducted following regulations, would have minimized the devastation of the civilian economy and the built environment. That by-the-book method of foraging involved a carefully controlled process of purchasing or pressing only the needed material and recording the transaction by issuing receipts or vouchers to the owner for adjudication after the war. One can find evidence that this actually happened now and then.

But it is very obvious that, more often than not, the process proceeded in a less orderly fashion. Officers often did not have the ability to control all their men; the troops had a tendency to want more food, better food, or just a change of diet now and then. The amount of unauthorized foraging was enormous, representing the mainstream way Federal soldiers lived off the countryside. The tendency to take more than needed, to laugh at the thought of giving receipts, and to wantonly burn dwellings and farm buildings was sometimes overwhelming. It is inevitable that a certain amount of pillaging and plundering would take place anytime an army entered enemy territory. Whether Union armies were more guilty of this than soldiers in any other war is an open question, but there is no doubt that it took place to a degree that shocked many observers and posed a real problem concerning discipline within Federal ranks.[2]

At the same time, foraging off the countryside certainly increased army mobility. Ironically, the Confederates employed it first in a spectacular way during Bragg's Kentucky Campaign. Federal commanders took notice and began a slow process of learning how to do it with their own armies. They made good use of this strategy before the end of the war, especially as a way to deal with the challenges of supplying operations in the Deep South. Most of the foraging conducted during the March to the Sea and through the Carolinas Campaign was done according to strict regulations laid down by Sherman beforehand. But there always was a certain percentage of every human population, whether civilian or military, who were inclined to violate every rule they could find and who were crafty about getting away with it. The worst cases of cruelty and pillaging in every campaign were perpetrated by a small minority of men in blue, and there was little opportunity for responsible officers to stop it. Even when relying mostly on well-established supply lines, these bad boys of the Union army pillaged and treated civilians with cruelty whenever they had the opportunity.

The Rebel army contained its share of bad boys, too, who plundered and hurt people at every opportunity. In addition, Confederate authorities were never able to create a stable, effective system of logistics and supply and faced many problems attending procurement, shipping, and distribution of material. As a result, Rebel armies relied more heavily on foraging from the countryside than did their Union counterparts and lived off their own countryside far more often than on enemy territory. They burdened their own people far more than the civilian society of the North, given their essentially defensive posture during the course of the war. The result generated a great deal of citizen anger at the Confederate army, which was supposed to protect rather than take advantage of them.

The Federal government had crafted a good system of supplying its army after the War of 1812. The Commissary and Quartermaster Departments were possibly the most effective government bureaus in the military system of pre–Civil War America. While the Confederate Commissary and Quartermaster Departments were modeled on this system, they merely reflected the form rather than incorporated the potential for growth and effectiveness that the Federal system possessed. The Rebel logistical and supply system lacked the protean quality of the Union system. Confederate authorities had the congressional authority to seize and operate railroad companies, but everyone from Jefferson Davis to the lowliest quartermaster was afraid to do this. The system of procuring food and forage was hopelessly muddled for a variety of reasons, as discussed in chapter 11. In no other area of the war could one see such a dichotomy between the operating style and effectiveness of Northern and Southern institutions as in the area of logistics and supply—the difference is stunning.

Even viewed within an international context, the Northern system of logistics and supply was the most advanced and efficient way to support armies developed thus far in history. The ability of Federal quartermasters to marshal privately owned river steamers and coastal vessels, totaling more than a thousand altogether at any one time in the war, and to make effective use of privately owned railroad corporations, readily seizing them when necessary, had an important effect on army mobility in the Civil War. Also, Federal armies used bigger wagon trains than was typical of armies operating in other countries even in the nineteenth century

The heavy-handed method of feeding armies from the countryside is an old story in world history, but the Civil War occurred on the threshold of a major shift in international history toward a truly modern, corporatist style of organizing men for war. The actual transition into the modern mode of warfare occurred during the fifty years between the end of the Civil War and the onset of World War I. Union commanders reflected modernizing trends nonetheless by striving to create a system of logistics and supply that was effective enough to serve all the needs of their field armies so as to lessen the necessity of living off the countryside. Even with the strategic raids of 1864–65, Federal armies relied more heavily on established lines of communications and lived off the countryside less than most field forces of the past. Yet they did need to forage to supplement their planned supply.

In contrast, armies raised to fight the great world wars of the twentieth century relied on well-developed channels of supply for virtually all they needed. There was rarely any need to rely primarily on civilian sources of food in the zone of operations during either war. Of course some degree of this occurred on a haphazard basis, for individual soldiers will always be interested in finding something to supplement or replace their army rations. But there was no need for regular or large-scale reliance on local food sources to feed modern armies in the twentieth century.

At the same time, politically and racially motivated devastation of the countryside in occupied territory became a horrifying feature of modern warfare during the 1940s both in Europe and Asia. Nazi ideology and the attitudes of Japanese militarists condoned utilizing scorched-earth policies, scouring the countryside for food to be shipped to the homeland, and securing civilian slave laborers from occupied territory. Sadly, even though the armies of World War II relied more heavily on secure lines of supply than ever before in history, this did not spare civilians in occupied territories from brutality, starvation, and murder.

"The art of subsisting troops during active operations in a hostile country, is one of the most difficult subjects connected with war," wrote Henry Halleck in his book *Elements of Military Art and Science,* originally published in 1846. Halleck pointed out that, historically, commanders had relied on a mix of established lines of supply and securing food from the area of operations. Modern military historians have confirmed that the mix has always been a factor in logistics and supply as long as organized warfare has existed. This certainly was true of Civil War armies as well.[3]

In the end, we cannot conclude that the Civil War was the first modern war, as so many people have argued. In areas such as strategy, tactics, and cultural attitudes toward combat, it was very consistent with the past. But we can conclude that in the area of logistics and supply, it was more advanced than in many other aspects of the conflict. Without that protomodern logistics-and-supply system, the North could not have won the war. In large part because they failed to meet many logistics and supply problems, the Confederates lost the war. Even though these aspects have largely been unexplored by historians for more than 150 years, Civil War logistics and supply were among the most important factors in determining the outcome of the conflict.

Notes

Abbreviations

ADAH Alabama Department of Archives and History, Montgomery, Ala.
ALPL Abraham Lincoln Presidential Library, Springfield, Ill.
BC Bowdoin College, Special Collections, Brunswick, Maine
CWM College of William and Mary, Manuscripts and Rare Books, Williamsburg, Va.
DU Duke University, Rubenstein Rare Book and Manuscript Library, Durham, N.C.
GLIAH Gilder Lehrman Institute of American History, New-York Historical Society, New York
KHS Kansas Historical Society, Topeka
LC Library of Congress, Manuscript Division, Washington, D.C.
LSU Louisiana State University, Louisiana and Lower Mississippi Valley Collections, Baton Rouge
MHM Missouri History Museum, St. Louis
MHS Massachusetts Historical Society, Boston
OR *War of the Rebellion: A Compilation of the Official Records of the Union and Confederate Armies,* 70 vols. in 128 parts (Washington, D.C.: Government Printing Office, 1880–1901; unless otherwise cited, all references are to series 1)
SOR *Supplement to the Official Records of the Union and Confederate Armies.* 100 vols. (Wilmington, N.C.: Broadfoot, 1993–2000)
TSLA Tennessee State Library and Archives, Nashville
TU Tulane University, Special Collections, New Orleans, La.
UM University of Michigan, William L. Clements Library, Ann Arbor
UNC University of North Carolina, Southern Historical Collection, Chapel Hill
USAMHI US Army Military History Institute, Carlisle, Pa.
UTC University of Tennessee, Special Collections, Chattanooga
UTK University of Tennessee, Special Collections, Knoxville
UW University of Wyoming, American Heritage Center, Laramie
YU Yale University, Sterling Memorial Library, New Haven, Conn.

Introduction

1. Balloch to wife, Nov. 14, 1862, George Williamson Balloch Papers, DU.

2. Sherman to Raum, Aug. 16, 1864, *OR*, 38(5):541; Sherman, *Memoirs*, 2:389.

3. Humphreys, *Yellow Fever*, 19, 27, 32; Steiner, *Disease in the Civil War*, 181–82, 189–90, 203–4.

4. Stevenson, *To Win the Battle*, 77–78.

5. Hagerman, *American Civil War*, 58-64, 70–79, 276–93; Hattaway and Jones, *How the North Won*, 716–18; Jones, *Civil War Command and Strategy*, 230, 217, 130, 137, 159, 201, 225, 254–55; Snell, "Union Lifeline," 74–97; Stoker, *Grand Design*, 157, 165, 330, 355–57; Murray and Hsieh, *Savage War*, 304–6, 313–15, 323–24, 415–18, 421–24, 443–48.

6. For example, see Lazenby, "Logistics in Classical Greek Warfare," and Erdkamp, *Hunger and the Sword*.

7. Examples of unpublished studies that bear fruitfully on the subject of logistics and supply are Harris, "Combat, Supply, and the Influence of Logistics"; Bailey, "Civil War Logistics"; and Galuszka, "Logistics in Warfare."

8 Scholarly studies of logistics and supply in wars other than the Civil War are numerous. Please see my fuller summary of them in *Civil War Logistics*, 1–16.

9. Engels, *Alexander the Great*, 9, 18–19, 22–23, 119–22. See also Lee, *Greek Army on the March*, 132–38.

10. Cashin, *War Stuff*, 3–8, 54–55, 112–13.

11. Halleck endorsement on conclusion of Buell Commission; and Granger testimony, Feb. 19, 1863, *OR*, 16(1):16, 451–52; Sherman to Guthrie, Aug. 14, 1864, in Simpson and Berlin, *Sherman's Civil War*, 694.

12. Gabel, *Railroad Generalship*, 8.

13. Moore, "Mobility and Strategy," 69, 77.

14. *Population of the United States*, xvi; Kennedy, *Preliminary Report*, 4.

15. *Population of the United States*, xlix.

16. Grehan, *Lines of Torres Vedras*, 102, 104, 176; Duffy, *Borodino*, 60.

17. For a discussion of Federal efforts to reduce the number of wagons allotted units in the field, see Hess, *Civil War Logistics*, 135–56.

1. War in the Upper South

1. Sherman to John Sherman, Jan. 8, 9, 1862, in Simpson and Berlin, *Sherman's Civil War*, 175, 184.

2. Sherman to John Sherman, Jan. 8, 1862, in Simpson and Berlin, *Sherman's Civil War*, 175; McClellan to Buell, Nov. 25, 1861; and Johnson and Maynard to Buell, Dec. 7, 1861, *OR*, 7:447, 480; McClellan to Buell, Dec. 29, 1861, *OR*, 1:899.

3. Buell to McClellan, Dec. 29, 1861, *OR*, 7:521.

4. Buell to Lincoln, Jan. 5, 1862, *OR*, 7:530–31; Lincoln to Buell, Jan. 6, 1862, in Basler, *Collected Works*, 5:91.

5. McClellan to Buell, Jan. 6, 1862, *OR*, 7:531.

6. Buell to McClellan, Feb. 1, 1862, *OR,* 7:931–32.

7. Annual Message to Congress, Dec. 3, 1861, in Basler, *Collected Works,* 5:37; Stanton to Hamlin, Mar. 22, 1862, *OR,* ser. 3, 1:942.

8. Sherman, *Memoirs,* 1:220.

9. Halleck to McClellan, Jan. 20, 1862, *OR,* 8:509; Hess, *Civil War Logistics,* 41–42.

10. Grant to Halleck, Jan. 29, 1862; and Grant to Julia, Mar. 1, 1862, in Simon, *Papers of Ulysses S. Grant,* 4:103, 307; Grant, *Memoirs,* 190.

11. Grant to Cullum, Feb. 19, 1862, in Simon, *Papers of Ulysses S. Grant,* 4:245.

12. John B. Anderson testimony, Buell Court of Inquiry, *OR,* 16(1):301; "John Byers Anderson."

13. Anderson testimony, Buell Court of Inquiry, *OR,* 16(1):301.

14. Anderson testimony, Buell Court of Inquiry, *OR,* 16(1):297, 300; John B. Anderson to brother, Apr. 26, 1862, Anderson Family Papers, KHS.

15. John B. Anderson to brother, Apr. 26, 1862, Anderson Family Papers, KHS.

16. Grant, *Memoirs,* 214, 256.

17. Sherman, *Memoirs,* 1:254, 257.

18. Cozzens and Girardi, *Military Memoirs of General John Pope,* 106–7.

19. Nevins, *War for the Union,* 2:112.

20. Ambrose, *Halleck,* 56; McPherson, *Battle Cry of Freedom,* 512; McDonough, *War in Kentucky,* 33, 35–36; Hess, *Banners to the Breeze,* 3–5.

21. Halleck to Stanton, June 9, 1862, *OR,* 10(1):671.

22. Stanton to Halleck, June 9, 1862, *OR,* 10(1):671; Halleck to Stanton, June 12, 1862, *OR,* 16(2):14.

23. Halleck to Stanton, June 25, 1862, *OR,* 16(2):62–63.

24. Sherman to John Sherman, [May 31, 1862]; and Sherman to Ellen, June 10, 1862, in Simpson and Berlin, *Sherman's Civil War,* 231, 240.

25. Brady, *War upon the Land,* 29–31; Scott to McClellan, May 3, 1861, *OR,* 51(1):370; Sherman to Halleck, June 26, 1862; Sherman to Hurlbut, June [30?], 1862; and Sherman to Kelton, Sept. 4, 1862, *OR,* 17(2):39, 58, 200.

26. Bell, "'Gallinippers' & Glory," 387, 392; Steiner, *Disease in the Civil War,* 171, 181.

27. William Preston to William Preston Johnston, June 14, 1862, Folder 20, Box 10, Johnston Papers, TU.

28. Williams, *Wild Life of the Army,* 89; Brown to Stephens, Feb. 25, 1862, *SOR,* pt. 3, 1:710.

29. Sherman to John Sherman, Aug. 13, Sept. 22, 1862, in Simpson and Berlin, *Sherman's Civil War,* 273, 301; Sherman to Grant, Oct. 4, 1862, *OR,* 17(2):260–61; Pettus to [Beauregard], May 1, 1862, *OR,* 52(2):309.

30. For a good map of the rail networks, see McDonough, *War in Kentucky,* 13.

31. Risch, *Quartermaster Support,* 401.

32. Dayton to Hurlbut, June 15, 1862; Special Orders No. 98, [Sherman's] Headquarters, June 20, 1862; and Sherman to Kelton, June 23, 1862, *OR,* 17(2):10, 20, 28.

33. McPherson to Halleck, June 29, 1862; and Dodge to Rochester, July 8, 1862, *OR,* 17(2):78, 81–82.

34. Pride to McPherson, July 11, 1862, George Greenwood Pride Papers, MHM.

35. Halleck to Stanton, July 7, 1862, *OR,* 17(2):78.

36. Special Field Orders No. 140, Headquarters, Department of the Mississippi, July 3, 1862, *OR,* 17(2):68–69.

37. McPherson to Halleck, Aug. 24, 1862, *OR,* 17(2):185.

38. McPherson to Halleck, Aug. 24, 1862, *OR,* 17(2):184–85.

39. Grant to Halleck, Oct. 5, 1862; and Special Orders No. 5, Headquarters, Thirteenth Corps, Department of the Tennessee, Nov. 1, 1862, *OR,* 17(2):262, 315.

40. Hess, *Banners to the Breeze,* 9–11.

41. Buell statement, Buell Commission, *OR,* 16(1):33.

42. Buell to Halleck, July 11, 1862, *OR,* 16(2):122–23; Buell statement, Buell Commission, *OR,* 16(1):32–33.

43. Buell statement and Darr testimony, Buell Commission, *OR,* 16(1):32–33, 602–3; Taylor, *"Supply for Tomorrow,"* 48–64.

44. Buell statement, Buell Commission, *OR,* 16(1):33; Daniel, *Days of Glory,* 93.

45. Buell statement, Buell Commission, *OR,* 16(1):32; Grant, *Memoirs,* 257.

46. Daniel, *Days of Glory,* 94, 96; McDonough, *War in Kentucky,* 43; Anderson testimony and Darr testimony, Buell Commission, *OR,* 16(1):299, 302, 604–5.

47. Anderson testimony, Buell Commission, *OR,* 16(1):297–98, 300–301.

48. Daniel, *Days of Glory,* 102–4; McDonough, *War in Kentucky,* 48–54: Hess, *Banners to the Breeze,* 12–13; Taylor, *"Supply for Tomorrow,"* 67; Fry to Crittenden, July 16, 1862; Buell to Rosecrans, July 28, 1862; and Wright to Miller, Aug. 7, 1862, *OR,* 16(2):162, 221–22, 281.

49. Daniel, *Days of Glory,* 105–6; Taylor, *"Supply for Tomorrow,"* 67; Buell to Halleck, Aug. 6, 12, 1862, *OR,* 16(2):266, 314–15.

50. Darr testimony, Buell Commission, *OR,* 16(1):604–5, 607.

51. Buell statement, Buell Commission, *OR,* 16(2):32; Daniel *Days of Glory,* 106.

52. Hess, *Banners to the Breeze,* 18, 20–22; Bergeron, *Reminiscences of Major Silas T. Grisamore,* 65; [Bragg] to Cooper, Aug. 1, 1862, *OR,* 16(2):741; Bliss to mother, Aug. 25, 1862, Robert Lewis Bliss Papers, ADAH.

53. Buell to Wright, Sept. 3, 1862; and Buell to Halleck, Sept. 14, 1862, *OR,* 16(2):476–77, 515; Anderson testimony and Darr testimony, Buell Commission, *OR,* 16(1):302, 605–6.

54. Bragg to Adjutant General, Confederate Army, Sept. 25, 1862, *OR,* 16(2):876.

55. Halleck to Thomas, Sept. 23, 1862, *OR,* 16(2):539.

56. Hess, *Banners to the Breeze,* 77–78, 80–91; Darr testimony, Buell Commission, *OR,* 16(1):606–7.

57. Bragg to Cooper, May 20, 1863, *OR,* 16(1):1093; Magee diary, Oct. 16, 1862, *SOR,* pt. 1, 3:221; Edward Clifford Brush Diary, Oct. 17, 19, 1862, Museum of the Confederacy, Richmond, Va.; copy of Semple to not stated, Nov. 28, 1862, Henry C. Semple Papers, UNC; Kirby Smith to Bragg, Oct. 22, 1862, *OR,* 16(2):975.

58. Bragg to Cooper, May 20, 1863, *OR,* 16(1):1094; Bragg to Davis, Oct. 23, 1862, *OR,* 52(2):382; Randolph to Lee, Oct. 25, 1862, *OR,* 19(2):682.

59. Buell to Halleck, Oct. 16, 1862, *OR,* 16(2):619.

60. Buell to Halleck, Oct. 17, 22, 1862, *OR,* 16(2):622, 637.

61. Halleck to Buell, Oct. 19, 1862, *OR,* 16(2):626–27.

62. Buell to Halleck, Oct. 22, 1862, *OR,* 16(2):636–37; Anderson testimony, Buell Commission, *OR,* 16(1):302.

63. Sherman to Guthrie, Aug. 14, 1864, *OR,* 39(2):248; Halleck endorsement on conclusion of Buell Commission, *OR,* 16(1):16; Buell statement, Buell Commission, *OR,* 16(2):32.

64. August Mersy to Henry Goedeking, Oct. 10, 1862, Engelmann-Kircher Collection, ALPL; George R. Elliott Diary, Oct. 3–6, 1862, Civil War Collection, TSLA; J. W. Harmon Memoirs, TSLA; charges, Rusk testimony, Bowen testimony, Lowry testimony, and conclusion, Van Dorn Court of Inquiry, *OR,* 17(1):415–16, 421, 439, 459.

65. Bragg to Cooper, Nov. 22, 1862; and Bragg to Davis, Nov. 24, 1862, *OR,* 20(2):417, 421.

66. Bragg to Cooper, Nov. 22, 1862; Bragg to Davis, Nov. 24, 1862; and Special Orders No. 28, Headquarters, Army of Tennessee, Dec. 18, 1862, *OR,* 20(2):416, 421–22, 453.

67. Rosecrans to Thomas, Feb. 12, 1863, *OR,* 20(1):189; Thomas to Rosecrans, Nov. 15, 1862, *OR,* 20(2):56; General Orders No. 2, Headquarters, Department of the Cumberland, Nov. 2, 1862; and Special Orders No. 178, Headquarters, Army of the Ohio, Oct. 30, 1862, Anderson Family Papers, KHS.

68. Rosecrans to Lincoln, Aug. 1, 1863, *OR,* 52(1):427.

69. Rosecrans to Halleck, Nov. 21, 1862, *OR,* 20(2):77; Bradley to mother, Nov. 12, 1862, Luther P. Bradley Collection, USAMHI; Fitch, *Annals of the Army of the Cumberland,* 279.

70. Rosecrans to Halleck, Nov. 17, 1862; Halleck to Rosecrans, Nov. 27, 1862; and Rosecrans to Halleck, Nov. 27, 1862, *OR,* 20(2):59, 102.

71. Garesché to Boyle, Dec. 5, 1862; and Guthrie to Rosecrans, Dec. 8, 1862, *OR,* 20(2):125, 141.

72. Wright to Cullum, Dec. 18, 1862, *OR,* 20(2):198–99.

73. Garesché to Crittenden, Dec. 25, 1862; Wright to Boyle, Dec. 29, 30, 1862; Wright to Pennock, Dec. 29, 1862; Wright to Tuttle, Dec. 29, 31, 1862; and Mitchell to Rosecrans, Dec. 30, 1862, *OR,* 20(2):235, 273–75, 282, 286.

74. Wright to Tuttle, Dec. 21, 1862; and Wright to Halleck, Jan. 5, 1863, *OR,* 20(2):286, 302.

75. Hess, *Civil War Logistics,* 256–57; Wheeler to Brent, Jan. 26, 1863, *OR,* 20(1):958–59; Mitchell to Rosecrans, Dec. 30, 1862, *OR,* 20(2):275.

76. Daniel, *Days of Glory,* 227.

77. Walker to mother, brother, and sister, Dec. 28, 1862–Jan. 1, 1863, James Walker Letter, LC; Otto, *11th Indiana Battery,* 22; Rosecrans to Halleck, Jan. 29, 1863, *OR,* 23(2):20–21; Daniel, *Days of Glory,* 225; Rosecrans to Stanton, Jan. 14, 1863, *OR,* 20(2):328; A. S. Bloomfield to father, Feb. 10, 1863, Battery A, 1st Ohio Light Artillery Regimental File, Stones River National Battlefield, Murfreesboro, Tenn.; unsigned letter to editor, Feb. 19, 1862, *Belmont (St. Clairsville, Ohio) Chronicle,* Mar. 5, 1863.

78. Fred Knefler to Wallace, Mar. 28, 1863, Frederick Knefler Letters, Lew Wallace Collection, IHS.

79. General Orders No. 3, Headquarters, Army of Tennessee, Jan. 11, 1863; and Circular, Jan. 14, 1863, Headquarters, Withers's Division, Jan. 14, 1863, *OR,* 20(2):494, 496–97; General Orders No. 38, Headquarters, Army of Tennessee, Feb. 16, 1863, *OR,* 23(2):636; Crittenden to

Bettie, Jan. 20, 1863, John Crittenden Collection, Auburn University, Special Collections and Archives, Auburn, Ala.

80. General Orders No. 9, Headquarters, Second Division, Left Wing, Jan. 8, 1863, *OR,* 20(2):309; Fitch, *Annals of the Army of the Cumberland,* 275, 279.

2. Grant and Vicksburg

1. Halleck to Sherman, Aug. 25, 1862, *OR,* 17(2):186.

2. Frank P. Blair Jr. to Judge, Dec. 6, 1862, Blair Family Papers, LC.

3. Grant to Halleck, Nov. 2, 1862; and Halleck to Grant, Nov. 3, 1862, *OR,* 17(1):466–67.

4. General Field Orders No. 2, Headquarters, Left Wing, Army of the Tennessee, Nov. 5, 1862; Special Field Orders No. 1, Headquarters, Department of the Tennessee, Nov. 7, 1862; and Special Field Orders No. 2, Headquarters, Department of the Tennessee, Nov. 9, 1862, *OR,* 17(2):321, 326, 331–32; Grant, *Memoirs,* 284.

5. Grant, *Memoirs,* 284; Grant to Sherman, Nov. 10, 1862, *OR,* 17(2):335–36.

6. Grant to Halleck, Nov. 12, 1862; and Halleck to Grant, Nov. 15, 1862, *OR,* 17(1):469–70.

7. Grant, *Memoirs,* 285–86; unnumbered order by Stanton, Oct. 21, 1862; and McClernand to Lincoln, Sept. 28, 1862, *OR,* 17(2):282, 849, 852–53; Niven, *Salmon P. Chase Papers,* 1:403–4; Halleck to Grant, Nov. 11, 1862, *OR,* 17(1):469.

8. Grant, *Memoirs,* 286.

9. Sherman to Halleck, Nov. 17, 1862, *OR,* 17(2):351.

10. Pride to Parsons, Nov. 17, 1862; Parsons to Grant, Nov. 20, [1862]; Allen to Halleck, Nov. 20, 1862; and Halleck to Allen, Nov. 22, 1862, *OR,* 17(2):352–53, 355–56.

11. Shea and Winschel, *Vicksburg Is the Key,* 38; Grant, *Memoirs,* 286; Grant to Hamilton, Nov. 26, 1862; and Grant to Sherman, Nov. 29, 1862, *OR,* 17(2):362, 367.

12. General Orders No. 2, Headquarters, Right Wing, Dec. 6, 1862, *OR,* 17(2):390.

13. Grant to Halleck, Dec. 4, 1862, *OR,* 17(1):472.

14. Halleck to Grant, Dec. 5, 1862, *OR,* 17(1):473.

15. Grant to Steele, Dec. 8, 1862, *OR,* 17(2):393.

16. Grant to Steele, Dec. 8, 1862, *OR,* 17(2):393.

17. Sherman to Porter, Dec. 8, 1862; and Grant to Pride, Dec. 19, 1862, *OR,* 17(2):392, 434.

18. Grant to Hudson, Nov. 15, 1862; and Grant to Mary, Dec. 15, 1862, in Simon, *Papers of Ulysses S. Grant,* 6:320, 7:44.

19. Throne, *Civil War Diary of Cyrus F. Boyd,* 83–84, 86.

20. Belknap, *Fifteenth Regiment, Iowa Veteran Volunteer Infantry,* 234–35; Gile to friends, Dec. 18, 1862, David Herrick Gile Correspondence, Civil War Manuscripts Collection, YU; Kraynek, *Letters to My Wife,* 42, 45.

21. Grant to Halleck, Dec. 25, 1862; and Van Dorn to Pemberton, Dec. 20, 1862, *OR,* 17(1):477–78, 503; Throne, *Civil War Diary of Cyrus F. Boyd,* 97–98.

22. Clark, *Downing's Civil War Diary,* 88–89.

23. Parsons to mother, Dec. 21, 1862, Folder 4, Box 31, Lewis Baldwin Parsons Papers, ALPL; Milligan, *Gunboats Down the Mississippi,* 106; Allen to Grant, Dec. 11, 1862; Sherman

to Gorman, Dec. 13, 1862; and Parsons to Halleck, Dec. 15, 1862, *OR,* 17(2):399, 409, 413–14; Parsons to Meigs, Oct. 15, 1865, *OR,* 52(1):709–10.

24. Parsons to [Halleck], Dec. 20, 1862; and Fitch to Halleck, Dec. 25, 1862, *OR,* 17(2):441, 480.

25. Parsons to [Halleck], Dec. 20, 1862, *OR,* 17(2):441; Parsons to mother, Dec. 27, 1862, Folder 4, Box 31, Parsons Papers, ALPL; Ferris, "Captain Jolly in the Civil War," 22–23.

26. Gile to friends, n.d., Gile Correspondence, Civil War Manuscripts Collection, YU.

27. McPherson to Grant, Dec. 20, 1862; and Denver to Stanton, Dec. 25, 1862, *OR,* 17(2):446, 484.

28. Grant to commanding officer of expedition down Mississippi, Dec. 23, 1862; and Special Field Orders No. 35, Headquarters, Thirteenth Corps, Dec. 29, 1862, *OR,* 17(2):463, 505–6; Grant to Kelton, Dec. 25, 1862, in Simon, *Papers of Ulysses S. Grant,* 7:105.

29. Coulter to not stated, n.d., *OR,* 17(1):301; Barber, *Army Memoirs,* 90.

30. Grant, *Memoirs,* 292–93; Grant to Halleck, Jan. 6, 1863, *OR,* 17(1):481; Pierce, *Second Iowa Cavalry,* 45; Grant to Halleck, Jan. 15, 1863, *OR,* 17(2):564.

31. Grant to commanding officer of expedition down the Mississippi, Dec. 23, 1862; and Grant to Quinby, Dec. 28, 1862, *OR,* 17(2):463, 504.

32. Grant, *Memoirs,* 292–93; Davies to Halleck, Dec. 23, 1862, Jan. 2, 1863; and Davies to Rawlins, Dec. 25, 1862, *OR,* 17(2):462–63, 482, 520; Davies to Rawlins, Jan. 9, 1863, *OR,* 17(1):549; Vance, *Report of the Adjutant General of the State of Illinois,* 6:339.

33. Grant to McClernand, Jan. 13, 1863, *OR,* 17(2):559; Gorman to Curtis, Jan. 3, 1863; and Fisk to Curtis, Jan. 10, 1863, *OR,* 22(2):13–14, 31; Allen to Grant, Jan. 10, 1863; and Allen to Halleck, Jan. 12, 1863, *OR,* 17(2):552, 556.

34. Throne, *Civil War Diary of Cyrus F. Boyd,* 99.

35. Grant to McClernand, Jan. 13, 1863; and McClernand to Grant, Jan. 18, 1863, in Simon, *Papers of Ulysses S. Grant,* 7:218–19, 232n; Porter to Welles, Jan. 18, 1863, *ORN,* 24:180.

36. Throne, *Civil War Diary of Cyrus F. Boyd,* 111–12, 114.

37. Grant to Halleck, Jan. 18, 1863; and Grant to Kelton, Feb. 4, 1863, in Simon, *Papers of Ulysses S. Grant,* 7:231, 281.

38. Grant to Wood, Mar. 6, 1863, in Simon, *Papers of Ulysses S. Grant,* 7:392.

39. Grant to Julia, Feb. 9, 1863, in Simon, *Papers of Ulysses S. Grant,* 7:309; Sherman to Porter, Feb. 19, 1863, David D. Porter Papers, MHM; General Orders No. 10, Headquarters, Fifteenth Corps, Mar. 7, 1863, *OR,* 24(3):89–90; Sherman to Ellen, Mar. 13, 1863, in Simpson and Berlin, *Sherman's Civil War,* 417; Sherman, *Memoirs,* 1:305.

40. Sherman to Wood, Mar. 15, 1863, *OR,* 24(3):109; Wood to Grant, Feb. 22, 1863; and Grant to McCulloch, Oct. 16, 1865, in Simon, *Papers of Ulysses S. Grant,* 7:393, 15:341–42.

41. Wright to Parsons, Mar. 11, 1863; and Parsons to Grant, Mar. 1, 1863, *OR,* 24(3):102–3, 115; Halleck to Grant, Mar. 5, 1863, in Simon, *Papers of Ulysses S. Grant,* 7:485; Halleck to Grant, Mar. 29, 1863, *OR,* 24(1):24.

42. Parsons to Grant, Mar. 16, 1863, *OR,* 24(3):115–16.

43. Allen to Halleck, Mar. 18, 19, 20, 1863; and Halleck to Allen, Mar. 19, 1863, *OR,* 24(3):120–22; Grant to Hurlbut, Mar. 19, 1863, in Simon, *Papers of Ulysses S. Grant,* 7:442.

44. Parsons to Grant, Mar. 16, 1863; and Allen to Halleck, Mar. 20, 1863, *OR,* 24(3):115, 122.

45. Halleck to Grant, Mar. 24, 1863, *OR,* 24(1):22; Grant to Halleck, Mar. 29, 1863, in Simon, *Papers of Ulysses S. Grant,* 7:484.

46. Grant to Allen, Mar. 26, 1863, in Simon, *Papers of Ulysses S. Grant,* 7:476.

47. Parsons to Allen, Apr. 4, 1863, *OR,* 24(3):172–73; Parsons to Grant, Apr. 11, 1863, in Simon, *Papers of Ulysses S. Grant,* 7:476–77.

48. Grant to Porter, Apr. 2, 1863; and Grant to McClernand, Apr. 2, 1863, in Simon, *Papers of Ulysses S. Grant,* 8:3–4, 56–57.

49. Grant to Halleck, Apr. 12, 1863, in Simon, *Papers of Ulysses S. Grant,* 8:53; McClernand to Grant, Apr. 13, 1863, *OR,* 24(3):190.

50. Grant, *Memoirs,* 314; Grant to Kelton, July 6, 1863; and Thomas to Stanton, Apr. 17, 1863, *OR,* 24(1):47, 517; Milligan, *Gunboats Down the Mississippi,* 149, 151–52; Ballard, *Vicksburg,* 192–202.

51. Pemberton to Chalmers, Apr. 18, 1863, *ORN,* 24:717; Grant to McClernand, Apr. 20, 1863, *OR,* 24(3):212; Grant to Halleck, Apr. 19, 1863, in Simon, *Papers of Ulysses S. Grant,* 8:91; Grant *Memoirs,* 314; Grant to Kelton, July 6, 1863; and Dana to Stanton, Apr. 20, 22, 1863, *OR,* 24(1):47, 77–78; "List of Boats destroyed on the Mississippi River and its tributaries from May 1st 1861 to the surrender of Genl. Kirby Smith's Army and the cessation of hostilities, June 2d 1865," Oversize Folder 7, Parsons Papers, ALPL.

52. Grant, *Memoirs,* 314; Grant to Kelton, July 6, 1863, *OR,* 24(1):47.

53. Grant to Julia, Apr. 28, 1863, in Simon, *Papers of Ulysses S. Grant,* 8:132; Milligan, *Gunboats Down the Mississippi,* 152–53, 156–57.

54. Grant, *Memoirs,* 321; McPherson to Rawlins, May 26, 1863; and Logan to Clark, May 26, 1863, *OR,* 24(1):634, 643; Record of Events, Battery G, 2nd Illinois Light Artillery, *SOR,* pt. 2, 8:408; Ballard, *Vicksburg,* 221–25.

55. Grant to Kelton, July 6, 1863, *OR,* 24(1):48.

56. Grant to Kelton, July 6, 1863, *OR,* 24(1):58; Grant to Hillyer, May 5, 1863; and Grant to Sherman, May 9, 1863, in Simon, *Papers of Ulysses S. Grant,* 8:163, 183; Grant to Sullivan, May 3, 1863, *OR,* 24(3):268.

57. Marquess to not stated, [May 1863], *OR,* 24(1):688; Sherman to Blair, May 4, 1863, *OR,* 24(3):271.

58. Grant to Sherman, May 3, 1863; and Grant to wife, May 3, 1863, in Simon, *Papers of Ulysses S. Grant,* 8:151–52, 155.

59. Sherman to Tuttle, May 5, 1863, *OR,* 24(3):274.

60. Grant to Hillyer, May 5, 7, 1863; Grant to Halleck, May 6, 1863; Grant to Bowers, May 5, 1863; and Grant to Sherman, May 8, 1863, in Simon, *Papers of Ulysses S. Grant,* 8:162, 168–69, 174–75, 178.

61. Grant to McClernand, May 7, 1863; and Grant to Sherman, May 9, 1863, *OR,* 24(3):280, 285–86; Grant to Pride, May 8, 1863, in Simon, *Papers of Ulysses S. Grant,* 8:181.

62. Macfeely to Grant, May 8, 1863; Grant to Bowers, May 9, 1863; and Grant to Sherman, May 9, 1863, *OR,* 24(3):281–82, 285–86; Grant to Hillyer, May 9, 1863, in Simon, *Papers of Ulysses S. Grant,* 8:186.

63. Grant to McPherson, May 11, 1863, in Simon, *Papers of Ulysses S. Grant,* 8:200.

64. Bingham to Grant, May 12, 1863, in Simon, *Papers of Ulysses S. Grant,* 8:155–56; Hawley to parents, May 18, 1863, Thomas S. Hawley Papers, MHM; Grant to Halleck, May 24, 1863, *OR,* 24(1):38.

65. Grant to Halleck, May 24, 1863, *OR,* 24(1):38.

66. Blair to Sherman, May 24, 1863, *OR,* 24(2):255; Kellogg, *War Experiences,* 34.

67. Tuttle to Sawyer, May 23, 1863; and Buckland to Sample, June 8, 1863, *OR,* 24(1):759, 761–62.

68. Tourtellotte to Martin, May 23, 1863, *OR,* 24(2):61.

69. Sneier to Sir, June 21, 1863, Samuel E. Sneier Letter, IHS.

70. Henry W. Tisdale Diary, June 30, 1863, Boston Public Library, Boston, Mass.; Barnard to father, June 19, 1863, William A. Barnard Collection, Archives of Michigan, Lansing.

71. Boughton to Friends at Home, May 21, 1863, Clement Abner Boughton Papers, UM.

72. Timothy Phillips Diaries, June 11, 1863, Wisconsin Historical Society, Madison.

3. Stockpiling Food at Vicksburg

1. Pemberton to Cooper, Aug. 2, 1863, *OR,* 24(1):290; Memminger, "Surrender of Vicksburg," 356.

2. Northrop to Walker, Apr. 15, 1863, *OR,* 24(3):990–91; Goff, *Confederate Supply,* 84–85; Moore, *Confederate Commissary General,* 144–47, 190.

3. Pemberton to Cooper, Aug. 2, 1862, *OR,* 24(1):288; Johnson to Northrop, Aug. 10, 1863, *OR,* 24(3):1051–52; Moore, *Confederate Commissary General,* 140–41, 183–84.

4. Pemberton to Cooper, Aug. 2, 1862, *OR,* 24(1):288; Cuney to Reed, Nov. 19, 1862, *OR,* 17(2):752.

5. Johnson to Northrop, Aug. 10, 1863, *OR,* 24(3):1051–52.

6. Moore, *Confederate Commissary General,* 206; Seddon to Pemberton, Jan. 18, 1863, *OR,* 17(2):839–40.

7. Pemberton to Cooper, Aug. 2, 1863, *OR,* 24(1):289; Reed to Johnston, Jan. 1, 1863, *OR,* 17(2):817; Reed to Pemberton, Jan. 31, 1863, *OR,* 24(3):609–10; Moore, *Confederate Commissary General,* 163, 184.

8. Thompson to Bowen, Feb. 22, 1863; and Reed to Stevenson, Mar. 3, 1863, *OR,* 24(3):639, 652.

9. Pemberton to Seddon, Mar. 19, 1863, *OR,* 24(1):299; Moore, *Confederate Commissary General,* 206.

10. Goff, *Confederate Supply,* 83–84; Moore, *Confederate Commissary General,* 206.

11. Pemberton to Chalmers, Apr. 18, 1863; and Thompson to Johnston, Apr. 20, 1863, *OR,* 24(3):765, 768; Memminger, "Surrender of Vicksburg," 356–57.

12. Pemberton to Cooper, Aug. 2, 1863, *OR,* 24(1):288; Reed to Key, Nov. 27, 1862, *OR,* 17(2):764.

13. Roach to Reed, Jan. 22, 1863, *OR,* 24(3):595.

14. "Memoranda Handed Maj. Theo. Johnston, Jan. 24, 1863," *OR,* 24(3):602.

15. Jones to Johnson, n.d., enclosed in response to Johnson to Jones, Jan. 21, 1863; and Johnson to Smith, Feb. 3, 1863, *OR,* 24(3):593, 615.

16. Reed to Johnston, Feb. 12, 1863, *OR,* 24(3):624.

17. Bradford to Mims, Mar. 20, 1863, *OR,* 24(1):300.

18. Ferguson to [Stevenson], Apr. 18, 1863; and Pemberton to Featherston, Apr. 20, 1863, *OR,* 24(3):762, 771; Broadwell to Pemberton, Mar. 17, 1863, and Johnston endorsement, Mar. 24, 1863; Pemberton to Koontz, Mar. 24, 1863; Pemberton to Stevenson, Apr. 8, 1863; and Pemberton to Bowen, Apr. 18, 1863, *OR,* 24(1):291, 304, 310, 313.

19. Pemberton to Cooper, Aug. 2, 1863, *OR,* 24(1):288.

20. Pemberton to Cooper, Aug. 2, 1863, *OR,* 24(1):289; Memminger, "Surrender of Vicksburg," 357.

21. Pemberton to Stevenson, Mar. 18, 1863; and Bradford to Mims, Mar. 21, 1863, *OR,* 24(1):298, 301.

22. Pemberton to Cooper, Aug. 2, 1863; and Taylor to [Wilson], Apr. 7, 1863, *OR,* 24(1):289, 309; Pemberton to Johnston, Apr. 17, 1863, *OR,* 24(3):752.

23. Memminger, "Surrender of Vicksburg," 357; Pemberton to Cooper, Aug. 2, 1863, *OR,* 24(1):289.

24. Reed to Theodore Johnston, Feb. 12, 1863, *OR,* 24(3):624; Johnson to Jones, Jan. 10, 1863, *OR,* 17(2):831.

25. Cammack note, Mar. 21, 1863; Carr to Willson, Mar. 29, 1863; and Wingate statement, Apr. 8, 1863, *OR,* 24(1):301, 305–6, 309–10.

26. Pemberton to Cooper, Aug. 2, 1863, *OR,* 24(1):292.

27. Reed to Key, Nov. 29, 1862, *OR,* 17(2):769.

28. Reed to Mims, Dec. 2, 1862, *OR,* 17(2):777; Reed to Thomas, Jan. 20, 1863; and Reed to [Devereux], n.d., *OR,* 24(3):591.

29. Northrop to Seddon, Jan. 23, 1863, *OR,* 24(3):634–35.

30. Johnson to Northrop, Aug. 10, 1863, *OR,* 24(3):1052.

31. Seddon to Pemberton, Mar. 12, 1863, *OR,* 24(3):664.

32. Reed to Cuney, Dec. 2, 4, 1862; and Reed to Smith, Dec. 23, 1862, *OR,* 17(2):776, 782, 802.

33. Pemberton to Theodore Johnston, Jan. 27, 1863, *OR,* 24(3):607.

34. Pemberton to Joseph E. Johnston, Apr. 17, 1863, *OR,* 24(3):752.

35. "List of stores in Vicksburg, Miss., December 15, 1862," *OR,* 27(2):797.

36. "Statement of subsistence stores on hand at the post commissary, Vicksburg, Miss., Jan. 15, 1863," *OR,* 17(2):837.

37. "Invoice of subsistence stores on hand at the post commissary, Vicksburg, Mar. 1, 1863, Capt. J. B. Smith," *OR,* 24(3):648.

38. "List of subsistence stores in Vicksburg, Miss., April 1, 1863"; and "Report of stores in Vicksburg, April 30, 1863, and stores shipped there from April 30 to May 14, 1863," *OR,* 24(3):709, 867–68.

39. "Report of stores in Vicksburg, April 30, 1863, and stores shipped there from April 30 to May 14, 1863," *OR,* 24(3):867–68.

40. Pemberton to Davis, May 2, 1863; and Theodore Johnston to Northrop, Aug. 6, 1863, *OR,* 24(3):815, 1047.

41. Wood to wife, June 21, 1863, Edward Jesup Wood Papers, IHS; Edwin C. Obriham to

sister, May 25, 1863; and Obriham to not stated, June 28, 1863, June and Gilbert Krueger Civil War Letters, Cornell University, Rare and Manuscript Collections, Ithaca, N.Y.

42. Atkins to Theodore Johnston, May 27, 1863, *OR,* 24(3):932.

43. Goodman to Joseph E. Johnston, May 31, 1863, *OR,* 24(3):938–39.

44. Maxwell to Harvie, May 29, 1863, *OR,* 24(3):933.

45. "Report of the number of rations on hand in Department of Mississippi and Eastern Louisiana, June 20, 1863 (exclusive of Port Hudson and Vicksburg)," *OR,* 24(3):968; Moore, *Confederate Commissary General,* 211.

46. Stevenson to Memminger, June 7, 1863; and "Many Soldiers" to Pemberton, June 28, 1863, *OR,* 24(3):953, 982–83.

47. "Rations in Vicksburg when surrendered, on July 4, 1863, per report of Capt. G. A. Woodward, assistant commissary of subsistence," *OR,* 24(3):869; Pemberton to Cooper, Aug. 2, 1863, *OR,* 24(1):292.

48. Ashbel Smith to Loughborough, July 10, 1863, *OR,* 24(2):392; Smith, *Reminiscences,* 27.

49. Watson to Cooper, Aug. 4, 1863, *OR,* 24(3):1043.

50. Abrams, *Full and Detailed History of the Siege of Vicksburg,* 78–79; Vindicus letter to editor, July 13, 1863, *Memphis Daily Appeal,* July 18, 1863; Bevier, *First and Second Missouri,* 208; Theodore Johnston to Northrop, Aug. 6, 1863, *OR,* 24(3):1047.

51. Silas Hemphill to brother and sister, June 9, 1863, Hemphill Family Papers, State Historical Society of Iowa, Des Moines.

4. Transportation Crisis in Appalachia

1. Hess, *Civil War in the West,* 187–98.

2. Rains to wife, Aug. 25, 1862, James E. Rains Letters, Civil War Collection, TSLA; Thomas B. Hall to father, Aug. 18, 1862, Walter King Hoover Collection, TSLA.

3. Wright to Halleck, Nov. 7, Dec. 18, 1862, *OR,* 20(2):24, 199.

4. Honnell to Eli, July 26, 1863, T. C. Honnell Letters, KHS.

5. Rosecrans to Lincoln, Aug. 1, 1863, *OR,* 52(1):427–28.

6. Special Field Orders No. 219, Headquarters, Department of the Cumberland, Aug. 10, 1863, Anderson Family Papers, KHS; Rosecrans to Halleck, Aug. 7, 1863, *OR,* 23(2):597; Taylor, *"Supply for Tomorrow,"* 123–24; Galuszka, "Logistics in Warfare," 113.

7. Galuszka, "Logistics in Warfare," 113.

8. Rosecrans to Halleck, Aug. 6, 1863, *OR,* 23(2):594; Rosecrans to Adjutant General of U.S. Army, Aug. 16, 1863, *OR,* 30(3):46; Rosecrans to Lincoln, Aug. 22, 1863, *OR,* 52(1):439; Cozzens, *This Terrible Sound,* 29–31.

9. Bragg to Johnston, Aug. 5, 1863, *OR,* 52(2):514.

10. Taylor, *"Supply for Tomorrow,"* 120–21.

11. Taylor, *"Supply for Tomorrow,"* 122; Galuszka, "Logistics in Warfare," 112–13, 121–22.

12. Taylor, *"Supply for Tomorrow,"* 150–51.

13. Galuszka, "Logistics in Warfare," 123–24, 127–28, 171–72.

14. Gilbert to Willcox, May 20, 1863, *OR,* 23(2):344–45.

15. Hess, *Knoxville Campaign,* 11.

16. Hess, *Knoxville Campaign,* 18.

17. Daniel, *Days of Glory,* 341.

18. Hess, *Civil War Logistics,* 191–98.

19. Scott to Stanton, Sept. 28, 1863; and Stanton to Scott, Sept. 28, 1863, *OR,* 29(1):175.

20. Howard to Henry Wilson, Dec. 27, 1863; and Howard to wife, Oct. 13, 1863, O. O. Howard Papers, BC.

21. Quaife, *From the Cannon's Mouth,* 266–67.

22. Scott to Stanton, Oct. 16, 1863, *OR,* 30(4):414.

23. Howard to mother, Oct. 7, 11, 1863, Charles Henry Howard Collection, BC; Meysenburg Journal, Oct. 4–15, 1863, Theodore Augustus Meysenburg Papers, MHM.

24. General Orders No. 337, Adjutant General's Office, War Department, Oct. 16, 1863; Halleck to Grant, Oct. 16, 1863; and Rosecrans to Halleck, Oct. 16, 1863, *OR,* 30(4):414; General Orders No. 1, Headquarters, Military Division of the Mississippi, Oct. 18, 1863; Grant to Thomas, Oct. 19, 1863; and Grant to Halleck, Oct. 26, 1863, in Simon, *Papers of Ulysses S. Grant,* 9:296, 302, 320.

25. Risch, *Quartermaster Support,* 403–4, 410; Taylor, *"Supply for Tomorrow,"* 168; General Orders (unnumbered), Headquarters, U.S. Quartermaster Department, Nov. 9, 1863, *OR,* 31(3):106–7.

26. Halleck to Grant, Oct. 20, 22, 1863, *OR,* 31(1):668, 698.

27. Taylor, *"Supply for Tomorrow,"* 157–60.

28. Lyon, *Reminiscences,* 128; Grant to Halleck, Oct. 26, Nov. 21, 1863; Grant to Julia, Oct. 27, 1863; and Grant to Jones, Nov. 17, 1863, in Simon, *Papers of Ulysses S. Grant,* 9:320, 334, 406, 428; Grant to Kelton, Dec. 23, 1863, *OR,* 31(2):29.

29. Kemmerly, "Dead Animals, Starving Men," 5, 8, 15–17, 19.

30. Grant to Kelton, Dec. 23, 1863, *OR,* 31(2):29; McCadden to sister, Oct. 25, 1863, Richard J. McCadden Letters, Civil War Collection, TSLA; Tourgée, *Story of a Thousand,* 263.

31. Grant, *Memoirs,* 417–18; Cozzens, *Shipwreck of Their Hopes,* 58–100; Daniel, *Days of Glory,* 367.

32. Wheeler, *Letters,* 430; Blair, *A Politician Goes to War,* 136–37, 140.

33. Donaldson to Meigs, Sept. 15, 1864, *OR,* 52(1):617–18.

34. Donaldson to Meigs, Sept. 15, 1864, *OR,* 52(1):618.

35. Donaldson to Meigs, Sept. 15, 1864, *OR,* 52(1):619.

36. Risch, *Quartermaster Support,* 401–2, 404; Special Orders (unnumbered), War Department, Oct. 19, 1863, Anderson Family Papers, KHS; Weber, *Northern Railroads,* 186–87.

37. Grant to Anderson, Nov. 1, 1863, in Simon, *Papers of Ulysses S. Grant,* 9:346–47; Anderson to Grant, Nov. 2, 4, 1863; and Grant to Anderson, Nov. 4, 6, 1863, *OR,* 31(3):16, 38–39, 65; [Dana] to Stanton, Nov. 4, 1863, *OR,* 31(2):56.

38. Meigs to Stanton, Nov. 16, 1863; Anderson to Reynolds, Nov. 22, 1863; and Anderson to Thomas, Nov. 28, 1863, *OR,* 31(3):162, 230, 264.

39. Grant to Julia, Nov. 14, 1863, in Simon, *Papers of Ulysses S. Grant,* 9:397.

40. Grant to Dodge, Nov. 21, 1863; Anderson to Grant, Nov. 22, 1863; and Grant to Anderson, Nov. 21, 23, 1863, *OR,* 31(3):219–20, 230, 237; [Dana] to Stanton, Nov. 21, 1863, *OR,* 31(2):63; "Death of L. B. Boomer," *New York Times,* Mar. 7, 1881.

41. Parsons to Rawlins, Oct. 2, 1863, *OR,* 30(4):28; Sherman to Rawlins, Oct. 24, 1863; and Grant to Sherman, Oct. 24, 1863, *OR,* 31(1):713–14.

42. Haines to Grant, Oct. 26, 1863; Sherman to Grant, Oct. 30, 1863; Phelps to Sherman, Oct. 31, 1863; and Sherman to Bingham, Oct. 26, 1863, *OR,* 31(1):740, 789, 798, 842.

43. Grant to Sherman, Nov. 5, 1863; and Sherman to Rawlins, Dec. 19, 1863, *OR,* 31(3):54–55, 570.

44. Grant to Bowers, Nov. 7, 1863; Sherman to Adjutant General, Washington, D.C., Nov. 8, 1863; and Sherman to Hurlbut, Nov. 9, 1863, *OR,* 31(3):74, 89, 101.

45. Thomson to Grant, Nov. 8, 1863; Dodge to Sherman, Nov. 11, 1863; and Barnes to Bane, Nov. 11, 1863, *OR,* 31(3):84–85, 119–20.

46. Dodge to Sawyer, Nov. 16, 1863; and Sherman to Grant, Nov. 19, 1863, *OR,* 31(3):170, 195.

47. General Orders No. 67, Headquarters, Left Wing, Sixteenth Corps, Nov. 12, 1863; General Orders No. 70, Headquarters, Left Wing, Sixteenth Corps, Nov. 16, 1863; and Dodge to Mizner, Nov. 27, 1863, *OR,* 31(3):132, 171, 261–62.

48. Carpenter to Eaton, July 18, 1865, in *How to Feed an Army,* 80.

49. Buck to friend and cousin, Dec. 2, 1863, W. G. Buck Letter, Virginia Polytechnic Institute and State University, Special Collections, Blacksburg.

50. Buck to friend and cousin, Dec. 2, 1863.

51. Grant to Hurlbut, [Nov.] 19, 1863, in Simon, *Papers of Ulysses S. Grant,* 9:416; Grant to Hurlbut, Nov. 10, 1863, *OR,* 31(3):113.

52. Edwards to Parsons, Dec. 13, 1865, in Parsons, *Reports to the War Department,* 50–51; Parsons to Meigs, Oct. 15, 1865, *OR,* 52(1):713; Le Duc, *Recollections,* 100–108.

53. Edwards to Parsons, Dec. 13, 1865, in Parsons, *Reports to the War Department,* 51; Le Duc to Reynolds, Oct. 28, 29, 1863, *OR,* 31(3):844, 849; Daniel, *Days of Glory,* 367; Meigs to Stanton, Nov. 16, 1863, *OR,* 31(3):162; Risch, *Quartermaster Support,* 414.

54. Symonds, *Report of a Commissary of Subsistence,* 121–22.

55. Hess, *Knoxville Campaign,* 109–11.

56. Fout, *Dark Days,* 236, 240.

57. Bowers to Grant, Nov. 6, 1863; and Bowers to Fitch, Nov. 9, 1863, *OR,* 31(3):64, 93.

58. Meigs to Foster, Dec. 23, 1863, *OR,* 31(3):476.

59. Hess, *Knoxville Campaign,* 179–95.

60. Howard to Mr. Gilman, Dec. 13, 1863, Howard Collection, BC.

61. Dodge, *Personal Recollections,* 141–42.

62. Granger to Thomas, Dec. 19, 1863, *OR,* 31(3):448.

63. Buckley to Mauran, Dec. 5, 1863, *OR,* 31(1):348–49.

64. Memorandum, Jan. 14, 1864, enclosed in Humphrey to Robertson, Dec. 2, 1879, in Robertson, *Michigan in the War,* 199.

65. Hazen to Whipple, Jan. 8, 1864, *OR,* 32(2):45–46.

66. Potter to Granger, Jan. 26, 1864, *OR,* 32(2):218.

67. Meigs to Foster, Dec. 23, 1863, *OR,* 31(3):476.

68. Fullerton to Granger, Dec. 24, 1863, *OR,* 31(3):483–84.

69. Bragg to Cooper, Dec. 28, 1863; and Longstreet to Brent, Oct. [?], 1863, *OR,* 30(2):37, 289–90; Bragg to wife, Sept. 27, 1863, Braxton Bragg Papers, MHM; Thomas W. Patton to mother, Sept. 28, 1863, James W. Patton Papers, UNC; Hess, *Braxton Bragg,* 169–90.

70. Jenkins to wife, Nov. 7, 1863, Micah Jenkins Papers, DU; Welborn to wife, Nov. 7, 1863, William Wesley Welborn Letters, Emory University, Manuscript, Archives, and Rare Books Library, Atlanta, Ga.; circular, Headquarters, Army of Tennessee, Nov. 1, 1863; and General Orders No. 212, Headquarters, Army of Tennessee, Nov. 18, 1863, *OR,* 31(3):622, 710–11.

71. Meigs to McCallum, Dec. 16, 1863; and Donaldson to Whipple, Dec. 23, 1863, *OR,* 31(3):422–23, 474.

72. Hooker to Chase, Dec. 28, 1863, *OR,* 31(2):342.

73. Donaldson to Whipple, Dec. 23, 1863; and "Railroad bridges and tunnels," comp. William E. Merrill, n.d., *OR,* 31(3):422–23, 474, 546–47.

74. Mizner to Grant, Dec. 3, 1863; Dodge to Grant, Dec. 9, 1863; Grant to Dodge, Dec. 9, 1863; Dodge to Sherman, Dec. 15, 1863; Sherman to Logan, Dec. 21, 1863; and Sherman to Halleck, Dec. 26, 1863, *OR,* 31(3):325, 366–67, 413, 459, 497.

75. Grant to Halleck, Dec. 17, 1863, OR, 31(3):429–30.

76. Grant to McPherson, Dec. 1, 1863; and Grant to Halleck, Dec. 7, 1863, in Simon, *Papers of Ulysses S. Grant,* 9:480, 500.

77. Halleck to Grant, Dec. 13, 1863; Grant to Halleck, Dec. 17, 1863; and Dana to Grant, Dec. 21, 1863, *OR,* 31(3):396, 430, 457–58; Grant to Halleck, Dec. 17, 1863, in Simon, *Papers of Ulysses S. Grant,* 9:534.

78. Grant to Julia, Jan. 2, 1863 [1864], in Simon, *Papers of Ulysses S. Grant,* 10:6; Dana to Grant, Jan. 10, 1864; Grant to Halleck, Jan. 15, 1864; and Sherman to Banks, Jan. 16, 1864, *OR,* 32(2):58, 99–100, 115.

79. Sherman to Banks, Jan. 16, 1864, *OR,* 32(2):115; Symonds, *Report of a Commissary of Subsistence,* 130.

80. Hunter to Stanton, Dec. 14, 1863, *OR,* 31(3):402.

81. Johnston to Beauregard, Jan. 13, 1864, *OR,* 52(2):596–97; Johnston to Davis, Jan. 2, 1864; and Johnston to Brown, Feb. 8, 1864, "Letters Sent, Aug 8, 1863–October 20, 1863," Box 5, vol. 4, Joseph E. Johnston Papers, CWM; Johnston to Brown, Jan. 25, 1864, *OR,* 32(2):612.

82. Johnston to Beverly Johnston, Feb. 15, 1864, Johnston Papers, CWM; Mackall to Ewell, Mar. 22, 1864, *OR,* 52(2):646.

83. Davis to Longstreet, Mar. 7, 1864, *OR,* 52(2):635; Hess, *Knoxville Campaign,* 232, 237–38.

84. Donaldson to Meigs, Sept. 15, 1864, *OR,* 52(1):620; Thomas to Anderson, Jan. 18, 1864; and Thomas to Townsend, Jan. 27, 1864, *OR,* 32(2):131, 237–38; Easley to wife, Jan. 15, 1864, Oscar Easley Civil War Letters, UTC; Rusling, *Men and Things,* 317–18.

85. Special Field Orders No. 12, Headquarters, Department of the Tennessee, Jan. 27, 1864, *OR,* 32(2):243.

86. Meigs to McCallum, Dec. 16, 1863, *OR,* 31(3):422–23.

87. McCallum to Stanton, Jan. 19, 1864, *OR,* 32(2):143–44.

88. McCallum to Stanton, Jan. 19, 1864, *OR,* 32(2):144–45.

89. McCallum to Stanton, Jan. 19, 1864, *OR,* 32(2):145.

90. McCallum to Stanton, Jan. 19, 1864, *OR,* 32(2):145; Weber, *Northern Railroads,* 190.

91. Risch, *Quartermaster Support,* 404; Donaldson to Meigs, Sept. 15, 1864, *OR,* 52(1):620; Haupt, *Reminiscences,* 290, 293; Weber, *Northern Railroads,* 188–89.

92. Leonard Eicholtz Diaries, Mar. 16, 27–31, Apr. 1–7, 14, 29, May 3, 5–6, 1864, UW.

93. Winslow to Parsons, Feb. 13, 1865, in Parsons, *Reports to the War Department,* 46–48.

94. Winslow to Parsons, Feb. 13, 1865, in Parsons, *Reports to the War Department,* 47.

95. Cox, *Military Reminiscences,* 2:109.

96. Donaldson to Meigs, Sept. 15, 1864, *OR,* 52(1):620; Weber, *Northern Railroads,* 189.

97. Galuszka, "Logistics in Warfare," 123; Hess, *Knoxville Campaign,* 183–84, 227.

98. *History of the Organization . . . Battery M, First Regiment Illinois Light Artillery,* 157–58.

99. *History of the Organization . . . Battery M, First Regiment Illinois Light Artillery,* 160.

5. Sherman and Atlanta

1. Sherman to Grant, Mar. 10, 1864, *OR,* 32(3):50; Sherman to Halleck, Sept. 15, 1864, *OR,* 38(1):61–62; Sherman, *Memoirs,* 2:31.

2. McCallum to Meigs, May 26, 1866, *OR,* ser. 3, 5:981–85.

3. McCallum to Meigs, May 26, 1866, *OR,* ser. 3, 5:981–85.

4. Donaldson to Meigs, Sept. 15, 1864, *OR,* 52(1):620.

5. Donaldson to Meigs, Sept. 15, 1864, *OR,* 52(1):620; Winslow to Parsons, Feb. 13, 1865, in Parsons, *Reports to the War Department,* 45–46, 48–49.

6. Donaldson to Meigs, Sept. 15, 1864, *OR,* 52(1):620–21.

7. Donaldson to Meigs, Sept. 15, 1864, *OR,* 52(1):621.

8. Sherman to Thomas Ewing, Aug. 11, 1864, in Simpson and Berlin, *Sherman's Civil War,* 689.

9. General Orders No. 6, Headquarters, Military Division of the Mississippi, Apr. 6, 1864, *OR,* 32(3):279; Sherman, *Memoirs,* 2:10.

10. Sherman, *Memoirs,* 2:10.

11. Donaldson to Meigs, Sept. 15, 1864, *OR,* 52(1):619.

12. Burt, "Sherman, Railroad General," 47–48; Sherman to Halleck, Sept. 15, 1864, *OR,* 38(1):62.

13. Sherman to John Sherman, Apr. 11, 1864; and Sherman to Dana, Apr. 21, 1864, in Simpson and Berlin, *Sherman's Civil War,* 619, 623; Sherman to Thomas, Apr. 24, 1864, *OR,* 32(3):469; Sherman to Webster, May 1, 1864; Lincoln to Sherman, May 4, 1863; and Sherman to Lincoln, May 5, 1864, *OR,* 38(4):3, 25–26, 33.

14. Sherman to Guthrie, May 1, 1864, *OR,* 38(4):4.

15. Sherman to Thomas, Apr. 25, 1864; and Thomas to Logan, Apr. 28, 1864, *OR,* 32(3):490, 521–22; Sherman, *Memoirs,* 2:8–9.

16. Sherman, *Memoirs,* 2:11–12.

17. Sherman to Sawyer, Mar. 28, 1864; and Sherman to Rawlins, Apr. 4, 1864, *OR,* 32(3):174, 247.

18. Brannan to Frank, Apr. 11, 1864, John M. Brannan Letters, New-York Historical Society, New York; Sherman to Butterfield, Apr. 15, 1864, William T. Sherman Letters, GLIAH; Sherman to Dana, Apr. 21, 1864, in Simpson and Berlin, *Sherman's Civil War,* 624; Sherman to Thomas, Apr. 24, 25, 1864, *OR,* 32(3):469, 490; Weber, *Northern Railroads,* 204; Cox, *Military Reminiscences,* 2:178–79.

19. Meigs to Thomas, Apr. 20, 1864, *OR,* 32(3):423; Donaldson to Meigs, Sept. 15, 1864, *OR,* 52(1):621–22.

20. Sherman to Thomas, Apr. 11, 1864; and General Orders No. 7, Headquarters, Military Division of the Mississippi, Apr. 18, 1864, *OR,* 32(3):323, 408.

21. Sherman, *Memoirs,* 2:22, 31; Sherman to Meigs, May 3, 1864, *OR,* 38(4):20.

22. Gibson to son, May 1, 1864, in Bigger, *Ohio's Silver-Tongued Orator,* 418; Fout, *Dark Days,* 303–4.

23. Sherman to Meigs, Apr. 26, 1864, *OR,* 32(3):503; Allen to Meigs, May 1, 1864, *OR,* 38(4):4; Donaldson to Meigs, Sept. 15, 1864, *OR,* 52(1):622.

24. Donaldson to [Meigs], May 1, 1864, *OR,* 38(4):10; Donaldson to Meigs, Sept. 15, 1864, *OR,* 52(1):622.

25. Daniel, *Days of Glory,* 390.

26. Sherman, *Memoirs,* 2:398.

27. McCallum to Meigs, May 26, 1866, *OR,* ser. 3, 5:989; Sherman to Stanton, Aug. 5, 1864; Special Orders (unnumbered), Adjutant General Office, Aug. 6, 1864; Johnson to Sherman, Aug. 7, 1864; and Donaldson to Sherman, Aug. 9, 1864, *OR,* 38(5):367, 391, 411, 434; Howland to mother, Aug. 28, 1864, Walter M. Howland Papers, DU.

28. McCallum to Meigs, May 26, 1866, *OR,* ser. 3, 5:988–89.

29. McCallum to Meigs, May 26, 1866, *OR,* ser. 3, 5:990.

30. Meigs to Grant, July 8, 1864; and Grant to Meigs, July 9, 1864, in Simon, *Papers of Ulysses S. Grant,* 11:196–97.

31. McCallum to Meigs, May 26, 1866, *OR,* ser. 3, 5:1002.

32. Donaldson to Meigs, Sept. 15, 1864, *OR,* 52(1):621.

33. Allen to Meigs, May 1, 1864, *OR,* 38(4):4; L. C. Easton to Hartz, May 20, 1864; and J. L. Donaldson to Hartz, May 20, 1864, Edward L. Hartz Papers, DU.

34. L. C. Easton to Hartz, May 15, 1864, Hartz Papers, DU; Special Field Orders No. 7, Headquarters, Military Division of the Mississippi, May 15, 1864, *OR,* 38(4):200.

35. Special Field Orders No. 11, Headquarters, Department of the Tennessee, May 16, 1864; Sherman to Halleck, June 2, 1864; Poe to [Sherman], June 8, 1864; Sherman to Halleck, June 11, 1864; and Special Field Orders No. 24, Headquarters, Military Division of the Mississippi, June 12, 1864, *OR,* 38(4):218, 385, 433–34, 454–55, 466; Sherman to Halleck, July 14, 1864; and Sherman to Smith, July 14, 1864, *OR,* 38(5):137, 141; L. C. Easton to Hartz, May 24, 1864, Hartz Papers, DU.

36. Haupt, *Reminiscences,* 289; Cox, *Atlanta,* 61.

37. Special Field Orders No. 8, Headquarters, Military Division of the Mississippi, May 16, 1864, *OR,* 38(4):216; Wright to McCallum, Apr. 24, 1866, *OR,* ser. 3, 5:951.

38. Wright to McCallum, Apr. 24, 1866, *OR,* ser. 3, 5:952; Hutchinson to father, June 7, 1864, Edwin Hutchinson Papers, LSU.

39. Sherman to Halleck, May 16, 1864; and Easton to Meigs, May 16, 1864, *OR,* 38(4):201, 214; Easton to Meigs, Aug. 18, 1865, *OR,* 52(1):698; Sherman to Halleck, July 6, 1864, *OR,* 38(5):65; Leonard Eicholtz Diaries, July 6–7, 1864, UW.

40. E. C. Smeed to Haupt, n.d., in Haupt, *Reminiscences,* 294–95.

41. E. C. Smeed to Haupt, n.d., in Haupt, *Reminiscences,* 296; Haupt's comment, ibid.

42. Sherman to Halleck, May 17, 1864; and Sherman to Webster, May 19, 1864, *OR,* 38(4):219, 249; Wright to McCallum, Apr. 24, 1866, *OR,* ser. 3, 5:951; Eicholtz Diaries, June 3–12, 1864, UW.

43. Easton to Meigs, Aug. 18, 1865, *OR,* 52(1):698; Wright to McCallum, Apr. 24, 1866, *OR,* ser. 3, 5:951; Haupt, *Reminiscences,* 296.

44. L. C. Easton to Hartz, June 8, 1864, Hartz Papers, DU; Julius E. Thomas Civil War Diary, June 7, 1864, UTK; West to Lee, Sept. 9, 1864, *OR,* 38(2):112.

45. Joseph Wheeler to Bragg, July [?], 1864, Braxton Bragg Papers, DU; Love to How, June 11, 1864; Milward to Moe, June 23, 1864; Steedman to Dayton, June 24, 1864; and McCook to Elliott, June 26, 1864, *OR,* 38(4):457, 580–81, 587, 596.

46. Sherman to Anderson, July 1, 1864; Sherman to Canby, July 7, 1864; and Sherman to Halleck, Aug. 17, 1864, *OR,* 38(5):4, 84, 547.

47. Raum to White, July 5, 14, 1864; and Lawyer to Estabrook, July 22, 1864, *OR,* 38(3):268–69, 466–67.

48. Sherman to Howard, Aug. 18, 1864, *OR,* 38(5):585; Neuman to Kind Friends, Aug. 21, 1864, James Neuman and Tripp Family Civil War Correspondence, Atlanta History Center; Wright to McCallum, Apr. 24, 1866, *OR,* ser. 3, 5:952.

49. Sherman to governors of Indiana, Illinois, Iowa, and Wisconsin, May 23, 1864; Hambright to assistant adjutant general, Department of the Cumberland, June 6, 1864; McPherson to Blair, June 7, 1864; and Special Field Orders No. 22, Headquarters, Military Division of the Mississippi, June 10, 1864, *OR,* 38(4):294–95, 425–26, 453; Thomas Civil War Diary, June 5, 29, 1864, UTK; Sherman to commanding officer at Allatoona, July 14, 1864; and Sherman to Tourtellotte, Aug. 16, 1864, *OR,* 38(5):140–41, 543.

50. Rousseau to Whipple, May 12, 13, 1864, *OR,* 38(4):154–55, 167.

51. Brown to Davis, June 28, 1864; and David to Brown, June 29, 1864, *OR,* 52(2):680–81; Cobb to Seddon, July 1, 1864; and Johnston to Davis, July 8, 1864, *OR,* 38(5):858, 869; Watts to Davis, July 4, 1864, in Crist, *Papers of Jefferson Davis,* 10:498; Joseph Wheeler to Bragg, July [?], 1864, Bragg Papers, DU.

52. Davis to Hood, Aug. 5, 1864, in Crist, *Papers of Jefferson Davis,* 10:586.

53. Modil Diary, Aug. 15, 18, 1864, George W. Modil Papers, Mississippi Department of Archives and History, Jackson; Smith to Sherman, Aug. 14, 1864; Sherman to Thomas, Aug. 15, 1864; and Sherman to Schofield, Aug. 15, 1864, *OR,* 38(5):501, 505–6, 511; McCallum to Meigs, Aug. 30, 31, 1864; and Donaldson to Meigs, June 30, 1865, *OR,* 52(1):612, 681; McCallum to Meigs, May 26, 1866, *OR,* ser. 3, 5:988.

54. Grant to Halleck, July 15, 1864, *OR,* 38(5):143–44.

55. Sherman, *Memoirs,* 2:98, 103–4; Castel, *Decision in the West,* 437–40; Sherman to Rousseau, June 30, 1864, *OR,* 38(4):648; Thomas to Sherman, Aug. 22, 1864, *OR,* 38(5):629; Evans, *Sherman's Horsemen,* 208–376.

56. Sherman to Ellen, June 30, 1864, in Simpson and Berlin, *Sherman's Civil War,* 660; Sherman to Halleck, July 6, Aug. 13, 1864; and Sherman to Thomas, July 20, 1864, *OR,* 38(5):66, 198, 482.

57. Sherman, *Memoirs,* 2:399.

58. Hartz to Easton, June 13, [1864], Letter Book, May 31st to July 18th, 1864, Edward L. Hartz Papers, LC; Easton to Hartz, June 28, July 1, 1864, Hartz Papers, DU.

59. J. L. Donaldson to Hartz, [May] 6, 26, 1864, Hartz Papers, DU.

60. Sherman to Webster, Aug. 4, 1864, *OR,* 38(5):351.

61. L. C. Easton to Hartz, June 28, 1864; and John Stewart to Hartz, June 30, 1864, Hartz Papers, DU.

62. Thomas Civil War Diary, May 22, June 1, 8, 14–15, 25, 29, July 1, 8–9, 11–12, 14, 16, 20, 22, 26–28, 1864, UTK.

63. Sherman to Webster, Aug. 4, 1864, *OR,* 38(5):351; L. C. Easton to Hartz, June 29, 1864, Hartz Papers, DU.

64. L. C. Easton to Hartz, May 20, 1864; J. T. Boyd to C. K. Smith, [May] 22, 1864; John Stewart to Hartz, June 17, 27, 1864; and J. T. Conklin to Hartz, June 21, 1864, Hartz Papers, DU.

65. J. Condit Smith to Hartz, June 10, 1864; unknown to H. M. Smith, June 11, 1864; L. C. Easton to Hartz, June 14, 25, July 6, 1864; and H. K. Skinner to Hartz, July 11, 1864, Hartz Papers, DU.

66. J. Condit Smith to Hartz, July 1, 1864; and L. C. Easton to Hartz, July 7, 1864, Hartz Papers, DU.

67. L. C. Easton to Hartz, June 9, 25, 1864; D. H. Rucker to Hartz, June 12, 1864; and W. D. Wood Jr. to Hartz, June 13, 1864, Hartz Papers, DU.

68. C. K. Smith to Colonel McKay, Aug. 8, 20, 23, 28, 1864, Civil War Quartermaster Reports, UTC.

69. Special Field Orders No. 8, Headquarters, Army of the Ohio, May 20, 1864; and Hascall to Campbell, May 23, 1864, *OR,* 38(4):273, 297–98.

70. Blair, *A Politician Goes to War,* 179; Lawson, "Hammontrees Fight the Civil War," 118.

71. Force Journal, July 12–13, 1864, M. F. Force Papers, University of Washington, Special Collections, Seattle; General Field Orders, Headquarters, Army of Tennessee, Aug. 12, 1864; General Orders No. 16, Headquarters, Ross's Brigade, Jackson's Cavalry Division, Aug. 14, 1864; and [Shoup] to Cleburne, Aug. 25, 1864, *OR,* 38(5):960, 963–64, 989.

72. Blair, *A Politician Goes to War,* 185; Thomas Civil War Diary, July 13, 17, 20, 22, 1864, UTK; Easton to Hartz, [May] 22, 1864, Hartz Papers, DU; Sherman to Webster, June 15, 1864, *OR,* 38(4):481; and Sherman to Halleck, Aug. 17, 1864, *OR,* 38(5):547. Evidence of cotton shipments north on the railroad can be found in E. Hade to Hartz, June 24, 1864; and L. C. Easton to Hartz, June 29, 1864, Hartz Papers, DU.

73. Gile to not stated, June 18, 1864, David Herrick Gile Correspondence, Civil War Manuscripts Collection, YU; Sherman to Grant, June 18, 1864, *OR,* 38(4):507.

74. Draft of Metzgar to Quartermaster General, U.S. Army, Aug. 22, 1864, John J. Metzgar Papers, UNC; Balloch to mother, Aug. 11, 1864, George Williamson Balloch Papers, DU; Henry Howland to Hartz, May 24, 1864; J. L. Donaldson to Hartz, May 24, 1864; and L. C. Easton to Hartz, June 9, 1864, Hartz Papers, DU.

75. "Report of artillery and infantry ammunition expended in the Army of the Cumberland during the month of August, 1864"; "Report of artillery and infantry ammunition expended in the Army of the Cumberland during the campaign commencing May 4 and ending September 8, 1864"; Wood to Fullerton, Sept. 10, 1864; and Fearing to Curtis, Aug. 16, 1864, *OR,* 38(1):171, 173, 386, 786; L. C. Easton to Hartz, June 24, 1864, Hartz Papers, DU; Logan to Clark, [Sept. 13, 1864], *OR,* 38(3):112.

76. Circular No. 1, Headquarters, Army of the Ohio, May 10, 1864; and Schofield to Sherman, June 27, 1864, *OR,* 38(4):132, 619.

77. Jennings to Burns, Sept. 13, 1864, *OR,* 38(2):832–33.

78. Sherman to Halleck, May 17, 1864; McCook to Elliott, June 2, 1864; and Stoneman to Humphrey, June 3, 1864, *OR,* 38(4):219, 387, 399.

79. Stickney to Rose, June 26, 1864, Clifford Stickney Collection, Chicago History Museum.

80. L. C. Easton to Hartz, May 5, 11, 20, 21, 31, June 16, 19, 26, 1864; R. W. Wetherell to Hartz, May 30, 1864; and John Stewart to Hartz, June 8, 26, 1864, Hartz Papers, DU; Hartz to Easton, June 1, 14, 1864, Hartz Papers, LC.

81. Easton to Meigs, Aug. 8, 1865, *OR,* 52(1):698–99; John Stewart to Hartz, June 30, 1864, Hartz Papers, DU; Hartz to Easton, July 10, [1864], Hartz Papers, LC.

82. Donaldson to Meigs, Sept. 15, 1864, *OR,* 52(1):621.

83. L. C. Easton to Hartz, June 11, 16, 17, 19, 22, June [?], 1864; and J. L. Donaldson to Hartz, June 22, 1864, Hartz Papers, DU.

84. J. L. Donaldson to Hartz, June 8, 21, 28, 29, 30, 1864, Hartz Papers, DU; Hartz to Easton, June 10, [1864], Hartz Papers, LC.

85. L. C. Easton to Hartz, May 30, June 24, 1864, Hartz Papers, DU.

86. Sherman to Ellen, July 9, 1864, in Simpson and Berlin, *Sherman's Civil War,* 664; Special Field Orders No. 29, Headquarters, Military Division of the Mississippi, June 26, 1864, *OR,* 38(4):601–2. Commissary H. C. Symonds also thought Sherman's officers were requesting far more food than justified by the number of troops reported in the field. See Symonds, *Report of a Commissary of Subsistence,* 158.

87. Beckwith to Commissary General of Subsistence, Aug. 23, 1864, *OR,* 52(1):594.

88. Special Field Orders No. 24, Headquarters, Military Division of the Mississippi, June 12, 1864, *OR,* 38(4):466; Butler, *Letters Home,* 139; Watkins to not stated, Aug. 24, 1864, John Watkins Papers, UTK; Smith, *Brother of Mine,* 233; John C. Brown Diary, May 15, June 12, 14, 1864, University of Iowa, Special Collections, Iowa City; David to wife, June 8, 1864, David Gilmer Watts and Clara Watts Papers, Atlanta History Center; Spencer to parents, June 22, 1864, Israel Spencer Letters, Civil War Collection, Stanford University, Special Collections and University Archives, Palo Alto, Calif.; Quaife, *From the Cannon's Mouth,* 339.

89. Hedley, *Marching through Georgia,* 122; Osborn, "Sherman's Carolina Campaign," 115; H. E. Collins to James Yeatman, June 24, 1864, *St. Louis Daily Missouri Democrat,* July 4, 1864.

90. Hedley, *Marching through Georgia,* 128–29; Cox, *Kiss Josey,* 218; draft of Metzgar to Quartermaster General, Aug. 22, 1864, Metzgar Papers, UNC.

91. Blank to [Gray], May 21, 1864, *OR,* 38(3):170; Randall to father, Aug. 23, 1864, Harrison E. Randall Letters, University of Notre Dame Rare Books and Special Collections, South Bend, Ind.; Trowbridge to wife and baby, July 25, 1864, George Martin Trowbridge Papers, Schoff Civil War Collection, UM.

92. Bartlett essay in Cook and Benton, *"Dutchess County Regiment,"* 140; Beasecker, *"I Hope to Do My Country Service,"* 282–83, 302; O'Connor to not stated, Sept. 7, 1864, *OR,* 38(2):229; Truman to Johnson, [July 17, 1864], in Graf, *Papers of Andrew Johnson,* 7:37.

93. Bradley to Mary, July 17, 1864, Luther P. Bradley Collection, USAMHI.

94. Lawton to Hewit, Sept. 13, 1864, *OR,* 38(2):578–79.

95. Goodman to Foye, Sept. 22, 1864, *OR,* 38(2):148, 153.

96. Sherman, *Memoirs,* 2:391–92.

97. H. E. Collins to James Yeatman, June 24, 1864, *St. Louis Daily Missouri Democrat,* July 4, 1864; Alanson B. Cone Memoir, July 9, 1864, New York State Library, Albany; diary, July 9, 1864, Albert M. Cook Papers, Syracuse University, Special Collections Research Center, Syracuse, N.Y.; Symonds, *Report of a Commissary of Subsistence,* 155.

98. Moore to Mary, July 25, 1864, John Moore and Robert Moore Letters, GLIAH; Stout to Erb, Sept. 14, 1864, *OR,* 38(1):471; Beasecker, *"I Hope to Do My Country Service,"* 313; Aten, *Eighty-Fifth Regiment, Illinois Volunteer Infantry,* 210.

99. Bradley to Mary, July 17, 1864, Bradley Collection, USAMHI; Eicholtz Diaries, May 18, 1864, UW; Thomas Civil War Diary, May 18, 1864, UTK; Moore to Howard, Sept. 28, 1864, *OR,* 38(3):55–56.

100. Dodge to Scott, Aug. 1, 1864, *OR,* 38(5):938.

101. Thomas B. Mackall journal, June 4, 1864 (McMurry transcript), Joseph E. Johnston Papers, CWM; Semmes to wife, May 30, June 7, 26, 1864, Benedict Joseph Semmes Papers, UNC.

102. Semmes to wife, Sept. 2, 4, 7, 1864, Semmes Papers, UNC.

103. Robinson to Friend Hunt, May 21, 1864, James Sidney Robinson Papers, Ohio Historical Society, Columbus; Metzgar to Carrie, Sept. 3, 1864, Metzgar Papers, UNC; W. P. Thornton to editor, July 31, 1864, *St. Louis Daily Missouri Democrat,* Aug. 9, 1864; Morse to Ellen, Aug. 9, 1864, Charles F. Morse Papers, MHS.

104. Special Field Orders No. 9, Headquarters, Military Division of the Mississippi, May 20, 1864; and Special Field Orders No. 15, Headquarters, Department of the Tennessee, May 20, 1864, *OR,* 38(4):271–73; Fullerton Journal, May 20–21, 1864, *OR,* 38(1):860; Hess, *Kennesaw Mountain,* 188–205; Sherman to Schofield, Aug. 9, 1864; and Sherman to Grant, Aug. 10, 1864, *OR,* 38(5):441, 447.

105. Sherman to Halleck, Sept. 4, 1864, in Simpson and Berlin, *Sherman's Civil War,* 697; Hood to Bragg, Sept. 3, 1864, *OR,* 38(5):1017.

106. Easton to Meigs, Aug. 8, 1865, *OR,* 52(1):699; Sherman to Grant, July 12, 1864; Sherman to Webster, Aug. 4, 1864; and Sherman to Stanton, Aug. 5, 1864, *OR,* 38(5):123, 351, 367; Sherman to Halleck, Sept. 15, 1864, *OR,* 38(1):62, 83–84; Sherman to Ewing, Aug. 11, 1864, in Simpson and Berlin, *Sherman's Civil War,* 689–90.

107. McCallum to Meigs, May 26, 1866, *OR,* ser. 3, 5:1001–2; Donaldson to Meigs, Sept. 15, 1864, *OR,* 52(1):622.

108. Sherman, *Memoirs,* 2:398.

109. McCallum to Stanton, Feb. 8, 1866, *OR,* ser. 3, 5:587.

6. Hood and Sherman in North Georgia

1. Sherman, *Memoirs,* 2:129.

2. Sherman, *Memoirs,* 2:130; Bradley to sister, Sept. 19, 1864, Luther P. Bradley Collection, USAMHI; Logan to Dayton, Sept. 20, 1864; and Howard endorsement, Sept. 20, 1864, and Sherman endorsement, Sept. 29, on Logan to Dayton, Sept. 20, 1864, *OR,* 39(2):428–29, 430.

3. Beasecker, *"I Hope to Do My Country Service,"* 317.

4. Sherman, *Memoirs,* 2:130; Grant to Halleck, July 15, 1864, *OR,* 37(5):143.

5. Easton to Meigs, Aug. 8, 1865, *OR,* 52(1):700; Sherman to Slocum, Sept. 3, 1864; and Sherman to Webster, Sept. 8, 1864, *OR,* 38(5):778, 830.

6. Sherman, *Memoirs,* 2:111; Sherman to Hood, Sept. 7, 10, 1864; Hood to Sherman, Sept. 9, 1864; Sherman to Calhoun, Sept. 12, 1864; and Halleck to Sherman, Sept. 26, 1864, *OR,* 39(2):414–16, 418–19, 480; Special Field Orders No. 67, Headquarters, Military Division of the Mississippi, Sept. 8, 1864; Sherman to Halleck, Sept. 9, 1864; and Sherman to Webster, Sept. 9, 1864, *OR,* 38(5):837–40.

7. Halleck to Grant, Oct. 2, 1864, *OR,* 39(3):25–26.

8. Grant to Halleck, Oct. 4, 1864, *OR,* 39(3):63–64.

9. McAlester Memorandum, Oct. 4, 1864, *OR,* 41(3):599–600.

10. Castel, *Decision in the West,* 550; Davis speech, [Sept. 23, 1864]; and Davis speech, Oct. 5, 1864, in Crist, *Papers of Jefferson Davis,* 11:61, 91–92.

11. Jefferson Davis to Hugh R. Davis, Jan. 8, 1865, in Crist, *Papers of Jefferson Davis,* 11:286; Castel, *Decision in the West,* 551.

12. Hood to Bragg, Sept. 21, 1864, *OR,* 39(2):860; Hood to Fry, Oct. 2, 1864, *OR,* 39(3):784; John W. Green to Govan, Nov. 29, 1886; and copy of John W. Green to wife, Oct. 2, 1864, Daniel Chevilette Govan Papers, UNC.

13. Mason to Stewart, Oct. 3, 1864; Mason to Lee, Oct. 4, 1864; and Hood to Bragg, Oct. 5, 1864, *OR,* 39(3):785.

14. Hood to Seddon, Oct. 7, 1864, *OR,* 39(3):801; French to Stewart, Nov. 5, 1864, *OR,* 39(1):818; Hess, *Civil War in the West,* 249–50.

15. Sherman to commanding officer, Allatoona, Oct. 3, 1864; and Mason to Iverson, Oct. 2, 1864, *OR,* 39(3):53, 783; Easton to Meigs, Aug. 8, 1865, *OR,* 52(1):700.

16. Lee to Davis, Sept. 19, 1864, *OR,* 39(2):846; Davis to Beauregard, Oct. 2, 1864; and Davis to Seddon, Oct. 2, 1864, *OR,* 39(3):782; Davis to Cooper, Oct. 12, 1864, *OR,* 39(1):796.

17. Beauregard to Cooper, Oct. 12, 1864, *OR,* 39(1):796; Vandiver, "General Hood as Logistician," 8.

18. Hood to Bragg, Oct. 8, 1864; and [Hood] to Elzey, Oct. 11, 1864, *OR,* 39(3):804–5, 812–13.

19. Johnson to Mussey, Oct. 17, 1864; and Lee to Mason, Jan. 30, 1865, *OR,* 39(1):717–21, 810–11.

20. Hood to Taylor, Oct. 16, 1864; and Mason to Jackson, Oct. 16, 1864, *OR,* 39(3):823.

21. Whitfield endorsement on Gaston to Grant, n.d., in Simon, *Papers of Ulysses S. Grant,* 16:467n; West to Lee, May 1, 1864, *OR,* 38(4):655.

22. Bullock to Forrest, Oct. 9, 1864; and Forrest to Taylor, Oct. 12, 1864, *OR,* 39(3):810, 815–17.

23. Beauregard to Cooper, Oct. 24, 1864, *OR,* 39(1):797; Brent to Richard Taylor, Oct. 23, 1864, Letter Book B, Oct. 23, 1864–Jan. 19, 1865, George W. Brent Papers, TU.

24. Bullock to Roddey, Oct. 23, 1864; Taylor to Forrest, Oct. 23, 1864; and Taylor to Brent, Oct. 27, 1864, *OR,* 39(3):846–47, 855.

25. Ross to Roddey, Oct. 28, 1864, *OR,* 39(3):864.

26. Forrest to Taylor, Oct. 21, 1864, *OR,* 39(3):838.

27. General Orders No. 1, Headquarters, Military Division of the West, Oct. 17, 1864; and Hood to Seddon, Oct. 19, 1864, *OR,* 39(3):824, 831; Hood to Cooper, Feb. 15, 1865, *OR,* 39(1):802.

28. Sherman, *Memoirs,* 2:163; Thomas to Sawyer, Jan. 20, 1865; Granger to Polk, Nov. 6, 1864; and Lee to Mason, Jan. 30, 1865, *OR,* 39(1):590, 696, 698–99, 811; Hood to Seddon, Oct. 31, 1864, *OR,* 39(3):870.

29. Howe, *Marching with Sherman,* 21.

30. Sherman, *Memoirs,* 2:158; Mason to Jackson, Oct. 16, 1864; Ewing to Cole, Oct. 18, 1864; Mason to Elzey, Oct. 19, 20, 1864; Hood to Taylor, Oct. 20, 1864; and Brent to Taylor, Oct. 23, 1864, *OR,* 39(3):823, 828–29, 832, 834–35, 844–45.

31. Semmes to wife, Oct. 10, 31, 1864, Benedict Joseph Semmes Papers, UNC.

32. Ewing to Cole, Nov. 4, 1864, and Cole's endorsement, Nov. 25, 1864, *OR,* 39(3):888–89.

33. Hood to Taylor, Oct. 30, 1864; and Hood to Beauregard, Nov. 8, 1864, *OR,* 39(3):868, 900.

34. Brent to Hood, Nov. 2, 1864; Williams to Bullock, Nov. 8, 1864; and Whitfield to Williams, Nov. 6, 1864, *OR,* 39(3):877, 902.

35. Whitfield to Williams, Nov. 6, 1864, *OR,* 39(3):902–3.

36. Gardner to Surget, Nov. 11, 1864, *OR,* 39(3):912.

37. Beauregard to Hood, Nov. 15, 1864, *OR,* 45(1):1210; Vandiver, "General Hood as Logistician," 9–11; Black, *Railroads of the Confederacy,* 265–66.

38. Sherman to Slocum, Oct. 29, 1864; Sherman to Steedman, Oct. 29, 1864; Sherman to Dana, Oct. 30, 1864; Halleck to Grant, Nov. 6, 1864; and Grant to Halleck, Nov. 6, 1864, *OR,* 39(3):494, 503, 527–28, 658; Thomas to Sawyer, Jan. 20, 1865, *OR,* 39(1):589.

39. Beauregard to Cooper, Nov. 3, 1864; Hood to Cooper, Nov. 9, 1864; and Hood to Davis, Nov. 12, 1864, *OR,* 39(3):880, 903, 913.

40. Brent to Hood, Nov. 17, 1864; Hood to Brent, Nov. 17, 1864; and Hood to Beauregard, Nov. 17, 1864, *OR,* 45(1):1215; Sword, *Confederacy's Last Hurrah,* 71–72.

41. McCallum to Stanton, Oct. 13, 1864; Granger to Polk, Oct. 10, 1864; Campbell to Hazzard, Nov. 24, 1864; and Forrest to Ellis, Oct. 17, 1864, *OR,* 39(1):507, 513–14, 521–23, 542, 544–45.

42. Forrest to Ellis, Oct. 17, 1864, *OR,* 39(1):548.

43. Rousseau to Thomas, Sept. 29, 1864; and Forrest to Ellis, Oct. 17, 1864, *OR,* 39(1):506–7, 546.

44. Kramer to Willett, Oct. 3, 1864; and Forrest to Ellis, Oct. 17, 1864, *OR,* 39(1):507–8, 547.

45. Forrest to Ellis, Oct. 17, 1864, *OR,* 39(1):547–49; Forrest to Taylor, Oct. 12, 1864, *OR,* 39(3):816.

46. Sipes to Polk, Oct. 3, 1864; and Rousseau to Thomas, Oct. 4, 1864, *OR,* 39(3):59, 81; McCallum to Stanton, Oct. 13, 1864; Wade to Hewitt, Oct. 3, 1864; Granger to Polk, Oct. 10, 1864; and Thomas to Sawyer, Jan. 20, 1865, *OR,* 39(1):507, 509–11, 517, 586.

47. Grant to Halleck, Oct. 13, 1864, *OR,* 39(3):240.

48. Forrest to Taylor, Oct. 12, 1864, *OR,* 39(3):815–16.

49. Thomas to Sawyer, Jan. 20, 1865; and Forrest to Surget, Jan. 12, 1865, *OR,* 39(1):589–90, 870–71; Howland report, Feb. 3, 1865; and Donaldson to Allen, Mar. 8, 1865, *OR,* 49(1):748–49, 871; Donaldson to Meigs, June 30, 1865, *OR,* 52(1):683.

50. Sherman to Grant, Nov. 6, 1864; and Sherman to commanding officer of all posts and stations, Nov. 6, 1864, *OR,* 39(3):659, 661; McCallum to Meigs, May 26, 1866, *OR,* ser. 3, 5:989.

51. Sherman, *Memoirs,* 2:144, 146; Sherman to Cox, Sept. 30, 1864, *OR,* 39(2):540.

52. Sherman to Cox, Sept. 30, 1864, *OR,* 39(2):540; Sherman to Grant, Oct. 1, 1864; Sherman to Howard, Oct. 2, 1864; and Wever to Smith, Oct. 3, 1864, *OR,* 39(3):3, 28, 50; "Abstract from Journal of Brig. Gen. Jacob D. Cox, U.S. Army, commanding Twenty-third Army Corps (temporarily) and Third Division, Twenty-third Army Corps," *OR,* 39(1):790.

53. Thomas to Sherman, Oct. 7, 1864; Corse to Thomas, Oct. 8, 1864; Thomas to Corse, Oct. 8, 1864; Ramsey to Wright, Oct. 8, 1864; Wright to McCallum, Oct. 8, 1864; and Wright to Thomas, Oct. 10, 1864, *OR,* 39(3):139, 152–53, 192.

54. Sherman to Thomas, Oct. 9, 1864; Sherman to Webster, Oct. 10, 1864; Sherman to Stanley, Oct. 10, 1864; and Sherman to Slocum, Oct. 10, 1864, *OR,* 39(3):170, 175, 177–78.

55. Sherman to Grant, Oct. 10, 1864, *OR,* 39(3):174.

56. Grant to Stanton, Oct. 13, 1864; Stanton to Sherman, Oct. 13, 1864; Grant to Halleck, Oct. 13, 1864; Sherman to Grant, Oct. 16, 1864; Grant to Sherman, Oct. 17, 1864; and Halleck to Sherman, Oct. 31, 1864, *OR,* 39(3):239–40, 304–5, 324, 529.

57. Sherman to Grant, Oct. 16, 1864; Sherman to Raum, Oct. 16, 1864; Warner to Halleck, Oct. 17, 1864; Perkins to Williams, Oct. 18, 1864; Perkins to Geary, Oct. 18, 1864; Thomas to Grant, Oct. 18, 1864; McCallum to Thomas, Oct. 18, 1864; Thomas to McCallum, Oct. 18, 1864; and Sherman to Halleck, Oct. 19, 1864, *OR,* 39(3):304–5, 309, 324, 348, 351, 353, 357; Thomas to Sawyer, Jan. 20, 1865, *OR,* 39(1):588.

58. Sherman, *Memoirs,* 2:158; Bright to Ramsey, Oct. 14, 1863; and Sherman to Halleck, Oct. 19, 1864, *OR,* 39(3):275–76, 358.

59. Sherman to Thomas, Oct. 16, 1864; Sherman to Schofield, Oct. [16], 1864; and Sherman to Thomas, Oct. 17, 1864, noon and 2 P.M., *OR,* 39(3):311, 333.

60. Sherman to Schofield, Oct. 17, 1864; Sherman to Halleck, Oct. 19, 1864; and Sherman to Wilson, Oct. 19, 1864, *OR,* 39(3):335, 357–58.

61. Sherman to Halleck, Oct. 19, 1864, *OR,* 39(3):358.

62. Sherman to Thomas, Oct. 19, 1864, *OR,* 39(3):365.

63. Sherman to Thomas, Oct. 20, 1864; Sherman to Grant, Oct. 22, 1864; and Sherman to Rosecrans, Oct. 29, 1864, *OR,* 39(3):377–78, 395, 494; Sherman to Ellen, Oct. 21, 1864, in Simpson and Berlin, *Sherman's Civil War,* 738–39.

64. Sherman to Easton, Oct. 19, 1864; Easton to Meigs, Oct. 23, 1864; and Wright to Thomas, Oct. 23, 1864, *OR,* 39(3):359, 409.

65. Reynolds to Perkins, Dec. 26, 1864, *OR,* 44:354; Bryant, *Third Regiment of Wisconsin Veteran Volunteer Infantry,* 273.

66. Sherman to Cox, Sept. 30, 1864, *OR,* 39(2):540; Bryant, *Third Regiment of Wisconsin Veteran Volunteer Infantry,* 273; Whittelsey to Easton, Jan. 20, 1865, *OR,* ser. 3, 5:399; Robinson to Robinson, Dec. 28, 1864; Summers to Whittelsey, Oct. 24, 1864; and Bloodgood to Kellam, Dec. 25, 1864, *OR,* 39(1):659–61, 682, 691; Blair, *A Politician Goes to War,* 208, 212; Circular, Headquarters, Twentieth Corps, Oct. 20, 1864; Robinson to Perkins, Oct. 20, 1864; Sherman to Thomas, Oct. 23, 1864; and Sherman to Halleck, Oct. 24, 1864, *OR,* 39(3):370–72, 408, 413.

67. Thomas to Sherman, Oct. 17, 20, 21, 1864, *OR,* 39(3):334, 379, 390–91.

68. Sherman to Thomas, Oct. 23, 26, 29, Nov. 2, 1864; Thomas to Sherman, Oct. 25, 29, 31,

Nov. 2, 1864; Sherman to Halleck, Oct. 27, 28, 1864; and Sherman to Beckwith, Oct. 28, 1864, *OR,* 39(3):408, 433, 448, 461, 476–77, 498, 535, 599–600; Sherman to Halleck, Jan. 1, 1865, *OR,* 39(1):583.

69. Sherman to Thomas, Nov. 11, 1864; and Thomas to Sherman, Nov. 12, 1864, *OR,* 39(3):746–47, 756.

70. Grant to Sherman, Nov. 1, 2, 1864; Sherman to Grant, Nov. 1, 1864; and Sherman to Poe, Nov. 1, 1864, *OR,* 39(3):576–77, 594.

71. Sherman to Halleck, Nov. 3, 1864; and Sherman to Grant, Nov. 6, 1864, *OR,* 39(3):614, 660.

72. Easton to Meigs, Aug. 8, 1865, *OR,* 52(1):700–701; Wright to McCallum, Apr. 24, 1866; and McCallum to Meigs, May 26, 1866, *OR,* ser. 3, 5:952, 988.

73. Easton to Meigs, Aug. 8, 1865, *OR,* 52(1):700; John Moore to Mary, Oct. 30, 1864, John Moore and Robert Moore Letters, GLIAH.

74. Easton to Meigs, Aug. 8, 1865, *OR,* 52(1):701.

75. Beckwith to Sherman, Oct. 30, 1864; and McCook to Sherman, Oct. 30, 1864, *OR,* 39(3):510–11.

76. Sherman to Easton, Oct. 31, 1864; and Easton to Beckwith, Oct. 31, 1864, *OR,* 39(3):529–30.

77. Easton to Sherman, Nov. 4, 1864; Sherman to Steedman, Nov. 4, 1864; Easton and Beckwith to Sherman, Nov. 5, 1864; and Dayton to Easton, Nov. 5, 1864, *OR,* 39(3):626, 632, 641–42.

78. Tindall to Thomas, Nov. 5, 1864, *OR,* 39(3):648.

79. William H. Osborn certificate, Nov. 15, 1864, George L. Reis Letters, UTK; Easton to Meigs, Aug. 8, 1865, *OR,* 52(1):702.

80. Easton to Meigs, Aug. 8, 1865, *OR,* 52(1):702; Sherman to Grant, Nov. 6, 1864; and Special Field Order No. 162, Headquarters, Department of the Tennessee, Nov. 9, 1864, *OR,* 39(3):661, 715; Wright to McCallum, May 20, 1865, Apr. 24, 1866; and McCallum to Meigs, May 26, 1866, *OR,* ser. 3, 5:29, 952, 988.

7. Hood's Tennessee Campaign

1. Hood to Seddon, Dec. 11, 1864, *OR,* 45(1):657.

2. Beauregard to Cooper, Apr. 15, 1865; Mason to Lyon, Nov. 18, 1864; Mason to Forrest, Nov. 20, 1864; and General Field Orders No. 35, Headquarters, Army of Tennessee, Nov. 20, 1864, *OR,* 45(1):650, 1221, 1227–28.

3. Hood to Beauregard, Nov. 25, 1864; Mason to Roddey, Nov. 25, 1864; and Mason to officer commanding at Corinth, Nov. 26, 1864, *OR,* 45(1):1245, 1249; Sword, *Confederacy's Last Hurrah,* 93–95.

4. Hood to Seddon, Nov. 27, 1864, and Northrop endorsement, Dec. 11, 1864; and Hood to Seddon, Nov. 28, 1864, *OR,* 45(1):1252, 1254.

5. Journal of the Army of Tennessee, Nov. 28, 1864; and General Field Orders No. 37, Headquarters, Army of Tennessee, Nov. 28, 1864, *OR,* 45(1):670, 1255.

6. Beauregard to Hood, Nov. 15, 18, 1864; and Brent to Hood, Nov. 17, 1864, *OR,* 45(1):1210, 1216, 1219.

7. Beauregard to Hood, Nov. 18, 20, 1864; Beauregard to Gardner, Nov. 18, 1864; Beauregard

to Taylor, Nov. 20, 1864; Brent to Maury, Nov. 22, 1864; Eldredge to Reid, Nov. 27, 1864; and Reid to Harvie, Nov. 29, 1864, *OR,* 45(1):1219, 1223, 1226, 1229, 1238, 1253, 1258–59.

8. Thomas to Wright, Nov. 14, 1864; Wright to Thomas, Nov. 14, 1864; Poteet to Moe, Nov. 16, 19, 1864; Moe to Poteet, Nov. 16, 1864; and Moe to Cruft, Nov. 17, 1864, *OR,* 45(1):883–84, 915–16, 925, 949; Leonard Eicholtz Diaries, Nov. 15–19, 1864, UW; Wright to McCallum, May 20, 1865, *OR,* ser. 3, 5:29.

9. Wright to McCallum, May 20, 1865; and McCallum to Meigs, May 26, 1866, *OR,* ser. 3, 5:29, 989; Thomas to Sawyer, Jan. 20, 1865; Thomas to Schofield, Nov. 20, 1864; and Thomas to Granger, Nov. 23, 24, 1864, *OR,* 45(1):33, 956, 1003–4, 1027.

10. Thomas to Sawyer, Jan. 20, 1865, *OR,* 45(1):34.

11. Whipple to Merrill, Nov. 23, 1864; Merrill to Whipple, Nov. 23, 1864; Granger to Thomas, Nov. 25, 27, 1864; Thomas to Merrill, Nov. 27, 1864; Merrill to Thomas, Nov. 27, 1864; and Thomas to Van Cleve, Nov. 25, 1864, *OR,* 45(1):1000, 1046–48, 1084, 1099.

12. Thomas to Schofield, Nov. 25, 1864; Thomas to Steedman, Nov. 25, 1864; Steedman to Thomas, Nov. 25, 1864; Polk to Milroy, Nov. 26, 1864; and Thomas to Rousseau, Nov. 29, 1864, *OR,* 45(1):1036, 1050, 1070, 1155.

13. Thomas to Steedman, Nov. 27, 28, 29, 1864; Steedman to Thomas, Nov. 28, 1864; and Thomas to Halleck, Nov. 30, 1864, *OR,* 45(1):1100, 1125, 1159, 1167.

14. Thomas to Thompson, Nov. 29, 1864; Thomas to Rousseau, Nov. 30, 1864; Rousseau to Thomas, Nov. 30, 1864; and Milroy to Thomas, Nov. 30, 1864, *OR,* 45(1):1162, 1186–87.

15. Eicholtz Diaries, Nov. 29–30, 1864, UW.

16. Hood to Cooper, Feb. 15, 1865, *OR,* 45(1):654.

17. Thomas to Halleck, Dec. 5, 1864, *OR,* 45(2):55; Thomas to Sawyer, Jan. 20, 1865, *OR,* 45(1):36.

18. Hood to Cooper, Feb. 15, 1865; Hood to Seddon, Dec. 11, 1864; and Journal of the Army of Tennessee, *OR,* 45(1):654, 658. 671; Hood to Beauregard, Dec. 6, 1864; and Hood to Maury, Dec. 6, 1864, *OR,* 45(2):653, 656–57.

19. Beauregard to Brown, Dec. 2, 1864; Smith to Brent, Dec. 6, 1864; and Brent to [Beauregard], Dec. 18, 1864, *OR,* 45(2):640, 656, 705.

20. Smith to Brent, Dec. 6, 1864; Taylor to Brent, Dec. 15, 1864; and "Subsistence stores in Mississippi and East Louisiana, Dec. 15, 1864," *OR,* 45(2):655, 693–94, 737.

21. Mason to Roddey, Dec. 5, 1864; and Hood to Beauregard, Dec. 13, 15, 1864, *OR,* 45(2):652, 655, 685, 690.

22. Thomas to Grant, Dec. 2, 1864; Grant to Thomas, Dec. 2, 1864; and Wright to McCallum, Dec. 5, 1864, *OR,* 45(2):17, 57; Eicholtz Diaries, Dec. 1–2, 1864, UW.

23. Thomas to Halleck, Dec. 1, 1864; Otis to Deuble, Dec. 2, 1864; and Rousseau to commanding officer at Chattanooga, Murfreesboro, Dec. 4, 1864, *OR,* 45(2):3, 27, 51; Thomas to Sawyer, Jan. 20, 1865, *OR,* 45(1):35–36.

24. Thomas to Sawyer, Jan. 20, 1865, *OR,* 45(1):45; Smith to Thomas, Dec. 13, 1864, *OR,* 45(2):177.

25. McDonough, *Nashville,* 149–53, 160–208, 225–66; Grant, *Memoirs,* 655–56, 659–60.

26. Hood to Cooper, Feb. 15, 1865; and Journal of the Army of Tennessee, *OR,* 45(1):655, 673; Mason to Stewart, Dec. 17, 1864, *OR,* 45(2):699.

27. Wood to Whipple, Jan. 5, 1865; and Fullerton, "Journal of the Fourth Army Corps," *OR,* 45(1):135, 157–58; Wood to Whipple, Dec. 17, 1864, *OR,* 45(2):233.

28. Thomas to Sawyer, Jan. 20, 1865; and Fullerton, "Journal of the Fourth Army Corps," *OR,* 45(1):41, 159.

29. Thomas to Sawyer, Jan. 20, 1865; and Fullerton, "Journal of the Fourth Army Corps," *OR,* 45(1):41, 159–60.

30. Fullerton, "Journal of the Fourth Army Corps," *OR,* 45(1):160–61; Wood to Whipple, Dec. 20, 1864, *OR,* 45(2):287.

31. Whipple to Donaldson, Dec. 20, 1864; Ramsey to Donaldson, Dec. 20, 1864; and Campbell to Ramsey, Dec. 20, 1864, *OR,* 45(2):285, 288.

32. Le Duc to Whipple, Dec. 20, 1864; Willett to Thomas, Dec. 20, 1864; and Schofield to Whipple, Dec. 20, 1864, *OR,* 45(2):285, 288; Fullerton, "Journal of the Fourth Army Corps," *OR,* 45(1):161.

33. Fullerton, "Journal of the Fourth Army Corps," *OR,* 45(1):161.

34. Ramsey to Wood, Dec. 20, 1864; Whipple to Schofield, Dec. 20, 1864; and Ramsey to Schofield, Dec. 21, 1864, *OR,* 45(2):287, 289, 301.

35. Van Duzer to Eckert, Dec. 21, 1864; Ramsey to Wood, Dec. 21, 1864; and Wood to Thomas, Dec. 21, 1864, *OR,* 45(2):299–300.

36. Ramsey to Schofield, Dec. 21, 1864, *OR,* 45(2):301.

37. Thomas to Sawyer, Jan. 20, 1865; Wood to Whipple, Jan. 5, 1865; and Fullerton, "Journal of the Fourth Army Corps," *OR,* 45(1):42, 136, 162.

38. Thomas to Sawyer, Jan. 20, 1865; and Fullerton, "Journal of the Fourth Army Corps," *OR,* 45(1):42, 162.

39. Thomas to Halleck, Dec. 23, 1864, *OR,* 45(2):319; Fullerton, "Journal of the Fourth Army Corps," *OR,* 45(1):162.

40. Sinclair to Wood, Dec. 24, 1864; Plum to Whipple, Dec. 25, 1864; Whipple to Wright, Dec. 25, 1864; Schofield to Thomas, Dec. 25, 1864; and Whipple to Schofield, Dec. 25, 1864, *OR,* 45(2):331, 346–47, 349–50.

41. Thomas to Halleck, Dec. 18, 1864; Whipple to Wright, Dec. 18, 1864; and Wright to McCallum, Dec. 18, 1864, *OR,* 45(2):249, 251–52.

42. Ramsey to Donaldson, Dec. 18, 1864; and Donaldson to Ramsey, Dec. 18, 1864, *OR,* 45(2):251–52; Eicholtz Diaries, Dec. 18, 1864, UW.

43. Thomas to Halleck, Dec. 19, 1864; Willard to Thomas, Dec. 19, 1864; Ramsey to Donaldson, Dec. 19, 1864; Schofield to Thomas, Dec. 19, 1864; Schofield to Whipple, Dec. 19, 1864; and Donaldson to Ramsey, Dec. 20, 1864, *OR,* 45(2):265–66, 268, 272, 286; Eicholtz Diaries, Dec. 19, 1864, UW.

44. Eicholtz Diaries, Dec. 20, 1864, UW.

45. Eicholtz Diaries, Dec. 21, 1864, UW.

46. Whipple to Eicholtz, Dec. 21, 1864; and Eicholtz to Whipple, Dec. 21, 1864, *OR,* 45(2):299.

47. Le Duc to Whipple, Dec. 21, 1864; and Whipple to Watkins, Dec. 21, 1864, *OR,* 45(2):297–98.

48. Eicholtz Diaries, Dec. 22, 1864, UW; Wright to Whipple, Dec. 22, 1864, *OR,* 45(2):309.

49. Ramsey to Wright, Dec. 22, 1864, *OR,* 45(2):310.

50. Eicholtz Diaries, Dec. 23–24, 1864, UW.

51. Donaldson to Whipple, Dec. 24, 25, 1864, *OR,* 45(2):330–31, 346.

52. Eicholtz Diaries, Dec. 26, 1864, UW; Wright to Whipple, Dec. 26, 1864; Schofield to Thomas, Dec. 26, 1864; and Thomas to Schofield, Dec. 26, 1864, *OR,* 45(2):357–58, 361–62.

53. Eicholtz Diaries, Dec. 27, 1864, UW; Wright to Whipple, Dec. 28, 1864, *OR,* 45(2):393.

54. Eicholtz Diaries, Dec. 28, 1864, UW; Schofield to Thomas, Dec. 28, 1864; and Whipple to Wood, Dec. 28, 1864, *OR,* 45(2):395, 394.

55. Donaldson to Thomas, Dec. 26, 1864; Joyce to Schofield, Dec. 26, 1864; Donaldson to Whipple, Dec. 28, 1864; Wright to Whipple, Dec. 28, 1864; Charles Thomas to George H. Thomas, Dec. 28, 1864; and Special Field Order No. 352, Headquarters, Department of the Cumberland, Dec. 28, 1864, *OR,* 45(2):356, 361, 391–93; Wright to McCallum, May 20, 1865, *OR,* ser. 3, 5:29–30.

56. Eicholtz Diaries, Dec. 29, 30, 1864, UW.

57. Wright to Thomas, Dec. 29, 1864; Watkins to Beaumont, Jan. 11, 1865; Watkins to Beaumont, Jan. 11, 1865; and Van Duzer to Eckert, Jan. 13, 1865, *OR,* 45(2):406, 570–71, 579; Eicholtz Diaries, Dec. 31, 1864, UW.

58. Thomas to Grant and Halleck, Dec. 17, 1864; Ramsey to Rousseau, Dec. 17, 1864; Thomas to Lee, Dec. 17, 1864; and Whipple to Granger, Dec. 17, 1864, *OR,* 45(2):229, 231, 243.

59. Thomas to Sawyer, Jan. 20, 1865, *OR,* 45(1):43; Whipple to Granger, Dec. 18, 1864, *OR,* 45(2):261.

60. Wright to McCallum, May 20, 1865, *OR,* ser. 3, 5:29.

61. Rousseau to Whipple, Dec. 21, 1864, *OR,* 45(2):304.

62. Donaldson to Whipple, Dec. 21, 1864; and Dana to Halleck, Dec. 21, 1864, *OR,* 45(2):297, 306.

63. Lockett to Alexander, Dec. 20, 1864, *OR,* 45(2):717.

64. "Journal of the Army of Tennessee," *OR,* 45(1):673.

65. Donaldson to Whipple, Dec. 22, 1864; and Granger to Whipple, Dec. 22, 1864, *OR,* 45(2):309, 318.

66. Whipple to Donaldson, Dec. 23, 1864; and Hood to Seddon, Dec. 25, 1864, *OR,* 45(2):320, 731.

67. Hood to Seddon, Dec. 25, 1864, *OR,* 45(2):731; "Journal of the Army of Tennessee," *OR,* 45(1):673–74.

68. Wilson to Whipple, Dec. 24, 1864; and Wilson to Whipple, Dec. 25, 1864, *OR,* 45(2):334, 351.

69. Fullerton, "Journal of the Fourth Army Corps," *OR,* 45(1):164–65.

70. "Journal of the Army of Tennessee," *OR,* 45(1):674.

71. Fullerton, "Journal of the Fourth Army Corps," *OR,* 45(1):165–66.

72. Whipple to Donaldson, Dec. 26, 1864; and Thomas to Schofield, Dec. 26, 1864, *OR,* 45(2):357, 362.

73. Schofield to Grant, Dec. 27, 1864; and Wilson to Whipple, Dec. 27, 1864, *OR,* 45(2):377–78, 380–81.

74. Thomas to Halleck, Dec. 27, 1864; and Whipple to Donaldson, Dec. 27, 1864, *OR,* 45(2):369–70, 373.

75. Lee to Thomas, Dec. 27, 1864, *OR,* 45(2):371.

76. Steedman to Whipple, Jan. 27, 1865, *OR,* 45(1):503, 505–6.

77. Steedman to Whipple, Jan. 27, 1865; and Palmer to Moe, Jan. 10, 1865, *OR,* 45(1):506–7, 643; Beauregard to Cooper, Jan. 22, 1865, *OR,* 45(2):804.

78. Dana to Thomas, Jan. 8, 1865; Dana to Stanton, Jan. 10, 1865; and Van Duzer to Eckert, Jan. 13, 1865, *OR,* 45(2):553, 566, 579.

79. Mason to Harvie, Dec. 26, 1864; Beauregard to Cooper, Jan. 2, 1865; Wintter endorsement, Jan. 21, 1865, on Brent to Taylor, Jan. 12, 1865; and Whitfield to Harvie, Jan. 16, 17, 1865, *OR,* 45(2):736, 753, 779, 787–88, 790.

80. Donaldson to Whipple, Dec. 29, 1864; Whipple to Donaldson, Dec. 29, 1864; and Donaldson to Meigs, Jan. 10, 1865, *OR,* 45(2):405, 561; McCallum to Meigs, May 26, 1866, *OR,* ser. 3, 5:989–90.

81. Brent to Mackall, Dec. 27, 1864; Brent to Beauregard, Dec. 27, 1864; Brent to Hood, Dec. 27, 1864; and Taylor to Adams, Dec. 27, 1864, *OR,* 45(2):739, 740–41.

82. "Journal of the Army of Tennessee," *OR,* 45(1):674; Harvie to Fleming, Jan. 14, 1865; Circular, Headquarters, Army of Tennessee, Jan. 14, 1865; and Mason to Stewart, Cheatham, and Stevenson, Jan. 14, 1865, *OR,* 45(2):782–83; Douglas J. Cater to Fannie, Dec. 15, 1864, Jan. 12, 1865, Douglas J. Cater and Rufus W. Cater Papers, LC.

83. McCook to Thomas, Dec. 23, 1864; Van Duzer to Eckert, Dec. 25, 1864; Donaldson to Whipple, Dec. 28, 1864; Milroy to Rousseau, Jan. 6, 1865; and Thomas to Halleck, Jan. 11, 1865, *OR,* 45(2):325, 347, 390, 527, 568.

84. Halleck to Thomas, Dec. 21, 1864; and Thomas to Halleck, Dec. 21, 1864, *OR,* 45(2):295–96.

85. Wood to Whipple, Jan. 5, 1865, *OR,* 45(1):137.

86. Thomas to Halleck, Dec. 29, 1864, *OR,* 45(2):403.

87. Halleck to Grant, Dec. 30, 1864, *OR,* 45(2):419–20.

88. Wood to Whipple, Dec. 30, 1864, *OR,* 45(2):423–24.

89. Halleck to Thomas, Dec. 31, 1864; Thomas to Halleck, Dec. 31, 1864; Whipple to Donaldson, Jan. 1, 1865; and Thomas to Wilson, Jan. 1, 1865, *OR,* 45(2):441–42, 471–72, 477.

90. Charles Thomas to George H. Thomas, Jan. 5, 1865; Sherman to Thomas, Jan. 21, 1865; and Thomas to Halleck, Jan. 24, 1865, *OR,* 45(2):511, 621–22, 627–28.

91. Wood to Donaldson, Jan. 10, 1865; and Sinclair to Kimball, Jan. 19, 1865, *OR,* 45(2):561, 615.

92. Grant to Halleck, Jan. 7, 18, 1865; and Whipple to Willett, Jan. 17, 1865, *OR,* 45(2):529, 603, 609–10.

93. Wilson to Whipple, Dec. 30, 1864, and Feb. 6, 1865, *OR,* 45(2):430–31, 513.

8. Strategic Raids in the Deep South

1. Easton to Meigs, Mar. 16, 1865, *OR,* ser. 3, 5:394; Easton to Meigs, Aug. 8, 1865, *OR,* 52(1):702; Sherman to Halleck, Jan. 1, 1865, *OR,* 44:8; Sherman, *Memoirs,* 2:177.

2. Sherman, *Memoirs,* 2:183.

3. Sherman, *Memoirs,* 2:182; Cook and Benton, *"Dutchess County Regiment,"* 140.

4. McWilliams, *Recollections,* 103.

5. Sherman, *Memoirs,* 2:183–84; Billings, *Hardtack and Coffee,* 241.

6. Special Field Order No. 120, Headquarters, Military Division of the Mississippi, Nov. 9, 1864, *OR,* 39(3):713.

7. Williams to Rodgers, Jan. 9, 1865, *OR,* 44:212.

8. Sherman, *Memoirs,* 2:181–82; O. P. Johnson to Sir, Jan. 10, 1865, Edward Louis Edes and Robert Thaxter Edes Correspondence, MHS; Howland to mother, Dec. 26, 1864, Thomas S. Howland Correspondence, MHS.

9. Hutchinson to mother, Dec. 16, 1864, Edwin Hutchinson Papers, LSU.

10. Sherman to Ellen, Dec. 16, 1864, in Simpson and Berlin, *Sherman's Civil War,* 768.

11. Sherman, *Memoirs,* 2:193.

12. Cobb to Davis, [Nov. 17], 1863, *OR,* 44:861; Bailey, *War and Ruin,* 67–69.

13. Sherman, *Memoirs,* 2:180; Howard to Dayton, Dec. 28, 1864; Davis to Rodgers, Dec. 31, 1864; and Williams to Rodgers, Jan. 9, 1865, *OR,* 44:76, 166, 210.

14. Gilmer to Seddon, Jan. 3, 1865, *OR,* 44:1012–13.

15. Gilmer to Seddon, Jan. 3, 1865, *OR,* 44:1012–13.

16. Hess, *Civil War Logistics,* 212–14.

17. Hill to People of Georgia, Nov. 18, 1864; Beauregard to People of Georgia, Nov. 18, 1864; and six members of Congress to People of Georgia, Nov. 19, 1864, *OR,* 44:867.

18. Circular, Headquarters, Cavalry Corps, Dec. 4, 1864, *OR,* 44:928; Dodson, *Campaigns of Wheeler,* 390.

19. Lawson to Davis, Dec. 27, 1864, *OR,* ser. 4, 3:967; Robert to Davis, Dec. 25, 1864; and Chesnut to Davis, Dec. 26, 1864, in Crist, *Papers of Jefferson Davis,* 11:252; Dodson, *Campaigns of Wheeler,* 387–89, 390–92; Wheeler to Bragg, Dec. 28, 1864; and General Orders No. 7, Headquarters, Cavalry Corps, Dec. 29, 1864, *OR,* 44:998, 1002–3.

20. Davis to Rodgers, Dec. 31, 1864, *OR,* 44:166–67.

21. Easton to Meigs, Aug. 8, 1865, *OR,* 52(1):702; Whittelsey to Easton, Jan. 20, 1865, *OR,* ser. 3, 5:400.

22. Sherman to Halleck, Jan. 1, 1865, *OR,* 44:13; Thompson, *Reconstruction in Georgia,* 28; *Statistics of the United States,* 298.

23. *Population of the United States,* 72–73. I excluded Chatham County, with its city of Savannah, from calculations to arrive at the population density of the counties lying close to the coast because it inaccurately skews the numbers. Sherman's march ended in that county, and the population of Savannah was not involved in producing foodstuffs that could be foraged by the Federals.

24. Hess, *Civil War in the West,* 262.

25. Hess, *Civil War in the West,* 262–63.

26. Easton to Meigs, July 22, 1865, *OR,* 53:44–45; Meigs to Stanton, Nov. 8, 1865, *OR,* ser. 3, 5:214–15; Weigley, *Quartermaster General,* 313.

27. Grant to Sherman, Dec. 6, 1864, in Simon, *Papers of Ulysses S. Grant,* 13:72–73.

28. Sherman, *Memoirs,* 2:206–7; Grant to Sherman, Dec. 18, 1864, *OR,* 44:740–41.

29. Grant to Stanton, July 22, 1865, *OR,* 34(1):44; Sherman to Halleck, Dec. 24, 1864, *OR,* 44:798–99.

30. Sherman to Lincoln, Dec. 22, 1864, *OR,* 44:783; Quaife, *From the Cannon's Mouth,* 355.

31. Easton to Meigs, July 22, 1865, *OR,* 53:45.

32. Easton to Meigs, July 22, 1865, *OR,* 53:45.

33. Chittenden, *Personal Reminiscences,* 246–48, 258, 266.

34. Sherman to John Sherman, Dec. 31, 1864, in Simpson and Berlin, *Sherman's Civil War,* 786.

35. Sherman to Ellen, Dec. 31, 1864, in Simpson and Berlin, *Sherman's Civil War,* 785; Sherman to Meigs, Dec. 25, 1864, *OR,* 45(2):512.

36. Sherman, *Memoirs,* 2:272; Grant to Sherman, Dec. 27, 1864, *OR,* 44:821.

37. Easton to Meigs, July 22, 1865, *OR,* 53:45–46.

38. Meigs Diary, Jan. 12, 1865, Montgomery C. Meigs Papers, LC.

39. Sherman, *Memoirs,* 2:269, 272.

40. General Field Orders No. 7, Headquarters, Department of the Tennessee, Jan. 30, 1865; Special Field Orders No. 14, Headquarters, Fourth Division, Fifteenth Corps, Feb. 11, 1865; Special Orders No. 4, Headquarters, Twentieth Corps, Feb. 13, 1865; Hazen to Woodhull, Feb. 22, 1865; Special Orders No. 55, Headquarters, Seventeenth Corps, Mar. 1, 1865; Special Field Orders No. 56, Headquarters, Army of the Tennessee, Mar. 8, 1865; and Special Orders No. 45, Headquarters, First Division, Fifteenth Corps, Mar. 13, 1865, *OR,* 47(2):171, 388–89, 410, 529–30, 632, 728, 809.

41. Kilpatrick to Dayton, Feb. 22, 1865, *OR,* 47(2):533.

42. Sherman to Wade Hampton, Feb. 24, 1865; and Hampton to Sherman, Feb. 27, 1865, *OR,* 47(2):546, 596–97.

43. General Orders No. 10, Headquarters, Fourth Division, Seventeenth Corps, Jan. 30, 1865; and Special Orders No. 38, Headquarters, Fifteenth Corps, Feb. 7, 1865, *OR,* 47(2):173, 331.

44. General Field Orders No. 9, Headquarters, Army of the Tennessee, Feb. 9, 1865; Howard to Blair, Feb. 20, 1865; and Circular, Headquarters, Army of the Tennessee, Mar. 4, 1865, *OR,* 47(2):360, 505–6, 677.

45. Morgan to McClurg, Mar. 29, 1865, *OR,* 47(1):487.

46. Sherman to Kilpatrick, Feb. 21, 1865; and Sherman to Stanton, Mar. 12, 1865, *OR,* 47(2):519, 793.

47. Sherman, *Memoirs,* 2:273–75.

48. Woods to Woodhull, Feb. 17, 1865, *OR,* 47(2):457; Howard, *Autobiography,* 2:121–22; Harwell and Racine, *Fiery Trail,* 129; Lucas, *Sherman and the Burning of Columbia,* 65, 68–69, 75–76, 83, 98, 102–3, 109, 118, 121–24, 127.

49. Special Field Orders (unnumbered), Headquarters, Military Division of the West, Jan. 23, 1865, *OR,* 45(2):805; "Conversation with South Carolina Delegation," [Jan. 9, 1865]; and Watts to Davis, Feb. 15, 1865, in Crist, *Papers of Jefferson Davis,* 11:298, 404; Longstreet to Lee, Feb. 2, 1865; and Special Orders No. 3, Headquarters, Armies of the Confederate States, Feb. 22, 1865, *OR,* 47(2):1078; Lee to Breckinridge, Feb. 19, 1865, *OR,* 47(1):1044.

50. Lee to Davis, Feb. 23, 1865, *OR,* 53:413; Lee to Johnston, Feb. 23, 1865, *OR,* 47(2):1256–57.

51. Lee to Johnston, Feb. 23, 1865; and Hardee to Johnston, Feb. 28, 1865, *OR,* 47(2):1257, 1290.

52. Dodson, *Campaigns of Wheeler,* 397–403; Circular, Headquarters, Cavalry Corps, Dec. 14, 1864, Jan. 14, 22, 23, 1865, General Orders, Civil War, Box 130, Joseph Wheeler Family Papers, ADAH, 205, 214, 217.

53. Whittelsey to [Meigs], Mar. 31, 1865, *OR,* ser. 4, 5:430; Williams to Dechert, Mar. 31, 1865, *OR,* 47(1):588.

54. Sherman, *Memoirs,* 2:241; Easton to Meigs, July 22, 1865, *OR,* 53:46; Wise to Meigs, Aug. 31, 1865, *OR,* ser. 3, 5:288.

55. Schofield to Sherman, Apr. 3, 1865, *OR,* 47(1):910–11; Garber to Meigs, July 10, 1865, *OR,* 53:54.

56. *Report of the Quartermaster General,* 113.

57. Geary to Perkins, Mar. 26, 1865, *OR,* 47(1):695, 697–98.

58. *Statistics of the United States,* 298, 309, 312.

59. *Population of the United States,* 358–59, 452.

60. Force to Cadle, Mar. 28, 1865, *OR,* 47(1):409; Schofield, *Forty-Six Years in the Army,* 346; Sherman to Schofield, Mar. 12, 1865; Sherman to Grant, Mar. 22, 1865; and Special Field Orders No. 69, Headquarters, Army of the Tennessee, Mar. 23, 1865, *OR,* 47(2):800, 950, 972; Sherman, *Memoirs,* 2:304.

61. Terry to Sherman, Mar. 14, 1865; and Sherman to Grant, Mar. 23, 1865, *OR,* 47(2):840, 969; Wright to McCallum, May 20, 1865, *OR,* ser. 3, 5:29–30; Sherman, *Memoirs,* 2:272.

62. Wright to McCallum, May 20, 1865, *OR,* ser. 3, 5:33–34.

63. Wright to McCallum, May 20, 1865, *OR,* ser. 3, 5:30–31.

64. Wright to McCallum, May 20, 1865, *OR,* ser. 3, 5:31–32, 36.

65. Sherman to Ellen, Mar. 26, 1865, in Simpson and Berlin, *Sherman's Civil War,* 837; Wright to McCallum, May 20, 1865, *OR,* ser. 3, 5:32.

66. Easton to Meigs, July 22, 1865, *OR,* 53:47–48; Wright to McCallum, May 20, 1865, *OR,* ser. 3, 5:32, 35–36.

67. Wright to McCallum, May 20, 1865, *OR,* ser. 3, 5:32.

68. Wright to McCallum, Apr. 24, 1866, *OR,* ser. 3, 5:970; Weber, *Northern Railroads,* 212.

69. Halleck to Grant, Dec. 30, 1864; and Grant to Halleck, Jan. 18, 1865, *OR,* 45(2):420, 609; Halleck to Sherman, Jan. 1, 1865, *OR,* 47(2):4.

70. Sherman to Thomas, Jan. 21, 1865, *OR,* 45(2):621–22.

71. Thomas to Halleck, Jan. 24, 1865, *OR,* 45(2):627–28; Thomas to Sherman, Feb. 5, 1864, *OR,* 49(1):653–54; Grant to Halleck, Dec. 8, 1864; and Grant to Sherman, Mar. 16, 1865, in Simon, *Papers of Ulysses S. Grant,* 13:83, 14:172–75.

72. Grant to Canby, Feb. 9, 1865; and Grant to Canby, Feb. 27, 1865, in Simon, *Papers of Ulysses S. Grant,* 13:397, 14:61–63.

73. Canby to Halleck, June 1, 1865, *OR,* 49(1):92–93; Sawtelle to Meigs, Dec. 13, 1865, *OR,* 53:607.

74. Sawtelle to Meigs, Dec. 13, 1865, *OR,* 53:606.

75. Osterhaus to Hinsdill, Mar. 23, 1865; and General Field Orders (unnumbered), Headquarters, Army and Division of West Mississippi, Mar. 23, 1865, *OR,* 49(2):67.

76. Granger to Canby, Apr. 13, 1865, *OR,* 49(2):348–49; Canby to Halleck, June 1, 1865: Grierson to Christensen, June 4, 1865, *OR,* 49(1):99, 300–301.

77. Wilson to Whipple, June 29, 1865, *OR,* 49(1):354–56.

78. Wilson to Whipple, June 29, 1865, *OR,* 49(1):356; Jones, *Yankee Blitzkrieg,* 28.

79. Jones, *Yankee Blitzkrieg,* 28, 69–91, 110–12, 132–39; Wilson to Whipple, Feb. 6, 1865, *OR,* 45(2):513.

80. Jones, *Yankee Blitzkrieg,* 185–86.

81. McCallum to Meigs, May 26, 1866, *OR,* ser. 3, 5:988.

82. Eicholtz to McCallum, Aug. 15, 1865, *OR,* ser. 3, 5:99–100.

83. Wright to McCallum, Apr. 24, 1866; and McCallum to Meigs, May 26, 1866, *OR,* ser. 3, 5:952–55, 988.

84. Stevens to McCallum, [July 1, 1865], *OR,* ser. 3, 5:88.

85. McCallum to Meigs, May 26, 1866, *OR,* ser. 3, 5:989.

86. McCallum to Meigs, May 26, 1866, *OR,* ser. 3, 5:988.

9. Rails and Rivers in the Trans-Mississippi

1. Piston and Hatcher, *Wilson's Creek,* 131–32.

2. Harding to Thomas, July 5, 1861, *OR,* 3:390.

3. Curtis to Carr, Dec. 28, 1861; and Curtis to Kelton, Jan. 9, 1862, *OR,* 8:473, 492.

4. Halleck to Curtis, Jan. 18, 1862; and Curtis to Kelton, Jan. 24, Feb. 1, 1862, *OR,* 8:506, 524, 540.

5. Special Orders No. 75, Headquarters Southwestern District of Missouri, Feb. 7, 1862, *OR,* 8:549.

6. Shea and Hess, *Pea Ridge,* 1–260.

7. Curtis to McLean, Mar. 17, 1862; and Halleck to Curtis, Mar. 19, 1862, *OR,* 8:622, 626.

8. Halleck to Steele, Mar. 1, 1862; and Steele to Halleck, Mar. 19, 1862, *OR,* 8:578–79, 627; Shea and Hess, *Pea Ridge,* 290–93.

9. Eugene A. Carr to Trumbull, May 22, 1862, Lyman Trumbull Correspondence, LC.

10. Shea and Hess, *Pea Ridge,* 284–306.

11. Curtis to Halleck, Aug. 6, 1862, *OR,* 13, 541.

12. Schofield to Grant, July 8, 1863; and Grant to Schofield, July 15, 1863, *OR,* 22(1):19–20.

13. Steele to Schofield, Sept. 12, 1863, *OR,* 22(1):474–75.

14. Steele to [Hurlbut], Aug. 26, 1863, *OR,* 22(1):473; Schofield to Halleck, Sept. 18, 1863; and Jacobi to Marsh, Sept. 19, 1863, *OR,* 22(2):539, 544.

15. Steele to Schofield, Sept. 12, 1863, *OR,* 22(1):476–77.

16. Schofield to Townsend, Dec. 10, 1863, *OR,* 22(1):15.

17. McNeil to Totten, Jan. 4, 1864, *OR,* 34(2):24; Adolf Engelmann to sister, Jan. 23, 1864, Engelmann-Kircher Collection, ALPL.

18. Graton to wife, Jan. 27–31, 1864, John R. Graton Correspondence, KHS; Lewis to Lewis B. Parsons, Feb. 20, 1864, J. V. Lewis Letter, MHM.

19. Adolf Engelmann to sister, Feb. 21, 1864, Engelmann-Kircher Collection, ALPL; Porter to Banks, Feb. 26, 1864, *OR,* 34(2):424.

20. Curtis to Insley, Feb. 29, 1864, *OR,* 34(2):468; Hunt to Comstock, Apr. 19, 1864, *OR,* 34(3):226.

21. Adolf Engelmann to sister, Mar. 20, 1864, Engelmann-Kircher Collection, ALPL; Owen to Hunt, Apr. 19, 1864, *OR,* 34(3):229.

22. Thayer to Rosecrans, May 26, 1864; and Thayer to Steele, May 28, 1864, *OR,* 34(4):50, 84.

23. Adolf Engelmann to Mina, Dec. 30, 1864, Engelmann-Kircher Collection, ALPL; Thayer to Green, Dec. 26, 1864, *OR*, 41(4):935.

24. Clayton to Steele, Nov. 26, 1864, *OR*, 41(4):692.

25. Adolf Engelmann to Mina, Dec. 30, 1864, Engelmann-Kircher Collection, ALPL.

26. McCallum to Meigs, May 26, 1866, *OR*, ser. 3, 5:991.

27. Halleck to Canby, May 7, 1864, *OR*, 34(3):491.

28. Sherman to Porter, May 3, 1864; and Sherman to Halleck, May 6, 1864, *OR*, 34(3):411, 479.

29. Porter to Sherman, Mar. 5, 1864, *OR*, 34(2):502.

30. Special Field Orders No. 2, Headquarters, Red River Expedition, Mar. 8, 1864; and Special Field Orders No. 6, Headquarters, Red River Expedition, Mar. 13, 1864, *OR*, 34(2):528, 584.

31. Stone to Beckwith, Mar. 16, 1864; Holabird to Welch, Mar. 17, 19, 1864; Welch to Holabird, Mar. 21, 1864; and Surget to May, Mar. 20, 1864, *OR*, 34(2):628, 635, 654–55, 679, 1060.

32. Porter to Stone, Mar. 21, 1864; Stone to Holabird, Mar. 25, 1864; and Stone to Beckwith, Mar. 25, 1864, *OR*, 34(2):678, 722.

33. Stone to Beckwith, Apr. 4, 1864, *OR*, 34(3):37.

34. Stone to Holabird, Apr. 4, 1864; Grover to Stone, Apr. 7, 1864; and Poole to Drake, Apr. 10, 1864, *OR*, 34(3):36–37, 71, 115.

35. Welch to Holabird, Apr. 12, 1864, *OR*, 34(3):140.

36. Kilby Smith to Hough, Apr. 16, 1864, *OR*, 34(1):380–82.

37. Porter to Sherman, Apr. 16, 1864; and Welch to Holabird, Apr. 23, 1864, *OR*, 34(3):172–73, 268.

38. General Orders No. 43, Headquarters, Nineteenth Corps, Apr. 27, 1864, *OR*, 34(3):307; Taylor to Anderson, Apr. 24, 1864, *OR*, 34(1):581.

39. Hunter to Grant, Apr. 28, 1864; Banks to Porter, Apr. 29, 1864; Matthews to Chandler, May 2, 1864; and Banks to Farragut, May 4, 1864, *OR*, 34(3):316, 333, 390, 427; Banks to Stanton, Apr. 6, 1865; and Bailey to Hoffman, May 17, 1864, *OR*, 34(1):209, 403–4.

40. Field Orders No. 27, Headquarters, Department of the Gulf, Apr. 26, 1864; Dwight to Porter, May 4, 1864; Porter to Banks, May 4, 1864; and Dwight to Beckwith, May 4, 1864, *OR*, 34(3):295–96, 428–29; Ullmann to Crosby, May 6, 1864, *OR*, 34(1):475; Brent to Surget, May 20, 1864, *SOR*, pt. 1, 6:354–59.

41. Caldwell to commanding officer, Forage Train Escort, May 1, 1864; Drake to Chandler, May 2, 1864; Dwight to Beckwith, May 7, 1864; Banks to Porter, May 9, 1864; Porter to Banks, May 11, 1864; McClernand to Warren, May 11, 1864; and Dwight to Warren, May 12, 1864, *OR*, 34(3):375–76, 390, 493, 513, 544, 546, 558; Banks to Stanton, Apr. 6, 1865; and Bailey to Hoffman, May 17, 1864, *OR*, 34(1):209, 403–4.

42. Chandler to Meigs, Dec. 26, 1864; and Becht to Malmros, May 25, 1864, *OR*, 34(1):236–37, 239, 241, 324.

43. Steele to Halleck, Mar. 12, 1864; and Circular, Headquarters, Third Division, Seventh Corps, Mar. 12, 1864, *OR*, 34(2):576–77.

44. General Field Orders No. 3, Headquarters, Salomon's Division, Mar. 25, 1864; and General Field Orders No. 3, Headquarters, First Cavalry Division, Mar. 27, 1864, *OR*, 34(2):729, 752–53; Henry to Meigs, May 12, 1864, *OR*, 34(1):679; Adolf Engelmann to sister, Mar. 20, 1864, Engelmann-Kircher Collection, ALPL.

45. Henry to Meigs, May 12, 1864, *OR,* 34(1):679–80.

46. Henry to Meigs, May 12, 1864; and Price to Boggs, May 7, 1864, *OR,* 34(1):679–80, 781.

47. Henry to Meigs, May 12, 1864, *OR,* 34(1):680.

48. Steele to Halleck, May 4, 1864; and Henry to Meigs, May 12, 1864, *OR,* 34(1):668, 680.

49. Clayton to Green, Apr. 26, 1864; Steele to Halleck, May 4, 1864; Henry to Meigs, May 12, 1864; and Price to Boggs, May 7, 1864, *OR,* 34(1):665, 668, 680, 781.

50. Steele to Halleck, May 4, 1864, *OR,* 34(1):668.

51. Halleck to Allen, May 3, 1864; and Allen to Halleck, May 3, 1864, *OR,* 34(3):410.

52. Green to Steele, Apr. 21, 1864; West to Andrews, Apr. 26, 1864; Carr to Sokalski, May 1, 1864; Andrews to Brush, May 3, 1864; and Green to Andrews, May 6, 1864, *OR,* 34(3):246, 297–98, 377, 415, 481.

53. Henry to Meigs, May 12, 1864; [Engelmann to Blocki], May 5, 1864; Dengler to Fuller, June [?], 1864; and Garrett to Gay, May 6, 1864, *OR,* 34(1):680, 727, 737, 741.

54. Steele to Halleck, May 4, 1864, *OR,* 34(1):670.

55. Henry to Meigs, May 12, 1864, *OR,* 34(1):681; Adolf Engelmann to Mina, May 4, 1864, Engelmann-Kircher Collection, ALPL.

56. Adolf Engelmann to Mina, May 8, 1864, Engelmann-Kircher Collection, ALPL.

57. Steele to Halleck, May 4, 1864; and Wheeler to Green, May 5, 1864, *OR,* 34(1):668, 676.

58. "Statement of wagons and mules captured and destroyed in the expedition of the Seventh Army Corps, Maj. Gen. F. Steele commanding," *OR,* 34(1):684; Halleck to Allen, May 6, 1864, *OR,* 34(3):480.

59. Halleck to Canby, May 7, 1864, *OR,* 34(3):491.

60. Canby to Halleck, May 28, 1864; Canby to Meigs, May 28, 1864; Canby to Steele, June 2, 1864; Christensen to Sawtelle, June 6, 1864; and Special Orders No. 202, War Department, Adjutant General's Office, June 9, 1864, *OR,* 34(4):73–75, 175, 242, 274.

61. Halleck to Canby, June 11, 1864, *OR,* 34(4):304.

62. Sawtelle to Christensen, June 11, 1864, *OR,* 34(4):305–6.

63. Hardie to Canby, June 13, 1864; Bailey to Christensen, June 21, 1864; and Bailey to Meigs, June 23, 1864, *OR,* 34(4):331, 481, 515.

64. Canby to Halleck, June 22, 1864; Canby to Hardie, June 24, 1864; and Canby to Meigs, June 24, 1864, *OR,* 34(4):498, 528–29.

65. Grant to Halleck, June 23, 1864; and Halleck to Canby, June 24, 1864, *OR,* 34(4):514–15, 528.

66. Grant to Rosecrans, Apr. 12, 1864; and Rosecrans to Grant, Apr. 12, 1864, *OR,* 34(3):145.

67. Owen to Hunt, Apr. 19, 1864, *OR,* 34(3):228–29.

68. Price to Boggs, Dec. 28, 1864, *OR,* 41(1):627, 638, 640.

69. Record of events, Company B, 12th Kansas, Jan.–Feb. 1865, *SOR,* pt. 2, 21:638.

70. Hill to Cole, June 5, 1864; and Thomas to Mason, Apr. 29, 1864, *OR,* 34(4):645, 663; McCulloch to Boggs, May 9, 1864; Thomas to Lanigan, Apr. 30, 1864; and McCulloch to Lanigan, May 8, 1864, *OR,* 34(3):813–15; Windham, "Problem of Supply," 153.

71. Brown, *Journey to Pleasant Hill,* 225.

72. Schaumburg to Boggs, Oct. 26, 1863, *OR,* 22(2):1049–53; Banasik, *Serving with Honor,* 135; "Consolidated report of clothing, clothing material, and camp and garrison equipage sold and issued to the officers and troops of the Trans-Mississippi Department by Maj. W. H.

Haynes, quartermaster, C. S. Army, and chief clothing bureau, Trans-Mississippi Department," *OR,* 34(4):658.

73. Franklin to Davis, Nov. 6, 1863, *OR,* 22(2):1058–59; General Orders No. 1, Headquarters, Trans-Mississippi Department, Jan. 9, 1864; Adams to Cooper, Jan. 29, 1864; General Orders No. 9, Headquarters, Price's Division, Feb. 9, 1864; and Barker to Garland, Jan. 26, 1864, *OR,* 34(2):849, 921–22, 957, 990.

10. Supplying the Army of the Potomac

1. Rucker to Meigs, Sept. 29 1863, *OR,* 51(1):1093.

2. Van Vliet to Marcy Aug. 2, 1862, *OR,* 11(1):156–57; McClellan to Thomas, Aug. 4, 1863, *OR,* 5:28.

3. McClellan memorandum, ca. Dec. 1, 1861, *OR,* 5:672–73.

4. Jewett, *Rise and Fall of the Confederacy,* 149.

5. McClellan to Thomas, Aug. 4 1863, *OR,* 5:27; Van Vliet to Marcy, Aug. 2, 1862, *OR,* 11(1):157–58; Ingalls to Meigs, June 26, 1862, *OR,* 11(3):262.

6. Van Vliet to Marcy, Aug. 2, 1862; and Clarke to Williams, Feb. 1, 1863, *OR,* 11(1):158, 167; Kautz Diary, *SOR,* pt. 1, 2:113; Wittenberg, *"We Have It Damn Hard,"* 19–20; Rucker to Meigs, Sept. 29, 1863, *OR,* 51(1):1095.

7. Clarke to Williams, Feb. 1, 1863, *OR,* 11(1):166–68.

8. Van Vliet to Meigs, May 7, 1862; and Ingalls to Meigs, July 18, 1862, *OR,* 11(3):149, 327; Clarke to Williams, Feb. 1 1863, *OR,* 11(1):176; Ingalls to Meigs, Sept. 28, 1863, *OR,* 19(1):104.

9. Van Vliet to Marcy, Aug. 2, 1862, *OR,* 11(1):158–59; Van Vliet to Meigs, May 23, June 5, 1862, *OR,* 11(1):162–63; Miller, "Scarcely Any Parallel," 134, 144–45, 154–59, 160–63.

10. Van Vliet to Marcy, Aug. 2, 1862; Ingalls to Marcy Feb. 17, 1863; and Clarke to Williams, Feb. 1, 1863, *OR,* 11(1):159, 165, 169; McCallum to Meigs, May 26, 1866, *OR,* ser. 3, 5:974.

11. Van Vliet to Marcy, Aug. 2, 1862; Ingalls to Marcy, Feb. 17 1863; and Clarke to Williams, Feb. 1, 1863, *OR,* 11(1):160, 165, 170; McCallum to Meigs, May 26, 1866, *OR,* ser. 3, 5:975.

12. McCallum to Meigs, May 26,1866, *OR,* ser. 3, 5:975.

13. Rucker to Meigs, Sept. 29, 1863, *OR,* 51(1):1095.

14. Ward, *That Man Haupt,* 118–19; Pickenpaugh, *Rescue by Rail,* 14–18; Risch, *Quartermaster Support,* 396–98.

15. Ward, *That Man Haupt,* 58–111.

16. Herman Haupt to [Cartwright], Apr. 30, 1862, Lewis Muhlenberg Haupt Family Papers, LC.

17. Herman Haupt to [Cartwright], May 5, 1862, Haupt Family Papers, LC; Haupt testimony, Dec. 6, 1862, Record of the McDowell Court of Inquiry, *OR,* 12(1):76.

18. Herman Haupt to [Cartwright], May 5, 1862, Haupt Family Papers, LC; Stanton to Haupt, May 28, 1862, *OR,* 12(3):274–75; Haupt testimony, Dec. 6, 1862, Record of the McDowell Court of Inquiry, *OR,* 12(1):76; Haupt, "Railroad Brigade," 467–68.

19. Ward, *That Man Haupt,* 120.

20. Ward, *That Man Haupt,* 121.

21. Haupt, *Military Bridges,* 8; McDowell note, Record of the McDowell Court of Inquiry, *OR,* 12(1):281n; Haupt, "Railroad Brigade," 466–67.

22. Haupt, *Reminiscences,* 193–94; Ward, *That Man Haupt,* 155.

23. Clarke to Williams, Feb. 1, 1863, *OR,* 11(1):171–72; Owen to Meigs, Sept. 19, 1863, *OR,* 51(1):106; Alexander Bliss, "Narrative," Bancroft-Bliss Families Papers, LC.

24. Ingalls to Meigs, Sept. 28 1863, *OR,* 19(1):101; General Orders No. 5, Headquarters, Army of Virginia, July 18, 1862, *OR,* 12(2):50.

25. Haupt, *Reminiscences,* 69–70; Halleck to Pope, Aug. 29, 1862, *OR,* 12(3):724; General Orders No. 19, Headquarters, Army of Virginia, Aug. 14, 1862, *OR,* 12(3):573.

26. Rucker to Meigs, Sept. 29, 1863, *OR,* 51(1):1096; Wool to Stanton, July 26, 1862; Pope to Meigs, Aug. 16, 1862; and Pope to Halleck, Aug. 16, 20, 1862, *OR,* 12(3):477, 576–77, 603; Haupt, *Reminiscences,* 73.

27. Pope to Haupt, Aug. 20, 1862; and Clary to Meigs, Aug. 26 1862, *OR,* 12(3):603, 677.

28. Pope to Halleck, Aug. 14, 1862; and Haupt to wife, Aug. 16, 1862, Haupt Family Papers, LC; Ward, *That Man Haupt,* 124–28; Haupt to Watson, Aug. 23, 1862; and Haupt to Lincoln, Aug. 30 1862, *OR,* 12(3):635, 637–38, 762.

29. Wright to Haupt, Sept. 17, 1862, *OR,* 12(3):813, 815.

30. Ingalls to Marcy, Feb. 17, 1863; and Ingalls to Meigs, Sept. 28, 1863, *OR,* 19(1):94–95, 102; Rucker to Meigs, Sept. 29, 1863, *OR,* 51(1):1096.

31. Meigs to McClellan, Sept. 9, 1862, *OR,* 19(2):225.

32. Haupt to Halleck, Sept. 27, 1862, *OR,* 51(1):867–69.

33. Meigs to Ingalls, Sept. 18, 1862; Meigs to Superintendents of Northern Central Railroad and Cumberland Valley Railroad, Sept. 18, 1862; Ripley to McClellan, Sept. 18, 1862; Du Barry to Stanton, Sept. 18, 1862; Ingalls to Haupt, Oct. 10, [1862]; and Haupt to Ingalls, Oct. 10, 1862, *OR,* 19(2):323, 327, 409.

34. Ingalls to Meigs, Sept. 21, 1862, *OR,* 19(2):339–30; McClellan to Halleck, Oct. 7, 1862, *OR,* 19(1):11.

35. Bliss, "Narrative," Bancroft-Bliss Families Papers, LC; McClellan to Lincoln, Nov. 7, 1862, *OR,* 19(2):549; Haupt to Heintzelman, Nov. 4, 1862, Letter Book, Haupt Family Papers.

36. Haupt to Burnside, Nov. 9, 1862; and Burnside to Haupt, Nov. 10, 1862, *OR,* 19(2):559, 565; McCallum to Meigs, May 26, 1866, *OR,* ser. 3, 5:975.

37. Haupt to Burnside, Nov. 9 1862, Letter Book, Haupt Family Papers, LC; Ingalls to Meigs, Nov. 6, 1862, *OR,* 19(2):549.

38. Meigs to Stanton, Oct. 25, 1862; and "Statement of clothing and equipment received at the different depots of the Army of the Potomac from Sept. 1, 1862, to October 31, 1862," *OR,* 19(1):22, 77.

39. Meigs to Stanton, Oct. 25, 1862; and McClellan to Thomas, Aug. 4, 1863, *OR,* 19(1):22, 80.

40. Haupt to Stanton, Nov. 18, 1862, Letter Book, Haupt Family Papers, LC.

41. Halleck to Stanton, Oct. 28, 1862, *OR,* 19(1):8.

42. McCallum to Meigs, May 26, 1866, *OR,* ser. 3, 5:975–76; Haupt to Meigs, Nov. 11, 1862, Letter Book, Haupt Family Papers, LC.

43. Haupt to Wright, Nov. 17, 1862; Haupt to Burnside Nov. 21, 22, 1862; and Haupt to Meigs, Nov. 29, 1862, Letter Book, Haupt Family Papers, LC.

44. Meigs to Burnside, Dec. 2, 1862, *OR,* 21:817–18.

45. Haupt to Burnside Dec. 5, 15, 1862; and Haupt to Wright, Dec. 11, 1862, Letter Book, Haupt Family Papers, LC.

46. Ingalls to Meigs, Dec. 25, 1862, and Meigs endorsement, *OR,* 21:884–85.

47. Meigs to Burnside, Dec. 30, 1862, *OR,* 21:916–17.

48. Gibbon, "Plan of a Winter Campaign," Nov. 30, 1862; and Franklin and Smith to Lincoln, Dec. 20, 1862, *OR,* 21:812–13, 868–69.

49. Meigs to Burnside, Jan. 12, 1863: *OR,* 21:966–67.

50. Meigs to not stated, sent to Halleck, Jan. 20, 1863, *OR,* 21:983.

51. Haupt to Wright, Dec. 30, 1862; Haupt to Burnside, Dec. 15, Jan. 17, 1862; and Haupt to Anderson, Mar. 28, 1863, Letter Book, Haupt Family Papers, LC.

52. Haupt, *Reminiscences,* 188–90; Ward, *That Man Haupt,* 153.

53. Woods to Sickles, May 21, 1863, *OR,* 25(1):396–97, 399; Hopkins to Ingalls, May 23 1863, *OR,* 25(2):559.

54. Wright to Haupt, May 13, 1863; and Haupt to Letterman, May 15, 1863, Letter Book, Haupt Family Papers, LC.

55. Halleck to Schenck, June 23, 1863; Meigs to Couch, June 29, 1863; and Thompson to Meigs, July 2, 1863, *OR,* 27(3):275–76, 411, 495; Haupt to Tilton, June 18 1863, Letter Book, Haupt Family Papers, LC.

56. Meigs to Ingalls, July 1, 1863; Ingalls to Meigs, July 1, 1863; and Smith to Stanton, June 30, 1863, *OR,* 27(3):472; Ingalls to Meigs, Aug. 28,1863, *OR,* 27(1):222.

57. Ward, *That Man Haupt,* 161–62; McCallum to Meigs, May 26, 1866, *OR,* ser. 3, 5:977; Thompson to Haupt, July 2, 1863; and Clough to Haupt, July 2, 1863, *OR,* 27(3):494–95.

58. Haupt to Stanton, July 7, 1864, *OR,* 27(1):22–23; Haupt to Halleck, July 4, 1863, *OR,* 27(3):521–22.

59. Haupt to Halleck, July 3, 1863; and Garrett to Halleck, July 9, 1863, *OR,* 27(3):511, 625.

60. Vollum to Surgeon General, July 25, 1863, *OR,* 27(1):26–28; McCallum to Meigs, May 26, 1866, *OR,* ser. 3, 5:977.

61. Ingalls to Meigs, July 4, 1863; Meigs to Ingalls, July 6, 1863; Rucker to Ingalls, July 6, 1863; and Howard to Warren, July 8, 1863, *OR,* 27(3):524, 569, 601; Haupt to presidents of twelve Northern railroads, July 6, 1863, Letter Book, Haupt Family Papers, LC.

62. Ingalls to Meigs, July 14, 1863; Meigs to Haupt, July 14, 1863; and Ingalls to Haupt, July 14, 1863, *OR,* 27(3):696–97; Ingalls to Meigs, Aug. 28, 1864, *OR,* 29(1):227.

63. Ingalls to Meigs, Aug. 28, 1864, *OR,* 29(1):227; McCallum to Meigs, May 26, 1866, *OR,* ser. 3, 5:976; Humphreys to officer commanding Eleventh Corps, Aug. 7, 1863; Heintzelman to [Kelton], Oct. 4, 1863; and Greene to Taylor, Oct. 2, 1863, *OR,* 29(2):12, 253–56.

64. Ingalls to Meigs, Aug. 28, 1864, *OR,* 29(1):227.

65. Ingalls to Meigs, Aug. 28, 1864, *OR,* 29(1):228; Meade to Halleck, Oct. 21, 1863, *OR,* 29(2):361.

66. Meade to Halleck, Oct. 20, 1863, *OR,* 29(2):358–59; McCallum to Meigs, May 26, 1866, *OR,* ser. 2, 5:976.

67. Ingalls to Meigs, Aug. 28, 1864, *OR,* 29(1):229; Batchelder to [Meigs], Sept. 15 1864, *OR,* 51(1):1221.

68. Haupt to Halleck, July 17, 1863; Haupt to Stanton, July 18, Sept. 5, 1863; and Stanton to Haupt, Sept. 14, 1863, Letter Book, Haupt Family Papers, LC.

69. Haupt to wife, Jan. 28, 1863, Letter Book, Haupt Family Papers, LC.

70. Haupt to Sickles, Nov. 13, 1862; and Haupt to Stanton, Nov. 15, 1862, Apr. 22, 1863, Letter Book, Haupt Family Papers, LC; Haupt to Burnside, Nov. 10, 1862, *OR*, 19(2):565.

71. Haupt to Halleck, Sept. 27, 1862, *OR*, 51(1):869–70.

72. Haupt to Lincoln, Aug. 7, 1863, Letter Book, Haupt Family Papers, LC.

73. Meigs to Wise, Apr. 16, 1864; Grant to Meade, Apr. 17 1864; and Wise to Meigs, Apr. 19, 1864, *OR*, 33:886, 889, 915.

74. [Meade] to Grant, Apr. 17, 1864, *OR*, 33:889–90.

75. Meigs to Grant, May 3, 1864; and Grant to Meigs, May 3, 1864, *OR*, 36(2):352.

76. Ingalls to Meigs, Aug. 28, 1864, *OR*, 36(1):277; [Wilson], "Feeding a Great Army," 149–50.

77. Ingalls to Meigs, Aug. 28, 1864, *OR*, 36(1):278.

78. McCallum to Meigs, May 26 1866, *OR*, ser. 3, 5:978; Abercrombie to Augur, May 13, 1864, *OR*, 36(2):737–38.

79. Rawlins to Abercrombie, May 20, 1864; and Ingalls to Meigs, May 25, 1864, *OR*, 36(3):26, 184; Sharpe, "Art of Supplying Armies," 74.

80. McCallum to Meigs, May 26, 1866, *OR*, ser. 3, 5:978; Ingalls to Meigs, Aug. 28, 1864, *OR*, 36(1):279.

81. Halleck to Grant, May 27 1864, *OR*, 36(3):245–46.

82. Grant to Stanton, July 22, 1865, *OR*, 34(1):18.

83. Halleck to Grant, June 7, 1864; and Grant to Biggs, June 12, 1864, *OR*, 36(3):665, 769.

84. Williams to Ingalls, June 19, 1864; and Ingalls to Meigs, June 27 1864, *OR*, 40(2):211, 463; Ingalls to Meigs, Sept. 28, 1865, *OR*, 51(1):251; Weigley, *Quartermaster General*, 313.

85. Ingalls to Meigs, Sept. 28, 1865, *OR*, 51(1):251–52.

86. Ingalls to Williams, June 28, 1864, *OR*, 40(2):479; Meade to Grant, Aug. 29, 1864; Ingalls to Duane, Aug. 29, 1864; and Ingalls to Meigs, Aug. 29, 1864, *OR*, 42(2):564, 566; McCallum to Meigs, May 26, 1866, *OR*, ser. 3, 5:978.

87. Grant to Stanton, July 22, 1865, *OR*, 34(1):19.

88. Ingalls to Williams, Aug. 4, 1864, *OR*, 42(2):40.

89. Haupt to Ingalls, July 14, 1863, *OR*, 27(3):696; McCallum to Meigs, May 26, 1866, *OR*, ser. 3, 5:978.

90. Stevenson to Stanton, Sept. 24, 25, 1864, *OR*, 43(2):168–69, 174.

91. Grant to Halleck, Sept. 27, 1864; Meigs to Grant, Sept. 27, 1864; and Grant to Meigs, Sept. 27, 1864, *OR*, 43(2):186–87.

92. Meigs to Grant, Sept. 27, 1864, *OR*, 43(2):187.

92. Stevenson to Stanton, Sept. 27, 1864, *OR*, 43(2):189.

93. Sheridan to Grant, Oct. 1, 1864; and Sheridan to Halleck, Oct. 1, 1864, *OR*, 43(2):249–50; J. H. Wilson to Grant, Oct. 4, 1864, Philip Henry Sheridan Papers, LC.

94. Stevenson to Stanton, Oct. 1, 5, 1864, *OR*, 43(2):253, 293.

95. McCallum to Meigs, May 26, 1866, *OR*, ser. 3, 5:977–78; Halleck to Meigs, Oct. 2, 1864; Grant to Stanton, Oct. 3, 1864; and Grant to Sheridan, Oct. 3, 1864, *OR*, 43(2):258, 266.

96. McCallum to Meigs, May 26, 1866, *OR*, ser. 3, 5:977–78; Sheridan to Grant, Oct. 7, 1864; Sheridan to Halleck, Oct. 11, 1864; Halleck to Sheridan, Oct. 25, 1864; Thom and Alexander to Halleck, Oct. 26, 1864; Garrett to Sheridan, Nov. 29, 1864; Moore to McCallum, Dec. 2, 1864;

and Orders (unnumbered), Headquarters, Sixth Corps, Dec. 2, 1864, *OR*, 43(2):308, 340, 465, 468, 697, 726–27.

97. *Report of the Quartermaster General*, 114.

98. Goulding, "Month on a Transport," 83.

99. Weber, *Northern Railroads*, 171–72.

100. Meigs to Stanton, Nov. 8, 1865, *OR*, ser. 3, 5:216; Ingalls to Brown, Jan. 5, 1865; Halleck to Grant, Jan. 8, 1865; Grant to Halleck, Jan. 9, 1865; and Grant to Meade and Ord, Jan. 13, 1865, *OR*, 46(2):39, 68, 74,113; Ingalls to Brown, Mar. 20, 1865, *OR*, 46(3):52.

101. Sheridan to Grant, Apr. 8, 1865, *OR*, 46(3):653.

102. Ingalls to Meigs, Sept. 28, 1865, *OR*, 51(1):255.

103. Ingalls to McCallum, Apr. 24, 1865, *OR*, 46(3):918; McCallum to Meigs, May 26, 1866, *OR*, ser. 3, 5:978.

104. McCallum to Meigs, May 26, 1866, *OR*, ser. 3, 5:978.

11. Feeding the Army of Northern Virginia

1. Moore, *Confederate Commissary General*, 85–130; Noland to Northrop, Mar. 27, 1862, *OR*, ser. 4, 1:1038–40.

2. Harman to Jackson, Mar. 10, 1863, *OR*, 12(1):722–23; Harman to not stated, n.d., *OR*, 19(1):960.

3. Hawks to Jackson, Feb. 6, 1863, *OR*, 19(1):961; Hawks to Jackson, Feb. 8, 1863; and Lock to not stated, n.d., *OR*, 12(1):720–21.

4. Ewell to Branch, May 14, 1862, *OR*, 12(3):890.

5. Lee to Johnston, May 13, 1862; and Cole to Johnston, May 13, 1862, *OR*, 11(3):513.

6. General Orders No. 68, Headquarters, Department of Northern Virginia, June 14, 1862, *OR*, 11(3):599.

7. Trimble to Faulkner, Apr. 10, 1863, *OR*, 12(2):723.

8. Lee to Davis, Sept. 3, 4, 5, 1862; and General Orders No. 102, Headquarters, Army of Northern Virginia, Sept. 4, 1862, *OR*, 19(2):590–94.

9. Lee to Davis, Sept. 7, 9, 1862, *OR*, 19(2):596, 602–3.

10. Longstreet to Chilton, Oct. 10, 1862; and Hill to Chilton, n.d., 1862, *OR*, 19(1):841, 1026; Lee to Randolph, Nov. 14, 1862, *OR*, 19(2):718.

11. Goff, *Confederate Supply*, 67.

12. Jewett, *Rise and Fall of the Confederacy*, 36.

13. Northrop memorandum, [ca. Nov. 1862], *OR*, ser. 4, 2:193.

14. Randolph to Lee, Nov. 14, 1862, *OR*, 19(2):716.

15. Lee to Randolph, Nov. 17, 1862; and Lee to Cooper, Nov. 18, 1862, *OR*, 21:1016, 1018.

16. Copy of Jefferson Davis to Browne, Nov. 12, 1862, William M. Browne Service Record, Compiled Service Records of Confederate General and Staff Officers and Non-Regimental Enlisted Men, M331, RG 109, National Archives and Records Administration, Washington, D.C.

17. Lee to Randolph, Nov. 17, Dec. 2, 1862, *OR*, 21:1016, 1041.

18. Crenshaw to Northrop, Jan. 12, 1863, *OR*, 21:1088–90.

19. Lee to Davis, Jan. 19, 1863, *OR*, 21:1096–97.

20. Dew to Perkins, Jan. 19, 1863, *OR,* 21:1097–98.

21. Lee to Davis, Jan. 23, 1863, and Northrop endorsement, Jan. 24, 1863, *OR,* 21:1110; Northrop endorsement on Lee to Seddon, Jan. 26, 1863, *OR,* 52(2):674–75.

22. Lee to Seddon, Jan. 26, 1863; and Lee to Jones, Jan. 27, 1863, *OR,* 25(2):596, 598.

23. Seddon to Lee, Jan. 28, 1863, *OR,* 25(2):599; Lee to Jackson, Feb. 7, 1863, *OR,* 52(2):678–79.

24. Longstreet to Lee, Mar. 24, 27, 1863; and Lee to Longstreet, Mar. 27, 1863, *OR,* 18, 942–44.

25. Lee to Seddon, Mar. 27, 1863, *OR,* 25(2):686–87.

26. Northrop endorsement, Mar. 28, 1863, on Lee to Seddon, Mar. 27, 1863, *OR,* 25(2):688.

27. Hess, *Civil War Logistics,* 136.

28. Northrop endorsement, Mar. 28, 1863, on Lee to Seddon, Mar. 27, 1863; and Seddon to Lee, Mar. 31, 1863, *OR,* 25(2):688, 693–94.

29. Pendleton to Cole, Mar. 31, 1863, *OR,* 25(2):695.

30. Longstreet to Hill, Apr. 2, 1863; and Longstreet to Seddon, Apr. 10, 1863, *OR,* 18, 956, 1002.

31. General Orders No. 52, Headquarters, Army of Northern Virginia, Apr. 5, 1863, *OR,* 25(2):708.

32. Lee to Seddon, Apr. 17, 1863, *OR,* 25(2):730.

33. Zachry to Gratton, May 8, 1863, *OR,* 25(1):981.

34. Stuart to Chilton, May 6, 1863; and Rodes to Pendleton, [May ?], 1863, *OR,* 25(1):887, 945.

35. "Record of a Court of Inquiry to investigate the evacuation of Winchester and Martinsburg," *OR,* 27(2):116; General Orders No. 45, Headquarters, Second Corps, June 15, 1863, *OR,* 27(3):895.

36. General Orders No. 72, Headquarters, Army of Northern Virginia, June 21, 1863; and Lee to Davis, June 25, 1863, *OR,* 27(3):912–13, 931.

37. General Orders No. 73, Headquarters, Army of Northern Virginia, June 27, 1863, *OR,* 27(3):943.

38. Reynolds to Butterfield, June 27, 1863, *OR,* 27(3):350; Brown, *Retreat from Gettysburg,* 35, 74, 387.

39. Brown, *Retreat from Gettysburg,* 388; Northrop to Lee, July 29, 1863, *OR,* 52(2):743; French to Northrop, Aug. 3, 1863, *OR,* 29(2):656–57.

40. Lee to Northrop, Aug. 5, 1863; and Lee to Seddon, Aug. 7, 1863, *OR,* 29(2):625, 628; Lee to Longstreet, Aug. 31, 1863, *OR,* 52(2):761.

41. Daniel to Seddon, July 30, Aug. 1, 1863, *OR,* 52(2):744, 747.

42. Lee to Lawton, Oct. 19, 1863, *OR,* 29(2):794.

43. Lawton to Lee, Oct. 12, 1863; and Lee to Seddon, Nov. 10, 1863, *OR,* 29(2):784–85, 830.

44. Lee to Seddon, Nov. 10, 1863; and Lee to Davis, Nov. 12, 1863, *OR,* 29(2):830, 832.

45. Lee to Seddon, Nov. 12, 1863, *OR,* 29(2):832–33.

46. Seddon to Lee, Nov. 14, 1863, *OR,* 29(2):835.

47. Seddon to Lee, Nov. 20, 1863; and Northrop to Lee, Nov. 22, 1863, *OR,* 29(2):838–39, 843–44.

48. Lee to Northrop, Nov. 23, 1863; and Lee to Bell, Dec. 22, 1863, *OR,* 29(2):844, 890.

49. French to Northrop, Jan. 12, 1864, *OR,* 46(2):1224–25.

50. Goff, *Confederate Supply,* 193–97; Lee to Northrop, Jan. 5, 1864, *OR,* 33:1064–65.

51. Lee to Northrop, Jan. 5, 13, 1864, *OR,* 33:1065, 1087–88.

52. Lee to Northrop, Jan. 5, 1864, *OR,* 33:1065.

53. Lee to Jones, Jan. 5, 21, 1864; and Lee to Davis, Jan. 11, 1863, *OR,* 33:1065, 1076–77, 1112–13.

54. Lee to Lawton, Jan. 18, 1864, *OR,* 33:1094.

55. Lee to Lawton, Jan. 19, 30, 1864, *OR,* 33:1098, 1131.

56. Lee to Lawton, Jan. 30, 1864, *OR,* 33:1131–32.

57. Lawton to Lee, Feb. 5, 1864, *OR,* 33:1146–47.

58. Lawton to Lee, Feb. 5, 1864, *OR,* 33:1147.

59. Lee to Seddon, Jan. 21, 22, Feb. 16, 1864, *OR,* 33:1113–15, 1181.

60. Northrop endorsement, Jan. 27, 1864, on Lee to Seddon, Jan. 22, 1864, *OR,* 33:1115–16.

61. Northrop endorsement, Mar. 6, 1864, on Lee to Davis, Jan. 11, 1864, *OR,* 33:1077.

62. Lawton to Lee, Mar. 31, 1864, *OR,* 33:1236–37.

63. Lawton to Lee, Mar. 31, 1864, *OR,* 33:1237.

64. Northrop to Cooper, Apr. 7, 1864, *OR,* 52(2):851–52.

65. General Orders No. 7, Headquarters, Army of Northern Virginia, Jan. 22, 1864, *OR,* 33:1117.

66. Lee to Seddon, Jan. 22, 1864; Lee to Davis, Apr. 12, 1864; and Lee to Bragg, Apr. 16, 1864, *OR,* 33:1114, 1275, 1285.

67. Lee to Seddon, Jan. 22, 1864, *OR,* 33:1114.

68. Jewett, *Rise and Fall of the Confederacy,* 150; Goff, *Confederate Strategy,* 213–14.

69. Jewett, *Rise and Fall of the Confederacy,* 150; Lee to Seddon, June 21, 1864; and Lee to Seddon, June 24, 1864, *OR,* 40(2):671–72, 684–85.

70. Lee to Davis, June 26, 1864, *OR,* 37(1):767; Northrop endorsement, June 16, 1864, on Ransom to adjutant general, June 12, 1864, *OR,* 36(3):899.

71. Lee to Seddon, July 1, 1864, *OR,* 40(2):709; Seddon to Lee, Aug. 23, 1864, *OR,* 42(2):1198–99; Woodward to Morgan, Sept. 16, 1864, *OR,* 42(1):27.

72. Jewett, *Rise and Fall of the Confederacy,* 42; Taylor, *Destruction and Reconstruction,* 247.

73. Younger, *Inside the Confederate Government,* 181.

74. Jewett, *Rise and Fall of the Confederacy,* 18–19.

75. Lee to Vance, Dec. 28, 1864, *OR,* 42(3):1334; Hoke to Lee, Dec. 25, 1864, *OR,* 46(2):1026–27; Henry to David, Dec. 26, 1864, in Crist, *Papers of Jefferson Davis,* 11:253.

76. Special Orders No. 309, Adjutant and Inspector General's Office, Dec. 30, 1864, *OR,* 42(3):1348–49; Seddon to Lee, Jan. 11, 1865, *OR,* 46(2):1034.

77. Seddon to Lee, Jan. 11, 1865, *OR,* 46(2):1034–35.

78. Northrop to Seddon, Jan. 11, 1865; Northrop endorsement on Seddon to Lee, Jan. 12, 1865; and Special Orders No. 9, Adjutant and Inspector General's Office, Jan. 12, 1865, *OR,* 46(2):1035, 1040–41.

79. Lee to Seddon, Jan. 11, 16, 19, 1865, *OR,* 46(2):1035, 1074, 1099.

80. Lee to Breckinridge, Feb. 8, 1865, *OR,* 46(1):382.

81. Northrop to Breckinridge, Feb. 9, 1865, *OR,* 46(2):1211–12.

82. Lee to Breckinridge, Mar. 9, 1865; French to St. John, Mar. 10, 1865; and Williams to St. John, Mar. 10, 1865, *OR,* 46(2):1295, 1297–98.

83. Lee to Johnston, Mar. 15, 1865; and Robinson to Otey, Mar. 18, 1865, *OR,* 47(2):1395, 1426.

84. Surdam, *Northern Naval Superiority,* 207.

Conclusion

1. For a full exploration of my argument, see *Civil War in the West.*

2. For an extended discussion of the rampant seizing of all manner of resources by the Federal army and the difficulty experienced by officers to control it, see Cashin, *War Stuff.*

3. Halleck, *Elements of Military Art and Science,* 89–96; Lynn, "History of Logistics and Supplying War," 20–22.

Bibliography

ARCHIVES

Abraham Lincoln Presidential Library, Springfield, Illinois
  Engelmann-Kircher Collection
  Lewis Baldwin Parsons Papers
Alabama Department of Archives and History, Montgomery
  Robert Lewis Bliss Papers
  Joseph Wheeler Family Papers
Archives of Michigan, Lansing
  William A. Barnard Collection
Atlanta History Center, Atlanta, Georgia
  James Neuman and Tripp Family Civil War Correspondence
  David Gilmer Watts and Clara Watts Papers
Auburn University, Special Collections and Archives, Auburn, Alabama
  John Crittenden Collection
Boston Public Library, Boston, Massachusetts
  Henry W. Tisdale Diary
Bowdoin College Library, Special Collections and Archives, Brunswick, Maine
  Charles Henry Howard Collection
  O. O. Howard Papers
Chicago History Museum, Chicago, Illinois
  Clifford Stickney Collection
College of William and Mary, Special Collections, Williamsburg, Virginia
  Joseph E. Johnston Papers
Cornell University, Rare and Manuscript Collection, Ithaca, New York
  June and Gilbert Krueger Civil War Letters
Duke University, Rubenstein Rare Book and Manuscript Library, Durham, North Carolina
  George Williamson Balloch Papers
  Braxton Bragg Papers
  Edward L. Hartz Papers
  Walter M. Howland Papers
  Micah Jenkins Papers

Emory University, Manuscript, Archives, and Rare Book Library, Atlanta, Georgia
William Wesley Welborn Letters
Gilder Lehrman Institute of American History, New York, New York
John Moore and Robert Moore Letters
William T. Sherman Letters
Indiana Historical Society, Indianapolis
Frederick Knefler Letters, Lew Wallace Collection
Samuel E. Sneier Letter
Edward Jesup Wood Papers
Kansas Historical Society, Topeka
Anderson Family Papers
John R. Graton Correspondence
T. C. Honnell Letters
Library of Congress, Manuscript Division, Washington, D.C.
Bancroft-Bliss Family Papers
Blair Family Papers
Douglas J. Cater and Rufus W. Cater Papers
Edward L. Hartz Papers
Lewis Muhlenberg Haupt Family Papers
Montgomery C. Meigs Papers
Philip Henry Sheridan Papers
Lyman Trumbull Correspondence
James Walker Letter
Louisiana State University, Louisiana and Lower Mississippi Valley Collections, Special Collections, Baton Rouge
Edwin Hutchinson Papers
Massachusetts Historical Society, Boston
Edward Louis Edes and Robert Thaxter Edes Correspondence
Thomas S. Howland Correspondence
Charles F. Morse Papers
Mississippi Department of Archives and History, Jackson
George W. Modil Papers
Missouri History Museum, St. Louis
Braxton Bragg Papers
Thomas S. Hawley Papers
J. V. Lewis Letter
Theodore Augustus Meysenburg Papers
David D. Porter Papers
George Greenwood Pride Papers

Museum of the Confederacy, Richmond, Virginia
Edward Clifford Brush Diary
National Archives and Records Administration, Washington, D.C.
William M. Browne Service Record, Compiled Service Records of Confederate General and Staff Officers and Non-Regimental Enlisted Men, M331, RG 109
New-York Historical Society, New York
John M. Brannan Letters
New York State Library, Albany
Alanson B. Cone Memoir
Ohio Historical Society, Columbus
James Sidney Robinson Papers
Old Court House Museum, Vicksburg, Mississippi
Philip Roesch Reminiscences
Stanford University, Special Collections and University Archives, Palo Alto, California
Israel Spencer Letters
State Historical Society of Iowa, Des Moines
Hemphill Family Papers
Stones River National Battlefield, Murfreesboro, Tennessee
S. Bloomfield Letters, Battery A, 1st Ohio Light Artillery Regimental File
Syracuse University, Special Collections Research Center, Syracuse, New York
Albert M. Cook Papers
Tennessee State Library and Archives, Nashville
George R. Elliott Diary, Civil War Collection
J. W. Harmon Memoirs
Walter King Hoover Collection
Richard J. McCadden Letters, Civil War Collection
James E. Rains Letters, Civil War Collection
Tulane University, Special Collections, New Orleans, Louisiana
George Brent Papers
Johnston Papers
US Army Military History Institute, Carlisle, Pennsylvania
Luther P. Bradley Collection
US Military Academy, Special Collections, West Point, New York
James Birdseye McPherson Papers
University of Iowa, Special Collections, Iowa City
John C. Brown Diary
University of Michigan, William L. Clements Library, Ann Arbor
Clement Abner Boughton Papers
George Martin Trowbridge Papers, Schoff Civil War Collection

University of North Carolina, Southern Historical Collection, Chapel Hill
Daniel Chevilette Govan Papers
John J. Metzgar Papers
James W. Patton Papers
Benedict Joseph Semmes Papers
Henry C. Semple Papers
University of Notre Dame, Rare Books and Special Collections, Notre Dame, Indiana
Harrison E. Randall Letters
University of Tennessee, Special Collections, Chattanooga
Civil War Quartermaster Reports
Oscar Easley Civil War Letters
University of Tennessee, Special Collections, Knoxville
George L. Reis Letters
Julius E. Thomas Civil War Diary
John Watkins Papers
University of Washington, Special Collections, Seattle
M. F. Force Papers
University of Wyoming, American Heritage Center, Laramie
Leonard Eicholtz Diaries
Virginia Polytechnic Institute and State University, Special Collections, Blacksburg
W. G. Buck Letter
Wisconsin Historical Society, Madison
Timothy Phillips Diaries
Yale University, Sterling Memorial Library, New Haven, Connecticut
David Herrick Gile Correspondence, Civil War Manuscripts Collection

NEWSPAPERS

Belmont (St. Clairsville, Ohio) Chronicle
Memphis Daily Appeal
New York Times
St. Louis Daily Missouri Democrat

BOOKS AND ARTICLES

Abrams, A. S. *A Full and Detailed History of the Siege of Vicksburg.* Atlanta: Intelligence Steam Power Presses, 1863.

Ambrose, Stephen E. *Halleck: Lincoln's Chief of Staff.* Baton Rouge: Louisiana State University Press, 1962.

Aten, Henry J. *History of the Eighty-Fifth Regiment, Illinois Volunteer Infantry.* Hiawatha, Kans., 1901.

Bailey, Anne J. *War and Ruin: William T. Sherman and the Savannah Campaign.* Wilmington, Del.: Scholarly Resources, 2003.

Bailey, Jarrod C. "Civil War Logistics: Effects of Logistics on the Pea Ridge Campaign." M.A. thesis, U.S. Army Command and General Staff College, 2015.

Ballard, Michael B. *Vicksburg: The Campaign That Opened the Mississippi.* Chapel Hill: University of North Carolina Press, 2004.

Banasik, Michael E., ed. *Serving with Honor: The Diary of Captain Eathan Allen Pinnell, Eighth Missouri Infantry (Confederate).* Iowa City: Camp Pope Bookshop, 1999.

Barber, Lucius W. *Army Memoirs of Lucius W. Barber, Company "D," 15th Illinois Volunteer Infantry, May 24, 1861 to Sept. 30, 1865.* Chicago: J. M. W. Jones Stationery and Printing, 1894.

Basler, Roy P., ed. *Collected Works of Abraham Lincoln.* 8 vols. New Brunswick, N.J.: Rutgers University Press, 1953.

Beasecker, Robert, ed. *"I Hope to Do My Country Service": The Civil War Letters of John Bennitt, M.D., Surgeon, 19th Michigan Infantry.* Detroit: Wayne State University Press, 2005.

Belknap, William W. *History of the Fifteenth Regiment, Iowa Veteran Volunteer Infantry, from October, 1861, to August, 1865.* Keokuk, Iowa: R. B. Ogden and Son, 1887.

Bell, Andrew McIlwaine. "'Gallinippers' & Glory: The Links between Mosquito-borne Diseases and U.S. Civil War Operations and Strategy, 1862." *Journal of Military History* 74, no. 2 (April 2010): 379–405.

Bergeron, Arthur W., Jr. *The Civil War Reminiscences of Major Silas T. Grisamore, C.S.A.* Baton Rouge: Louisiana State University Press, 1993.

Bevier, R. S. *History of the First and Second Missouri Confederate Brigades, 1861–1865.* St. Louis: Bryan, Brand, 1879.

Bigger, David Dwight. *Ohio's Silver-Tongued Orator: Life and Speeches of General William H. Gibson.* Dayton, Ohio: United Brethren, 1901.

Billings, John D. *Hardtack and Coffee; or, The Unwritten Story of Army Life.* Boston: George M. Smith, 1887.

Black, Robert C., III. *The Railroads of the Confederacy.* Chapel Hill: University of North Carolina Press, 1952.

Blair, William Alan, ed. *A Politician Goes to War: The Civil War Letters of John White Geary.* University Park: Pennsylvania State University Press, 1995.

Brady, Lisa M. *War upon the Land: Military Strategy and the Transformation of Southern Landscapes during the American Civil War.* Athens: University of Georgia Press, 2012.

Brown, Kent Masterson. *Retreat from Gettysburg: Lee, Logistics, and the Pennsylvania Campaign.* Chapel Hill: University of North Carolina Press, 2005.

Brown, Norman D., ed. *Journey to Pleasant Hill: The Civil War Letters of Captain Elijah P. Petty, Walker's Texas Division CSA.* San Antonio: University of Texas Institute of Texan Cultures, 1982.

Bryant, Edwin E. *History of the Third Regiment of Wisconsin Veteran Volunteer Infantry, 1861–1865.* Madison, Wis.: Democrat Printing, 1891.

Butler, Watson Hubbard, [ed.]. *Letters Home: Jay Caldwell Butler, Captain, 101st Ohio Volunteer Infantry.* N.p., 1930.

Burt, Jesse E. "Sherman, Railroad General." *Civil War History* 2, no. 1 (March 1956): 45–56.

Cashin, Joan E. *War Stuff: The Struggle for Human and Environmental Resources in the American Civil War.* New York: Cambridge University Press, 2018.

Castel, Albert. *Decision in the West: The Atlanta Campaign of 1864.* Lawrence: University Press of Kansas, 1992.

Chittenden, L. E. *Personal Reminiscences, 1840–1890, including Some Not Hitherto Published on Lincoln and the War.* New York: Richmond, Croscup, 1893.

Clark, Olynthus B., ed. *Downing's Civil War Diary.* Des Moines: Historical Department of Iowa, 1916.

Cook, S. G., and Charles E. Benton, eds. *The "Dutchess County Regiment," (150th Regiment of New York State Volunteer Infantry) in the Civil War: Its Story as Told by Its Members.* Danbury, Conn.: Danbury Medical Printing, 1907.

Cox, Florence Marie Ankeny. *Kiss Josey for Me!* Santa Ana, Calif.: Friis-Pioneer, 1974.

Cox, Jacob D. *Atlanta.* New York: Charles Scribner's Sons, 1882.

——. *Military Reminiscences of the Civil War.* 2 vols. New York: Charles Scribner's Sons, 1900.

Cozzens, Peter. *The Shipwreck of Their Hopes: The Battles for Chattanooga.* Urbana: University of Illinois Press, 1994.

——. *This Terrible Sound: The Battle of Chickamauga.* Urbana: University of Illinois Press, 1992.

Cozzens, Peter, and Robert I. Girardi, eds. *The Military Memoirs of General John Pope.* Chapel Hill: University of North Carolina Press, 1998.

Crist, Lynda Lasswell, ed. *The Papers of Jefferson Davis.* 11 vols. Baton Rouge: Louisiana State University Press, 1971–2003.

Daniel, Larry J. *Days of Glory: The Army of the Cumberland, 1861–1865.* Baton Rouge: Louisiana State University Press, 2004.

Dodge, Grenville M. *Personal Recollections of President Abraham Lincoln, General Ulysses S. Grant and General William T. Sherman.* Denver: Sage Books, 1965.

Dodson, W. C., ed. *Campaigns of Wheeler and His Cavalry, 1862–1865.* Atlanta: Hudgins, 1899.

Duffy, Christopher. *Borodino and the War of 1812.* New York: Charles Scribner's Sons, 1973.

Engels, Donald W. *Alexander the Great and the Logistics of the Macedonian Army.* Berkeley: University of California Press, 1978.

Erdkamp, Paul. *Hunger and the Sword: Warfare and Food Supply in Roman Republican Wars (264–30 B.C.).* Amsterdam: J. C. Gieben, 1998.

Evans, David. *Sherman's Horsemen: Union Cavalry Operations in the Atlanta Campaign.* Bloomington: Indiana University Press, 1996.

Ferris, Ruth, ed. "Captain Jolly in the Civil War." *Bulletin of the Missouri Historical Society* 22, no. 1 (October 1965): 14–31.

Fitch, John. *Annals of the Army of the Cumberland.* Philadelphia: J. B. Lippincott, 1864.

Fout, Frederick W. *The Dark Days of the Civil War, 1861 to 1865.* N.p.: F. A. Wagenfeuhr, 1904.

Frank Leslie's Scenes and Portraits of the Civil War. New York: Mrs. Frank Leslie, 1894.

Gabel, Christopher R. *Railroad Generalship: Foundations of Civil War Strategy.* Fort Leavenworth, Kans.: U.S. Army Command and General Staff College Press, 1997.

Galuszka, Douglas H. "Logistics in Warfare: The Significance of Logistics in the Army of the Cumberland during the Tullahoma and Chickamauga Campaigns." M.A. thesis, Command and General Staff College, 2005.

Goff, Richard D. *Confederate Supply.* Durham, N.C.: Duke University Press, 1969.

Goulding, Joseph H. "A Month on a Transport." In *Vermont War Papers and Miscellaneous States Papers and Addresses for Military Order of the Loyal Legion of the United States,* 79–97. Wilmington, N.C.: Broadfoot, 1994.

Graf, LeRoy P., ed. *The Papers of Andrew Johnson.* 16 vols. Knoxville: University of Tennessee Press, 1967–2000.

Grant, Ulysses S. *Personal Memoirs of U. S. Grant.* 2 vols. in 1. New York: Viking, 1990.

Grehan, John. *The Lines of Torres Vedras: The Cornerstone of Wellington's Strategy in the Peninsular War, 1809–1812.* Staplehurst, Kent: Spellmount, 2000.

Hagerman, Edward. *The American Civil War and the Origins of Modern Warfare: Ideas, Organization, and Field Command.* Bloomington: Indiana University Press, 1988.

Halleck, H. Wager. *Elements of Military Art and Science; or, Course of Instruction in Strategy, Fortification, Tactics of Battles.* New York: D. Appleton, 1862.

Harris, Jason T. "Combat, Supply, and the Influence of Logistics during the Civil War in Indian Territory." M.A. thesis, University of Central Oklahoma, 2008.

Harwell, Richard, and Philip N. Racine, eds. *The Fiery Trail: A Union Officer's Account of Sherman's Last Campaigns.* Knoxville: University of Tennessee Press, 1986.

Hattaway, Herman, and Archer Jones. *How the North Won: A Military History of the Civil War.* Urbana: University of Illinois Press, 1983.

Haupt, Herman. *Military Bridges: With Suggestions of New Expedients and Constructions for Crossing Streams and Chasms.* New York: D. Van Nostrand, 1864.

——. "The Railroad Brigade." In *Battles and Leaders of the Civil War,* vol. 6, edited by Peter Cozzens, 466–76. Urbana: University of Illinois Press, 2004.

——. *Reminiscences of General Herman Haupt.* Milwaukee: Wright and Joys, 1901.

Hedley, F. Y. *Marching through Georgia.* Chicago: Donohue, Henneberry, 1890.

Hess, Earl J. *Banners to the Breeze: The Kentucky Campaign, Corinth, and Stones River.* Lincoln: University of Nebraska Press, 2000.

——. *Braxton Bragg: The Most Hated Man of the Confederacy.* Chapel Hill: University of North Carolina Press, 2016.

——. *The Civil War in the West: Victory and Defeat from the Appalachians to the Mississippi.* Chapel Hill: University of North Carolina Press, 2012.

——. *Civil War Logistics: A Study of Military Transportation.* Baton Rouge: Louisiana State University Press, 2017.

——. *Kennesaw Mountain: Sherman, Johnston, and the Atlanta Campaign.* Chapel Hill: University of North Carolina Press, 2013.

——. *The Knoxville Campaign: Burnside and Longstreet in East Tennessee.* Knoxville: University of Tennessee Press, 2012.

History of the Organization, Marches, Campaigns, General Services and Final Muster Out of Battery M, First Regiment Illinois Light Artillery. Princeton, Ill.: Mercer and Dean, 1892.

Howard, Oliver Otis. *Autobiography of Oliver Otis Howard.* 2 vols. New York: Baker and Taylor, 1907.

How to Feed an Army. Washington, D.C.: Government Printing Office, 1901.

Howe, M. A. DeWolfe. ed. *Marching with Sherman: Passages from the Letters and Campaign Diaries of Henry Hitchcock.* Lincoln: University of Nebraska Press, 1995.

Humphreys, Margaret. *Yellow Fever and the South.* New Brunswick, N.J.: Rutgers University Press, 1992.

Jewett, Clayton E., ed. *Rise and Fall of the Confederacy: The Memoir of Senator Williamson S. Oldham, CSA.* Columbia: University of Missouri Press, 2006.

Jones, Archer. *Civil War Command and Strategy: The Process of Victory and Defeat.* New York: Free Press, 1992.

"John Byers Anderson." Wikipedia. Last edited Sept. 23, 2019. https://en.Wikipedia.org/wiki/John_Byers_Anderson.

Jones, James Pickett. *Yankee Blitzkrieg: Wilson's Raid through Alabama and Georgia.* Athens: University of Georgia Press, 1976.

Keegan, John. *The American Civil War: A Military History.* New York: Alfred A. Knopf, 2009.

Kellogg, John Jackson. *War Experiences and the Story of the Vicksburg Campaign.* Washington, Iowa: Evening Journal, 1913.

Kemmerly, Phillip. "Dead Animals, Starving Men, and Treacherous Anderson Road: 1863 Siege of Chattanooga." *Tennessee Historical Quarterly* 77, no. 1 (Spring 2018): 2–35.

Kennedy, Joseph C. G. *Agriculture of the United States in 1860.* Washington, D.C.: Government Printing Office, 1864.

———. *Preliminary Report on the Eighth Census, 1860.* Washington, D.C.: Government Printing Office, 1862.

Kraynek, Sharon L. D., [ed.]. *Letters to My Wife: A Civil War Diary from the Western Front.* Apollo, Pa.: Closson, 1995.

Lawson, Lewis A. "The Hammontrees Fight the Civil War: Letters from the Fifth East Tennessee Infantry." *Lincoln Herald* 78, no. 3 (Fall 1976): 117–24.

Lazenby, J. F. "Logistics in Classical Greek Warfare." *War in History* 1, no. 1 (1994): 3–18.

Le Duc, William G. *Recollections of a Civil War Quartermaster.* St. Paul, Minn.: North Central, 1963.

Lee, John W. I. *A Greek Army on the March: Soldiers and Survival in Xenophon's Anabasis.* New York: Cambridge University Press, 2007.

Lucas, Marion Brunson. *Sherman and the Burning of Columbia.* College Station: Texas A&M University Press, 1976.

Lynn, John A. "The History of Logistics and Supplying War." In *Feeding Mars: Logistics in Western Warfare from the Middle Ages to the Present,* edited by John A. Lynn, 9–27. Boulder, Colo.: Westview, 1993.

Lyon, Mrs. Adelia C., ed. *Reminiscences of the Civil War.* San Jose, Calif.: William P. Lyon Jr., 1907.

McDonough, James Lee. *Nashville: The Western Confederacy's Final Gamble.* Knoxville: University of Tennessee Press, 2004.

———. *War in Kentucky: From Shiloh to Perryville.* Knoxville: University of Tennessee Press, 1994.

McPherson, James M. *Battle Cry of Freedom: The Civil War Era.* New York: Ballantine, 1988.

McWilliams, John. *Recollections of John McWilliams, His Youth, Experiences in California and the Civil War.* [Princeton, N.J.: Princeton University Press, 1921].

Memminger, R. W. "The Surrender of Vicksburg: A Defence of General Pemberton." *Southern Historical Society Papers* 12 (1884): 352–60.

Miller, William J. "Scarcely Any Parallel in History: Logistics, Friction, and McClellan's Strategy for the Peninsula Campaign." In *The Peninsula Campaign of 1862: Yorktown to the Seven Days,* 2: 129–88. Campbell, Calif.: Savas Woodbury, 1995.

Milligan, John D. *Gunboats Down the Mississippi.* Annapolis, Md.: Naval Institute Press, 1965.

Moore, Jerrold Northrop. *Confederate Commissary General: Lucius Bellinger Northrop and the Subsistence Bureau of the Southern Army.* Shippensburg, Pa.: White Mane, 1996.

Moore, John G. "Mobility and Strategy in the Civil War." *Military Affairs* 24, no. 2 (Summer 1960): 68–77.

Murray, Williamson, and Wayne Wei-Siang Hsieh. *A Savage War: A Military History of the Civil War.* Princeton, N.J.: Princeton University Press, 2016.

Nevins, Allan. *The War for the Union.* 4 vols. New York: Charles Scribner's Sons, 1960.

Niven, John, ed. *The Salmon P. Chase Papers.* 5 vols. Kent, Ohio: Kent State University Press, 1993–98.

Official Records of the Union and Confederate Navies in the War of the Rebellion. 30 vols. in 2 series. Washington, D.C.: Government Printing Office, 1894–1922.

Osborn, Hartwell. "Sherman's Carolina Campaign." *Western Reserve University Bulletin* 15, no. 8 (November 1912): 101–19.

Otto, John. *History of the 11th Indiana Battery.* Fort Wayne, Ind.: W. D. Page, 1894.

Parsons, Lewis B. *Reports to the War Department, by Brev. Maj. Gen. Lewis B. Parsons, Chief of Rail and River Transportation.* St. Louis: George Knapp, 1867.

Pickenpaugh, Roger. *Rescue by Rail: Troop Transfer and the Civil War in the West, 1863.* Lincoln: University of Nebraska Press, 1998.

Pierce, Lyman B. *History of the Second Iowa Cavalry.* Burlington, Iowa: Hawk-Eye Steam Book and Job Printing, 1865.

Piston, William Garrett, and Richard W. Hatcher III. *Wilson's Creek: The Second Battle of the Civil War and the Men Who Fought It.* Chapel Hill: University of North Carolina Press, 2000.

Population of the United States in 1860. Washington, D.C.: Government Printing Office, 1864.

Quaife, Milo M., ed. *From the Cannon's Mouth: The Civil War Letters of General Alpheus S. Williams.* Detroit: Wayne State University Press, 1959.

Report of the Quartermaster General of the United States Army to the Secretary of War, for the Year Ending June 30, 1865. Washington, D.C.: Government Printing Office, 1865.

Risch, Erna. *Quartermaster Support of the Army: A History of the Corps, 1775–1939.* Washington, D.C.: Center of Military History, 1989.

Robertson, John, comp. *Michigan in the War.* Lansing, Mich.: W. S. George, 1882.

Rusling, James F. *Men and Things I Saw in Civil War Days.* New York: Eaton and Mains, 1899.

Schofield, John M. *Forty-Six Years in the Army.* New York: Century, 1897.

Sharpe, Henry G. "The Art of Supplying Armies in the Field as Exemplified during the Civil War." *Journal of the Military Service Institution of the United States* 18 (January 1896): 45–95.

Shea, William L., and Earl J. Hess. *Pea Ridge: Civil War Campaign in the West.* Chapel Hill: University of North Carolina Press, 1992.

Shea, William L., and Terrence J. Winschel. *Vicksburg Is the Key: The Struggle for the Mississippi River.* Lincoln: University of Nebraska Press, 2003.

Sherman, William T. *Memoirs.* 2 vols. New York: D. Appleton, 1875.

Simon, John Y., ed. *The Papers of Ulysses S. Grant.* 24 vols. Carbondale: Southern Illinois University Press, 1967–2000.

Simpson, Brooks D., and Jean V. Berlin, eds. *Sherman's Civil War: Selected Correspondence of William T. Sherman, 1860–1865.* Chapel Hill: University of North Carolina Press, 1999.

Smith, Hampton, [ed.]. *Brother of Mine: The Civil War Letters of Thomas and William Christie.* St. Paul: Minnesota Historical Society, 2011.

Smith, Ralph J. *Reminiscences of the Civil War.* [San Marcos, Tex., 1911].

Snell, Mark A. "Union Lifeline." In *The Ongoing Civil War: New Versions of Old Stories,* edited by Herman Hattaway and Ethan S. Rafuse, 74–97. Columbia: University of Missouri Press, 2004.

Statistics of the United States (including Mortality, Property, & c.), in 1860: Compiled from the Original Returns and Being the Final Exhibit of the Eighth Census, under the Direction of the Secretary of the Interior. Washington, D.C.: Government Printing Office, 1866.

Steiner, Paul E. *Disease in the Civil War: Natural Biological Warfare in 1861–1865.* Springfield, Ill.: Charles C. Thomas, 1968.

Stevenson, Robert. *To Win the Battle: The 1st Australian Division in the Great War, 1914–18.* Cambridge, UK: Cambridge University Press, 2013.

Stoker, Donald. *The Grand Design: Strategy and the U.S. Civil War.* New York: Oxford University Press, 2012.

Supplement to the Official Records of the Union and Confederate Armies. 100 vols. Wilmington, N.C.: Broadfoot, 1993–2000.

Surdam, David G. *Northern Naval Superiority and the Economics of the American Civil War.* Columbia: University of South Carolina Press, 2001.

Sword, Wiley. *The Confederacy's Last Hurrah: Spring Hill, Franklin, and Nashville.* Lawrence: University Press of Kansas, 1993.

Symonds, H. C. *Report of a Commissary of Subsistence, 1861–65.* Astor Place, N.Y.: J. J. Little, [1888].

Taylor, Lenette S. *"The Supply for Tomorrow Must Not Fail": The Civil War of Captain Simon Perkins Jr., a Union Quartermaster.* Kent, Ohio: Kent State University Press, 2004.

Taylor, Richard. *Destruction and Reconstruction: Personal Experiences of the Late War.* New York: Longmans, Green, 1955.

Thompson, C. Mildred. *Reconstruction in Georgia: Economic, Social, Political, 1865–1872.* Gloucester, Mass.: Peter Smith, 1964.

Throne, Mildred, ed. *The Civil War Diary of Cyrus F. Boyd, Fifteenth Iowa Infantry, 1861–1863.* Baton Rouge: Louisiana State University Press, 1998.

Tourgée, Albion W. *The Story of a Thousand: Being a History of the Service of the 105th Ohio Volunteer Infantry, in the War for the Union from August 21, 1862, to June 6, 1865.* Buffalo, N.Y.: S. McGerald and Son, 1896.

Vandiver, Frank. "General Hood as Logistician." *Military Affairs* 16, no. 1 (Spring 1952): 1–11.

Vance, J. W., ed. *Report of the Adjutant General of the State of Illinois.* 8 vols. Springfield, Ill.: H. W. Rokker, 1886.

War of the Rebellion: A Compilation of the Official Records of the Union and Confederate Armies. 70 vols. in 128 parts. Washington, D.C.: Government Printing Office, 1880–1901.

Ward, James A. *That Man Haupt: A Biography of Herman Haupt.* Baton Rouge: Louisiana State University Press, 1973.

Weber, Thomas. *The Northern Railroads in the Civil War, 1861–1865.* New York: Columbia University Press, 1952.

Weigley, Russell F. *A Great Civil War: A Military and Political History, 1861–1865.* Bloomington: Indiana University Press, 2000.

———. *Quartermaster General of the Union Army: A Biography of M. C. Meigs.* New York: Columbia University Press, 1959.

Wheeler, William. *Letters of William Wheeler of the Class of 1855, Y.C.* Riverside, Cambridge, Mass.: H. O. Houghton, 1875.

Williams, Frederick D., ed. *The Wild Life of the Army: Civil War Letters of James A. Garfield.* Lansing: Michigan State University Press, 1964.

[Wilson, Thomas]. "Feeding a Great Army." *United Service* 2, no. 2 (February 1880): 149–59.

Windham, William T. "The Problem of Supply in the Trans-Mississippi Confederacy." *Journal of Southern History* 27, no. 2 (May 1961): 149–68.

Wittenberg, Eric J., ed. *"We Have It Damn Hard Out Here": The Civil War Letters of Sergeant Thomas W. Smith, 6th Pennsylvania Cavalry.* Kent, Ohio: Kent State University Press, 1999.

Younger, Edward, ed. *Inside the Confederate Government: The Diary of Robert Garlick Hill Kean.* New York: Oxford University Press, 1957.

Index